INDEPENDENTS STRUGGLE

Michael Darlow is one of Britain's leading TV directors, producers and writers. After starting as an actor, his first short film was spotted by the documentary pioneer John Grierson and shown on TV and at the 1960 Edinburgh Film Festival. He then worked at the BBC in Bristol, at ATV and Granada, before becoming a freelance in 1969.

Michael's drama, documentary, arts and music programmes have won awards around the world, including BAFTAs, an Emmy, and Gold at the New York Film and Television Festival. They include *Auschwitz The Final Solution*, *The World at War*, *Johnny Cash in San Quentin*, *The Barretts of Wimpole Street*, and *Bomber Harris*. He has ranged from pop music to classics by Ibsen, Marivaux and Hazlitt, from a BBC adaptation of Dostoyevsky's *Crime and Punishment*, to modern authors including Michael Frayn, Robin Chapman, Nigel Williams and David Mercer. He is a Fellow of The Royal Television Society and was awarded the society's Silver Medal in 2000. He has been a member of many TV industry committees and taught at the National Film and Television School, the National Short Course Training Programme, for the BBC, LWT and in Europe.

He is the author of *Terence Rattigan: the Man and his Work* (Quartet Books, 2000). He lives in Wiltshire where he and his wife keep rare breed Soay sheep.

Independents Struggle

The programme makers who took on the TV establishment

MICHAEL DARLOW

QUARTET BOOKS

First published in 2004 by Boa Ms Limited
in association with Quartet Books Limited
A member of the Namara Group
27 Goodge Street, London W1T 2LD

A catalogue record for this book is available from the British Library

ISBN 0704381559

Typeset by Antony Gray
Printed and bound in Great Britain by Creative Print and Design

For Sophie

Contents

Acknowledgements

Working on this book has been like going on a journey. I set out thinking that I knew the terrain reasonably well, but quickly discovered that I did not know large stretches of it at all. I therefore wish, at the outset, to express my sincere thanks to the literally dozens of people who gave so generously of their time to fill in the gaps in my knowledge. They are so numerous and their help has been so extensive that I cannot hope in the space available to thank them all. That said, I am still left with the difficult task of deciding who to mention by name.

I cannot fail to express my deepest and ongoing gratitude to all those who were my colleagues and friends during the protracted struggles described in this story. Their fortitude and patience then, and their generosity and eagerness to help while I have been working on this book were, and have continued to be, an enormous source of strength and encouragement. Out of many colleagues, I wish particularly to thank Sophie Balhetchet, Paul Styles and John Woodward, who were my closest colleagues and confidantes for more than a decade and who, to this day, remain friends in whom I have absolute trust. I am also especially grateful to my many mentors, of whom many have become colleagues and friends. Out of a long list of those who inspired me and from whom I learned a huge amount, I think immediately of Phillip Whitehead, Christine Fox, Iain Bruce, Nicholas Garnham, David Elstein, Michael Jackson, David Norris, Michael Peacock, Anthony Smith and Janet Walker. There were others who are, alas, now dead – Maurice Hatton, Caroline Heller, Udi Eichler and Simon Hartog.

One of the heart-warming things about working on this book has been the response of so many who could be said to have been our opponents during some of the battles described. They have been extraordinarily generous with their time and encouragement. They have been unfailingly candid and painstaking in their willingness to provide facts, unearth papers and make themselves available to me. All, I believe, have been united by a shared commitment to the truth and, above all, to good broadcasting. Again, it is hard to single out individuals, but I must acknowledge a special debt of gratitude to those who, in addition to their generous help on this project, were my bosses and encouragers during my career in television – Sir Denis Forman, Sir Paul Fox, David Plowright, Michael Grade, Alasdair Milne, Sir Bill Cotton, Brian Tesler and Chris Rowley.

Considering the controversial nature of many of the events, and the passions which some of them aroused, it is surely remarkable that almost without exception everyone whom I approached agreed to help me. A full list of those whom I have interviewed at length, together with a list of some of the many others whose brains I have picked along the way, appears with a bibliography at the end of the book. Specific sources are acknowledged in the text itself. Unfortunately I failed to make contact with a few of those I would have liked to be able to talk to. They included Sir Michael Checkland, Iain Bruce and David Shaw. Just two people turned me down, and then for understandable reasons. Both Lady Thatcher and Lord Hurd had too many other commitments, Lord Hurd adding, with characteristic modesty, that his memory was 'less than brilliant'.

With the two exceptions I have mentioned, I made it a general rule that I would not interview politicians, as the majority of those most closely concerned with these events have already published memoirs and because of a deep-seated desire among some politicians to present themselves as having been unfailingly in the right over controversial events. I felt that it would better serve my purpose to examine the actions of politicians and what they said at the time, rather than risk confusing matters by paying too much attention to the motives which they might ascribe to their actions and utterances long afterwards. I recognise that this is in some ways an arbitrary decision on my part, particularly as I have been at pains to try to understand the motives of the programme makers, heads of broadcasting organisations and broadcast regulators. I suppose my decision is based on the belief that broadcasters of whatever stripe are generally more to be trusted than politicians and that I feel more confident about my ability to distinguish between when broadcasters are telling the truth and when they are trying to improve on it.

I also decided not to interview career civil servants. It seemed to me invidious to single out individuals. Similarly, except where the individual had already been named by others or spoke out under his or her own name in public at the time, I have attempted to maintain their anonymity. However, the position of Lord Griffiths of Fforestfach (Professor Brian Griffiths) was rather different. As Head of the Number 10 Policy Unit during the latter half of the 1980s he was a senior policy adviser to Margaret Thatcher rather than a career civil servant and had a special role in the formulation of broadcasting policy. I am extremely grateful to Lord Griffiths for agreeing to talk to me, particularly as I believe that this is the first time that he has agreed to be interviewed about his work at Number 10. I am grateful to him as well for drawing my attention to a number of writings and lectures of relevance to my research.

In addition to those I have already mentioned, many other people have, in addition to talking to me, put at my disposal private and previously unpublished papers. Among the many who helped me in this way, I particularly wish to thank Neal Ascherson, Mike Dibb, David Graham, Lord Macdonald of Tradeston (Gus Macdonald), Colin Thomas and John Wyvver. I am especially grateful to John Whitney who, in addition to meeting me, responding to a long list of written questions and giving extremely generously of his time, has allowed me to quote from the private diary which he kept during his years as Director-General of the IBA; to Sir Alan Peacock, who chaired the committee which enquired into the financing of the BBC in the mid-1980s, who went to considerable lengths to meet me, drew my attention to a number of little-known but important published sources and arranged for me to attend a range of seminars and lectures dealing with different aspects of broadcasting at the Institute of Economic Affairs. In addition to acknowledging the source of all the illustrations in the book in the ususal manner, I wish to particularly thank the many people who have helped me in my search for pictures and generously gave me permission to reproduce material. I am particularly grateful to Steve Clarke for permission to use cartoons drawn by him for *Open Secret*, Colin Thomas and others who produced *samizdat* material that circulated within the BBC in the early 1970s, Christine Fox and Neal Ascherson who were responsible for much of the material published by the Free Communications Group, PACT and BECTU which granted me permission to reproduce photographs originally published by their predeccessor organisations, the AIP and the ACTT, Richard Paterson and Louise Watson of the BFI, Jill Donnellan and Sue Shephard.

I have received a great deal of help from institutions, their officials, archivists, librarians and staff. I am particularly indebted to Janet Moat and Andrew Lockett of the British Film Institute. Janet, with Anthony Smith's enthusiastic endorsement, guided me through the unique collection of private papers held in the Anthony Smith Collection at the Institute. Andrew gave me great encouragement in the latter stages of my work, arranging to have my manuscript read by an expert in television history and making available to me his detailed notes. I am especially indebted also to the Royal Television Society, and to Clare Colvin, the Society's Archivist, who was tireless in finding articles and papers, retrieving video and audio recordings of the Society's events, copying them for me and generally guiding me through the Society's archival treasure trove. I acknowledge the generous assistance of the Producers' Alliance for Cinema and Television, PACT, and of Shaun Williams, its former Chief Executive, who made available to me the records of PACT and its forerunners, the British Film and Television Producers' Association, the Association of Independent Producers and the Independent Programme Producers' Association. Shaun and PACT's staff were indefatigable in tracking down documents and retrieving them from storage. I wish to thank Bridget Cass, the Administrator of the Campaign for Quality Television, who drew my attention to various of the Campaign's publications and research papers and made them available to me, and Barrie MacDonald of the Independent Television Commission for unearthing and sending to me copies of various IBA and ITA publications. I am similarly indebted to the Royal Society of Arts, the Broadcasting, Entertainment, Cinematograph and Theatre Union and the Conservative Party for generously providing me with documents and information. Among many libraries I wish to thank three in particular – Cambridge University Library, the London Library and the British Library.

Over the years many people have cajoled and encouraged me to set down the story of the rise of independent television producers in Britain. But it was Naim Attallah, the Chairman of Quartet Books, who, by his infectious enthusiasm, gave me the final impetus to actually do it. This was reinforced by Piers Blofeld and Jeremy Beale, my editors at Quartet. Both have been unfailingly kind, encouraging and patient, particularly as the process of research and writing stretched to fill double the time that I had originally forecast and the book's length grew in proportion. My warmest thanks also go to my assistant Debbie Slater, who has been tenacious in unearthing facts and figures, checking my errors and bringing order to my manuscript. I wish also to acknowledge my special debt to Sophie Balhetchet, Ray Fitzwalter, Richard Moxon, Shaun Williams and John Woodward who not only took time out of busy careers to read my completed manuscript and draw my attention to the errors but to discuss a number of the issues raised in it with me at length.

Finally, and above all, I want to thank Sophie, my wife. She encouraged me to embark on this book and continued to enthuse me throughout its long gestation. Over the last forty years she has lived with and supported me through many of the events described. Through much of the 1980s it was she who carefully fished papers relating directly to this story out of the wastepaper basket after I thought I would have no further use for them. It was she who then kept them safe, realising that I or someone else might want them some day. Without Sophie I would in all probability not have got through many of the events described. Without her instinct for preserving written records and artefacts much of the irreplaceable material on which this book is based would no longer survive. I therefore dedicate this book to Sophie as a small, and all too inadequate, token of many years of abiding love and gratitude.

MICHAEL DARLOW, *November 2003*

INDEPENDENTS STRUGGLE

Introduction

I have worked in television for over forty years. My first professional television engagement was as an actor playing the head boy of a school in a BBC play transmitted live, as all plays were in those days, on New Year's Day 1959. As the director cut to his first shot of me, a close-up on my face, the elderly actress with whom I was playing the scene forgot her lines. As a result my first screen utterance was a hastily invented line intended to get us back onto the play's plot. It may not be thought surprising, therefore, that as soon as the opportunity presented itself I opted for spending as much time as I could behind the camera making programmes, rather than in front of it performing in them. However, within a few years of entering television I came increasingly to question how it was that some programmes got made and others did not, who got to make such decisions and how they got their authority, why some people were given the opportunity to make programmes or express opinions and some were not, how the programmes were made and the relationship between the way programmes were made and whether they got made at all. The more I learned about the answers the more I questioned those answers.

Coming into television in the early 1960s I was far from alone in questioning such things. At that time many of the assumptions about society, which had underpinned the way in which broadcasting had been set up and controlled ever since the start of radio and the creation of the BBC in the early 1920s, were under challenge. Many of the new generation of film and television makers who entered the industry in the 1960s felt as I did. They found that too often they and their programmes came off a poor second to the needs or whims of the executives, politicians and money men who ran television. Increasingly we came to believe that the whole system of control and funding in film and broadcasting was inappropriate to the needs and aspirations of the new age; that the BBC and ITV networks, controlled and run respectively by narrow elites of predominantly middle-class Oxbridge-educated men and a handful of show business agents and impresarios, no longer adequately met the range of needs and tastes of the viewing public or of society at large. As a result we began to search for ways of making the media in which we worked more accessible and participatory, open to a much wider range of possible ideas, films and programmes – drama, entertainment, documentary and current affairs, even to forms and content not so far seen or invented. In searching we sought to create a freer and more open arena in which to realise our own creative ideas.

Anthony Smith, a key player in this story, has described the successive campaigns waged by programme makers between the late 1960s and the mid-1980s as 'a liberation struggle'. Their later campaigns have been described, with admiration or disapproval depending on who was speaking, as a story of how 'radicals on the margin' became 'the mainstream' and as 'one of the most successful lobbies in British political history'. Whatever one thinks of those campaigners, whether one admires what they did or not, there is no denying that they played an essential role in changing British television and bringing about what we now have.

In view of this it seems strange that while there have been numerous books about television, about the BBC, ITV and other broadcasters, there has, so far as I know, been no book devoted exclusively to exploring the role of programme makers in challenging the broadcasting status quo in the 1960s, deflecting the course of development of television in the 1970s, in the creation of Channel Four, in the emergence and growth of the independent programme production sector, or to their influence on crucial government decisions about broadcasting in the 1980s and 1990s, and to their probable role in the broadcasting and new media of the future. Of course parts of the story have been touched on in various television histories and books about broadcasting, in broadcasters' memoirs and political biographies. Nevertheless, this, I believe, is the first time that the story has been told as a narrative whole and from the inside. There seem to be two principal reasons why the story has not been told before. One was undoubtedly a wish to protect some of those involved. The other was the deliberate decision of some of us not to tell it. We feared that we might need to do some of the same things again, employ the same methods and call on the same contacts in future struggles. But times change. There is no longer a need to protect the identities of individuals involved. The campaigners have moved on. It will not be they who will conduct future struggles aimed at liberating and improving broadcasting.

Technological and other changes taking place in broadcasting today are every bit as profound and far reaching as anything that was happening in the 1960s. A new generation of young, aspirant programme makers wanting to protect and enhance the quality and diversity of television, wanting to win space and freedom in a new environment to make the programmes they want to make and say the things they believe need saying, will need to fight new campaigns. So, by describing the inside story of earlier programme makers' struggles, I hope that in addition to contributing to a better understanding of important events in recent broadcasting history, I may be able to help a new generation of idealistic programme makers to learn, to take encouragement and be warned by the successes and mistakes of earlier broadcasting campaigners.

Because of my involvement in events described in this book I cannot pretend to be entirely objective about them. Nevertheless, and particularly in light of the story with which I began, I think that I owe it to my readers to make this promise: I undertake not to make things up for the sake of getting back onto the plot. I will try not to improve on my own or my friends' role in the story and I will endeavour to exercise my duty to be fair and report both sides, while at the same time not attempting to disguise my own views. If, in spite of my best efforts, this sometimes seems an unduly subjective or exaggerated account, I can only plead that the issues involved were often as controversial, the emotions aroused as high and the events themselves sometimes as unlikely as the plot lines of the dramas, soap operas and music-hall sketches which I at one time appeared in and later directed.

I

Free Communicators – The 1960s

'Some men see things as they are and say why.
I dream things that never were and say why not.'

A favourite saying of Robert Kennedy's,
quoted by Senator Edward Kennedy at the memorial service
after Robert Kennedy was assassinated in June 1968

Among the less remembered events in Britain in the summer of 1968 were a revolt
of members of the British Film Institute led by a struggling but high-principled
film maker called Maurice Hatton, the coming together of an obscure media
pressure group called the Free Communications Group and the start of new,
eight-year ITV franchises.

* * *

It is hardly surprising that three such seemingly disparate events are remembered
today by only a handful of people. Even at the time they barely registered beyond
the circle of those directly involved in them. In the first six months of 1968 there
were so many other, more momentous events to claim people's attention. In
January Alexnder Dubček had become First Secretary of the Czech Communist
Party. Political dissidents had started to be freed, restrictions on writers, artists and
broadcasters were being lifted. Backed by the regimes of Tito in Yugoslavia and
Ceauçescu in Romania, 'the Prague Spring' was dawning. By early summer, despite
continuing pressure on Dubček from Moscow, it appeared that 'Communism
with a human face' might really be possible in eastern Europe.

In March 1968 the US government announced the death of the 20,000th
American serviceman in the war in Vietnam. Three days later an American army
unit, led by a Lieutenant Calley, massacred a hundred defenceless Vietnamese
men, women and children in the village of My Lai. Across the United States anti-
war demonstrations escalated in scale and violence. At the end of March US

7

President Lyndon Johnson astonished the world by announcing that he was standing down from the US presidential election due that autumn. Five days later, on 4 April, the Nobel Prize-winning black American leader, Martin Luther King, was shot dead by a white assassin as he stood on his hotel balcony in Memphis, Tennessee. Rioting broke out across America. Shops and homes were ransacked, more than five thousand fires were started, 70,000 soldiers and National Guardsmen were called in. Over the next five days 24,000 people were arrested, thirty-six blacks and four whites were killed. In early May a Poor People's March set out for Washington. On 5 June Robert Kennedy, the leading Democrat candidate for the presidential election, was shot dead by a Palestinian Arab in a Los Angeles hotel where he was holding a primary election victory rally.

Just across the English Channel in May 1968 agitation among students on the university campus at Nanterre on the outskirts of Paris escalated into a nation-wide campaign of direct action against the government of President de Gaulle. Riot police responded to peaceful protestors with tear-gas and bullets. Barricades went up in the centre of Paris and on 13 May workers across France came out in support of the students. A general strike began.

One small, but high-profile catalyst in the lead up to the 'May Events' in France had been the action of leading French film makers in protest at the Gaullist government's intervention in the affairs of the French cinema. On 14 February about 3,000 cinema enthusiasts, led by the stars of the French New Wave and its leading directors François Truffaut and Jean-Luc Godard, had protested in the Place du Trocadéro, outside the Cinémathèque (France's equivalent of the British Film Institute and the National Film Theatre), against the sacking of its inspirational veteran head, Henri Langlois, and his replacement by a Ministry of Culture nominee. Langlois was the man to whom France's leading film makers and cineastes attributed the rejuvenation of the French cinema over the previous decade. Langlois's offence seemed to be that he was a free spirit. This was compounded by the fact that he had refused to hand over the Cinémathèque to the government for use during state visits or for the purposes of government propaganda. Langlois had argued back. The Cinémathèque's first duty, he said, was to show as many films as possible to as many people as it could manage. The sacking of Langlois was part of a wider crackdown in the arts intended to silence dissent and establish government control over all the principal outlets of creative and political expression in France. This extended to relieving of their posts France's leading composer and conductor, Pierre Boulez, the leading actor and theatre director Jean-Louis Barrault (dismissed because he had discussed grievances with the students who had occupied his Odéon Théâtre rather than simply opposing them on behalf of the authorities) and the head of the state broadcasting organisation ORTF.

On 14 February the protestors outside the Cinémathèque had been surrounded by thirty busloads of riot police, who had moved in and broken up the demonstration with considerable force. Both Godard and Truffaut had been injured. French television did not even report the incident, dismissing it with a reference to an official government communiqué which spoke of a 'disturbance' caused by a few 'hotheads'.

As the general strike and student protests spread across France in the second week of May 1968, Truffaut, perhaps the least political of French film makers, was asked about the role of the state in the cinema: 'The state plays the role of oppressor. It treats the cinema like it treats the people – despising the young and the old, and exploiting the rest.' On 17 May, building on the organisation established by the Cinémathèque protestors, all branches of the French film industry came together in Paris under the aegis of a new organisation called the États Généraux du Cinéma to hold the first in a series of excited and heated debates. They demanded radical reform of the French film industry and to the role of the state within it. The following day Truffaut, Godard, Lelouch and others travelled south to Cannes where the annual international film festival was in full swing. They invaded the main stage, sabotaged the projection equipment and demanded the closure of the festival in the name of the États Généraux du Cinéma. Later Truffaut told people that what pleased him most about the whole of the 'May Events' was the idea that 'people were not going to obey, were never again going to obey'.[1]

In addition to the upheavals in America, Czechoslovakia and France there were riots and anti-government protests in countries as economically and politically far apart as Poland, Italy and Mexico – there had even been a small public demonstration in support of imprisoned writers in Moscow.

*　　*　　*

Against a background of such momentous events elsewhere in the world, it was hardly surprising that the three seemingly unimportant and unrelated events in Britain which I recalled at the start of this chapter paled into insignificance. When Maurice Hatton and his fellow BFI member protestors staged their revolt in early

June 1968, they were probably almost as much influenced by recent events in France, by the protests of film workers and the excited meetings of the États Généraux du Cinéma in Paris, as they were by their own specific grievances against the policies of the British Film Institute.

In 1968 the BFI was in receipt of an annual government grant of £400,000 from the Department of Education and Science. With this, plus the modest subscriptions of its members, it operated both the National Film Archive and the National Film Theatre. It also maintained a specialist library devoted to all aspects of film making and screen culture. The BFI acted as a vital resource and meeting ground for cineastes and young, would-be film makers – in 1968 there was no National Film School and few specialised film courses. The prime duty of the BFI was, in the words of its constitution, to promote and encourage the 'art of film'. This the Institute did mainly through its programme of film exhibitions, publications and work in education. In addition to all this, since 1952 the BFI had had a small fund with which it could finance the production of films which might not otherwise get made – initially called the Experimental Film Fund, latterly the BFI Production Board. Over the previous fifteen years this fund had helped to finance early films by many young film makers who had subsequently gone on to enter the mainstream film and television industries and win wider recognition.[2] They included Karel Reisz, Tony Richardson, Ken Russell, Jack Gold, Claude Goretta, Alain Tanner, Jon Irvin and many others who were to play leading roles in this story.

The money available to this production fund was extremely limited – about £10,000 each year. With this it could normally fund some fifteen short films a year – occasionally it might part-fund a longer feature film with other co-production partners. Those who got grants often shot, edited and wrote the films themselves. If the director needed to employ any other technicians the BFI had an arrangement with the main film union, the ACTT,[3] under which full union rates did not have to be paid. It went without saying that the film maker himself worked unpaid. Only in the unlikely event of his film being shown commercially in cinemas or on television and then going on to make a profit did the film maker receive any money.

There was no shortage of people eager to get BFI funding. Between two and four thousand people applied to the BFI Production Board each year. As the 1960s had progressed ever more people from a growing range of social backgrounds and wider spectrum of aesthetic and political viewpoints aspired to make films. For those on the political left cinema was of particular interest. In the 1960s many remembered that Lenin himself had told his followers in the early idealistic years immediately after the Russian Revolution, when he and his fellow revolutionaries had been trying to forge a new culturally and socially progressive state out of the sprawling, down trodden Russian Empire, 'Film is the most important art for us.' By 1968 the new generation, inspired by the films and utterances of film makers from other countries such as Jean-Luc Godard and Chris Marker, or motivated by the writings of Raymond Williams which highlighted the centrality of popular cultural forms in reforming society, were eager to bring fresh aesthetic and political values to British cinema. What they saw in Britain was a cinema dominated to an extent unequalled elsewhere in Europe by safe commercialism, subjugated to the commercial requirements of the two major British film distributors, Rank and ABC, and in thrall to the values of Hollywood. Ninety per cent of films registered as British were financed with American money.

To the aspiring young film makers of 1968 the conventional feature film industry remained remote, as closed to new entrants as it was to new ideas. It was true, as defenders of the British cinema were quick to point out, that since the 1950s some new subject matter, new performers and new directors had broken through into the commercial mainstream with films such as *Saturday Night and Sunday Morning* (1960) and *A Taste of Honey* (1961). But this had largely been on the back of the commercial success of the Royal Court Theatre, of John Osborne's *Look Back in Anger* and Joan Littlewood's Theatre Workshop. The gulf between the aspirations of the growing body of eager, young would-be film makers and their fulfilment still remained as wide as ever. Even those determined, ingenious and lucky enough to succeed in getting a short film made, even those who did better still and had their films selected for showing in a club cinema or on television, were usually no nearer to being able to enter the conventional film industry and make films that would be shown in high-street cinemas. Even success in the precariously small art-house cinema sector generally counted for nothing with the commercial film industry. No matter how much praise a film might win at festivals or the critical attention it might gain as a result of a few showings at Derek Hill's New Cinema Club, it was no passport into the feature film industry for its struggling director. It was not even a limited entry permit. Not only was the British commercial feature film industry irredeemably cautious and conservative, the industry trade unions maintained strict control over who could work in the industry.

A would-be new entrant to the feature film industry, even to a junior technical grade such as assistant film-editor or a junior job in a camera crew, found the doors to the industry effectively closed. One of the BFI's policy objectives was to establish a national film school, of similar standing to those in Poland and the USA, which would offer high-calibre training qualifying its alumni to work in the film industry. In 1968 only two film technicians in the previous three years had entered the industry from such schools as then existed in Britain.[4] The main technicians' union, the ACTT, mindful of the extensive cutbacks in feature film production and work for technicians which had followed the introduction of commercial television in 1955, maintained what amounted to a 'closed shop'. Any would-be film maker seeking work in the feature film industry, even in the most junior technical grade, let alone as a director, faced a catch-22 situation: in order to be considered for a vacancy in a studio or a one-off job on a particular production, he, or unusually she, had to be a member of the union – to 'have a ticket'. But in order to be eligible for union membership you already had to have a job in a recognised union grade. Only if it could be shown that no existing union member could be found who was available and willing to do the job, might a non-member be considered for the post and, with it, for membership of the union.

Even supposing the aspirant film maker cleared all these hurdles, he was still faced with an array of obstacles. New entrants to the union were usually restricted for a period of two years to working in the same job, or grade. Even after this 'probationary period' had expired, individual union shops or committees could put restrictions on an individual's movement between jobs or kinds of work. It often seemed that, having got in themselves, members of the union became determined to make sure that no one else followed them.

As a consequence of the double stranglehold maintained over the mainstream feature film industry by conservative bosses and protectionist trades unions, would-be film makers had to devise other means of getting their films made and seen, and to find other ways of getting into the industry. Sponsored film making was the route in for many. Major companies and government agencies such as Shell, the Ford Motor Company, the National Coal Board and the Central Office of Information maintained their own small film-making departments which made short films for use in company training programmes, the dissemination of information within the organisation or for external promotion of the company and its products. Although these film-making departments were unionised, they were small and the jobs within them less sought after by the feature film technicians. As a result opportunities sometimes arose for non-union members to apply successfully for jobs in them. Once in, the person would be eligible for union membership and, because the departments were small, opportunities for advancement and for learning a number of different skills were greater. In addition to big companies that maintained their own film-making departments, there were other companies, institutions or campaign groups that occasionally wanted short films made – CND, Oxfam, British Rail and the Reed paper company all sponsored notable short films during the 1950s and 1960s. The films of the Free Cinema Movement – such as *We Are the Lambeth Boys* and *Every Day Except Christmas* – which gave early breaks to directors like Lindsay Anderson, Karel Reisz and Tony Richardson, had been made through sponsorship. As a result of such sponsorship a number of small independent companies had sprung up. Often run on co-operative lines, they produced films for sponsors and supplied facilities – camera and sound equipment, editing rooms or crews to others. Many of these little companies were in Soho, in the narrow streets and up the rickety staircases of buildings formerly occupied by the clothing trade. Those who worked in them were generally like-minded, that is to say left-minded. Geographically and politically close to each other, eking out a living between one commission and another, they tended to eat in the same small Soho restaurants and drink in the same pubs. Here they discussed new projects, agreed to lend each other equipment, swapped news and debated the latest political developments. Around this loose nucleus floated a fluctuating cloud of freelances, aspirant film makers and beginners. Insecure but united in their enthusiasm for films and film making they made up an admirably tolerant, open and progressive community. With their shared sympathies and common insecurity, individuals and companies often combined together to help each other to get their films made. Many a new project or professional relationship was forged as a result of a chance meeting in the Intrepid Fox, or fresh industry campaign planned in eager conversation in the George in Wardour Street.

The history of this informal network of personal, unfunded or semi-funded film making has been documented by Margaret Dickinson in her book *Rogue Reels*.[5] Dickinson herself entered the film industry as a general trainee in the film department of Siddeley Engines in Bristol in 1965. Describing her own experience working as a cutting-room assistant at MGM in 1966, she says that of the twelve assistant film editors that she knew, three were 'making their own unfunded experimental films' in their spare time. In 1968, when she was editing a film at Dateline, a small independent company in Soho established four years earlier by one of the original members of the Free Cinema Movement, John Fletcher, Dickinson found that 'all the people permanently associated with the company had worked for free on their own or other people's productions, and the cutting rooms were regularly borrowed at evenings or weekends by people making unfunded films, practices no one regarded as unusual'.

Maurice Hatton, the prime mover in the BFI members' revolt in the summer of 1968, was himself a typical member of this loose community of film makers and the revolt itself largely stemmed from their frustrations. While working as a photographer for the arts pages of the *Guardian* in the early 1960s, Hatton had met the journalist Bruce Page, then working on 'The Londoner's Diary' at the *Evening Standard*. Page shared a flat with two friends, one of whom, Jon Irvin, was an assistant film editor at J. Arthur Rank. (Irvin and Bruce had originally met when each of them had stopped to barrack a National Front speaker outside Earls Court tube station.) At the time when Hatton met Bruce, Irvin was twenty-three years old and had just been awarded one of the coveted BFI Experimental Film Fund grants to make a film about the annual Miners' Gala and street parade in Durham. Hatton, who was twenty-five, was eager to work on film and told Page that he would love to work on Irvin's film. As a result Hatton was taken on as a fourth cameraman. He, Irvin, another friend and Richard de la Mare, the grandson of the poet, set up a company together through which to make the film. Among the company names on offer to them through their solicitor had been Mithras. 'Richard told us that Mithras was the sun god in Greek mythology and was generous to women – and we felt that! So we chose that one.'[6] Using a 16 mm hand-held Arriflex camera Hatton turned out to be as adept with a movie camera as he had been with a press camera. 'Maurice got wonderful stuff. He didn't hold back and observe, he got into the middle of it and went with the flow.'

Irvin and Hatton's film proved a considerable critical success, winning a British Academy Award. More short films had followed and in 1964, in the run-up to the general election, Mithras won the contract to make films for the Labour Party. But even though they were relatively successful, not enough money came in from their company's film making to support all four partners. They survived by all chipping in everything they earned, from whatever source, to a joint pot from which they each drew £50 per week.

By the spring of 1968 Hatton was attempting to set up a 90-minute fiction film. He had got together a few thousand pounds and some film stock and with this he approached a number of young technicians and actors, offering each £30 a week to work on his film. Among those who agreed was a quiet young man called Stephen Frears, who since coming down from Cambridge had worked at the Royal Court as an assistant to Lindsay Anderson and with Karel Reisz on his film *Morgan: A Suitable Case for Treatment*, as an assistant director. Another was Charles Stewart, a 29-year-old lighting cameraman. He recalls, 'Maurice didn't have enough money – he would never tell us how much he had got – but he just went ahead and blagged laboratories into doing the lab work and equipment suppliers into letting us have stuff.'

It is worth briefly outlining the plot of Hatton's film, as it provides an insight not only into Hatton's own attitudes but into the prevailing atmosphere and politics of many of those who were later to play crucial roles in this story. Entitled *Praise Marx and Pass the Ammunition*, Hatton's film was set in the present – that is in the spring of 1968. While putting the case for radical social change in Britain, it was at the same time an ironic take on the futility of much contemporary revolutionary activity. It provides an interesting and not entirely complimentary picture of the intensely self-absorbed small revolutionary groups that proliferated in the late 1960s, groups of the kind that Hatton and those involved in the small independent film production community knew well. The plot concerns the activities of one such small revolutionary group – 'The Revolutionary Party of the Third World' – membership rising twenty-five. Called upon by his party to go to Paris to take part in the 'May events', the film's protagonist, Dom (played by a young John Thaw), returns injured – not because of taking part in any heroic revolutionary struggle, but because he has jammed his hand in a door. When the film was released in the late autumn of 1969 (at Derek Hill's New Cinema Club), Jan Dawson, reviewing it for the BFI's magazine *Sight and Sound*, wrote that it represented a very considerable achievement by Hatton. On a total budget of only £25,000 (less than one tenth of the cost of a modest feature film at the time), he had 'succeeded in capturing the full, self-absorbed, conspiratorial flavour of radical politics among the Suez generation . . . combining dedicated intellectual activity with tortuous apologies for their own gracious living'. Although in France and Czechoslovakia the revolutionary path may appear straight, Dawson observed, 'on the home front it is still a question of selecting the slogan for the latest poster and agitating on the margins of minor industrial disputes'.[7]

Hatton's film, like most films made for the cinema, had been shot on 35 mm film. However, by the late 1960s the survival of the informal, activist community of film makers to which people like Hatton and Irvin belonged, largely depended on recent advances in the quality of 16 mm film stock and equipment. Over the previous decade a new generation of lightweight 16 mm cameras and portable sound tape recorders, pioneered in France, Switzerland and America, had been introduced. Allied with dramatic increases in the sensitivity of film stock, these had transformed the way in which films could be made. Crucially for the small production companies around Soho, the television companies had decided that this new generation of equipment and film stocks was of sufficiently high quality to be used in the making of television programmes.[8] In consequence many small companies in Soho were able to survive largely by hiring out their equipment and services for making location inserts for television dramas and documentaries. The increased contact that came about was to prove an important factor in transmitting aesthetic and political ideas between those working in the independent film community and those working in television. As well as offering young film makers a means of economic survival, these technical advances seemed to open up tantalising new possibilities for both documentary and fiction. Frustrated in Britain, they looked ever more enviously across the Channel to France and to other European countries with governments and cultural institutions which had film policies that took account of their own cultural and local needs.

The result was that by the late 1960s an increasingly unreasonable weight of expectation and frustrated idealism had become concentrated on the BFI, on its choice of films for exhibition at the National Film Theatre and its regional film theatres, on its educational work and the operation of the National Film Archive, and particularly on its small production fund. Discontent had been fermenting among the BFI's membership for some time. For more than a year there had been a growing volume of complaints about the BFI's governors. Their critics accused them of allowing the commercial cinema bosses among their number to exert undue influence on the Institute's cultural activities and on its attitude to the work of film makers who operated outside the commercial mainstream.

The BFI's governors were appointed by the minister with responsibility for the arts in the Ministry of Education. Late in 1967 two BFI governors, Lindsay Anderson and Karel Reisz, had resigned. Anderson and Reisz had made little secret of their unhappiness with the internal functioning of the Institute and let it be known that they thought that an external inquiry was needed.

The assault launched on the BFI by Hatton and his colleagues in early June

1968 went much further than previous attacks. Claiming that the Institute was being run by a small clique and was out of touch with the new generation, they put forward proposals for a reformed organisation to take its place. In an open letter to Jennie Lee, the minister responsible for the arts in Harold Wilson's Labour government, they not only attacked the BFI's proliferating bureaucracy and inefficient use of its resources, demanding an inquiry, but called for altered priorities in the BFI's allocation of funds, a greater concentration on the work of British film makers and the creation of a new organisation to be called Cinetec International. Between them, the signatories to the letter lined up by Hatton and his colleagues constituted a formidable cross-section of progressive figures in the arts – film, theatre and television. They included Tony Richardson, John Schlesinger, Clive Donner, Paul Rotha, Joan Littlewood, Susannah York, Sean Kenney, Ken Loach and Tony Garnett.

When the letter was published it gained wide support from other screen publications, from young film makers and students. The Institute's response, fronted by BFI governor and leading documentary film maker from an earlier generation, Edgar Anstey, claimed that the real problem with the BFI was that its finances were inadequate for the amount of work it was called upon to perform.

A few weeks later the Arts Minister, Jennie Lee, responded with an open letter of her own. She dismissed the protest, calling the letter 'a rather odd way of going about things'. Pointing out that government aid to the Institute had trebled in the four years since Labour had come to power, she acknowledged that with all the calls on the BFI's funds there had still 'unfortunately not been much over to help young film makers'. But, she insisted, she had not 'been backward' in discussing the BFI's financial needs with the Treasury. The BFI's problems, she said, 'must be overcome as soon as more funds can be found'.[9]

Later that autumn the governors instigated a series of open meetings at the National Film Theatre about different aspects of the BFI's work. The intention, the governors said, was to allow members to ask questions and voice their complaints. The meetings, however, were poorly attended and petered out. The Director of the Institute, Stanley Reed, concluded that members were not seriously interested in the points raised by Hatton's group and that support for the protestors was not as widespread as it had seemed.

The significance of the Hatton-led BFI revolt was not so much what it achieved; it could fairly be said to have achieved nothing (although a further revolt by many of the same people three years later did win concessions). Its significance lay in the way in which it had brought together a community of interest around specific demands and in the nature of those demands.

*   *   *

'Returning that summer from "the Paris May", full of German revolutionary theory and fervour, I heard from Gus Macdonald that he wanted to talk to me' – Neal Ascherson, who was the foreign correspondent of the *Observer*. In the spring and early summer of 1968 Ascherson had covered protests, revolts and student uprisings all over Europe. He was, therefore, somewhat surprised when he met Macdonald (a young journalist and television researcher) and a colleague in a Fleet Street pub to discover that what they wanted to talk about were the lessons to be learnt from recent events at ORTF – the French state broadcasting organisation – and the de Gaulle government's absolute determination to retain control of broadcasting.

The problems at ORTF had arisen independently of the rest of the wave of protests and strikes across France. Just as the protests had been beginning in the spring of 1968 a report about ORTF, previously ordered by the French Senate, had been published. The *Diligent Report* (after its chief architect André Diligent) had criticised bias in ORTF's news. (ORTF was under the direct control of the French government to a far greater degree than the BBC or most of the other state broadcasters in the democratic world and ORTF journalists had long resented the level of government interference in their work). As the wave of protests had swept across France matters at ORTF had come to a head. On the evening when a report on the student strike at the Sorbonne by the prestigious ORTF current affairs programme *Panorama* was due to be transmitted, officials from the French Ministries of Education and Information had driven to the ORTF studios and given orders that the programme was not to be transmitted. The workers at ORTF, led by many of French television's best-known journalists and reporters, had responded by going on strike. The strikers had gained widespread popular support, being hailed as heroes at well-attended mass meetings in towns all across France. Despite threats and the mounting of a skeleton service, the Gaullist government had been unable to force the strikers into submission for eleven weeks. Even then the strikers had only returned to work following government promises of reform. But, once the government had re-asserted its control, it had ordered that ORTF be 'compressed'. One hundred journalists were sacked or moved to jobs in the provinces.

Macdonald told Ascherson that he saw the events at ORTF as of more significance than the success of the student movement in igniting a nationwide wave of strikes. The 'desperation of the regime in France to recapture broadcasting', he told Ascherson, was 'very revealing'. Surely, the French government's actions showed that the regime recognised that capture of the media offered a direct route to the mobilisation of the working class? Ascherson's response must have disappointed Macdonald and his colleague: 'It hadn't really occurred to me that capture of the media was that important.'[10]

Today the mood and language of that pub conversation may seem outlandishly apocalyptic and revolutionary. Yet, as recalled by Ascherson, it accurately reflects the discourse and ideas of a large body of young and articulate people who were politically, socially and creatively active at the time. As with the young film makers, a variety of factors going back to the end of the Second World War had contributed to this mood. More than twenty years of European peace, full employment, unparalleled prosperity and universal secondary education, combined with growing access to cheap, convenient foreign travel, the spread of television, exposure to international tastes in popular music, fashion, films and magazines had produced a youth with tastes and attitudes which were very different from those of their parents. Ideas and tastes that caught the imagination of the new generation of one country could rapidly enthuse their contemporaries in others. Although there had been no upheavals to match the scale of those in France or the divisions caused in America by race and the Vietnam war, by the time that Ascherson and Macdonald met to discuss *les événements de Paris* in their London pub there was growing evidence of conflict in Britain. In 1967, the year when the Beatles' *Sergeant Pepper* had been released, the year of the 'Flower Power Summer', there had been a student sit-in at the London School of Economics resulting in the intervention of the police. There had been a currency crisis, followed by devaluation of the pound after which the Prime Minister, Harold Wilson, had had to appear on television to assure the nation that it did not mean that 'the pound in your pocket' was worth one penny less. In January 1968 the government had announced large cuts in public expenditure. These were followed by big tax increases. In March 25,000 people, mostly students, had marched on the American Embassy in Grosvenor Square chanting 'Ho Ho Ho Chi Minh!'[11] and demanding an end to the Vietnam War. While still not remotely approaching the violence in Paris or the USA, the protestors had thrown firecrackers in among the horses of the mounted police guarding the embassy. When the police charged, the protestors rolled marbles under the hooves of the horses. This caused outrage among respectable older people, who seemed more concerned about the welfare of the horses than of the students or even the police. A total of 177 policemen were hurt and 246 protestors were charged with offences. The whole spectacle was watched by millions on national television.

The following month Barbara Castle, the Secretary of State at the Department of Employment, was charged by Harold Wilson with reforming the trades unions and reducing the number of unofficial 'wildcat' strikes.[12] That spring, as the strikes and student protests in Paris reached a climax, student protests broke out at Oxford, Cambridge, Essex, Sussex, Manchester and Aston universities and at art colleges in Guildford and Hornsey.[13] The immediate causes of the student protests varied, but all had in common a desire for a greater student voice in determining the curriculum and in matters of discipline.

It was no coincidence that British students' demands were similar to demands voiced by students across Europe and the United States. By the late 1960s there existed, to an extent that would previously have been impossible, what Joan Bakewell (herself an icon of the age) describes as a 'general international intellectual and creative, often oppositional, mafia interested in freedom – freedom of expression, freedom to live life on their own terms'.[14] In their conversation in that London pub in the summer of 1968, Neal Ascherson and Gus Macdonald were reflecting this new climate. Although some people in positions of power would later try to claim that their meeting, and more specifically the group that eventually came together as a result of it, represented something sinister or revolutionary, Ascherson and Macdonald were doing no more than exploring what lessons recent events might hold for young and progressive-minded people in their own fields – broadcasting and the press.

The fact that Ascherson and Macdonald should meet in a pub to discuss ideas in the way that they did was itself an illustration of the way in which the new interest in freedom of expression and in ideas perceived in some quarters as oppositional was, by 1968, bringing together people from different backgrounds. Only a generation earlier the differences between Ascherson and Macdonald would almost certainly have kept them apart. Ascherson was thirty-five years old. After education at Eton and King's College, Cambridge, and national service in the Royal Marines, he had quickly won recognition as a journalist with the *Guardian* and the *Observer*, becoming its Central European correspondent. In

1968 he was made the *Observer*'s East European correspondent. Macdonald, by contrast, was still in his twenties. He had left school at fifteen to become an apprentice marine fitter in a Clyde shipyard, becoming a shop steward by his early twenties. He had been a member of the Young Socialists National Committee and the leader of the Gorbals and Govan Young Socialists in the 1950s. In his mid-twenties he had got a job as circulation manager of *Tribune* magazine and moved to London. There he wrote occasional leaders for *Tribune*, became editor of *Anti-Apartheid News* and began to work part-time with Bruce Page on the *Sunday Times' Insight* team. In 1967 he had been offered two jobs, one by Harry Evans on the *Sunday Times*, the other by Granada Television with their new current affairs programmes research bureau. When the Granada executive re-sponsible for setting up the bureau, David Plowright, heard that the *Sunday Times* was also after Macdonald, he had told his Granada boss, Denis Forman, to send the company's executive aircraft to fetch Macdonald down to Manchester: 'He's a working-class socialist, that'll clinch it,' said Plowright. Macdonald does not remember that any aircraft actually came to take him to Manchester. What really clinched his decision to go to Granada, he says, was that while he was waiting around to see Forman and Plowright it was suggested that he might like to join some young Granada producers who were watching films with a group of visiting Chinese. This was when the Maoist Cultural Revolution was at its height in China and Granada was eager to get permission to enter the country with cameras. When Macdonald sat down at the back of the darkened viewing theatre the film on the screen was showing heroic Chinese soldiers, swords drawn, entering a dark and evil capitalist atomic cloud. The Granada producers were manfully suppressing any tendency to giggle at this ludicrous scene and being intensely polite to their Chinese guests. 'This could be an interesting place to work,' Macdonald had decided.[15] By the summer of 1968, when Macdonald and Ascherson met in that pub to discuss *les événements de Paris* the differences between them mattered less than the things that united them – a shared socialism, a serious concern with the media and a conviction that fundamental change was needed.

That year, 1968 was the one in which television finally overtook the press as the most important medium of news. At the end of his life Dennis Potter would describe the period from the late 1960s into the 1970s as television's 'golden age'. 'But,' Potter added, 'we wouldn't have thanked you for telling us so.'[16] Looking back today, it does indeed seem a golden age. At the BBC *The Wednesday Play* was at the pinnacle of its achievement – the years 1965–8 saw new plays from Potter himself, from David Mercer, John Hopkins, Jim Allen, Alan Plater and many more, directed and produced by brilliant programme makers such as Ken Loach, Jack Gold, Tony Garnett, James McTaggart and Kenith Trodd. The titles alone conjure up a sense of television's golden, lost past – *Alice, Stand Up Nigel Barton, Vote Vote Vote for Nigel Barton, Where the Buffalo Roam* (all by Potter), *And Did Those Feet, In Two Minds, The Parachute, Let's Murder Vivaldi, On the Eve of Publication* (Mercer), *The Lump* (Jim Allen), *Up the Junction* (Nell Dunn), *Cathy Come Home* (Jeremy Sandford) and John Hopkins' quartet *Talking To a Stranger* which George Melly, writing in the *Observer*, called 'the first authentic master-piece written directly for television'.[17] To those who bemoaned the state of the film industry, people working in television could confidently respond: 'The British film industry is alive and well, and living in television.' Even series intended primarily as popular entertainment such as *Z Cars* and *The Forsyte Saga* seemed to aspire to new levels of creative and social relevance. Comedy included *Till Death Do Us Part* and *Dad's Army* as well as *The Morecambe and Wise Show*. Personal documentary and arts films flourished – Ken Russell's portrait of the dancer Isadora Duncan, *Isadora* (1966), and his film about Delius, *Song of Summer* (1968); Tony Palmer's Beatles film *All My Loving* (1968) and the series *One Pair of Eyes*. The distinguished theatre critic T. C. Worsley said such work deserved the same respect as major new works for the theatre or cinema.[18] So why were Dennis Potter and his contemporaries so reluctant to acknowledge that they were living through some kind of golden age? Why were they so rebellious? In order to begin to understand one has to look back briefly to what had happened to broadcasting since 1960.

In 1960 ITV had been on the air for just over four years. After a rocky start, it had grabbed 70% of the available television audience from the BBC. In the same year Hugh Carleton Greene had been made Director-General of the BBC and the government (led by Prime Minister Harold Macmillan) had set up a commit-tee of inquiry, under the chairmanship of Sir Harry Pilkington the head of a family glass-making firm, to look into the whole future of broadcasting and the possible allocation of a new, third television channel. As the new Director-General of the BBC, Greene had set himself two immediate tasks – to win back BBC television's share of the audience to a level of at least 50:50 with ITV and to persuade the Pilkington Committee that the BBC should be given the right to operate the new third television channel. To this end Greene had set about opening 'the windows and dissipating the ivory tower stuffiness which still clung to some parts of the BBC'. He aimed 'to make the BBC a place where talent of all sorts, however unconventional, was recognised and nurtured'.[19] In pursuit of those aims Greene had got rid of older, more cautious people and promoted younger, more adventurous ones. Old programmes had been scrapped and new ones introduced – *Z Cars* in contrast to *Dixon of Dock Green*,[20] *Maigret*, *Steptoe and Son*, *Gallery*, Ken Russell's *Elgar* and *That Was The Week That Was*.

Greene's campaign, which he himself would later describe as a form of 'psychological warfare' (he had been Head of the Psychological Warfare Department during the Malayan emergency in the 1950s), was aimed at 'unselling ITV' in order to build up the standing of the BBC. He was so successful that when the Pilkington Committee reported in June 1962, the BBC had been garlanded with praise and ITV condemned as an unmitigated, tasteless disaster. As a result the BBC had been given the immediate go-ahead to start BBC-2.

When adverts had appeared in the national press in March 1963, inviting people to apply to work for the new BBC-2, they had revealed a huge dammed-up reservoir of frustrated young people all eager to work in television. At least 10,000 people had replied to the adverts and over 6,000 sent in completed application forms. From these the BBC selected some 700 people for interview. Finally slightly over 400 had been given jobs. Over the next few months the age of the people working around the BBC could be been seen to drop as these new people, and others brought in in accordance with Greene's new policies, had taken up their posts. Many of these new recruits had come more or less direct from university. Once inside the BBC, they had started to live what one of them has called 'a protected lifestyle', in which there was time and an enthusiasm for a 'continuous debate' about the nature and purpose of broadcasting. Like many of the aspirant film makers then scrabbling around to establish a toehold in the film industry, many of those who had joined the BBC in the early 1960s were influenced by the thinking of Raymond Williams and his ideas about culture. Williams argued that, in contrast to much of Europe, the BBC itself had only come into existence as an non-commercial public service institution independent of detailed state supervision as a consequence of Britain having had an unusually compact and cohesive ruling class, and a clear idea of both the national culture and of the national interest. However, by the early 1960s that ruling class was under challenge and the cultural consensus was breaking down. In 1956, when Jimmy Porter had raged in *Look Back in Anger* at the values of the old ruling class and culture, educated members of the younger generation had stood and cheered. As a result, by the end of the 1960s, as one of the intake that joined the BBC at the start of BBC-2 put it, 'The lunatics had taken over the asylum.' Carleton Greene was sympathetic to the mood of this new generation. Indeed, his assistant Colin Shaw, who had played a key role in recruitment for BBC-2, asserts that 'The asylum was better for being taken over.'[21]

Even after BBC-2 started, the numbers employed by the BBC had continued to grow rapidly – rising by 40% between 1960 and 1968. But the BBC's system of promotions, staff appointments, gradations of pay and status had remained very much the same as it had been ever since the 1920s when the founding Director-General, Sir John Reith, had modelled it on the system in operation in the civil service. Although there were pockets of the BBC where a more freewheeling and self-governing style of personnel and resources management prevailed – in the single plays and arts documentary departments, for instance – throughout most of the rest of the Corporation an armed forces or civil service model still persisted. George Orwell was famously said to have based *Nineteen Eighty-Four* on his experiences while working in the BBC in the 1940s. By 1968 such a system had become hopelessly inappropriate as a means of retaining the loyalty of a creative and often iconoclastic workforce.

A couple of my own early experiences of the BBC may give an idea of what I mean. In 1963 I, like thousands of others, applied to work for BBC-2. As I had worked in the theatre and already made a couple of short 16 mm films I was invited to appear before the final selection board. Asked to talk to them about some of my programme ideas, I rattled on for some minutes about whatever two or three programmes I was most burning to make at that moment. When I finally paused for long enough to draw breath one of the panel said heavily, 'Yes. Well. The trouble with you, Mr Darlow, is that you only seem to want to make programmes about things that you either know rather a lot about or care rather a lot about.' With more honesty than good interview technique, I shot back, 'Yes, and the trouble with the BBC is that it is full of people making programmes about things that they neither know anything about nor care anything about.' Needless to say, I was not offered a job. However, a documentary series producer at the BBC in Bristol, who had seen one of my short films, asked me to make a film for him. A few months later he asked me to return to the BBC to make more films. But when I got there I found that, without me being told, the series I had been going to work on had been cancelled and I had been assigned to work on a game show. The BBC management's reasoning was that someone of the correct grade was needed to fill the role, I was the right grade, so I would do it. Consulting me in advance did not come into it. I served the minimum time on my contract and left.

The 1960s were an era of corporate and organisational giantism. An era when it was believed that one giant organisation run from the centre must be more efficient than a number smaller self-managing units. Harold Wilson and Labour had got into office in 1964 on a promise of bringing 'the white hot heat of the technological revolution'. Groups of ailing British manufacturing companies had been amalgamated into single giant corporations run from the centre in pursuit of efficiency. The BBC had not remained exempt from such fashions. However, as departments had grown and management become more remote, creative people had found the system becoming less and less responsive. The self-defeating inflexibility of the system became strikingly apparent in 1965 when three of its brightest younger television executives, Donald Baverstock, Controller of BBC-1, Alasdair Milne, the head of the programme group responsible for *Tonight*, *That Was The Week That Was*, *The Great War* series and many more, and Antony Jay – like Milne and Baverstock a former editor of *Tonight* – left and set up their own independent production company – JBM. They got work making films for a computer company and supplying services to a couple of ITV companies. However, when they approached the BBC and asked about JBM making pro-grammes for the Corporation they were rebuffed: 'We don't need you.' The BBC was fully staffed with people of its own. Three very experienced producers, who had until then been regarded by the BBC and their creative colleagues as among the most talented and important creative liberating influences inside the BBC, were superfluous.[22] By the late 1960s things had reached such a point that when David Attenborough, the Controller of BBC-2, told the Drama Department that he wanted to cancel a returning series he was told that he couldn't. The sets were already being built by the scenery department and they couldn't be stopped.

Today it is sometimes hard to credit just how old-fashioned Britain had remained until well into the 1960s. When Kenneth Tynan had uttered the word 'fuck' on television in *BBC-3*, a late-night satirical show, on 13 November 1965 it had seemed that the nation was about to have collective heart attack. The fact that he had used the word in a neutral way to illustrate a serious point was irrelevant. Newspaper headlines trumpeted 'Insult to Womanhood' and a *Daily Express* correspondent called it 'the bloodiest outrage' he had 'ever known'. MPs called for the dismissal of the Director-General and the Prime Minister had had to answer questions. As recently as the end of 1960 the prosecuting counsel in the *Lady Chatterley's Lover* trial had been able to ask in all seriousness if jurors would 'approve of your young sons, young daughters – because girls can read as well as boys – reading this book'. Was D. H. Lawrence's novel ' . . . a book that you would have lying around in your house? Is it a book that you would even wish your wife or your servants to read?' For all the 1960s' remembered permissiveness, Mary Quant miniskirts, the Beatles and girls on the Pill, homosexual acts between consenting adults in private had not been decriminalised until 1967 and it was the end of 1967 before women were granted a limited right to seek a medical abortion. Theatre censorship, introduced in the reign of James I and carried out by an official of the royal household, the Lord Chamberlain, continued in force until July 1968.

Just how out of touch with the new post-war generation many of those in positions of responsibility remained was highlighted by their attitudes towards women. Even in the late 1960s a woman like Joan Bakewell, who presented the low-budget late evening BBC-2 television programme *Late Night Line-Up*, was a rarity. Although sometimes dismissively described by the press as 'the thinking man's crumpet', Bakewell's intelligence was recognised and she was not expected to conceal it simply because she was a woman. The normal attitude that prevailed was graphically revealed by what happened when Bakewell and some of her female colleagues from the BBC Presentation Department went to see their boss to suggest that a woman should sometimes read the news. 'It will never happen', they were told, their voices and clothes would be too distracting. As the delegation left, Bakewell said, 'We'll be back!'[23]

As a woman in a high-profile job who was recognised as both attractive and intelligent, Bakewell and her show's fame spread beyond the narrow confines of the British intelligentsia. When Václav Havel, the Czech dissident writer and one of the leaders of the Prague Spring, arrived unannounced at Heathrow and was stopped by immigration officials who wanted to know what he was doing in Britain, he told them that he had come to be interviewed by Joan Bakewell on *Late Night Line-Up*. He was immediately waved through. Nevertheless there still remained limits as to what even someone of Bakewell's fame and intellectual standing was permitted to discuss on the air. When she interviewed Daniel Cohn-Bendit, one of the French student protest leaders, she and her colleagues were summoned by their BBC boss and accused of 'trying to overthrow the democratically elected government of this country'. 'No,' Bakewell replied, 'we are trying to explore ideas from every point of view.'

However, despite the rumblings of possible future revolt among the staff, and whatever the irritations, bureaucracy and the occasional Orwellianisms of the management, the vast majority of those who worked for the BBC still knew that the overriding purpose of the whole institution was to make the best programmes of every kind to the highest standards. They still had ample reason to believe that their bosses, people of the calibre of Greene, Huw Wheldon, Michael Peacock, David Attenborough, Humphrey Burton and Sydney Newman, were as excited by programmes as they were themselves.

Whatever the pressures might be inside it, throughout the 1960s the most serious pressures on the BBC had come from outside it. Above all they had come from Harold Wilson and the Labour government. Ever since the creation of the BBC by Sir John Reith in the 1920s, the relationship between it and the government had been ambiguous, the BBC being, at the same time, both the state broadcaster and editorially independent of the government. At times of national crisis, particularly when crises had involved divisions within the country itself, this had led to tension between the BBC and whatever government was in power. As the historian A. J. P. Taylor had commented on the first, and defining, test of the BBC's position in relation to the government at the time of the General Strike in 1926: 'The vaunted independence of the BBC was secure as long as it was not exercised.'[24] Since 1960, when Greene had taken over as Director-General, determined to blow away the traditional stuffiness of the BBC and 'open the windows' to new ideas and the new generation, there had been a series of rows between the Corporation and the government or those who saw themselves as being in positions of moral authority. This series of incidents had served to raise in the minds of people like Ascherson, Macdonald and those who had recently come into broadcasting the whole question of just how independent of government and the establishment broadcasting really was.

The first big test of the relationship between the BBC under Greene and the government had come while Macmillan was still Prime Minister with the start of *That Was The Week That Was* in November 1962. Fathered by Greene himself with Alasdair Milne, produced by Ned Sherrin and introduced by a young David Frost, *That Was The Week That Was* was an entirely new kind of television programme, made up, as a BBC internal management memo put it, of 'new sketches, new songs, new and barbed portraits of leading political figures and new lyrics which embodied sharp comments on the contemporary social scene'.[25] Taking its cue from the cabaret clubs of Berlin during the Weimar Republic and many of its writers and performers from *Beyond the Fringe*, the Cambridge Footlights Club, the newly launched Establishment Club and the satirical magazine *Private Eye*, *TWTWTW* or *TW3* as it soon became popularly known, was at the centre of controversy from the start. This was not least because it was so popular. Originally expected to appeal to a small sophisticated audience of two to three million, it quickly started to draw a loyal audience of six to ten million and, at its height, of twelve million. For a late night show this was astonishing. Angus Wilson summed up the reasons for the loyalty the programme inspired among the generation which came of age in the early 1960s: 'The audience know the actors are with them against authority, the people who push them around, or try to stop them enjoying themselves; to laugh with *TW3* gives you certainty you're laughing at the bullies, the fakes and the killjoys.'[26]

"Stop laughing, you fool - they're taking the mickey out of people like us."

Anton in *Punch*, 20 March 1963

Yet in spite of its astonishing success the show had been taken off after only thirteen months. Ostensibly the reason for dropping it had been the imminence of the 1964 general election. While millions had loved *TW3*'s refreshing irreverence, wit and vitality, an increasingly vocal minority had been offended by what they saw as its smutty jokes and blasphemous attitude to authority and matters they held sacred. The programme had first arrived on people's screens towards the end of a long period of Conservative government, at the moment when the moral and social climate in the country was beginning to change and as a series of government crises and ministerial scandals became public. As the series progressed, Greene had had to defend the programme with increasing frequency at meetings of the BBC Board of Governors – over sketches about the Profumo scandal (John Profumo, the Secretary of State for War in Macmillan's government had been found out using the services of Christine Keeler, a high-class prostitute who was also consorting with a military attaché at the Soviet Embassy), jokes about the monarchy (the Governors, who by and large were drawn from the ranks of the nation's 'great and good', told *TW3*'s producers that mocking the 'mummery surrounding the crown' was 'fair game', but mocking the Queen herself or members of the Royal Family was 'going too far') and disparaging cracks about politicians. The Governors were up in arms when, in October 1963, following Macmillan's resignation, Willie Rushton appeared on the programme as Macmillan tearfully singing 'The Party's Over' and enraged again when, after it was announced that Sir Alec Douglas-Home was to succeed Macmillan as Prime Minister, the programme commented in the words of Disraeli that he was 'a pleasant man who had foreseen nothing and was qualified for nothing'. When the programme's presenter, David Frost, joked that, with Home and Wilson as the leaders of the two main political parties, the choice now before the British electorate was between 'Dull Alec and Smart Alec', politicians on all sides were outraged. One Conservative MP even called for the BBC to be impeached for holding MPs up to ridicule. After thirteen months, and in spite of the programme's continued popularity, the show was taken off.

The pressure on the BBC came not only from those whose authority its programmes questioned or mocked, but from those who were shocked by the new candour over morals, sex and the nation's institutions. In 1963, after a programme in which Dr Alex Comfort had defended premarital sex (he had suggested that a chivalrous boy was 'one who takes contraceptives with him when he goes to meet his girlfriend'), Mary Whitehouse, a Midlands school teacher with connections to the Moral Rearmament Movement, had approached the BBC and asked to meet Greene. When the BBC refused to see her or to change its policies, Whitehouse and her supporters had called a mass meeting in Birmingham town hall and launched a 'Clean Up TV' campaign. They had issued a manifesto condemning the BBC for undermining Christian family values and promoting a new morality of 'disbelief, doubt and dirt'. Their outrage increased still further when the BBC started transmitting a series of single plays called *The Wednesday Play* in October 1964. One that particularly provoked them was *Alice*, written by Dennis Potter. It explored the repressed sexual undertones of *Alice in Wonderland*. In less than six months Mary Whitehouse and her supporters had collected 365,000 signatures on a petition to Parliament calling on the BBC to institute 'a radical change of policy and produce programmes which build character instead of destroying it, which encourage and sustain faith in God, and bring Him back to the heart of the British family and national life'.[27]

Such shows of public concern affected the attitude of politicians. While Macmillan had been comparatively relaxed about the satirists' portrayals of him as some kind of unworldly left over from the Edwardian era, Wilson, when he came to power in October 1964 with a parliamentary majority of only four seats, already harboured deep suspicions of the BBC. He believed that it was biased against him. The BBC was in urgent need of a substantial increase in its licence fee. But Wilson had used the BBC's shortage of money as a lever with which to exert influence over BBC programmes. By 1965, when the BBC announced that, 'in the public interest', it would not transmit Peter Watkins' *The War Game*, it had seemed that Wilson's attempts to control the BBC were working. *The War Game* was a realistic dramatic reconstruction of the effects of dropping a hydrogen bomb on Britain. Watkins and the film's makers believed that in a democratic country that lived under the shadow and protection of the hydrogen bomb, the public had a right to know what the effects of using it might be. The BBC had known that the film was likely to be controversial and was unlikely to win favour with the military. Nevertheless it had authorised its production. However, with the film complete and the Labour Party, which was deeply divided over the whole issue of the nuclear deterent, now in power with a tiny majority, the BBC had laid on a private viewing for representatives of the Ministry of Defence, the Home Office and the Chiefs of Staff. They had been predictably unhappy with what they saw. Two months later, and without any formal request from the government, the BBC governors decided to ban the film. One of them wondered, in a private note to his colleagues, what would have been the fate of Christianity if Watkins had 'shown in advance to the followers of Jesus a documentary showing the details of his inevitable crucifixion'.[28] In the public row that followed Peter Watkins had resigned from the BBC.

Even after Harold Wilson and the Labour government had been returned with a greatly increased majority in the April 1966 general election, Wilson's distrust of the BBC had continued unabated. On his way back to London from his Huyton constituency after the election he had refused to take part in a live BBC interview from his train, and once back in Downing Street had summoned the Chairman and Director-General to a secret meeting (so secret that they were instructed not to enter through the front door of Number 10), during which he had aired a string of what he called 'grievances' against the BBC and accused it of conspiring against him. Not long afterwards Tony Benn, a senior member of Wilson's cabinet, had publicly broached the possibility of removing Greene from the director-generalship by exercising his ministerial powers to appoint or remove BBC governors. He had also proposed that the BBC could be funded, at least in part, by advertising.

The morale of people working in broadcasting had reached a new low in July 1967 when, following the death of the BBC's Chairman Lord Normanbrook, Wilson had appointed Lord Hill, the Chairman of the Independent Television Authority, to take his place. Hill was a former Conservative politician who had first come to prominence during the war as the Radio Doctor, in which role he had broadcast little homilies on such things as the efficacy of prunes for ensuring regular bowel movements. To people inside the BBC Wilson's action appeared to be pure spite. The Vice-Chairman wrote later that 'It was the end of the BBC as I knew it', and probably 'the most shattering day' in the Corporation's whole history. Greene recorded that his first reaction was 'How can I work with a man for whom I have the utmost contempt?'

Hill had been received at the BBC with thinly veiled hostility. David Attenborough, the Controller of BBC-2, had told him that when staff had received news of his appointment their reaction had been 'just as if Rommel had been put in charge of the Eighth Army'. Hill had asked if that meant that they doubted whether he was a good general? Attenborough had replied, 'No. They know that you are. But they need to be convinced that you are fighting on the same side.'

On the day that he had appointed Hill, Wilson had told a cabinet colleague, 'Charlie Hill has already cleaned up ITV, and he'll do the same to the BBC now I'm appointing him chairman.'[29]

On arrival at the BBC, Hill had immediately made it clear that he intended to be a much more interventionist chairman than his predecessors. One of his first acts had been to meet Mary Whitehouse. To many in the BBC just agreeing to meet Whitehouse seemed a betrayal. Both Normanbrook and Greene had always refused to meet her.

People both inside and outside the BBC had suspected that in appointing Hill, Wilson's real intention had been to force Greene's premature resignation as

'And here's the four-letter word that caused the biggest shock of all – H-I-L-L!'

Whitworth in *Sheffield Morning Telegraph*, 28 July 1967
by permission of the Sheffield Telegraph

Director-General. So, when in July 1968 it was announced that Greene was to step down early there was dismay inside the BBC and a storm of press comment. It was widely held that Greene had been pushed, that the programme values that he had stood for had become untenable with Hill's arrival and that there had been a great row between them. That it later emerged that none of the wilder speculation was correct and that the timing of Greene's resignation probably owed more to Greene's impending divorce than to differences with Hill over

BBC policy did nothing to affect the heavy clouds of suspicion and conspiracy theory that now engulfed broadcasting and the BBC in particular.

It was at this moment of mounting crisis, with broadcasting sinking beneath an all-pervading tide of gloom and suspicion, that Ascherson, Macdonald and his colleague met in their pub to discuss the relevance to what was happening in Britain of recent events across the Channel in the French state broadcasting organisation, ORTF. Their initial meeting was followed by others involving Bruce Page and Alex Cockburn. By the autumn about a dozen people in all, drawn from journalism, television, the cinema, publishing and even the theatre, had become involved in trying to draw up a statement of principles and a plan of action. Their discussions reflected their shared concern that all the media were falling inexorably into the hands of fewer, ever more powerful businessmen and corporations; that at the same time their work was becoming subject to steadily greater control by government; that editorial and creative decision-making were becoming progressively further removed from the writers, producers, directors and others who worked in the media and from the concerns of the public whom they were supposed to serve.

One of the things that had impressed Ascherson, while he had been working in Germany for the *Observer*, had been the system of workers' representation in industry and the extent to which the workforce had a say in the management of the enterprises in which they worked. He had drawn inspiration from the example of those German newspapers where management and staff jointly drew up editorial principles for the paper. During *les événements de Paris* the workers had briefly instituted a similar system at ORTF. These principles generally included provisions guaranteeing that no journalist would be forced to 'write against his conscience, or be penalized for refusing to do so', a say for journalists in appointments and advance information about the management's financial plans. This contrasted with the situation in Britain where wealthy magnates like Lord Thomson or Robert Maxwell bought up titles, changed their editorial policies and formats, hired and fired editors and journalists at will. (Rupert Murdoch had not yet arrived on the British scene although, unseen, he was already buying up shares in the *Mirror*'s holding company.)

As Macdonald, Ascherson and their colleagues' discussions about the possible formation of an action group and drawing up a manifesto continued into the autumn of 1968, despondency over what was happening in the BBC deepened still further. Shortly after becoming Chairman, Hill had called in a firm of outside consultants (a practice in vogue since Wilson had become Prime Minister) to examine the BBC's administration and use of resources. Hill argued that if the BBC was ever going to get the licence fee increase that it now desperately needed, he would have to demonstrate that it used its money efficiently. In September McKinsey & Co. (the consultants called in by Hill) submitted their initial report. Although they found that the Corporation was generally efficient, they recommended that the BBC introduce a whole new tier of management and tighter controls over spending and its use of resources.

In October 1968 Wilson renewed his attack on the BBC at the Labour Party Conference, again accusing it of bias against him. The party greeted Wilson's attack with wild applause.[30] This was followed two weeks later by a widely reported speech, made by Tony Benn to a meeting of his Bristol constituency party, on the role of the media. In a long speech to a thinly attended meeting, which dealt mainly with broadcasting, and with the BBC in particular, one short sentence stood out and was picked up by the press: 'Broadcasting is really too important to be left to the broadcasters.' Benn had been arguing for access to the airwaves for a wider range of viewpoints and people, unmediated by the editorial priorities of the BBC. Rightly or wrongly, his words were interpreted as a thinly veiled threat by a senior member of the government to the editorial integrity of the BBC and of broadcasters in general.[31] As Benn must have anticipated, a headline-grabbing public row broke out. The broadcasters – BBC, ITV and individual producers – responded that no matter what Benn might think, broadcasting was a great deal too important to be left to the mercy of politicians.

What eventually emerged in the late autumn of 1968 from the meetings and discussions of Macdonald, Ascherson and their friends was not a tight-knit revolutionary cell seeking to capture the media in order to ignite a working-class uprising, nor even a group with a clearly defined political programme – although detractors would later accuse it of being both of those things – but something much more open-ended and informal, the Free Communications Group (FCG). Although broadly left wing, the group would eventually include members with a spectrum of political views, ranging from Marxists through all shades of socialist and liberal opinion to people from the left of the Conservative Party.

The FCG's statement of principles, drawn up in the meetings of the group's originators over the preceding months, reflected their concern over recent events in broadcasting and the press, their disenchantment with the politicians' view of the media and with their bosses' reaction to Benn's most recent attack.

It stated boldly that 'The Free Communications Group believes that communications are too important to be left to proprietors, shareholders, professional communicators and Boards of Governors. We therefore intend working towards democratic control of all media, by the people and the workers in the industry.' They committed themselves to 'defending the openness of the media against the menace of bureaucratic encroachment' and 'to encouraging participation and control of the media through democratic decision making. In this battle cameramen and producers, reporters and compositors are fighting as trustees of an increasingly manipulated public . . . ' In articles introducing the first two editions of the FCG's journal *Open Secret*, the group's founders amplified their fears and their aims. 'People who work in newspapers and television, despite the competition between them, have many aims and interests in common. We have a common interest in the quality, organisation and control of the huge communications industry in this country . . . an interest which stretches beyond newspapers and television and radio into every sphere of communications and society.' Warning that 'The media are now largely locked up in enormous multimedia concerns which administer a portfolio of holdings in every branch of the industry . . . ', they cited the way in which large newspaper groups, such as Thomson and the *Mirror*, had already expanded into magazine and book publishing, television, advertising and newsprint; how ITV companies used their enormous profits to expand across other areas of entertainment, into publishing, garages, flower rental and even grocery stores. They accused the BBC of being 'a rigid and fiercely hierarchic state, with all the minute gradations, checks, protocols and rungs for which the Chinese Imperial Civil Service was once justly famous' and of subservience and 'self-effacement before the establishment'. They expressed an equally low opinion of the US media. They deplored the fact that decisions about programmes, policy and appointments 'always devolve to owners, politicians and upper management; upper management being, as we know, always finks, passing the buck till it is safely stowed in the company safe. The whole debate about what free communications can be has never really taken place. It has been surrendered to Royal Commissions and pieties about nationalisation.' The FCG, they continued, did not intend to wait passively for the millennium and a change in the structure of society; it intended ' . . . to launch a campaign to inaugurate ideas about democratic media which have never got above ground in previous debate'. The FCG, they announced, would publish the undisclosed facts about the media. The editorial in the first edition of the group's journal, *Open Secret*, ended with this declaration: 'The energy of the communications industry is in those who run it – who produce the news and entertainment. The Free Communications Group intends to transform that energy into power'.[32]

I was one of dozens of young programme makers attracted to the FCG as soon as its ideas became known. Phillip Whitehead, the editor of ITV's *This Week*, was another: 'The FCG grew out of a feeling that everywhere Mammon was in the ascendant'.[33]

* * *

The third of the 'forgotten' events of the summer of 1968 recalled at the beginning of this chapter was the start of new eight-year ITV contracts. Nowhere was Mammon more in evidence in 1968 than in ITV.

Commercial television, ITV, had begun in September 1955 following a successful four-year campaign by Norman Collins, a former Controller of BBC Television, to persuade the government that in a democracy the BBC's monopoly in broadcasting was essentially unhealthy. He had argued that its monopoly should be broken in order to increase creative and journalistic freedom and to extend public choice. Collins had been supported by an influential wing of the Conservative Party, led by John Profumo, and backed by others with more material and less lofty motives – advertisers, television set manufacturers and show-business tycoons. Those who had opposed Collins, on the grounds that the purposes of broadcasting were too important to be subordinated to the needs of advertising, had included the churches, the universities and most of the Labour Party. One of the people who had written to the Beveridge Committee opposing the introduction of commercial television had been Sidney Bernstein, the proprietor of Granada Theatres, a family chain of cinemas.[34] He had told the committee that 'the right of access to the domestic sound and television receivers of millions of people carries with it such great propaganda power that it cannot be entrusted to any persons or bodies other than a public corporation or a number of public corporations'.[35] Collins himself had recognised that if commercial television did no more than give the public exactly what it wanted, the result 'would be a perfectly appalling service . . . If we provided that it would be deplorable.'[36] As a result of such fears, commercial television had been placed under the supervision of a statutory authority – the Independent Television Authority (ITA) – which was to keep advertising interests at arm's length from those who controlled the programmes and to prevent any one broadcaster or individual becoming too powerful. The service was provided by fourteen programme contracting companies which were each given a licence of limited duration to operate in one area of the country. So that there should be no mistake as to its lofty ideals, the whole service was known as ITV – *Independent* Television – rather than commercial television.

ITV had opened on 22 September 1955 with the rich and portentous tones of Leslie Mitchell, voice of thousands of cinema newsreels, announcing 'This is London' and a rendering of Elgar's Cockaigne Overture from Sir John Barbirolli and the Hallé Orchestra. The first advert had been for Gibbs SR toothpaste and featured a pretty girl and a block of ice. Speeches from an inaugural dinner in the Guildhall had been followed by a quiz show hosted by Hughie Greene, the proposal scene from Wilde's *The Importance of Being Earnest* featuring John Gielgud and Dame Edith Evans, some boxing, four and a half minutes of news read by Christopher Chataway and a variety show which, as the *Manchester Guardian* commented, was 'up (or some would say down) to BBC standards'.

So much for the high-mindedness that had surrounded the concept of ITV at the start. After the first night it had been downhill and downmarket all the way. The companies which had won the first contracts lost money at an alarming rate during ITV's first year and for a time it had looked as if one or more would go bust. Promises that the companies would be made to compete with others were forgotten in a scramble to survive. With the ITA alternately encouraging them or choosing not to look, the four largest ITV contractors, Lew Grade's ATV (in which Norman Collins had become a director), Associated-Rediffusion, ABC and Granada had entered into a series of undertakings under which they agreed to collaborate rather than compete. The companies carved up the network between them, supplying programmes to each other at notional cost. (Bernstein had quickly overcome his scruples, writing to the Labour Shadow Home Secretary, Herbert Morrison, that although he still thought 'the country would be better off' without it, if there was 'to be commercial television in this country, we think we should be in'.)

By 1956, with commercial television's transmitter coverage spreading and the programmes going steadily downmarket, the audience had started to build. 'Let's face it once and for all. The public likes girls, wrestling, bright musicals, quiz shows and real life drama ... we gave them the Hallé Orchestra, the Foreign Press Club, floodlit football and visits to the local fire station. Well we've learned. From now on, what the public wants it's going to get,' said Roland Gillette of Associated-Rediffusion. The ITA, charged with maintaining programme standards and regulating the contractors, far from discouraging them, had taken on their critics. 'If you decide to have a system of people's television, then people's television you must expect it to be, and it will reflect their likes and dislikes, their tastes and aversions, what they can comprehend and what is beyond them,' Sir Robert Fraser, the Director-General of the Independent Television Authority, told those who were dissatisfied with ITV and its programmes. 'It is not really television with which they are dissatisfied. It is with people.'[37] And 'people', in their millions, had loved it. From an audience of fewer than 200,000 when it started in September 1955, by 1957 ITV's audience had reached 4 million. Whereas in 1955 the advertisers had spent just £2 million buying advertising time on ITV, by 1959 they were spending £58 million. In one of the most ill-judged and costly one-liners in history, Roy (Lord) Thomson, chairman of Scottish Television, had boasted that 'a contract to operate a commercial television programme company is like having a licence to print money'. By 1960, when Sir Hugh Carleton Greene had taken over as Director-General of the BBC, ITV had been attracting twice as many people as the BBC.[38]

* * *

The Pilkington Committee, set up by the Macmillan Conservative government in July 1960, had been in part a response to the success of ITV. Greene's campaign to 'unsell ITV' to the Pilkington Committee had stressed the broadcaster's influence on the moral values and attitudes of society. The BBC's policy, Greene had told the committee, was to provide programmes over 'the widest possible range of content and treatment' rather than simply to provide programmes whose sole objective was to entertain or relax the audience.

When it had reported in June 1962, the Pilkington Committee had condemned ITV under two headings: disquiet and dissatisfaction. Disquiet because ITV did not seem to recognise, or refused to take adequate account of 'the power of the medium to influence and persuade'; dissatisfaction on account of the narrow range of programmes offered by ITV and what the committee interpreted as their paucity of quality and ambition. The committee had dismissed ITV's claim that television was merely 'a mirror of society', accusing it of abrogating the broadcaster's responsibility to determine what that mirror was to reflect. 'Is it to reflect the best or the worst in us?' the committee had asked. 'One cannot escape the question by saying that it must do both.' If the broadcaster was to show both, he had a responsibility to show the worst in such a way that it would 'be recognised for what it is'. The committee had rejected the idea that the alternative to 'giving the public what it wants' was 'giving the public what someone thinks is good for it' as a false antithesis and 'a gross over-simplification' of the complex problems that broadcasters faced in deciding what programmes to provide.

The committee had reserved its harshest judgement for the ITA itself. It had 'misconceived its relationship with the programme contractors', seeing itself as their advocate, excusing and defending them rather than controlling them. The ITA had told the committee that it saw its relationship with the contractors as one 'between friends and partners'. The Authority sought, it had told the committee, to persuade and influence, giving friendly advice and encouragement, rather than directions. The ITA's case had been seriously undermined when its own first chairman, Sir Kenneth Clarke, had told the committee that the Authority was 'entirely wrong' to see its relationship with the companies in this way. The committee had concluded that for the companies to be 'regarded as principals and the Authority as their spokesman is unsatisfactory'. The Authority must 'be master, and must be seen to be master'.[39]

The Pilkington Committee called for radical changes to ITV. In future the Authority should plan the programmes, sell the advertising, buy programmes from the companies to make up the schedule and pay over any surplus income to the Treasury.

However, neither the government nor the press had been convinced. 'The Piffington Report' was how the *Daily Sketch* had described the committee's judgement on ITV. The *Daily Mirror* claimed that the report in effect told the public to 'Go to Hell!' But press reactions had been nothing as compared to reactions inside the ITV companies themselves. Peter Cadbury, Chief Executive of Westward Television, had publicly burnt Sir Harry Pilkington in effigy along with copies of his report. Denis Forman of Granada had read the report with mounting horror: 'It seemed to find everything to do with ITV bad, everything to do with the BBC good. Until now any article that was critical of Independent Television, no matter how hard it had slammed into quiz shows, advertisements and so on, had always qualified its condemnation with the words "except for Granada". But in the Pilkington Report there was no "except for Granada" . . . Granada's dedication to politics and to serious social issues were not mentioned. Nor were Granada's plays.' As Forman's fury mounted he had called his chairman Sidney Bernstein. 'I know, I know, I know,' Bernstein had replied, 'it's disgraceful. But don't let's fool ourselves – it's going to change the face of television.'[40]

By painting the BBC too uniformly white and ITV so irredeemably black the report had spoiled its own case. Forman's reaction, while partisan, was to some extent justified. Simply because it was more lively, more down to earth and approachable in its programmes and in its presentation, the arrival of ITV had improved British television as a whole. It had forced the BBC to change and Greene had acknowledged this when he set himself the task of letting a blast of fresh air into the BBC. It was Granada that had successfully challenged the convention that had prevented the proper reporting of elections by giving full coverage to the Rochdale by-election in 1958. It was ABC which had instigated the ongoing series of contemporary plays under the generic title *Armchair Theatre*, commissioned from British writers many of whom were until then barely known – among them Alun Owen, Bill Naughton, Clive Exton, Angus Wilson and Harold Pinter, whose first television play, *A Night Out*, was transmitted in May 1960.[41] It was A-R and Granada who, with the BBC's *Tonight*, had woken up current affairs programmes with *This Week* and *Searchlight* (the forerunner of *World in Action*). It was the ITV news, presented by 'newscasters', who wrote their own scripts, conducted their own interviews and had a hand in selecting the news, that had finally brought the BBC news into the modern world (the first ITV newscasters were Christopher Chataway, Robin Day and – unheard of – a woman, Barbara Mandell). Until the advent of ITN the BBC's head of news had clung to the belief that rules of precedence required that BBC bulletins lead on royal stories, no matter how dull. In short, ITV had prepared the ground on which Greene and the BBC had been able to build.

It had been unrealistic to imagine that any government would risk the wrath of the electorate by making radical changes to anything so popular as ITV. Just a week after Pilkington reported, the government had issued a broadcasting white paper which had ignored almost all of the committee's recommendations for restructuring ITV. A government bill followed which authorised the BBC's second television channel and extended both the BBC charter and the life of the ITA until 1976. However, the Pilkington Committee's findings could not be ignored altogether, so the powers of the ITA had been strengthened and a levy introduced on the ITV companies' profits (later changed to a levy on the ITV companies' income). Sidney Bernstein's initial assessment of the likely effect of the

Pilkington Committee Report proved remarkably accurate. It did change the face of television. From then on the ITA had had to be seen to be more active in its supervision of ITV. The companies, in addition to amassing audiences, had had to win brownie points with their programmes. In spite of the hefty new levy imposed by the government on their profits, the companies' programmes had improved.

When Lord Hill had become chairman of the ITA in July 1963 he had discovered that the Pilkington Committee had been all too correct in its assessment of the attitude of Fraser and the Authority to the ITV companies. 'Robert Fraser was utterly devoted to this child of his creation, finding it difficult to see anything wrong in his growing offspring . . . [The companies] needed to be cosseted. Fraser saw ITV as one big happy and prosperous family.'[42]

Hill had immediately set about changing the ITA and sharpening its attitude to the companies. He set up a committee, under his own chairmanship, to study the ITV schedule in advance and in detail. ITA interventions over programme content and the schedule had increased. Soon, however, younger programme makers and some of the more adventurous company executives around the network had begun to suspect that many of Hill's interventions were made not so much out of a desire to improve the service as to make it more acceptable to people in authority, to the narrow-minded and conservative. Granada, in particular, with its left-leaning, crusading image, came under the Authority's cosh. Shortly after Hill's arrival the Authority had decreed that all *World in Action* programmes were to be vetted by its officials in advance of transmission. The result had been warfare between the *World in Action* team and the ITA. Investigative programmes on defence spending, inadequate government backing for the British squad at the Olympic Games, the living conditions of blacks in South Africa, the repressive Portuguese regime in Angola, drugs procurement in the National Health Service, the Vietnam War, Mandy Rice-Davies[43] talking to girls at her old school and a major three-part series, *What Price Peace?*, had all been banned or substantially altered on the ITA's orders. Contrariwise, when Granada had refused to broadcast the Queen's Christmas message, the ITA had forced it to do so. Tim Hewat, *World in Action*'s editor, an ebullient Australian and former *Daily Express* journalist, had demanded to know from the ITA why programmes should be suppressed for telling the truth? The suspicion, voiced by the press as well as by the *World In Action* production team and programme makers across the network, was that the answer lay in the fact that the programmes contained implied criticism of the government. In private Hewat dismissed the ITA as 'silly buggers' and continued to delight in running rings round them. Things had reached a height of absurdity in 1965 over a quasi drama-documentary called *The Entertainers* made by two of the very best programme makers in the business – Denis Mitchell and John McGrath – featuring some northern night club performers and a striptease act. The ITA, having previewed the programme, had pronounced two scenes obscene and demanded that they be cut. Granada had refused and withdrawn the programme. Nine months later Granada had resubmitted it. This time the ITA had passed it for transmission, one member of the Authority expressing 'satisfaction that the offending scenes had been cut'. In fact the programme had not been altered.

It was not only Granada or its current affairs and documentary programme makers which had come into conflict with the ITA. The Authority's interventions in drama seemed equally perverse. Harold Pinter's *The Lovers*, deemed unsuitable for those who were young or unmarried, had been consigned to a late evening slot, some regional companies refusing to transmit it at all for fear of offending their viewers. But at least *The Lovers* had been transmitted, unlike Graham Greene's *The Complaisant Lover*. When the ITA had demanded cuts in the play and the company producing it, ATV, agreed, Graham Greene had withdrawn it. The play had later been produced by the BBC uncut. Nevertheless, despite such displays of censorship and prurience, Hill had improved ITV.

Hill's last act as Chairman of the ITA had been to preside over the selection of new ITV programme contractors for the period due to start at the end of July 1968. Following the drubbing it had received at the hands of the Pilkington Committee, in selecting the new contractors the ITA had seen itself as being as much on trial as those competing for the franchises. The Authority had wanted not only to exercise its power, but to have been seen to exercise it.

The first step had been to modify the contract areas so as to achieve a more equal division of power and income between the companies. The number of contract areas was increased from fourteen to fifteen and in future there were to be five, rather than four, network companies. The Authority made little secret of the fact that it would favour those applicants who promised the best schedule.

When the advertisements inviting applications for the new franchises had appeared on 28 February 1967, they had sparked off what the press called a 'Gold Rush'. By 15 April, the date by which applications had to be in, a total of thirty-six had been received.

In six of the franchise areas there was no competitor to the incumbent contractor. The largest number of applications was for the new Yorkshire area, a seven-day-a-week franchise carved out of the eastern side of the old Granada area. The contract eventually went to a consortium headed by a former RAF pilot Ward Thomas – soon to gain an unfortunate reputation for inviting executives for a flip in the company jet as a means of softening them up before firing them ('unfortunate' because it seems to have been baseless – for a start Yorkshire did not own a company jet, although it did later acquire a helicopter). Ward Thomas's Controller of Programmes was Donald Baverstock, the former Controller of BBC-1 who had left to set up a production company with Antony Jay and Alasdair Milne but then been refused work by the BBC.

Another contract which excited particular interest was the award of the franchise for Wales and the West of England to Harlech Television. It was headed by Lord Harlech, a former British ambassador to Washington, and featured a star-studded list of famous Welshmen – Stanley Baker, Geraint Evans, Harry Secombe, Wynford Vaughan Thomas and Richard Burton with Elizabeth Taylor. The award of the contract would, the ITA believed, 'offer a welcome means for the expression of their cultural patriotism'.[44]

However, the ITV franchises which excited most press attention were the two for London – one for weekdays from Monday to Friday evening, the other for the weekends, Friday evenings through to the end of Sunday. Hill and the members of the Authority had been particularly concerned to improve the image of ITV's programmes at the weekend when, in the words of the ITV official history, 'opinion formers and other people of public power and influence were thought most likely to be viewers'.[45] The award of the weekend contract had been seen as *the* test case for the ITA. By the closing date of 15 April the Authority had received three applications for the contract.

The obvious front-runner was ABC, headed by Howard Thomas – who had devised the BBC's prestigious wartime radio series, *The Brains Trust*, been the producer who had made Vera Lynn 'The Forces' Sweetheart', the impresario behind the 1953 Coronation film and prime mover in making ABC one of the original big-four ITV network contractors. Since 1955 ABC had provided ITV programmes at the weekends in the Midlands and the North of England. It had been a pioneer of adult education and televised religion on ITV, had produced the arts series *Tempo*, *Armchair Theatre* and *The Avengers*.

The other serious contender for the franchise had been a consortium hastily put together by David Frost and a former Conservative junior minister and first editor of ITN, Aidan Crawley – The London Television Consortium.[46] Frost had first considered the idea of mounting a challenge for the London weekend franchise during an Associated-Rediffusion staff party in January 1967. Much of the talk at the party had been about the forthcoming ITV contract round. In his speech announcing the winners of a raffle Frost had added a topical joke – there would be a special extra prize this year, the ITV contract for Yorkshire. Frost says that later that evening he had had a flash of inspiration: 'Why not go for London? Why follow the pack and set your sights only on Yorkshire? London at the weekends could be vulnerable, and the talent needed for a winning bid might respond more readily to the idea of London. I knew I would.'[47]

Following his success with *That Was The Week That Was*, Frost had become one of the most talked about celebrities in the country, seemingly able to invite anyone from Prime Minister Wilson down to take breakfast with him at the Connaught Hotel and not be refused. Frost, in somewhat the same way as others involved in making programmes, had believed that 'It was time for people with talent to get much more involved in the day-to-day programming decisions that ruled their lives.' Frost's charm, energy and powers of persuasion were legendary and by the time the London Television Consortium's application had arrived at the ITA on 14 April 1967, Frost, Crawley and Clive Irving (a former managing editor of the *Sunday Times* who was to be responsible for the company's current affairs and documentary output), had brought together an array of talent and a basket of programming ideals so impressive that Lord Hill had been driven to say that it was 'an understatement to say that the Authority liked this application . . . here was a group which would bring new thinking, fresh ideas and a lively impetus to weekend broadcasting . . . It had to have its chance whatever the repercussions.'[48]

Frost's biggest coup, 'the grand prize' as he would later put it, had been to enlist Michael Peacock, the first Controller of BBC-2 and subsequently of BBC-1, as his consortium's Managing Director. The Deputy Managing Director was to be Dr Tom Margerison, the Science Editor of the *Sunday Times*. Others included Humphrey Burton, Head of Music and Arts at the BBC, to head the consortium's Drama, Music and Arts output; Frank Muir, the man behind many of the BBC's most successful comedy programmes, to head the consortium's Entertainment Department with input from the writers Ray Galton and Alan Simpson, creators of *Hancock's Half Hour* and *Steptoe and Son*. The Family Programmes Unit was to be overseen by Doreen Stephens, Head of BBC Television's Family Programmes

Department. The group had stressed their belief that those who knew about television, cared about television and made the programmes broadcast on television, ought to have an effective voice in the broadcasting companies (together with a generous share of the company's equity). At the same time Frost and Crawley had lined up an extremely impressive array of city and business backing. The chairmen of Bowaters, of Pearl Assurance and the *New Statesman*, the chief executives of the London Cooperative Society, Samuel Montagu, Leyland Motors and GEC had all agreed to join the board. Major financial backers included the Imperial Tobacco Pension Trust, Lombard Banking and Weidenfeld and Nicholson. In the wings was John Freeman, a former Labour junior minister, who, after resigning with Harold Wilson and Aneurin Bevan from Attlee's Labour government in 1951 over the introduction of health charges, had become famous, in the words of Kingsley Martin, 'for showing the public his backside' as the inquisitor in the BBC's interview series *Face to Face*. Significantly, in view of what was to happen, Freeman had not actually joined the group, but was poised to become its Deputy Chairman as soon as he had completed his term as British High Commissioner in India.

The consortium's eighty-page confidential franchise application opened with a ringing statement of the group's beliefs: 'The applicants represent a programme making capacity with a proven record in both Independent Television and the BBC. These programme makers have been united by a common belief that the quality of mass entertainment can be improved while retaining commercial viability.' It had continued by saying that the company's programme policy was 'in harmony with the commercial policy and it is a basic tenet of this application that a higher proportion of the company's revenue will be spent on programmes than has normally been the case . . . The applicants make no claims in this document which they feel they cannot fulfil.'[49] The group had outlined plans for major new one-hour plays on Sunday evenings, a drama series on Fridays, a Frost programme on all three days, a 45-minute news review on Sunday afternoons, a regular arts programme, religious programmes and religious services, adult education programmes on fringe medicine, a series devoted to the fascinations of the British Museum and a crusading programme about the state of the river called *Poor Father Thames*. The 'first, and inherent, principle of the Company's programme philosophy', the consortium had told the ITA, was 'respect for the creative talents – for those who . . . conceive and make television programmes'.

The Frost team's formal interview at the ITA had, according to the merchant banker David Montagu, gone so well that at the end they had received 'what almost amounted to a standing ovation'. Frost and Peacock told the Authority that they had a new conception of what weekend broadcasting should be, that there was room at the weekends for a deeper analysis of the week's events as well as for light entertainment, that current affairs and plays had a place in weekend programming. Hill and his colleagues had wanted to believe that people were no less intelligent at the weekend than they were during the week, and that if serious Sunday newspapers could succeed, so could serious television. The Authority would say later that the company represented 'the greatest concentration of talent in one company ever seen in British television'.[50] It was an endorsement that would prove hard to live up to.

Having decided to award the London weekend contract to the Frost–Crawley consortium (its name changed to London Weekend Television), the Authority had not been inclined to do the unthinkable and deprive ABC of its contract altogether. So Hill had pushed ABC into a shotgun marriage, in which it was the dominant 51% to 49% partner, with the existing London weekday contractor Associated-Rediffusion (which had given an extremely bad formal interview but was felt to have given good service since ITV started). The resulting new company, called Thames, had been given the London weekday franchise.

Within weeks of awarding the new contracts Hill had been moved by Wilson to the BBC. As a result he would not be around to cope with the fruits of his handiwork. By the time that Ascherson and Macdonald met in their Fleet Street pub, only days before the new contractors were due to start broadcasting, there were clear signs that things had started to go dreadfully wrong.

Notes

1. Quoted in C. G. Crisp, *François Truffaut*, November Books Ltd, London, 1972.
2. The author and a colleague received a grant of £250 in 1963 from the BFI Experimental Film Fund to help finance an early short film.
3. The Association of Cinematograph and Television Technicians, previously the ACT – the extra 'T' had been added after the introduction of commercial television.
4. The best known at the time were probably the film courses at the Slade and the London Film School.
5. *Rogue Reels: Oppositional Film in Britain, 1945–90*, edited by Margaret Dickinson, British Film Institute, London, 1999.

6. Jon Irvin, interviewed by the author in August 2001.

7. Jan Dawson, *Sight and Sound*, London, Vol. 3, No. 4, Autumn 1969. Many of those who were associated with Mithras and its films later became well known. Jon Irvin directed a number of outstanding television dramas in the 1970s and early 1980s before moving on to direct major international feature films. Stephen Frears also achieved success in television drama and then moved on to directing feature films, among which were *My Beautiful Laundrette* and *Dangerous Liaisons*. The film's lighting cameraman, Charles Stewart, is today one of Britain's leading documentary director–cameramen.

8. Lightweight video equipment was still in its infancy, while the standard outside broadcast units equipped with two inch videotape recorders, which were the only alternative to film for pre-recording material outside, were both costly and cumbersome. In 1963 the BBC had made its first play using an outside broadcast unit and video tape – a production of T. S. Eliot's *Murder in the Cathedral*, recorded in Canterbury Cathedral. Granada Television had pioneered the use of video recording for documentaries and in 1964 *A Wedding on a Saturday*, directed by Norman Swallow, recorded by using lorryloads of outside broadcast equipment, had won the prestigious *Prix Italia*. But generally the spontaneity-crushing effects of the use of the cumbersome OB equipment far outweighed any claimed benefits.

9. An account of the BFI revolt is included in Ivan Butler's *To Encourage the Art of Film*, Robert Hale & Co, London, 1971.

10. Neal Ascherson, interviewed by the author, February 2001. Neither Ascherson nor Lord Macdonald can now remember who the third person who took part in the conversation was. There is also doubt about the venue of their meeting. Ascherson now thinks it may have been in a Soho pub.

11. The name of the leader of Communist North Vietnam.

12. In fact, by international standards, Britain lost comparatively few working days to strike action in the mid-1960s. However, what mattered to Wilson was public perception and this, egged on by the popular press, was that the country's economy was being crippled by greedy and irresponsible industrial militants.

13. By 1968 there were four times as many students coming out of university with humanities degrees than there had been as recently as 1960.

14. Joan Bakewell, interviewed by the author in December 2000.

15. David Plowright gave me his side of how Macdonald was recruited to Granada when I interviewed him in October 2000. Lord Macdonald told me his version of the same events when I interviewed him in June 2001.

16. Dennis Potter, interviewed by Melvyn Bragg in *Without Walls*, Channel Four Television Corporation, 5 April 1994.

17. A judgement confirmed by its re-showing on BBC-4 in the summer of 2003.

18. Quoted in Worsley's collected criticism, *Television: The Ephemeral Art*, 1970.

19. Sir Hugh Carleton Greene, *The Third Floor Front. A View of Broadcasting in the Sixties*, Bodley Head, London 1969.

20. In fact *Dixon of Dock Green* clung on for another fourteen years, but *Z Cars* made the running for future cop series and regularly outperformed *Dixon* in the ratings.

21. Colin Shaw, interviewed by the author in October 2000. The BBC-2 recruit quoted is Nicholas Garnham, interviewed by the author in November 2000.

22. Alasdair Milne interviewed by the author in October 2000. Talking to older BBC people for this book they were unanimous in regarding Jay and Milne, in particular, as among the most important liberating forces in the BBC during the first half of the 1960s.

23. Joan Bakewell, interviewed by the author in December 2000.

24. *English History 1914–1945*, A. J. P. Taylor, Oxford University Press, London, 1965. There was no doubt in the mind of the BBC's founder, Sir John Reith, about the true nature of the relationship between it and the government. Immediately after the General Strike he noted in his diary, 'They know that they can trust us not to be really independent.'

25. Quoted in *Governing the BBC* by Asa Briggs, British Broadcasting Corporation, London, 1979.

26. Quoted by Briggs, *op. cit.*

27. From a petition to the House of Commons presented in 1965 by 'residents of Bromsgrove and other places'.

28. Sir Robert Lusty, quoted in *The History of Broadcasting in the United Kingdom, Vol. V, Competition*, Asa Briggs, Oxford University Press, Oxford, 1995. Recently Tony Benn told Patrick Murphy, who was working on a book about Watkins, that, in his role as Postmaster General in Wilson's government, he was told to communicate to the BBC a ban on *The War Game*.

29. Richard Crossman, *Diaries of a Cabinet Minister, Vol. Two*, Hamish Hamilton Ltd and Jonathan Cape Ltd, London, 1976.

30. In January 1969 Hill invited Wilson to lunch with the governors and senior staff in order to try to heal the rift. Hill recorded in his diary afterwards: 'He was friendly, confident and chatty. Clearly he wanted to bury the hatchet (leaving himself free to dig it up).' As a senior colleague of Hill's who was present at the lunch put it afterwards: 'He has buried the hatchet but marked the spot.' A week later Wilson was complaining again. Hill, *op. cit.*

31. The full text of Benn's speech and details of the ensuing row are contained in the Benn diaries, *Office Without Power: Diaries 1968–72*, Tony Benn, Century Hutchinson Ltd, London, 1988.

32. Quotations from the statement of the FCG's aims come from a number of such statements debated or published by the FCG in early editions of its magazine, *Open Secret*, and from an undated version in the author's possession. The statement of FCG aims which appeared in the first edition of *Open Secret* in June 1969 is also reprinted in *British Broadcasting*, compiled by Anthony Smith, published by David & Charles (Holdings) Ltd, Newton Abbott, 1974.

33. Phillip Whitehead, interviewed by the author. Whitehead had stood unsuccessfully as a Labour candidate in the 1966 general election.

34. The Beveridge Committee, appointed by the Labour government in 1949 to consider the future of broadcasting, had come down against commercial television.

35. Quoted in *Persona Granada: Some Memories of Sidney Bernstein and the Early Days of Independent Television*, Denis Forman, André Deutsch Ltd, London, 1997.

36. Norman Collins, quoted in *Britain in the Sixties: Communications*, Raymond Williams, Penguin Books Ltd, London, 1962.

37. From a speech given by Sir Robert Fraser at the Manchester Luncheon Club on 17 May 1960 and quoted in *Independent Television in Britain, Vol. 3*, by Jeremy Potter, Independent Broadcasting Authority & Independent Television Companies Association, Macmillan Press Ltd, 1989, and Roland Gillette, quoted in *Tomorrow's Television*, by Andrew Quicke, Lion Publishing, Berkhamsted, 1976.

38. At one point ITV claimed to be attracting four times as many viewers as the BBC.

39. *Report of the Committee on Broadcasting, 1960*, chaired by Sir Harry Pilkington, Cmnd. 1753.

40. Forman, *op. cit.*

41. *A Night Out* was watched by 6,380,000 people. Later Pinter calculated that for one of his stage successes to be seen by that many people it would have to run for 38 years.

42. *Behind the Screen – The Broadcasting Memoirs of Lord Hill of Luton*, Sidgwick and Jackson Ltd, London, 1974.

43. One of the girls involved in the Profumo scandal.

44. *Independent Television in Britain, Vol. 2, Expansion and Change 1958–68*, by Bernard Sendall, Independent Broadcasting Authority & Independent Television Companies Association, Macmillan Press Ltd, London, 1983.

45. *Ibid.*

46. The third contestant for the London weekend franchise, headed by a facilities and recording company, TVR, seems never to have been in the running.

47. *David Frost, An Autobiography: Part One – From Congregations to Audiences*, David Frost, HarperCollins Publishers, London, 1993. The complete story of the Frost/LWT bid for the London weekend contract is well told in Frost's own book, also in *Running the Show: 21 Years of London Weekend Television*, David Docherty, Boxtree Ltd, London, 1990. I have also drawn on accounts in Hill, *op. cit.*, Sendall, *op. cit.* and interviews which I conducted with Michael Peacock and Brian Tesler.

48. Hill, *op. cit.*

49. Reprinted in *Open Secret*, No. 1.

50. Jeremy Potter, *op. cit.* and *Independent Television in Britain, Vol. 4, Companies and Programmes 1968–80*, 1990.

2

Mammon and the 'Open Secret':
Calls for change – 1969 to 1970

'The LWT affair called into question most of the fundamentals of Independent Television: the methods and morals of contract awards; the role and competence of the Authority; the pattern of regionalism; inter company relationships; and the philosophy of programming.'

ITV official history.[1]

The first hint of trouble came immediately after the announcement by the ITA of the contract awards. At the press conference David Frost told reporters that LWT hoped to give the public 'what they will grow to want'. Michael Peacock went further: 'The present weekend programmes are bland, featureless and tasteless' and added, 'You won't have to be a moron to get something out of London Weekend Television.'[2] It was hardly a remark calculated to endear him to the companies which had been supplying ITV's weekend programmes until then, companies such as Bernstein's Granada or ATV, run by the redoubtable Lew Grade. Because of the ITV networking system Peacock was going to have to work with these men. They would construct the network's weekend schedule together.

A week before the contract decisions were announced, *The Economist* had raised the question of how the ITA reached its decisions, asking why it was that the ITA could make far-reaching commercial and cultural decisions 'without any serious public discussion whatever'.[3] Other critics began to question the ITA's system of confidential franchise applications, secret interviews and unexplained decisions. Was it right that such important decisions about a valuable public asset of vital interest to millions of viewers should be made by 'a bunch of amateurs' in private?

Despite generalised boasts about the cornucopia of challenging programmes that LWT would bring the weekend public, exact details of what the consortium had promised the ITA had remained secret. Nevertheless, expectations were fanned by press rumours and the confident statements and pub talk of LWT insiders. More star names were added to LWT's list of those already signed up to make its programmes. Derek Granger, a former drama critic and senior producer with Granada; Jimmy Hill to mastermind the sports output, and a trio of top BBC drama people associated with *The Wednesday Play* – James McTaggart, Tony Garnett and Kenith Trodd. When they had first been approached they had, according to Trodd, taken 'a snooty, leftist attitude. We said that we would only join as a collective.'[4] They had got round the problem by signing up through their own company, Kestrel Productions.

However, once 'the first dizzy flush' of success began to dissipate, the members of the LWT consortium began to take in the enormity of what they had taken on. In little over a year, by 2 August 1968, they would have to acquire or build and equip studios and offices, take on hundreds of staff and create a stockpile of programmes. Not only were they going to have to learn to work with each other, they were going to have to learn to work with their money men and with the other members of the ITV network.

One of the first things that Michael Peacock and his team were going to have to do was to reach an agreement with the trade unions. The main technicians' union in ITV was not the comparatively easygoing ABS, which operated in the BBC, but the film technicians' union, the ACTT. By the 1960s the ACTT and the other film unions had established an even more creativity-crushing stranglehold over ITV than they already exercised over the film industry. This had come about in the period leading up to ITV going on the air in 1955, when the original ITV contractors had needed, like LWT now, to stockpile programmes in advance of beginning transmissions. In the 1950s, before the advent of video tape recording, the companies had had no alternative but to shoot on film any programmes that were not going to be transmitted live. To this end, Associated-Rediffusion's boss, Captain Tom Brownrigg, had made arrangements to shoot a series of programmes in the film studios at Shepperton. The ACTT had promptly told Brownrigg that, as it was the union which represented technicians at Shepperton, he would have to enter into an agreement with it. If he didn't there would be no filming. Brownrigg, who, according to one of his ITV colleagues, saw little distinction between running a television company and commanding a battleship, had recognised that he was outgunned. Accordingly he had struck his colours and signed up Associated-Rediffusion with the ACTT. With a precedent thus established, the ACTT and the other film unions had then lodged claims for recognition with all the other ITV contractors. Eventually, after protracted negotiations, it had been agreed that technicians working in ITV were to be employed 'under terms no less favourable than such staff would have enjoyed had they been employed under the terms' operated by the film producers' trade association, the BFPA.

Within a few years ITV had acquired a deserved reputation for being an industrial relations minefield of inter-union demarcation disputes, exorbitant overtime rates, overmanning and restrictive practices. Because of ITV's vulnerability to strike action (if a station's programmes were blacked out it lost the airtime it could have sold to advertisers for ever and could not re-sell it at a later date), once established in commercial television the unions had been in an unusually strong position to extort ever more advantageous terms from the companies. As the years went by, the union had imposed ever more arcane rules over manning and job demarcation. Once ITV's initial financial difficulties had been overcome and the money had started to pour in, the unions had been able to act like armed bank robbers in a Klondike boom town without a sheriff. When challenged they had, with some justification, responded that the companies, instead of putting their large profits back into programmes, had diversified into other unrelated activities.

One graphic example from my own experience of the way in which union attitudes pushed up costs in ITV and held back creative and technical progress concerned a helical-scan camera unit purchased by Granada after the success of its first documentaries produced on video tape in the early 1960s by Norman Swallow and Denis Mitchell. Swallow's *A Wedding on Saturday* had won numerous awards, including the most coveted of all, the *Prix Italia*. It had been made using a cumbersome outside broadcasting unit, equipped with two-inch videotape recording machines and bulky outside broadcast cameras of the kind used to cover sports events. Helical-scan recording equipment and lightweight cameras, which had only recently become available, employed portable-¾ inch gauge recording machines. As a result, instead of requiring an outside broadcasting unit consisting of one or more large trucks and a large team of men to operate it, all the equipment needed could be loaded into one estate car and operated by a three-man crew consisting of a camera operator, a sound man and a recordist, one of whom could double as the driver. Seeing this as a way forward for television documentary-making, Granada purchased a kit of helical-scan equipment, mounted appropriately onto a gleaming new Ford Granada estate car, and recruited Denis Mitchell and Norman Swallow to work with a team of enthusiastic young acolytes[5] to make a series of what they hoped would be ground-breaking documentaries under the generic title *This England*. However, the gleaming new helical-scan camera unit never left the spot outside a scenery bay inside Granada's Manchester studio complex where it had been proudly parked after delivery. The unions demanded a manning agreement for the unit so prohibitively expensive and excessively overmanned as to completely negate all the advantages of using it. As a result the shining new Granada estate, decked out in the company's tasteful blue-grey livery, its technically advanced little camera sitting on top of it, sat reproachfully unused next to an internal passageway leading from the production offices to the studio canteen. Slowly it gathered dust, as month after month negotiations between management and unions dragged on to no avail. Meanwhile Mitchell, Swallow and their team got on with making *This England* on 16 mm film. Months turned to years and the tyres of the Granada slowly deflated, along with the programme makers' and management's hopes. Finally, shortly before I left Granada in 1969, the Granada estate and its helical-scan unit disappeared – presumably whisked away by a shamefaced and frustrated management – leaving a rectangular accretion of grime and discarded snack wrappers around the still shiny patch of floor where it had stood. We never did make a *This England* documentary on helical scan, and an important advance in documentary technique was delayed until the coming of video Hi-8 and mini-digital camcorders in the 1990s.

Having gained recognition in ITV, the ACTT had imposed a closed shop. As a result, by the 1960s people wishing to work in ITV faced much the same catch-22 situation as those who aspired to work in the film industry. Apart from a few people taken on with the union's agreement as trainees or researchers, all applicants for a job in ITV had to possess a union card. Trainees and researchers could be offered probationary union membership, which entailed restrictions on what work the person could undertake. For instance, when I was offered my first contract in ITV in 1964, I was granted a probationary union ticket which, although I had directed in the BBC and in the theatre, barred me from directing anything for at least two years. In the long run it did not particularly matter to me as I was fortunate to be able to work with a number of the very best directors and producers in the industry, people whose work I had long admired. Even so, ridiculous situations could arise. Early one morning when I turned up on a location at the Horse Guards' barracks where, as the programme's researcher, I had with some difficulty arranged to film one short sequence for an hour-long ATV documentary, I was told that the director was unwell and would not be able to come in that morning. He had asked me to make sure that the scene which we had planned was shot. I discussed the simple sequence of shots with the cameraman and the other members of the crew, who then shot it. However, when the crew got back to ATV's studios and news of the morning's events leaked out, there was the most terrific row with the union. A researcher on a restricted ticket (me) had 'directed' a sequence. For a while it looked as if the programme would be 'blacked' and I would lose my union card. In the end it blew over. I was allowed to stay in the union and the documentary was completed as planned. I was (still am) a committed trade unionist, but I vowed that once the opportunity came, I would work to get the worst and most anti-creative of the union's practices altered. There were many more of my generation who felt the same.

There was also strict demarcation between what tasks could be undertaken by members of which union. I remember during a camera rehearsal when I was a young actor appearing in my first ITV play in 1959, I heard the director ask for a drinking mug which was in front of me on the table around which we were sitting to play the scene to be moved a little to the right or left so that it would not block the shot. Without thinking I leant forward, as I would have done in the theatre, to move the mug. But before my hand could reach it my fellow actors hissed at me urgently, 'Don't do that, they'll all walk out on strike!' Seconds later a props man appeared out of the shadows and moved it the required few inches. Over time such petty restrictions built up a reserve of resentment against the unions, particularly among younger people such as researchers, trainee directors and producers, many of whom were coming into television direct from university, journalism and the theatre.

In 1967, with the announcement of the winners of the new contracts, many people working in ITV became fearful for their jobs. As a result industrial relations worsened and there was a series of wildcat stoppages at companies around the network. The ACTT demanded that before the new contractors recruited any new staff they must engage all the union members who were being made redundant by the companies which were losing their franchises. With the ACTT maintaining its closed shop across the whole of ITV, the employers ultimately had no alternative but to accede to the union's demand. LWT, which had been planning to take on 600 staff at basic rates of pay determined by the company, was forced to take on 900 at rates of pay very much higher than it had expected.

Difficulty with the unions was only one of the problems that beset LWT in the run up to going on air. Today Peacock admits that he and his colleagues were 'profoundly naïve'. They had underrated the importance of the federal nature of the network system in ITV. The sort of programmes LWT was planning, however welcome they might have been to Lord Hill, were unlikely to please Lew Grade. Worse, Lord Aylestone (better known as Herbert Bowden, a workhorse Labour politician who, after war service as a Special Constable and a stint in the RAF Police, had risen to the level of Chief Whip and Leader of the House), the man appointed by Wilson to succeed Hill as Chairman of the ITA, was not the man to carry through the kind of changes planned by Hill. He liked ITV's game shows and chorus girls. Offered the choice of the chairmanship of the ITA or of the BBC by Wilson, he had indicated a preference for the ITA because he felt he 'could much more easily work with Robert Fraser and the ITA than with Hugh Carleton Greene and the BBC.'[6]

Even Granada which, unlike some of the other network companies, had welcomed the appointment of LWT as a potential ally inside the Network Programme Committee in battles to get their serious programmes scheduled in good slots, soon fell out with Peacock and his team. It was just as important to Granada as to Lew Grade and the other network companies that ITV retained large audiences at the weekend. Denis Forman of Granada says, 'We had an appalling time with Peacock and Margerison. They were going to have the best programmes ever.' He claims that when Granada offered LWT *Coronation Street* for their weekend schedule they turned it down: 'They said they were going to do better than that. So we said to ourselves "They're intolerable." After that we simply said, "Piss off." '[7]

Relationships inside LWT itself deteriorated almost as rapidly as those with the other companies in the network. For a start, Frost's role in the company was far from straightforward. He was barred from becoming an executive director of the company under ITA rules that forbade anyone who was expected to appear in a company's programmes from also taking an active role in its control. Shows fronted by him – *Frost on Friday*, *Frost on Saturday* and *Frost on Sunday* – were to be the new company's main identifying feature. In addition, his company, Paradine (Frost's middle name), was to supply packaged programmes featuring expensive stars like Tommy Cooper, Danny La Rue and Ronnie Barker to LWT. On top of this, Frost still had outstanding commitments as a performer elsewhere. Frost had probably originally envisaged himself running the company. However, in practice this could not work. In fact, in the rush of putting together the LWT bid for the ITA, far too many things seem to have been left ill-defined. The result was that clashes between Frost, Michael Peacock and Cyril Bennett, the Programme Controller, began almost as soon as LWT had been awarded the franchise. There were also difficulties between the professional television executives and the non-broadcasters on the company board. 'Michael Peacock was offensive from an early stage,' according to one anonymous board member. Another called him 'an arrogant young man of immense abilities, but he made it clear that he was not going to be influenced by the Board as far as programmes were concerned'.[8] Although neither Peacock nor Crawley had run a commercial company before, not all of the blame for the internal difficulties at LWT can be laid at Peacock's door. He could be direct, even brusque, but he had had a brilliant career at the BBC and people had found him by no means impossible to work with. Perhaps, as David Docherty suggests in his book about LWT, it would have helped if other key executives in the company, particularly Tom Margerison and Clive Irving, had been more supportive of Peacock and if his chairman, Crawley, had been firmer with the high-powered businessmen on the board. Those businessmen, the great captains of Wilsonian British industry, Lords Campbell, Crowther, Hartwell and Stokes, the Hon. David Astor and the Hon. David Montagu, Sir Arnold Weinstock and Evelyn de Rothschild, had never seemed the most likely people to settle down readily to the often tedious business of running what was, by their standards, a small company – even in so supposedly glamorous an industry as television. Things would almost certainly have turned out better if John Freeman had become the deputy chairman as had been assumed at the time of the company's ITA application. One of the factors that had persuaded Peacock to throw in his lot with Frost had been the prospect of working with Freeman. Peacock admired and respected Freeman, who was the godfather to one of his children. However, Harold Wilson had asked Freeman to become the British Ambassador to the USA and Freeman had gone to Washington rather than the modest LWT headquarters in Savile Row.

For the moment, however, the tensions inside LWT remained hidden from the outside world. Whispers of difficulties did leak out during the winter of 1967 and spring of 1968, but they remained only whispers. The impression given to the rest of the television industry remained one of overweening self-confidence, coupled with generous budgets and high salaries. In May 1968, as revolts by students, peace protestors, workers and intellectuals flared around the world, Michael Peacock announced 'a programme revolution'. LWT, he told an expectant press conference, would spend more per programme hour than any ITV company to date. In fact, because of the problems LWT had had with the unions, the company had only just been able to start recording the vital stock of programmes that it needed by the date of its first transmission, Friday 2 August 1968.

*   *   *

On Monday 20 May, in what could have been a portent, the first of the new clutch of ITV contractors went on air – Harlech Television in Wales and the West of England. The previous incumbent, TWW, outraged that it had been deprived of its contract, had (in the words of the official ITV history) 'retired in a huff' two months early. The Chairman of the ITA, Lord Aylestone, travelled down to Cardiff for the much-heralded 'first night of the new ITV'. It turned out to be a monumental disaster, marked by technical mishaps, climaxing in the non-appearance of the station's two biggest stars – Richard Burton and Elizabeth Taylor. So much for expressions of 'cultural patriotism'.

The rest of 'the new ITV' did not fare much better when it went on air on Monday 29 July. On that day ITV's interim national agreement with the ACTT expired. Months earlier the union had lodged a claim for a 7% rise in pay rates and a reduction in the working week from 40 to 35 hours which, taken together, amounted to an increase of almost 30%. The companies had responded with an offer of just 2.5%. There matters had stuck, deadlocked. As a result, on the new ITV contractors' first night, 29 July, Thames, the new London weekday contractor, was taken off the air for almost two hours. The ITV network had then lurched forward for the rest of the week until 7 p.m. on Friday 2 August, when LWT was due to take over. Bang on time LWT launched into its first announcement – '*We Have Ways of Making You Laugh!*' And then the screen went black. The ACTT had pulled the plugs on the station's first show, an offering from Frank Muir's Entertainment Unit. How much were grand promises going to be worth now?

For the next two weeks ITV limped on with an improvised service, played out by managers operating video machines. LWT had intended to rely heavily on its three live Frost shows each weekend. But with the technicians refusing to work they could not be done. After two days of having the programme taken off the air by the ACTT, the LWT management decided that they would not to be cowed. If the technicians wouldn't put out the Frost show the bosses would do it themselves – they had all been programme makers. The Programme Controller, Cyril Bennett, became the show's producer, doubling as the floor manager. Bennett's driver became a cable operator. Michael Peacock was hauled out of fruitless negotiations with the union to direct the programme – allowing Frank Muir, doing the studio warm-up, to quip: 'The Managing Director is managing to direct.' Away from the studio furious union members sat at home trying to spot strike-breakers. The next day Alan Sapper, the union's Assistant General Secretary, angrily told a *Daily Sketch* reporter: 'Not only is this action contrary to the ITA regulations . . . this equipment can be quite dangerous if inexperienced technicians handle it. They are walking on a knife edge, taking their lives in their hands.'[9] The following day someone stuck up a studio notice reading: 'Beware. Killer Cameras!' The strike lasted for two weeks. Even then no new national agreement was concluded until March 1969, when the union won a rise of 13% over three years.

While all this was going on tragedy unfolded overseas. Warsaw Pact tanks rolled over the border into Czechoslovakia and Soviet paratroops put an end to the Prague Spring. In Chicago, outside the Democratic Party Convention, Mayor Daley's police beat up anti-Vietnam War demonstrators.

Seemingly oblivious to the trouble they were now in with both the unions and the other ITV companies, a week after the strike ended LWT put out *The Franchise Trail*, a musical satire on the quest for riches of a bunch of prominent people going in search of an ITV franchise. The satire was feeble and the music little better. The title song contained this verse:

> You can dream of Eldorado, you can dream of pirate gold
> You take a gun and rob the Royal Mail.
> But I'll be a boardroom bandit, I'll be rich before I'm old,
> I'll pack my bags and ride the franchise trail.[10]

Peacock had expected, following conversations with Lord Hill when LWT was appointed, that the basis on which the ITV network companies supplied programmes to one another would be changed so as to accurately reflect the true cost of producing the programmes. But with Hill's departure these promises were forgotten. The companies continued as before, exchanging programmes according to a points system which was meant to reflect the percentage that each company had of ITV's total Net Advertising Revenue (NAR). This took no account of the fact that the type of programmes being produced by LWT were often much more costly than those ITV had made previously. As a result LWT was losing out financially. To make matters worse, while ITV's weekday audience was holding up well, the weekend audience in the LWT area began to plunge, and with it the income earned by LWT from the selling of its advertising airtime.

On 9 September ITV's old guard struck. 'I got where I am by knowing what I hate, and I know I hate David Frost,' Lew Grade was reported to have told the Network Programme Committee.[11] What Lew Grade really hated, and what the other ITV bosses hated as much as he did, was what LWT's programmes were doing to ITV's audience ratings. Possibly worse from Grade's point of view, posh LWT programmes had replaced audience favourites such as his own *London Palladium* variety shows in the weekend schedule. Until 1968 the four original network companies ATV, A-R, ABC and Granada had been able to carve up the network between themselves without much outside interference. Although there had sometimes been disagreements and a good deal of tough horse-trading between the bosses, the schedule had generally been constructed through a series of bilateral discussions, often on the phone, between individuals – Lew Grade calling one of the Bernsteins or Howard Thomas, doing a deal between them on the placing of a programme or series, then calling the other two majors and squaring things. But as soon as LWT and Yorkshire arrived relations deteriorated. Denis Forman, who convened the new Programme Controllers Committee, recalls that at its first meeting things got so heated over an allegedly broken promise about a programme scheduled in a Friday peak-time slot that Cyril Bennett of LWT took his jacket off and challenged Donald Baverstock of Yorkshire to 'come outside'. Soon the controllers were joined by their respective managing directors with, as Forman describes it, 'Lew Grade in the van pounding the table in his customary stye'. The meeting ended in disarray. After that Forman laid down strict ground rules and insisted that at future meetings there should be an invigilator from the ITA 'to ensure a better standard of behaviour in class'.[12]

Before LWT began, its executives had assumed that because of the reputation of the team they had assembled to make its programmes, the company would be given disproportionate access to network slots. The other ITV companies quickly disabused Peacock and his colleagues of this idea. The other companies had no interest in playing LWT's upmarket specials and one-off dramas in weekend peak time against the aggressive scheduling of the new Controller of BBC-1, Paul Fox. When he joined the Frost bid Humphrey Burton had seen himself playing the role of a 'Trojan Horse bringing culture to the masses'. But Granada already considered itself to be the network's supplier of upmarket drama and arts programmes. LWT was now in a fight – a fight it was bound to lose unless the ITA intervened.

To its dismay the beleaguered LWT management found that the ITA never did intervene, unless it was to ban or to express its displeasure with some LWT programme, or to avoid incurring the displeasure of the government. In one particularly notorious instance, in November 1968, the ITA took off LWT's *Mrs Wilson's Diary* (based on a regular column in *Private Eye*) because of a sketch depicting a very drunk George Brown (Wilson's Foreign Secretary, who was often described in *Private Eye* and elsewhere as 'tired and emotional' or 'as tired as a newt'). Both the ITA's Chairman, Lord Aylestone, Wilson's former Chief Whip, and the Director General, Robert Fraser, formerly a socialist journalist (although to young programme makers like myself his one-time socialism seemed impossible to detect), had, it seemed, taken 'great exception' to the offending sketch.

By the winter of 1968–9, with the national economy in recession, advertising expenditure depressed, LWT meeting resistance to its programmes from audiences and the other ITV controllers, and rows between Frost and Peacock, morale and revenue in the company plummeted. Now not only were the management falling out with each other, the board was falling out with the management. The captains of industry were becoming mutinous. In the words of one of them, it was 'clear that the executives had no idea about money, no control, no idea about numbers'.[13]

The programme people were in trouble too. On its very first assignment, an investigation into drug pushers in Brixton, four members of Clive Irving's Public Affairs Unit were arrested on suspicion of supplying cannabis. A storm blew up when the Kestrel team made a programme showing the work in Africa of the Save the Children Fund in a bad light. LWT's chairman, Aidan Crawley, who took a particular interest in the work of the Fund, was deeply embarrassed when the Fund came to him to complain. *The Inquisitors*, a series planned as a replacement for the long-running *Avengers*, was found to be so awful that it had to be dropped before ever getting on the air.

In an attempt to counter the antipathy of viewers, early in 1969 LWT shifted to a more populist programme schedule. Lew Grade's London Palladium shows came back at peak time on Sundays, complete with Jack Parnell's Orchestra and The Palladium Dancers. But still viewers stayed away. In February Humphrey Burton penned a memo to Cyril Bennett with a copy to Peacock, expressing mounting discontent among LWT's programme makers. Reminding him of the high promises they had made to the ITA and the high ideals with which the founding programme maker members of the company had come together, Burton wrote: 'something has gone crucially wrong with our company.' Deploring the unoriginal programming, increasing reliance on showbiz and narrowly focused narrative drama, Burton continued, 'we didn't join forces only to make money, now did we?' Bennett replied tersely that until the programme makers had secured high ratings the company could not afford to 'spend time, energy or manpower on shows that push back the television frontiers.'[14]

The problems confronting ITV as a whole increased further in March. The 1,265-feet high Emley Moor transmitter on the Yorkshire moors between Leeds and Manchester collapsed, depriving the six million viewers in the newly created Yorkshire Television franchise area of ITV pictures. In the budget the government announced substantial increases in the Exchequer Levy paid by the companies to the government from their gross advertising incomes. This, at least, did provoke a response from the ITA. Its Chairman and Director-General spoke out in public against the increases.

However, the ITA continued to do nothing about the state of LWT's programmes or to make the company stick to its promises. In April, dismayed by its cost and lacklustre programmes, Peacock and Bennett disbanded Clive Irving's Public Affairs Unit. With this, dissension inside LWT became public. Members of the Public Affairs Unit protested and the press and other programme makers accused LWT of reneging on the promises made when it won the franchise. But what precisely were those promises? Still no one, except the Authority and those who had penned LWT's original eighty-page franchise application, knew. The franchise application and details of LWT's lofty promises remained secret.

Late in May Ben Whitaker, who was the MP for Hampstead where some of the members of the now jobless Public Affairs Unit lived, wrote to Lord Aylestone expressing the 'disquiet of both the public and some ITV employees' at the 'apparent failure' of certain ITV companies to adhere to undertakings given on programme quality, undertakings upon which, Whitaker pointed out, they had 'obtained their franchises'. What means, he wanted to know, were there of making LWT adhere to its undertakings? A few days later Aylestone's extended reply, drafted in the unmistakably circumlocutory style of his Director-General, Sir Robert Fraser, revealed only that while the Authority paid 'careful regard' to the 'general character of a company's declared programme intentions', it might not attach 'great weight' to its specific proposals. The Authority, he continued, 'does not . . . exact undertakings' over particular programmes nor about the amount of any one genre of programme that a company will produce. Instead the Authority relied, he told Whitaker, on the fact that the companies drew up their schedules in consultation with the Authority and could only operate with schedules that had its prior approval. LWT's successive programme schedules had had 'the Authority's approval from the start'.[15] Not satisfied, Whitaker wrote again. Was there not even a broad obligation on a successful applicant to adhere to the general principles upon which the company had won its contract?

Now the Free Communications Group intervened, forcing the whole issue of the LWT franchise and its programme promises into the open. Three months earlier the FCG had held its first public meeting, attended by 150 people from the press, radio, television and film making. During the meeting the organisers had said that they hoped to ferret out hidden stories about the crisis in the communications industry and asked for help so they could publish details in the group's journal *Open Secret*. With discontent rising to near mutiny among senior programme staff at LWT, the FCG had been given a copy of the original eighty-page confidential LWT franchise application. This the FCG now published in the first edition of *Open Secret*. Because the FCG included a lot of successful journalists, *Open Secret* was circulated not only inside newspaper offices, studios and cutting rooms, but put on sale by newsagents and specialist book shops. Publication of the LWT franchise application produced an immediate storm of press coverage. LWT was severely criticised for failing to stick to its promises, and the ITA was hounded for failing to do anything about it. A few days later, when Cyril Bennett faced the press to announce yet another, even more populist, revised programme schedule, he was forced to defend his company's record. 'The first duty of a commercial station', he said, 'is to survive.' Milton Schulman, writing in the *Evening Standard* under the headline 'The Scandal of London Weekend', riposted that LWT's 'first duty is suicide'.

In August, with Peacock away on a much-needed holiday and so unable to defend himself, the captains of industry and representatives of 'the great and good' on the LWT board, frustrated by the company's continuing lack of profits and stung by the criticism heaped on them since the FCG's publication of the secret franchise application, turned on Peacock. On the evening of his return, Sunday 7 September 1969, Peacock was summoned to his chairman Aidan Crawley's home in Chester Square and told that he must resign forthwith. Cyril Bennett, he was told, would be going as well. But Peacock was not the kind of man to walk meekly out of the company that he had done so much to set up without demur. The next day there was an almighty row at a board meeting and one of its members, Lord (Jock) Campbell, was deputed to look into the matter. By now word had got round the company and several of the star names whose inclusion in the original contract application had helped to secure the company's franchise made it clear that they would resign unless Peacock was re-instated. Nevertheless when Campbell reported back that Peacock had the overwhelming support of the programme staff, the board, fearing that it would become a laughing stock, again decided that Peacock must go. Meanwhile at the ITA, Sir Robert Fraser wrote privately to Lord Aylestone to inform him about what was going on: ' . . . I need hardly say that this will not be very good for the Authority. It will revive the whole question of the selection of programme companies, for there is little doubt in my mind that LWT owes its appointment far more to the inclusion of Michael in the group than to any other single factor. I can remember how he dominated the interview with his consistent and brilliant talk.'[16]

Yet despite this endorsement of Peacock's pivotal role in the award of the contract to LWT, the ITA did not intervene. Nor did David Frost, the person responsible for luring Peacock away from the BBC in the first place. Frost was working in New York when he got an urgent phone call from Clive Irving informing him that Peacock was being fired. Frost says that he 'immediately saw the need for it, and felt that, once taken (the decision), had to be adhered to'.[17] He flew back to London for a day and a half between his engagements in New York, talked to virtually everyone involved including Cyril Bennett, but not, it seems, to Peacock himself, and then, convinced that the sacking should take its course, simply flew back to New York. However, the rest of the dissident star-name programme makers were not to be so easily deflected from defending Peacock and asked to meet Sir Robert Fraser to voice their concerns. They were refused.

On 19 September the LWT board confirmed Peacock's dismissal publicly and announced that Dr Tom Margerison would become the company's new Chief Executive. One of the protestors later recalled that on hearing this, 'We all fell about laughing.' Margerison had, in comparison to Peacock or Bennett, virtually no programme-making experience. The press, meanwhile, had a field day. Peacock's resignation made the front page of every national newspaper. The *Evening Standard* reported that, as they drove away from their board meeting, the shamefaced chairman and directors of the company hid their faces from the cameras.

The next day six of LWT's senior programme executives and the three Kestrel executives resigned. Frank Muir, Doreen Stephens, Terry Hughes, Derek Granger, Joy Whitby, Tony Garnett, James McTaggart, Kenith Trodd and Humphrey Burton all went.[18] Burton, who had emerged as the leader of the protestors, summed up his fellow rebels' attitude thus: 'We thought, "You can't sack him because you haven't asked us, and without us you wouldn't have the franchise in the first place." '[19] At hastily convened meetings throughout the company 500 employees pledged their support to Peacock and threatened to black out the company's programmes. Within days 800 ACTT members across ITV had signed a petition. Questions were tabled in the House of Commons and there were calls for a full public enquiry.

A week later Lord Aylestone, commenting on what had happened at LWT and the ITA's failure to intervene, said that the Authority had no right or inclination to instruct the boards of ITV companies about whom to employ or dismiss; if directors were not permitted to manage their own affairs there would not be a self-respecting board left in the whole of ITV. LWT had been 'subjected to criticism altogether excessive in relation to its faults'.[20]

Two years earlier, while Michael Peacock had been clearing his desk in the BBC Television Centre in preparation for joining David Frost's consortium in the bid for the LWT contract, David Attenborough had presented him with a cigarette lighter. Knowing how prone he was to losing lighters Attenborough had said, 'You'll have lost it by the time you ask to come back.'[21] Now, pitched unceremoniously out of LWT with just one year's salary by way of compensation, Peacock found that like Alasdair Milne and Antony Jay before him, the BBC did not want to know him: 'I was made to kneel in the snow.'[22] Apart from a few short consultancies and research jobs, Peacock was out of work for two years. When the BBC did eventually agree to allow Peacock to do some work for them, it was made clear to him that he could never again expect to be a part of the BBC's senior management. He was not even to be allowed to attend departmental meetings. It seemed an uncalled-for insult to a man who, until he threw in his lot with David Frost, had been widely tipped as a future Director-General.

However, Peacock was down, not out. A decade later he would be back, playing a crucial role on the side of rebel programme makers.

* * *

The fall-out from the LWT affair was to infect broadcasting for the next decade. The idea that putting programme people in charge of ITV companies might be a solution to the shortcomings of ITV or a means of alleviating the frustrations of programme makers had been seriously discredited. On the other hand, the Free Communications Group, by obtaining a copy of LWT's original franchise application and publishing it, was itself now thrust firmly into the spotlight. Not only had the group achieved its intention of getting the ITA held up to ridicule in the national press and caused people to question the whole way in which the media were administered, regulated, owned and run in Britain, it had also stimulated interest in the Group's own views. In the weeks following its publication of London Weekend's franchise application, the FCG's aims were discussed in almost every Sunday and daily newspaper and in the weeklies. It even got good coverage in the foreign press and on radio. Three leading members of the Group were invited onto *Late Night Line-Up* to outline the Group's aims.

The result was to increase greatly the number of people joining the FCG. Within months membership was well into the hundreds, eventually reaching over 700. In addition to young radicals, those drawn to the group included a substantial number of older and well-respected journalists and television producers. Many of the people involved in the Hatton BFI revolt the previous summer joined the group, together with people working in publishing and even a few from the theatre. Initially, the FCG had no money except what it could raise from selling *Open Secret* (at four shillings a copy), membership subscriptions (£2 per year to include all publications, but members were encouraged 'to contribute £3 or £5') and whatever volunteers could scrape together from supporters and sympathisers in the way of contributions in kind, such as use of the phone, paper, duplicating equipment, desk space, rooms to meet in. For the first year of its existence the FCG had no paid staff. Later the steering committee appointed Christine Fox, a researcher at Thames who had worked as a journalist in Scotland and for the *Daily Mail*, as the organiser at a salary of £30 a week. Her first task was to apply to the Rowntree Trust for a grant to pay her salary and open a small office. By its fifth edition *Open Secret* was able to announce 'Our busking days are over!' The Rowntree Foundation had agreed a grant of £6,000 to the FCG spread over three years and to provide secretarial help and an office in a narrow street close to Charing Cross station.

By 1970 the FCG had become established as the main forum through which a growing number of journalists, programme and film makers, unhappy with developments in their own industries, could channel their discontent and work towards planning reform. The FCG was now run by a council, the composition of which fluctuated in number – a minimum of twenty, but sometimes as many as thirty, depending on need and the number of people able to devote sufficient time. The council had specialist sections covering the press and publishing, television, radio, film and the theatre. In addition to Gus Macdonald, Neal Ascherson, Bruce Page and Alex Coburn, those who joined the FCG included many who were already well known or would later become well known in their own fields – Phillip Whitehead, Editor of the ITV weekly current affairs programme *This Week*, Stuart Hood, a former Controller of Programmes at BBC Television, Jonathan Steele, a leader writer on the *Guardian*, Bill Webb, Literary Editor of the *Guardian*, Michael Wolfers, Africa correspondent of *The Times*, Claire Walsh, publicity manager of Penguin Books, Tim Fell, West End theatre organiser of the actors' union Equity, Roger Graef and Maurice Hatton, David Elstein, Nicholas Garnham, Colin Thomas, Richard Broad, Geoff Dunlop, Steve Morrison and Maxine Baker, who all went on to become well known in television. At least half of the television membership came from the BBC and ranged from senior producers to trainees, assistant editors to cameramen. Members were drawn from most of the ITV network television companies, notably Granada, Thames and LWT.[23] There were also members from provincial newspapers and regional television stations. In addition, more or less autonomous FCG groups sprang up in major centres outside London. There was a particularly lively group in Bristol under the title FreeProp.

By the time of the Free Communications Group's second public meeting in July 1969, it was sufficiently well known to get a cabinet minister, Tony Benn, to address it. But Benn, giving what Phillip Whitehead described as 'a superb imitation of a public school history master who has mixed up his periods', turned out to have little to add to the media debate beyond a repeat of his by now infamous views about the control of broadcasting and a litany of already familiar, imprecise Labour Party policy formulations about giving more broadcast airtime and press coverage to the expression of a greater range of opinions. The FCG members in the hall responded by giving him the bird. They told him in no uncertain terms that, while they were certainly not hostile to the principle of encouraging the inclusion of a much wider range of opinion in what was seen and read, the Labour Party's policy was simply not good enough. What was needed was a radical overhaul of the whole way in which broadcasting was organised. In his diaries Benn describes himself as fighting back as hard as he could and greatly enjoying it. He says that after presenting his lecture he 'got absolutely hammered by these guys, who like all left-wingers, were totally pessimistic and said nothing could or would be done'. He described the FCG as 'highly revolutionary – a sort of Maoist Group'.[24]

The belief that the Free Communications Group was some kind of extreme left-wing group bent on revolution gained wide currency, particularly among those who ran television or owned newspapers. The newspaper owners were particularly worried by its influence and its promotion of the idea of journalists' rights to consultation over editorial policies. The Newspaper Proprietors Association became so concerned about the activities of the FCG that they secretly sent a delegation to Downing Street to seek Harold Wilson's help in getting the group closed down.[25] Many prominent members of the FCG became convinced (and remain convinced to this day) that the FCG was placed under surveillance by the security services and infiltrated. If so, it was a reaction which was out of all proportion to any threat posed by the activities of the FCG and said rather more about those responsible for the surveillance than about the FCG itself. Benn's description of the FCG as a highly revolutionary, 'sort of Maoist group' is simply wide of the mark. There were certainly a number of Marxists in the FCG, of quite a wide range of complexions, among them Trotskyites and syndicalists (some of the FCG's policies were syndicalist in spirit). But most FCG members were probably fairly mainstream Labour Party supporters (I doubt if the majority of them were even Party members, except through the affiliation of the trade unions to which more or less everyone working in the press or broadcasting had to belong). Phillip Whitehead, who was one of the members of the FCG's Council, says that 'the FCG was divided between the old Communists like Caroline Heller, those who wanted Gosplan (the Soviet economic planning commission) applied to broadcasting, and the others who thought merely that broadcasting needed the intervention of the state between the broadcasters and the forces of commerce'. There were a few members of the Conservative Party among the FCG's members and many who had no party affiliation. What really characterised the group and its members was a shared anti-authoritarianism.

They had, as Dr Johnson said of Milton, 'not so much the love of Liberty as the repugnance to Authority'. The FCG's journal, *Open Secret*, which included cartoons and was laid out in a style reminiscent of *Private Eye*, was itself testimony to the members' sense of fun, to their delight in mocking the pompous, the greedy and the over-powerful. *Open Secret*, reporting in its third issue on an FCG conference on possible future structures for the administration of broadcasting, ended by quoting approvingly from an essay by Stuart Hall: 'The error was and is always to see the alternatives as confined to either bureaucratic, administratively top-heavy, executive orientated, paternalistic broadcasting organised in a mono-lithic unit; or robber-baron, advertising conscious, programme starved, profit-orientated contracting companies: the one given a licence to improve minds under the charter, the other a licence to print money under the Act . . . The need in broadcasting was, is now, and continues to be the need to transcend this set of alternatives.'[26] This seems as clear a statement of the goals of the FCG as its members ever produced. Political differences between members of the FCG were generally sunk in pursuit of a common goal – a freer, more plural broadcasting, press, cinema, theatre and publishing. Phillip Whitehead sees the FCG as a product of its time: 'We wanted it and we wanted it now. It was very much a baby-boomers' crusade.'[27]

In retrospect it is clear that one of the most important things that the FCG achieved was to establish a unique forum in which programme makers from the BBC and ITV, journalists and film makers could meet, learn from each other's experience and together discuss possible solutions to the problems that con-fronted them. None of the other industry institutions, such as the Royal Television Society, the Society of Film and Television Arts (later BAFTA) or the trade unions, offered quite the same focus. Ideas were developed, campaigning techniques honed and working relationships forged during the four years of the FCG's existence which would be the foundation of some of the most important broadcasting industry campaigns of the next twenty years.

* * *

At the very moment in September 1969 when problems in ITV – the dismissal of Michael Peacock and the resignation from LWT of nine of its leading pro-gramme makers – were making all the headlines, the BBC faced a new crisis. In April 1969 Charles Curran, regarded by even his colleagues in the BBC as an austere and colourless administrator, had taken over from Hugh Carleton Greene as Director-General. Programme makers suspected that Curran had been chosen in preference to other more colourful candidates with a proven commitment to programmes and programme makers in order to appease Harold Wilson and to do Hill's bidding. Reporting on Curran's appointment, even one of the BBC's own news programmes, *The World at One*, had questioned whether Curran would be any more than 'Hill's tame poodle'.

The first major issue that Curran had to deal with was *Broadcasting in the '70s*, the final report by the consultants McKinsey & Co. into the BBC's finances and use of resources. Published on 10 July 1970, it provoked a storm of protest. Although most of its proposals related specifically to radio (reorganisation of the four national radio channels – Radios 1, 2, 3 and 4 – major changes in the BBC's regional structure, reduction of the number of BBC house orchestras from nine to five), it was widely recognised that the real issues concerned the future of the BBC itself. The next day the press pointed accusingly to the fact that *Broadcasting in the '70s* was really about money. The *Sunday Telegraph*'s headline read 'BBC plan ducks vital issues of cost', while the *Sun*'s heading read 'BBC need money, not an axe'.[28] The BBC house union, the ABS, rejected the report and threatened industrial action. The reaction of younger, more politicised programme makers to *Broadcasting in the '70s* was summed up by Nicholas Garnham, a BBC producer and a member of the FCG. The effect of the report was to pin financial responsibility on to producers at the very point at which creative responsibility was being removed from them: 'What is happening is a normal process of industrial growth . . . BBC television is no longer a cottage industry. It is now entering the mass production phase and producers are becoming mere wage-slaves.'[29] One week after the report was published the Government announced that there would be no immediate increase in the BBC licence fee, renewing speculation that the BBC was to be forced to take advertising.

The first concerted protest against the proposals contained in *Broadcasting in the '70s* came not from inside the BBC but from a new group based at the address of the Royal Institute of British Architects, just up the street from the BBC's Broadcasting House headquarters. In a slim booklet entitled *Crisis in Broadcasting*, the Campaign for Better Broadcasting denounced *Broadcasting in the '70s* as a 'disaster policy . . . a masterpiece of devious and subtle generalisation' which, in capitulating to accountants' logic, had claimed to put broadcasting first and money second, while in fact doing the reverse. The manifesto was backed by a letter signed by twelve of the Campaign's leading lights – Sir Adrian Boult, Sir

Tyrone Guthrie, Sir Roland Penrose, Professor Max Beloff, James Cameron, Dr John Kendrew, Frank Kermode, George Melly, Jonathan Miller, Henry Moore, Peter Shepheard and the Reith lecturer G. M. Carstairs. Other famous names in the arts were soon added to the list – the poets John Betjeman and C. Day Lewis, Geraint Evans, Harold Pinter, J. B. Priestley, Michael Redgrave and Harry Secombe.

By October the BBC faced the first ever strike by members of its house union, the ABS, backed for the first time by the 2,000 ACTT members who worked in the BBC. Rather than taking blanket action, they targeted selected programmes. One day the Petula Clark show was blacked out and on the next filming of Zola's *Germinal* was stopped, followed by blackouts of *24 Hours* and *Nationwide*. The strike was not directly about *Broadcasting in the '70s*. It was about pay, particularly the salaries of the vital monthly paid staff who were the Corporation's backbone. But inevitably the two issues had become entwined. Curran's response to the union action was to have a notice posted on all BBC noticeboards stating that the proposals in *Broadcasting in the '70s* were to be implemented without consultation.

The reaction was immediate. A joint statement was issued by the ABS and the ACTT, by the actors' union Equity and the MU, the musicians' union, calling for a public enquiry to be held before any proposals were implemented. As the Head of Programmes in the BBC's North Region warned Curran, 'Discontent that was smouldering on the floor' was now 'ready to blaze into anger'. Mass meetings were held in BBC studios up and down the country. The strike became total.

In Bristol, home of one of the most active FCG groups – Bristol FreeProp – two hundred people from every kind of job in the BBC crammed into Studio B and elected a joint action committee. In the weeks that followed they set up working parties and practical seminars in which they hammered out possible new organisational structures for broadcasting. They also tried out new, more collective methods of working, experimenting with role swapping on productions. They shot programme exercises in which secretaries took on the role of the director and directors filled the roles of production secretaries. Over time the management in Bristol even allowed them to use BBC resources for these exercises. Among those who became involved in this were two students who were in Bristol on a course – Steve Morrison and John Willis – both later to become heads of broadcasting organisations. The young ACTT shop steward who was the organiser of Bristol FreeProp, Colin Thomas, remembers: 'There was a real buzz. When we got 200 at the meeting in Studio B we thought it is really happening. Now things will change. But, of course, they didn't!'[30]

The strike itself was settled ten days after it had begun, when Curran backed down and invited the government to intervene. Barbara Castle set up a Court of Inquiry which, criticising the BBC for its lack of communication, told the BBC to improve its offer.[31]

As Hill was to write in his memoirs later, 'What had begun as a revolt against changes in radio generally, and the Third Programme in particular, was developing into a fundamental attack on the system, BBC and ITV alike.'[32]

One strand in that attack came from a commission of enquiry set up by the ACTT to look at the whole television industry and suggest possible alternative structures. FCG members had been instrumental in getting the ACTT to establish the commission and a leading FCG member, Caroline Heller, was taken on by the union as its organiser.[33] Another strand was the launch of the 76 Group at a meeting in the House of Commons on 18 November 1969. Chaired by the Labour MP Brian Walden, the meeting opened with a speech by Stuart Hood, the former Controller of Programmes in BBC Television. It demanded the setting up a new royal commission to look into the organisation of broadcasting after 1976, when the BBC Charter and the ITV Act were both due to expire.

The idea of such a campaign had come out of a gathering in Phillip Whitehead's London flat. Again, many of the 76 Group's founders were leading lights in the FCG – Richard Broad, David Elstein, Nicholas Garnham and Cate Haste, in addition to Whitehead and Hood. Because the 76 Group was a single issue group, with a limited but focused objective, it was able to draw support from across a surprisingly wide spectrum of interests. LWT rebels such as Doreen Stephens, Kenith Trodd and Humphrey Burton were joined by leading figures from the other arts, including the conductor Sir Charles Groves and Delius's former amanuensis, Eric Fenby. In addition to Labour MP Brian Walden there was a Conservative, John Costello. It seemed that the BBC itself tacitly supported the Group's aims. Curran told senior BBC managers that he had no wish to prevent Corporation staff from supporting the 76 Group's activities as long as they did not act in 'any organisational or public relations capacity' or sign any policy statements issued by the group.

A letter signed by founder members of the 76 Group told potential supporters

that it had been launched 'to represent the views of men and women professionally employed in television and radio' who were 'united by a common concern'
over the future of broadcasting and 'dismay at recent events in both I.T.V. and the
B.B.C . . . we feel that the structures of both B.B.C. and I.T.V. must be radically
examined. On the one hand, control by the I.T.A. has shown itself too feeble to
influence programme policy, while control at the B.B.C. is over centralised and
bureaucratic.' The Royal Commission should, the organisers said, include representatives of those who work in television.[34]

It soon became evident that the 76 Group, the Campaign for Better Broadcasting, the strikes and other protests were having an impact. Early in December John
Stonehouse, the Minister of Posts and Telecommunications, told MPs during a
debate on the BBC and *Broadcasting in the'70s* that, although he had not reached
any conclusion about a new inquiry into broadcasting, he was considering
prospects for some sort of commission or inquiry into the long-term future of
broadcasting after 1976.

The groups' response was to step up their campaigns. In February 1970 a letter
protesting against the proposals in *Broadcasting in the'70s*, signed by over one
hundred BBC staff producers, was published in *The Times*. This was followed over
the next few days by similar letters from other BBC staff members. The government reacted by softening its position still further. In a statement in the House of
Lords, Lord Shackleton said that while he would 'greatly regret' any form of
public enquiry into broadcasting at this time, he did not know what would happen
if pressure for one continued to mount.

Unsurprisingly, the 76 Group pressed on. It held a packed meeting on BBC
premises at Kensington House, the home of the BBC Television Arts and
Features departments off Shepherd's Bush Green, and elected a committee which
included Whitehead, Trodd, Burton and Hood. The following month the 76
Group and the Campaign for Better Broadcasting placed a joint advertisement in
the *Guardian* headed 'Crisis in Television and Radio: A Royal Commission *Now*'.
This was signed by 102 of the most distinguished names from academia, the arts,
politics and broadcasting. To others who had already declared their hands, were
added the names of Michael Ayrton, Jim Allen, Professor Alan Bullock, Lord
Beaumont of Whitley, Brigid Brophy, Alan Bennett, Nevil Coghill, Len
Deighton, E. M. Forster, Arthur Koestler, Raymond Leppard, James McTaggart,
Daniel Massey, David Mercer, George Melly, Dennis Potter, Dame Flora
Robson, George Steiner, Milton Shulman, Philip Toynbee and John Wain. The

advertisement deplored the financial stringency to which the BBC had been subject in recent years and the burden on ITV resulting from the imposition of the Exchequer Levy. Calling for a royal commission to be set up at once, it accused current BBC performance of bearing 'little relation to the undertakings implicit in the BBC evidence to the Pilkington Committee', and the ITV companies of making programmes subservient to profits and breaking explicit promises made to the ITA in their franchise applications. The ITA had failed 'to exercise the powers laid upon it by the Television Act when confronted with the shortcomings of the Companies'. The managements of both ITV and the BBC, the advertisement's authors claimed, had lost the confidence of those who worked for them.[35]

In another paper, the group drew attention to the decline in the number of BBC producers in permanent posts and the increase in the use of freelances and those on short-term contracts. The sense among programme makers of being oppressed by what a popular book of the time, *Up the Organisation*, described as an insane, bureaucratic machine was all too often heightened by the interventions of the regulatory bodies such as the ITA and the BBC Governors. In one instance a team of ITA officials appeared at the Thames studios on the day of transmission of a *This Week* programme detailing the connections between a Labour MP and the colonels' junta in Greece and personally oversaw the making of cuts which, as Jeremy Isaacs, the programme department head, Phillip Whitehead, *This Week*'s editor, and John Morgan, the programme's reporter, noted furiously, had the effect of completely emasculating it.

The ITA, it seemed, after the fall-out from the LWT affair, the failure of HTV to live up to its franchise promises and the criticisms made of it as far back as the Pilkington Report, was belatedly determined to show the government that it was not a toothless watchdog. In one January weekend in 1970 LWT received reprimands from the Authority over no fewer than four programmes. Saturday's programmes, they were told, had been 'tasteless and witless', the sitcom 'contained too much dirt'. *Frost on Sunday* was 'too often smutty and suggestive' and the arts programme, *Aquarius*, contained 'frontal shots' of nudity.

Perhaps as a result of this sort of thing, the ITA seemed to enjoy a relatively easy ride with the Wilson government. Not so the BBC, even with Hill in charge. In December 1969 Wilson once again flew into an irrational rage, this time over a BBC *Panorama* programme dealing with the shameful role played by Britain in standing aloof as thousands starved to death in the Nigerian breakaway state of

Biafra. Television pictures of starving children had shocked people at home in Britain much as pictures of the brutality of the war in Vietnam had shocked Americans. As soon as the programme was over, a furious Wilson rang the BBC Director-General, Curran, at home and told his secretary to phone Lord Hill to order him to present himself in Downing Street next day. Ignoring the fact that the programme had been scrupulously balanced with appropriate spokesmen from both government and opposition, Wilson launched into a paranoid litany of every grievance and supposed slight he had ever suffered at the hands of the BBC, adding that the Corporation had even precluded his wife, Mary, from appearing on screen 'because Ted Heath was a bachelor'. The more he thought about it, he told Hill, the more he became convinced that the BBC was prejudiced against him. The BBC 'was failing to perform its duty as a public service'. This had led him, he continued, 'to re-think his whole relationship with the BBC'. Once the tirade had finished the long-suffering Hill tried to calm him down, telling Wilson that it 'both astonished and depressed' him that the Prime Minister should 'see in the BBC a conspiracy against him'.[36]

In Wilson's anger at the BBC, the ITA and the ITV companies saw an opportunity to persuade the government to lessen the tax burden on themselves. Since July 1969, when the increased Exchequer Levy had come into effect, most of the companies had been returning reduced dividends to their shareholders, some making no profit at all and a few even making a loss. The companies had reacted by instituting heavily publicised economies. Apart from the viewers, the people who bore the brunt of these economies were those who made the programmes. As a result programme makers' disenchantment with their managements increased. Grampian (the contractor for the north of Scotland) closed its Edinburgh studio. Tyne Tees reduced local programmes by a third, concentrated the work of its three studios into one and made part of its staff redundant. Peter Cadbury of Westward (who had burnt Harry Pilkington in effigy after the publication of his committee's report in 1962), flamboyant as ever, was reported to be ready to hand his franchise back to the ITA. (A row with his fellow directors pretty quickly changed his mind.) Yorkshire mothballed its outside broadcast unit. Across ITV programme expenditure was curtailed.

Harlech even sent a delegation to the ITA's offices in London in December 1969 to tell the Authority that because of the Levy they were being 'forced' to abandon their programme promises. Fraser's reaction, rather than insisting that they stick to what they had promised, was to sympathise. Scottish Television announced that Levy payments of £750,000 had pushed them into a trading loss. This was, of course, the company whose founder Roy Thomson had boasted a few years earlier that being granted an ITV licence was equivalent to being given a licence to print money. Programme makers who had watched money made in the good years taken out of television to acquire and build businesses which made toys, provided motor insurance, sold wine, published comics, ran restaurants and operated motorway service stations were less than sympathetic. Nevertheless, it was their programme budgets and their jobs which were now on the line.

The government remained understandably mystified. How could companies that had until recently been so lucrative that they could compare themselves to the Royal Mint so quickly reach a point at which one of the most profitable of them could argue that payment of three-quarters of a million pounds would, in just one year, drive it to the brink of insolvency? The volume of advertising on the screen remained, for all to see, virtually unchanged – the number of minutes of advertising sold had fallen by about 1%. So in April 1970, at the same time as announcing a reduction in the Exchequer Levy – intended to reduce by £6 million the total of £29 million currently being paid by the companies and targeted to give relief to the smaller ITV companies in particular – the government also announced that it had instructed the National Board for Prices and Incomes to carry out a thorough investigation into ITV's costs and revenues.[37]

Sensing that the tide was all the time turning their way, the 76 Group, the FCG and the other groups stepped up their pressure for a full royal commission on broadcasting still further. Finally, in what seemed like testimony to how effective the FCG and the 76 Group had by this time become, on 14 May the government announced that Lord Annan, the Provost of University College, London, would chair an inquiry into the long-term future of broadcasting after the expiry of the ITV Act and the BBC Charter in 1976. The announcement bore all the signs of a decision made in haste. No other names of members of Annan's committee were given, none had been decided on. Nevertheless, it seemed like a victory for the campaigners.

Just four days after the announcement Wilson called a general election.

Notes

1. Potter, *op. cit.*
2. Docherty, *op. cit.*
3. *The Economist*, 3 June 1967.
4. Quoted in Docherty, *op. cit.*
5. These included Mike Newell, Michael Apted, Peter Jones, Michael Beckham, Mike Grigsby and Leslie Woodhead. The author was hired by Granada to work with Mitchell and Swallow as the series researcher.
6. Lord Aylestone, quoted in Sendall, *op. cit.*
7. Sir Denis Forman and Michael Peacock, interviewed by the author in the autumn of 2000. Peacock denies that LWT were offered *Coronation Street*, but the evidence tends to suggest that they were. The fact that Peacock does not believe that such an offer was ever made may perhaps be taken as further evidence of the degree of misunderstanding between LWT and the other ITV companies.
8. Quoted in Docherty, *op. cit.*
9. *Daily Sketch*, 5 August 1968.
10. *The Franchise Trail* by Nemone Lethbridge, commissioned by London Weekend Television Ltd, 1968. The lyric for the title song is included in *British Broadcasting*, compiled and edited by Anthony Smith, David & Charles (Holdings) Limited, Newton Abbott, 1974.
11. *Sunday Times*, 23 December 1968. Grade would later write to the *Sunday Times* denying that he had ever used these words and saying that he did not hate David Frost. There is little doubt, however, that he hated what LWT was doing.
12. Forman, *op. cit.*
13. Docherty, *op. cit.*
14. Quoted in Docherty, *op. cit.*
15. Correspondence between Ben Whitaker and Lord Aylestone, quoted in Potter, *Independent Television in Britain, Vol. 3.*
16. Potter, *Independent Television in Britain, Vol. 3, op. cit.*
17. *David Frost, An Autobiography: Part One*, HarperCollins Publishers, London, 1993.
18. Four of those who had originally signed the letter to the board threatening to resign changed their minds and decided to stay.
19. Quoted in Docherty, *op. cit.*
20. Lord Aylestone, address to Scottish Centre of the Royal Television Society, 26 September 1969. Quoted in Potter, *Independent Television in Britain, Vol. 3.*
21. Frost, *op. cit.* The lighter story, as told by Frost, may have grown with repeated telling down the years.
22. Michael Peacock, interviewed by the author in November 2000.
23. The author was a member of the FCG Council for most of its existence.
24. Tony Benn, *Office Without Power: Diaries 1968–72*, Century Hutchinson Ltd, London 1988. Entry for July 1969.

25. Years later Lord Macdonald (Gus Macdonald) was told about the NPA delegation by Joe Haynes.

26. Unidentified quote from Stuart Hall in *Open Secret* article in Nos. 2 & 3, p. 16.

27. Phillip Whitehead, interviewed by the author in November 2000.

28. *Sunday Telegraph*, 13 July 1969, *Sun*, 11 July 1969.

29. *The New Priesthood, British Television Today*, by Nicholas Garnham & Joan Bakewell, Allen Lane, The Penguin Press, London, 1970.

30. Colin Thomas, interviewed by the author in October 2000.

31. The eventual settlement was 4%, which was in breach of the ceiling of 3.5% set by the government under its Prices and Incomes policy.

32. Hill, *op. cit.*

33. Heller had been a script writer with the Shell Film Unit and, in the mid-1960s, organiser of the Short Film Makers' Campaign. She later married another leading member of the FCG, Nicholas Garnham.

34. Letter, undated, from the 76 Group, inviting recipients to become members. Some members of the FCG viewed the 76 Group with suspicion because, by pursuing its strictly limited objectives through the Labour Party, it seemed to be substituting only a very diluted version of the FCG agenda for the wholesale change to the entire system sought by the FCG's more radical members.

35. Advertisement paid for by members of the Campaign for Better Broadcasting and the 76 Group published in the *Guardian*, 17 March 1970.

36. See Hill, *op. cit.*

37. The National Board for Prices and Incomes, set up by Wilson in 1965, had been given the task of controlling inflation.

3

Stop ITV-2! – 1970 to 1972

Against expectations, Labour lost the general election held on 18 June 1970. While the campaign was in progress the economy, which had seemed to be picking up in the first half of the year, suddenly appeared to go into reverse. A BBC *Panorama* programme two weeks into the campaign featured a former Governor of the Bank of England and a Labour-leaning industrialist who agreed on the seriousness of the economic situation. Just three days before the polls, monthly balance of payments figures were published showing a serious deficit. Labour voters, disappointed by Wilson's failure in government to live up to the glowing promises made in 1964 and 1966, stayed at home in their millions.[1] Among the long catalogue of excuses later given by Harold Wilson to explain his defeat was a strike by Granada technicians which had blacked out ITV programmes across Lancashire for the entire period of the campaign.

In January 1970 the leaders of the Conservative Party had held a conference at a hotel in Surrey, Selsdon Park, at which they had decided finally to close the door on post-war consensus politics. They had decided to cut back hard on state spending, intervention and regulation in industry, and come down in favour of giving free rein to market forces and curbing trade unions. When announced, this conversion to an older, seemingly long-dead species of Conservatism had been greeted with mockery. 'Selsdon Man' had seemed no more convincing than 'Piltdown Man'. Today 'Selsdon Man' can be seen as the father of the Iron Lady.

Less than a week after his election victory, Edward Heath named Christopher Chataway as the new Minister of Posts and Telecommunications. On the same day the *Sun*, which since October 1969 had been owned by Rupert Murdoch, reported that the BBC was to be 'cut down to size'. ITV would be left to do the popular programmes while the Corporation would concentrate on the serious programmes and culture.[2] One month after being appointed, Chataway announced the indefinite postponement of the Annan Inquiry. Instead, he informed the House of Commons, 'I propose to ask my Television Advisory

Committee to undertake a study designed to identify the main technical questions and report to me early in the new year.' Only then would he consider whether an inquiry into the structure of broadcasting after 1976 was necessary, and if so what form such an inquiry should take.

The broadcasting campaign groups, which until the election had appeared to be winning concessions, were now back to square one. In some ways worse: the 76 Group's and FCG's most effective spokesman, Phillip Whitehead, had been elected as Labour MP for Derby North and effectively removed from the scene. Although he could work within the Labour Party and sound off in the House of Commons, as a new-boy MP he would need time to find his feet. For as long as the Conservatives were in power any views that Whitehead might express would likely be dismissed as opposition sniping and would be unlikely to influence Conservative policy.

*   *   *

For all its shortcomings and in spite of the fact that their managers had lost the confidence of so many of those who worked in it, the previous few years had demonstrated the possibilities of television, in particular to those idealistic young people who had come into the industry over the previous decade. I can remember the moment about half-way through the 1960s when I said to my closest professional colleague, a friend with whom I had been planning a new regional theatre, that over the next few years there would be more opportunities to create exciting and original new work in television than in the theatre. Having secured a toehold in television, I had decided to devote my energies to trying to realise some of those possibilities, and I advised him to do the same. Dozens of my contemporaries in television had made similar decisions.

As the 1960s ended and the 1970s began, the 'insane, bureaucratic production machines' of both the BBC and ITV were still managing to make a lot of excellent and original programmes. In October 1969 the BBC broadcast the first of many editions of *Monty Python's Flying Circus*. On New Year's Day 1970 the BBC transmitted the first episode of *The Six Wives of Henry VIII* and the following day on ITV there was the first edition of LWT's arts programme *Aquarius*. In February the BBC had Ken Russell's *Dance of the Seven Veils* and ITV Adrian Cowell's brilliant *The Tribe That Hides from Man*. In May ITV transmitted the first of Granada's important anthropological series *Disappearing World*.

However, being able to see the possibilities only made the failures of courage

79

by the BBC and ITV stand out worse. Having seen what could be done we were even more frustrated by our bosses' apparent fear of upsetting governments or the moral puritans supporting Mary Whitehouse, of tackling the unions when they blocked creative advances and of alienating audiences.

An important factor that contributed to the emergence of the Free Communications Group had been the growth of freelancing. By 1969 the BBC Television Drama Department alone produced almost 400 hours of drama, consisting of 650 separate productions. Yet there were fewer than twenty staff drama directors and only about thirty staff drama producers to cover all those productions. As a result the Drama Department had come to depend to an increasing extent on freelance directors, working on short contracts, to direct specific productions. In the year April 1969 to March 1970, 116 hours of single plays were produced by the BBC, with the Single Plays Department alone calling on up to 100 freelance directors. Similar developments were occurring in arts, documentary and features departments in both the BBC and ITV. It suited managers not to have to keep as many people on their books, and it suited the new breed of programme makers who, as the Director of Programmes at BBC Television, David Attenborough, put it, were 'free voices . . . not interested in the ethos of any broadcasting organisation . . . interested only in his own programme . . . speaking in the language of video tape or film, and finding places where his voice (can) be heard whether it is on the BBC, on ITV, or . . . in the commercial cinema, or the underground cinema'.[3] Such people (of whom I was one) constituted an important part of the FCG's membership. To them freedom of expression mattered more than any broadcasting institution, political or economic theory.

One of the things that particularly alarmed members of the FCG was the way in which the power of the ITV companies, and the patronage of those who ran them, had steadily expanded until it reached into every area of the entertainment industry and could affect the whole of a programme maker's or performer's professional life. The third edition of *Open Secret*, which appeared early in 1970, was largely devoted to 'the Grade Dossiers', an examination of the Grade family and its network of interlocking show-business interests. Back in 1966 a *Sunday Times* article had gone so far as to suggest that the government should legislate to curb the hold which the three Grade brothers, Lew Grade, Leslie Grade and Bernard Delfont,[4] exerted over so many branches of the entertainment industry. Between them they controlled a network of theatrical agencies, theatres, cinema and TV interests, which the *Sunday Times* believed gave them an unhealthy influence over whole swathes of the British entertainment industry and over the careers of those employed in it, from Laurence Olivier to casino and theatre managers, from television producers to leading film lighting cameramen.

Grade brother Lew was the Managing Director, Chief Executive and undisputed power behind the ITV Midlands contractor ATV. Brother Leslie headed the Grade Organisation, through which he owned or controlled a clutch of the most important talent and artistes booking agencies, together with a string of influential music publishing businesses, theatrical managements, a chain of cinemas, theatres and record companies. So powerful had the Grades' theatrical agencies become that, at the time of the 1966 *Sunday Times* article, the actors' union Equity had complained to the government that the control exercised by the Grade family over the employment prospects of actors in theatre, television and films was so extensive that it amounted to a monopoly. Since the *Sunday Times* article the Grades' show business interests had increased still further.

The third Grade brother, Bernard Delfont, was perhaps the most powerful of all. He was one of the most influential directors of EMI (Electrical and Mechanical Industries, 'the most powerful entertainment organisation in the country', as it told its shareholders in its 1969 annual report) which, through its acquisition in 1968 of the Associated British Picture Corporation, also controlled Thames Television. By 1969 EMI had become so ubiquitous in the music, record and show business industries that the Board of Trade had started asking questions about its potential to operate a cartel. Under pressure, EMI sold off the talent agencies in the Grade Organisation. The biggest of these were London Management and London Artists. The stars on their books included Laurence Olivier, John Gielgud, Noel Coward, Dirk Bogarde, Kenneth More, Brigitte Bardot, John Osborne, Ian Carmichael, Frankie Vaughan, Bruce Forsyth and Princess Margaret's husband, Lord Snowdon. When the deal disposing of London Management was announced, with due razzmatazz at a press conference at the Café Royal on 28 October 1969, it was revealed that two of the men controlling the company that was to acquire the organisation had been colleagues of Lew and Leslie Grade's while they had been building it up. Another of the men controlling the company that was to acquire the agency was Leslie Grade's own 26 -year-old son, Michael. Next morning the newspapers carried glowing accounts of Grade junior's entrance onto the show-business stage. 'Mike makes the Grade' headlined the *Daily Mail*, above a photograph of young Grade sporting fearsome sideburns and brandishing a cigar (his uncle Lew's trademark pose for photographers always featured him holding an enormous cigar and uttering some ever more outlandish superlative about his latest show).

The attention of the ITA had also been drawn to the power of EMI, in particular to its control of Thames Television. As a result the Authority pressed it to dilute its holding. A month after the sale of London Management, EMI announced that Forte's Holdings and British Lion (Holdings) would each be taking up '20–25 per cent of new voting equity in Thames Television Holdings'.[5] 'This', as the *Open Secret* commented tartly, 'may fool the Independent Television Authority' but would fool no one who looked at the directorships, share holdings and interlocking financial and family interests behind the deal. As things stood, *Open Secret* continued, EMI shareholders could 'sleep easily . . . [as] EMI's interests will be well looked after in the new deal'. Bernard Delfont would continue not only to be a director and extremely influential shareholder in EMI, he was on the board of Forte's Holdings, while in turn Charles Forte, founder and boss of the clutch of Forte companies, was on the board of Delfont's Bernard Delfont Ltd. *Open Secret* called for an investigation by the Monopolies Commission.

In order to explain what this complex web of related interests, cross-shareholdings and family connections meant in practice, *Open Secret* imagined a Londoner going on an evening out. It drew attention to each of the times during the evening that he would use the services, buy the products or otherwise encounter companies having a Grade, Delfont or Littler as a director, or which were subsidiaries of larger companies of which one of them was a director (the Littler brothers were rivals and sometimes partners of the Grade brothers in many ventures) by highlighting them in bold type. As he sets out the imaginary Londoner leaves his children at home playing contentedly with toys bought for them from **Century 21 Toys Ltd** and reading a **Joe 90 and TV 21** comic. Before he leaves he switches on an episode of *The Saint*, being transmitted by **Thames Television**. He then sets out in his car, insured by **Eagle Star Insurance**. Arriving in the West End he chooses between eating at one of the chain of **Grill and Griddle** restaurants or splashing out at the **Café Royal**. The wine he has with his meal has been supplied by the **Hungarian State Wine Cellars Ltd** and is finished off with a **Puritan Maid** ice cream and a cup of **Kardomah** coffee, while the restaurant's background music comes courtesy of **Muzak**. He now opts to see either a film at his local **ABC** cinema, which is quite likely to be showing a film made by the **Associated British Picture Corporation**, or he can go to one of the **twelve West End theatres**, accounting for some 40% of the commercial theatre seats in the West End, controlled by companies with Grades or Littlers on their boards. In the provinces the powerful **Moss Empires** and **Stoll Theatres** chains were wholly owned subsidiaries of Lew Grade's ATV, with Prince Littler as Managing Director of both chains, while the **EMI** theatres such as the **Grand**, the **Opera House** and the **Winter Gardens** in Blackpool all came under Bernard Delfont as head of the company's Entertainment Division. The show the Londoner sees is quite likely to have been produced by London's most powerful producing management **H. M. Tennent** and to star artists from **London Management**. If later he wants to go to a floor show there is the popular **Talk of the Town** on the corner of Charing Cross Road and Leicester Square where, as earlier at the theatre or cinema, the costumes for the show may well have been supplied by one of London's main costumiers, **Monty Berman's**, and the equipment used in the show very probably came from **General Building and Theatre Equipment Ltd**. Were he to opt to go bowling instead he could go to either **Ambassador** or **Transworld Bowling (UK) Ltd** and still be in the Grade embrace. On the way home he can stop off for a quick snack at a **Forte** cafe. Back at home he can put on a record, likely to be from the **EMI** stable – **Parlophone**, **His Master's Voice**, **Columbia**, **Harvest**, **Capitol** or **Stateside**, or he can play a tape which may well have been manufactured by **EMI**. Meanwhile the television is still showing programmes from **Thames Television** and, even if he switches to the BBC, the video tape and equipment transmitting the programme have quite probably been supplied by **EMI**. As the FCG writer concluded, 'You are not the only guy to have had a great evening.'[6]

The *Open Secret* articles on the Grades concluded by saying that even if the laws which were supposed to curb the monopoly power of organisations such as the Grades were reformed so as restore a greater degree of commercial competition, they would be ineffective against the growing power of international entertainment industry corporations around the world, and against the threat that these increasingly posed to the free flow of ideas, attitudes and information which are the foundation of individual freedom.

The Grades were perhaps the most extreme case, but the other ITV companies had also used the massive profits of the 'licence to print money' days to diversify into all kinds of other areas. Granada, for instance, was in everything from hotel and motorway service stations, to publishing, theatres, cinemas and bingo halls, from office furniture and television rentals to a plastic flower rental business.

With such concentrations of power reaching right across the entertainments industry those who campaigned for reform risked seriously damaging their careers. Just belonging to the Free Communications Group, the 76 Group or other such organisations, particularly if the person could be identified with specific protests or articles which highlighted the failings of the system, or if he or she made programmes which caused ructions, could land the person involved in trouble. Troublemakers, or people who were regarded as 'politically unsound', found their careers blighted. Although the whole story did not come out until later, it was known that there was a brigadier from the security services based in Broadcasting House, whose job it was to vet people being considered for BBC posts and to maintain confidential files on programme makers. The files of those deemed 'unsuitable' were stamped with an inverted fir tree symbol. Among those whose files were marked in this way were a number of talented writers and producers who had opposed the Vietnam War, Chinese speakers and those who had supported left-wing causes.[7]

In ITV there was a more informal, but equally effective system for weeding out people regarded as troublemakers. For instance, when I fell out with Granada in 1969 over a programme featuring the Country and Western singer Johnny Cash giving a concert for prisoners in San Quentin prison in California, I faced a potentially career-threatening situation. Granada's proprietor, Sidney Bernstein, demanded cuts in a sequence which combined interviews with a murderer and the executioner, with shots of the jail's empty gas chamber. He had become jumpy over the issue of violence in programmes following a public row over scenes in a Granada drama in no way connected with my programme. This was the third time in less than two years that Bernstein had intervened personally and de-manded idiosyncratic and arbitrary changes, without warning or, as I saw it, good reason, at a very late stage in a programme of mine. In this and the previous instance his intervention had come after the programme had been edited and approved for transmission by other senior Granada executives. This time I resigned from the company rather than agree to what I believed were damaging and unnecessary cuts. Unfortunately, the press got hold of the story when, after promoting the programme, Granada suddenly removed it from the schedules.[8] Hearing that I was leaving Granada, Jeremy Isaacs, the Controller of Features and Current Affairs at Thames, invited me to lunch to discuss making a programme for him about Charles Dickens. When Isaacs got back to his office he found a note on his desk from his managing director, Howard Thomas, saying that if a programme maker called Darlow sought work at Thames he was not to be hired. Isaacs, who had worked at Granada, simply wrote on the note: 'Sorry, too late. I've already hired him' and returned it to Thomas. I was extremely lucky. My career in television could, under different circumstances, have ended at that point. Others, more deserving than me, who had defended much more important programmes than mine or put their names to alternative broadcasting policies which those in charge saw as being against their commercial or institutional interests were often much less fortunate.

Jeremy Isaacs was one of a small number of television executives in ITV and the BBC who was known to stand up for programmes and programme makers against unreasonable demands from management. As a result he inspired enormous loyalty from programme makers. A demonstration of this occurred early in 1970 when his department at Thames got permission to take cameras into South Africa to make two programmes about life there. When the first, which linked the national obsession with rugby to racism and an unsavoury brand of Afrikaner triumphalism, was transmitted, word quickly spread round his department that Thames had received a strong complaint from South Africa House. The complaint, it seemed, carried with it a thinly veiled threat that if the second programme, which was about the employment policies of certain British companies operating in South Africa, gave as much cause for offence to the government in Pretoria as the first, reprisals might be taken against the business interests of certain of Thames's major shareholders. One of Thames's corporate shareholders held a bus operator's franchise in South Africa and a subsidiary of another was at that moment bidding for a major equipment contract for the new South African television service. The staff feared that the Thames board would now insist on the second programme being withdrawn or substantially altered. So, without being bidden, every available researcher in the Features and Current Affairs departments immediately dropped whatever he or she was doing and turned to uncovering the business interests of every member of the Thames board, and compiling a list of their interests in South Africa. Within hours the Thames board was acquainted with the fact of the list's existence and that it could be made available to the press, in which event it might cause considerable embarrassment. No one doubted that Jeremy Isaacs would do everything in his power to defend the programme but the Thames researchers believed that they might be able to strengthen his hand. Their action was as much a demonstration of loyalty to Isaacs as a defence of the programme. The precise sequence of events thereafter now seems lost in the mists of time and diplomatic memory loss on the part of the main players. But the programme was transmitted unmutilated.[9]

*   *   *

Chataway, the new minister responsible for broadcasting, was one of the very few ministers ever to come into the job with sufficient first-hand experience of the medium to merit the respect of those who worked in it. In his youth a distinguished international long-distance runner, he had been one of the original team of newscasters at ITN when it started in 1955 and later a reporter for the BBC's *Panorama*. Where Harold Wilson was known to have an enmity for the BBC, Christopher Chataway was viewed by programme makers as potentially an ally of ITV. At a press conference after announcing the scrapping of the Annan Committee, Chataway told reporters that by doing away with the inquiry he was freeing broadcasters from inhibitions about planning for the future. This was widely interpreted as a green light to the ambitions of those who had been lobbying for a start to commercial radio, an easing of Pilkington-inspired regulation of ITV and as a sign that the government would support any proposal by the ITA to use the long-vacant fourth television channel.[10]

However, such hopes received a rude setback when the National Board for Prices and Incomes published its report on ITV's finances in October 1970. Although it forecast that ITV's costs and revenues would continue to worsen until at least the mid-1970s and highlighted the effect which the increased Exchequer Levy on advertising income had had on the companies' profitability, the Board held back from recommending a reduction in the Levy. Nor, which would have been better for the companies, did the Board recommend reforming the whole basis on which the Levy was assessed. The Board considered the possibility of establishing a second ITV channel, but concluded that a second competitive ITV channel would only exacerbate the existing contractors' already serious problems. As to giving the existing ITV companies a second, complementary channel this, the NBPI concluded, was simply too fraught with commercial uncertainty.[11]

The ITV companies, led by Granada's Denis Forman, and their advocate the ITA, could be said to have done rather too well in putting across their case for a reduction in ITV's tax burden. As a result of Forman and Fraser's pleading the Board had concluded that what the companies needed was not a risky second channel nor even a further immediate cut in the money they paid to the Treasury, but greater long-term security so that they could bear down on their costs, restructure their advertising rate cards and improve the way in which they sold advertising airtime. The Board recommended that rather than the periodic round of new contract awards, such as had taken place in 1967–8, company contracts should be renewed automatically unless a contractor had twice been warned by the ITA that its performance was unsatisfactory. There should, the Board advised the Authority, be a rationalisation of the system so as to get rid of duplication of facilities and under-used studio space. This should be achieved through a reduction in the number of contractors or mergers between them. In addition the companies were urged to get their costs and industrial relations under control. Costs in ITV had gone up by 9.5% in 1968 and by a further 21.4% in 1969.

The NBPI's Report on ITV was its swansong. Shortly afterwards the Heath government abolished it. However, the financial information and details of the inner workings of the ITV system contained in the NBPI's last report would provide campaigners with evidence and ammunition for use against ITV for years to come.

*   *   *

With the election of the Heath government industrial relations in ITV, which were already pretty dire, got even worse. The strike at Granada during the election, to which Wilson in part attributed his defeat, had been triggered by an ACTT claim for a 12.5% wage increase in return for agreeing to work a new duty roster associated with the re-equipment of Granada's studios. The union justified its claim on the grounds that its members' 'productivity' was to be increased. But the management, for once, had stood firm and the strike had lasted for four weeks, costing Granada £750,000. But three days after the election Granada caved in. The unusual feature of the strike was not that it had occurred or that Granada had caved in, but that an ITV management had held out for four weeks. David Plowright, who had recently become Granada's Programme Controller, says that throughout the 1960s and 1970s Granada did not fight as strongly as it should have done over industrial relations. In any case, he adds, 'If we had done we would have been isolated by the other companies. The mood in that time was that advertising airtime perishes very quickly. We didn't apply the same rigour to dealing with bad industrial relations practice as we did to getting controversial programmes on the air. Peaceful industrial relations took precedence over innovative programme making.'[12]

In August 1970, only six weeks after the Granada strike had been settled, the

87

ACTT submitted a claim for a pay rise across the network for working in colour. While there might just conceivably have been some justification for a claim on behalf of cameramen, lighting directors or designers, it was hard to see that any case could be made for technicians who were completely unaffected by the changeover to colour, such as sound engineers. That, however, did not deter the union. It demanded a 10% increase for those directly affected and 5% for everyone else. When the managements did not accede to their demands the unions called a strike. It began on 13 November 1970. Unfortunately, at that moment, Lew Grade at ATV was in the middle of making three expensive colour productions for delivery to American television. Unwilling to default on his contract, Grade broke ranks with the other ITV companies and entered into a settlement with the ACTT.

Denis Forman describes union/management confrontations at this period as being like a ritual war dance. Following each new demand from the unions there would be well-worn cries of 'Ridiculous' and 'Disgraceful' from management, followed by choruses of 'Stand Firm, Show of Strength, No Compromise and Management Must Manage'. These in turn, Forman says, would be followed by panic and far-fetched solutions aimed at avoiding expense. After which other companies would be consulted: ' "What does Lew think?" – most commonly, "Pay up and keep the show on the road." "Can the Authority do anything?" (No they never can.) "Has the Minister been advised?" "Yes, the Minister has been told but won't help." '[13] A deal would then be done giving the unions more or less everything they wanted. In return, ITV's screens rarely went dark and the advertising revenue continued to roll in uninterrupted.

As we have seen, union bloody-mindedness and management ineptitude not only increased costs, they set back the cause of adventurous programme making. Granada's uniquely valuable, award-winning anthropological series *Disappearing World* was eventually killed off, largely due to union rules that made it prohibitively expensive. In most ITV companies, a director and crew setting out for some remote overseas location in a tropical forest or wilderness, perhaps to record the life of some isolated and endangered primitive tribe, could be 'on the clock' in union terms, from the moment they 'left base' on their way to the airport until they returned home at the end of a trip weeks or even months later. Any hours 'on the clock' over the forty or so per week stipulated in the union agreement would entitle members of the crew to 'time off in lieu' or payment at overtime rates. Directors usually received 'time off in lieu' and as a result many could only make one film in a year in spite of being paid as if they had been working for all of it. The technicians were generally paid at overtime rates for such hours. These escalated in multiples of two for each period 'worked' over the prescribed number of hours or whenever there had not been a minimum '10-hour break' between shooting calls. Thus a cameraman or recordist could be being paid at a rate of 8, 16 or even 32 times his normal hourly rate by the end of a long shoot or stay out on location (these multiple rates were referred to as rates of 8T, 16T or 32T, etc.). The result was that ITV series such as *Disappearing World* became prohibitively expensive to produce.

By the early 1970s the new contractors, Thames, Yorkshire and LWT, had acquired even worse reputations for poor industrial relations than their older counterparts. While Frank Cvitanovich was making the BAFTA award-winning documentary *Beauty, Bonny, Daisy, Violet, Grace and Geoffrey Morton* on a York-shire farm for Thames Television in 1974, his crew managed to clock up an astounding amount of overtime (reputed to have reached a figure calculated at a rate of 64T), because one of the Shire horses featured in the film refused to foal for four whole days because of the presence of the camera. Thames was notorious for its overmanning and demarcation disputes, particularly in its Teddington studios, where most of the company's drama and light entertainment was produced. At Thames, unlike Granada, the unions still insisted that all personnel going on flights of longer than two hours duration travelled first class. In 1970, shortly after I joined Thames to make a documentary, I had lunch with Denis Forman. He enquired how I was finding life at Thames. 'Fine,' I replied, 'but I am finding it a bit confusing. So far I have managed to identify three people who seem to be the Head of Film.' 'Oh, I don't find that surprising at all,' replied Forman cheerfully. 'We have just done a comparison of our costs at Granada with Thames, and we find that they employ three times as many people as we do to make exactly the same number of hours of programmes.'

The company with the worst reputation of all was Yorkshire. Paul Fox, who left the BBC in July 1973 to become Managing Director of Yorkshire, described the pressure exerted on the company by the ACTT and the ETU (the electricians' union) as the worst in the whole ITV system. Stories about Yorkshire abounded. One concerned a crew sent to Saudi Arabia to make a documentary about the life of the Bedouin. After weeks of painstaking negotiation the director had obtained permission from a tribe who roamed the desert Empty Quarter of southern Saudi Arabia to film the life of the women in the tribal harem. This was potentially a considerable coup and the crew were duly flown out from their hotel in Riyadh to a desert airstrip where, after negotiation with union representatives, it had been agreed that they could stay for one night prior to being ferried out in Land-Rovers to meet up with the Bedouin tribe. The next day, after some hours of driving across the Arabian sands in the piercing heat, the director and his crew made their appointed rendezvous with the Bedouin. As anyone who has travelled or worked in Arabia will testify, things progress with due decorum and good manners in the desert. Thus, on their arrival the director and his crew were invited to take coffee and some refreshment with the tribal sheikh and his most senior elders. An hour elapsed, and then another, while pleasantries were exchanged and excellent perfumed coffee was consumed. The director, knowing the ways of the desert and having come by pre-arrangement for the specific purpose of filming in the harem, knew better than to be the first to broach the subject of the purpose of their visit. He knew that when he deemed the moment fit the sheikh would broach the subject and invite the director and his cameraman to film. However, the cameraman, more aware of the union rules and the special concession that had been made by the union that allowed them to be there at all, quietly caught his director's attention and pointed to his watch. In accordance with the agreement made with the union, they would have to leave shortly in order to get back to the airstrip in time to meet up with the light plane that was to take them back to their hotel in Riyadh for the night. So, tentatively and as politely as he could, the director introduced the subject of their visit into his conversation with the sheikh. The sheikh happily picked up the director's hint and courteously invited the director and his crew to set about their filming. However, by this time there was only a little over one hour remaining before the appointed time of departure. So, with all the unpacking and preparation necessary before they could shoot, and the nervousness and embar-rassment of the ladies in the harem who were totally unused to the presence of strange men in the form of a film crew, the poor director had succeeded in shooting very little before he had to make his apologies to the sheikh and take his leave. A once-in-a-lifetime opportunity had been wasted. For their part, the sheikh and his followers were so surprised by their guests' behaviour that news of what had happened spread across the desert like wildfire, which was how I learned about it. I was working with a film crew, living in tents in the desert more than one hundred miles away across the border in Oman and was told the story just two days later.[14] We were making a film for a private sponsor rather than for television and so were permitted by the union to live in tents without having to return to a hotel each night. Even so, on union insistence we had had to engage a second, unneeded sound man whom it had been impractical to take with us into the wild places of Oman, and we had therefore had to leave him on full pay in England for the duration of the shoot.

As well as rows over pay, manning and working practices, there were disputes over political objectives. In these, producers and directors were frequently at one with the unions; indeed it was often the producers, directors and researchers who were the most vocal advocates of such union policies. One such policy was the blanket ban on working on programmes other than news or current affairs in apartheid South Africa. This led to a major controversy in 1973 over an account of the life of Baden Powell, founder of the Scout movement, to be written and performed for Thames as a quasi-drama documentary by the idiosyncratic Welsh actor Kenneth Griffith. Because of the ban on filming in South Africa the ACTT prevented it from being made. When the ACTT banned their members in the BBC from working in Greece on the drama series, *The Lotus Eaters*, in protest against the rule of the colonels' junta, the BBC took the union to court for 'inducing its employees to break their contracts'. The court ruled in favour of the BBC. Political bans and strikes of this sort caused serious rifts inside the ACTT itself. Divisive issues included the nationalisation of the film industry and workers' control in broadcasting. While highly paid but casualised technicians who worked mainly in feature films tended to be opposed to the more radical policies, the more secure, regularly employed technicians working in television tended to support them.

The sort of repeated industrial disputes endemic in ITV were exactly the kind of trade-union behaviour which Heath and his Conservatives had made it clear they would put a stop to. Within weeks of taking office, the new government announced that in future it would not intervene to settle industrial disputes. Free-market principles were to determine which industries survived and which went to the wall. In future the government would not subsidise 'lame ducks'. In December 1970 the government unveiled its new weapon in the anticipated battle with the trade unions – the Industrial Relations Bill. Quickly passed into law despite a Conservatives' Commons majority of only thirty, the Industrial Relations Act promised tough sanctions against striking trade unionists. Unions would have to go through an officially sanctioned procedure before they could call their members out on strike. Unions or trade union members who failed to do this would be hauled in front of the courts and might be sent to prison.

This measure, followed by the Heath government's first budget which cut *6d* off the standard rate of income tax and slashed £330 million from public expenditure, entailing cuts in council housing and the end of free school milk (the minister entrusted with implementing the last measure was Margaret Thatcher, earning her the protestors' soubriquet 'Thatcher, Milk Snatcher!'), provoked a wave of strikes and protests across the country. In February 1971 more than 1.5 million people went on strike in protest against the Industrial Relations Bill. At the same time unemployment rose to 800,000, the highest for more than thirty years. Publication of the Industrial Relations Bill led to a further increase in the membership of the Free Communications Group. Fighting the Bill, and lending the support of film makers to the campaign against it, became a cause in itself for many FCG members. FreeProp, the FCG group in Bristol, produced a twenty-minute agitprop film called *Know Your Enemy* for use by trade unionists, socialist organisations and community groups in heightening opposition to the Bill. Employing techniques that harked back to the *Agitprop* films made in Russia immediately after the Soviet Revolution, it featured villainous capitalist bosses having their evil way with the workers and people's property.

Colin Thomas, one of the leading members of FreeProp who helped to make the film, remembers that, by this time, the attitude of many programme makers working in the BBC was openly oppositional: 'It came to distract you from doing your best work. If you made a programme that upset the BBC it was almost a good programme for that reason alone.' When Thomas made a documentary about a leek grower who was also a shop steward at Vickers he ran into trouble with his BBC channel controller because the programme included an interview in which the shop steward said, 'It is very easy to be insubordinate if you are a shop steward at Vickers.' After arguing his case with the channel controller, Thomas was allowed to keep the line in the programme. When the programme went out Lord Hill received a letter from the chairman of Vickers which started, 'My dear Charles, I write to you more in sorrow than in anger, but when programmes like this go out it is not surprising that the BBC has so few friends . . . ' A copy of the letter was attached to Thomas's personnel file.[15]

Dissent inside the BBC gave rise to a particularly rich vein of cheeky *samizdat* which began to circulate inside the Corporation from early 1971. This *samizdat* included mock-up editions of the BBC's house magazine *Ariel*, produced in the appropriate format and typeface, bearing titles such as *Burial* or *Shit*. These looked like a cross between an official government report, complete with a graphically modified royal coat of arms in which two workmen are bashing the lion and unicorn and an amended BBC motto reading: 'If you don't hit it, it won't fall!' Such scurrilous publications, packed with in-jokes and satirical articles owing much of their inspiration to magazines such as *Private Eye*, drew on the skills of a range of graphic artists, comedy writers and top-flight journalists working in the BBC. Packed with cartoons and sharp comment, they achieved a quality and inventiveness that rivalled the BBC's own publications. One of these *samizdat* publications was produced as a facsimile of the *Radio Times*. Its front page carried photographs of the BBC's newsreaders Robert Dougall, Richard Baker and Kenneth Kendall, graphically altered to make them look like The Mad Hatter, Mickey Mouse and Adolf Hitler. In the top right-hand corner was a roundel proclaiming 'NEW REDUCED PUBLIC SERVICE'. Its programme pages listed shows such as *It's a Knock-Out!*, with a billing promising a fun set of new games ' . . . designed to have everybody competing against everybody else. "Grab That Contract" – in which freelances compete to make innocuous pro-grammes for the largest possible audience with the smallest possible budget . . . ' and answers to 'viewers' letters' which included a 'handy glossary of BBC terms' such as '**Violence**. This is a term used to describe the activities of football hooligans, students, bank robbers, Rhodesian blacks, kidnappers, Young Liberals, sex maniacs, miners, male nurses, pickets and demonstrators, etc. It is intended to cancel out the issues involved so as to concentrate on superficial aspects in order to discredit any cause and lump together serious social upheaval with ordinary crime. However, it is not to be confused with the activities of the forces of **Law and Order**, who don't commit violence because they are the forces of law and order . . . Since this concept may be a little confusing, an easy rule of thumb to apply is: those out of uniform are violent; those in uniform are not.' Another definition was '**Public Service Broadcasting**. Broadcasting in the service of Big Government and Big Business, but for which neither Big Government nor Big Business have to pay.' It also featured full-page photographs of Lord Hill and Charles Curran, stripped except for tight briefs, posed as Charles Atlas muscle men.

BBC management made repeated attempts to curb such material. As a result the methods used to distribute the material became almost as inventive as the *samizdat* itself. Colin Thomas was one in a network of people in different parts of the BBC who organised its distribution. A contact in the Television Centre would get in touch with Colin and say that there were twenty copies of whatever new *samizdat* item was concerned and Colin would provide the names of twenty suitable people in the building or unit where he was working. These people would then be sent copies, read them and spread them around innocently to others so that they could share the joke. In time these publications became highly prized and each new edition would be passed eagerly from hand to hand, even on the executive sixth floor of the BBC Television Centre. Realising this, the people

Pages from a mock-up of the *Radio Times*, produced and circulated
by dissidents inside the BBC in the early 1970s

Popular newsreaders of the day

BBC Chairman, Lord Hill

BBC Director-General, Charles Curran
Permission to use pictures from the mock-up of *Radio Times* given by
Colin Thomas and Bill Mather on behalf of the BBC Bristol dissidents

behind the *samizdat* arranged for one publication to be produced in shorthand so that executives eager to know its contents would have to ask their secretaries to read it to them. Another item was distributed in the form of a jigsaw. Colin Thomas claims that as the publications continued and the BBC became more anxious to stop them, private detectives were hired to find out who was responsible and force them out of the Corporation. The members of Colin Thomas's group responded by adopting code names to disguise their identity.

One particularly effective piece was a seven-inch extended play record produced to mark the enforced retirement in the aftermath of the McKinsey reports of the veteran 'radio ballad' producer Charles Parker. On a sleeve bearing the BBC Records logo and headed 'Special Anniversary Release', the record featured 'Charles Parker, A Radio Producer and His Sacking Group'. The recording took the form of a radio sketch–comedy show opening with an announcer saying 'This is a benefit performance for Charles Parker – a cost benefit performance for Charles Parker by McKinsey and Co.' The sketches included Charles Parker, played by an actor, being given his annual personnel interview. The personnel officer refers to the fact that Parker has won the *Prix Italia*, adding distastefully, 'That's foreign isn't it?' He also notes disapprovingly that Parker has made programmes praising black people. In another sketch the 'Charlie Hill mob' moves in and beats up 'that Commie bastard Charles Parker'. In the final sketch Parker's colleagues are drinking in the BBC Club. All wring their hands over Parker's fate, but end up deciding to do nothing to support him.[16]

In addition to satirising their bosses, lampooning the organisations in which they worked and publishing the unpublished and uncomfortable facts about them, both the FCG and the 76 Group put forward new or alternative ways of managing broadcasting in the public interest. Understandably, many of those in power in broadcasting did not like what groups such as the FCG, the 76 Group and, a little later, the TV4 Group said. So they attempted to discredit them. Dr Tom Carbery, a Scottish academic who had become a member of the ITA in January 1970, described the membership of these groups as being 'the disgruntled, the disenchanted and the failed'. The official history of ITV for this period claims that the groups 'all tended to be influenced by the same authoritarian Marxist element, at that time stridently articulate within the Labour Party, the trade union movement and Polytechnic departments of sociology'.[17] For Carbery to say that the members of these groups were the disgruntled and the disenchanted was stating no more than the obvious, but to suggest they were people who had failed was to betray the fact that he either did not know who the members of such groups were or refused to face the facts. By the early 1970s not only did the groups include Conservative and Labour MPs, successful producers and journalists, the former or current editors of *Panorama*, *This Week* and *World in Action*, a former controller of BBC television and heads of arts, documentary and drama programmes from network ITV companies and the BBC, they included people who had won some of the most prestigious awards in broadcasting including the *Prix Italia*, Emmys and BAFTAs. Many would later head television channels, programme departments, even whole broadcasting organisations and major British institutions. There were equally distinguished people in the groups from the worlds of print journalism and publishing. As for the charge that they were under the influence of authoritarian Marxists, that, as we have seen, is simply rubbish. My own memory, as a rather ordinary, middle-of-the-road member of the Labour Party and a committee member of both the FCG and the TV4 Group throughout much of the groups' existence, is not of them being dominated by authoritarian Marxists or authoritarian anything elses. The one thing, sometimes the only thing, that we were nearly all agreed on was our opposition to authoritarianism in all its forms.

*　　*　　*

In October 1970 Sir Robert Fraser, Director-General of the ITA, retired and was replaced by Brian Young. Young, an old Etonian, was the son and grandson of colonial governors. He had been a surprise appointment. A brilliant scholar, he had progressed from being an assistant master at Eton to being headmaster of Charterhouse by the time he was thirty. When he took over at the ITA he was forty-eight and had been running a charity, the Nuffield Foundation. The press greeted Young's appointment by describing it as the most extraordinary since Caligula made his horse a consul. It is reported that at a party Young introduced himself to the journalist who had penned that particular piece with the words, 'May I introduce myself? I am Caligula's horse.'[18]

Brian Young had not originally even been considered for the job, and when appointed was widely reported not to know anything about television. *Broadsheet*, the 76 Group's journal, lampooned Young's appointment under the heading 'A Surprise Appointment – Ex-TV Man Lands Top Teaching Job'. The article opened: 'There is some surprise in academic circles at the appointment of Sir Lew Grade, 63, as the Headmaster of Charterhouse . . . The governors have rejected complaints by Old Carthusians that Sir Lew is unfit for his new post, having never taught in a school. They point out that he has owned one for the past year . . . "I know nothing about teaching, but that's show-biz," he quipped. Asked if his views were influenced by Aristotle, he replied, "I haven't seen much of him since he married Jackie, but the Greeks have something to teach us about making money." '

According to the official history of ITV, Young had been recruited 'to exercise a more interventionist leadership'[19] and one of the most urgent and intractable problems that confronted Young on his appointment was the ongoing crisis at LWT. A month after he took over, LWT announced that it had made a loss of £67,000 in the year (in fact it had made a profit of £2.92 million, but had had to pay Exchequer Levy of £2.99 million. LWT's losses had been made worse, although they did little to publicise the fact, because of a decision to invest in a television recording company which resulted in LWT having to write off £400,000). LWT's programmes still fell a long way short of the promises made in its franchise application. During the summer before Young arrived, Lew Grade had approached the ITA and suggested that ATV might solve LWT's financial problem by entering 'into some form of association' with it. Shortly after Young took over, Granada too had approached the ITA and proposed some kind of association with LWT. Young responded that under no circumstances would the ITA allow two of the big five ITV companies to merge.

Out of sight, LWT's shares had begun to fall into the hands of Rupert Murdoch, who now owned both the *News of the World* and the *Sun*. By late 1970 under Murdoch's ownership, the *Sun*, which as the *Daily Herald* had been a serious Labour-supporting newspaper, was headed fast downmarket, its first bare-breasted 'Page Three Girl' appearing on 17 November 1970. It was widely believed that Murdoch had a score to settle with LWT which arose from a television interview with David Frost a year earlier in which Frost had grilled Murdoch in front of a hostile studio audience. As Murdoch had stormed out of LWT after the programme he was reported to have said: 'LWT has made a powerful enemy tonight.'

In the summer of 1970, having apparently received some encouragement from LWT's chairman and managing director, and knowing that there was likely to be a substantial number of LWT shareholders eager to sell their shares (they included former executives who had left at the time of Peacock's enforced resignation), Murdoch and his legal adviser Lord Goodman had had lunch with

Fraser. Murdoch had told Fraser that he had been in touch with LWT's major shareholders and that he estimated that 63% of LWT's shares were for sale. What, he wanted to know, would be the ITA's attitude if he were to buy them? There is some conflict about the exact nature of Fraser's response, but whatever he did say, it had not warned Murdoch off buying the shares.

By November Murdoch had acquired a substantial slice of LWT's stock and joined the LWT board. With money still pouring out of LWT as a result of its continuing losses and the costs of constructing and equipping its new South Bank studios, the new managing director, Tom Margerison, and some of the other executives were eager to encourage him. With his financial resources and experience in the media, they believed that Murdoch would be able to turn the company around. By the beginning of 1971 Murdoch, having put still more of his own money into LWT, was attending meetings of the executive directors and devoting part of his time to sorting out the company's day-to-day problems. On 20 January 1971 Stella Richman, the new LWT Programme Controller, reported to the LWT board that after her first 'bad and disappointing' year in the job there were fourteen problems facing the company which were 'currently insurmountable'. To Murdoch bad results coupled with defeatism were unacceptable. Richman was fired. Margerison followed her a month later. Murdoch, presiding over an executive committee of the company and acting, according to Margerison, 'much as one would expect the chief executive to act', now seemed to be in charge in all but name.

Once again LWT's fat was well and truly in the public fire. Phillip Whitehead, Stuart Hood, Alan Sapper (General Secretary of the ACTT) and Barry Took (one of the executives who had left LWT) headed a six-man delegation to the ITA. When Young refused to meet them, Whitehead raised the issue in the House of Commons, commenting that the position at LWT showed 'what value could be placed on assurances given to the ITA'. Chataway, as the minister responsible for broadcasting, responded that it was not up to him to decide what action should be taken, that was the responsibility of the ITA. The press was now in full cry. 'Lost Weekend – Chapter Three' trumpeted the *Evening Standard*. *The Times* printed an angry letter from Clive Irving demanding a full ITA inquiry into how so much power had come to be transferred into 'the hands of a non-executive director who nevertheless calls the tune'.[20] Murdoch's reaction was to dismiss Irving as David Frost's front man – 'His Master's Voice'. In future, Murdoch suggested, LWT might not be able to afford Frost's fees.

The ITA was now on the horns of a dilemma. Solicitors confirmed that the changes at LWT 'constitute an event affecting the nature and characteristics of LWT which, if it had occurred before the signing of the programme contract, would have induced the Authority to refrain from entering into the contract and which entitled the Authority to determine the programme contract'.[21] However, if the Authority were to terminate LWT's contract it would throw LWT into chaos, put the workforce out of work and throw the whole ITV network into confusion. Where were the programmes provided by LWT to come from? Even if the other ITV companies could, in time, fill the void, the balance of power between them, and the whole system's finances, seemingly so carefully adjusted at the last franchise round, would be back in the melting pot. The FCG had repeatedly called for the ITA to be given real teeth so that it would manage to regulate ITV effectively and be able to meet just such a crisis as this. It had proposed providing the ITA with the nucleus of its own programme-making capacity so that it would be 'ready to make programmes at very short notice'.[22]

True to form, the ITA did nothing beyond making noises. The day after Clive Irving's letter appeared in *The Times*, the Authority announced that it had sent a sternly worded letter to LWT telling the company that it had six weeks in which to put its house in order, to prepare a new programme submission and appoint a new Managing Director and Programme Controller. Or else, it was implied, the ITA would take away LWT's contract.

Luckily for the Authority its threats were not put to the test. John Freeman, who had been Frost and Peacock's original choice as chairman of LWT, was now due to become free from his duties as British Ambassador in Washington; Frost, with Murdoch's agreement, contacted him. On 9 March an extremely relieved Lord Aylestone was able to tell Chataway that Freeman would become both Chairman and Chief Executive of LWT.

On 22 April an LWT team, headed by Freeman, faced the ITA in its headquarters in Brompton Road. Freeman told the Authority that despite all the setbacks the company still believed in the ideals of its original application and that, with every prospect of being able to place its finances on a sounder footing, there was 'no reason why LWT should not now realise its full creative potential'. The next day the Authority announced, with evident relief, that LWT's contract was now secure. Everyone slapped everyone else on the back and looked forward to a glorious future.

Since that time the widely accepted view has been that LWT went on to fulfil its original promises, that Freeman presided over a great flowering of talent and that the ITA did well not to deprive LWT of its licence. However, examination of LWT's actual programme record, despite some very good individual pro-grammes and a brief golden period in the late 1970s shortly after Michael Grade became Controller of Programmes, shows that LWT never really consistently lived up to the promises contained in its original franchise application. LWT did not effect the change in either ITV or the weekend schedule which it had held out.[23] For that failure both the ITV system and the Authority's stewardship of it must be held responsible. However, it is hard to see what else the Authority could have done in February, March and April 1971 other than issue threats. It is fortunate that the ITA never had to act on those threats. If it had, the Authority would have been revealed to all as an even more mangy animal than it already appeared. If Murdoch had not been amenable, despite the rough handling he had had in the press, to being moved to the side, the Authority would have been forced to limp back into its kennel growling ineffectually.

The result of the LWT affair, all three chapters of it, was to demonstrate beyond contradiction that the ITA and the whole ITV system was in need of serious examination, followed by major overhaul or, at the least, substantial adjustment. The public demonstration of the existing system's weaknesses strengthened the hands and the resolve of the FCG and the 76 Group.

*   *   *

The dramatic events in broadcasting in the early months of 1971 were being played out against a backdrop of even more disturbing events beyond it. Three days before the Authority met to re-interview LWT, unemployment in Britain reached its highest since 1940. In January 1971 postmen had gone on strike for the first time ever, and in February that symbol of all things sound and British, Rolls-Royce, had been declared bankrupt. In March Bangladesh declared its independence from Pakistan, triggering the indiscriminate slaughter of hundreds of thousands of Bangladeshis by the Pakistani Army and a massive refugee crisis across the border in India. In April a BBC reporter working on *24 Hours*, Bernard Falk, was sent to prison for four days for contempt of court after refusing to answer questions in court about IRA men he had interviewed. Curran, the Director-General of the BBC, responded by banning all interviews with IRA men except those undertaken with his express permission. The extent of the government's and the security forces' over-anxiety about the media, about those working in it and their interest in the troubles in Ireland and elsewhere, seemed to be reaching even greater heights. In January the security forces raided Cinema Action, a small, London-based group set up by people who had been involved in the strike at ORTF in May 1968. Independent, but left-wing, Cinema Action's sin seemed to be that it had filmed in Londonderry and among those organising protests against the Heath government's Industrial Relations Bill.

In this unpromising climate Young, together with the heads of the ITV companies, had continued to press the government for further relief from the Exchequer Levy. At the same time the BBC had continued to press its case for an increase in the Licence Fee. At last, on 15 February, the day when the country changed over from pounds, shillings and pence to decimal coinage, 'Decimalisation Day', when the main focus of press attention was elsewhere, the government responded. Chataway announced in the House of Commons that he was increasing the BBC Licence Fee by £1, to £7 for black-and-white sets and £12 for colour. At the same time he halved the ITV Levy, promising a full review of the basis on which it was charged.

In lobbying the government to get the Levy eased, the ITA had promised the government that it would secure an improvement in ITV's programmes. However, although upmarket programmes might please regulators, critics and even MPs, they might also drive away downmarket viewers. The companies' aversion to highbrow programmes in peak-time slots had been at the root of many of LWT's problems. It appeared an irresolvable problem. But the companies and the ITA had a solution ready and waiting – a second ITV channel. This would not only give the companies somewhere to play new 'quality' programmes, it would reduce the pressure to show existing Authority-'mandated' programmes on the main ITV channel in peak hours – programmes such as the weekly current affairs programmes *This Week* and *World in Action*, weekday and weekend plays, the minimum thirteen peak-time serious documentaries each year and arts programmes such as LWT's *Aquarius*. With some or all of these dumped on a second channel (there was already a button on most of the new sets marked 'ITV-2'), ITV would be able to take on the BBC and its two channels head-to-head. They would also be able to charge advertisers premium rates for targeted audiences on the new channel.

In February 1971, ten days before Chataway announced the reduction in the Exchequer Levy and only weeks after the ITA had sanctioned Murdoch becoming the biggest shareholder in LWT, 'new boy' MP, Phillip Whitehead, had lunch with 'new boy' Director-General of the ITA, Brian Young. 'I remember the exact date – it was the day that my son was born and Rolls-Royce went bust', Whitehead recalls. Young described to Whitehead his plans for the future of ITV and for a new ITV-2: 'He was telling me how his ideas were all going to be the best for everyone, even for someone like me. I had a feeling of unreality. I thought, where had I heard all this before? And then I remembered the Central African Federation – Rhodesia and Nyasaland. And then I thought, but of course, Brian Young comes from that world, colonial administration. His brief was to hand it all over to the white man.'[24]

However, there were still a number of problems which would have to be overcome before Young could realise his plans. Ever since its creation in the 1950s ITV, and in particular the ITA in the person of its Director-General Sir Robert Fraser, had talked in terms of an eventual second ITV service which would compete with rather than be complementary to its first service. The issue had last been seriously addressed by the government in 1966, when the Labour government had decided that a second ITV service could not be afforded for at least another three years. Nothing more had been heard of it and in May 1970 the ITA had unobtrusively dropped the idea of a second competitive service. On 13 May 1970, the day before the official announcement by the outgoing Labour government setting up an inquiry into the future of broadcasting under the chairmanship of Lord Annan, Fraser had secretly asked the ITV companies at a meeting of ITV's Standing Consultative Committee for estimates of the additional costs if a second ITV channel were authorised. This, he had suggested, might be run like BBC-2, as a complementary service to ITV-1, transmitted for approximately 35 hours per week in peak times, with the programmes produced predominantly by the five main network companies.

What, one may wonder, had Fraser been up to? At the very moment at which he made his request to the ITV companies for estimates of the costs of a second service, he, the Authority and the companies had been engaged in what they were promoting as a life-and-death campaign for the very survival of the single ITV channel against the crushing burden of the Exchequer Levy. The official history ascribes Fraser's conversion from a long-held 'belief in the virtues of competition' to a complementary second ITV channel to financial realism and a desire for better programmes. He was prompted, we are told, by a realisation that a new inquiry into broadcasting would put the whole issue of what to do with the long vacant fourth channel back into the melting pot.[25] Whatever the precise balance of reasons for Fraser's seemingly Damascene, and for the moment little-publicised, conversion, from that moment on the idea of a competitive second ITV channel had been dead.

However, the publication of the National Board for Prices and Incomes Report in October 1970 had dealt the prospects for an early go-ahead for a complementary ITV-2 a serious blow. In pleading their case for an easing of the burden of the Exchequer Levy, the ITA and the companies had perhaps rather over-egged the pudding. The NBPI, in addition to concluding that a second competitive commercial service would further damage the finances of the existing companies, had doubted the ability of the ITA to ensure that the companies would really run any second ITV channel as a complementary service. If the Authority failed to ensure this, the report had said, 'the second service could to a large extent become subject to popular programming, with the total television audience possibly tending to divide itself in roughly equal shares between the three "popular" channels and a minority audience viewing BBC-2. Such a distribution would give ITV a greater share of the total audience and would be the most favourable outcome for it. Even so, the financial out-turn would be extremely uncertain.'

With no decision on the Levy, the ITV bosses had continued to pile on the agony. In October 1970 Howard Thomas of Thames had said that the financial situation of the companies called for urgent action. Three firms of accountants which had reviewed the companies' revenue and expenditure had forecast that 'within two or three years ITV would, on the present basis, no longer be a financially viable system'. In December, after publication of the NBPI Report, Aidan Crawley, the Chairman of LWT, had criticised the gloomy predictions contained in the report as too optimistic! Even if the Levy were abolished altogether, Crawley had said, for the whole of the coming decade the industry would still be having difficulty 'in earning the 25% on equity capital before tax which Mr Jones (the Chairman of the NBPI) considers desirable . . . Instead, therefore, of being a goose laying an endless succession of golden eggs, ITV has become a high risk industry.'[26]

In light of such prophecies of ongoing financial doom, it came as something of a surprise when, in June 1971, little more than three months after the government had lifted just half the burden of the Levy, an article appeared in the Thames staff magazine written by none other than Howard Thomas, headed 'Thames Wants ITV-2'. Thomas warned of the creeping threat of BBC-2 to ITV's ratings and of a loss of revenue resulting in 'a non-viable ITV system'.

(Again? So soon?) The only fair solution, Thomas opined, was for ITV to have a second complementary channel: 'Only by having two simultaneously planned channels can we maintain our present edge on the BBC.' The way Thames saw it, Thomas told his staff, was for ITV-1 to be like the *Daily Express* and for ITV-2 to function like the *Daily Telegraph*, 'offering a different range of programmes to a different audience and attracting new kinds of advertising. This does not mean that ITV-2 would be in any sense a "minority" service. There would need to be a full quota of entertainment although we would want to use ITV-2 as a try-out ground for programme experiments and for new concepts and new ideas. It is essential that ITV-2 should be operated by the existing contractors.' New contractors, Thomas warned, would inflate costs to an impossibly high level and 'debase programme standards to the lowest level'. The cost, he estimated, would be approximately £20 million a year, '£10 million of which would come from reducing the Levy to zero. The remainder would come from advertisers, mostly new to television and probably at the expense of the Sunday newspaper supplements. The date? If our campaign succeeds we could begin ITV-2 in Autumn 1973; at worst Autumn 1974.'[27]

Even allowing for a sharp and unexpected upturn in sales of advertising airtime, such a timely resurrection in ITV's financial fortunes smacked, and not only to cynical programme makers in groups such as the FCG and the 76 Group, a little too much of the miraculous. Even inside the main ITV technicians' union, the ACTT, whose television members and unemployed film technicians seemingly had most to gain from ITV-2, the name of Lazarus was widely invoked. Any programme makers who still doubted that Thomas's article was part of a long-prepared joint campaign by the companies and the ITA had those doubts dispelled three weeks later by an open letter from Brian Young addressed to people working in ITV. Under the heading 'ITV-2', Young invited views. His letter began: 'Independent Television is likely to need a second channel before long – to give a better service to the viewer, to make an outlet for more creative work, and to compete successfully with the BBC. But what would be the best arrangements for ITV-2?' The similarities between the reasons given by Young for an ITV second channel and those voiced by Thomas were striking. 'The ITA', Young said, 'has begun to examine this question in a joint working party with the Managing Directors of ITV companies. It would now be valuable to have an expression of views, however informal, from anyone or any body of people, working in Independent Television who may have something to contribute to the discussion.' Young explained that suggestions should be based on two assumptions: that ITV-2 would be complementary to ITV-1 rather than competitive with it – 'only in this way can we fully enlarge our range and increase the choice for the viewer' – and that since ITV's total audience share could not be dramatically increased, 'some way needs to be found of financing two services from an amount nearer to our present income than twice that income'. He asked for contributions by 30 September. These would be incorporated into a discussion paper for a one-day conference for invitees from ITV to be held late in October. Young's letter ended: 'The present intention is not to have a public debate, but rather to make sure that anyone in ITV who wants to do so has a chance to join in the collective discussion of the shape and character which a second service might have.'[28]

This was remarkable indeed from a service which only months earlier was so financially strapped that it had claimed that it could no longer fulfil its public service obligations without the risk of going bust! Yet in telling the programme makers as much as he had in his letter, Young was still not telling them the half of it. Unknown to the programme makers, a schedule for the new service had already secretly been drawn up by the controllers of the five network companies and representatives from the five medium-sized companies – Anglia, Harlech, Scottish, Southern and Tyne Tees. This, when later it became public, revealed that it was the result of 'several meetings' specifically devoted to drawing up plans, preparing a case and formulating ways of countering opposition. Young later suggested that such meetings, under the aegis of the ITA, had been going on since the autumn of 1970 and had been prompted by an article in the *Sunday Times* in July 1970 by one of ITV's leading documentary producers, Peter Morley. Morley had said that ITV 'must have' a second 'specialised' channel, completely complementary to ITV-1. These two channels should be scheduled so as 'to make sure of consistently high ratings' for ITV. This would free commercial television from the 'ratings tyranny' and, by breaking the deadlock between quality and profitability, enable ITV for the first time to provide the service required of it by Parliament. It would also provide additional creative outlets for people such as himself.[29]

With the arrival of Young's letter in July 1971, it was clear beyond doubt to the programme makers in the FCG and the 76 Group that a well-laid ITV/ITA plot was afoot. Although at the time we were unaware of it, there can be little doubt that the plan to get ITV its second channel went back at least to Fraser's volte-face on a competitive ITV-2 in May 1970, and had never been off the agenda for long, since ITV started in the 1950s. Nevertheless, even as late as the summer of 1971, the amount of work that had gone into ITV's campaign to win its second channel remained a closely guarded secret.

If Young and the companies thought that promises of 'a better service to the viewer' and 'an outlet for more creative work', coupled with an invitation to those working in ITV to submit proposals, would be enough to win over sceptical programme makers, the press, the public and even some of their own colleagues, they were in for a rude surprise. Peter Cadbury, the flamboyant boss of the tiny West of England contractor Westward, responded immediately to Young's letter with a public attack on ITV's plans. Under the plans envisaged by Thomas and Young, the five network companies would be the major beneficiaries in any re-apportionment of income resulting from ITV-2. Therefore, said Cadbury, they should bear the brunt of the increased costs. At the same time the smallest companies, which were likely to suffer a fall in advertising revenue during the roll-out period for the new service, should be shielded from any resulting losses. Cadbury voiced a long-held complaint of the smallest ITV companies: 'For years we in the regions have been virtually excluded from the network not because our programmes are inferior but because the screening of a regional programme excluded a programme produced by a network company. The actual cost to us of providing, for example, *The Potter's Art*, will be minimal; but the satisfaction of getting our productions on a national network will give a fillip to all concerned.' Cadbury then went on to propose either a genuinely free second ITV service which would carry no advertising or a second service based on a modified form of regional competition with ITV-1.[30] Doubts were also cast on ITV's proposals by the advertisers, who wanted the ITV companies' monopoly in the sale of television advertising broken.

On 31 July, the day on which the lead story in the press was the dramatic take-over by Jimmy Reid and the shipbuilding workers of their bankrupted workplace on the Upper Clyde, *The Times* carried a report by Chris Dunkley headlined 'Power game behind scenes of television' (*The Power Game* was a hit ITV drama series). Spelling out the cynicism behind Thomas's and the companies' advocacy of ITV-2, Dunkley described the campaign being mounted by the independent television contractors as a totally unequal contest 'with the ITA and the commercial companies on one side, and on the other a few individuals and lobby groups'. Those opposed to the ITA and independent television companies were, Dunkley said, understandably reticent over opposing their bosses when they were apparently holding out promises of employment for their unemployed colleagues. By contrast, Dunkley continued, 'Little reticence is shown by the independent companies' lobby which is highly organised, fresh from its victory in reducing the government levy, and in an advanced state of readiness.'

As Dunkley had suggested, technicians and programme makers felt inhibited over expressing their objections to ITV's plans. Some 11,000 people were in full-time employment in ITV and many more worked for it on short-term or freelance contracts, a large proportion of whom were both opinionated and articulate, yet barely fifty (including those who like Peter Cadbury had re-sponded publicly) replied to Young's invitation to submit ideas in writing. That so many people did not want to stick their heads above the parapet was, for reasons that have been explored, understandable. Nevertheless in August, using the ACTT's magazine *Film and Television Technician*, Caroline Heller, the union's TV Commission Officer, spelt out the reservations of many who felt inhibited about speaking out in person. Simply to accept the ITA's and the companies' claim that 'natural justice' demanded that the fourth and last avail-able colour television channel should go to ITV so that it could have two channels to match the BBC's two channels, was, Heller said, not good enough. It was difficult to come to any conclusion about the best use of the last immediately available television channel 'until all the other alternatives have been fully and openly discussed'. No decision should be made ahead of the full legislative review that would have to take place prior to the renewal of the BBC Charter and the Independent Television Act in 1976. Something more imaginative than simply handing over the fourth channel to ITV so that the companies could compete head-to-head with the BBC was called for. She concluded, 'This is the time at which ACTT members have a very special responsibility to use their professional imagination and experience in defence of the true potential of broadcasting, the public interest and the quality of their own jobs.'[31]

In September the Federation of Broadcasting Unions, which included the unions representing the performers as well as the technicians' unions, responded to Young's letter with one of their own saying that it would be unwise to make any decision on the future of the fourth television channel before there had been a full consideration of a range of alternative uses to which it might be put.

However, the companies were not going to be deflected by either adverse press comment or the hostility of those who worked for them. On 23 September Lord Renwick told the Annual General Meeting of ATV's shareholders that the company would 'continue to press for this highly desirable extension of the national broadcasting service'. Days later Lord Harlech told his shareholders that ITV's future would be 'seriously jeopardised' unless they could match the BBC's two channels with two of their own. In the *Guardian* John Freeman, answering questions from Peter Fiddick in what was billed as 'his first interview since becoming Chairman of LWT', held out a vision of ITV-2 as a haven for open-ended discussion programmes on a vast range of ideas. Claiming to sympathise with programme makers who 'feel frustrated because they can't themselves run the media', Freeman said, 'but I am afraid I do take the slightly regimental view that newspapers have to be run by editors and television companies by pro-gramme controllers'. He concluded, 'I believe the adding to (ITV's existing channel) of a complementary channel would liberate the whole thing and lead to an improvement of quality on the first channel.'[32]

Two weeks later, on 13 October, under a front-page headline 'ITV Big 5 planning for another channel', *The Times* revealed the existence of the ITV Programme Controllers' 'Strictly Confidential' ITV-2 Outline Schedule. This revelation caused the ITV lobby huge embarrassment. Not only did it confirm the accusations that the ITA had been colluding with the companies for months in preparing a carefully orchestrated campaign to secure the fourth channel for ITV, the schedule also revealed that the companies were aiming specifically to challenge and take audiences from BBC-2. The proposed ITV-2, rather than the cornucopia of new, original programmes and alternative viewing promised to the public over the past months by the companies, would consist largely of more of the same. To prove the point *The Times* report included an almost complete breakdown of the intended schedule. Asked to comment, the ITA was reduced to saying that in the months since the schedule had been drafted amendments had been made. *The Times* highlighted the fact that the ITA and the companies had gone ahead with preparing their plans despite the fact that neither the Minister, Chataway, nor the government, had given 'any indication as to possible uses of Britain's fourth and, in the foreseeable future, last available television channel'. *The Times* added that the Free Communications Group, the 76 Group and 'the freelance director/producer lobby are anxious to publicize the danger of the fourth channel being granted virtually automatically to the present commercial contractors. Mr Nicholas Garnham, a member of all three of these groupings, summarises their attitude in the comment: "The ITA is collaborating in the covert carve-up of a scarce national asset." '[33]

The ITV managing directors' draft schedule showed that no fewer than 13 out of the planned 35 hours of programmes each week would be made up of films, film series and repeats. Another 3 hours would be light entertainment and game

"Listen! — we dump Hughie Green, sign up Hugh Carleton Greene and then we've got 'Opportunity Knocks' for eggheads, right?"

Open Secret, No. 7, by kind permission of Peter Clarke

shows. The schedule was quite explicitly targeted to compete with BBC-2. The proposed start time was 7.15 p.m.: '7.15 is suggested because of the possibility of a fifteen-minute news bulletin being scheduled from 7.15 to 7.30 which would get on the air ahead of BBC-2 Newsroom.' Elsewhere the document marshalled the arguments to be used by ITV company executives in presenting the case for ITV-2. The first of these was 'The survival of ITV and the maintenance of programme standards in the face of increased competition from two BBC services'. Other arguments suggested in the document for giving ITV a second channel were the need 'to improve ITV's public service,' 'the need to expand television', to stimulate new programme ideas and to experiment and 'provide more outlets for a growing surplus of creative and productive talent'. Recognising the existence of freelance 'production talent whose creative energies cannot be absorbed by the present structure of television', the television bosses continued, 'Their resistance to corporate bodies and consensus opinion is likely to be a factor in the ITV-2 debate. Whether they represent formidable opposition or not remains to be seen, but it is reasonable to suppose that a second ITV channel would be required to show we were capable of providing opportunities for a growing number of independent programme makers, while maintaining the editorial and statutory responsibilities of the companies and the ITA.'[34]

Three days later the *Sunday Times* ran a devastating leader article headlined 'ITV-2: A Case Not Proven'. Dismissing ITV's claims that their motive for wanting ITV-2 was to improve the range and quality of the programmes available to the public, the *Sunday Times* leader writer said the companies' real motive was commercial self-interest. 'The companies would doubtless make promises – they are making them already. But past evidence offers no reason for believing the assertion of any commercial television contractor that it will give priority to public service . . . any suggestion that ITV-2 would resemble BBC-2 should be treated with the blackest scepticism.' This was not because those promoting it were dishonest but because, no matter what the ideals of those involved, commercial television's driving priority had to be profit. On top of this there was the major problem of the ITA. 'The ITA is meant to be a regulatory body, and hence act as custodian of the public interest. It has a poor record of authority and independence.' The last franchise round had been a scandal. 'It remains shocking, if not very surprising, to find the ITA apparently acting in consort with the companies at this crucial period. Instead of holding the ring between alternative strategies, it seems to have adopted a position which excludes all but one strategy. If ITV-2 is created, and even if it is not, a minimum condition must be the recasting of the Authority into a relevant body.'[35]

The ITV document had wondered just how formidable the opposition of the 'production talent' was. Over the next few weeks it became all too evident.

Programme makers' pent-up aspirations and frustrations now focused down to one simple determination: 'Stop ITV-2!' To these people it was intolerable that companies which had broken so many of their promises and the ITA which had abjectly failed to hold the companies to those promises, should now expect simply to be handed a second channel with which to drive the BBC downmarket.

By 2 November 1971, when Young held his one-day consultation on ITV-2 for people working in ITV, he did so against a background of vocal criticism. The unions having refused to take part, Young had had to resort to inviting union members working in ITV to participate as individuals. In the hostile atmosphere that had been engendered it was remarkable that the consultation brought together people from as wide a range of interests as it did. Individual trade unionists did sit down with ITV company bosses, producers with members of the Authority. David Elstein, a 26-year-old producer at Thames and a member of both the 76 Group and the FCG, found himself sitting next to the 26-year-old John Birt (recently moved from being joint editor, with Gus Macdonald, of *World in Action* to become producer of *The Frost Programme* at LWT). Birt, in turn, found himself sitting next to Lew Grade. The consultation went on all day. Young opened proceedings by telling those present that the intention of the day was to help the Authority in preparing a submission to the Minister of Posts and Telecommunications. Peter Morley (author of the article which had seemingly so influenced Young), speaking, he claimed, 'as an independent producer', kicked off the discussion. It was comparatively unimportant, Morley said, who actually made the programmes. The important thing was for television to keep expanding, to utilise under-used capacity, labour and the great wealth of material which wanted and needed access to a channel. By utilising the studios and facilities that already existed, the companies or independent producers could bring ITV-2 'within the bounds of practical financing' and provide adequate access to those who currently felt themselves to be cut off from television.

Much of the consultation was taken up with discussion of how the new channel was to be controlled. Was it to be through an extension of the existing arrangements for ITV-1? By the creation of an ITV-2 Limited which would sell the advertising and be owned by all the companies jointly? By the ITA or some combination of the two which might perhaps include outside participation? Or was it possible that ITV-2 could be run directly by the ITA which would purchase or commission programmes from the ITV companies or outside agencies and then schedule them? There was considerable dissent during the meeting between the big five companies and the ten smaller regional companies over who should make the lion's share of the programmes and who should exercise the greatest control over the channel. Young, according to one participant, tried rather hastily to move the discussion on to safer areas. Nevertheless David Elstein and the other members of the independent pressure groups who had managed to get invitations persisted in pressing the case for a channel which would not be scheduled by the existing ITV companies at all.

Young had said that he did not intend to have a public debate on the fourth channel. The Free Communications Group decided that in that case they would hold it for him. A week after the ITA's consultation *Time Out* ran a double-page spread above a photograph of the dinner-jacketed heads of the ITV companies and ITA, posed as for a veteran football team picture, captioned in bold black letters: 'Are We Going To Let These Old Men Run TV4?' It announced a joint Free Communications Group/*Time Out* conference, sponsored by the Post Office Union. All the organisations and individuals who had submitted evidence to Pilkington, together with dozens of social and political organisations and individuals with an interest in television, had been invited. The conference should, *Time Out* claimed, 'be one of the most representative ever held'. It was to be held the following Saturday, 13 November, in the newly opened Central Polytechnic building in Marylebone Road, opposite Madame Tussaud's, and would be preceded by a demonstration of the most modern TV equipment, alternative TV systems, cable TV and video recording equipment. It was to close with a festival of 'Forgotten Films' and banned programmes.

A briefing document, on paper headed in huge letters 'TV4?' followed in much smaller type, by ' . . . or ITV-2?', was sent to hundreds of organisations and

Accompanying an article about forthcoming FCG/*Time Out* TV4 Campaign conference
Time Out, 12–18 November 1971. Every attempt has been made
to contact the owner of this picture if not *Time Out*

individuals by the Free Communications Group organiser, Stacey Marking. This emphasised the opposition that already existed to the ITA/ITV proposals. The ITA, the ITV companies and the professional organisations connected to ITV, the briefing paper pointed out, had already held many meetings. These discussions, it said, were 'called by broadcasters for broadcasters. They have perpetuated the split between the broadcasters who control the media and the people who watch and listen. The heart of the debate on TV4 is the desire to make television more democratic. Its future should not be discussed in closed shop professional conferences.'[36]

The conference itself was attended by more than two hundred people. Although most were television professionals or people connected with broadcasting in some way, it was by no means only a meeting 'called by broadcasters for broadcasters', nor a gathering made up exclusively of those on the political left. As well as the professional broadcasters, those from the broadcasting unions (the ABS, the ACTT and the NUJ) and pressure groups (both the FCG and the 76 Group), there were members of Mary Whitehouse's National Viewers and Listeners' Association, members of the Conservative Bow Group, Stephen Murphy (the Secretary of the British Board of Film Censors), Richard Neville, the Labour MP John Golding, Dr Tom Margerison (the former managing director of LWT), Chris Dunkley of *The Times*, representatives of the National Union of Teachers and Professor Hilde Himmelweit from the London School of Economics. Stacey Marking told the conference that Brian Young had been invited to attend but had refused, saying that he felt that 'the ITA would not be in a position to answer the questions that were certain to be raised'.

Anthony Smith, who had recently resigned as the editor of the BBC's *24 Hours* current affairs programme and left the BBC, warned the conference that, 'The ITV companies want a chaotic discussion so that they can pluck the only apparently viable alternative.' Among politicians, he said, there was 'a unanimity of coinciding opportunisms' – the Tories liked inactivity so that they could get on with making profits, while Labour was 'apathetic except for periodic vendettas against the BBC'. (There had recently been a new BBC/Labour Party row.) Smith called for a fourth channel which did not set out, like the existing channels, 'to provide editorial unity' but was so constituted as to provide for the greatest possible 'catholicity' of taste, expression and viewpoint.

Other speakers included Phillip Whitehead, Stuart Hall (Director of the Centre for Contemporary Cultural Studies at Birmingham University), Jay

Blumler (Director of Leeds University Centre for TV Research), and leading programme makers including Tony Garnett and Philip Donnellan.[37]

As someone who attended the conference and spoke at it, I recall it as being both refreshing and exhilarating because of the very diversity of views expressed. It was, one felt, the first time that such a cross section of people had sat down to discuss television together. As well as the powerful sense of outrage, there was often an infectious sense of fun to the proceedings. It was in many ways a unique occasion, unmatched at least until the best years of the debates at the Edinburgh International Television Festival between 1977 and the mid-1980s. That the discussion was focused around one self-contained issue, the future of the fourth channel, helped. What happened to the channel, the potential opportunities it presented, taken together with the proposals of the ITV companies, opened up the whole debate about the control, funding, organisation, accountability, uses and potential of television. Of course, such a broad spectrum of opinion was never going to agree over such a wide range of issues, but on the central issue before the conference, consensus was reached. A public inquiry into television must be held as soon as possible; the remaining television frequencies must not be allocated before such an inquiry had reported; and, in the words of the conference's final resolution, 'there is need for the discussion of the need for a new channel at all'. This unanimous resolution opposed the allocation of 'the fourth and last television channel' to the ITA and the current commercial television contractors. A new campaign – the TV4 Campaign – (based at the address of the FCG) was born.

On the following Tuesday twenty-five people from the TV4 Campaign staged a demonstration outside the ITA's headquarters in Brompton Road while inside the members of the Authority held an Authority meeting. The demonstrators handed in a petition containing the conference resolution. One of the demonstrators was Phillip Whitehead: 'We were all over the *Evening Standard*. We thought we were awfully clever.'[38] A few days later 400 out of 500 delegates at the national conference of the National Union of Students in Margate, representing more than 60 universities and colleges, signed the TV4 Campaign's petition and passed a resolution calling on the minister to delay his decision on the allocation of the fourth channel and to set up a royal commission.

Within four weeks the campaign had set up a network of regional representatives, mounted a campaign in the press, launched a national petition by sending out 10,000 copies, each with space for twenty-five signatures, and produced an eighteen-page pamphlet, *Opportunities for the Fourth Channel*. The pamphlet summed up the motives behind the campaign by saying that its intention was to let the British people know 'what a great place could be found for their interests on the fourth channel. The Church (the BBC) and the King-and-Barons (ITV) must move over: it is time we had a Parliament.'[39] The campaigners were determined to seize the moral high ground from what they portrayed as the machinations of Mammon.

Demonstrators outside the ITA on 16 November 1971
Time Out, 26 November–2 December 1971. Every attempt
has been made to contact the owner of this picture if not *Time Out*

Within days of its launch, the campaign succeeded in introducing its petition into the House of Commons. On 2 December five Labour MPs, including Phillip Whitehead and John Golding, presented an Early Day Motion which quickly attracted the signatures of more than one hundred MPs. The Early Day Motion, like the TV4 Campaign petition, called for a public inquiry into the structure of broadcasting and demanded that the fourth channel should not be allocated to the ITV companies. In addition to the National Union of Students, every member of the Executive of the Post Office Engineering Union, of the National Union of Journalists, together with Laurence Olivier, the Director of the National Theatre and his two Deputy Directors, Michael Blakemore and John Dexter, signed the TV4 Campaign's petition, as did Kenneth Tynan, Professor Frank Kermode, Ken Russell, Arnold Wesker and Tony Benn. Yet still Brian Young refused to meet the TV4 Campaign to debate the issues.

When the ITA had submitted its proposals to the government in early December they were virtually unchanged from those drawn up by the ITV managing directors and the ITA in the summer, except that the role of the Authority in scheduling the second channel so as to ensure that it was complementary to ITV-1 had now been given stronger emphasis. The Authority urged the government to reach a quick decision. When the ITA's submission was made public on 8 December, it was greeted in the press with a hail of hostile leading articles. By mid-December *The Times*, the *Financial Times*, the *Guardian*, the *Daily Telegraph*, the *Daily Mail*, the *Sunday Times* and the *Sun* had all called for a public inquiry before any decision was reached. Not one national newspaper now backed the ITA's plans.

With public interest in the issue running extremely high, Chataway, speaking in the House of Commons on the day when the ITA submission was published, said that he was unable to give any undertaking not to allocate the fourth channel before there had been a public inquiry. Whitehead responded by telling Chataway that many people working in broadcasting regarded the timing of the ITA's proposals as a deliberate attempt to set up ITV-2 before any public inquiry.

The Commons returned to the issue a week later in a debate on the Consolidated Fund Bill (a technical measure allowing a range of issues to be aired). Whitehead again called for a public inquiry. Golding supported him, saying that he was annoyed at the way in which the ITV companies had ganged up to try to gain control of the fourth channel. He hoped that the Minister would 'refuse to join that conspiracy'. By now even some Conservative MPs were expressing unease at the way in which the companies and the ITA had acted. But Chataway still refused to be drawn. He said only that the government did not have a closed mind. The issue had not been settled.

Public expressions of hostility to the ITA's proposals continued unabated. A week later the *New Statesman*, under the headline 'Free Speech – TV Style', reported on an attempt by a group of producers working in ITV to organise 'a round robin to *The Times* opposing the ITA's/Brian Young's proposals for ITV-2' who had been stopped 'when their programme controller invited them to have a look at their contracts. These specifically forbade "writing for possible publication anything concerning our business or the television industry generally".' In the same edition of the *New Statesman* a leading article castigated the ITA's proposals. Headed 'Greedy TV Tycoons', it said that 'Opposition to a commercial fourth channel is total.'[40]

If people had but known it, ITV's chances of snatching the fourth channel before there could be an inquiry were already doomed. On 9 December, the day on which Chataway had told Whitehead in the House of Commons that he could give no guarantee that the fourth channel would not be allocated before a public inquiry had been held, he had privately told Lord Aylestone, Chairman of the ITA, that unless there was a measure of public agreement, which clearly there was not, he believed that the fourth channel could not be allocated before 1976. By 19 January 1972 the pressure on the government to make its position clear could be put off no longer. Announcing that he was lifting remaining government restrictions on broadcasting hours – this would benefit ITV by allowing the companies to fill the additional airtime with low-cost programmes and at the same time sell additional advertising and so increase their income – Chataway said that proposals on the fourth channel recently submitted to him by the ITA had 'prompted the expression of a number of different views in Parliament and elsewhere concerning, for example, the possibility of reserving the fourth network for a specialised service or of organising a fourth service on some different basis. I am not persuaded that the time has come to allocate the fourth network.' (Labour cheers)[41]

Notes

1.   Some 2 million potential Labour voters failed to cast a vote.
2.   *Sun*, 24 June 1970. Rupert Murdoch had been 'allowed' by the print unions to take over the *Sun*, formerly the trade union backed *Daily Herald*, in October 1969, ten months after his acquisition of the *News of the World* and only one year after his arrival in Britain.

3. Interview with David Attenborough, quoted in Garnham and Bakewell, *op. cit.*
4. Delfont had adopted the name in 1929 when he was working as a dancer in order to avoid confusion with another dance act.
5. *Daily Telegraph* financial pages, 7 November 1969, quoted in *Open Secret*, Nos 2 & 3.
6. *Open Secret*, Nos 2 & 3.
7. The details finally came out in an *Observer* article on 17 August 1985.
8. The programme, *Johnny Cash In San Quentin*, was eventually transmitted with only very minor cuts, but by that time I had quit Granada.
9. As I have indicated, the precise details of the story are now lost, but I vividly remember going into Thames, which I had recently joined, on the morning in question to find all the researchers missing and being told the details pretty much as outlined. Other points have been clarified by people who were at Thames at the time.
10. In opposition Chataway had been a vocal supporter of the local commercial radio lobby and, had they not been defeated in the 1964 general election, it had been widely forecast that the Conservatives would have sanctioned a start to ITV-2. They had been inhibited from doing it earlier by Pilkington's criticism of ITV.
11. *National Board for Prices and Incomes, Report No. 156, Costs and Revenues of Independent Television Companies*, HMSO 1970, Cmnd. 4524.
12. David Plowright, interviewed by the author in November 2000.
13. Forman, *op. cit.*
14. The story as told here is more or less as we received it in our desert encampment. Conversations with colleagues later suggested that, while some details may have become amplified during the story's transmission via the desert telegraph, its essential details were correct.
15. Colin Thomas, interviewed by the author in October 2000.
16. Charles Parker, who left the BBC in December 1972, was widely regarded as one of the most brilliant and original radio producers of all time. He was in the pioneering line of radio, film documentary and feature producers who explored the poetic potential of the two media, particularly through the lives and speech of working people. It was a line of descent which included Humphrey Jennings, Dylan Thomas, Laurence Gilliam, Douglas Cleverdon, Louis MacNeice, Denis Mitchell, Philip Donnellan and later Paul Watson.
17. Dr Tom Carbery in *Independent Broadcasting No. 6*, November 1975 and Potter, *op. cit., Vol 3*.
18. See Potter, *op.cit., Vol. 3*.
19. *Ibid.*
20. Letter from Clive Irving, published in *The Times*, 25 February 1971.
21. Legal opinion quoted in Potter, *op. cit.*
22. *Open Secret*, Nos 2 & 3.
23. In fairness it should be noted that a few years later the Annan Committee, while castigating the ITA for its handling of the crisis, judged that under Freeman LWT had finally come 'to match in performance what its application had promised.' Sir Denis Forman is among the ITV bosses of that time who has said that he feels that

Murdoch was treated shabbily by the ITA, in effect being told that 'he was a colonial bastard unworthy of holding an ITV contract.'

24. Phillip Whitehead, interviewed by the author in November 2000. Rhodesia and Nyasaland had been joined together by the British colonial administration in 1953 to form the Central African Federation. In 1959 disturbances led by the African nationalist leader Dr Hastings Banda were put down by the British using methods, the Devlin Commission later judged, worthy of a police state.

25. See Potter, *op. cit.*, *Vol 3*. Reports of what happened at the momentous Standing Consultative Committee meeting on 13 May 1970 were subsequently confirmed to Stephen Lambert by the Deputy Director-General of the ITA of the time, Bernard Sendall. See Lambert, *Channel Four: Television with a Difference?*, British Film Institute, London, 1982.

26. Howard Thomas and Aidan Crawley, quoted in *TV4: A Report on the Allocation of the 4th Channel – Prepared by the A.C.T.T. Television Commission*, ACTT, London, November 1971.

27. *Thames Television Newsletter*, 7 June 1971.

28. Open letter from Brian Young, Director-General of the ITA, to people working in ITV, dated 30 June 1971.

29. Morley's article, which appeared in the *Sunday Times* on 5 July 1970, under the heading 'ITV'S SECOND CHANNEL', prescribed almost everything that the ITV companies could have wished for; indeed, it reads as if it could have been written by them as a blueprint for maximising their profits and driving down the BBC's viewing figures.

30. Message to staff from Peter Cadbury in *Westward Television Newsletter*, July 1971. The extent to which the smaller companies' programmes were excluded from the network by the five big companies went well beyond the requirements of making up a viable network schedule. The author can recall being shocked went he first became a member of Granada's programme committee in 1968 and a programme was offered by one of the regional companies: 'If we are going to transmit shit,' said one of the senior executives on the committee, 'then we are going to transmit our own shit.' The actual merits of the programme concerned were not discussed at all.

31. Caroline Heller, "Happy People with Happy Problems", *Film and Television Technician*, August 1971.

32. Lord Renwick and Lord Harlech, AGMs and Annual Reports to shareholders quoted in the ACTT TV4 report, *op. cit.* and the *Guardian*, 1 October 1971.

33. *The Times*, 13 October 1971.

34. *ITV-2*, published as an appendix to the ACTT TV4 report, *op. cit.*

35. *Sunday Times*, leader article, 17 October 1971.

36. *Time Out*, 12–18 November 1971 and undated *TV4?* circular distributed by the Free Communications Group and *Time Out*.

37. The presence of so many academics, many of whom spoke, was a symptom of the growing interest in the media as a field for serious study. In the early 1970s today's profusion of media studies courses, research departments and fellowships did not exist.

38. Phillip Whitehead, interviewed by the author in November 2000.
39. *Opportunities for the Fourth Channel: A Memorandum on TV4* published by the TV4 Campaign, December 1971.
40. *New Statesman*, 24 December 1971.
41 *Hansard*, House of Commons debates, 19 January 1972.

4

Must the Media Moguls Win? – 1972 to 1974

If there ever was a 'golden age' in British television it was the decade which lasted roughly from 1972 until the coming of the new ITV contracts in 1982. After that there was one final golden flush following the start of Channel Four. To be sure, by the 1970s the excitement and originality of Hugh Carleton Greene's early years as Director-General of the BBC in the 1960s was missing – the early *Wednesday Plays* – Loach, Garnett, Potter, Mercer *et al* – the irreverence of *That Was The Week That Was* and the achievement of series such as *The Great War*. Nevertheless, throughout the 1970s, as sales of colour sets started to increase and with them licence fee income, the BBC was able to make brilliant and original programmes which we still remember today. At the same time the ITV companies, flush with money as a result of the changes made to the Levy in the spring of 1971 and an upturn in advertising, remained determined to prove themselves worthy of a second ITV channel. Many of the senior executives now running the ITV companies had themselves worked in the BBC. They, together with such men as Forman and Plowright at Granada and Bob Heller at ATV, were as proud to compete with the BBC in the quality of their programmes as the money men behind them were pleased to compete for audiences. Throughout the 1970s and 1980s three flagship current affairs shows were transmitted each week in peak time – *Panorama* on BBC-1 and *World in Action* and *This Week* on ITV. In addition to the many BBC documentaries, ITV usually ran at least one major documentary each week, often in peak viewing time before 10 p.m. Of course there was *Coronation Street* and the cardboardy (and that did not apply to the sets alone) *Crossroads* on ITV. Despite *General Hospital* and *Softly Softly* (and *Dixon of Dock Green*, a folksy BBC police survivor from the 1950s which continued until 1975), the networks were not clogged up every evening with soaps and returning series set in hospitals, fire and police stations in the way that they are today. Throughout the 1970s in most weeks ITV showed at least two single plays in peak time, while the BBC produced about a hundred single plays every year plus numerous original series such as *Pennies from Heaven* and adaptations of literary classics. Shaun Sutton and the other heads of drama defended their output fiercely. While he was Controller of BBC-2 Aubrey Singer said that if he attempted to cut a single play 'it was Armageddon on the sixth floor', because of the fierceness of the Drama Department's defence of its output.[1] By the 1970s the single play, commissioned from writers working specifically for the medium such as Dennis Potter, David Mercer, Trevor Griffiths and Jack Rosenthal, had come to be widely recognised as the closest that television had come to creating its own original art form. A selection of titles (arbitrarily selected and perhaps unfairly weighted towards drama – the titles of drama programmes seem to lodge more easily in the memory of this writer than documentary titles) – demonstrates how from 1972 onwards, ITV, with only one channel, easily matched in quality the BBC with two:

Search for the Nile (BBC 1971), *Edna, The Inebriate Woman* (BBC 1971), *Country Matters** (Granada 1972), *Stockers Copper* (BBC 1972), *Long Day's Journey into Night* (ATV 1973), *The World at War** (Thames 1973), *The Ascent of Man* (BBC 1973), *Anthony and Cleopatra* (ATV 1974), *The Opium War Lords* (ATV 1974), *Jennie** (Thames 1974), *Rising Damp** (Yorkshire 1974), *Shoulder to Shoulder* (BBC 1974), *Edward the Seventh** (ATV 1975), *The Naked Civil Servant* (Thames 1975), *Johnny Go Home** (Yorkshire 1975), *Fawlty Towers** (BBC 1975), *The Evacuees* (BBC 1975), *Days of Hope* (BBC 1975), *Rock Follies** (Thames 1976), *Glittering Prizes* (BBC 1976), *I, Claudius* (BBC 1976), *Hard Times* (Granada 1977), *Shooting the Chandelier* (BBC 1977), *Edward and Mrs Simpson** (Thames 1978), *Pennies from Heaven* (BBC 1978), *Licking Hitler* (BBC 1978), *Law and Order* (BBC 1978), *The Knowledge* (Thames 1979), *Tinker, Tailor, Soldier, Spy* (BBC 1979), *Death of a Princess* (ATV 1980), *Cream in My Coffee* (LWT 1980), *Caught on a Train* (BBC 1980 – which starred Dame Peggy Ashcroft, who in the same year was also in a BBC production of Ibsen's *Little Eyolf*), *Brideshead Revisited* (Granada 1981), *United Kingdom* (BBC 1981), *Whoops Apocalypse* (LWT 1982), *Boys from the Black Stuff* (BBC 1982), *Home Sweet Home* (BBC 1982).

All those shown with an asterisk reached the 'Top Twenty' in the weekly audience ratings, demonstrating that it was possible to make programmes that were both good and popular.

Yet for many young, creatively ambitious programme makers these years were to prove an intensely frustrating time, strengthening their conviction that 'there must be a better way'. In part this was a result of increasing tensions in British society. Shortly after taking office in 1970, Heath had declared a state of emergency because of a national dock strike. By that autumn strikes had reached the highest level since the General Strike of 1926. A particular source of trouble for broadcasters was the deepening conflict in Northern Ireland. Programme makers saw it as their duty to report what was going on in Ireland and to include views from all sides. The government and the authorities in Northern Ireland had grave doubts about this. The result was repeated rows.

Early in 1972 a particularly bitter argument erupted over a programme called *A Question of Ulster*. The programme, which went out live, was a three-hour-long and extremely sober attempt to examine all points of view in the Irish question, included Republicans and Paisley's Protestants. The only people excluded were representatives of the IRA and the Protestant paramilitaries. Before the transmission both the Northern Ireland authorities and the Heath government, in the person of the Home Secretary Reginald Maudling, brought pressure to bear on the BBC not to go ahead with the programme. A young BBC producer working on *The Money Programme* later recalled how he watched 'that fundamental clash of principle between a government which believes it has the right to determine what is in the national interest and a broadcasting authority which feels that its role in a democracy is to report, to inform, and to represent the wide range of opinion existing in the country'.[2] That young producer was Roger Bolton, who would later become embroiled in the biggest ever row between the government and a broadcaster over a programme about Ulster.

Hill and the BBC stood firm over *A Question of Ulster* which, when it went out as planned on 5 January 1972, was watched by 7 million people, including more than two-thirds of the population of Ulster. More than half of them continued watching until the programme finished three hours later after midnight. As a result Ulster enjoyed one of the most trouble-free nights it had had for weeks. Afterwards even the politicians who had objected to it beforehand, praised the programme for its unsensational even-handedness and for allowing people of all persuasions to express their views without bullying from a presenter or hectoring by a studio audience.

The biggest row of all, probably the biggest since the Suez crisis in 1956, had occurred in June 1971. This did not involve the conflict in Ireland but the *amour-propre* of politicians, and in particular of the BBC's old adversary Harold Wilson. *Yesterday's Men*, timed to coincide with the first anniversary of Labour's 1970 election defeat, dealt with the experience of political defeat and the difficulties, both personal and political, of former members of the Wilson government who found themselves in Opposition. Trouble blew up a month before the scheduled transmission of the programme, when David Dimbleby interviewed Wilson. As part of the programme's examination of how former cabinet ministers coped with the sudden loss of income resulting from defeat, Dimbleby asked Wilson about his earnings (reported in the press to be between £100,000 and £250,000) from the publication and serialisation in the *Sunday Times* of his memoirs. At first Wilson was evasive, but when Dimbleby repeated the question Wilson blew up saying that he did not think that how much he had been paid was 'a matter of interest to the BBC or anybody else'. How did Heath pay for his ocean-going yacht, Wilson asked, 'Did you ask that question? Did you ask him how he was able to pay for a yacht? Have you asked him that question?' Wilson demanded that the questions about how much he had been paid for his memoirs be cut out of the programme and, after some discussion, Dimbleby and the producer, Angela Pope, agreed. Wilson added that he did not want to read about this part of the interview in the press nor about the fact that he had asked for it to be cut: 'If this film is used or if this is leaked, then there is going to be a hell of a row.'[3] However, the story did leak and one week before the programme was due to be transmitted a version of what had happened was printed in the London *Evening Standard*. The following day the story was taken up by all the national papers. Wilson and his colleagues were further enraged when they learned that the programme's intended title was – *'Yesterday's Men'* – a phrase that had been used by the Labour Party during the 1970 election campaign as a jibe to describe the Conservatives. Worse still, the *Radio Times* promotion for the programme included a verse from the satirical songs commissioned for the programme from the Liverpool group, the Scaffold. Dimbleby and the producer, Wilson claimed, had assured him that this would be a responsible and serious programme. Now Wilson wanted it stopped.

Threats of legal action and an injunction to halt transmission followed. As the row hotted up, culminating on the night before transmission in a face-to-face row between Curran and Wilson at a party given by Wilson in his room in the Commons, it focused down to an issue of three changes in the programme demanded by Wilson – the title must be changed, the last remaining question from Dimbleby about his earnings from his book must be cut, as must photographs of Wilson's three houses (pictures which implied that Wilson was a wealthy man, rather than the beer-drinking, pipe-smoking man of the people which he had been at pains to present to the electorate). On the morning of the transmission Hill and those members of the BBC Board of Governors who were in Broadcasting House met and previewed the programme. They decided that

"I'll tell you how much I made from my memoirs --
if you'll tell me how much Heath paid you to ask ..."

Unpublished cartoon, by kind permission of Peter Clarke

the remaining reference to Wilson's earnings from his book should be cut, but that the title of the programme and pictures of his houses must remain. They confirmed that the programme would be transmitted that night as scheduled. By viewing the programme before transmission, and by making it public that they had done so, the Governors had become involved in the day-to-day programme decision-making of the BBC in a way which had not happened before. This set a dangerous precedent.[4]

When the programme was transmitted reaction was mixed. To many people, particularly the younger generation, it seemed an enormous fuss about very little. Much of the press and the older generation condemned the programme's makers for trivialisation and lack of respect towards senior politicians. Within days of the transmission the BBC held an internal inquiry which acknowledged that mistakes had been made. But at the same time Hill, defending the BBC, gave a public undertaking on behalf of the Governors to do nothing that could put at risk the independence of the BBC. Broadcast journalism, he said, had special obligations 'but it cannot surrender to any individual or party or government – any more than can the press – its right of independent editorial judgement'.[5] The distinguished broadcaster Robert Kee, writing five weeks after the transmission, provided probably the best summing-up of the views of the majority of programme makers and most of the audience: 'From all the apparently never-ending exchange of memoranda and counter-memoranda about *Yesterday's Men* what emerges clearly is that the Labour leaders' principal complaint is that they were made to look silly. The complaint has substance. But do they not in fact on occasion look silly? . . . Disrespect plays a not inconsiderable part in any healthy democracy's attitude to its politicians. It is the duty of a healthy Fourth Estate to reflect some of it. Let us now have a *Today's Men* on the Tories.'[6] However, among the plethora of editorials on the affair, a leader in *The Times* was probably of more long-term significance than all the rest put together. Described as 'magisterial' – younger programme makers might have thought the word 'pompous' more apposite – *The Times* leader proclaimed that the programme was too shallow to be tolerated: 'Its attitude towards politics was utterly trivial, the attitude of the gossip column or the political novelette.' There had been no serious discussion of the significance of any political issue – 'The leading Labour politicians were all treated as though the great questions of public affairs played no part in their lives . . . Ambition and money are not the only motivation of human life, surely not even at Television Centre. This view of political affairs is, to put it frankly, the view of immature young people.'[7] That *Times* leader was written by William Rees-Mogg who, ten years later under Margaret Thatcher, would be made Vice-Chairman of the BBC.

During the 1970s the BBC under Hill and Curran still generally stood up for its programme makers against attacks from governments and the establishment, at least in public. The same could not be said of the ITA over in ITV. Anxious to get the Levy reduced and then to win a second ITV channel, the ITA frequently appeared to programme makers to be their most conspicuous enemy. Too often the Authority seemed bent on curbing the controversial, censoring just criticism of the powerful and hobbling investigative journalism. Granada's *World in Action*, consistently the best British television current affairs programme and the only one regularly to equal the best investigative newspaper journalism, was regularly in trouble with the Authority.

Tim Hewat, the great, ebullient founding editor of *World in Action*, had called the Authority's handling of programmes 'non-sensical', its senior officials 'silly people' (in private he would probably have said 'fuckers') and the officer who most frequently dealt with programmes 'a prick' – sentiments with which most young programme makers would have heartily agreed. Denis Forman suggested that Sir Robert Fraser's actions had been motivated by fear – 'fear of what the press would say, fear of public opinion, fear of displeasing our lords and masters in Westminster'. Any hope that things might change as a result of Young taking over from Fraser had soon been dashed. As Forman observed, his technique was different but the results were the same: 'He believed that by reasoned argument he could persuade an opponent to accept the right view (his) on any topic . . . Brian believed that on the whole governments were good, democracy worked and civil servants were not corrupt.'[8] [The parenthesis is Forman's]

So in 1971, when *World in Action* investigated Idi Amin's military takeover of Uganda in a programme called *The Man Who Stole Uganda*, and portrayed Amin as corrupt, despotic and cruel, Granada was back on the carpet. The Foreign Office was furious (Amin was British Army-trained and seen as a bulwark against his Communist rival Milton Obote) and Lady Cohen, the widow of a former British Governor, and other prominent persons who knew the country well, were up in arms and protesting that Amin was a fine man and a friend of Britain. Although the ITA could not doubt the accuracy of the facts reported in the programme, Granada was told that it 'had erred through sins of omission'. By concentrating only on what was demonstrably wicked the viewer had received a very distorted picture. Granada responded that in the case of a regime as evil as Amin's, impartiality was out of place. Unsurprisingly, this cut no ice.[9]

The constraints on television, and in particular the control exercised over it by a narrow group of political, commercial and social power brokers were graphically demonstrated again early in 1973. *World in Action* had recruited a young reporter from the Bradford *Telegraph and Argus* called Ray Fitzwalter, who had recently won the 'Young Journalist of the Year' award, to undertake a one-hour special investigation into the affairs of John Poulson, a north-country architect who had gone spectacularly bust and whose bankruptcy proceedings were then being heard in a Wakefield court. Poulson had built up a lucrative architecture and engineering business through a network of companies operating both in Britain and overseas. Fitzwalter's investigation led him right to the top of the two major political parties and implicated senior civil servants, powerful businessmen and trade union officials in a complex web of corrupt dealing, bribery, deceit and the dishonest use of influence. Poulson's close associates included Reginald Maudling, who had been Heath's Home Secretary until mid-1972. Maudling had been the chairman of two of Poulson's overseas companies. Another close associate of Poulson's was the disgraced former Labour leader of Newcastle-upon-Tyne Council, a powerful and charismatic character called T. Dan Smith, who had masterminded a massive building and regeneration programme in the city. Smith had used his influence to assist Poulson's companies in winning lucrative contracts while at the same time being on Poulson's payroll. Smith was also a director of Tyne Tees Television. When the officers of the IBA (the Independent Television Authority had become the Independent Broadcasting Authority in 1972) saw the programme ahead of transmission, their reaction was, in Denis Forman's words, 'one of shock and disbelief'. The programme was banned. The Director-General, Young, then referred the banning to a full meeting of the Members of the Authority. The Authority confirmed the banning 'permanently' and 'irreversibly'. In order to justify the ban, the Authority cited a general provision, seldom-used, if ever, of the Television Act giving the Authority editorial freedom to reject any programme of which it disapproved. The national press now went to town on the IBA, drawing attention to the close connections between three Authority Members and those heavily implicated in the Poulson case – Baroness Sharp, Sir Frederick Hayday and Baroness McLeod. Sharp had been a top civil servant in the Ministry of Housing and had appeared as the only character witness on behalf of T. Dan Smith at his trial for bribery at the Old Bailey a year earlier. Sir Frederick Hayday was an influential union official with close links to Poulson's network, and Baroness McLeod was the widow of Maudling's former cabinet colleague Iain McLeod.

On what should have been the day of transmission, Granada asked to meet the Members of the Authority so that they could view the programme together and discuss it. Granada was brusquely turned down. That night in place of the *World in Action* programme the ITV network showed a film – *The Flight of the Snow Goose*. Pickets now appeared outside the IBA's headquarters opposite Harrods and the ACTT's General Secretary, Alan Sapper, reaffirmed the union's opposition to censorship in whatever guise. Unless the Authority changed its decision, the union announced, in future weeks ITV would be blacked out at the time when *World in Action* would normally be screened. The IBA did now agree to meet Granada and see the programme. Forman has recorded that when the lights went up after the viewing in the Authority's tiny preview theatre, Baroness Sharp was heard to say, 'Poor Dan, this film will ruin him.' The Authority would still not change its mind and continued to ban the transmission. The following Monday, at the time when *World in Action* should have been on air, screens across ITV were blacked out.

So things continued for three months, with Forman determined that the programme should go out and Baroness Sharp equally determined that it should not. By the time the Authority relented and let the programme go out, the time that had elapsed and the changes that had been made to the programme to appease the IBA had blunted its impact.[10]

Another major row, over a very different kind of programme, broke out just as the battle over the Poulson programme was beginning. It was over a film made by the photographer David Bailey about the American pop artist Andy Warhol. This had been commissioned by Bob Heller, who was responsible for documentary and current affairs programmes at ATV. Heller was a remarkable man, one of the great unsung heroes of British television. An American who had worked on the legendary American series *The March of Time* and, probably as a result, fallen under the suspicion of the witch-hunting anti-Communist Senator McCarthy and his House Un-American Activities Committee, Heller had been brought over to Britain on the recommendation of Ed Murrow by Sidney Bernstein in 1955 to head the programme side of Granada Television. After falling out with Bernstein (Bob always claimed that he was the only man ever successfully to sue Bernstein, but I have never found any confirmation of the story), Heller had joined Lew Grade at ATV. Generously funded by Grade to raise the company's prestige by contributing major one-hour current affairs or documentaries to the network for twelve weeks in the year, Heller had engaged a succession of distinguished and challenging film makers to make films with teams of their own choice. Heller guarded this creative freedom and his closeness to Grade tenaciously. Intensely secretive, with his domed forehead and glasses, Heller reminded one of the American comedian Phil Silvers as the scheming Sergeant Bilko in the hit 1950s–60s US TV series of that name. On top of his other talents, Heller mixed the best dry martini in London.

From the 1960s onwards Heller had commissioned a dazzling series of award-winning films including Adrian Cowell's *The Tribe That Hides from Man*, about a tribe living deep in the Brazilian jungle, Anthony Snowdon's *Born to Be Small* and a series of films from John Pilger. He had hired Denis Mitchell and Norman Swallow when they left the BBC to set up their own company and also Peter Batty when he became an independent. Under Heller, ATV became 'the best refugee camp in the land' for television programme makers who were in trouble because of their work or their political views. Almost any programme maker, more or less whatever their views, who Bob felt had a proven track record and one of whose programmes had recently been banned or who had refused to accept censorship of his work and quit, could expect a phone call from Bob. Having himself suffered censorship and intimidation because of his views, Heller used his position to help others in similar difficulties. I alone was bailed out no fewer than three times between 1964 and 1970 when my work got me into trouble with the people I was working for. I was only one among dozens of film makers who received the typical telephone rescue call from Bob. 'You need a job?' the unmistakable voice would ask in a low, slow drawl. A call from Bob might mark the birth of a new project or a couple of weeks on a wild-goose chase to somewhere such as Mexico, with a useful fee at the end of it, plus a helpful cash advance if you needed it. From 1972 onwards, Charles Denton, a young producer who had himself been in trouble over a programme he had made for Granada with John Pilger about the disillusion of American GIs fighting in Vietnam (Sir Robert Fraser had accused them of 'outrageous left-wing propaganda'), had joined Bob Heller, becoming first his deputy and then taking over from him when he retired in 1974.

The way in which Heller and Denton ran the documentary department at ATV and the way in which they engaged film makers more or less mirrored the way in which people worked in the independent film sector. By running their department in this way they demonstrated that something similar to the independent film sector could work successfully in television. Together Heller and Denton put down an important marker for the way in which a new fourth channel might commission programmes.

The programme Heller had commissioned from Bailey about Andy Warhol had been scheduled for transmission on the ITV network on Tuesday, 16 January 1973 at 10.30 p.m. On the Sunday before transmission the *Sunday Mirror* carried the headline 'Andy Warhol shocker for ITV'; the *News of the World* trumpeted 'This TV Shocker is the worst ever', adding 'Millions of viewers will find it offensive'. The programme, already passed by the IBA for transmission 'outside family viewing hours', readers were eagerly informed, contained four-letter words and a naked lady who used the nipple of one of her ample breasts as a paint brush. The Festival of Light (a moralising extension of Mary Whitehouse's pressure group, the National Viewers and Listeners Association), claiming to stand for 'moral purity and Christian values', whose supporters included four bishops, Lord Longford and Cliff Richard and had a couple years previously drawn a crowd of 35,000 for a rally in Trafalgar Square, now alighted on the Warhol programme. One of their number, Ross McWhirter, broadcaster and editor of the *Guinness Book of Records*, applied for a court injunction to restrain the IBA from transmitting the programme. The court threw out his application, but McWhirter immediately applied to the Court of Appeal, where Lord Denning upheld his injunction. A long and complex series of legal arguments ensued. While these continued, members of the Festival of Light and the National Viewers and Listeners Association orchestrated a campaign of telephone calls and letters to the IBA and the ITV companies urging them to drop the programme. The argument quickly escalated beyond a simple row over the fate of one fifty-minute documentary (which neither McWhirter nor the Appeal Court had seen) and became a battle of principle over the concept of freedom of expression – freedom of speech versus the rights of an individual. As Chris Dunkley wrote in the *Financial Times*, McWhirter's injunction was 'one small step for Ross McWhirter and one massive retrograde stride for British television in particular and the concept of free speech in general'.[11]

As the legal arguments dragged on and the concern already felt by programme makers deepened, Sir Hartley Shawcross, the Chairman of Thames Television (a former Labour Attorney General whose political views had shifted to the right), told a reporter that from all that he had heard about the programme (he, like the majority of those who were now pontificating about it, had not actually seen it), he was glad of McWhirter's injunction because it would spare Thames from the distasteful task of transmitting the programme. The response of Thames's programme makers was fury. They issued a round-robin statement, signed by 287 Thames employees, publicly dissociating themselves from Shawcross's remarks: 'We wish to make it clear that the present high standing of Thames's reputation is based in large part upon the creative freedom we have hitherto enjoyed.'[12] Eventually, after much legal argument turning not on the merits of the programme but on the right of the IBA to decide whether to transmit the programme and the standing of the procedure used by McWhirter in bringing his action, the Court lifted the injunction. As a result, on 27 March 1973 the Warhol programme was transmitted. Following all the fuss, the programme was seen by 14 million viewers. A survey afterwards revealed that most had been bored rather than shocked by it and that 84% thought it a lot of fuss about nothing.

Such rows, and the many lesser ones which did not become public, served to heighten the resolve of progressive programme makers that a better way had to be found to get programmes made and broadcast.

*   *   *

The divisions in society had continued to deepen, between left and right and between moderates and extremists in morals and art, between feminists and campaigners for sexual liberation, even between members of the same political party. Three weeks after the transmission by the BBC of *A Question of Ulster* in January 1972, British troops had opened fire on civil rights marchers in Londonderry on what became known as Bloody Sunday. A month later the IRA bombed Aldershot; a month after that the Stormont Parliament was suspended and direct rule of Northern Ireland by the government in London was instituted. In the second week of January 1972 a strike of coal miners had begun and by the end of the month unemployment had risen to over a million (in those days an unheard-of figure which was thought to spell certain political and economic disaster). In early February, as a result of the continuing miners' strike, there were power blackouts and the government declared a State of Emergency. In May there was a work-to-rule on the railways and in July another dock strike.

Following all the discussion of the allocation of the fourth channel and the rows over television programmes, in August 1972 the House of Commons Select Committee on the Nationalised Industries produced a new report on ITV and the IBA's stewardship of it. The Committee's report was almost as critical of the IBA and ITV as the Pilkington Committee had been ten years earlier. It criticised the Authority's secrecy, particularly in its handling of the HTV and LWT franchise applications and of the companies' subsequent failure to live up to their programme promises. The Select Committee said that the fourth channel should not be allocated before there had been a comprehensive inquiry into broadcasting as a whole and other alternatives for its use had been examined. Audience ratings were not an adequate measure of what constituted a good broadcasting service. The existing ITV service needed greater programme innovation and diversity, with more access for the public 'freer from the editorial controls of the professional broadcasters'.

The report, which was unanimous and signed by as many Conservative as Labour members, was widely seen as a triumph for the programme makers and radicals organised by the FCG and the 76 Group. Invited to present evidence to the committee, they and their supporters had repeatedly criticised the IBA. Asked by the committee about the IBA's handling of Rupert Murdoch's 35% shareholding in LWT, Caroline Heller, who appeared before the Committee as a member of the ACTT delegation, said simply, 'We are unable to see any substantial difference between the rotten programmes that existed before and the ones that are put out now.' The FCG's representatives had been even more scathing: 'Our criticism of the IBA is that throughout its existence it has quite simply failed to exercise the authority with which it is entrusted . . . The IBA seems to cling with a childish naivete to the notion that commercial TV companies are "free enterprise" institutions and that therefore the commercial logic of their operations must not be interfered with. So they allowed the companies to suck huge sums of money out of television in the late '50s and early '60s, but when the going got temporarily rough they rushed to the companies' aid in demanding a reduction of the Levy.' The FCG argued for root and branch change to the whole set-up to make television more open and democratic.

The vision of what broadcasting could be, held out by people like Nicholas Garnham, Anthony Smith and groups such as the FCG, and the reality of ITV, despite some good and courageous programmes, were by now light years apart. In the ITV official history for this period, Jeremy Potter describes the proprietors and senior executives of the ITV companies: 'Like medieval barons, they rode up to the capital from their territorial fiefdoms to show their faces in the corridors of power, pay court to their sovereign lords and plot among themselves.'[13] Clearly those 'barons', whether in television or the press, were not going to tolerate rebellion or challenges to their power by the peasants of the FCG. The barons now called on every means available to put the peasants down.

At the beginning of the year, after Chataway had announced that he was not going to make an immediate award of the fourth channel to ITV, members of the FCG had gleefully calculated that while it had cost the ITV companies hundreds of thousands of pounds to mount their campaign to win ITV-2, it had cost the FCG just £126 to stymie them – a sum arrived at, as I recall, by adding the cost to us of organising the public meeting at the Central London Polytechnic to what it had cost us in postage to send out information and petitions to potential supporters. There were to be no such gleeful calculations after the FCG's success with the House of Commons Select Committee on the Nationalised Industries. That summer, as the Committee's report was published, the FCG magazine *Open Secret*'s lead story told of the sudden withdrawal of the group's funding by the Rowntree Trust. Members' suspicions focused on the overlapping financial interests of individual Rowntree trustees and leading members of the Newspaper Proprietors' Association. The FCG had been active in newspapers, promoting the introduction to British newspapers of West German-style workers' participation in the management and editorial decision-making, and in goading the previously compliant National Union of Journalists into a more proactive stance. Members of the FCG did not need reminding that many newspaper owners also had major financial interests in commercial television – Rupert Murdoch and the Thomson Organisation were only the most prominent examples. Such proprietors had reason to resent the FCG's role in blocking their plans for ITV-2, the embarrassment and difficulty the Group had caused them by acts such as publishing the LWT franchise application and its evidence to the Select Committee on Nationalised Industries. Publicly the reason given for the withdrawal of the Rowntree Trust's money was that the activities of the FCG had become too overtly political and so fell outside the terms of the Trust's charitable aims. But when Neal Ascherson made private enquiries among senior people with connections in the Rowntree Trust it became clear that the heat was being turned up on the Trust itself on account of its support for groups putting forward socialist or Marxist solutions to a whole range of issues. Some Trustees apparently feared that sensational press exposés would start to appear alleging that money provided by the Trust for educational work by liberation movements in Portuguese Africa was being used by the Marxist guerrilla movement in Mozambique, Frelimo, to buy arms. A further concern, Ascherson and some of his colleagues in the FCG suspected, was the possibility that some FCG funding had made its way to Radio Free Derry, a pro-Republican radio station in Londonderry. 'In the great scheme of things,' Ascherson's contact told him, 'support for Frelimo is more important.' Ascherson recalls, 'I was very moved really and had to agree that continuing support for the anti-colonial struggle in Portuguese Mozambique was more important.'[14]

Although there was optimistic talk of the FCG continuing, of concentrating on a reduced number of issues where it had already had most success, nothing came of it. The reality was that the FCG could not continue without funding.

It was not only the withdrawal of its Rowntree Trust funding that caused the FCG's demise. Neal Ascherson dates the start of the FCG's problems to 1970 when it first received the grant: 'Once the FCG had got money from Rowntree and got an office in Craven Street the voluntary effort dropped off. As we could pay someone to do the work people felt that *they* need no longer bother.' Or as another member of the FCG put it at the time, 'Getting the Rowntree money was the kiss of death.' Ascherson believes that by 1972 there was a widespread perception among the sort of people who belonged to the FCG 'that things had changed, that we were now entering a period of terrific union struggle – that many of the things we believed in would be done by trade union power. Many of those who were more to the left believed that the industrial conflict that resulted from Heath's policies would precipitate the showdown that would transform society. Others viewed Heath's policies with alarm and concentrated on stopping ITV-2.'[15] Christine Fox, the FCG's longest serving organiser, says that by the end it was no longer possible to contain all the different political views inside the one group. 'It should have been possible to have an FCG view on any issue, but it was impossible to contain all the different groups. Whatever you said was unacceptable to one faction or another – the WRP, the IS, moderate socialists or people who were just left of centre. It was very important to concentrate on what you'd been set up to do, to have an immediate response. But by the end it was about time for it to finish.'[16] The sense of shared purpose, which in 1968 had united Marxists and Trotskyites with moderate members of the Labour Party and liberals (with or without a capital 'L'), had broken down by 1972.

The FCG had, in any case, served its purpose. Created in response to specific events in 1968 and drawing its strength from the prevailing mood of that time, by 1972, in very different circumstances and a changed political atmosphere, it was no longer relevant. In addition to its obvious achievements as a campaigning organisation, the FCG had largely succeeded in realising Gus Macdonald's original intentions for it. It had raised awareness among people working in television of the importance of the structure and underpinning political assumptions that lay behind the organisations in which they worked. It had proved to producers and programme makers that they could affect the policies and political decisions which impacted on their professional lives. A generation of programme makers had learned how to lobby effectively. Working associations and friendships had been forged between programme makers from different programme disciplines and companies, and between programme makers and journalists, which would endure to serve them in future campaigns. The FCG disappeared, but reverberations from it (albeit often unrecognised) would sound down through the broadcasting battles of the next fifteen years.

*　　*　　*

Following publication of the Select Committee on the Nationalised Industries Report in August 1972, the IBA issued a lengthy rebuttal of the Select Committee's criticisms and once again pressed its claim for a second ITV channel. At the same time different groups within broadcasting started to come forward with their own solutions to the ills of broadcasting and recommendations for what to do about the vacant fourth channel.

First in the field had been the Association of Broadcasting Staff (ABS). In January 1972 a letter from Tom Rhys, President of the ABS (the main BBC union) had been published in *The Times*. He revealed that his union had sent a proposal to the Minister suggesting the creation of an entirely new kind of broadcasting organisation to run the fourth channel – the National Television Foundation. Unlike existing broadcasting organisations it would take programmes from a variety of sources. 'BBC-1 and -2 and ITV-1 and -2 would be mirror images of each other . . . the National Television Foundation will provide the new type of impresario which British television needs . . . it will provide a fresh outlet for talent and energy.'[17] Amid the clamour of argument at that moment over preventing Chataway from allocating the fourth channel to ITV, Rhys's proposal had gone largely unnoticed. However, a few months later Anthony Smith, who had played a significant role in the initial genesis of the idea, had returned to the proposal and developed it further. By then Smith had left the BBC and become a Fellow at St Antony's College, Oxford.

The idea for a National Television Foundation had originally grown out of discussion at ABS meetings in the BBC in the summer and autumn of 1971. Smith describes his own role in the initial genesis of the idea as that of amanuensis to the programme makers and technicians who developed the proposal. However, this seems unduly modest. Although there is no doubt that a lot of the ideas did come from others, there is also ample evidence that Smith's own input into the development of the idea was considerable and went well beyond simply putting the ideas of others into words and turning the whole into a coherent proposal. Smith largely attributes his own initial thinking on the subject to a book, *Television: A Personal Report*, written by Robin Day back in 1961 at the time of the Pilkington Committee. Day had written that what disturbed him was that 'everybody appears to be thinking of television's future as first and foremost a question of *control*. How to stop this, restrict that, prevent the other . . . But I believe that it is wrong to start by seeing the issue as one of control. I see it primarily as one of *freedom*: how can television be built into the broadest possible platform of democratic opinion?' Day went on to describe a broadcasting system which would commission a wide variety of individuals or groups to present programmes on a basis of merit and diversity of opinion. He foresaw a broadcasting organisation which would commission a considerable number of small, independent, freelance groups of producers and journalists in much the same way as books or articles expressing independent opinions are commissioned by a publisher or magazine. The organisation suggested by Day would, he said, 'be different in character from the BBC or the ITA. It would originate, but not control. It would select but not supervise. It would be a publisher, not producer.'[18]

In a full page article in the *Guardian* in April 1972 Smith described his own vision for a National Television Foundation. In his proposals, Robin Day had been talking primarily about journalism and current affairs programmes. Smith and his ABS colleagues had extended this idea to cover the whole range of programmes. 'The system of broadcasting had been based on this idea of a homogeneous society,' says Smith. '1968 had revealed there was no homogeneity to what was wanted from programmes and in our society any more.' He had also been impressed by what had been happening in the theatre since the first appearance in London of Brecht's Berliner Ensemble, the success of the Royal Court, the rise of Joan Littlewood's Theatre Workshop and the resultant flowering of new talent and new writing among people from all sorts of different backgrounds. In his own field of documentaries and current affairs, Smith said 'for every current affairs programme that was made there were ten more that were forbidden'. New technology, small cameras and video recorders were beginning to suggest that 'things could be done in another way, that programmes could be made differently'. As Smith saw it, 'The unions supported the bosses in keeping the system as it was, through restrictive practices, through keeping new kinds of people out and by traditional and established ways of making programmes.'[19] What was needed, Smith wrote in the *Guardian*, was 'a system of controlling television so that it will respond to the frustrations currently being expressed among the public, the political community, and the television workers themselves . . . that will be able to respond also to the frustrations not yet expressed, flexible enough to introduce ideas into the television industry in answer to grievances which have not yet even been generated. We need an institution which isn't an institution, which does not collect, as a response to its own historical battles, a set of its own vested interests and habits which it has to fight to protect.'

To realise this utopian concept, Smith proposed a charitable foundation. Rather than the equivalent of a newspaper editorial office, he proposed a group of trustees who would distribute airtime to ideas on the basis of spread rather than balance, whose aim would be to supplement rather than to compete. They would accept or commission programmes from a variety of sources, from interest groups and organisations as well as from programme makers or groups and companies of programme makers, even from the staff of other broadcasters 'which are not able to house the particular idea or person concerned'. The total cost of such a set-up, Smith estimated, would be about £20 million a year, or about the same as the scheme proposed by the ITV companies. This money would come from sponsorship by government ministries, large organisations, unions and companies, from a government grant, 'block' (as opposed to 'spot' advertising), programme sales and publishing, and from licences or subscriptions 'paid directly by the viewer to the programme maker'.[20] Smith followed his first *Guardian* article with others as more people contributed additional ideas and as he developed his own ideas further.[21]

Smith's proposal was particularly welcomed by the increasing body of younger would-be programme makers eager to get into television and by frustrated programme makers who felt that their more way-out ideas could find no outlet through the BBC and ITV companies. It also found favour with propagandists of many complexions, with trade unionists who felt they were unreported or unfairly reported by the existing channels, with the likes of Tony Benn, with the growing body of feminists who understandably felt they were misrepresented and patronised by the predominantly male governed channels and even with bodies such as Mary Whitehouse's National Viewers and Listeners Association who felt that their case was never properly put on television. One person with whom it did not find favour was the former Director-General of the BBC, Hugh Carleton Greene, who appeared in a *Late Night Line-Up* interview and gave his backing to ITV-2. He later modified this a little, suggesting that the National Television Foundation should perhaps share a bit of ITV-2.

For their part, the advertisers continued to press for a second commercial television channel which would break ITV's monopoly in the sale of television advertising airtime. They produced a number of plans, the most important of which argued for the rapid allocation of a fourth channel which would sell advertising in competition to ITV. In March 1973 Sir John Eden, the new Minister for Posts and Telecommunications, told the Advertising Film Ball at the

Dorchester Hotel that he hoped to be able to announce plans for the fourth channel in 1974. His announcement was greeted with cheers.

That same month, March 1973, Sir John Eden published the government's response to the Report of the Select Committee on the Nationalised Industries. He brushed aside the Committee's stern criticisms of ITV and its calls for a full public inquiry into the future of broadcasting. The technical committee set up by Chataway having advised the government that there were unlikely to be any significant technical developments in television warranting major changes in the organisation of broadcasting before 1981, there was, he said, 'no cause in the current decade to alter the structure of broadcasting', so there was no cause to hold a further formal inquiry into broadcasting. However, he continued, that was not necessarily a reason to put off a decision on the allocation of the fourth channel. He would welcome views on the various ideas that had already been put forward and 'constructive suggestions' from those who had not already put forward their ideas. He called for these before the end of July 1973. He did not know how long it might take him to work through these ideas but, he said, he hoped 'to make substantial progress with it in the remaining part of the year'. John Grant, speaking for the Labour Party, responded: 'The future of broadcasting is far too important to leave to the government of a commercially sponsored party.' A new Labour government, he warned, would not be bound by the Tory government's decisions. He pledged that, if re-elected, Labour would re-instate the Annan Committee.[22]

As was to be expected, Eden's announcement triggered off a plethora of special pleading and proposals from individuals and interest groups – some altruistic, more the veiled expression of vested interest. At the end of July the ITV companies launched a new campaign to win their second channel with a new submission to the Minister. 'To operate an additional television channel the prime needs are: 1. Programmes 2. Production facilities 3. Finance. Only ITV can provide all three.' ITV was now prepared, the companies announced, to accommodate parts of other ideas into their scheme. They would provide facilities to 'other programme makers and groups who are lacking facilities and finance' so that they too could contribute programmes to the channel through a new 'independent production board'.[23]

Two of the most interesting and significant of the dozens of other proposals sent to the Minister came from private individuals. The first came jointly from David Elstein and John Birt and the other from Jeremy Isaacs.

The genesis of the Elstein–Birt proposal went back to the conference called by Brian Young at the ITA in November 1971 when Birt and Elstein had found themselves sitting next to each other. After Eden's statement in the House of Commons Elstein and Birt had got together to discuss ideas. Elstein's interest ever since he joined the Free Communications Group and became a founder member of the 76 Group had, by his own account, been purely that of a concerned broadcasting insider. He had not had much to do with the TV4 Campaign, the initiatives based on political and social principle or the work of Caroline Heller and the ACTT Television Commission. To him the fourth channel was important because 'it was the last, and only opportunity for the foreseeable future of achieving something that was different and better'. His intervention with Birt into the debate at this stage was, Elstein says, 'quite narrow. It was concentrated just on the fourth channel rather than the broader issues to do with broadcasting as a whole or freedom of expression. We took an insider's rational, pragmatic, professional view.'[24] After mulling over their thoughts, it was Elstein who composed the letter which they sent jointly to the Minister on 20 May 1973. The basis of their submission was 'that if TV4 is allocated, then it should be run as a form of ITV-2 under the IBA. But the new channel should *not* be run by the existing ITV companies, though they would be able to contribute to it. The aim of the scheme is to get the benefits of complementary planning of two channels, whilst spreading the creative and scheduling functions more than has been thought possible up to now ... ITV-2 would be run as a nationally networked channel, by an independent Programme Controller appointed by the IBA. The Controller would have a number of departmental heads under him, and between them they would commission and buy programmes wherever they chose – not just from the existing ITV companies ... ITV-2 would be financed, indirectly, by advertising. The existing companies would have the right to sell the advertising on ITV-2 in their own areas, and would pay a proportion of their income to the IBA to cover ITV-2's running costs.' Elstein and Birt argued that letting ITV sell the advertising on ITV-2 would remove the problem of the two ITV channels damaging the quality of each other's programmes which would arise if they competed to sell advertising.[25]

To many of their campaigning colleagues Birt and Elstein's scheme looked dangerously like the proposal of the IBA and ITV companies. It certainly did not meet the desire to achieve a plurality of programming decisions as outlined in proposals for a National Television Foundation. On his copy of the Birt–Elstein letter, next to the proposal for a single Programme Controller to schedule the channel, Smith scrawled 'Aubrey Singer *again*'. (Singer, the BBC's Head of Features, seemed to his critics to embody, both in his person and through his BBC role, some of the less attractive features of the ITV moguls.) In September Elstein and Birt followed up their submission to Sir John Eden with a second letter taking account of some of the other proposals that were by then doing the rounds. Since their original submission, they said, four main alternatives for the fourth channel had emerged: 'Non-allocation; an educational channel; a National Television Foundation; or a form of ITV-2.' Ignoring non-allocation, they went on to politely rubbish each, except their own, in turn. An educational channel, they said, was problematic. How would it compare in 'cost-effectiveness and cost-benefit . . . with books, radio, cassettes and so on as a means of education'? A National Television Foundation, they depicted, as some kind of cuckoo in the nest, particularly if the fourth channel were split between it and ITV as some people were now suggesting. The philosophy behind the two ideas was completely different and, they implied, more or less impossible to reconcile. 'The most detailed and practical proposals still appear to us to involve a form of ITV-2.' The ITV companies, they said, now appeared to accept that 'a significant proportion of ITV-2's programmes would come from outside the present system'. It was, however, crucial that the Programme Controller be independent of the ITV companies. They set out a management chart for an independent, non-profit-making corporation, answerable to the IBA, with its own chairman, governors and chief executive. 'Television at the moment has two significant needs.' The first was for more access, but as 'very much part of the *present* system' and not as a minority or 'ghetto' element. 'The second need is for the creative forces within the present system to be liberated from the restrictions imposed by the requirements of the institutions which presently employ them.' They could not predict, they said, what programmes 'might emerge from such a system'. But, as examples, they cited a number of programmes shown recently on BBC-2 including *Monty Python's Flying Circus* and Marcel Ophuls' four-hour documentary *Le Chagrin et la pitié*.[26]

Birt and Elstein thought they were getting somewhere when they received a summons to see the Minister. However, their illusions were dispelled immediately they were shown into Sir John Eden's office. Introducing them, the senior civil servant in the Broadcasting Department of the Ministry of Posts and Telecommunications, Jolyon Dromgoole, said, 'Minister, Mr Birt and Mr Elstein to see you.' Looking up to greet his visitors, Sir John Eden was clearly surprised. 'Oh. I thought I was seeing Bert Aylestone.'[27]

Unlike Birt and Elstein, who went to considerable pains to publicise their submission, going so far as to get it published in *Broadcast*, the letter from Jeremy Isaacs to the Minister was confidential. Isaacs was the Controller of Features at Thames Television, run by Howard Thomas, one of the leading advocates of ITV-2. After Thomas's earlier threats against staff who spoke out against his plans for ITV-2, it would have been a serious embarrassment if one of his senior executives publicly came forward with alternative proposals. In private, however, Thomas was prepared to live with the fact that Isaacs had different views from his own – Thames was not a totalitarian regime, or as Isaacs puts it: 'We lived in a freer state than that'. Isaacs felt that as a senior programme executive he had a responsibility to speak up. 'I'm not part of that rabble-rousing lot, but I didn't think that the people who ran ITV should have power over it. I didn't believe either that it should be run by the IBA as it was too conservative and saw its job as stopping things from going out.'[28] Isaacs' plan shared a number of important features with the Birt–Elstein scheme. His proposed channel would have a programme controller, independent of ITV, to schedule it. It was to be a separate channel under the direct control of the IBA rather than the companies, but it would be funded by the ITV companies through a levy paid to the IBA in return for being granted rights to sell the advertising on the channel. Beyond that the whole emphasis of the Isaacs proposal was different from the Birt–Elstein plan. Isaacs' letter started: 'The fourth television channel is a public asset which should be used and not wasted.' While acknowledging that ITV had a strong claim to ITV-2 on simple grounds of parity with the BBC, Isaacs argued, 'But ITV's interest is not necessarily the public's interest.' The government should only make the fourth channel available if 'it will lead to wider choice of programmes, add to the services which broadcasting provides, and offer the possibility of a genuinely new experience on British television'. The controller should invite programme offers from all the ITV companies and from independent producers 'in broad proportions agreed with the IBA and subject to periodic review'. While there should be some entertainment programmes on the channel, there should be a 'heavy emphasis' on programmes 'catering for the interests of minorities of viewers'. Summing up, he concluded: 'ITV should have access to ITV-2, but only on terms that guarantee the public not a mirror image of BBC-1 and BBC-2, but a widening range of broadcasting . . . A government which effected this extension to British television would convey a lasting benefit of which it might be properly proud.'[29] Isaacs saw the fourth channel as 'an opportunity to do something at an angle to both the BBC and ITV . . . It was a sense that change was needed. It should be a change that empowered the programme makers. The vital thing was that ITV should not control it. It reflected my sense of the constant tension between what ITV said it was going to do and what it did do.'[30]

Other potentially influential ideas came from the Standing Conference on Broadcasting (SCOB). SCOB was in a sense a skeleton of the FCG, re-created in intellectually heavyweight but politically anaemic form. It was created early in 1973 with funding, again from the Rowntree Trust, but this time through the Acton Society. The first name given to SCOB was the Alternative Annan, but this lacked the requisite *gravitas*. It consisted of twenty-seven people who, although some of them had had direct recent experience of broadcasting as programme makers or executives, were in the main academics or trade union officials. How they were selected is unclear, but they appeared, to outsiders at least, to be self-selecting. Chaired by Professor Roy Shaw, the Professor of Adult Education at Keele University (and from 1975 Secretary of the Arts Council), its secretary was the ubiquitous Caroline Heller. Other familiar names from the FCG or other campaigns included Nicholas Garnham (now Head of the Department of Communication Studies at the Polytechnic of Central London), Stuart Hall (Deputy Director of the Centre for Cultural Studies at Birmingham University), Dr Jay Blumler (of the Centre for Television Research at Leeds University), Professor Hilde Himmelweit (Department of Social Psychology at the LSE), Professor Stuart Hood (now at the Department of Film and Television at the Royal College of Art), Anthony Smith (St Antony's College, Oxford), Colin Young (the Head of the newly opened National Film School), the critic Milton Schulman, Alan Sapper (General Secretary of the ACTT), John Morton (General Secretary of the Musicians' Union), Tony Hearn (General Secretary of the ABS), Bob Hamilton (also of the ACTT) and Phillip Whitehead MP. In 1973 both Hood and Whitehead were working on Jeremy Isaacs' Thames series, *The World at War*. It gives some idea of the circles-within-circles nature of some of these groupings and of how small, in a sense, television was, that others working for Isaacs on *The World at War* at the time included Neal Ascherson, David Elstein and me.

By the summer of 1973 SCOB had drawn up an impressive schedule of meetings and research projects on issues relating to the 'social and political implications' of developments in broadcasting 'with the aim of stimulating constructive discussion between broadcasters, politicians and outside academic commentators'. As its executive committee reported to members, 'We are hoping to arrange a series of dinners at which members of the Standing Conference will have the opportunity of meeting people with interesting personal views on broadcasting policy.'[31]

SCOB was clearly intended to bring influence to bear by dint of its powerful academic credentials and connections. By July it seemed to making encouraging progress. Caroline Heller had written to Sir John Eden raising 'the matters of principle' over Thames Television's self-interested public intervention in the debate over the allocation of the fourth channel. Professor Himmelweit had had discussions with Brian Young about criticisms of the IBA's supervision of the ITV companies. SCOB had also made arrangements to present its views on the fourth channel informally to the Under-Secretary at the Ministry of Posts and Telecommunications. SCOB told the government 'that the fourth channel should not be allocated to ITV-2. That the fourth channel should only be allocated within the context of a comprehensive investigation into national broadcasting needs and resources. That the Minister should be urged to set up a series of studies and experiments' to identify such needs and priorities and how best to meet them.[32]

Sadly, SCOB was no substitute in terms of its political effectiveness for the now-disbanded FCG or the 76 Group (effectively in abeyance since Eden's decision to extend the lives of the BBC Charter and the IBA). As a result, there was now no large, organised body of people commanding the kind of popular support necessary to mount an effective political campaign against the ITV companies' renewed drive to get ITV-2. Albeit by default, the all-important consensus that only eighteen months earlier Chataway had said was essential before he could award ITV its second channel might now plausibly be claimed to exist by those pressing for ITV-2. It could even be argued that some of those, such as Elstein, who had previously been calling for an inquiry, were now calling for a form of ITV-2. On 3 August 1973 Anthony Howard raised the alarm in a powerful article in the *New Statesman*. Headed 'Must the Media Moguls Win?' he began: 'Whether we like it or not, one of the major, lasting decisions for the future of broadcasting in this country is about to be taken. By "the turn of the year" – a suitably vague, evasive phrase that the government now seems determined to clasp to its bosom – an announcement is due to be made about whether or not a fourth television channel shall be launched . . . There has been no public debate, no popular agitation, hardly even the slightest manifestation of concern from anyone except those most intimately involved. I am sure this suits the government and the Tory Party very well. I am equally certain that it is likely to end up suiting the rest of us extremely badly.' Turning to the companies' renewed campaign to grab the fourth channel, Howard asked, 'Yet what response has this classic, avaricious attempt at a capitalist coup produced? . . . From the Labour Party two conference resolutions, from the BBC a quiet and necessarily defensive memorandum . . . From the self-appointed guardians of participation in the trendier parts of the media a scarcely suppressed bored yawn. The end-result threatens to be that – unless someone gets a public protest or, preferably, a popular outcry going very speedily – we shall shortly see yet another case of legalised daylight robbery.' Lamenting the fact that even the apparently well-informed parts of the public seemed prepared to accept at face value the ITV companies' claims that they were the only people able to pay for a fourth channel, Howard ended with a warning: 'If the government . . . gets away with making the one available new means of communication yet another part of the capitalist apparatus, the rest of us will have consented to be treated like Victorian children – occasionally, at appropriate times of day, permitted to be seen but never, except with the express agreement of our elders and betters, allowed to be heard.'[33]

But Howard warned in vain. Opponents of the ITV companies' plans began to fight among themselves in public. Ten days after Howard's warning Nicholas Garnham launched a scathing attack on ITV's plans in the *Guardian*'s letters page, but at the same time took the opportunity to rubbish Anthony Smith's National Television Foundation. He called the Smith proposal an 'all-things-to-all-men, you-name-it-we-will-do-it solution to the problem of the fourth channel.' Garnham said he imagined that 'endorsement by the commercial television companies is a kiss of death which this scheme cannot long survive' and accused Smith of 'tinkering at the edge' of the existing system in a way which was merely 'diversionary', putting off the day when real structural change of the entire broadcasting system might be brought about. Creating a National Television Foundation was 'like building a small village in which to eke out a living at the mercy of the feudal barons, rather than laying siege to their fortresses. We cannot solve the structural problems of British broadcasting by expansion.'[34] Clearly stung, Smith responded in kind: 'It would be a pity if discussion of the use of the fourth television channel disappeared into an arid more-radical-than-thou contest between supporters of the various rival proposals. Nicholas Garnham illustrated aptly the way in which some of those opposed to ITV-2 are currently diverting themselves towards a kind of revolutionary inertia, in which good arguments against ITV-2 are frittered away by useless insistence on "solving the structural problems of British television" first.' Implying that Garnham was being politically naïve if he thought that a decision on the fourth channel would be delayed for the length of time needed to achieve the kind of major structural upheaval in broadcasting which he was advocating, Smith pointed out that the fourth channel provided the one available opportunity to create a new kind of institution to run television while not interfering with any real structural changes if these came about. Smith repudiated the ITV companies' attempt to graft some of the National Television Foundation's ideas onto their own plans for ITV-2, and slapped down Garnham and the ITV companies together for deliberately misrepresenting the fundamental nature of what his proposals entailed. The National Television Foundation 'involves something rather more than "tinkering at the edges" ', Smith pointed out. 'It involves introducing the concept of a public right to broadcast outside the processes of editorial supervision which hamper existing broadcasting. It makes room for kinds of experiment which broadcasting authorities shun.'[35]

That autumn, while former allies sniped at each other, while SCOB held discreet dinner party discussions and others who had campaigned so actively only eighteen months earlier against ITV-2 either temporised with the commercial companies or did absolutely nothing, the ITV company chiefs rubbed their hands together and confidently awaited the allocation of their long-dreamed-of second channel.

That there was no announcement giving the go-ahead to ITV-2 in late 1973 nor early in 1974 owed nothing to the programme makers or the former activists of the FCG and the 76 Group. It owed everything to outside events. In October 1973 the Arabs attacked Israel, triggering the Yom Kippur War. A bloodier and longer struggle than previous wars between the Arabs and Israelis, during it the Arab oil producers of OPEC brought pressure to bear on Israel's Western allies by cutting oil supplies. In Britain (North Sea oil did not come on-stream until 1975), already wracked by industrial unrest, high inflation, record balance of payments deficits (£1.5 billion in 1973), bomb attacks by the so-called Angry Brigade and escalating Northern Irish terrorism, the result was disastrous. When, in November, the miners put in another large wage claim and declared an overtime ban, Edward Heath responded by declaring a national state of emergency. In mid-December Heath, for the second time since he became Prime Minister, introduced a three-day working week. There were electricity blackouts and television was required to close down at 10.30 p.m. each evening. In January 1974 the miners called a national strike and Heath replied by calling a 'Who Governs Britain?' general election. It was held on 28 February 1974 and Labour won, just – by 301 seats to 297, with the Liberals, Nationalists and others holding the balance of power. Harold Wilson was once more Prime Minister, but this time of a minority government.

Notes

1. Told to the author by Shaun Sutton in 2001.
2. *Death on the Rock and Other Stories*, Roger Bolton, W. H. Allen & Co. Plc, London 1990.
3. Taken from a transcript of the relevant section of the interview reproduced in Lord Hill's memoirs, *op. cit.*
4. In the manner characteristic of the British system in such matters, there was a complex legalistic, almost theological, argument over whether in meeting as they had, not in a formerly convened meeting of the full Board of Governors but as a group within it, and discussing particular changes to the programme, the Governors had created a precedent. Had they crossed a line from passing impartial judgements, to assuming final editorship of the BBC? A year later Anthony Smith concluded in an article in the *New Statesman* (16 June 1972) that the long-held practice whereby the BBC Governors exercised no executive function, having responsibilities which were general and not particular, was finally buried by the *Yesterday's Men* affair, with the result that the constitutional pattern of the BBC was overturned for ever.
5. From the report of the BBC Governors printed in *The Listener*, 15 July 1971.
6. Robert Kee, 'Views' section, *The Listener*, 22 July 1971.
7. *The Times*, 19 June 1971.
8. Forman, *op. cit.*
9. Readers will remember Phillip Whitehead's comment about Young's family connections with British colonial rule. One of the Members of the Authority was Baroness McLeod, widow of Iain McLeod, who as a minister had been deeply involved in Uganda becoming independent within the Commonwealth.
10. T. Dan Smith did wind up behind bars, but that would probably have happened regardless of Granada's film. Successive court cases over the next two years vindicated Granada's programme and highlighted the IBA's censorship. The changes made to the programme by Granada to appease the IBA were presentational rather than factual.
11. Quoted in Potter, *op. cit.* Date of original article not cited.

12. Quoted in Potter, *op. cit., Vol.3.*

13. Potter, *op. cit., Vol. 4.*

14. Neal Ascherson, interviewed by the author in February 2001 and *Open Secret* No. 9, summer 1972. The truth or otherwise of the suspicion about FCG money going to Radio Free Derry now seems lost in the mists of time, but a number of former members of the FCG Committee believe that it probably was. The truth of the allegations about Frelimo and Rowntree is questionable, but any press story could have been damaging to Rowntree even if untrue.

15. Neal Ascherson, interviewed by the author in February 2001.

16. Christine Fox, interviewed by the author in October 2000.

17. Letter from Tom Rhys, President of the Association of Broadcasting Staff, published in *The Times*, 5 January 1972. In addition to BBC staff the ABS represented some of those who worked for the IBA.

18. Robin Day, *Television: A Personal Report*, Hutchinson & Co Ltd, London, 1961. Anthony Smith also ascribes part of his thinking to the influence of Stuart Hood, the former Controller of BBC Television, who after his sudden resignation from the BBC in 1965 had for a while, with his partner Jill Mortimer, shared Smith's house.

19. Anthony Smith, interviewed by the author in September 2000.

20. *Guardian*, 21 April, 1972.

21. When I interviewed Smith for this book he told me that he always intended the idea to grow through people adding their own ideas to what he had written. Peter Fiddick, who commissioned Smith's first article in the *Guardian*, was, in Smith's words, 'a great help and a key influence' on the proposal. Smith sent copies of the article to two hundred people and asked for their ideas. These he digested and then did another article, and so on. There were, Smith says, about six articles in all.

22. *Hansard*, 3 May 1973.

23. Submission to the Minister of Posts and Telecommunications by the Independent Television Companies Association 27 July 1973.

24. David Elstein, interviewed by the author in November 2000.

25. Letter from John Birt and David Elstein to Sir John Eden, Minister of Posts and Telecommunications, 20 May 1973.

26. Letter from John Birt and David Elstein to Sir John Eden, Minister of Posts and Telecommunications 25 September 1973.

27. David Elstein, interviewed by the author in November 2000.

28. Sir Jeremy Isaacs, interviewed by the author in October 2000.

29. Submission to the Minister of Posts and Telecommunications from Jeremy Isaacs, 25 June 1973, reproduced in *Storm Over 4: A Personal Account*, Jeremy Isaacs, George Weidenfeld & Nicolson Ltd, London 1989.

30. Sir Jeremy Isaacs, interviewed by the author in October 2000.

31. Report of executive committee of the Standing Conference on Broadcasting, dated July 1973, included among Anthony Smith's papers held at the British Film Institute.

32. Minutes and notes relating to SCOB, held among Anthony Smith's papers at the British Film Institute.

33. Anthony Howard, 'Must the Media Moguls Win?', *New Statesman*, 3 August 1973.

34. Letter by Nicholas Garnham in the *Guardian*, 17 August 1973. Garnham's own plan called for a broadcasting system in which all the television channels were split and brought under the control of democratically elected bodies.

35. Letter from Anthony Smith published in the *Guardian* on Saturday, 18 August 1973.

5

Annan and After – 1974 to 1979

Wilson, already suspected from his previous administration and the row over *Yesterday's Men* of harbouring Lizzie Borden-like views on the correct relationship between hatchets and broadcasters,[1] moved control of broadcasting to the Home Office, the government department responsible for prisons and the police. However, many of the fears that this might have aroused were allayed by the fact that the new Home Secretary was Roy Jenkins, who in Wilson's previous administration had been responsible for a string of liberal reforms over such things as theatre censorship and the law on homosexuality. On 10 April, in a written parliamentary answer to a question from Phillip Whitehead, Roy Jenkins announced the resurrection of the Annan Committee. It was 'To consider the future of the broadcasting services in the United Kingdom . . . and to propose what constitutional, organisational and financial arrangements and what conditions should apply'[2] to all of the broadcasting services. It was anticipated that it would take about two and a half years to report. At the same time the ITV Levy was restructured yet again, from a payment based on a percentage of advertising income to a percentage of profits. This was intended to encourage the companies to spend more money on programmes.

*   *   *

A good deal of politicking, mischief and attempted general horse-nobbling usually surrounds government reports, white papers and the like, but the amount involving the Annan Committee was greater than normal. First, there was a considerable behind-the-scenes tussle over its membership. The press called for the committee to be composed of experts, people who knew something about broadcasting from the inside rather than the inept and amateurish people who had conducted too many previous inquiries – 'Please, not Billy Wright again' (the former England football captain who had been a member of the Pilkington Committee), pleaded Peter Fiddick in the *Guardian*.[3] The government, however, was reluctant to have any programme makers at all on the Committee and only backed down when Annan said that he would have 'difficulty in continuing to serve' as chairman unless 'at least two expert programme makers' were included. On the other hand, Annan was reluctant to have any serving MPs on the Committee. But Roy Jenkins insisted, a decision Annan later conceded was wise because of the intensity of political interest in the inquiry. In the end, fifteen members were chosen to deliberate with Lord Annan. The two MPs were Phillip Whitehead, an obvious choice in view of his knowledge and proven interest over a long period, and Sir Marcus Worsley, the Conservative MP for Chelsea, who had worked for the BBC earlier in his career. A second person with strong Tory connections was also chosen, Sara Morrison, a Vice-Chairman of the Conservative Party. As was to be expected, there were representatives from Scotland and Wales, a couple of trade unionists, someone who could speak for the ethnic minorities, a businessman, the Director of the Consumers' Association, a scientist, a novelist and a brace of educationalists, one of whom was the ubiquitous Professor Hilde Himmelweit.

The major behind-the-scenes struggle was over the choice of professional broadcasters to serve on the Committee. Shortly after Jenkins' announcement Jolyon Dromgoole, the civil servant in the Broadcasting Department of the Home Office dealing with appointments to the Committee, had visited Anthony Smith at his country cottage to sound him out about joining it and Smith had accepted with some alacrity. However, later, when the names were announced, Smith's name had not been among them. Piecing together what had happened with Phillip Whitehead afterwards, Smith discovered that immediately before the names were to be announced the list had been sent round to Downing Street for Wilson's personal approval, normally a formality. But Wilson had vetoed Smith's appointment. One reason for Wilson's veto seems to have been connected with the *Yesterday's Men* affair three years earlier and the fact that Smith had been the editor of *24 Hours* at the time when the programme went out, even though he had had nothing to do with the programme itself. Another, more powerful reason went back to an incident in 1972. At the time of the Prague Spring in 1968 Smith had got to know many of the leaders of the country's democracy movement and after the Soviet invasion he had kept in touch with them. In 1972 Harold Wilson had gone to Czechoslovakia and made a speech in which he said that the time had come 'to let bygones be bygones'. Smith had arrived in Czechoslovakia a few days after Wilson's speech and a number of his dissident friends had told him how appalled they were by what Wilson had said. When he arrived back in England Smith had told Phillip Whitehead how upset his Czech friends had been by Wilson's speech and Whitehead advised him to write to Wilson about it. Smith wrote what he describes as a 'coruscating letter' to Wilson 'telling him what a terrible thing he had done. I got back a long letter from Wilson, listing in typical Wilson fashion, all the wrongs and misunderstandings of which he, Wilson, had been a victim. My card seems to have been marked by Wilson from that moment onwards.' So Smith was not a member of the Annan Committee and, it seems, at Lord Annan's personal request to Roy Jenkins, Antony Jay replaced him. (Jay, it will be remembered, had left the BBC in the mid-1960s and set up an independent production company with Alasdair Milne and Donald Baverstock.) In gaining Jay, a brilliant broadcaster with valuable insights and ideas of his own (he had recently written a monograph on the future of the BBC advocating mature reflection before any reform),[4] the committee did not exactly lose Smith. Not only did Smith submit his National Television Foundation proposals to the Committee, he was invited by Annan to undertake a number of important studies on behalf of the Committee.

When ITV saw the names of those who had been selected to sit on the committee, the companies and some Authority Members and staff demanded that their Chairman, Lord Aylestone, write to the Home Secretary to complain. In the words of the official history, 'the dice were so heavily loaded' against ITV that 'a protest seemed called for'. The particular object of their complaint was Whitehead. Not only was he a sitting MP who had helped to formulate Labour Party policy hostile to the current set-up in ITV, he had been a founder member of the 76 Group, the FCG and of SCOB. However, Aylestone was reluctant. His letter, not sent until a month after the names became known, was clearly half-hearted. It referred to his 'natural reluctance to complain about the referee before the game began'. Presumably fearful that by complaining about the composition of the Committee he would merely antagonise its members without succeeding in changing them, and mindful of the hammering that ITV had taken from the Pilkington Committee, Aylestone confined himself to observing that in committees of this sort, 'ITV is always in danger of having no-one who can speak for it with experience.' Unsurprisingly, Aylestone's complaint got nowhere.

Thousands of letters poured in to the Committee and 750 communications from both individuals and organisations were circulated to each member. In addition the Committee spent twenty-five days hearing oral evidence from individuals and organisations, visited all fourteen ITV companies, the IBA, Broadcasting House, most of the BBC's local and regional centres and stations, where they talked to staff as well as management. They also visited experimental cable stations in Bristol, Swindon, Sheffield and Wellingborough. Anthony Smith undertook a comparative study on behalf of the Committee into 'the relationship of management with creative staff in broadcasting organisations in France, Canada, West Germany and the UK'. In all the Committee held forty-four formal meetings to discuss evidence and prepare its report.

The Labour Party organised what almost amounted to a pre-emptive strike on the Committee.

In May 1974, between Roy Jenkins' announcement of the resurrection of the Annan Committee and the publication of the names of those who were to serve on it, the Labour Party's Home Policy Committee published what it described as a Green Paper or, to avoid any confusion with government publications, a policy 'discussion paper' on the media. *The People and the Media* was intended, it said, to 'assist' the Annan Committee 'in its deliberations'. When the paper was published twenty-nine people were listed as having played an active part in its formulation. They included many who had been active in the campaigns of the previous few years. Among them were Labour MPs Tony Benn, John Grant, John Golding and Phillip Whitehead, plus Neal Ascherson, Christine Fox, Nicholas Garnham and Caroline Heller of the FCG, Roy Lockett, Alan Sapper and Bob Hamilton of the ACTT. Unsurprisingly, the paper's views coincided in large measure with views already expressed elsewhere. Basing its recommendations on the premise that: 'The plain fact is that our broadcasting, for all its reputation and achievements, is now characterised by closed and autocratic institutions and marked resistance to wider public involvement in its decision making processes', and citing the findings of the Select Committee on Nationalised Industries in support of its case, *The People and the Media* listed seven essential requirements for public service broadcasting in the contemporary context – a larger number of broadcasting units distributed throughout the country, central funding (including the collection of advertising revenue) which was free of political and commercial pressure, separation of advertising revenue from programme making and scheduling, internal democracy within a framework of public accountability, elected representation on broadcasting management bodies, democratic determination of broadcasting policy and independent complaints procedures. In order to realise these principles, the paper recommended the creation of two national bodies, one of which would advise the Minister, undertake research and keep broadcasting policy and development under continuous review; the other, consisting of ministerial appointees and elected representatives, would be responsible for the overall administration and funding of all broadcasting. The BBC and ITV as such would be swept away and replaced by two publicly owned television corporations which would each run two channels. These would be funded with money raised through advertising and direct taxation (the Licence Fee, being a form of regressive taxation, would be phased out and replaced by direct government funding). 'Programme making itself', the document said, 'would be carried out by a wide variety of dispersed *programme units* reflecting the creative talent of all parts of the UK.'[5] The ACTT submitted proposals along similar lines, so similar that Annan would later say he suspected that they had been written by the same people.

Although initially impressed by the academic credentials of SCOB, Annan soon came to entertain suspicions that it too was some kind of front for Labour Party policy. SCOB opened its submission with the assertion that the existing system of broadcasting in Britain had 'manifestly failed'. Unlike the Labour Party, SCOB wanted the fourth channel left unallocated. In trying to arrive at a unanimous set of recommendations SCOB had had a blazing row, amounting to a split, during which Dr Jay Blumler and Anthony Smith had accused their colleagues of wanting too much centralised control of the broadcasting institutions and not giving enough space or freedom for the individual, the dissenting voice or the alternative view. Although the disagreement mainly centred on the narrow issue of the allocation of the fourth channel, it revealed a fundamental difference in philosophical outlook – a difference which by this time was opening up all over the left on a whole range of issues and would lead eventually to the split in the Labour Party and to its impotence throughout the 1980s.

The showdown with his colleagues in SCOB was to have a lasting effect on Smith. Until then he had seen himself as a fairly conventional member of the political left, but 'It made me realise that I wasn't on the left – that I did believe in a more American kind of free-expression.' Smith had insisted that the fourth channel must be governed in a different way and according to a separate philosophy from the other channels. But to Heller, Garnham and other members of SCOB this would have the effect of letting both the BBC and ITV 'off the hook of reform. As the main channels of broadcasting were (under Smith's scheme) going to remain ITV and the BBC, channel four would be just a side issue.' To them the main thing was to reform the governance of the main channels. 'It wasn't a dispute between revolutionaries and reformers. We were all reformers. We just thought different things important. Tony Smith and co. were on the side of "leave it to the creators" whereas we had the view that if it was public money then the audience had a right to have a say. The creators were, in the end, just another special interest group. In the real world there has to be some compromise between the two.'[6]

In December 1974 Smith submitted an extensively refined summary of his National Television Foundation proposal to the Annan Committee. In it he again stressed that the fourth channel had to be placed outside the control of either the BBC or the IBA so as to achieve 'a form of institutional control wedded to a different doctrine from the existing broadcasting authorities, to a doctrine of openness rather than to balance, to expression rather than to neutralisation'.[7] When Smith and Blumler appeared before the Annan Committee to give oral evidence they both stressed that they wanted a body that would counter 'a widely shared feeling that British broadcasting is run like a highly restricted club – managed exclusively by broadcasters according to their own criteria of what counts as good television and radio'. A producer's independence, Smith told the committee on another occasion, 'is not a personal privilege, it is a responsibility exercised on behalf of the public'.[8]

As was to be expected, the evidence presented to the Annan Committee by the broadcasters aimed to protect and enhance their own positions. The ITV companies' and IBA evidence, although it talked optimistically about increased creative opportunities for those who worked for them, amounted to a rehash of the proposals they had put to the Conservative government a year earlier. 'The Authority believes that the introduction of ITV was a public benefit and that the introduction of ITV-2 . . . will be of similar benefit.'[9] The ITV companies' evidence, prepared and presented through the companies' trade association, the ITCA, was a model of concision, lucid argument and good prose. In the climate of the time and after the mauling ITV had received from Pilkington, the Annan Committee posed a real threat to ITV. In order to meet this threat, the companies had set up a special committee made up of six company chief executives. It was chaired by ITV's master diplomat Denis Forman ('the acceptable face of ITV' as one former FCG member called him). It included two former real politicians, John Freeman, Labour, and Lord Windlesham, Conservative, together with the head of Independent Television Publications, Jeremy Potter,[10] a Tyne-Tees expert on advertising, and Bill Brown of Scottish Television to look after the smaller company and regional interest. As was to be expected, their evidence stressed what they saw as the strengths of the ITV system – its regional diversity and the improvements in the quality of their programmes since the Pilkington Report. At the same time it played down ITV's weaknesses – high costs, duplication of resources and personnel, its piratical network scheduling system. The companies argued their by now familiar case for being given a second channel: 'A second ITV channel is necessary if ITV is to provide a fully comprehensive service and cater better for minorities.' They also got in some shots at the IBA's control over the schedule and its interference in programmes.

The BBC, having come so well out of the Pilkington inquiry twelve years earlier, could not realistically expect to gain much more than a pat on the head from Annan and a recommendation to further expand its radio services. What it did not want was the kind of radical restructuring being proposed by the pressure groups. Nor did it want ITV to be given control of a second commercial channel. The new chairman of the BBC, Sir Michael Swann, formerly Principal and Vice-Chancellor of Edinburgh University, knew Annan from the academic world and was therefore moderately confident that he would tend to side with the kind of reasoned argument put forward by the BBC rather than with the commercial claims of ITV or the untried radical schemes of politically motivated pressure groups. This feeling, reinforcing a sometimes overweening pride bolstered by its success with the Pilkington Committee and the congratulatory mood engendered by the celebration of the BBC's fiftieth anniversary a year earlier, encouraged over-confidence in the Corporation. The BBC's evidence was presented in the form of a four-inch-high pile of smug and wordy foolscap papers packed with lofty quotations from Milton, Shakespeare, and perhaps incongruously (certainly unwisely) advice from Lord Hill. The BBC's actual appearance before the Annan Committee was by most accounts a disaster. Annan and Huw Wheldon, the Managing Director of BBC Television, already knew and, according to Alasdair Milne, hated each other. Wheldon spoke too much, for too long and lectured Annan on the principles of good broadcasting. Annan responded, also at length, reminding Wheldon sternly of the deficiencies of the BBC's own management. The Annan Committee's meeting with the BBC took in lunch. For this Wheldon had, according to Milne (now back at the BBC as Director of Programmes), uncharacteristically laid on 'the most exotic fare'. As a result Annan and the Committee members munched their way through BBC lobster, while registering undisguised 'disenchantment with the way BBC Television was being run'.[11]

However, one piece of BBC evidence to the Annan Committee was to have far-reaching consequences. This was a proposal put together by Colin Shaw on use of the vacant fourth channel. Shaw was the Chief Secretary of the BBC. In his early years in the BBC he had written plays and features for the BBC in Leeds and Manchester, working with some of the great creative figures in radio. After reading for the Bar in his spare time, Shaw had moved into administration, playing a key role in the recruitment of programme makers at the start of BBC-2. He had then become assistant to Hugh Carleton Greene and had written speeches for him and later for Lord Hill. Shaw was widely regarded by colleagues as the most politically wily and astute man in the BBC. Sir Michael Swann, the BBC's Chairman, once referred to him as 'The Thought Police'.[12] Shaw had persuaded the Director-General, Curran, to let him set up what became known as 'The Unthinkable Committee'. A small group, which included the Controllers of BBC-2 and Radio 3, the committee's purpose was, as its name implied, to think the unthinkable. It had decided that the whole BBC television operation had become too big and unwieldy and, as a result, was becoming increasingly uncreative – much the same thought that had increasingly exercised the programme makers since the late 1960s. 'People who had been creative for five or ten years had ceased to be. Yet they continued to be paid and to have an office. The BBC had lots of people who were no longer useful. It was an example of the inertia of large organisations.' What Shaw appeared to have in mind was to induce producers who were creatively spent to leave the BBC and become independent producers or freelances, thus freeing the BBC of the ongoing costs of keeping them on the staff while at the same time making them available to work for the BBC when and if needed. The event which crystallised for Shaw the scale of the BBC's problem was the moment (see Chapter 1) when David Attenborough, as Controller of BBC-2, had wanted to cancel a returning drama strand but had been told by the Drama Department that this would take fifteen months to implement as the people and resources for it had already been allocated. 'This is absurd,' decided Shaw. In turning its attention to the evidence to be presented to the Annan Committee, the Unthinkable Committee knew that one of the BBC's main objectives must be to prevent ITV gaining a second channel with which to take on the two BBC channels head to head. In Milne's phrase, 'We reckoned there had to be an escape route.' Having studied Anthony Smith's proposals for the National Television

Foundation, the Unthinkable Committee persuaded the BBC to propose that the fourth channel should be turned over to a television foundation along the lines proposed by Smith. As Shaw saw it: 'Our evidence to Annan was a way to choke off ITV-2, but it was also a way of bringing about something which I wanted anyway – greater creativity and scaling down.'[13]

When ITV learned about the BBC's evidence it was furious. It launched a bitter attack on the BBC's proposals in an unsigned article in the IBA's magazine *Independent Broadcasting*. It accused the BBC of being worse than 'unctuous and misleading' because it had said that ITV's case for a second channel 'seems based more on under-used capacity than unmet need'. Commenting (in a way which today carries a particular sting), the anonymous article's author says that in describing the Television Foundation as acting in a manner analogous to the proprietor of a railway track 'deciding the routes and the timetables, but looking to other bodies to supply and finance the trains', the BBC's proposals overlook the fact that 'this would be an odd way to run a railway, and quite certain to fail'. The IBA heaped scorn on the idea of independent producers being able to supply any significant part of the material for such an enterprise: 'Cynics might ask who these producers are whose material is at present kept from the networks; and it might be argued, without cynicism, that the producers' best hope would be not for any organisational change but for the BBC to have increased revenue, and ITV to have increased air-time as well.'[14]

Much of the evidence pouring into the Annan Committee reflected the results of a decade of cross-fertilisation of ideas, aesthetic and political values between those in the relaxed, open and democratic world of small independent film making, the sort of people who had been involved in the Hatton–BFI revolt and those who worked in the much more hierarchical and layered world of the broadcasting institutions. The evidence also reflected a more general reawakening of concern with personal creativity and the values and quality of individual lives. E.F.Schumacher's *Small Is Beautiful: A Study of Economics as if People Mattered* had been published in Britain in 1973. It ran through sixteen re-printings and new editions in five years. The evidence gathered during the Annan Committee's visits to BBC programme departments and regional centres, and a great volume of the evidence that came in from people who worked in the BBC and the ITV companies, tended to support the idea of smaller scale, self-managing, production units, and the pluralist values embodied in the proposed National Television Foundation.

Producers in the features and arts departments of the BBC, based in Kensington House in Shepherd's Bush, angered their managers by submitting their own detailed proposals to Annan. They told the Committee that while they accepted the need for financial stringency in the BBC, they felt 'strongly that real control, artistic as well as financial, has moved further and further away . . . producers often feel accountable rather than responsible'. The BBC, the Kensington House staff believed, 'is expected to do what is, in fact, no longer possible. It attempts to express a consensus view of society that no longer exists'. Making much the same point as Colin Shaw, they said that the BBC's organisation and financial system tended to 'inhibit much of the creative energy of the BBC's staff', choking experiment and creativity. They made a series of specific proposals to rectify these problems, including greater devolution of control over programme decisions and finance, and increasing the number of opportunities for programme makers from outside the Corporation to make programmes for the BBC. They made a specific case for setting up a number of small, integrated multi-role production units inside the BBC which would operate alongside the existing major genre production departments. Technicians would be integrated into these units along with producers and other production staff. The units would then operate much as if they were small independent production companies within the BBC, working across a wide range of programmes directly commissioned by the channel controllers. Later Alasdair Milne set up a study group chaired by Paul Bonner to look at this idea. Although the study group concluded that establishing such units was likely to benefit the BBC and increase job satisfaction, opposition elsewhere in senior management prevented it from being tried.[15]

Time and again BBC producers talked to Annan about the 'gulf or lack of communication between management and staff'. Colin Thomas, drafting evidence for the Annan Committee on behalf of ACTT members employed by the BBC, started with the words 'IMAGINE – A NEW BBC' and continued by saying that the BBC Charter should not be renewed on its present terms. The BBC, according to Thomas and his colleagues, should be reorganised so that each BBC centre was more locally accountable to the community it served. In the same spirit as the Kensington House staff, the ACTT members called for an internal re-organisation of the BBC which would result in each of the centres and departments in the BBC becoming self-managing on a democratic and participatory basis.

These groups, and the others like them in the ITV companies, were telling the

Annan Committee not that they necessarily wanted to leave their ITV companies or the BBC, but that they wanted to work in a similar way to the people in the small independent film companies in Soho. At the same time they wanted to continue to enjoy financial security for both themselves and their programme budgets. They did not necessarily want to become freelances, but they did want to work in the way that directors did for Bob Heller and Charles Denton at ATV, where programme makers could generally choose which cameramen and other key technicians they worked with. Alternatively, they wanted to operate in ways that had been tried in the experimental workshops at the BBC in Bristol and in weekend workers' control workshops organised by the ACTT. Small was indeed beautiful; self-management and the responsibility over money and standards that came with it was a price felt to be well worth paying in return for the creativity and self-fulfilment that it would bring. The opponents of such ideas inside BBC and ITV managements accused them of irresponsibility, jeering that they wanted all the advantages of operating as small independent producers without the financial risks.

By the time the Annan Committee had finished hearing evidence, the gap left in the programme makers' lobbying machinery by the demise of the FCG and the 76 Group had begun to be filled by new pressure groups. The first of these, the Independent Filmmakers Association (IFA), might be said to have been a direct descendant of the protesting independent film makers who, led by Maurice Hatton, had campaigned for radical reform of the BFI in 1968. They aimed to marry radicalism of content with radicalism of form and often with radicalism of film-making practice as well. The IFA was born in the autumn of 1974 out of an angry reaction by film makers to a BBC programme, hosted by Melvyn Bragg, which showed a series of short clips from films made by independent film makers. Furious that their work had, in their view, been grossly misrepresented, they called a protest meeting and sent off a letter to the BBC demanding another programme in which they would be consulted about the films shown. Aubrey Singer, the newly appointed Controller of BBC-2, replied that he was 'not having that kind of film on *my* television'.[16] Ignoring the fact that the BBC was meant to be a public service rather than the private fiefdom implied by Singer, the film makers called a meeting and formed an association to act as a forum and lobby group. Although suspicious of television, the film makers recognised that a new fourth channel might, if it were operated in a way that was radically different from the existing channels, provide a useful outlet for their work and a source of funds.

Another new pressure group was the Association of Producers and Directors (ADP). It, like others, told Annan that the BBC had 'failed dismally to resist pressure' from the government over programmes. The birth of ADP was a reflection of the rapid changes that by the mid-1970s were taking place in the way in which programmes were made and the way in which the broadcasters engaged those who made them. A decade earlier the majority of programmes had been transmitted live or, where they were pre-recorded, they had still been shot in multi-camera studios and transmitted after only minimal editing. Growth in the use of fast 16 mm film and lightweight film cameras, and in studio videotape recording machines and electronic editing, meant that by the mid-1970s pre-recording of drama, documentaries and even some light entertainment programmes, often on location, followed by detailed editing of a complexity akin to that in cinema films, was commonplace. As a result the most sought-after directors and producers could pick and choose what programmes they made, moving from company to company and project to project. Although at the beginning of the decade only the most successful producers and directors could afford to freelance in this way, by the middle of the decade freelancing was much more widespread. Bob Heller's documentary department at ATV had found that, because it only had to fill a documentary slot on sixteen weeks in the year, there was a double advantage in hiring freelances. Not only did it gain the added prestige of being able to claim that it only engaged the best to make its documentaries, it had the added economic advantage that ATV did not have the cost of keeping a full complement of producers, directors and production staff on the payroll all the year round. As the ability to engage freelances increased and the economic advantages to the broadcasters became apparent, so the practice had grown until it extended well beyond those producers and directors with the greatest reputations. It extended to technicians as well – notably researchers, cameramen and sound recordists. From the point of view of the technicians it facilitated easy movement between work on cinema films and in television. However, while the rates of pay in feature films were sufficient to tide a freelance technician over during gaps between engagements, the rates in television, although higher for freelances than for staff technicians, were not sufficient to ensure a decent living unless the technician could get regular engagements without long gaps between them. This could be particularly difficult for directors as only a very few of them could expect to work on feature films and, unlike the technicians, they did not receive overtime payments while they were working.

Their creative life expectancy might, as Colin Shaw had noted, be only a few years. The union agreements negotiated with the broadcasters, particularly in the ACTT, were geared overwhelmingly towards the requirements of technicians rather than towards directors or producers, and towards the permanently employed rather than freelances. As a result freelances, particularly directors and producers, had started to campaign inside the union to have their interests given the same weight by union negotiators as the interests of permanently employed technicians.

The increased use of film and video recording had also resulted in an increase in the number of programmes that were repeated or sold overseas. One of the directors' and producers' demands was for a system of repeat and residual payments, based on a percentage of their original fees or the sale price of the programme. David Elstein, then working on the staff at Thames Television on the weekly current affairs programme *This Week*, had been particularly active inside the ACTT over the issue. He cited the case of a person like Peter Graham Scott, who had been the original producer and creator (with the writer John Elliott) of the hit drama series *Mogul* (*The Troubleshooters*), which had run for some eighty episodes on BBC-1. In Britain he was treated, in Elstein's phrase, as 'simply a hired hand' who gained no financial reward from the success of what he had created, whereas if he had been working in American television he would have had an ongoing entitlement to income from the success of the series. Even if he had never produced another successful programme he could probably have retired on the continuing income from that one hit series. Elstein, frustrated at his continuing failure to get the union to take a sufficiently robust stand with the employers over the issue of residual and repeat payments, invited a number of prominent producers and directors, mainly in drama – Alvin Rakoff, Piers Haggard, Verity Lambert, Jon Scoffield and others – to a meeting at his home in Highbury. The result was the formation of ADP. Intended mainly as a ginger group inside the union, it carried with it the thinly disguised threat that it could become a breakaway directors' and producers' union.

ADP made two submissions to the Annan Committee. The first stressed the importance of producers and directors to good programmes and their claim to an ongoing financial interest in their creative work. The second, at the particular urging of Elstein, restated the case made by Elstein and Birt a couple of years earlier for an ITV-2 with a separate and independent Controller of Programmes.

The most significant of new pressure groups was AIP – the Association of

Independent Producers. It did not come into being until March 1976, by which time the Annan Committee had nearly finished hearing evidence. AIP's birth was almost accidental. A young and enthusiastic would-be film producer called Richard Craven was attending a weekend class in public speaking at a seaside hotel (his wife attended evening classes several times a week and Craven had decided he had better enlist in one himself). In one exercise each member of Craven's class was given half an hour to prepare a case for something, followed by ten minutes in which to make a speech advocating it to fellow class members. The class was to act as a panel of imaginary bankers who would award money to the person who was most persuasive. In his half-hour of preparation Craven thought up a new association of independent producers to challenge the Rank and EMI production and distribution duopoly which, with the American major studios, continued to dominate the perpetually crisis-ridden British film industry. Craven's new association would, he argued, bring into being a new, vibrant indigenous British film industry. The question 'What to do about the British film industry?' had been much in the air. In the previous three years British feature-film production had shrunk by almost 40%. The ACTT had called for the complete nationalisation of the film industry under workers' control and in September 1975 the Labour Party had published a long-nurtured policy discussion document on the Arts which had argued that government policy on the film industry should no longer be based on purely commercial considerations but should recognise film's importance in cultural terms.[17]

In his ten-minute speech to his fellow participants at the weekend public speaking course, Richard Craven had set out how to create and finance an association of film producers which would bring the ideas now swirling around for the re-invigoration of the indigenous British film industry to fruition. Naturally enthusiastic and emotional in all things, Craven's impassioned oratory had won the imagined money from his fellow course participants hands down. Five minutes later Craven had turned his enthusiasm to other things and forgotten all about his association of independent producers. However, the next day, waiting on the station platform to return home, one of the course participants had approached him and asked when he planned to start the association. Craven confessed that he had had no serious intention of doing so, it was just an idea he had dreamed up for the exercise. But spurred on, Craven had returned to London and started to make phone calls and then to write letters. The response he got was so enthusiastic that he called a meeting. Having gone to the ICA and asked to hire a small room on a quiet evening, he was astonished when he arrived on the evening in question, 10 March 1976, to find a dense crowd milling around in the ICA. They were all eager producers or would-be producers who had turned up for the meeting. The result was the birth of AIP.

Within months Craven's whole working life was taken up with AIP. Opening a small office costing £8 per week in Wardour Street, the fledging association soon started to attract attention. Just weeks after starting the association Craven was astonished to receive a phone call from the Prime Minister's office inviting him to lunch at the Athenaeum with Harold Wilson and Lady Falkender. The government, under Wilson's personal supervision, was preparing policy pro-posals intended to reform the whole film industry, leading to the setting-up of a British Film Authority and perhaps, eventually, to full nationalisation. Wilson wanted it to be known that he had consulted the young turks of the industry as well as the tired old hands. Within six months of starting, AIP had enlisted 350 subscription-paying members and received the offer of an unconditional one-off donation of £5,000 from Lord Bernard Delfont (ennobled earlier in the year) to enable it to rent a bigger office and take on a small permanent staff. To the members of AIP, with their sights set on making small- to medium-sized-budget films, the role of television was more central than to the more radical film makers of the IFA. By July 1976, barely four months after Craven had called that first meeting at the ICA, AIP had hammered out and published a submission to the Annan Committee.

Perhaps mercifully for the members of the Annan Committee, who had by then had to plough through hundreds of wordy and ponderous submissions from all kinds of organisations, AIP's submission amounted to a cogent and clearly reasoned five pages backed by clear figures. They argued that, as film and television were inextricably linked, the traditional rivalry between the two should be ended and replaced by co-operation, with television setting up a new autonomous fund (operated along lines already operating in West Germany) from which films for distribution in both the cinema and on television could be financed. On the fourth television channel, AIP argued that it must 'broaden the base of cultural activity' in the country rather than 'duplicate and compete with what is being produced on the other three channels'; that it must foster new talent, ideas and skills, allowing them access to the channel on an ongoing basis. 'We therefore wholeheartedly support the ADP submission . . . that the fourth television channel should invest no money in productive capacity . . . but should act simply as a distribution channel for independent production.' AIP believed that the channel should be administered by the IBA and financed from a combination of a levy on the excess profits of ITV and the sale by the channel of advertising airtime. Specifically AIP wanted the fourth channel to be required to finance 25 'realistically budgeted' British feature films each year 'made for dual release in the cinemas and on television'.[18]

The submission by AIP must have been one of the last to be taken into consideration by the Annan Committee because by the autumn of 1976 its members were eager to reach final conclusions and start writing their report. What had held them back was the late arrival of evidence from the Treasury on the BBC licence fee. The delay to the Treasury evidence was the result of a full-scale financial crisis. By 1974 inflation had reached 28% and, although the government had instituted a series of public expenditure cuts, deficits had continued to escalate. By the summer of 1976 James Callaghan, who had succeeded Wilson as Prime Minister after the latter's surprise retirement in March 1976, and his Chancellor Denis Healey had been forced to go to the IMF for a $3 billion loan. In return the government had been forced to make still deeper public expenditure cuts in an attempt to hold down inflation.

When the Annan Committee finally published its report in March 1977 it backed away from plans to split up the BBC, the majority of the committee's members believing that the risks involved were too great to justify the possible gain, settling instead for severe criticism of the BBC's creativity-stifling bureaucracy, hoping that this would be sufficient to make the BBC managers see the error of their administrative ways. 'Whereas in the BBC manning agreements with the unions compare favourably with those in most ITV companies, management is by comparison top-heavy. Some of us suspect that the plethora of executive jobs is the result of discovering ways of promoting producers when they have given all they can and need to be replaced by younger men. Others believe that it is part of the natural disease of bifurcation from which bureaucracies spring. It is a disease we believe which has led to the resignation from senior positions in the BBC of over two dozen of the best known names among producers, editors and more senior executives, only four of whom have subsequently returned.'[19] Suggesting that there might be even more fundamental reasons for 'the bureaucratic fog' which 'envelop[s] the upper slopes of the BBC', the Committee traced the possible causes back to the BBC's staff grading system and the assertive management systems put in place as a result of the McKinsey investigations and *Broadcasting in the '70s*. The Committee had been impressed by the evidence presented to them by the BBC programme makers at Kensington House and concluded ' . . . we are convinced that communications in the BBC are far from being what they should be. Many producers told us that there is a gulf or lack of communication between management and staff.' Accordingly the Committee recommended the creation of smaller production units to replace the BBC's large programme genre departments. Reminding the Corporation that both *That Was The Week That Was* and *Z Cars* had been created as a result of a cross-fertilisation of ideas and methods between people from different disciplines, the Committee stressed the need for better communication between units and departments and more creative cross-fertilisation. The Committee also pointed out that the BBC, in claiming to inhabit 'the middle ground' in programmes and ideas, should not confuse this with 'a neutral zone. It should be the BBC's aim to ensure that many different views are heard; and, if their own producers echo each other, to commission work from independent producers.' (ITV was also told that it should be more open to the work of independent producers.) The Annan Committee's report, while admonishing the BBC for failings highlighted by dis-enchanted programme makers, also went out of its way to praise the Corporation's programmes. On the whole, the Committee said, the BBC had overcome its Aunt Edna image of the 1950s, except for 'some affliction of feebleness [which] had struck the current affairs output. Time and again people in the BBC attributed this palsy to the effect of the row over *Yesterday's Men*.' The Committee went on to regret the lack of courage in the BBC's investigative journalism, which it compared unfavourably with the journalism of Granada's *World in Action*: 'We have the impression that the fault lies at the top. The younger generation of producers is bubbling with ideas which are not allowed to surface.'

The IBA and the ITV companies, having made a good presentation to the Committee, did not receive the kind of hammering that they had received from Pilkington fifteen years earlier. But despite being praised for its lack of bureau-cracy and the improved quality of many of its programmes, ITV did not get the prize they had campaigned for almost continually over the previous seven years – ITV-2. Instead, at the urging of Whitehead (who Annan later described as 'the hero' of the committee), the Report recommended that the fourth channel should be run by a separate authority set up for the purpose and operated in accordance with the spirit of Anthony Smith's National Television Foundation. The distinctiveness of this new channel, and the departure that its creation would represent from what had gone before, was highlighted in the name suggested for it by the Committee – the Open Broadcasting Authority. The new channel was to act as a publisher of other people's ideas. It was to be pluralist rather than monolithic and must aim at celebrating difference rather than feigning consensus. The Report pointedly quoted Anthony Smith who, drawing on the words of Rousseau, had written: 'If I am free to say anything I want to say except the one thing I want to say then I am not free . . . If the medium is to be managed, how can there be any democracy? . . . In broadcasting . . . a single prohibition imposed on a national Broadcasting Authority or within it tends to corrode the whole output.'

The Committee said that programmes for the OBA were to come from three different sources: educational programmes, including those of the Open University which would be transferred from BBC-2; from the ITV companies which had stressed that they had the spare studio capacity, the cash, and frustrated producers eager for the opportunity to spread their creative wings; and above all, 'from a variety of independent producers. We attach particular importance to this third category as a force for diversity and new ideas . . . We stress that we see the new Authority as a publisher, which commissions programmes. Its aim should be to encourage productions which say something new in new ways.'[20]

The least convincing part of the OBA plan, even to many of those programme makers who most welcomed it, was the suggested financing. The Committee believed that it would cost between £25 and £40 million at then current prices. Stressing that if the channel was to be plural so should be the sources of its finance, the Committee pointed out that £3.5 million was already available from Department of Education funding for the programmes of the Open University which the new channel would be taking over from BBC-2. A second, and it seemed to outsiders unlikely, block of money was to come from bodies such as the Arts Council, the TUC, the CBI, charities and sponsorship – 'unlikely' because each of these providers was either habitually short of money for its own work or likely to want to attach editorial strings either to the channel's whole output or to any programmes that they supported. Funding from these sources would, critics thought, tend to result in worthy and safe programmes rather than the kind of bold and innovative work envisaged by the Committee. The third source of funding was to be block advertising – by which it was assumed the Committee meant long blocks of adverts of perhaps fifteen or twenty minutes rather than the short spots which were the norm on ITV. Such advertising, which was to be sold by the OBA itself, rather than by the ITV companies, was likely to prove unattractive to advertisers as compared to the spot advertising already available on ITV. It would therefore be likely to raise only comparatively meagre amounts of revenue.[21] Anthony Smith had suggested that an additional, and probably crucial, portion of revenue should come from a government grant in the form of a percentage of the ITV Exchequer Levy paid over directly to the new channel. Members of the Committee were divided about this and in the end came down against it. Denying ITV its ITV-2 and then taking the money off the companies to pay for the OBA, particularly at a time of economic stringency, was just too bold.

When the Annan Committee Report was published on 23 March 1977, six months later than originally envisaged, it was widely seen as a triumph for Anthony Smith, Phillip Whitehead and the years of campaigning by small, shifting groups of committed programme makers.

Phillip Whitehead and Lord Annan at a press conference on the Annan Committee
Courtesy of *Morning Star*, 25 March 1977

A title for the whole Annan Committee period – from the resurrection of the committee in 1974 until the fall of the Labour government in 1979 – could be 'All Talk and No Action'. While the Annan Committee was sitting, there was a great deal of talk; once its report had been published there was still no action. Had the report appeared even six months earlier things just might have been different. But by March 1977 there was a maximum of only two and a half years to go before there had to be another general election. Just enough time, if the government was really determined, to prepare and publish a White Paper, allow time to consult on it, draft a fairly simple bill and push it through Parliament; just time, but only if the changes made to the structure of broadcasting were fairly straightforward. The proposals in Annan were anything but.

Things outside broadcasting, the 1976 IMF loan crisis and the consequent delay in the crucial Treasury evidence, had delayed the report's appearance, and now it was things outside broadcasting that would determine the report's fate. Callaghan's government, having secured its IMF loan and introduced severe public spending cuts, faced a rising tide of industrial unrest. In March 1977, the month in which the Annan Report appeared, one million working days were lost through strikes. The deepening divisions in the country were reflected in the Labour Party and the government, which were becoming steadily more polarised between the moderate right of the party under Callaghan and the Bennite left. Since Wilson's second election win in October 1974 the government had lost a series of by-elections, mainly to nationalist candidates, and by 1977 was only hanging on to power through an agreement with the Parliamentary Liberal Party – the Lib-Lab Pact. In what might almost have been interpreted as a symbolic gesture, a couple of months after the Annan Report was published, the Queen's Silver Jubilee celebrations in May 1977, which were to have been ITV's biggest ever outside broadcast, were blacked out by 38 Thames Television production assistants. They were insisting on additional payments in breach of the government's pay code in return for accepting new technology which required them to note start and stop times during studio video recording (an operation already routinely carried out by PAs in the BBC). The Sex Pistols, whose record for the Jubilee contained the refrain 'God Save the Queen, Fascist Regime', were not the only party-poopers that summer!

The press generally damned the Annan Report with qualified praise. The heading to a leader in *The Times* summed up the general view – 'Fair audit but weak blueprint'. Almost everyone commented unfavourably on the Committee's proposals for financing the new fourth channel. In the House of Commons debate on the Report William Whitelaw, the Conservative Shadow Home Secretary, attacked the proposed OBA. He disliked new bodies, he said, because they lead to more bureaucracy and cost, 'but I certainly appreciate the Committee's purpose . . . It wanted, as I understand it, that when a fourth channel was introduced it would provide programmes of different sorts, that minority interests would be catered for, and that independent producers would have greater opportunities. The thinking behind the Open Broadcast Authority was, therefore, both original and imaginative.' But, he went on, 'It has a fatal flaw – its financing.' As the new channel would be heavily reliant on the IBA and the ITV companies for many of its transmission and technical services, the 'sensible' thing to do was to give the fourth channel to the IBA and the ITV companies, but on conditions that meant that the new channel would realise the Committee's purposes. He concluded, 'ITV-2 is the only means of using the fourth channel reasonably quickly . . . and on a sure financial basis.'[22] Lord Annan, delivering the Royal Television Society's annual Fleming Lecture a month earlier, had already dealt with this line of reasoning: 'If the fourth channel becomes ITV-2 it will become a weapon in the ratings war and lose any individuality it otherwise may have had.' New kinds of broadcasting required new kinds of authorities. 'But if the IBA ran the channel almost inevitably they would be under pressure to allot all the prime viewing time every night to the ITV companies.'[23]

MPs seemed to have trouble grasping either the idea that anything 'new' was possible or the concept of a channel that was complementary to all three of the existing channels. Nevertheless, and despite the government's difficulties, Merlyn Rees, the new Home Secretary, although perhaps not the most charismatic or recognisably forceful member of the Cabinet, made a determined start to implementing the Annan Committee's recommendations.[24] He announced that he required comments on the report by 1 July.

As soon as the Annan Report had been published the ITV companies had launched an assault upon it. This was now continued in formal comments submitted on their behalf by the ITCA to the Home Secretary. They rubbished the OBA by saying that all the new and innovative programmes suggested for the new channel could be made not only as well, possibly better, by the ITV companies, but could be provided at less risk to the public purse. Six hours out of the forty hours of programmes planned for their proposed ITV-2, they assured the Home Secretary, could come from independents. Both channels would be scheduled together to ensure that they were complementary. Competition between the OBA and ITV would, they said, be far more harmful to good programming than any competition between ITV and the BBC. If given the go-ahead they could provide the additional service immediately.

The IBA, also keen to wrest control of the fourth channel for ITV, adopted a more conciliatory approach. The Authority now talked of creating a separate planning group for the fourth channel, made up of representatives from both network and regional companies, from providers of educational programmes and independent producers. This group, which would have a single full-time executive, would be responsible for scheduling ITV-2: 40% of the programmes would come from the five network companies, 10–15% each from the educational providers, ITN, sport, and from the regional companies, and 15% from independent producers. The IBA's ITV-2 would be complementary to ITV-1 but more independent in its choice of programmes. The new sophistication in the IBA's approach could be ascribed, at least in part, to Colin Shaw, the wily BBC tactician who had drafted the Corporation's cunning suggestions on the fourth channel for the Annan Committee. Shaw had joined the IBA just days after the Annan Report was published.[25]

Every bit as worrying for the campaigners was the attitude of their own trade union, the ACTT. The attitude of a vocal and relevant union affiliated to the TUC, such as the ACTT, could be expected to carry considerable weight within the Labour government when it came to reach decisions over broadcasting. The 1977 annual conference of the union, held at the TUC on 3 April, came too soon after the publication of the Annan Report for its recommendations to be the subject of formal motions and policy decisions at the conference. Instead the union's Television Vice-President, a likeable veteran of the Granada camera department viewed by younger programme makers as a union old lag, moved an emergency motion saying that because the Annan Report was of such enormous importance to the industry there must be a special conference of the union before 1 July to formulate the union's response. The short debate that followed made it abundantly clear that the permanently employed technicians in ITV were extremely hostile to both the OBA and to the idea of more independent production for ITV. The General Secretary, Alan Sapper, wound up the debate with a fiery speech claiming that, if enacted, the Annan proposals would 'destabilise the employment and financial basis of ITV'. He warned the union to be ready to adopt 'a confrontational position'.[26]

Two months later, in June 1977, without warning or notice, the Executive Committee of the Union's General Council, which was dominated by ITV company staff, held a meeting and decided by a vote of 8 to 6 to drop the one-day conference, to oppose the OBA and Annan's proposals on ITV. Armed with this dubious authority (it was alleged that the meeting of the union executive at which the decision was taken had been inquorate), the union's executive submitted the ACTT's formal response to the Annan Report to the Home Office. It rejected the OBA and gave its backing to ITV-2 with 'new and stringently enforced safeguards'.

The pro-Annan campaigners inside the ACTT were furious and there was a row in the union's governing body, the General Council. Stuart Hood, by then a Senior Lecturer in Media and Communications and a representative of the union's

Young radicals? Demonstration against political censorship in programmes about Northern Ireland outside the IBA. Far left, with long hair and glasses, John Birt. Centre, holding out a leaflet, David Elstein. To Elstein's left, Alan Sapper, ACTT General Secretary. Jack O'Connor, the ACTT's Television Organiser, is just visible behind and to Sapper's left.

Film and Television Technician, April 1977,
by kind permission of the BECTU Photographic Archive

small Edtech Branch, questioned the way in which the union's policy had been arrived at. I and others, including some representatives of technicians employed at Granada, joined in, accusing the union of forming 'an unholy alliance' with ITV and the IBA. David Edgar, the playwright, who represented the Writers' Section of the union, mocked the union's policy for relying on the IBA to prevent the ITV companies from dominating the new channel: 'To ask ITV for safe-guards is liking asking brewers to organise a campaign for the abolition of alcohol.' However, the General Secretary, Sapper, although admitting that 'in some senses ITV-2 is ideological anathema; commercialism is not public service broadcasting', made a robust defence of what the executive had done: 'The interests of our actual membership in ITV are at stake. The OBA proposals are a real threat to employment and programme standards on ITV-1.' The other ITV shops and the Laboratory Branch supported him and again they won the day.[27]

The author speaking at ACTT Annual Conference, 3 April 1977

Film and Television Technician, May 1977,

by kind permission of the BECTU Photographic Archive

Only days after this a still more violent row broke out at a mass meeting of some 200 members of the union's Film Branch in St Pancras Town Hall. At issue was a proposal for the ACTT to amalgamate with the ABS – the union which represented staff at the BBC. Although most of the union's officials, the permanently employed members in ITV, and the freelances who worked in television were in favour of amalgamation – it would create one powerful broadcasting union, unify rates of pay and conditions across broadcasting and, important to the television freelances in particular, allow much greater freedom of movement between jobs for people to work in both the BBC and ITV – most of the technicians who worked in film studios were violently opposed to it. They feared that it would lead to feature-film production being flooded with ex-BBC technicians, eager to work on movies and therefore prepared to work on less stringent pay rates and conditions.

For some years Film Branch meetings had been becoming steadily more unruly as the branch had become politically more polarised between left and right. The issues of amalgamation with the ABS had become conflated and confused with other issues to do with casualisation and union policies over the renting-out of film studios without permanently employed film crews – in the jargon 'four-wallers'. The woman chairing the meeting in St Pancras Town Hall was widely believed to be associated with the small body of Trotskyites who had gained an influence inside the branch that far outweighed their numerical strength and even before the St Pancras Town Hall meeting began, rumours were circulating that some people had come with the intention of causing trouble. Early in the debate someone proposed a motion of 'No Confidence in the Chair' from the floor. When the 'Chair' refused to accept the motion all hell broke loose. People on the floor tried to invade the platform and seize the microphone, bent on physically ejecting the 'Chair' and her fellow committee members from the stage. She, however, clung steadfastly to the microphone, so becoming the only person who could still make herself heard above the hullabaloo. At this point an alternative microphone and public address system miraculously appeared in the body of the hall. For some minutes pandemonium reigned as two parallel meetings were conducted simultaneously – old Stalinists who had been silent in the union for years, speaking out on the same side as a body of film technicians known to have close links with the employers' organisations and the Conservative Party. Not long afterwards the meeting broke up in confusion amid calls for the police to be summoned. A small body of confused, mostly conventional Labour Party supporters like myself, who had watched this display in a state of mounting dismay, walked away from the hall together. Christine Fox, formerly organiser of the FCG, remembers that evening as clearly as many of the rest of us: 'I was deeply shocked. It was like we had read was happening in Equity. After that we thought we have got to be more active. We have got to get on these committees.'[28] That evening we firmly made up our minds that we must strive to return the union to the sort of functioning democracy which it palpably no longer enjoyed. Never a formal group, in fact no more than acquaintances with a shared understanding, many of the people whose minds were made up by events that evening in St Pancras Town Hall were the same people who had been members of the FCG, who had taken part in the various campaigns to open up broadcasting, and were now members of AIP. Today Roy Lockett, then the union's Research Officer and editor of the union's journal, traces the start of the slow change in the union over the next few years, which eventually transformed and modernised it, to that evening meeting in St Pancras Town Hall.[29]

However, change took a long time. A year later ACTT policy on the fourth channel still backed ITV-2. In December 1978 the front-page headline of the ACTT's magazine, in bold letters and outlined in red ink, proclaimed: 'Broadcasting Unions Totally Opposed to OBA.'[30]

*   *   *

While battles continued inside the union and arguments raged over the correct response to Annan, an event of less immediately obvious, although ultimately equal importance to the fate of the fourth channel took place. In August 1977 the first full Edinburgh International Television Festival was held.[31] It was intended to be a television equivalent of the film festival which had run since just after the war as an adjunct to the annual Edinburgh Festival of the Arts. It was another of the brain-children of Gus Macdonald. Macdonald had been the Vice-Chairman of the Edinburgh Film Festival for some years – 'We kept doing special events on Fassbinder and the American brats and such like and it used to irritate me that there was never any equivalent on the British. I would say, "There's work at least as good going on here all the time. What's going on in TV drama is much more radical than anything being shown in the cinema – work by people like Trodd, Loach and Garnett." But they would say, "Oh, that's only television." There was that cinéastes' snobbery. And I would retort with things like Peter Fiddick's phrase, "The British cinema is alive and well – it's living in television." In the end they said, "Go on then, you set something up on television." And that's where the TV Festival came from.'[32] Where the Free Communications Group had been designed to act as a catalyst to a more free, open and democratic process of decision-making and control in broadcasting on the political and management level, so the Edinburgh International Television Festival was intended to provide a more open and inclusive arena for the discussion and exploration of the medium on the creative level. It took the form of a symposium in which programme makers from all over television, from the BBC, the ITV companies, freelances and independents, took part as equals. It was not to be an event at which people scrambled for prizes (at the EITF, unlike at other film and television festivals, there were no prizes) or jockeyed to broker deals. The idea quickly developed such momentum that television executives started to turn up as well. However, in Edinburgh executives were expected to drop their status and take part in the debates as equals with programme makers both high and low – 'All guns to be checked at the door', as Macdonald would jokingly announce at the start of each session.

The Edinburgh International Television Festival of 1977 opened with a keynote lecture given by Marcel Ophuls, the great French documentarist whose series about the Nazi occupation of France, *Le Chagrin et la Pitié*, had been shown to great acclaim in Britain a few years previously. He attacked the frequency with which unimaginative puritans had been put in charge of television around the world. However, most of the week was taken up with topics related to television drama. On the fourth day a showing, followed by a discussion, of Dennis Potter's play *Brimstone and Treacle*[33] (banned nine months earlier by the BBC) transformed the Festival, making it headline news. After the showing Potter gave a lecture in which he launched into the creative sterility of the medium: 'A preoccupation with *styles* of production has almost completely blanked out more meaningful debate, such as that about the choices between "naturalism" and its alternatives – choices that have too often been reduced to discussion about techniques. Perhaps the lack of a long critical tradition, the inevitable confusion of roles and purposes which make the word "television" a plural noun . . . the continued ignorance and Philistinism of its planners and administrators have together brought about this sterility . . . Never in the entire history of drama in all its forms has so much been produced for so large an audience with so little thought.'[34] Having seen *Brimstone and Treacle* and listened to Potter's lecture, the audience was in a state of suppressed rage over the banning of the play. Alasdair Milne who, as Director of

Programmes, was the BBC executive responsible for banning the programme, had sat at the back of the hall during Potter's speech. He was on holiday in Scotland and had decided that he ought to come and speak for himself. Milne had believed that although the play, which had been referred up to him by the Controller of BBC-1 at the last moment, was fine it could not be shown because of the violence. Milne's decision, as he later explained, was influenced by the fact that when it was made the Annan Committee was still sitting and the Labour government was much exercised by public concerns about sex and violence on television and its effects.[35] The debate following Potter's speech quickly worked itself into a fine fury. Speaker after speaker denounced the BBC for its cowardice, while Milne gamely tried to explain his decision. Jeremy Isaacs, Director of Programmes at Thames Television since 1975, where he had been responsible for a string of bold and innovative dramas including *The Naked Civil Servant* and *Rock Follies*, sat on the floor in the centre of the hall throughout most of the debate. Near the end he leapt to his feet and proposed that a strongly worded protest should be sent to the Chairman of the BBC on behalf of everyone attending the festival. His proposal was adopted with acclaim. The *Brimstone and Treacle* session, although widely reported in the press, did not change the mind of the BBC. The play remained untransmitted for a further ten years. However, the row, and the press coverage that it provoked, transformed the Festival. For the next decade it became *the* ideal arena for any campaigner wishing to advance a newsworthy broadcasting cause.

*   *   *

It has to be remembered that, in the great political scheme of things, broadcasting is comparatively unimportant and the money involved relatively trivial, at least when set beside matters such as the Health Service or national defence. As a result, responsibility in government for broadcasting policy has always been placed either in the hands of a junior minister and a small department in one of the great departments of state, such as the Home Office, or placed in the hands of a less influential member of the cabinet running a smaller ministry such as Posts and Telecommunications. Yet at the same time broadcasting excites great interest; the press like it because it generates stories that sell newspapers but also fear it as a competitor; politicians alternately court it and seek to control it (Wilson had been a classic example); everyone, because they watch and listen to it, has views about it. Like the prostitute in the moral arena who is damned for exercising power without responsibility, broadcasting in the political arena is condemned to be treated as simultaneously both unimportant and vital. The result is to give us governments which give insufficient effort to thinking through broadcasting policy but ministers who are all too eager to interfere and pontificate.

By September 1977 Merlyn Rees had handed over the detailed preparation of government policy and drafting of the anticipated Broadcasting White Paper to Lord Harris, the junior minister in the Home Office and a small team of civil servants in the Broadcasting Department. It was anticipated that their draft would be submitted to the cabinet by the end of the year and that a Broadcasting White Paper would be published early in 1978. A new broadcasting bill could then be prepared for submission to Parliament during the next Parliamentary year, starting in the autumn of 1978.

Lord Harris and his civil servants swiftly and quietly rejected almost all of the Annan Committee's proposals, leaving the entire television system in the hands of the bureaucracies which already controlled it. The OBA was ditched as impractical and potentially expensive. Encouraged by the Treasury, which was still struggling with the economy and more than usually unwilling to support anything that might cost money, Harris and his officials drafted two alternative plans for the fourth channel – one followed closely the model for ITV-2 proposed by the ITV companies and the other the plan most recently submitted by the IBA.

At this point the drama surrounding the fate of the fourth channel became still more bizarre and convoluted. In December, as expected, Merlyn Rees handed over his department's draft White Paper to Number 10, together with a suggested list of ministers who should make up the Cabinet Committee to examine it in detail. But someone in the Cabinet Office, knowing of his interest in the issues, leaked the draft to Phillip Whitehead. Whitehead, no admirer of the performance of Merlyn Rees as Home Secretary – 'He was never in charge of his department'[36] – was horrified by the Home Office's proposals and immediately set to work lobbying sympathetic members of the cabinet to get the draft thrown out. He succeeded. The draft was rejected in the cabinet and the membership of the Cabinet Committee was changed to include ministers sympathetic to the kind of radical change proposed by Annan. Roy Hattersley, William Rodgers and Tony Benn joined the Cabinet Committee and Callaghan himself elected to chair it. The burial of the Home Office's pro-IBA/ITV draft of the White Paper was later explained away by Shirley Littler, who became Under-Secretary in charge of the Broadcasting Department in the Home Office at about the time when the Home Office draft was thrown out, with the words that it was 'generally speaking regarded as too dull, cautious and orthodox'. This, while it may have been true, omitted the most salient fact – that the draft flew flat in the face of both the Annan Committee's recommendations and declared Labour Party policy. In January 1978, very shortly after taking over in the Broadcasting Department, Shirley Littler went with Merlyn Rees and her Civil Service boss in the Home Office, Robert Armstrong (later famous for having been 'economical with the truth' during in the Peter Wright/*Spycatcher* affair – it must be something civil servants inhale with the air they breathe in Whitehall!), for an 'exchange of views' with the IBA. When Rees asked the IBA how Annan's intentions for the fourth channel could be realised other than by establishing the OBA, the Authority's officials assured him 'at length' that this could be done by giving the channel to the IBA. This, they stressed, was not the same thing as giving it to the companies. The IBA officials later recorded the impression that Rees and the Home Office officials would have been happy to accept their advice. However, as he was leaving, Rees informed the IBA officials that the contents of the White Paper and any legislation were now 'largely out of his hands'. Other of his cabinet colleagues 'had views' on broadcasting.[37]

By the time that the White Paper on Broadcasting emerged from the Cabinet Committee on 26 July 1978, the chance of the government being able to draw up a comprehensive broadcasting bill and enact legislation before an election had clearly gone. There had to be a general election by October 1979 at the latest. Nevertheless, the White Paper, despite the continuing opposition of Home Office officials, resurrected Annan. It proposed that the fourth channel should be operated by a new authority, the OBA. It was 'to explore the possibilities of programmes which say something new in new ways. The aim will be to widen the choice available to viewers by providing programmes . . . not intended to compete with programmes on existing channels . . . The talent exists in this country to respond to the challenge which this opportunity offers.' The service was to include programmes which 'cater for minority tastes and interests, particularly those not adequately catered for on the existing three television services . . . The character of the fourth channel service will be determined not only by the *kinds* of programmes it contains but also by the *sources* from which its programmes will be obtained.' There was to be a wide variety of such sources, but the programmes were to come 'in particular [from] producers from outside the existing broadcasting organisations'. The OBA was to act 'in some sense as a publisher', and be run in such a way as to allow for 'a degree of complementary scheduling with ITV'. It was to be funded, as proposed by Annan, by sponsorship and block advertising, but also by spot advertising. Despite continued Treasury opposition, financial assistance would be provided by the government 'especially in the early years'.[38] Priority was to be given to providing a Welsh-language service in Wales. In addition to all this, the White Paper called for the establishment of a veritable quangocracy of boards and councils to supervise and meddle in the different bits of the existing broadcasting services.

In the debate in the House of Commons which followed publication of the White Paper, William Whitelaw repeated that his party agreed with the basic aim of having the fourth channel 'provide different kinds of programmes from those on the existing channels'. However, he was totally opposed to a separate authority to run it on grounds of cost to the taxpayer. The fourth channel should be placed in the hands of the IBA, he said, but should have 'a separate programme planning board on which the main ITV companies would not have a majority'. Other Conservatives, including John Gorst and Julian Critchley, the Chairman of the Conservative Media Committee, were even more outspoken than Whitelaw in their condemnation of the OBA. They still wanted the fourth channel to be handed over to the IBA and the ITV companies. Gorst said that 'the proposals for an OBA quango contain very nearly all the known evils of broadcasting plus many untried ones, particularly sponsorship and a lack of balance in programmes'. Critchley (by now regarded by many programme makers as the ITV companies' chief apologist in the House of Commons) wanted to know what authority the OBA would enjoy over its programme makers? The Liberals, led by David Steel, sided with Whitelaw. They, too, called for the OBA to be contained in the IBA. When Phillip Whitehead spoke he accused Whitelaw of 'humbug'. He asked if the 'spokesman for the Conservative Party – the party of competition and free enterprise – has objected to a new outlet in broadcasting because it threatens vested interests with which the Conservatives are allied?'[39]

The ITV companies, appalled at the prospect of not gaining control of the fourth channel, openly denounced the White Paper. Typical was an outspoken attack in a letter to *The Listener* from Paul Fox, Managing Director of Yorkshire Television: 'In addition to the privilege of paying the Exchequer Levy of more than £60 million a year, we are now being asked to make programmes for our competitor . . . We are a programme company – not a facility company for other people's programmes. Of course, we have the capacity, the ability and, indeed, the will to make more programmes . . . But to hand them over to a competitive service to be scheduled by a London-based bureaucrat who has not been involved in the making of the programmes and who will simply add it to the rest of the OBA ragbag is presuming a little too much on our goodwill.'[40]

While the Annan Committee had been sitting, there had seemed no particular need to fill the void left by the demise of the FCG and the 76 Group. However, once the committee's report had been published and it became clear that its recommendations were far from certain to be enacted, all those who had campaigned since the late 1960s for the reform and opening-up of broadcasting realised that if they wanted to wrest anything from the Annan Report and all their years of hard work, they were going to have to go back into action. A new campaigning group was needed. One obvious vehicle for this was the Association of Independent Producers – AIP. In February 1978, with its immediate financial future secured by the one-off unconditional donation from Lord Delfont, it had recruited two extremely bright and presentable young women as administrative officers (so presentable that their appointment, together with pictures of them, had featured in the *Evening Standard*'s *Diary* page). One, Clare Downs, already had experience of doing promotional work in the film industry. The other, Sophie Balhetchet, was twenty-two and had graduated from Oxford with a first the previous summer. It was her first job.

Sophie Balhetchet and Clare Downs shortly after their appointment as Administrators by AIP

Courtesy of PACT

By April 1978 AIP had been persuaded to call a meeting to bring together all those who over the previous decade had campaigned to prevent ITV gaining control of the vacant fourth channel. The meeting's organisers included Roger Graef and Phillip Whitehead, who had been leading lights of the FCG, Anthony Smith, the father of the National Television Foundation proposal and Iain Bruce, who had been active in the ACTT over the fourth channel. The meeting, held on a Saturday morning, had been called in what seemed an unlikely venue – the Churchill Hotel in the heart of London's West End. About sixty people turned up, almost filling but certainly not over-filling, the hotel's function room. Rising to start the meeting, Phillip Whitehead took in the room, its business executive furniture and decor and the incongruity of the motley and generally radical group of people who were congregated there. Calling to mind Churchill in the summer of 1940, and his pledge to continue to fight and never surrender, he said, 'This is perhaps an appropriate place to hold this meeting.' He explained that the organisers had in mind creating a new campaign to fight for a fourth channel independent of ITV and dedicated to the principles outlined by Annan. Within a couple of hours a new, independent campaign group had come into being – the Channel Four Group. AIP, the ADP and the more radical IFA (the Independent Filmmakers' Association) were each to have representatives on its steering group, along with individuals with campaigning experience, useful industry profiles and relevant contacts. Iain Bruce became the new group's first, unpaid organiser.[41]

From its start, the Channel Four Group was marked by its pragmatism. While it intended to campaign for the OBA solution for the fourth channel, its members were less concerned about its precise form of organisation than that it be independent of the other broadcasters, that it have its own controller and compile its own programme schedule, dedicated to plurality rather than to consensus, to innovation, experiment and new voices, to serving minorities rather than maximising audiences, and that it be free of editorial constraint and unnecessary censorship. The channel must be a publisher of other people's work rather than a producer of its own, having minimal staff and few facilities, commissioning from a variety of sources, most of them independent.

As the autumn of 1978 advanced, and industrial unrest in the country continued to mount in the face of a continued government clampdown on wages, as the date of a general election drew inexorably closer and the fate of the OBA continued to hang in the balance, Iain Bruce took AIP's young organiser Sophie Balhetchet aside: '"The fourth channel", he told me, "is the *real* issue." He made this really powerful speech to me – "This is the big issue. This is going to be the real thing. You should be involved in this."' AIP, Bruce told Balhetchet, needed to do more than it already had to assist the Channel Four Group. As a result Balhetchet set about persuading AIP that, while the fourth channel was not strictly a film issue, the association ought to act as the umbrella for the Channel Four Group. To Balhetchet: 'Broadcasting was much more important politically and culturally than getting more independently-produced films made.' She had originally responded to AIP's advertisement for an administrative officer because AIP had seemed to her very much a case of the little man against the powerful commercial duopoly – the two distributors which controlled most of what was seen in British cinemas. 'That appealed. I believe in opportunity. I don't like bullies. I have a fantastic sense of natural justice. And I suppose I found this anarchic, spirited group of people great fun. It was a chance to meet some great film makers, mavericks, so to me great people. It was an incredibly broad church. I can remember being incensed that TV sets were manufactured with an ITV-2 button – you already have one licence to print money. You want another?'[42]

That winter Sophie Balhetchet succeeded in persuading the members of AIP that the group should act as the umbrella for the Channel Four Group, providing it with desk space and use of a telephone in its new offices. She herself began to devote most of her time to the battle for the fourth channel.

Members of the Channel Four Group also started privately to target leading Tories, especially those known to be sympathetic to the interests of small businesses and the freeing-up of what they called the enterprise culture. They tried to win these Conservatives over to the idea of independent producers as small businessmen and potential entrepreneurs. For the time being, however, little was said about these initiatives or their results even inside the Channel Four Group itself. Phillip Whitehead and his fellow campaigners knew that behind the scenes the ITV companies and the IBA, with active assistance from Whitehead's arch-Tory Commons opponent Julian Critchley, had been deliberately targeting Shadow Home Secretary Willie Whitelaw with the aim of winning him over to the case for ITV-2. All too conscious of the fact that the Labour government stood in serious danger of losing the forthcoming general election before any broadcasting bill establishing the OBA-run fourth channel could be enacted, Whitehead and his friends were privately casting about for ways of influencing Conservative Party thinking so as to offset the worst results of a possible Conservative victory. Whitelaw, who had said he was sympathetic to many of the ideas in the Annan Report, was one obvious target. However, his prescription for the new channel still seemed likely to produce ITV-2 'by the back door'. What Whitehead needed was somebody with potentially even more influence with Mrs Thatcher than Whitelaw. That person was Keith Joseph, who with Margaret Thatcher had set up the Centre for Policy Studies, the think tank from which nearly all the new policies adopted by the Conservative Party since Mrs Thatcher had become its leader had originated. Joseph was the philosopher and theoretician of what came to be called Thatcherism, of its commitment to self-reliance, the freedom of the individual and the removal of obstacles to the success of small businesses. In her memoirs, *The Downing Street Years*, Lady Thatcher says that during her years in opposition after the fall of the Heath government, Keith Joseph had made a remark that had reverberated powerfully in her mind. He said 'I have only recently become a Conservative', meaning she says 'that for his first twenty years in politics, many of them at the top, he had been a sort of moderate Fabian'. It was this remark which had led to the establishment of the Centre for Policy Studies and thence to her conviction that it was 'the job of government to establish a framework of stability' and then to leave individual families and businesses 'free to pursue their own dreams and ambitions'.

For Whitehead, a moderate member of the Labour Party, who had himself once been a 'working class Conservative', Joseph appeared the ideal target. But as a Labour MP, it was likely to be counter-productive if Whitehead tried to talk to Joseph himself. The obvious person for that task, Whitehead decided, was Anthony Smith, author of the idea of a National Television Foundation, out which had grown the concept of the OBA. Better still, Smith was a socialist who had recently come to the conclusion that he did not really belong on the left because he believed in 'a more American kind of free expression'. The opening to Joseph came through one of Whitehead's friends at Thames Television, Udi Eichler. A producer in the documentary and current affairs department with an eclectic range of contacts and sympathies, Eichler was a supporter of the Channel Four Group. Among Eichler's interests was membership of a little-known Conservative think tank (other members were said to include Kingsley Amis). Whitehead asked Eichler to invite Anthony Smith to go and talk to them. After Smith's talk the group rejected his ideas about the OBA but, Smith recalls, had been very interested in what he had to say about producers creating new businesses that would supply programmes to the new channel. When the meeting was over Eichler suggested that Smith should meet Keith Joseph. Smith recalls that when he went in to see Joseph, probably just after Christmas 1978, there was also 'a sort of very junior acolyte' present who made the drinks – Norman Lamont. Joseph seemed very interested, particularly when Smith explained that under his foundation/publisher model Channel Four would be both controllable in the way that the other three channels were but at the same time would create opportunities for producers to establish new small businesses. Smith painted a picture in which new entrepreneur–producers would set up production companies in their garages and create new jobs. He remembers that at one point Joseph turned to Lamont enthusiastically and asked, 'Norman, why aren't we doing this?' This meeting led shortly afterwards to another, this time with Willie Whitelaw.

For the time being there was no way of knowing what the effect of Smith's advocacy had been. Very few people, even in the steering group of the Channel Four Group, ever heard about the meetings at all. However, Smith is convinced that they were an important element in persuading Whitelaw and the Conservative government to set up Channel Four in the way in which they eventually did.[43]

*　　*　　*

'If you are the Home Secretary and you are facing a situation of civil unrest you are not going to push through legislation which is controversial.'[44] During the winter of 1978–9 – The Winter of Discontent – the OBA and broadcasting reform were finally and irretrievably overtaken by outside events. The Callaghan government, still only hanging on to power with the support of the Liberals, now faced a wave of industrial disruption unmatched since the General Strike of 1926. During the summer the government had announced its intention to limit pay settlements to 5% but this had been thrown out by the Labour Party Conference that autumn. Ford workers went on strike and won a 17% rise. They were swiftly followed by demands from haulage workers who, having turned down 13%, wanted 22%, and BBC technicians, who threatened to black out the Christmas Day showing of *The Sound of Music* unless they got a 15% rise. They got 12.5% and the transmission went ahead, netting the BBC an audience of eighteen and a half million, the second highest rating that Christmas.

On 10 January 1979, returning from a meeting of European leaders in the West Indies, Callaghan was asked by reporters to comment on the crisis. He was reported, inaccurately, to have replied 'Crisis – what crisis?' Crisis or no, on

22 January 1.5 million service workers came out on strike, followed over succeeding weeks by selective strikes of others. Television news showed pictures of uncollected and decomposing rubbish piling up in the streets, while lurid press accounts talked of bodies going unburied. On 28 March Scottish Nationalist MPs, angry about the results of a referendum on devolution, tabled a motion in the House of Commons of no confidence in the government's handling of the industrial situation. The Labour government fell by one vote.

Notes

1. "Lizzie Borden took an axe, And gave her mother forty whacks."
2. *Hansard*, 10 April 1974.
3. *Guardian*, 10 June 1974.
4. My sources for appointments to the Annan Committee include interviews I conducted with Anthony Smith and Phillip Whitehead, a Granada Guildhall Lecture given by Lord Annan in 1977, published in *Television Today and Tomorrow*, Granada Publishing, London, 1977, *The Ulster Television Lecture: The Politics of a Television Inquiry*, delivered by Lord Annan on 25 May 1981 and published by Ulster Television Ltd, Briggs, *op. cit.*, Potter, *op. cit.*, Vol. 3 and Lambert, *op. cit.* Whitehead confirms the truth of the story of Smith's appointment to the Annan Committee being blocked personally by Wilson on account of the Czech incident. Antony Jay's monograph on the future of the BBC was entitled: *Public Word and Private Words or What Shall We Do about the BBC?* published in November 1972 by the Society of Film and Television Arts.
5. *The People and the Media*, published by the Labour Party, London, 1974.
6. Interviews with Anthony Smith and Nicholas Garnham conducted by the author in September and October 2000.
7. Anthony Smith, *The National Television Foundation – a Plan for the Fourth Channel*, reprinted in *The Shadow in the Cave*, Quartet Books, London, 1976.
8. *Report on the Future of Broadcasting*, Chairman Lord Annan, 1977, Cmnd. 6753 and 6753-1.
9. *IBA Evidence to the Committee on the Future of Broadcasting*, September 1974.
10. Jeremy Potter was later the author of Volumes 3 and 4 of the ITV official history, *Independent Television in Britain*.
11. Account of the BBC's meeting with the Annan Committee is based on interviews by the author with Alasdair Milne, Phillip Whitehead and Milne's account in *DG: Memoirs of a British Broadcaster*, Hodder & Stoughton, London, 1988. Wheldon, it seems, generally organised only the most meagre meals when BBC staff met on the premises to discuss business.
12. See *The Last Days of the Beeb* by Michael Leapman, Allen & Unwin, London, 1986.
13. Colin Shaw, interviewed by the author in November 2000.

14. *Independent Broadcasting*, March 1976.
15. The scheme's opponents claimed that such units threatened centralised internal control of the BBC.
16. Quoted in Dickinson, *op. cit.*
17. The author was a member of the Labour Party Committee that produced the policy document.
18. *Submission to the Committee on the Future of Broadcasting by the Association of Independent Producers: On Co-operation between the Film and Television Industries*, 14 July 1976.
19. Among those who left the BBC were Hood, Jay, Baverstock, Smith, Peacock and Paul Fox. Milne was one of the few who had returned. David Attenborough had given up his executive role to return to programme-making, albeit for the BBC.
20. *Report of the Committee on the Future of Broadcasting*, Chairman: Lord Annan, presented to Parliament, March 1977, Cmnd. 6753 and 6753-1.
21. It later emerged that what the Committee had had in mind was single adverts running two or three minutes rather than the fifteen- or thirty-second adverts which were the staple of ITV.
22. *Hansard*, 23 May 1977.
23. Lord Annan, *RTS Fleming Lecture*, 28 April 1977.
24. Merlyn Rees succeeded Roy Jenkins as Home Secretary when Jenkins left the government and went to Brussels as President of the EEC Commission, after losing to Callaghan in the Labour Party leadership contest following Wilson's resignation.
25. Colin Shaw has confirmed to the author that he did play a part in preparing the IBA's formal Home Office response to the Annan Report. He recalls that, having written important sections of the BBC's evidence to Annan, in his first few months at the IBA he was "playing ping-pong" against himself.
26. Alan Sapper, quoted in report of ACTT Annual Conference in *Film And Television Technician*, May 1977.
27. Quotations from a report in *Film and Television Technician*, December 1977.
28. Christine (Fox) Benson, interviewed by the author in October 2000. British Actors' Equity, the actors' trade union, had been riven by a series of widely publicised rows between Trotskyites and supporters of Militant on one side and more moderate trade unionists on the other.
29. Lockett's promotion to Deputy General Secretary of the union in 1979 was part of that process.
30. *Film and Television Technician*, December 1978.
31. There had been smaller scale weekend events in 1975 and 1976, when the revered BBC drama producer James McTaggart had given a lecture and a group of drama producers and directors had discussed television drama. 1977 was the first time that the festival lasted for a week.
32. Gus Macdonald (Lord Macdonald of Tradeston), interviewed by the author in June 2001.
33. In *Brimstone and Treacle* the Devil, in the guise of a personable young man, insinuates himself into the household of a family with an inert, brain-damaged girl, rapes her

and, in so doing, restores her understanding that it was her father who caused her injuries when he ran her down in his car speeding away from having sex with her best friend. A fine and disturbing play, even if some people judged it to be below Potter's very best. It raised deeply serious and fundamental moral and religious questions. The BBC production, because of its tight and claustrophobic small screen domestic intensity, was infinitely more powerful and immediately relevant than the later cinema version.

34. Quoted from a lecture by Dennis Potter given at the 1977 Edinburgh International Television Festival in an article called *Middle-Aged, But Not Grown Up* by the author, published in *Film and Television Technician*. In my article I commented after the quotation from Potter's lecture that 'What Potter says about drama applies equally to the other disciplines in television.'

35. Alasdair Milne, interviewed by the author in October 2000.

36. Phillip Whitehead, interviewed by the author in January 2001.

37. See the official ITV history, Potter, *op. cit.*, *Vol. 3*. Shirley Littler's (Lady Littler) explanation of why the Home Office draft of the White Paper was thrown out is contained in an essay by her about the setting-up of Channel Four in *The Making of Channel 4*, edited by Peter Catterall, Frank Cass Publishers, London, 1999. Lady Littler later became Director-General of the IBA. After the Labour government fell, Lord Harris, the junior minister responsible for the draft White Paper, became a director of the ITV company Westward. Shortly afterwards a board room coup ousted Westward's flamboyant Chairman, Peter Cadbury, and appointed Harris in his place.

38. *White Paper on Broadcasting*, July 1978, Cmnd. 7294.

39. *Hansard*, 26 July 1978.

40. Paul Fox, *The Misbegotten Fourth Child*, *The Listener*, 17 August 1978. Fox had left the BBC to join Yorkshire Television in 1973.

41. The author took part in the Churchill Hotel meeting and became a member of the Channel Four Group steering group.

42. Sophie Balhetchet, interviewed by the author in November 2000.

43. The story of this sequence of previously unreported meetings is based largely on interviews conducted by the author during 2000 with Anthony Smith and Phillip Whitehead, coupled with other bits of published circumstantial evidence.

44. Phillip Whitehead, interviewed by the author in January 2001.

6

Cut to Thatcher: We're all free marketeers now! – Summer of '79

For the programme makers the summer of 1979 was bleak. A whole decade of argument, campaigning and risk to their careers had got them nowhere. On 3 May the Conservatives had won the general election with an overall majority of 44. Margaret Thatcher entered Downing Street quoting St Francis of Assisi: 'Where there is discord, may we bring harmony. Where there is error, may we bring truth. Where there is doubt, may we bring faith. And where there is despair, may we bring hope.' It seemed unlikely that she would bring harmony, truth, faith or hope.

Broadcasting policy had not figured in the Conservatives' election manifesto and was little raised in the campaign. The election had been fought on Labour's record on the economy and against a background of mounting IRA terrorism. A Tory poster featuring a dole queue and the heading 'Labour Isn't Working' was the election's most potent symbol. Eleven days later, on 15 May, the new government announced in the Queen's Speech that a bill would be introduced to extend the life of the Independent Broadcasting Authority and give it responsibility – 'subject to strict safeguards' – for the fourth television channel. No further details were given – the announcement ran to just thirty-nine words and was sandwiched between policies on stricter immigration controls and the Official Secrets Act. However, the new Home Secretary William Whitelaw's views were already known. In an article in the Royal Television Society Journal published immediately before the election he had reiterated his party's firm opposition to the OBA and had specifically endorsed the last IBA, Colin Shaw influenced ITV-2 proposals. Having won the election, the only people now likely to influence Whitelaw would be the IBA, other Tories such as Julian Critchley and Sir Paul Bryan, and above all, Margaret Thatcher. Their influence seemed certain to favour the ITV companies.

Any lingering doubt about the thrust of the new government's policies was removed a month later. On 14 June Sir Geoffrey Howe introduced his first budget. Income tax and higher rate taxes were cut, public expenditure slashed, VAT jacked up sharply and Monetarism, in the form of control of the Public Sector Borrowing Requirement, introduced. 'The Market' would rule and entrepreneurs were to be its princes.

*　　*　　*

The entrance of Thatcher seems an appropriate point at which briefly to halt the onward march of events and review where some of the leading dramatis personae who still had a major part to play in the story were in the summer of 1979. Among the original BFI and FCG protestors of 1968 most, like me, were still pursuing careers as film and television programme makers either inside the BBC and major ITV companies or, increasingly, as freelances moving from project to project and company to company. A few, like Roger Graef, had achieved a degree of fame. With the success of his 1972 series, *The Space Between Words*, Graef had become recognised as one the country's leading documentarists. Colin Thomas, on the other hand, had publicly resigned from the BBC in the summer of 1978 over the censorship of a series he had been working on about Northern Ireland and, temporarily unable to find work in England, had gone to work for RTE in Dublin.[1] Some had left the business altogether, while a significant number of others had moved into academe – Nicholas Garnham had been Head of the Department of Communications at the Central London Polytechnic since 1972. He was now a Governor of the BFI, elected by the members under reforms instituted following a renewed campaign by Hatton and the protestors. He had married Caroline Heller, who continued to write extensively on media-related issues but had largely dropped out of active campaigning. After leaving the BBC in 1971 Anthony Smith had been a fellow of St Antony's College, Oxford, until 1975 and worked as freelance, writing copiously on media issues. In 1979 he was appointed Director of the BFI.

Phillip Whitehead had been re-elected as MP for Derby North. Gus Macdonald, who had been appointed the editor of *World in Action* in the early 1970s (initial doubts over his suitability for the post on account of his political views having been overcome), was by 1979 one of Granada's most senior producers and a member of the company's programme committee. David Elstein edited Thames Television's weekly current affairs programme *This Week* from

1974 until 1978, but by 1979 faced mounting trouble with his management over his involvement in the fourth channel debate and some of the controversial investigative programmes for which he was responsible. Jeremy Isaacs had left Thames in September 1978 after a sensational row with Thames's combative Managing Director, Bryan Cowgill, in circumstances described as 'something between resignation and the sack'. The row had centred on a *This Week* programme on an Amnesty International Report about the RUC's treatment of prisoners at the Castlereagh Interrogation Centre. It had been banned by the IBA, and Isaacs had responded by authorising the use of six minutes from the programme by the BBC. Since leaving Thames Isaacs had worked as one of a growing band of quasi-independents, making programmes for the BBC, Scottish Television and Television New Zealand. In 1979 he had been made a Governor of the BFI and had become Chairman of its Production Board, the successor to the Experimental Film Fund.

Of the other broadcasters, Michael Peacock, after being fired from LWT in 1969 with just one year's salary as compensation, had initially found life difficult. In eighteen months he had earned just £500 (at LWT his salary had been £12,000). The BBC having refused to take him back before he had been 'made to kneel in the snow' for an extended period, he had got involved in making training films. By the mid-1970s he had become involved in commercial radio and then been a senior film company executive with Warner Brothers, first heading their UK operation and then going to the United States. He had returned to Britain in 1976 and had expanded his training film company, Video Arts. By 1979, the company, which he ran with Antony Jay, had become one of the most successful makers of training films in the country and had recently added a television production arm. Alasdair Milne was back in the BBC and was, by 1979, Managing Director of Television. Paul Fox, another of the executives who, as Annan commented unfavourably, had defected from the BBC, was now Managing Director of Yorkshire Television. Colin Shaw now held the key position of Director of Television at the IBA. Charles Denton who, after becoming Bob Heller's deputy, had succeeded him as Head of Documentaries and Features at ATV, was by 1979 Controller of Programmes. Sir Denis Forman, following a spell as Chairman of the BFI during which he had instituted many of the reforms called for by Hatton and his fellow protestors, had been knighted in 1976. He was now both Chairman and, with David Plowright, Joint-Managing Director of Granada Television. Michael Grade, Leslie's son and Lew's nephew, following his highly publicised 1969 Café Royal entry into the family business, had moved across to television in 1973, becoming head of LWT's entertainment programmes. In 1977 he had been promoted to Controller of Programmes. In a coup bearing all the hallmarks of the Grade family style, in the spring of 1979 he had lured Dennis Potter and Kenith Trodd, still smarting from Milne's refusal to show *Brimstone and Treacle*, away from the BBC to LWT, where it was planned they would make six plays through their independent production company, Pennies From Heaven Ltd.[2] This was another quasi-independent production deal, although reportedly more lucrative than the ones Jeremy Isaacs had done with the BBC, Scottish Television and Television New Zealand. Under each of these deals the independent contracted to supply key personnel while the broadcaster provided the equipment, facilities and crews.

Among the politicians, the only ones that counted for broadcasting were Margaret Thatcher and William Whitelaw, possibly with Keith Joseph in the background.

* * *

The first event after the election of any significance for the fourth channel campaigners was a piece of old business left over from 1977. The campaigners had remained determined to overturn the ACTT's dubiously arrived at anti-OBA policy. Their only real chance of doing so in a way that would prevent Alan Sapper and the union's Television Branch from ignoring them was through a vote at the union's annual conference. In 1979 this was due to be held over the weekend of 19 and 20 May in St Pancras Town Hall (venue of the rowdy Film Branch meeting eighteen months earlier). After months of patient lobbying inside various branches and union shops the campaigners had managed to get two motions on to the conference agenda. One, to be proposed by Iain Bruce, said that union policy on the fourth channel could not be allowed to stand because the special conference agreed by the ACTT's 1977 Annual Conference had not been held. The other, more substantial one, was in the form of an Emergency Motion to be moved by David Elstein on behalf of union members employed by Thames Television.

Elstein's motion coupled safeguarding the jobs of technicians working in the ITV companies with the prospect of more work for ACTT members in laboratories and film production by calling on the union both to campaign in defence of the present ITV structure and for the creation of a fourth channel that was 'neither controlled nor dominated by the present ITCA companies' and drew 'the majority of its programmes from a variety of British independent production sources other than the existing ITCA companies'. When Elstein rose to propose his Emergency Motion and start what was likely to be the major

David Elstein moving the emergency motion to reverse union
policy on the fourth channel at the ACTT Annual Conference
in Camden (St Pancras) Town Hall on 19–20 May 1979
By kind permission of the BECTU Photographic Archive

debate of the conference, the atmosphere in the hall was already highly charged. Elstein began: 'What is at stake is not just jobs, not just the structure of an industry, but the quality of free expression in our society.' To a union that professed, even if it did not always practise, a strong commitment to the principle of free speech, this was a powerful argument that it would be difficult for the ITV shops simply to ignore. However, the crucial thing for the campaigners was to gather enough conference votes from film and laboratory members to overturn the union's existing policy. Elstein therefore went on to explain that if the new channel were given to the existing ITV companies only about 1,000 new jobs would be created, and that only about half of those would be ACTT jobs. Whereas, said Elstein, 'common sense dictates that by looking outside the existing contractors far more new jobs are bound to be created, either in existing facilities companies, or in new production houses, set up to ACTT standards to meet the new demand for programmes'. Many of these new jobs would, he said, be permanent. 'The fourth channel offers a chance for de-casualisation by encouraging the growth of new permanent employers.' Handing the fourth channel to the ITV companies would encourage them to maximise their audience, driving every serious programme off BBC-1 and downgrading BBC-2. The union's support for ITV dominance of the fourth channel was, Elstein said, 'a recipe for a disastrous decline in the quality of British television'.[3]

Elstein's motion was seconded by Charles Stewart, the cameraman who had been so closely associated with the work of Maurice Hatton and Roger Graef. He told the conference that the ITCA companies were celebrating over the new government's fourth channel decision. It guaranteed them a secure monopoly and therefore 'secure profits'. However, it quickly became clear that we campaigners were not going to get things all our own way. Representatives of technicians permanently employed in ITV angrily denounced Elstein's motion. Speaker after speaker said that giving the ITV companies the fourth channel would maintain stability, improve job satisfaction and increase the number of creative outlets. It would mean less pressure from 'facility house vultures' who did not match ACTT crewing and wage rates.

Sensing that Elstein and his supporters were nevertheless likely to win the vote, the union's General Secretary, Alan Sapper, approached Elstein in a coffee break and asked him to remit his motion to the union's General Council for further consideration. Elstein refused. 'I'm not letting you off the hook this time,' he said. 'I'm pushing it to a vote. The ACTT may want control of the channel, but that is like saying the printers of the *Daily Mirror* should have control of the paper.'[4] When the debate restarted, union officials resorted to warning the conference of the danger of a split in the union if the motion was passed. The TV organiser, a hard-drinking Irishman called Jack O'Connor who had repeatedly made clear his antagonism towards freelancing, painted a lurid picture of the consequences for the membership of a split between those who were permanently employed in television and the people in all the other branches. Winding up the debate from the platform, Sapper warned delegates that it would be 'tragic for the union' if conference delegates passed the Emergency Motion in the face of the hostility of the TV Branch: 'It would be highly dangerous for the TV Branch to be driven into a corner with a policy that they believe very seriously affects their employment prospects.' Iain Bruce retorted by asking, 'Who needs guarantees most?' Freelances had suffered increasing discrimination over several years. In his closing speech Elstein told Sapper that his remarks about the danger of dividing the union were nothing more or less than a threat. 'What kind of blackmail is going on here?' he asked. A Television Branch representative spoke last, revealing the true depth of hatred and division which had built up in the television shops. Accusing freelances of not paying their full union dues, but of being content to ride on the backs of their brothers in the ITV companies, he said: 'I spoke about unity. I don't know why, but it's going to be war.' Nevertheless, when the motion was put it was passed by 111 votes to 55.[5]

Even with a new, anti-union government it was an important victory. It boosted the morale of the Channel Four Group at a time when their prospects looked bleak. It showed the campaigners that they could still get their act together and mount a successful campaign, even in the hitherto hostile territory of trade union politics. Later that summer the union held a conference on how to implement its new policy on the fourth channel, which took as its starting point a paper prepared by the union's newly promoted Deputy Secretary, Roy Lockett. The conference passed off amicably, marking the beginning of a new mood in the union. Lockett was one of a new breed of trade union officials who had started to enter the ACTT in the late 1970s and early 1980s. He had studied at Ruskin College and later got a degree at Oxford. His views coincided much more closely with those of the campaigners. He had himself worked tirelessly inside the union to get it to recognise the training provided by the National Film School. His growing influence inside the union would have an important bearing on later battles to realise the possibilities of Channel Four.

It was one thing for the Channel Four Group campaigners to win a victory inside the union, but likely to be quite another to win similar victories in the world of real politics. Three weeks after the ACTT conference, Colin Shaw, the

Director of Television at the IBA, addressed the Broadcasting Press Guild. Shaw revealed that the IBA was already having detailed talks with the government about the shape of the new channel and that the government was likely to adopt a plan very close to the one put forward by the IBA in its original response to the Annan Report. Despite the change of government, the officials in the Broadcasting Department of the Home Office were still mostly the same officials who had been there under the previous government. The new government's plan looked suspiciously like the one put forward under the Callaghan government by Lord Harris and his Home Office officials. In his speech Shaw had spoken of 'Channel Four' but had made it clear that he expected it to be known as 'ITV-2'. On the vital issue of the scheduling of the new channel Shaw said little beyond repeating the IBA's commitment to 'complementarity' with ITV, adding that this did not mean that 'the scheduling arrangements' between the two channels would necessarily be the same. But, he said, 'the big questions revolve around the role of the programme companies and the independent producers'. Conceding that the 'visibility' of the independent producers was 'greater than it was', Shaw continued, 'I am sure we must try to distinguish between the individual producer, for whom the OBA was tailor-made, and the independent company whose instincts may be as resolutely commercial as that of any programme contractor.' Independents tended, he suggested, to be more interested in single major programmes, significant plays, short drama series or documentaries, than in the run-of-the-mill bulk programming on which any television channel principally depended. 'Keeping the screen alight for many hours a week calls for a regular provision of programmes which in turn calls for resources and organisation which are hardly compatible with "independence" in the way in which that term has often been used recently. So the new channel, while it must welcome the contribution of the independent producers and ensure that they play their part in the scheduling of the service, will have need of the programme companies for what the Authority sees as a substantial contribution.' Shaw reiterated that the Authority believed that the sale of advertising on the two channels should remain in the same hands.[6]

Three weeks later Sir Brian Young, the Director-General of the IBA, deepened the campaigners' gloom. Addressing delegates to an international television festival at BAFTA, he said that, in discussing the fourth channel, the Annan Committee had appeared to identify the new channel's needs in almost exactly the same terms as the IBA in its proposals for ITV-2. In proposing the creation of the

OBA, the Annan Committee had been engaged in doing no more than 'throwing the dogmatists a bone'. But since the election circumstances had changed. It was not only the victory of the Conservatives at the polls, Sir Brian said, but 'the sheer logic of sensible decisions' that had 'brought back, as the basis for forthcoming legislation, the IBA's plan for the fourth channel'. The tone of Young's speech suggested that he viewed the freelance and independent production sector as no more than also-rans in the new channel. In deciding the structure of the new channel, in addition to consulting the ITV companies the IBA would, Young said, want to talk to 'new kinds of participant, such as the independent producers'. Perhaps, he ventured, BAFTA might speak for them?[7] To many freelances that seemed downright insulting. BAFTA, however honourable its attempts to be some sort of forum for debate, was chiefly associated with its annual programme awards. These were seen by a lot of programme makers as unduly subject to the influence of the major broadcasters. After nine years in the job, Young seemed to the campaigners to be no more in touch with programme makers than he had when *Open Secret* had lampooned his appointment in 1970.

By one of the ironies of fate that so often seemed to spur the campaigners on at crucial moments in the campaign, the top award at the international television festival which Sir Brian Young had been addressing was won by an independent producer called Christopher Nupen who, because he had no reliable television market for his programmes in Britain, had to rely on sales to the German station ZDF in order to make them. Two days after Sir Brian's speech Nupen was on the same BAFTA stage. He described how he had had to mortgage his house in order to make *Itzhak Perlman: Virtuoso Violinist*, widely accepted as one of the finest music films ever made, because no British broadcaster would put up the money for him to make it. Nupen was taking part in a BAFTA presentation, organised by the Association of Directors and Producers (ADP), under the title 'Who Are the Independents?' The IBA, the ITV companies, Conservative MPs and Home Office civil servants had repeatedly made hay with the claims of independent producers, deriding their ability to supply the bulk of programmes for the fourth channel. They had repeatedly asked sneeringly 'Who are they?', before going on to assert that there were very few independents and that those that there were worked in only a narrow range of programmes. The ADP presentation was an attempt to banish this caricature once and for all. A large contingent of journalists had been invited, together with the Deputy Director of Television at the IBA, David Glencross, and four Home Office Broadcasting Department civil servants.

Elstein recalls 'I kept my eyes on the four Home Office officials all through. They were the key audience. We had to get it through to the Home Office and the IBA that it was not a high risk proposition, independents supplying Channel Four.'[8] During the presentation, extracts were shown from nineteen programmes made by independents, none of which had received any finance from the BBC, ITV or bodies such as the Arts Council. Each programme maker introduced the extract from his or her own work and the audience were told repeatedly how the BBC and ITV refused even to view independent productions and, whenever an independent's programme succeeded in winning overseas awards, offered their makers only derisory sums for screening them on British television. The programmes screened ranged from a major series being made by Michael Peacock and Antony Jay's company Video Arts for the American public service broadcasting network PBS about the political and economic theories of Mrs Thatcher's favourite economic guru, Milton Friedman, to a seven-minute animation film by Bob Godfrey, from Alan Parker's *No Hard Feelings* and John Cleese in an adaptation of a Chekhov short story, to Nick Downie's current affairs documentary *Front Line Rhodesia*. Downie, a gifted and courageous cameraman–reporter, told the audience how, although his previous two films had won prizes, he had still been unable to cover their costs 'because of the cartel operated by ITV and the BBC' against buying independent productions. As a result he had had to pawn most of his equipment to finance his next project.

The problem with this sort of event was that, while it produced good news copy and increased sympathy for independents such as Downie and Nupen, it could also be used to reinforce the point made by Colin Shaw in his address to the Broadcasting Press Guild – the independents might usefully add to the mix of programmes on ITV-2 but they could not be regarded as a sufficient source for the supply of the volume and kind of programmes needed to keep any channel on the air for forty or fifty hours a week, week in and week out, fifty-two weeks a year. For some people, events such as the BAFTA presentation, and the hype that surrounded it, only reinforced the impression that the independents were little more than a bunch of whingers who were good at PR.

At the BAFTA presentation one programme maker had told the IBA's David Glencross, 'A different channel has to mean entirely different people taking all the programme production decisions.' But this was the rub. If the ITV companies were going to supply the bulk of the programmes and sell the advertising, as both Young and Shaw had confirmed and as seemed implicit in all that Whitelaw and the Conservatives had said both before and since the election, then no matter what the scheduling arrangements might be on paper, in practice the companies would, in very short order, be in complete control of the channel. In its formal response to the Annan Report two years earlier, the IBA had conceded, as a sweetener, that independents should provide up to 15% of the programmes on the new channel. Shaw and Young were now trotting out this figure again. Some independents, particularly the more established ones who survived by supplying programmes for overseas markets or packaged drama series to the ITV companies, seemed ready to accept that, with the Conservatives now in power, the fourth channel campaigners had lost. They believed that there would be no independent or separate fourth channel and that the independents should grab what was now on offer. They should concentrate their efforts on trying to up the percentage a bit and improving the terms on which ITV-2 would buy their programmes so as to ensure that they would get paid enough to cover the full costs of production, leaving producers with sufficient rights to make a profit from overseas sales. It was a seductive argument: better to secure a substantial toehold from which the independents might grow than to risk antagonising Whitelaw and the IBA in a fight over principle that could not be won and so risk losing everything.

It is easy to forget that, unlike the ITV companies, the IBA and the Home Office, all of which had full-time, highly qualified staff backed by generous budgets, committed to working towards ITV-2, the independents and would-be independents were all busy programme makers, giving their time to campaigning between struggling to make a living and keep their careers going. The Channel Four Group struggled to keep a single-room office open and pay the expenses of its single organiser. It only succeeded in bridging the shortfall between its members' subscriptions and its costs thanks to the support of AIP, which was itself continuously short of money. The previous November the AIP journal, reduced to a single sheet of folded A4, had carried the single headline 'The Last Ditch. SEND £5 NOW – SAVE AIP'. Iain Bruce had had to give up being the Channel Four Group's organiser owing to his professional commitments and the need to earn a living. He had been replaced by the only volunteer, Frank Brown, a former executive with an ITV company defeated in the 1968 franchise round.

Such was the state of affairs a few weeks after the election when a small group of Channel Four Group members, including myself, was sitting around one evening in the dingy AIP office in Great Pulteney Street, gloomily assessing dashed prospects. Someone said something like – 'Didn't the Conservative manifesto have a lot of stuff in it about the importance of small businessmen? Well, as independent producers, wouldn't we be small businessmen, running our own companies and making television programmes?' And, yes, Whitelaw, the IBA and even the ITV companies had referred to finding room on a second ITV channel for programmes made by 'independent producers'. Might there not be something here on which we could build rather than mutely accepting what little seemed currently on offer? Might this not be used as the basis for a renewed campaign? (It seems unlikely that any of those present that evening knew of Anthony Smith's meetings with Keith Joseph and William Whitelaw six months earlier. If any of us did know then we must have dismissed them in the light of what Whitelaw had said since.) In the days that followed, a copy of the Conservative election manifesto was obtained and its contents scrutinised. There was, indeed, a whole section on improving the lot of small businesses and on their importance to the economy. More discussions followed, and over the next week or two old ideals were re-born, but disguised behind a new language borrowed from Thatcher's lexicon – enterprise, small business and 'The Free Market of Ideas'.[9] It was a frail enough chance, but it seemed worth a go. If we were to have any chance of succeeding we were going to have to work fast. A full meeting of the Channel Four Group was called for 20 June.

By the time that the full Channel Four Group meeting took place it had attracted a good deal of interest. As a result the usual campaigners were joined by representatives of some of the larger established independent production companies. Michael Peacock of Video Arts spoke at some length, telling the meeting that having examined various models currently being mooted for the fourth channel, he was in favour of a model being put forward by a former Managing Director of Yorkshire Television, under which the fourth channel would be run by a sixteenth ITV company. As *Broadcast*'s reporter put it: 'His position hardly endeared him to the ADP people there, particularly as he made it clear he had little time for the sort of ideas that people like David Elstein had in mind for the channel.' The 'second front', as *Broadcast*'s correspondent termed the big companies which had all of a sudden started to evince an interest in the fate of the fourth channel, 'has not been greeted with wild enthusiasm by those of the Channel Four Group . . . The fear is that the alliance of these large production houses could militate against the small independents – and against more experimental programmes – because the big production companies which recoup on American sales can sell their product more cheaply to the fourth channel.'[10]

Those of us who had been deeply involved in the battle for the fourth channel for many years had all along feared precisely the kind of public split in the carefully fostered unity of our campaign which now seemed to loom. Many also felt an understandable resentment that large companies, which had kept aloof during all the years when people had repeatedly risked their careers in order prevent the ITV companies from snatching the fourth channel, were, now that there seemed some immediate prospect of some new opportunities opening up, coming forward like carpetbaggers. Worse still, they seemed intent on telling the people who had got the campaign this far what to do. It was widely rumoured that a group of big companies, including Peacock's Video Arts and the Robert Stigwood Organisation, had put up £50,000 to engage the services of the publicist who had worked on the Heath government's campaign for EEC membership, to promote a big-company vision of the fourth channel.[11]

The meeting ended by agreeing to hold another meeting a month later to thrash out a text on Channel Four for submission to the Home Office. Those present agreed to stump up £1,000 in individual donations to fund 'the next (and last) six months of the campaign'. The AIP magazine's report noted that the Channel Four Group had elected a new steering group and agreed to 'pressure the Home Office to include a separate Schedule to the Bill which clearly defines the IBA obligations for the fourth channel, especially concerning independents' contribution (UK grass-roots type, not Hollywood conglomerate subsidiaries), finance and production decision control and complementary scheduling not meaning a "slave" system to support the ITV-1/BBC-1 ratings street fight.' Frank Brown, the Channel Four Group's new organiser, was quoted as saying, 'It's for real this time. The shape of ITV for the next ten years or so will be decided by Parliament this autumn.'[12]

We were all too aware of the enormity of the task we were taking on. To have any hope of succeeding we needed a dedicated team of the sharpest, most energetic people we could find. Central to all we did would be the group's full-time organiser. Increasingly Sophie Balhetchet, I and others in the small inner circle of the campaign questioned whether the Group's new organiser, Frank Brown, nice and well-meaning though he was, was really the right man for the kind of street fight that we were now going to have to get into. We needed somebody young, someone single-minded and, when need be, ruthless, able to find his way around among new contacts and use the new voguish language of Thatcherism with conviction. Where to find someone at short notice, with the necessary qualities and able to work full-time for very little money?

A few months earlier two of Nicholas Garnham's media studies students from the Central London Polytechnic had been to AIP to interview Sophie Balhetchet and some of the Association's members for their final year theses. One student in particular, who my wife described at the time as 'looking underfed and in need of looking after', had made a powerful impression on Balhetchet. 'He had a way of extracting information from people that was voracious. Talk about pumping people.'[13] His name was Michael Jackson. He had an absolutely single-minded interest in everything to do with television. He and Balhetchet, who shared an interest in television history and the new kinds of television shows which were then becoming popular, had continued to meet. By July, when it became clear that the Channel Four Group was going to mount one last all-or-nothing push to try to wrest the fourth channel from the control of ITV, Balhetchet had become convinced not only that Brown was not the man for the job, but that Michael Jackson was. 'I worked out precisely how to get Brown out and my boy Jackson in.' She sent Jackson off to see Iain Bruce, who seemed equally impressed. Then she arranged for Jackson to meet a cross-section of the Channel Four Group committee. At the same time we checked him out with Nicholas Garnham. Garnham's verdict was that Jackson was unique – more focused on his goals than any other student he had ever had, and very bright indeed.

Jackson was taken on at £30 per week and Brown was eased aside. As soon as he took over, Jackson started to work feverishly drumming up funds, preparing leaflets, writing letters: 'I didn't know you could pay someone to address envelopes so I did them all myself.' Jackson's impressions coming new into the small inner circle of the Channel Four Group that summer are revealing. 'No one was a considerable figure, and people were risking their careers by speaking out. Iain Bruce had a really hungry desire for Channel Four and Sophie Balhetchet had youth and politicking on her side, while David Elstein had his two brains working.' His opinion of the broadcasters and their programmes was very low. 'We were pushing against this monolithic edifice which was very conservative, very inefficient and had awful unions. The choice of programmes was very narrow – there were no plays about gays; there were no coloured people and there were no women on screen or in positions of authority. It wasn't healthy.'[14]

In preparation for the crucial July Channel Four Group meeting, David Elstein wrote a devastating critique of the ITV companies' case for ITV-2. He rubbished the companies' twin claim that, as they were going 'to pay for ITV-2' (providing the channel's budget in return for selling the advertising airtime), they had the right, 'in natural justice', to control its schedule; that, as they already made most of the programmes for ITV, they must be recognised as the 'natural' suppliers of programmes for ITV-2. 'If, in 1954, the ITA had looked to the "natural" source of programmes for its new channel, it would have taken 75% of its output from the BBC', which, as Elstein pointed out, 'would have defeated the whole purpose

Michael Jackson shortly after he joined
the Channel Four Group as its organiser
Courtesy of PACT

of the new channel'. The ITV companies' argument was equally ridiculous now. 'Why', he asked, 'does the IBA apparently believe that it would be more difficult now than it was in 1954 to find new sources of programmes? After all, in 1954, Sidney Bernstein was running cinemas, and Lew Grade a talent agency. Does the IBA believe that no new Bernsteins and Grades could emerge today?' When the ITV companies advanced their case for a second channel in 1971 they had claimed that they could make the programmes for it with their under-utilised facilities and with their creatively frustrated staff. This argument for control of the channel had since collapsed with the admission by the companies that they would only be able to produce the programmes for a second ITV channel by double-shift working in their studios and through extensive use of overtime. The

IBA's claim that in order for the programmes on the new channel to be complementary to those on ITV-1 they must come from the same source was, Elstein claimed, nonsensical – 'Common sense suggests that the opposite should be just as much the case . . . the channel can as easily draw its programmes from new sources as old ones. In theory, a schedule complementary to ITV could be compiled from the BBC's programmes.' Elstein ended his critique with a list of demands and safeguards. The fourth channel must be genuinely 'independent' of ITV and of the commercial contractors. This must be a new channel, free to choose its programmes 'on merit' without regard to the wishes of the existing ITV contractors. It must be headed by a controller, appointed by the IBA and independent of the ITV companies. The channel must pay the full production cost of programmes made for it by independent producers. In turn, these producers must be free to make programmes by whatever means they deemed appropriate and not be forced to rely on the ITV companies' personnel or facilities.[15]

I also wrote a short internal Channel Four Group paper in preparation for the meeting. This concentrated on the kind of campaign we were going to have to conduct. I had been away from the campaign a lot during the previous nine months due to a heavy schedule of productions but, I said, coming back fresh to it since the government's announcement in the Queen's Speech, I detected a dangerous shift in the Group's concerns and public pronouncements. Perhaps owing to the fact that we had now both lost the fight for the OBA and simultaneously won our demand for airtime for independent productions, we had been distracted from our central demand – a fourth channel 'whose programme content and schedule was separate from and independent of the existing three channels'. Instead, we had been drawn into arguments about precise percentages of airtime to be given to independents, into definitions of what constituted an independent and of the capacity of independents to produce specified numbers of hours or particular genres of programmes. 'We seem in danger of forgetting that the Channel Four Group remains a lobby not a legislating body.' For the Group to be drawn into such arguments damaged the Group's credibility. 'The pursuit of principle is replaced by the unattractive spectacle of transparent vested self-interest.' We were in danger of being perceived as 'a motley, raucous array of would-be filmmakers lobbying competitively for a slice of the action. Meanwhile the fat cats of the ITCA smile silkily, offer 15% . . . of air-time . . . to squabble over, while quietly preparing to take full control themselves.' The Channel Four Group and its predecessors, right back the original campaigns of the FCG, the 76 Group and the TV4 Campaign, owed their success to being able to articulate one simple, readily understood demand around which a whole spectrum of interests and the general public had been able to unite. In challenging the control of the existing television duopoly, we had demanded something that went beyond the self-interest of any group of disaffected media professionals or commercial production houses – 'wider access, greater freedom, more variety and new blood in the name of the cultural, democratic and social health of the whole community'. We must, I argued, return to pressing 'single-mindedly for our original central demand: a fourth channel on which control of programme content and schedule is independent of the existing commercial franchise holders. This is a demand which is still achievable under the terms of government policy as so far expressed; it still commands public support as well as a powerful lobby inside the IBA itself.' Urging the campaign not to dissipate its energies on subsidiary issues, I ended: 'We should not be fighting about a percentage for Independents, but for total independence for the Channel.'[16]

'References to "a war situation" and to dangers of "sharks basking in very rich water" were heard at a well-attended but fairly chaotic Channel Four Group – er, well, discussion last Monday.' Thus *Broadcast* began its report of the crucial Channel Four Group meeting on 23 July at the Ivanhoe Hotel in Bloomsbury.[17] While everyone at the meeting seemed able to agree with my call to stop ourselves from being sidetracked into arguments about definitions and percentages of programmes and to concentrate instead on the central issue of a fourth channel independent of the ITV companies, they had been divided over the specific proposals and safeguards outlined in Elstein's paper. To most of us who had been over the ground a lot of times during the previous ten years, Elstein's proposals seemed pretty uncontroversial. Even so, they were too much for some of the big-company new entrants into the discussion. Their stance served to reinforce suspicions that they were only in it for what they could get out of it for themselves. However, no one wanted an open split in the campaign. As a result, the meeting ended by agreeing to leave decisions about the text of any submission to the Home Office in the hands of the steering group.

The campaigners had long been stigmatised by opponents as 'dogmatists' to whom, as Sir Brian Young had put it in his BAFTA speech, Annan had thrown a bone. They had been identified with the Left and, indeed, many of them were, like me, active members of the Labour Party who still looked to the day, probably four or five years hence, when Thatcher's small majority would be wiped out and

Labour would return to power. Our problem was how we were to bring the same pressure to bear inside the new Conservative government that we had previously been able to bring to bear inside the Labour Party. Here, in particular, the new big-company entrants to the campaign might be useful. Once again David Elstein made a start. He led a delegation of high-profile programme makers from ADP, including Christopher Nupen and Mark Shivas (producer of the BBC's *The Six Wives of Henry VIII* and the BBC's 1979 award winner *On Giant's Shoulders*), to meet the Conservative Backbench Media Committee. They stressed the greater incentive on independents to maximise overseas sales of their programmes as compared to the ITV companies which made most of their money from the sale of domestic advertising airtime. In addition Elstein had been involved in a soirée organised by Richard Price (a former head of overseas sales at Granada and one-time Conservative Parliamentary candidate, who now owned one of the very few really successful independent programme sales companies).[18] Among the Conservative MPs who attended the soirée had been Leon Brittan, who as Minister of State at the Home Office would be responsible for much of the detailed work on the broadcasting bill.

One other person who was to have a key role in the coming battle over the fourth channel committed his thoughts to paper in the weeks immediately prior to its commencement. That person was Colin Shaw, the Director of Television at the IBA. On 10 August 1979 he wrote privately to a colleague in the United States, laying out his assessment of the state of the broadcasting scene in Britain in the aftermath of the Conservative election victory.[19] Writing about the fourth channel and the 'strict safeguards' which the government in the Queen's Speech had said were to be a condition of awarding it to the IBA, Shaw wrote that he felt certain that this would mean fewer programmes would be permitted from the five major companies than on ITV and that more would come from the ten smaller regional companies. 'Protection for independent producers, whose work would have been, in an ideal world, the lifeblood of the Open Broadcasting Authority', along with protection for 'educational programmes of a more or less formal kind' also seemed to Shaw to be reasonably assured. The system of horse trading in programmes between the five major companies in the ITV network, which took no real account of the true cost of a programme, would have to be ended on the fourth channel in order to allow both the regional ITV companies and independent producers to offer programmes to the channel on an equal basis with the major ITV network companies.

Turning to the problem of the independent producers, Shaw again pointed, as he had in his lecture to the Broadcasting Press Guild in June, to the disparities between the bigger commercial producers and the smaller freelances. 'Some of these people talk very grandly of the scale on which they might contribute to the Fourth Channel – 50%, some of them say, should be ours by right. Others are more modest, accepting that the 15% of which the Authority has talked, is the right amount to begin with. They ask not for rights as much as for the willingness to consider expansion should they prove a success.' But, Shaw went on, 'expansion, if no more time is available and none will be at peak times, can only be at the expense of those who provide the network's bread-and-butter, that is the programme companies, and they cannot be asked to tool up for an increased output, only to be asked soon afterwards not to offer so much'. Shaw concluded by forecasting that the problems created by all these contending interests would ensure that 'the pot will go on boiling more or less continuously for the next sixteen months or so'.[20] Shaw's letter not only reveals his real thoughts on the eve of the decisive battle for Channel Four, it neatly states the dilemma facing the programme makers of the Channel Four Group and the reason why Elstein, Whitehead, I and others who thought like us, believed that we had no alternative but to fight single-mindedly for a channel on which, from the outset, the majority of the programmes came from independents and over which the ITV companies could not exercise control.

By another of those accidents of timing on which this story seems so often to hinge, on the day that Colin Shaw wrote to his colleague in the United States, a major industrial dispute broke out in ITV, blacking out the entire network. The ACTT and the ITV companies had been in negotiation over a new national agreement since early June. The union claimed that while prices had climbed by over 70% since 1975 their wages had increased by less than 50%. 'Only an increase above 20% will re-establish the purchasing power lost over four years of pay policy,' the union claimed.[21] In the same period, according to the union, ITV companies' share values had risen by 1,593%, their dividends by 161% and their profits by 189%. The companies, who had a particular need not only to stand firm but, at a time when decisions were being made that would determine their futures, also to be seen by the new government to be standing up to the unions, had responded with a 'final offer' of 15%. The unions riposted with a total, and very public, blackout of ITV.

* * *

' . . . All the key people involved in the new channel are playing their cards extremely close to their chests and are not revealing what they are. Firm proposals have to be made by the end of October. This blueprint will then be presented to the Home Office and we can expect to see the government's own proposals for legislation on ITV-2 placed before Parliament before the end of the year. So the time for argument, if it's to have any chance of being effective, is now.' Thus George Scott, the veteran BBC presenter, introduced the edition of BBC-1's *The Editors* devoted to the prospects for the forthcoming fourth channel, on Sunday 26 August 1979, the eve of the Edinburgh International Television Festival. Following a short compilation made up from some of the independent productions which had been shown in the presentation at BAFTA, Scott introduced a studio discussion on the fourth channel involving Julian Critchley (Chairman of the Conservative Backbench Media Committee), Alasdair Milne (Managing Director of BBC Television), Stuart Wilson (author of the proposal to set up the fourth channel as if it were a sixteenth franchise contractor), Mike Townsin of the advertising agency Young and Rubicam, and me, as a would-be independent and member of the Channel Four Group. With ITV blacked out by the ACTT neither the IBA nor the companies had been willing to provide a spokesman. Turning to Critchley and referring to the fact that he, and he claimed Whitelaw, had always supported an extension of ITV to run the fourth channel, Scott asked if this was likely to change. Critchley responded, 'Anything could happen, but it won't. Quite clearly ITV-2 is going to be in the Bill very much as we expect it to be. Therefore, what we ought to be discussing are the safeguards and the proportion of the different programmes shown by the different people in ITV-2.' Were the independents now going to be satisfied with 15% of programmes on the new channel, Scott wanted to know. No, we were not, I said, but to put the issue like that was to make us seem no more than another vested-interest group. 'I think there is a more important issue . . . If you give the new channel to the people who already control a channel you are almost bound to get more of the same. The health of broadcasting demands that it be independent of the existing people so that it can offer a different choice.' Milne, Wilson and Townsin joined in to support me. So Critchley took another tack. Turning to me, he said, 'The independent producers have been one of the most successful lobbies in British political history. Their lobbying owes a great deal to the skills of Phillip Whitehead and David Elstein . . . when one looks at the number of independent producers one actually marvels at the skill of that political lobby, because there are, in fact, hardly any of them at all.' Wilson, with the authority of a former managing director of Yorkshire Television, told Critchley that it was a matter of opportunity. Once there was a market for the independents' programmes, plenty of independents would appear, both from new entrants to the industry and from within ITV and the BBC. Milne chipped in, saying he thought that it was 'a marvellous idea'. But how much financial risk were the independents going to have to bear? (Milne, of course, had experienced the financial problems of being an independent when he left the BBC to set up an independent company with Baverstock and Jay.) Wilson said that it must go into the Bill that independents would get paid the full cost of production for their programmes and be left with the rights to sell programmes overseas so that they could build up businesses attractive to investors. I said that the new channel was not necessarily for people like me who were already able to work for the BBC and ITV, but for new people and people with new ideas. 'If it were the wrong channel it would be better not to have it.'[22]

However, this was but a polite skirmish before the real battle which was due to begin next day. The campaigners had realised ever since re-launching their campaign earlier in the summer that the one major public opportunity for them to influence both the public and the government before any irrevocable decision was made would be at that year's annual Edinburgh International Television Festival. Well-sourced rumour suggested that Home Office civil servants would be present, together with officials from the IBA and senior executives from the ITV companies. So the Channel Four Group had made up its mind to intervene in every debate during the week-long Festival, no matter what the topic, to bring the discussion back to the subject of the fourth channel. The weeks leading up to the Festival had turned into a race against time for the campaigners and their new 'organiser', Michael Jackson.

By the time the Festival opened on 27 August the small inner group of activists, led and co-ordinated by Jackson, was ready. A new thirteen-page position paper had been prepared – *TV4: The Case for Independence*, which carefully set out the arguments and the historical background to the Channel Four Group's case. The issue of the 'strict safeguards' mentioned in the Queen's Speech was examined – their importance, the paper said, 'must not be underestimated'. The recurring crises in the British film industry were cited as a warning of the consequences of repeated government failure 'to protect and encourage the expansion of the film industry. If TV4 is not to resemble the British film industry, if TV4 is to be truly independent of duopoly control, then the "strict safeguards" will need to ensure that the channel is politically, culturally and economically free of dominant ITV influence.' Turning to the IBA's plans, the paper said, 'Independents reject the IBA's plan for a 15% quota for independent production on TV4 not out of greed or self-aggrandisement but because conceding 15% of the channel' to independents would still leave the ITV companies in control of the channel. The IBA would have the power to make TV4 'properly independent. But', the paper asked, 'will it use that power?' Recalling the LWT debacle, the Channel Four Group doubted that it would. A checklist of things needed in the legislation to ensure that the IBA would use its power to secure the true independence of new channel followed. The fourth channel must be run by a board charged with the duty to uphold the principles of the channel. The members of the board need not be representative but rather should be people who had demonstrated 'an awareness of and concern for the television medium and the society it serves'. They should appoint a Programme Controller who must not be under any obligation to commit any specific quota of hours to the ITCA companies or their subsidiaries. It would be the duty of the controller 'to draw programmes from diverse sources . . . encourage new programme making ventures . . . purchase at least half its programmes from programme makers having no direct or indirect association with any ITCA contractor'. The money paid for programmes must properly reflect the full production costs of the programmes. Funding for the channel should come from advertising revenue collected by an agency or agencies under the supervision of the IBA. The channel should not acquire its own production facilities beyond those needed to keep it on the air and the Programme Controller must have complete freedom over the schedule of programmes on the channel.[23]

By the time the Edinburgh Television Festival opened, a small army of Channel Four Group speakers had been briefed and a whole range of leaflets prepared. Before each session Michael Jackson, Sophie Balhetchet and others were to dash into the venue as soon as the doors were opened and, before the audience could take their places, place an appropriately tailored sheet of facts, issues and questions on each chair. Back in AIP's cramped London offices, relays of other volunteers were standing by to type and roneo fresh leaflets and press releases to be rushed to Edinburgh on overnight trains as need arose. If the campaigners failed to make a sufficiently powerful and united impression now, Edinburgh would probably be their last throw.

As we travelled up to Edinburgh on Monday 27 August in time for the first set-piece event of the festival, the prestigious McTaggart Lecture to be delivered by Jeremy Isaacs at 6 p.m. in the hall of classically austere Georgian Edinburgh's Royal College of Physicians, news started to come in of the assassination by the IRA of Lord Mountbatten and members of his family on their boat off the coast of County Sligo. Approaching the Royal College of Physicians delegates were confronted by pickets of striking ACTT members bearing placards reading 'No ITV-1: Why?' or 'It's a Lock-Out!' Looking around inside the hall as the last of the two hundred or so delegates took their seats, we campaigners noted with satisfaction that officials from the Home Office Broadcasting Department were, as forecast, discretely dotted about the auditorium. The next four and a half days were to be 'do or die'.

The Festival was being held under the general title 'Television in the 80s' and the air of expectancy had been building for weeks. As already explained, Isaacs enjoyed a charismatic reputation among programme makers, built not only on the programmes for which he had been responsible in his years at Thames, but on his commitment to courageous journalism, innovative programme making and his consistent defence of programme makers. He inspired a loyalty among the programme makers who had worked for him unequalled, in my experience, by any other television executive in Britain. The manner of his leaving Thames a year earlier in the row over the Amnesty Castlereagh Interrogation Centre programme had served to enhance that reputation. His executive experience, his reputation and the fact that he was now 'available', made him the obvious front-runner for the post of Controller, if indeed there was going to be one, of the fourth channel. The MacTaggart Lecture would provide Isaacs with an ideal platform from which to set out his vision for the new channel. It was assumed he would use it to build an irresistible claim to the top job. Paul Bonner, the Festival chairman, and Colin Shaw, who was a member of the Festival Committee, had deliberately chosen Isaacs to deliver the lecture in the expectation of stirring up a good debate.

Plunging into his lecture, Isaacs came straight to the point. Quoting the words of the Queen's Speech about the IBA being given responsibility for the fourth channel ' – subject to strict safeguards – ', Isaacs said, 'The words "subject to strict safeguards" appear in parenthesis, almost as if they were inserted in the Gracious Speech as an afterthought. No one has yet made clear precisely what the safeguards will be, or, indeed, what it is they are intended to protect from whom.'

As responsibility for the channel had been handed to the IBA, it was reasonable to assume, he said, that the new channel would be set up more or less in accordance with the successive submissions made by the IBA over the previous ten years, each of which had been made on behalf of ITV and advocated ITV-2. So it was ITV-2 that we would have. Those who had argued for an OBA, who had argued for pluralism as the best way of extending and improving British broadcasting, who advocated the creation of a 'publisher' broadcaster in preference to yet another producer/broadcaster on the ITV/BBC model, may have won the argument, Isaacs said, but they had 'lost the vote'. The idea behind the OBA, that 'broadcasting systems should see themselves as publishers rather than authors, remains and ought to influence our practice', but those who wish to continue to argue for the OBA were wasting 'their energy and our time.' They also wasted their breath who continued to argue for a fully competitive fourth channel, competing all out for audiences and advertising against ITV-1. There still remained, Isaacs believed, a broad consensus among all political parties that 'the social purposes of British broadcasting are worth fostering. Our television is not, and I hope never will be, organised to suit advertising claims first, and all other claims after.'

Before turning to his own prescription for the fourth channel, Isaacs entered a stout defence of the quality of ITV as a public service broadcaster within a fully regulated system and of the BBC as 'still the best television service in the world'. He argued powerfully that it was the duty of the politicians to give the BBC the licence fee increase that it now so desperately needed in order that it could maintain the quality of the service. The BBC, he said, had been undermined and under-funded ever since the founding of BBC-2 in 1964. The practice in recent years by successive governments of awarding the BBC inadequate licence fee increases to last just one year after which the BBC had to apply all over again was 'no less than a national scandal . . . I say this to Mr Whitelaw. It is the BBC which sets the standard of television in this country. If the BBC is not strong the whole system is in peril.' So the first of the 'safeguards' talked about in the Queen's Speech should be a safeguard for the system as a whole – 'to grant the BBC the long-term licence fee increase it desperately needs'.

Isaacs then turned to his own prescription for the new 'fourth channel'. He said he wanted a channel which 'extends the choice available to viewers; which extends the range of ITV's programmes; which caters for substantial minorities presently neglected . . . which encourages worth while independent production . . . We want a fourth channel that will neither simply compete with ITV-1 nor merely be complementary to it. We want a fourth channel that everyone will watch some of the time and no-one all of the time. We want a fourth channel that will, somehow, be different.' Rhetorically asking, 'Can all these objectives be realised on ITV-2?', he answered that he believed they could, but 'I have to say I would not be optimistic if the channel were run by the IBA's proposed planning group, or by the Companies' Programme Controllers' Group enlarged. If the channel is to have a different flavour it needs a different chef.' Isaacs recommended that the channel have its own controller independent of the companies, but answerable to a board on which both the IBA and the companies were represented, which would plan not just the independents' contribution but the whole of ITV-2. The channel should be funded by a levy on the companies, paid in return for being given the right to sell the advertising on the new channel as well as on ITV-1. Isaacs suggested that a realistic target share of the total TV audience would be 10%.

Turning to the independent producers, he urged them to be modest in both their demands and their expectations. 'ITV-2 should provide access for a guaranteed number of hours each week for genuine independent producers. By "minimum" I mean that the volume can be increased if the need is there, or if sufficient programmes of originality and merit are on offer. By "genuine" I mean producers capable of conceiving and realising such programmes. Independent producers . . . cannot have, either individually or jointly, any automatic right to air-time. Under any procedure I can envisage, someone will have to select from what they offer.' That said, they should receive a 'fair price' for their productions. He was dismissive of the argument that once there was a demand for the programmes of independents the capacity to produce them – the producers, technicians and facilities – would appear to meet that demand. It would take time. 'Skilled film lighting cameramen, and all the back-up craftsmen and women that make up film and OB crewing are in high demand and short supply. Start work for the fourth channel tomorrow, and watch the bottlenecks build up,' he warned.

We campaigners listened with growing dismay as Isaacs rubbished one by one the central tenets of the programme makers' case ever since the Free Communications Group and the first appearance of Anthony Smith's proposal for a National Television Foundation. 'Independent producers do not represent a great new untapped source of energy and ideas. Many of them are gainfully employed at this time in the BBC or ITV. Their problem outside will be to assemble behind their projects, when they have backing for them, the people and facilities that will make them happen.' The creation of the fourth channel would, Isaacs conceded, suck into television a new influx of programme makers but, he seemed to imply, it would happen too slowly and would never be enough. 'Better by far, for all concerned, that the independent production sector begins modestly, supplying only what it knows it can supply with people and facilities it knows are there, than blows itself up early to unrealistic dimensions.'[24]

By the time the delegates reached the Edinburgh bars that evening, Isaacs' speech was being described as 'the best public job application ever made'. It seemed certain to please the IBA – and particularly any IBA appointments board seeking an ITV-2 chief executive – and the BBC; it also seemed likely to reassure the Home Office. Programme makers, too, welcomed his sentiments about the funding of the BBC, about the need to maintain broadcasting regulation, to defend the public service ethos against the commercial imperative, his desire to see a higher profile for black Britons and for women, and his call for more programmes that catered for the young. However, to us campaigners, what he had said about the role of the independents in the fourth channel was a massive disappointment. Isaacs had not put an actual figure on the percentage of independent production which he expected to see on the new channel, but as he had referred specifically to the latest IBA proposals for ITV-2, it had to be assumed that the figure he had in mind was, like the Authority's, around 15%.

In a Festival session the next morning the Head of Network Productions at BBC Birmingham summed up Isaacs' speech as 'A fine radical speech advocating more of the *status quo*'. One of the ITV executives responsible for the companies' original submission to the Annan Committee pointed out, with evident satisfaction, that the current proposals for independent productions were exactly what they had been under the ITV and IBA proposals put forward six or eight years earlier. Questioned by the campaigners, Isaacs dashed their expectations still further, forecasting that initially independent producers would only be capable of supplying some 10% of the channel's demand for programmes. Dissent, as the *Observer* reported, was loud and clear. Andrew Brown, producer of one of the most highly praised series made under Isaacs' aegis at Thames, *Rock Follies*, asked: 'If 60% of the programmes come from the existing ITV companies, how can it be different?'[25] Others wanted to know, 'How different was different?'; Isaacs' response was, 'Different, but not that different.' The effect of Isaacs' speech and his remarks the following day on the programme makers in the audience in

Edinburgh was appalling. I had always been one of Isaacs' strongest admirers, but addressing him from the floor, I said: 'While we're thinking small, the ITV companies will be getting larger.' As a result the independents would miss their chance for ever. Isaacs conceded that continuity of work was an important element in the achievement of excellence, so it might be unwise to start too small. Whereupon an ITV executive, Jeremy Wallington, jumped in to tell the independents to look at some of the less glamorous areas of programme making, rather than trying to concentrate on big-money, peak-time blockbusters. Isaacs added that it would be better for them to be 'magnificent specialists rather than mediocre all-rounders'.[26]

As the Festival progressed, the campaigners stuck to their plan of action. They intervened in every debate, turned every discussion to the subject of the fourth channel; to how vital it was that control of the channel was independent of the ITV companies, to the benefits to the channel and to broadcasting as a whole that would flow from it acquiring programmes from the widest diversity of sources, free of the domination of the ITV companies. Michael Jackson was proving every bit as energetic and effective as Sophie Balhetchet had anticipated. Each morning he would go down to Waverley Station in Edinburgh as soon as the Red Star parcels office opened to pick up fresh batches of leaflets for the coming day's debates, despatched on the overnight train by the volunteers back in AIP's London office. Balhetchet remembers that at the start of the Festival Michael Jackson had suddenly become nervous when faced with all these people who he had previously only heard about. But by the second day he had mastered any nerves and was handing out leaflets, buttonholing delegates and co-ordinating the Channel Four Group's speakers without flagging.

Turning the other Festival sessions to the fourth channel and the claims of the would-be independent producers was not too difficult. On the second day, after the discussion of Isaacs' speech, debate centred on the 'industrialisation' of television. The debate took as its starting point a paper by Anthony Smith which opened, 'It's about five years now since people started saying that an "industrial" mood had taken over British television, that it had ceased to feel like a primarily creative activity, or like a primarily public service.' (Most of the programme makers in the hall would probably have dated it earlier, around the time of *Broadcasting in the '70s* at the BBC and the 1968 ITV strike.) Saying that some people put this down to overlarge units, some to the end of expansion, some to anonymous managements, swollen bureaucracy or swollen profits, Smith added that others put it down to 'a spirit of concentrated venality [that] has entered the body of television and is slowly eating its heart out'.

Smith should have been joined on the platform by the General Secretaries of the ACTT and the ABS, but Alan Sapper of the ACTT had gone to London for further negotiations over the ITV strike, taking the rest of the ACTT delegation with him. A senior Yorkshire Television drama producer voiced the secret thoughts of many when, speaking from the floor, he denounced both management and unions as 'mean-spirited, greedy bastards' who were 'as happy as pigs in shit. They love the stalemate.' Michael Grade, the only ITV network company senior executive present, then got up and, introducing himself with a characteristic joke as, 'LWT, resting', bemoaned the lack of understanding on both sides. The solution to television's industrial relations problems was, he suggested, for more producers and directors to 'get off their arses' and involve themselves in negotiations. That, I told him angrily, was an irresponsible suggestion. 'You're asking us to become stalking horses for management.' Seizing their cue, the campaigners leapt in, pointing out that the frustrations of producers and directors, like those of technicians, were mainly down to greedy, short-sighted management attitudes which did not allow technicians to become sufficiently creatively involved in the productions that they worked on. The cameraman, Charles Stewart, pointed out that ever since the 1960s one of the programme makers' central demands had been an end to the artificial distinction made by television managements between 'creative' personnel, producers and directors, and technicians, who were employed as members of staff and treated as units of labour, interchangeable between one kind of production and another with scant regard to individual talents or opportunity for becoming more creatively involved in the productions on which they worked. Paul Bonner pointed out that, because of shortage of funds, no trial of the BBC's internal proposals for small integrated production units, designed to alleviate these very problems, had ever been attempted. All of which led Anthony Smith and others back to the fourth channel and the possibility that, provided it was run on the lines advocated for the OBA and in the proposals put forward by the Channel Four Group, it could offer a way forward.

By the end of the second day the campaigners could feel that things were going pretty much according to plan. But on day three things changed sharply. Word got out that six drama producers who had done 'packaging deals' with broadcasters, under which they supplied scripts and certain key creative personnel and then used the broadcasters' facilities and technicians to shoot and edit their programmes, had sent a telex to the chairwoman of the IBA, Lady Plowden, and to Sir Brian Young, with copies to William Whitelaw and the Home Office, offering to put their expertise at the disposal of the IBA over the central issues relating to the fourth channel – the volume of production to be supplied by independents and the basis on which such programmes were to be paid for. 'We, the undersigned producers', they wrote, 'wish to participate in the channel four debate . . . We are all interested in supplying independently-produced drama programmes to channel four and would like to help in the establishment of a flourishing independent television production community in Britain. We are available now and would appreciate an early meeting.' Questioned by journalists, they had denied that they were setting up a fresh consortium to feed on 'possible pickings' from the fourth channel. One of them, Mark Shivas, told a reporter from *Broadcast*, 'We all have good track records and felt that we could form a more effective lobby as a small group than as part of a larger one.'[27] None of these people was a member of the Channel Four Group, although some had taken part in earlier campaigns to block ITV-2. They included Kenith Trodd (who, with Dennis Potter and their company Pennies From Heaven Ltd, had recently signed an agreement to produce plays for LWT), Andrew Brown, Tony Garnett and Stella Richman, the short-lived LWT Controller of Programmes fired by Murdoch in 1971. To the leaders of the Channel Four Group they looked ominously like another bunch of would-be carpetbaggers. Their emergence highlighted once again the necessity of preventing those campaigning for the fourth channel from arguing with each other and the need to concentrate everyone's efforts on fighting for the central issue, the creation of a channel that was not dominated by ITV, was free to select its programmes on merit from a wide variety of sources and to control its own schedule. The members of this new producers' group made no secret of the fact that they regarded the demands of the Channel Four Group as the 'pie-in-the-sky'.

When Phillip Whitehead called for the Festival to make minimum recommendations on the percentage of the new channel's programmes to be supplied by independents and on the financial conditions to apply to the channel's purchase of such programmes, he provoked an angry reaction from people working for the broadcasters. People the campaigners would normally have regarded as kindred spirits laid into the would-be independents. They also felt frustrated, they said, because their boldest and most innovative programme ideas were not being accommodated by the companies on ITV-1. For the campaigners to claim that the new channel should be used for new voices and new ideas belittled their ideas and their work, threatening to confine them to ITV-1 for ever. Gus Macdonald tried to calm them down, warning that too often those who worked on the staff of ITV companies appeared to act as auxiliaries to those companies, often revealing a worrying 'conspiracy of interest' with their managements. The effect of creating a truly independent fourth channel, Macdonald said, should be just as dramatic, and beneficial, for programme makers inside ITV companies as for those outside them.

The author, front row left, and Phillip Whitehead, unidentified delegate, right of her, with his head lowered, Michael Jackson and, behind him, Michael Grade; standing, the producer W. Stephen Gilbert during the debate.

Courtesy of *Broadcast*

During the week a number of other potential contenders for the job of Controller of the new channel seemed to try to stake their own claims to the top job. Anthony Smith had provided the focus for one important debate, Brian Wenham, the Controller of BBC-2, was much in evidence during a number of sessions, as was Paul Bonner, who was chairing the whole Festival. Giving a lecture on censorship, John Birt too appeared bent on staking a claim. Birt's thinking had clearly moved a long way towards the ideas of Anthony Smith since he had written his letter with David Elstein to Sir John Eden back in 1973. His lecture ended with a rallying call which, on paper if not exactly in delivery, should have united the campaigners and radicals in support of a John Birt candidacy: 'When the fourth channel is housed in the inevitable rather tatty tower block, may I suggest an inscription to be placed over the door. A slogan for broadcasting in the eighties of just five words: LET ALL VOICES BE HEARD.'[28] Although in its report on the festival the *Observer* hailed Birt as 'the hero of the week' and 'at 34 the Peter Pan of television', he did not inspire the kind of loyalty among programme makers inspired by Jeremy Isaacs. However, Isaacs had now put that loyalty under severe strain.

An official from the Home Office was billed to appear on the platform as a member of the panel on the final morning of the Festival. But by the time the expectant delegates had assembled to hear what he might say, the civil servant had thought better of it. Gus Macdonald had to announce to the crowded hall that the Home Office had decided to save what it had to say for a speech due to be delivered by the Home Secretary at the Royal Television Society's Cambridge Convention in two weeks' time.

Gus Macdonald tells delegates that the Home
Office representative has decided not to appear
at the final session of the Festival.

Courtesy of *Broadcast*

Michael Grade at the rostrum

Courtesy of Broadcast

Platform during final debate of the Festival (left to right: David Glencross of the IBA, Colin Young chairing the debate and Robin Scott, Deputy Managing Director, BBCtv. Beside him, an empty place for the Home Office representative.

Courtesy of Broadcast

Notes

1. The row had centred in particular on a shot of a headstone bearing an inscription which included the words 'murdered by the British Army'.
2. The company's name was taken from the triumphantly successful series of the same name written by Potter and produced by Trodd, shown by BBC a year earlier.
3. Report of speech by David Elstein in *Film and Television Technician*, June 1979.
4. Told to the author by David Elstein in an interview in November 2000.
5. Report of ACTT 1979 Annual Conference, *Film and Television Technician*, June 1979.
6. *Aspects of Channel Four Programming*, text of a speech by Colin Shaw to the Broadcasting Press Guild 6 June 1979, reprinted in *Independent Broadcasting*, the journal of the IBA, Number 21, August 1979.
7. *The IBA and Channel Four*, lecture delivered by Sir Brian Young on 26 June 1979 at the BAFTA International Television Festival, reprinted in *Independent Broadcasting*, Number 21, August 1979.
8. David Elstein, interviewed by the author in November 2000.
9. No record of that crucial informal meeting seems to exist but it must have taken place in late May or early June 1979.
10. *Broadcast*, 2 July 1979.
11. This rumour was referred to as a fact during an IBA/ITV drama seminar a few weeks later.
12. Report in the July 1979 edition of *AIP & Co.*
13. Sophie Balhetchet, interviewed by the author in December 2000.
14. Michael Jackson, interviewed by the author in October–November 2000.
15. Internal paper by David Elstein for the Channel Four Group, dated 7 July 1979, a copy of which is in the author's possession.
16. Paper by the author for the Channel Four Group, dated 8 July 1979.
17. *Broadcast*, 30 July 1979.
18. Price had stood as a 'very Left-wing' – Price's description – Conservative candidate in the 1970 general election.
19. Letter from Colin Shaw to Michael Rice, Programme Director, Aspen Institute, Washington, DC, dated 10 August 1979, held in the Anthony Smith papers at the British Film Institute.
20. Letter dated 10 August 1979, from Colin Shaw at the IBA to Michael Rice, Programme Director of the Aspen Institute, Washington, DC, a copy of which is held in the Anthony Smith papers at the BFI.
21. *Film and Television Technician*, 1979.
22. *The Editors*, transmitted on BBC-1 on 26 August 1979.
23. *TV4: The Case for Independence*, a position paper prepared by the Channel Four Group, London, 1979.
24. From the text of The 1979 McTaggart Lecture, delivered by Jeremy Isaacs and reproduced in the Official Programme of the Edinburgh International Television Festival 1980, published by *Broadcast*.

25. *Observer*, 2 September 1979. The remaining 40% would, it was assumed, be made up of programmes from the ITV regional companies, news, educational material produced for the Open University, material bought in from the USA and elsewhere, plus whatever percentage remained for the independents.

26. I have drawn on reports of the debate in the *Observer*, 2 September 1979, *Broadcast*, 10 September 1979 and recollections by Isaacs, myself and others who took part.

27. *Broadcast*, 10 September 1979.

28. From *Freedom and the Broadcaster*, a lecture by John Birt, given in memory of Clive Goodwin at the 1979 Edinburgh International Television Festival and reproduced in the Official Programme of the 1980 Edinburgh International Television Festival, published by *Broadcast*.

7

Battle for the Bill – 1979 to 1980

Whatever else they might have achieved at Edinburgh, the members of the Channel Four Group had made it clear that in spite of the changed political situation they were not going to go away. Inside the ITV companies this had been noted. Early in August Gus Macdonald had taken part in an internal conference of senior Granada executives on the consequences of the introduction of the fourth channel. He had warned his colleagues about what he saw as a dangerous complacency among ITV executives and a tendency to dismiss the independents. He had urged his colleagues to view the independents not as enemies but as possible allies in the battle to reduce costs, introduce more flexible systems of working, bring in new blood and fresh ideas. ITV needed the talents of such people, not their hostility. Immediately after Edinburgh, Macdonald's boss, Sir Denis Forman, sent him a note. He had noted what he had said and agreed that the 'companies are foolish to regard the Independents as anything but allies'. But, Forman said, since then things have changed. Since Edinburgh the independents' 'posture' has become clear.[1]

Returning to London, I wrote to David Glencross at the IBA. Although I wrote privately I indicated that I was confident that what I said coincided with the views of other Channel Four Group campaigners. I told him that on the financing of the new channel my view had shifted somewhat in the light of Edinburgh, and now coincided with that of Jeremy Isaacs. The most secure way, I now believed, to ensure both the channel's financial viability and its independence, would be to extend the payments made by the ITV companies under the Exchequer Levy system to include a sum sufficient to meet the costs of the fourth channel. In return the companies should be granted the right to sell the advertising on the new channel, thus maintaining their monopoly over the sale of television advertising airtime. I had been worried and saddened, I told him, that talented programme makers inside ITV felt threatened by the independents. It would be the duty of independents like myself to strive for a genuinely independent fourth channel which would offer opportunities to good programme makers inside the companies to make programmes which their employers would not contemplate showing on ITV. I concluded by giving Glencross my own rather gloomy forecast of what would actually happen over the fourth channel. The ITCA companies, and their subsidiaries such as ITN, would expand their capacity so as to enable them to supply the vast majority of the new channel's programmes. The independents would be 'guaranteed a small percentage of airtime (say 15%) with the intention that this should be increased when they have "proved" themselves'. This they would do quite quickly, but by then the increased 'output levels in the ITCA companies will have become established norms which . . . neither management nor unions will then be willing to cut back to make way for new and developing independent production'. A solution to the problem might be to slowly increase the total number of hours of broadcasting on the new channel after it started. Even so, the result was likely to mean new independent production being ghettoised in slots outside peak viewing hours.[2] A few days later Glencross replied: 'Try and be a little less gloomy about Channel Four! It just might be the success story of the 1980s.'[3]

*   *   *

The Royal Television Society's biennial Cambridge Convention was by tradition the occasion at which Home Secretaries outlined to the industry their government's thinking about the future direction of any legislation. Over the weekend of 14 to 16 September, the new Home Secretary, William Whitelaw, was expected to outline the plans of Margaret Thatcher's government for ITV-2.

In those days (and to some extent still) the RTS Cambridge Convention was an exclusive gathering where broadcasting's establishment talked to itself and to its political masters in an atmosphere redolent of the participants' youth – living in draughty college rooms, dressing up in the evenings to eat dinners of uneatable food in college dining rooms, preceded by grace and followed by sometimes puerile after-dinner speeches, passing any unfilled hours by forming parties to go punting on the Backs. The RTS Cambridge Convention in 1979 was not, therefore, a place where delegates were likely to be troubled by the presence of many upstart would-be independent producers or disaffected programme makers. The campaigners could only hope that their efforts in Edinburgh and over the previous ten years had been enough.

When the Home Secretary rose to address the assembled suits he made it clear that he did not intend to publish another White Paper. He indicated that what he was about to say would set out the essence of what would be contained in a new broadcasting bill. Whitelaw opened with reassurance. Talks were already advanced to secure the future funding of the BBC; the BBC Charter and the life of the IBA were both to be extended; there was, as expected, to be no OBA, the fourth channel would be the responsibility of the IBA. Competitive advertising on the fourth channel was out, it would 'inevitably result in a move towards single-minded concentration on maximising audiences for programmes, with adverse consequences for both the commercial channels and before long for the BBC as well'. Whitelaw then turned to the government's prescriptions for the fourth channel and the crucial issue of the 'strict safeguards' referred to in the Queen's Speech. 'I start from the position that what we are looking for is a fourth channel offering a distinctive service of its own . . . there must be programmes appealing to and, we hope, stimulating tastes and interests not adequately provided for on the existing channels.' He knew that the existing channels had identified some of these so-called minority interests but he was convinced 'there is much more of worth which could be done'. It would not be right to try to specify the proportion of programmes which would come from various sources. 'But the fourth channel should not be dominated by the network companies. There will, therefore, be a substantial contribution from the regional, as opposed to the network, ITV contractors and from the independent producers.' Independent producers had 'a most important role to play' and the fourth channel must provide a fair return on their products. 'It is important that independent producers not only have new opportunities to see their programmes broadcast, but that they receive a fair negotiated market price for what they are selling.' He did not intend to spell out the details yet, but 'the arrangements for the acquisition of programmes for, and the scheduling of programmes on, the fourth channel will need to be separate from that for ITV-1'. The channel would be expected to extend the range of programmes available to the public and 'to find new ways of serving minority audiences and to give due place to innovation'. Not only would the new channel not be expected to compete with ITV for audiences, the two services together would not be scheduled so as to obtain for each the largest possible audience. (ITV executives had talked of ITV-2 aiming for 25% of the audience which Alasdair Milne had said would amount to a declaration of war on the BBC.) Last in Whitelaw's list of 'strict safeguards' came the most important of all for the independent producers – the IBA would be expected 'to make arrangements for the largest practical proportion of programmes on the fourth channel to be supplied by organisations and persons other than the companies contracted to supply programmes on ITV-1'.[4] The government wanted the new channel to be on the air in three years' time – in the autumn of 1982.

'This speech naturally disappointed the big ITV companies' is how Shirley Littler (the senior civil servant in the Home Office's Broadcasting Department) describes the reaction of the ITV bosses to what Whitelaw had said. This is a considerable understatement. Although relieved that they were going to keep their monopoly on the sale of advertising, they were appalled that they were not to get control of the channel or to supply the vast majority of the programmes for it. To many ITV executives Whitelaw's words came as a bombshell. John Freeman seems to have reacted particularly badly. Shirley Littler remembers him asking her how deeply Whitelaw was committed to entirely separate scheduling for the new channel and explaining to her the advantages of complementary scheduling in maximising audiences for the ITV system. She says, in a character-istic piece of civil servicese, 'I was non-committal, but interested in his professional advice.'[5] Speaking during the debate after Whitelaw's speech, Freeman, in pressing the companies' case for complementary scheduling, declared that any other arrangement would be 'a recipe for muddle, friction and failure'.[6]

The ITV companies were not alone in their confusion. Even the few independent producers who were present seem not to have grasped the full significance of what Whitelaw had said. The IBA, it appears, had itself not been warned of what Whitelaw was going to say. David Glencross admits that he was surprised – 'I had thought in terms of ITV-2.'[7] Sir Denis Forman, who had seen quite a lot of Whitelaw in the weeks leading up to the speech, says, 'The IBA had totally lost touch with what was going on politically.'[8]

After Whitelaw had spoken, it fell to Colin Shaw to make the immediate formal response on behalf of the IBA. He describes himself as having been 'not intellectually unprepared' for Whitelaw's speech – 'I had not the slightest sympathy with the idea that ITV-2 should be the creature of the companies. I brought with me from the BBC a suspicion of the ITV companies. ITV, like the BBC, was too big and cumbersome. I also had the view that the unions were too powerful and helped to stifle creativity.'[9] Even so, as we know from Shaw's letter to his American colleague only a month earlier, he had not expected Whitelaw to go as far as he had over the separation of the fourth channel from ITV or to lay such a heavy stress on the importance of the role of independent producers. As a result, in his response Shaw signalled one immediate retreat from the position taken by the IBA's Director-General, Sir Brian Young, in his BAFTA speech in June. Then Young had talked of the new channel having 'many constituents' including ITN, the independent producers, education and the ITV companies' and of its schedules being arrived at by a series of 'committees and bodies and boards'. Now Shaw accepted that the new channel would need a single controller rather than some kind of panel – 'This is, I realise, a recipe for megalomania on a scale unparalleled since Diaghilev or Randolph Hearst. Unlike these megalomaniacs, however, this controller will be accountable in this world rather than the next.' At the same time the channel would have to be distanced from the IBA and operate with an independent budget. 'The IBA must not appear to be the judge of ITV-1 and the co-inspirator of ITV-2,' he said.[10]

It was Freeman who, as well as being Chairman of London Weekend Television, was chairing the Convention, had the final word. He was almost certainly expressing the fears of all his colleagues in ITV when, in summing up at the end of the Convention, he reminded the assembled ranks of broadcasting's establishment that the Report of the Annan Committee had been entitled *The Future of Broadcasting*. 'It might', he said, 'have been called *Institutional Television: The Final Ten Years.*' This was greeted with laughter. Laughter betraying fear?

When news of what Whitelaw had said reached the campaigners they were elated. The years of campaigning and the work on the Annan Committee seemed to have paid off. Although Whitelaw claimed later that he had made up his mind about what he wanted to do over the vacant fourth channel by the time that the Conservatives got into power in May 1979, the evidence suggests that the efforts of the campaigners in the few weeks between the election in May 1979 and Whitelaw's speech at the Cambridge Convention in September, together with the initiatives taken by Anthony Smith and others before the election to win over people like Keith Joseph, had substantially changed the government's mind. Whitelaw's statement was a big advance on the policies outlined in his article published in the Royal Television Society's Journal immediately before the election and on the bald statement in the Queen's Speech.

However, substantial worries remained for the campaigners. As the anonymous author of the report in the RTS Journal on the proceedings of the Cambridge Convention commented, whatever arrangements were put in place for the fourth channel, pressure was still likely to come 'from the existing franchise holders, which wish to protect their investments and profitability'. The new channel was still to be the responsibility of the IBA and it was going to be known as 'ITV-2'. In 1962 the Pilkington Committee had branded the IBA the ITV companies' advocate rather than their regulator. The campaigners still feared that, despite Whitelaw's words, the IBA would attempt to aid and abet the ITV companies in hijacking Whitelaw's ideas, subtly turning them so as to realise their own long-cherished ambitions for a channel with which to compete head-on with the BBC. In addition, as we have seen, as the possibility of real programmes, and with them real money, had drawn nearer, potential splits had started to appear in the campaigners' own ranks. Anyway, what proportion was 'the largest practical proportion' of programmes? In Edinburgh Isaacs had suggested it might be as little as 10%, while the IBA had still not budged beyond 15%. It might be fine to talk about the independents 'starting modestly' and of their share of programmes growing once they had 'proved' themselves. But for reasons we have explored, starting small would, in practice, almost certainly mean staying small. In my letter to Glencross after Edinburgh I had told him that the Channel Four Group was exploring means by which they could quantify the actual production capacity of the independent sector in order to demonstrate that our claims were based on 'something much more substantial than assertion and faith in history'. Events such as the BAFTA screening organised by Elstein had shown, for those who were either so blinkered or ill-informed that they did not already know it, that independents and freelances could make good programmes and that currently they got a raw deal from the broadcasters. The task now, which was becoming ever more urgent, would be to demonstrate that we could make programmes in sufficient volume and across a broad enough range to meet at least half the requirements of a whole television channel.

The debate inside the IBA on how ITV-2 should be set up and run was already well advanced by the time Whitelaw spoke in Cambridge and the Authority's officials had no intention of being deflected. Less than two weeks after Whitelaw's Cambridge speech the IBA held a long-planned consultation, one of the aims of which, it was claimed, was to quantify the capacity of the independent sector. About 150 people turned up, a number which Lady Plowden, who chaired the IBA, admitted to those present surprised her. The IBA, she confessed, had underestimated the likely response from independent producers. In fact, about a third of the people at the consultation could, fairly, already be said to be 'independent producers'. Most of the rest were freelances, aspirants and other interested parties – such as the Independent Filmmakers' Association, which had put forward its own case for special arrangements for 'innovative and experimental work' through the creation of a 'foundation', which would receive 10% of the channel's budget. Although the IBA's consultation did little to really quantify the potential capacity of the independent sector, the fact that enough people had turned up to elicit an admission of surprise from Lady Plowden perhaps did more than anything that was said to start the long process of loosening the impression in the minds of those running the IBA, fostered by the ITV companies and bolstered by Isaacs, that the independents did not 'represent a great new untapped source of programmes'.

The campaigners immediately set about trying to loosen it still further. *TV4 Whom?*, the lead article in the edition of the AIP magazine immediately following Whitelaw's Cambridge speech, declared: 'It is fundamental that "the largest practical proportion" means the *majority* of programmes, not the 15% of airtime which the IBA originally and grudgingly conceded to independent producers.'[11] Michael Jackson started sending out dozens of copies of a Channel Four Group statement intended for publication as an open letter to the Home Secretary. Jackson invited people to sign it and contribute £10 towards costs. Referring directly to Whitelaw's speech and his injunction that the fourth channel must 'find new ways of serving minority and specialised audiences' and give due place to innovation, the statement said, 'We, the undersigned, wholeheartedly endorse the spirit of your address.' Whitelaw's speech, it asserted, challenged the IBA to come up with 'a radically different approach to broadcasting in this country'. It went on to list key issues identified by Whitelaw which would determine the character of the new channel – that the 'arrangements for the acquisition and scheduling of programmes . . . will need to be separate from ITV; that the largest practical proportion of programmes' would need to come from sources other than the ITV companies, that the channel must have adequate and assured finance for the commissioning of programmes from independent producers and that the IBA must prevent a ratings war between ITV and the fourth channel. It then listed a set of principles that the signatories wanted incorporated into the legislation in order to protect the independence of the new channel. These included a management board for the channel answerable to the IBA; a programme controller who, once appointed, should 'have no connection whatsoever with the BBC or ITV' and who must be free 'to schedule independently of the ITV companies in consultation with the IBA'. The open letter also called for 'a progressive build-up of hours for TV4 with a majority of the channel's programmes to come from sources wholly independent of the BBC and ITV', and guaranteed finance to fund the channel's programme needs 'so that no organisation has a lien on programme time'.[12] When the statement appeared, as a half-page advertisement in the *Guardian* on 10 October, headed *The Fourth Television Channel: An Open Letter to the Home Secretary*, it included the names of almost four hundred signatories – prominent programme makers, campaigners, organisations involved in films, broadcasting and the arts, production and facility companies, together with politicians, trade unionists, academics, journalists and even senior people in ITV companies and the BBC. Among them were David Attenborough, Ballet Rambert, Tony Benn, James Cameron, a branch of British Actors' Equity, Richard Eyre, Tony Garnett, the Greater London Arts Association, Richard Hoggart, John Hurt, Tom Jackson, Gus Macdonald, Leo McKern, Mike Leigh, Michael Meacher, David Mercer, Molinaire Ltd, Christopher Morahan, The Moving Picture Company, Dipak Nandy, Lord Seebohm, the Society of Authors and The Robert Stigwood Group.

The numbers prepared to put their names to the open letter were impressive in themselves, but more important still were the range of views represented and the breadth and depth of both talent and potential production capacity. The advertisement demonstrated that the Channel Four Group, by promoting a set of clear principles, had assembled a range and volume of support that it would be difficult for the IBA simply to ignore. The signatories included not only some of the most respected creative talent in the industry but many of the biggest facility and production companies outside the BBC and ITV. It might not precisely quantify the independent sector's production capacity, but it ought to go a long way towards substantiating the claim that, given time, independent producers would be able to provide at least half of the programmes for the new channel.

But the IBA and the ITV companies were not idle either. As Michael Jackson and the campaigners were collecting signatures and £10 subscriptions for their advertisement, the IBA was preparing a set of detailed proposals for submission to Whitelaw and had invited the ITV companies to prepare a confidential memorandum setting out their ideas in the light of what he had said. The companies had set to with a will. In a nod to Whitelaw's ideas for 'safeguards', the companies proposed that the channel should be owned by a trust, to be owned jointly by the IBA and themselves. This trust would appoint a board of ten governors to run the channel. In addition to a chairman and deputy chairman there would be one with special responsibility for education and two with responsibility for independent production. The remaining five would come from the ITV companies – two from the major network companies and three from the smaller regional companies. Scheduling of the channel was to be complementary and subservient to the needs of ITV-1. They justified this on grounds of their 'experience in the various intricacies of scheduling'. They clearly still regarded the role of independent producers as peripheral, assuming that they would contribute no more than 10–15% of output. On top of this they rejected any idea of the channel putting up any seed money or development costs for programmes from independents: 'ITV-2 should never become involved in prospective or retrospective finance or development before a proposal is put and accepted.'[13]

Two days after the Channel Four Group's open letter to the Home Secretary appeared in the *Guardian* I received a phone call from the secretary of my old boss, the Chairman of Granada Television, Sir Denis Forman. Would I like to come up to his office for a drink at the end of the day? Despite my publicly acrimonious departure from Granada ten years earlier, my personal relations with Sir Denis had remained cordial and I had continued occasionally to work for Granada on a freelance basis. No indication was given as to the purpose of this meeting but I was in little doubt that it was intended as more than a social visit. It seemed to me unlikely that it was about a job and, knowing that Sir Denis was deeply involved in the ITV companies' campaign for ITV-2, I guessed that it would turn out to have something to do with the fourth channel and my role in the campaign. But what? I was puzzled. We met at 5 p.m. on a Friday in Sir Denis's modest but comfortable office above Granada's headquarters in Golden Square, looking down on that iconic thoroughfare of the Swinging Sixties, Carnaby Street, which by 1979 was a tatty tourist trap characterised by its purveyors of overpriced souvenirs. Once the whiskies were poured and pleasantries completed, Sir Denis turned to what he had in mind. None of my private speculations ahead of the meeting had prepared me for what he now suggested. With every outward semblance of being serious, he said that he wished to become a member of the Channel Four Group. After all, he said, he was entirely in favour of the creation of the fourth channel. It was the sort of dramatic moment, rich in irony, which I knew Sir Denis secretly enjoyed. Deciding that one piece of disingenuousness deserved another, I replied that I felt sure that my colleagues in the Channel Four Group would be delighted to accept him as a member of the group. But, I felt that I had to point out to him that membership did carry with it certain public commitments to central planks of the Group's policy. The most important of these were that Channel Four must be controlled by a board totally separate from the ITV companies, run by a chief executive who was independent of the ITV companies and scheduled independently of ITV. If signing up to these policies was not an embarrassment to him, I felt certain that my colleagues would be happy to welcome him – with open arms and in public! Sir Denis seemed totally unfazed by this and when we parted he assured me that he would think about all that we had said over the weekend.

On the Monday morning a hand-delivered note arrived at our home from Sir Denis. He had thoroughly enjoyed our conversation, he told me. At his time of life, he continued, 'I am positively unembarrassable'. However, upon reflection, he felt that his application to join the Channel Four Group 'might perhaps embarrass others – such as my colleagues and maybe some of yours'. Could we, therefore, 'defer' his application 'for the time being'? He might well ask me, he said, to re-activate it when the time was right. 'In one matter I know we are both completely at one, which is that the new channel must offer new talent an opportunity whether through independents or through the companies. We are going to need all the support we can get for this point of view.'[14] Although I did not spot it at the time, Sir Denis has recently explained to me that, in addition to being a ploy, his suggested application to join the Channel Four Group was intended to signal to the independents that Granada considered itself independent of the ITV companies over the issue of the fourth channel.

On the day that I met Sir Denis, 19 October 1979, the ACTT/ITV strike ended in ignominious defeat for the ITV companies. After ten weeks, during which the entire ITV network (with the exception of the tiny Channel Islands station) had been closed down, the technicians had finally settled for an increase of 45%, which amounted to roughly treble the last 'new final offer' of 15% made by the companies to the unions in July. Michael Grade, then the Controller of Programmes at LWT, is today in no doubt that it was this ten-week strike that was the seminal event in the battle over the fourth channel between the independents and the ITV companies – 'We had blank screens. I don't think the independents would have happened had it not been in the interests of the Baroness (Mrs Thatcher) . . . That was the background and the context.'[15] By the late 1970s the 'Spanish practices' of trade unions inside ITV had become a byword for greed and all that was wrong with British industrial relations. Stories of the exorbitant sums earned by technicians in ITV in overtime, of rigging of the shift patterns and of holding managements up to ransom with threatened walk-outs that would black out the network had spread well beyond the industry. Michael Grade would not have been accused by his colleagues in ITV managements of exaggeration when he put it in his autobiography that 'A kind of collective madness had infected the entire industry and distorted any rational sense of priorities.' In his memoirs he repeats stories familiar in many companies of cameramen so incompetent that they could barely get a shot in focus who it was impossible to fire because of the power of the unions, of videotape engineers who earned £100,000 a year at 1979 prices by fixing the shift rostering system, and repeats a popular industry joke of the period: 'What is the difference between an Arab oil sheikh and an LWT video engineer?' 'The Arab oil sheikh doesn't get London weighting.'[16] As the strike had dragged on without a settlement, the companies had started to blame each other for the mounting losses in advertising revenue. In the end it had been, as Sir Denis Forman described it, 'the old story of brave talk in the boardrooms ("time for a showdown") giving way in due course to panic in the face of unacceptable losses and a final scramble for the best deal that could be got'. The ITV companies' capitulation had done them immeasurable harm in the eyes of Mrs Thatcher, who had set her sights on getting management to stand up to unions and finding means of curbing union power. For ten weeks ITV screens had been blank, a continuous provocation and reminder to Mrs Thatcher, her ministers and their constituents of the ITV companies' abysmal performance in industrial relations, an emblem of the so-called 'British disease' which the Conservative government had been elected to cure. We independents knew that our case for a new way of making television programmes and a channel which did without old institutions held captive by the unions must look ever more appealing to Keith Joseph and Mrs Thatcher.

* * *

The BBC was also in hot water with the government. The press had picked up a story about a *Panorama* film crew who, while working on a programme about the IRA, had received an anonymous phone call informing them that if they got down to a village called Carrickmore they 'might see something interesting'. On arrival the crew, led by director David Darlow (no relation) and reporter Jeremy Paxman, had found a roadblock where masked armed men were stopping cars. There was nothing particularly unusual about such incidents in Northern Ireland. The unit had filmed it and then got on with the rest of their story. Although neither the programme nor any of the footage that the BBC crew had shot had been transmitted, rumour of the incident leaked out and three weeks later, on 8 November, reached the London press which ran a series of exaggerated stories under lurid headlines accusing the BBC of stage-managing the incident in order to film it. '*Panorama* – Dupes of the Air' ran a *Daily Mail* headline, while the *Daily Express* screamed 'BBC Outrage'. Thus provoked, Mrs Thatcher ordered William Whitelaw to leave a Cabinet meeting to telephone the Chairman of the BBC Governors and express her anger. That afternoon at Prime Minister's Question Time in the House of Commons Mrs Thatcher denounced the BBC, saying that 'It is time the BBC put its own house in order.' She added that the incident seemed to be a matter for the Director of Public Prosecutions. Following this the BBC was made, under the provisions of the Prevention of Terrorism Act, to hand over the uncut rushes of the filming to the police. It was the first time that the Act had been used to curb the activities of journalists in this way and it set a dangerous precedent. The incident itself seemed fairly quickly forgotten, but its memory lingered both in the mind of Mrs Thatcher and on the BBC records of two people shortly to feature in this story, Roger Bolton, the editor of *Panorama*, and John Gau, the BBC's Head of Current Affairs.

*   *   *

When the IBA published its proposals for the fourth channel in mid-November, the members of the Channel Four Group were outraged.

As was to be expected, the IBA repeated the principles enunciated by Whitelaw, but combined them with large elements of its own thinking and of the confidential proposals submitted to the Authority by the ITV companies. There were no more than a few nods in the direction of the ideas of the Channel Four Group. The main elements of the IBA plan were that the channel 'should extend the range of programmes available to the public; that there should not be competitive selling of advertising on the two channels; that the channel's budget should not necessarily be limited to the revenue earned from advertisements shown on it; that arrangements for planning and scheduling should not be dominated by the big ITV companies; and that, while the number of programmes from the regional ITV companies and ITN should be increased, there should be the opportunity for as many programmes as practical to be supplied from sources other than the ITV contractors'. Reiterating Colin Shaw's point at Cambridge about the IBA not wishing to be seen as 'the judge of ITV-1 and the co-inspirator of ITV-2', the Authority proposed establishing a separate company with its own board to run the channel. A board of twelve to fourteen members was proposed, to be 'chosen by the Authority after consultation'. In addition to an independent chairman and deputy chairman, the members would 'broadly represent', but not be delegates of, those likely to provide programmes for the service – four from the ITV companies 'which, as well as providing some of the programmes for the Fourth Channel, will be providing virtually all its budget'; five 'would be able to speak on behalf of other potential suppliers of programmes.' The company would have 'a considerable degree of independence – but it would be subject to the ultimate control of the Authority' which would retain responsibility for appointing the non-executive members of the board, would set the channel's annual budget, and approve the programme schedule so as to ensure co-ordination of the schedules of ITV-1 and the fourth channel. The schedule, the Authority said, would be 'intended to complement ITV-1'. The IBA confirmed that the channel should not make its own programmes but 'commission and acquire' programmes from others. The document made no commitment on the vexed issue of the price that would be paid for the programmes, saying only that it would 'need to provide a continuing incentive to independent producers and to ITV companies to supply programmes', that 'no artificial, pre-determined tariff rate for programmes or types of programme would govern purchases' and that the person responsible for the financial control of the channel 'would be able to obtain the cost figures involved in programme production where required and appropriate'. The Authority said that they expected money for the channel to be 'tight' and that 'programmes will not all be able to have the budgets that are sought for them'. The channel's annual budget of £60–£80m would be provided through an annual 'fourth channel subscription' paid to the IBA by the ITV companies in return for the right to sell the advertising on the fourth channel. Although in the early years the income from the sale of advertising time on the fourth channel might not meet the full cost to the companies of this subscription, the Authority anticipated that in time the fourth channel would add between a fifth and a quarter to the total advertising revenue earned by the ITV companies.

The Authority hoped that the channel would, from the outset, be on the air for 45–50 hours a week. On the contentious issue of where the programmes were to come from, the IBA spelled out that 'there should be no quotas, or rights to contribute, for anyone'. The programme controller would select programmes on the basis of quality. However, 'a possible pattern at the start would be that between

15% and 35% of the output would come from independent producers, with between 25% and 40% coming from the major ITV contractors, a further 10% to 20% from the regional ITV contractors, up to 15% from ITN, and 5% to 14% from foreign sources'. As the independents immediately realised, this meant that up to 75% of the programmes would come from ITV, leaving only 25% to be shared between independents and cheap imported programmes. It gave independents virtually no chance of achieving the 35% floated as a possible maximum in the IBA's proposals.

It had already been announced that the IBA intended to advertise in December 1979 for new contractors to run ITV-1 franchises from 1982. Consequently, the IBA now asserted, it needed what amounted to general agreement to its proposals for the fourth channel by December 1979 in order that 'those who are to consider applying for one of those contracts . . . know, in general terms, what arrangements the Authority has in mind'. In addition the Authority also wanted to press ahead with appointing a shadow board for the new channel – 'With the proposed start of the service being now less than three years ahead . . . the Authority is likely to establish special consultative arrangements during the early part of 1980 to ensure that, when the Bill is passed, the Fourth Channel can go ahead with all possible speed.'[17]

Immediately after reading the IBA's proposals, which were entitled *The Fourth Channel: The Authority's Proposals*, I scrawled this bitter note on the front of my copy in reference to a decade of struggle devoted to preventing the ITV companies from gaining control of the fourth channel: 'We stopped them coming in through the front door; Whitelaw slammed the back door; we must now stop them coming up through the floorboards in disguise. We were encouraged, but now the IBA have blown the wall down so that they can drive in in their limousines – see Pilkington for the IBA/ITCA relationship.' In the next few weeks I would reiterate those immediate reactions repeatedly in a series of angry speeches attacking the IBA proposals. I was by no means alone in my feeling of outrage. Not only did the IBA's proposals fall significantly short of the kind of vision set out in Whitelaw's speech, it was clear that the Authority hoped to get its ideas for the fourth channel approved in principle before the bill setting it up had even been published, let alone considered by Parliament.

The IBA was certainly bold. To the campaigners the Authority once again seemed intent on hijacking the new channel on behalf of the ITV companies rather than using it as a genuine opportunity to respond to the possibilities set out in the

Annan Report and echoed by Whitelaw. By its insistence that the new channel's role would be to 'complement' ITV-1, the IBA appeared to reject the Annan Report's proposal that the new service should not merely be 'complementary' to ITV but complementary to all three existing channels. By fudging the issue of the price to be paid for programmes the IBA had not only not failed to lay down as a principle that the Channel should meet the full cost of programmes, it had ignored successive submissions by the campaigners and left the door open to the ITV companies to make below-cost deals with the channel. As a result of saying that the channel would start up by broadcasting for 45–50 hours a week and then saying that it expected up to 40% of the programmes to come from the ITV majors, a further 10%–20% from the smaller ITV companies, up to 15% from ITN and perhaps 14% from overseas, the IBA had left very little room for independent productions and very little opportunity to expand later, once they had, as suggested in the summer speeches of Young, Shaw and Isaacs, 'proved themselves'. By changing the 15% of programmes which the Authority had suggested in previous plans might come from independents to read 'between 15% and 35% ', the IBA was offering something or nothing, probably nothing. The IBA proposals had used Whitelaw's words 'the largest practical proportion' in reference to the volume of programmes to be supplied by the independents, but then interpreted that as meaning the kind of figure they had first thought of. It certainly came nowhere near the formulation set out in the Channel Four Group's half-page advertisement in the *Guardian*, which had specified that the 'largest practical proportion' must in practice mean 'a majority'. Back in August, in his private letter to his American colleague, Colin Shaw had accurately encapsulated the problem of how to accommodate the aspirations of the independents once the companies had tooled up for increased production. Then he had suggested that some room for manoeuvre might lie in the area of educational production, but this nod was not even mentioned in the IBA document.

In one telltale phrase the IBA document actually referred to its new proposals as being for 'a channel of the kind suggested over the last eight years by the Authority'. Beside this on my copy I wrote in capitals 'GIVE AWAY'. Such suspicions seemed confirmed when the ITV companies immediately issued a statement saying that they were 'reassured'. The Channel Four Group's response was a press statement saying that the IBA proposals were 'unacceptable'. The IBA had 'outlined an ITV-2 instead of the genuinely independent TV4' promised by the Home Secretary. The IBA's proposals would lead to 'a fourth channel on the cheap, allowing major companies and multi-national conglomerates to dominate the channel'. What the IBA had presented, as nearly as changed circumstances allowed, was no more than their old proposals, dating in origin all the way back to 1971, skilfully re-worded and re-spun by Colin Shaw. Despite all the references in the document to the 'fourth channel', they amounted to 'ITV-2 by the back door'.

Aware that drafting of the broadcasting bill must already be well advanced, the Channel Four Group urgently set about trying to get the IBA's proposals challenged by as wide a range of interests as possible. On 27 November the secretaries, chairman or organisers of eight different groups professionally involved in broadcasting signed a joint letter to the 'Chairman' of the IBA, Lady Plowden. The BBC union – the Association of Broadcasting Staffs, the Writers' Guild of Great Britain, the Society of Authors, the Association of Directors and Producers and the Women's Film and Broadcasting Group joined with the IFA, AIP and the Channel Four Group left Lady Plowden in no doubt about their views: 'In the light of the IBA's recent proposals . . . we would like to express collectively our alarm and dissatisfaction with the IBA's current position. We would therefore hope to meet with you at the earliest possible opportunity to express our views to you personally.'[18] The December edition of AIP's journal carried an article by Michael Jackson giving a detailed comparison between the ideas outlined in Whitelaw's Cambridge speech and the proposals of the IBA. The Channel Four Group, he said, believed that the channel should not open until the IBA can fulfil Mr Whitelaw's requirements. As the battle for the fourth channel moved to Parliament, the Channel Four Group would 'be trying to convince MPs from all parties of the discrepancies between the statement of the Home Secretary and that of the IBA'.[19]

On Monday 3 December I chaired a meeting, sponsored by Conservative, Labour and Liberal MPs, in a committee room of the House of Commons addressed by representatives of the eight organisations that had signed the joint letter to Lady Plowden. Launching the Channel Four Group's response to the IBA proposals, I delivered an angry attack on the IBA's plans, calling them ' . . . a cause for scandal and alarm. In effect these proposals appear perilously close to an attempt by a statutory authority to subvert the declared policy of the responsible Minister.' I accused the IBA of 'bidding to replace the Home Secretary's outlined intentions with a thinly disguised version of their own, and their masters', old plans for ITV-2.' I said that over the years this plan, in its various guises, had been rejected by a royal commission and governments both Conservative and

Labour. The company the Authority was proposing should run the fourth channel would be controlled by a board which 'to put it mildly would be prone to domination by the ITCA companies, a company to run a service the great majority of whose programmes would be supplied by those same ITCA companies', companies which would also be selling the advertising on the channel. 'If that is not a recipe for handing over control of the fourth channel to those companies I don't know what is. When the IBA justifies such an arrangement on the basis that it is the companies who will be providing most of the money for the channel this is simply shallow semantics.' The money paid by the companies in the Fourth Channel Levy would come from their profits and therefore most of it would in reality be money that would otherwise being going to the Treasury in the form of ITV Exchequer Levy. This point had already been picked up by others, not least by Sir Michael Swann, the Chairman of the BBC. It was reported that over dinner with Mrs Thatcher at Number 10, Sir Michael had raised the question of the burden on the Treasury of the IBA's fourth channel plans. It was reported that as a result she had asked the Treasury to investigate how more of the initial start-up costs of the channel could be loaded onto ITV and leave less to be borne by the Exchequer.

Reminding the MPs and journalists assembled in the House of Commons committee room of the Pilkington Committee's charge that the IBA acted more as the ITV companies' spokesman than as their regulator, I drew attention to a recent Radio 3 interview given by Howard Thomas of Thames, in which he had referred to the fourth channel as 'my second channel'. Rather than the innovation spoken of by the Home Secretary and the acquisition and scheduling of programmes separated from ITV, the IBA proposed 'complementary scheduling' – the very phrase used in the Authority's rejected proposals to Annan. The Home Secretary, I reminded them, had not been frightened of the idea of 'something different rather than more of the same' nor of putting different people in charge of the channel in order to achieve that. So why had the IBA come forward with these proposals? 'Why? Because like the dog on the gramophone record it recognises its Master's Voice, rather than the Minister's.' I called on Parliament to teach the IBA 'which voice is really that of its master and which is really that of the dog food manufacturer'. Over the years, I concluded, various people had said that broadcasting was too important to be left to other people whom they thought of as irresponsible – 'Today I am saying that the future of our television is too important to be left simply to the IBA.'[20]

Phillip Whitehead followed me, calling the IBA's proposals 'an affront' and 'a gross betrayal of many people right across the political spectrum'. They meant 'ITV-2 by the backdoor'. The Conservative MP, Michael Morris, raised once again the unhealthy continuance of the ITV companies' monopoly over the sale of television advertising. The Channel Four Group's document went through the IBA proposals and rejected them step by step. The IBA, by leaving only a month for discussion, was attempting to rush its proposals through before they could be adequately scrutinised. Not only would the proposed board be prone to undue influence by the ITCA companies, the concept of a representational board would result in 'hostility, division and in-fighting when what is required of a board is a clear, coherent and shared view of the Channel's duties, with no individual interest prevailing over loyalty to the channel as a whole . . . Channel Four should not be a service company (like ITN) but a separate structure and its board should protect the ethic of the channel rather than represent suppliers of product.' No one with an interest, direct or indirect, in supplying programmes to the channel should sit on its board. As a 'mark of the channel's "independence from all others" it should be named "TV4" '.[21]

Two weeks later *Time Out* and the Channel Four Group staged a joint 'TV4 Conference' at the ICA. It was attended by two hundred independent and would-be independent programme makers. The aim: 'To put the case against the IBA proposals.' By then a copy of the ITV companies' confidential submission to the IBA had leaked out. As a result the Group was able to make a point by point comparison between the companies' proposals and the IBA's. The ITCA's schedule provided for just six hours each week of independent productions, placed in clearly defined slots in the schedule where they would play against the most popular programmes on ITV-1. Michael Jackson highlighted one phrase in particular from the ITCA document: 'On the nature of ITV-2 there is a large measure of agreement between the ITV companies and the IBA.' There certainly was. Addressing the ICA conference, which was chaired by Udi Eichler and had opened with a presentation by Jonathan Dimbleby, Phillip Whitehead called for the IBA to be publicly 'put on the rack' for its proposals. He reported the words of one anonymous ITV executive who had recently said that no matter how they set up the channel 'within a couple of years we will control 80% of it'.[22] I told the meeting that this was our last chance: 'We have to make MPs and others get up and protest.' At the time it was suggested that Phillip and I had gone too far in our outbursts against the IBA, and in truth I almost certainly had. Nevertheless, the anger and frustration were real. We saw ourselves as engaged in the final battle in a war that had already lasted ten years. It seemed essential that the programme makers' strength of feeling and purpose was clearly expressed. The IBA had to know that not all the programme makers could be silenced or intimidated by their employers. The IBA had to be made to realise that lame excuses and justifications on the basis of doubtful expediency, such as the Authority had produced over its failure to hold LWT to the promises made in its franchise application, would be ruthlessly highlighted and challenged in the case of Channel Four. We were not going to go away until we had a fourth channel that was more open and free, that provided opportunities for programme makers and voices of all kinds and did not exist simply to serve the ITV companies and their shareholders.

One of the reasons that I was playing a more prominent role in the public presentation of the campaigners' case at this point was because my recent work had given me a fleeting prominence that I had not had before. During the summer a three-part adaptation of *Crime And Punishment*, directed by me and starring John Hurt, had been transmitted on BBC-2 and that autumn virtually the whole of a Sunday evening on BBC-1 had been given over to a three-hour - long drama written by Ian Curteis and directed by me, *Suez 1956*, which had dramatised the political events and international collusion surrounding the Suez crisis. A week or two after the transmission word reached me that William Whitelaw, who had served with many of the people portrayed in the play, had watched it and commented favourably. Using this opening, I wrote to him. In more measured tones than I had employed in some of my recent speeches, I outlined the concerns of my colleagues in the Channel Four Group. I told him that I had been much heartened by his speech at the Royal Television Society and then incensed by the IBA's proposals. I told him that people who, like myself, made television programmes were far from convinced that more television always meant better television and that to follow the IBA's prescription for the fourth channel was likely to lead to an 'inevitable decline in the standards and cultural independence of all British television, both BBC and ITV'. It would be better to have no fourth channel than one which led to having 'more of the same programmes and a new ratings battle'.[23] Whitelaw's reply was reassuring. He made it clear that specific duties in relation to the new channel would be laid on the IBA and that the Authority would be expected to report on its fulfilment of those duties. 'Domination of the channel by the ITV companies' would be ruled out by safeguards in the Bill.

Invited to contribute an article to *The Listener*, I had written under the title *Gadarene Rush for ITV-2*: 'A new acrimony has turned the fourth channel debate into a battle.' Undeterred by Whitelaw's RTS speech, the Authority had continued to work on a set of proposals which would have the effect of handing control of the new channel to the ITV companies. Criticising the IBA's proposals, I said that there must be time for second thoughts. 'The IBA's eagerness for a Gadarene rush into their own wholly inadequate version of it seems astonishing.' Reminding readers of the IBA's record of failed stewardship of ITV, I concluded that 'the future of British television is too important to be left to the IBA, and it is to be hoped that the Home Secretary and individual MPs will repudiate its disastrous policy'.[24]

The following week Colin Shaw responded in an article, *ITV-2: Some Swine, Some Rush*. He assured readers that although the Authority's estimates of the percentages of the total number of hours of programmes transmitted by the channel were arrived at as a result of consultations with the various potential suppliers and the Authority's assessment of their relative strengths, these estimates 'were not intended to bind the fourth channel company. It may reach different conclusions based upon its own consultations. The company will not be bound by any quotas, or by any draft schedules which may now be in circulation. (A reference to the recently leaked draft schedule proposed by the companies.) It will have to ensure, however, that each source of supply is fairly represented in the schedules sent to the Authority for approval.' Shaw said that part of the 'protection' offered to independent producers would lie in the scheduling arrangements – 'It would *not* [author's emphasis] be treated in scheduling matters as a junior partner in the Authority's services, free to act only in reaction to the plans of the first independent television channel. The requirement to avoid competition between the two channels . . . does not, in the Authority's view, call for a relationship of that kind.' On the composition of the channel's board Shaw used words very similar in spirit to those contained in various of the Channel Four Group's own submissions – 'Freed from some of the preoccupations of a normal commercial undertaking, [they] should be drawn primarily from those with a professional concern in broadcasting.' Only the chairman and vice-chairman would be drawn 'from the ranks of the great and the good'. Five would speak on behalf of potential suppliers of programmes apart from the programme companies, while the four from the programme companies would 'not necessarily [be] drawn from company boardrooms'. He concluded, 'Perhaps it is Mr Darlow's experiences with *Suez* which have led him to suspect collusion between the IBA and the companies. I doubt myself whether, in recent months, the programme companies have felt all that much colluded with . . . Those of us who have worked closely on the IBA's proposals would not attach our names to anything likely to wreak the damage to British television suspected by Mr Darlow. On the contrary, we believe that the IBA's proposals, evolving further in the months to come, offer a way forward to some at least of the things to which, I think, he also subscribes.'[25]

Shaw's apparent concessions in his *Listener* response to me seem to some extent to reflect the struggle which had been going on for some time behind the scenes inside the IBA itself. *Broadcast* magazine's report of the *Time Out* – Channel Four Group conference at the ICA a month earlier had said that an IBA 'mole' had been present. The so-called 'mole' was Chris Rowley who many of us had known for years. He had been a senior member of Jeremy Isaacs' team at Thames and had produced a programme which I had directed starring Leo McKern about the painter JMW Turner. Subsequently Rowley had moved to the IBA to become the TV Schedules Officer. In this post Rowley had become one of the most important day-to-day links between the IBA and the ITV companies. Back in the summer of 1978 he had written an internal IBA paper for Sir Brian Young proposing that the fourth channel should be set up as a separate entity – 'a third force . . . to encourage innovation', as advocated by Annan, while at the same time giving the ITV companies a stake in its success by allowing them to collect all the advertising revenue. From the start Rowley had had rather more confidence than his Authority colleagues in the independent producers' capacity to supply a sub-stantial proportion of the channel's programmes. After all, he had worked with and had continued to be friends with many of them. He had helped to set up the 'consultation' with independents held by the IBA at which Lady Plowden had confessed to surprise that so many independents had turned up. Rowley believes that that meeting and a succession of others that he arranged for officers and Members of the Authority with independents had an important cumulative effect – 'staff and therefore Authority Members did not believe in the *practicality* [Rowley's emphasis] of the independent sector: it might be sensible in theory in the long term but who were the people? I once added up the independent producers I had met and did a note on it. I've forgotten how many it was – 200, 300, 500 – i.e., massive to dubious officers. But it was also important that I had "successful" people there – not just the slightly way-out experimental people whose films I ran at the IBA with bewilderment on a weekly basis.' Rowley had argued with Shaw about the actual wording of the IBA document in respect of the role of independent producers. Rowley had wanted a clear minimum number of hours or percentage of independent production included: 'Colin and I argued for many hours over three or four weeks . . . I lost and put up with the not very clear Colin compromise as at least it was indicative of a largish amount.' Rowley remembers that he had not been helped by Jeremy Isaacs, 'who, although he had just made the independent production *A Sense of Freedom*, kept saying to me that there were no such things as independent producers'.[26]

The business of quantifying what Whitelaw had termed 'the largest practical proportion' and establishing that that could be at least 51% of the new channel's output had continued to be a major preoccupation for the Channel Four Group. Since Whitelaw's Cambridge speech Michael Jackson had organised scores of visits for individual MPs, members of the IBA and IBA officers to facility companies and the big producers, in an effort to convince them of the latent capacity of the independent sector. Mike Luckwell, whose Moving Picture Company was the largest facility company and supplier of equipment for the production of commercials in the country, could always be depended upon to put on a dazzling display of technical wizardry and the most up-to-date electronic equipment. MPs in particular liked the feeling that such visits gave them an insight into the reality behind show business glamour. They liked rubbing shoulders with the stars and Jackson played on this. Luckwell's company had made the live-action sequence for the Beatles' *Yellow Submarine*. Luckwell was exactly the kind of successful entrepreneur who Keith Joseph and the new Conservative government wanted to encourage. On top of all this, he had already defeated the ACTT by taking the union to court when, in an attempt to get him to adopt union pay scales and crewing arrangements, it had threatened to black commercials made and distributed around the ITV network by his company. After his victory in court Luckwell had told Alan Sapper and Jack O'Connor, the union's television officer, that he would make sure that they were both personally bankrupted if they ever threatened him again. According to Luckwell, O'Connor was 'very shocked – he had never been spoken to like that before'.[27]

Although it was not apparent to the campaigners at the time, by its efforts between January 1979 and January 1980 the Channel Four Group had, little by little, changed the perception within the IBA. Colin Shaw describes what happened thus: 'There was a prising apart to establish Channel Four and its board as separate from ITV.' Shaw's deputy at the IBA, David Glencross, says that what the Group's campaign achieved between the Conservative election victory in May 1979 and the publication of the Broadcasting Bill in February 1980 was that it 'loosened up the IBA framework, rather than dramatically changing it'.[28] The evidence suggests that politically the Group achieved even more. Whitelaw had always professed an enthusiasm for many of the underlying ideas that had informed the Annan Committee's proposed OBA. However, many, probably most, of his party had been against these principles and had favoured ITV-2, or something very close to it – ITV-2 with a dash of independent production to spice things up a bit and keep the companies on their toes, especially in their dealings with the unions. The ACTT strike in the autumn of 1979 (and events before that such as the Thames PAs' action that blacked out ITV's coverage of the Queen's Jubilee in the summer of 1977) had undoubtedly played into the campaigners' hands. Michael Grade's assessment may well be correct – that the timing of the strike and the companies' eventual capitulation was the seminal event in deciding what happened. Keith Joseph's espousal of the entrepreneurial aspects of the independents' case was obviously crucial, particularly in winning over Mrs Thatcher. In Whitelaw's rather cautious article in the March/April 1979 edition of the RTS Journal he had concentrated on the institutional independence of all television channels from the state and spoken only of 'greater opportunities for independent producers'. He had specifically commended the plan put forward by the IBA in the summer of 1977 after publication of the Annan Report. Just how far the government had moved in the year since Whitelaw had written that article became apparent when it published its long-awaited Broadcasting Bill on 6 February 1980.

*　　*　　*

'The Channel Four Group welcomes the enlightened and forward-looking Broadcasting Bill published today. We see it as a vindication of our battle for an independent fourth channel' were the opening words of a press statement released by the Channel Four Group on 6 February 1980. Sir Denis Forman, speaking as the Chairman of the ITCA's Service Two Policy Working Party on the same day, said, 'The companies welcome the Bill without reservation.' But Sir Denis immediately added, 'Any reservations we may have are confined to the way in which the Bill may be interpreted.'[29] Accepting that 'the companies will not get Service 2 in the form that they originally wanted it', Sir Denis said that the companies now accepted that the form of control and operation of the new channel would be in the hands of the IBA. This, unsurprisingly, was precisely the aspect of the Bill which still most worried the campaigners. 'The history of the fourth channel debate', the Channel Four Group's press statement continued, 'has been punctuated by the neutralising effect the IBA has had on the government's proposals. The IBA must not erode the excellent objectives of the Bill.'

Reporting the publication of the Bill and reactions to it, *Broadcast* quoted the Conservative Chairman of the Parliamentary Media Committee, Julian Critchley: 'The debate at Westminster, if not elsewhere, will turn upon the degree to which programmes shown on Service 2 will include those of independent producers.'[30] The Bill, which *Broadcast* described as 'couched for the most part in terms of considerable ambiguity', extended the life of the IBA until 31 December 1996 (with a further extension until 2001 if needed), required the IBA to establish a subsidiary to operate the new channel – described in the Bill as 'Service 2'.[31] The programmes in 'Service 2' were 'to contain a suitable proportion of matter calculated to appeal to tastes and interests not generally catered for by Service 1 . . . to ensure that a suitable proportion of the programmes are of an educational nature . . . [and] to encourage innovation in the form and content of programmes; and to give Service 2 a distinctive character of its own.' A proper balance and wide range of subject matter was to be maintained as between the two ITV services. The importance attached by the government to the volume of programmes to be obtained from independents was highlighted by the duty placed on the IBA 'to secure that . . . a substantial proportion of the programmes broadcast in Service 2 are supplied otherwise than by persons of either of the following descriptions, namely a TV programme contractor and a body corporate under the control of a TV programme contractor.' The IBA was to be required to report annually on the way in which it had discharged each of the above duties. The ITV companies were to have the right, 'in consideration of payments made to the Authority' to provide the advertisements in their own areas. Income received by the companies from selling the advertising on 'Service 2' was to be included with their other income for the purposes of calculating the amount of Exchequer Levy which each paid. The new service was also to provide 'a suitable proportion of matter in Welsh'.[32] This last provision was to trigger a passionate response from the Welsh, who had been promised that Welsh language broadcasting on television was to be concentrated in one service. The Conservative government had gone back on that pledge and Welsh nationalists responded with a campaign of civil disobedience and attacks on transmitters. Gwynfor Evans, the President of Plaid Cymru, issued an extremely credible threat that unless the government changed its mind over a Welsh-language television service he would go on hunger strike and starve himself to death. His threat was believed and the government backed down, introducing amendments late in the passage of the Bill through Parliament which created a Welsh Fourth Channel Authority (S4C). But that is a separate story.

The ITV official history would later describe the 1980 Broadcasting Bill as meeting the most important demands of the independent producers 'in preventing the companies from dominating the channel'.[33] So, in a sense, it did. Yet the Bill still left a great deal to the discretion of the IBA. 'The Bill is based on a false premise,' said Phillip Whitehead. 'That the IBA can be trusted to prevent the emergence of what the companies, with supreme impertinence, persist in calling ITV-2.'[34] In its first press statement after the Bill's publication the Channel Four Group repeated what it had said after Whitelaw's Cambridge speech – the 'substantial proportion' of programmes that was to come from 'persons other than television programme contractors' could 'only mean a majority'. The AIP magazine concluded that the Channel Four Group had won on a lot of issues 'in principle'. But, AIP's editorial continued: 'The distance between enabling legislation that says nothing about the appointments to the fourth channel board, says little about scheduling and advertising and gives no indication what is to be understood by a "substantial" proportion of programmes from independents – and interpretation by the IBA, is very great.'[35]

Opening the House of Commons debate on the Bill, Whitelaw moved to allay such fears, 'I know that a number of honourable Members will be concerned lest the fourth channel is dominated by the ITV companies, particularly perhaps the network companies. I would not be prepared to countenance this.'[36]

When Parliament settled down to going through the Bill clause by clause, the Channel Four Group and its allies at Westminster concentrated their energies on trying to narrow the distance between Whitelaw's stated intentions and the IBA's room to use the legislation to further the aims of the ITV companies. A list of amendments, under the name of Michael Jackson, was prepared for sympathetic MPs to move. These aimed to make the arrangements for the acquisition and scheduling of the channel not only separate from ITV-2, but 'independent of' them as well. The independents wanted it stipulated that there must be 'equality of treatment and a fair market price' for all who supplied programmes to the channel, be they independents or ITV companies. The Channel Four Group proposed a tightening up of the definition of an independent – the wording in the Bill simply excluded TV programme contractors or bodies corporate 'under the control of a TV programme contractor'. The Channel Four Group wanted to tighten this to exclude any body 'with any financial connection' with a TV programme contractor. The Channel Four Group wanted the Bill to legislate for the word 'substantial', as applied to the proportion of programmes to be supplied by independents, to come, over time, to mean 'the majority'. Finally, in order to mark publicly the fact that the new channel was intended to be a separate entity from ITV, they wanted its name changed from the uninspiring 'Service 2' to 'Channel 4'.[37]

Throughout March and on into the summer, as detailed scrutiny of the Bill proceeded in Parliament, Jackson, Balhetchet or Iain Bruce, sometimes all three, were in attendance at almost every sitting at which the fourth channel was discussed. However, although Leon Brittan, the Home Office minister charged with piloting the Bill through the Commons, gave further government reassurances about the intentions behind the wording in the Bill, he would not budge on the wording itself. The government maintained that its intentions were plain and that the IBA would be expected to act on them. To prescribe exact quotas or minima would be to risk undermining the government's prime purpose – that programmes shown on the channel should be chosen on the basis of merit rather than predetermined criteria. On top of which quotas or percentages set at this stage were likely to become out of date as the channel developed. Nevertheless, as a result of a Channel Four Group amendment, put forward by Phillip Whitehead, the IBA's 'second service' was renamed the 'Fourth Channel'. During the Standing Committee's discussion of the Bill, Whitehead also put forward an amendment proposed by the IFA, which, since the Edinburgh Television Festival, had been pressing for a foundation to be set up by the channel, but at arm's length from it, which would facilitate the making of innovative and experimental films. The IFA proposal gained support from both Labour members of the Standing Committee and from a number of Conservatives. Leon Brittan rejected it, but in doing so said that he shared the concern of the whole Committee that the Fourth Channel should encourage innovation and experiment. How this was done, however, had to be a matter for the IBA and the channel. The IBA would 'have to work out carefully how they will discharge a serious obligation imposed by Parliament with bipartisan support'.[38]

When the Bill, with its Commons amendments, reached the House of Lords on 24 July 1980, Lord Annan gave his own reactions to what the government and others had made of his handiwork in the three years since his Committee's report.

'I want to give a warm welcome to the Bill and to congratulate the Home Secretary upon standing firm on a number of matters on which he must have been under strong pressure to yield,' he said. Whitelaw had 'got it right' by resisting both the claims of the ITV companies to their own second channel and of the advertisers, and the monetarists in the government, who wanted a fully competitive fourth channel. 'Some of our Lordships may ask if I mourn the extinction of the Open Broadcasting Authority. I answer not at all. The Open Broadcasting Authority was born from an idea of Mr Tony Smith, who, I may say, is one of the few good academic experts on broadcasting. They are not all that numerous, I fear. It was he who talked about setting up a foundation to run the fourth channel. Our committee took that piece of dough and began to bake it. I do not think that it got very far in the baking before we had to finish our report. The new fourth channel is really the same loaf, only now it is done to a turn.'[39]

Notes

1. Memo from Sir Denis Forman to Gus Macdonald, September 1979.
2. Letter by the author to David Glencross, Deputy Director of Television at the IBA, 7 September 1979.
3. Letter from David Glencross, Deputy Director of Television at the IBA, to the author, 11 September 1979.
4. From a transcript of the text of the speech given to the Royal Television Society by the Rt. Hon. William Whitelaw on 14 September 1979. Published by the Royal Television Society, London.
5. See Catterall, *op. cit.*
6. Report of RTS Cambridge Convention 1979, RTS Journal, November–December 1979, Vol. 17, No. 12.
7. David Glencross, interviewed by the author in October 2000.
8. Sir Denis Forman, interviewed by the author in October 2000.
9. Colin Shaw, interviewed by the author in November 2000.
10. RTS Journal, November–December 1979, Vol. 17, No. 12. Report of 1979 Cambridge Convention.
11. *AIP & Co*, No. 21, October 1979.
12. From *The Fourth Television Channel: An Open Letter to the Home Secretary*, from The Channel Four Group, published in the *Guardian* on 10 October 1979.
13. *ITV-2: The Fourth Channel*, a confidential memorandum from the ITV companies to the IBA, October 1979, quoted in *Channel Four – Television with a Difference?* by Stephen Lambert, British Film Institute, London, 1982.
14. Letter from Sir Denis Forman to the author, 22 October 1979. Talking to Sir Denis Forman recently about the incident he cheerfully admitted to the element of

disingenuousness in his application for membership of the Channel Four Group, adding that he thoroughly enjoyed attempting the ploy.

15. Michael Grade, interviewed by the author in November 2000.

16. *It Seemed Like a Good Idea at the Time*, Michael Grade, Macmillan Publishers Ltd, London 1999.

17. *The Fourth Channel: The Authority's Proposals*, a news release from the Independent Broadcasting Authority, 12 November 1979.

18. Letter to Lady Plowden, 27 November 1979.

19. *IBA's Smoke Screen* by Michael Jackson in *AIP & Co*, December 1979.

20. Speech delivered by the author on 3 December 1979 to launch *The Fourth Channel: A Reply to Proposals by the Independent Broadcasting Authority* by the Channel Four Group.

21. *The Fourth Television Channel: A Reply to Proposals by the Independent Broadcasting Authority* by the Channel Four Group, 3 December 1979.

22. Speech by Phillip Whitehead, delivered at the ICA on 17 December 1979 and included in *Look Here*, a television programme shown by LWT on 6 January, 1980, and reported in *Broadcast*, 7 January 1980. *Broadcast*'s estimate of 200 attendees at the conference appears to have been somewhat overgenerous. My recollection suggests a number nearer to 100 or 150.

23. Letter from the author to the Rt Hon. William Whitelaw, MP, the Home Secretary, 12 January 1980.

24. *Gadarene Rush for ITV-2* by the author, *The Listener*, 24 January 1980.

25. *ITV-2: Some Swine, Some Rush*, by Colin Shaw. *The Listener*, 31 January 1980.

26. From a letter by Chris Rowley to the author, 1 December 2000.

27. Mike Luckwell, interviewed by the author in November 2000.

28. Colin Shaw and David Glencross, interviewed by the author in October and November 2000.

29. Report of a press conference given by the ITCA, *Television Today*, 14 February 1980.

30. *Broadcast*, 11 February 1980.

31. The idea that this subsidiary should be a company, owned by the IBA, seems to have originated with the Home Office lawyers while the Bill was being drafted. (See the paper *Establishing the Regulatory Framework* by Lady Littler, published in Catterall, *op. cit.*) Making it a company offered certain legal advantages and reduced the possibility of Parliamentary argument about the channel's precise institutional form.

32. *Bill 139*, HMSO, February 1980.

33. Potter, *op. cit.*, *Vol. 3*.

34. Quoted in *Broadcast*, 18 February 1980.

35. *AIP & Co*, No. 23, February 1980.

36. *Hansard*, 18 February 1980.

37. From an original undated Channel Four Group note and list of proposed detailed amendments prepared following a meeting at the House of Commons with a group of MPs.

38. *Hansard*, Standing Committee E, Broadcasting Bill, 24 April 1980.

39. *Hansard*, 24 July 1980.

8

Fo(u)r What and Whom? – 1980 to 1981

Today it is easy to forget that in its first years the Thatcher government was far from secure. Ever since the 'thirteen wasted Tory years' of Conservative governments that had followed Attlee's post-war administration after 1951, governments had come and gone. Even Harold Wilson never managed more than six consecutive years in power. In 1979 and 1980 there was no reason to suppose that Mrs Thatcher would be any different. Even Callaghan's replacement by Michael Foot as leader of the Labour Party in November 1980 did not immediately alter expectations. There were splits in the Conservative Party which at that stage looked potentially as serious as any which had so far surfaced in the Labour Party. The Conservatives had got in after the Winter of Discontent on the slogan 'Labour Isn't Working'. By the middle of 1980 it was clear that Conservative government wasn't working either. That autumn the number of unemployed rose from 1.5 million to 2 million and inflation touched 20%. Even inside the government there were calls for increased public spending and a return to the Keynesian economic policies pursued by both Conservative and Labour governments since the war. Thatcher dismissed such calls, labelling the Ministers who made them 'wets'. In the government's Autumn Statement even deeper public expenditure cuts were announced. At the Conservative Party conference that autumn Mrs Thatcher mocked the 'wets', declaring, 'U-turn if you want to. The lady's not for turning.' (A line supplied for her by the playwright Ronald Millar.)

This was the political context which informed the campaign waged by the Channel Four Group between the summer of 1979 and mid-1981. Even if they had wanted to, the campaigners could not afford to antagonise the Labour Party. Equally vital was the campaigners' relationship with the trade unions. As we have seen, although most of the activists were politically on the left, one of their objectives was to reduce the level of restrictive practices which hampered their work as programme makers. Neither the Channel Four Group, nor its parent AIP, were formal trade associations or employers' organisations. Over the years

AIP had put out a number of feelers to see if the unions, in particular the ACTT, could be persuaded to enter into discussions about creating new working agreements that might allow more cinema films to be produced in the UK. But these feelers had been rebuffed. The unions feared that any agreement with AIP would threaten the relationship they already had with the major film producers' association, the BFPA, and undermine the lucrative agreements that they had with the British arms of the American major film producers. In addition, animosities had grown up between some of the more high-profile members of AIP and some officers and individual members of the ACTT's General Council. By late 1979, as it became clear that Channel Four was going to become a reality and that independent producers would be making some of its programmes, it had also become clear to some of us who were active in both the Channel Four Group and the ACTT that it was unlikely that the unions would ever be induced to recognise AIP as a body with which to negotiate the working agreements needed by independents if their programmes were to be transmitted by the new channel. Would-be independent producers feared that union intransigence might prove fatal. Channel Four programme budgets were expected to be substantially lower than those available to the BBC and ITV, so unless the independents could use smaller crews and more modern flexible equipment they would be unable to make anything but the most simplistic and basic mass-produced studio material for the new channel.

By February 1980, as the Broadcasting Bill started to make its way through Parliament, no progress had been made on this vital issue. Unless a way could be found to resolve the problem, all the independents' hopes might be strangled before the channel was born. Iain Bruce, who had been elected to the General Council of the ACTT the year before and was treasurer of the Channel Four Group, and I, with a few other trusted members of the Channel Four Group committee including Sophie Balhetchet, the campaign's official link to AIP, began to discuss ways in which the problem might be overcome. One solution might be to create a trade association, separate both from the campaign and the BFPA, which could represent producers making programmes for the fourth channel. This body, dealing only in trade issues, might do more than negotiate agreements with the unions, it might represent producers in their dealings with the fourth channel and, because it confined its activities to trade matters alone, might unite all the different groups of producers, including those who did not subscribe to all the aims of the Channel Four Group. It was decided that as a first step Iain and I should seek a private meeting with the ACTT's General Secretary, Alan Sapper.

Late on the afternoon of Friday 21 March, Iain and I met Sapper and his deputy Roy Lockett in Sapper's wood-panelled office in the union's headquarters overlooking Soho Square. Iain and I put it to them that the Fourth Channel (Whitehead's amendment to the Broadcasting Bill replacing the name 'Service 2' with the name the 'Fourth Channel' had been accepted by the government that very week) was clearly going to come into existence within two years and that independent producers were going to be making a lot of the programmes broadcast by it. We suggested to them that, in view of Mrs Thatcher's declared policies towards unions and restrictive practices, they had no more interest in creating a situation in which the unions could be bashed for killing the new channel at birth than we had in creating an unholy free-for-all in which it would become impossible to budget the cost of productions in advance. If that happened the channel would either collapse or become a paradise for producer con men and cowboys. It was immediately clear that we had touched a chord. They agreed that what was needed was a mechanism or a forum through which national agreements covering such things as rates of pay, hours and conditions of work, appropriate alike to the needs of their members and of independent producers, could be negotiated. They also accepted that it would be inappropriate for the independent producers to work through the mechanisms and under the agreements that already covered ITV. Quite apart from major disagreements of principle between the independents and the ITV programme contractors, the independents were likely, for the first few years at least, to be small companies working on single productions or series without any guarantee of ongoing work. On the other hand the ITV companies, and the union agreements they worked to, were based on fixed studios employing permanent staffs with established patterns of promotion and an ongoing flow of production governed by a system of rostered hours. The arrangements in cinema film production were equally inappropriate. Not only had the Channel Four Group grown up under the wing of AIP, an organisation specifically committed to liberating film production from the dead-hand and extravagant labour practices of the BFPA, itself an organisation dominated by the British arms of the major American film companies and the film subsidiaries of the ITV companies, the union agreements applicable to feature films would be as inappropriate to independent production for the Fourth Channel as those covering the ITV companies. Films made for the cinema engaged large crews on high wages based on budgets which would simply be unavailable for programmes made for the Fourth Channel.

However, Sapper and Lockett knew that any proposal for a new agreement covering independent productions for the new channel was likely to encounter opposition inside the union. According to Lockett, the ACTT was in a way two unions – 'the strong collective bargaining one and the radical wing that had started the (union's) Television Commission run by Caroline Heller'. On the one side Sapper and Lockett would have trouble with the traditional film technicians who would see any agreement with the independents that provided for smaller, more flexible crewing arrangements and lower rates of pay, as a threat to the existing, lucrative agreements they had with the BFPA. On the other side the television technicians were likely to oppose anything that sanctioned an extension of freelancing. Jack O'Connor, the union's Television Organiser, had repeatedly proclaimed that the television shops in ITV 'will fight to the death against freelancing'. It was less than a year since the union's 1979 annual conference at which Sapper had warned that David Elstein's motion on independents and the fourth channel risked splitting the union. When Elstein's motion was passed, a senior ITV shop steward had glared at the union's freelance television members and declared, 'It's going to be war!'

We suggested that it might help if there was a trade association, distinct from both the BFPA and the ITV companies association (the ITCA), that was not AIP and which covered all the producers who made programmes for the new channel. The union could then negotiate with this new body. One of the recurring nightmares of all the trade unions operating in show business was producers and promoters who took on union members, performers or technicians, and then disappeared or dissolved their companies before paying them. To overcome this recurring problem the unions had set up a system of escrow deposits, guaranteed by the various film and theatre producers associations, under which deposits on minimum fees were paid in to a closed account in advance of commencement of production and only refunded to the producer after he had paid what he owed. We suggested that one of the things that an independent producers' trade association might do would be to set up such a system or get the channel itself to guarantee technicians' payments provided that the producers making the programmes belonged to the association and worked in accordance with agreements made between it and the unions. We stressed that these agreements could not be the same as those that applied to feature films nor could the conditions of employment be similar to those in the ITV companies. This they accepted. However, they said, it would help them in squaring things inside the union if any agreement was based on a precedent, preferably an already existing agreement. There was one agreement, little used and not very widely known, that might be applicable – the Short Films Agreement. This was designed for low-budget training and instructional film production and allowed for much-reduced crewing and more flexible working arrangements than for feature films. It dated back to the heyday of British film making before the advent of commercial television. It ought to be possible to extend it to cover television productions made for the fourth channel by independent producers. By happy chance I had recently completed an industrial training film for Michael Peacock's company Video Arts made under this agreement and had found it a completely liberating experience, flexible and adaptable as the changing circumstances of the production had required. It had been in startling contrast to the experience I was then going through in shooting a drama for Thames. One evening while shooting a short dialogue scene for the Thames drama on one camera involving three men sitting in a stationary car, I had counted sixty-seven people queuing at the catering truck. When I had questioned the numbers with the Thames production manager he seemed unconcerned – 'Oh, that's about normal for this sort of scene,' he had assured me cheerfully.

Because the Short Films Agreement was already in use within the union, it would be more difficult for either the film technicians or the members of the ITV shops to oppose its use. However, the first requisite was an independent producers' trade association with which the union could negotiate and which was willing to use this agreement. Iain and I promised to go away and put in train the setting-up of an independent television producers' trade association.

Our meeting with the union officials, and meetings which followed, had to be conducted in complete secrecy. If news of what we were proposing got out before both we and the union officials were ready there would be storms of protest from both militant members of the union and from members of AIP, the Film Producers' Association and the IFA (some of whose members believed that the kind of film making they hoped that the new channel would foster should not be subject to conventional wage or workplace bargaining at all). Three weeks after that first private meeting with Sapper and Lockett, notices appeared in the trade press announcing that a meeting called by Iain Bruce, myself and six others, including Sophie Balhetchet, Michael Jackson, David Puttnam and Mark

Shelmardine, was to be held at 7 p.m. on Wednesday 30 April at the Hyde Park Hotel, 'to see if there was a necessity for a new trade association to represent the interests of independent producers.' As the trade press noted, all those calling the meeting were members of either AIP, the Channel Four Group or the Association of Producers and Directors.

As seven o'clock approached, the eight of us who had called the meeting, together with Colin Young whom we had invited to chair it, waited somewhat apprehensively to see who, if anyone, would turn up. Although Colin Young was a member of the Council of AIP he, unlike Richard Craven, was known to believe that it should not attempt to become a trade association. At the same time, we believed that Young was a suitably neutral figure, with a known sympathy for the idea of the fourth channel. Young had witnessed many of the debates and campaigns over the fourth channel since he had returned to Britain in 1970 from the United Sates to become the first head of the National Film School. 'What attracted me to those debates was that they were goal orientated – they were aimed at a result which was not what our lords and masters wanted. It was in that sense very like what I had experienced in the States in the 1960s.'[1]

A function room in the ultra-respectable, nineteenth-century splendour of the Hyde Park Hotel in Knightsbridge seemed a somewhat incongruous setting for a meeting called by campaigners, many of whom had, until recently, been widely written off as hotheads, dangerous Marxists and outsiders. I could only remember one other occasion when I had entered the hotel, and that was when I had been one of a small group of film and television directors invited by the Foreign Office to meet some distinguished Polish film makers. The sense of unreality was heightened by the fact that earlier in the day, only a few hundred yards further along Knightsbridge, five armed men had seized the Iranian Embassy in Princes Gate and were at that moment holding twenty-one people hostage inside it, including a London policeman and a two-man BBC news team. Outside the security forces, who had surrounded the building, were waiting to see if it would be necessary for the SAS to storm it. It seemed possible that no one at all might turn up to our meeting. But by just after seven o'clock about seventy were sitting patiently waiting for it to begin. Many were people whom we already knew, freelance producers and directors working in television and campaigners who had been involved in the various lobbies and pressure groups down the years. There were also a few who were on the staff of the broadcasters and must, we assumed, either be there as spies for their bosses or be considering leaving. However, we were particularly interested in the few who had turned up from facility companies and the larger independent production companies, companies which were mostly involved in making training films, commercials or promotional films for corporate clients – companies such as Video Arts. These companies had so far largely kept aloof from our campaigns. Prominent among them were Mike Luckwell, already a friend and supporter, and Michael Peacock, the Managing Director of Video Arts, who had taken a strategically positioned seat on the centre aisle about halfway back. Did this mean that at last 'the big boys' were going to come out to play with the young upstarts? Curiously, through oversight or pressure of our other work (at that time I was actively working on two productions and was also going back and forth to Paris for meetings about the script of a feature film), we had not planned how to conduct the meeting. We had simply left it to Colin Young. But Colin, having been not much more than an interested spectator of the campaign until this point, had no precise idea of what was expected either. So after calling the meeting to order he turned to me, sitting in the audience. Could I explain what the meeting was about?

Unprepared, I went to the front and, ear half-cocked for the sound of explosions from the Iranian Embassy, explained that it seemed to those calling the meeting that if independent producers were to realise their ambition to supply a substantial proportion of the programmes shown on the new channel they were going to need their own properly constituted trade association which could negotiate standard terms of trade for them with Channel Four and establish working agreements with the trade unions – the technicians and the performers. This required a new trade association, specifically created for that purpose. Others who had been involved in calling the meeting followed me, adding to what I had said and trying to allay any fears among representatives of the established companies that this was some sort of plot by a bunch of left-wing hotheads. Like Lady Plowden of the IBA eight months earlier, John Gau (who, although he was still Head of Features at the BBC, had come along to the meeting) remembers that he was amazed at how many people were there: 'I had been conditioned to the BBC and broadcasters' view that there weren't any independents.'[2] As more and more people joined in the discussion, Iain Bruce and I waited to see what Michael Peacock might say. To succeed we knew that we needed the big boys on our side. Of course having Luckwell, Shelmardine and Puttnam was a help (this was before Puttnam produced the Oscar-winning *Chariots of Fire*, so he was not yet the force that he would become). Nevertheless, Peacock, because of the positions he had held and his experience, would give any independents' trade association the authority that it would need. The alternative, to have the big established independents working separately from us, and perhaps perceived as working in competition with us or even against us, might prove fatal. Peacock remembers that 'Lots of people spoke from all ends of the spectrum – some fairly naïve things were said. But I sensed for the first time that there must be a trade association, that it should be properly constituted and that the terms of trade with Channel Four were vital.'[3] Peacock had learned what he calls 'the reality of being an independent' when Video Arts had tried to negotiate a deal with the BBC to make a series about Milton Friedman (part of which had been included in the BAFTA showing of independents' work in the summer of 1979). He had had 'a real upper and downer' with the BBC negotiator. In the end Video Arts had done the series for PBS in America and the BBC jointly, but not before they had had to agree to the BBC re-cutting their six programmes into four and re-editing them to 'suit what they saw as their style'. As a result, Peacock spoke up in favour of establishing a trade association. After about two hours and with still no sounds of explosions from further along Knightsbridge, the meeting agreed that a new independent producers' trade association should be formed. It was to be called, initially at least, the Independent Television Producers' Association.[4]

The new association would endeavour as soon as possible to turn itself into 'the foremost body representing the interests of independent programme producers for television'.[5] Its aims were to include many of the goals of the Channel Four Group – to secure the largest practicable, and a growing, proportion of the programme budget and hours on the fourth channel for programmes produced by independent producers; to secure adequate funding for these programmes on the basis of sound contractual and financial terms; to ensure that independent producers who made programmes for the new channel were genuinely independent of the ITV companies. An interim working party was appointed to bring the new association into existence. Its members were to be Colin Young, Mike Luckwell, Alan Bell, Michael Peacock, Iain Bruce and me, Simon Hartog of the IFA and Christopher Morahan, a former BBC Head of Plays and one of the most respected drama directors in television. There was no doubt in my mind or of my close colleagues that the person who should eventually become the new trade association's first chairman was Michael Peacock. On returning to Video Arts after the meeting Peacock said to his colleague Antony Jay, 'This is important. I am going to have to devote a good deal of time to this.'

Over succeeding weeks, as the steering committee laboured, with meetings three or even four times a week, to bring IPPA (the name of the association was changed from the ITPA to the more user-friendly IPPA, the Independent Programme Producers' Association) into formal existence, membership grew rapidly to over one hundred companies and soon-to-be companies. The association quickly became recognised as the body through which the IBA, the Home Office and later the embryo board of Channel Four negotiated with independent producers. By June it was able to issue a formal statement of Aims and Objectives. Among the things that the Association was committed to securing was that the Fourth Channel: 'a. Discriminates positively in favour of independent production; b. Agrees prices with independent producers which fairly reflect the real costs of productions and wherever possible pays the entire cost of production; c. Recognises that a genuine independent production cannot be one financed in whole or in part by any ITV contractor, its parent, associated or subsidiary companies.'[6]

* * *

IPPA still had no Fourth Channel with which to negotiate anything. Nor, until there was a channel and the way in which it would commission programmes had become a little clearer, could the association try to come to concrete terms with the unions. In February Lady Plowden had invited Edmund Dell to become chairman of a panel of 'consultants' who, once the Broadcasting Bill had passed through Parliament, would become the Board of the Fourth Channel. Dell, as Secretary of State at the Board of Trade in the Callaghan government, had been a member of the cabinet committee which had considered the Annan Report, but on his own admission, had played no part in the arguments over it. There were, in his view, already enough experts on the committee – 'particularly Bill Rogers and Tony Benn, and I had other things to do'. Enticed by Lady Plowden's assurance that the chairmanship of the new channel was 'the last big job in television' but that it would only take him away from his new job in the city for one or two days a week, Dell had accepted her invitation 'with an enthusiasm undimmed by an entire ignorance of what the chairmanship would involve'.[7] When Dell's appointment was announced a rumour rapidly spread around the television industry that he did not even possess a television set. That, as Dell later explained, was amusing but not quite true – 'I had bought my first TV set in April 1979, ten months before Lady Plowden's visit. It is true that my mind was not clouded with much knowledge about television and that I did not know personally or even by name any of those whose important function it is to produce TV programmes rather than present them. Thus my nomination was a typical British amateur appointment but I would not entirely rule out the possibility that the IBA was right in its choice in the peculiar circumstances of Channel Four.'[8] Perhaps as a foil to Dell, the IBA invited Sir Richard Attenborough, actor, film producer and Chairman of Capital Radio, to become Deputy Chairman.

While Lady Plowden was enlisting Dell and Attenborough, the Director-General of the IBA, Sir Brian Young, had written to a number of bodies representing potential suppliers of programmes for the fourth channel, inviting them to suggest names of people for consideration for the Board of the Fourth Channel Company. AIP and the Channel Four Group had continued to argue against having even a 'loosely representative' board for fear of conflicts of interest if board members were both custodians of the channel and potential suppliers of its programmes. Initially both groups therefore delayed any reply. But in April, when the Broadcasting Bill had more or less completed its passage through the House of Commons, they accepted that they had lost this argument and put forward some names. Among the names they put forward as having 'the trust of independent producers', were a number of those involved in setting up IPPA. As 'representatives of the ITCA companies with a "demonstrable concern for the character of the new channel" ', AIP suggested Udi Eichler and Gus Macdonald together with Anthony Smith and one member of the Annan Committee, Sara Morrison.

Nevertheless, the independents remained suspicious of the whole 'representative' board concept and of the IBA's motives. When Sir Brian Young rang up Roger Graef and asked him to be a member of the board he replied, 'No, it's a carve up. It looks like ITV-2 to me.' But Young pressed him, inviting him to come round to meet him. Graef continued to play hard to get and said that he was not free until Saturday morning. When Young said that they really wanted him to be on the board of the fourth channel, Graef remembers saying, 'Well, I don't trust you.' To which Young responded that if Graef would not do it they would invite an MP or Gus Macdonald. Eventually, when he discovered that both Anthony Smith and Sara Morrison had been invited, Graef was reassured and agreed to join the board.

Young was having equal difficulty with the ITCA companies which still expected that five out of the board's ten members would come from ITV.

However, the IBA was adamant. It insisted on adhering to Whitelaw's intention that the new channel would not be under the control of ITV. Only four out of ten of the board would come from ITV. The companies' irritation was increased still further when they learned that the IBA intended that two of these four were not to be ITV managing directors but senior programme makers. In the ensuing row some ITV companies considered instituting a total boycott of the channel. In the end the IBA agreed to compromise – three board members were to be ITV managing directors – William Brown of Scottish, David McCall of Anglia and Brian Tesler of LWT – while the fourth ITV 'representative' was to be Joy Whitby, Head of Children's Programmes at Yorkshire, one of the LWT executives who had resigned in the wake of Michael Peacock's sacking. When the names of the Fourth Channel 'consultants' were announced by the IBA at the end of June, the campaigners started to relax and feel that perhaps the IBA really had changed and would not be party to the ongoing efforts of ITV to gain control over the fourth channel. Tesler was known to many of the programme makers in the Channel Four Group and was felt to be 'one of the good guys'. Joy Whitby was also held in high esteem as an excellent programme maker and because she had stuck to her principles in the LWT affair. Along with Graef, Smith and Morrison, the board of Channel Four might really be 'independent' in the real sense of the word and not merely in its 'I'TV meaning.

*   *   *

'Going to the IBA was like visiting the headquarters of the British Empire – all that oak panelling and oil paintings. There was wood everywhere' was Michael Jackson's impression from our increasingly frequent visits that summer to the Authority's headquarters opposite Harrods. On 20 May, three weeks after IPPA's inaugural meeting at the Hyde Park Hotel, Jackson, Iain Bruce, Mike Luckwell and I with two dozen or so other independent producers joined a hundred facilities and studio owners, film financiers and guarantors at an all-day IBA Consultation on production facilities for the Fourth Channel.

Invited to speak first on behalf of the independents, I was at last able to say that we were encouraged by what we saw as a new attitude of openness in the IBA towards the ambitions and potential of the independent sector. Colin Shaw made it clear that the IBA now accepted that a significant quantity of independent facilities already existed which could be available for use in the fourth channel. What the Authority wanted to know was whether these facilities matched the needs of the independent producers and if anything was needed. Mike Luckwell assured them that sufficient film and videotape facilities already existed. Iain Bruce added that the ITV companies had no spare capacity and would have enough difficulties in meeting the demands placed on them for programmes by the fourth channel without having to worry about making facilities available to the independent sector as well. I assured them that, by and large, independents did not want to use their big conventional studio complexes with fixed plant and the tied technicians who worked in them. Independents wanted the freedom to work on location with the latest lightweight film and video equipment and editing facilities.

When the possible attitude of the unions to crewing arrangements and pay for productions for the Fourth Channel was raised Iain Bruce and I, terrified that premature public discussion might undo what we had achieved in our meeting with Sapper and Lockett, hastily deflected the discussion into safer waters, explaining that these issues were already being actively explored by the recently established independent producers' trade association.[9]

*   *   *

In spite of what was said at the IBA consultation, Michael Peacock found out that Lady Plowden and Edmund Dell were privately still not convinced that independent producers would be able to supply more than a tiny fraction of the programmes. Despite the example of independent production houses in America, they did not believe that British independents would be able to operate as profitable, ongoing independent businesses of the kind that they believed would be essential to guarantee the channel a continuing supply of programmes. Realising that the independents had still failed to establish their credibility, Peacock told Michael Luckwell that he and his Moving Picture Company, which operated its own studios, facilities and equipment and had a permanent staff of technicians, was the one person who might convince Plowden and Dell that the independents could deliver. So Luckwell set about impressing a fresh stream of visitors – Dell, Plowden, members of the shadow Channel Four board and senior IBA officials. While showing them round his Soho premises Luckwell repeatedly stressed the ongoing and profitable nature of his company's operation, making and servicing television programmes, commercials, promotions, industrial and instructional videos day in and day out the year round. His visitors often seemed surprised that the Moving Picture Company was such a large and well-oiled machine.

By now concern had begun to focus on who was to be the channel's first Chief Executive. A week after the IBA consultation advertisements appeared for a Chief Executive who 'will be responsible for the whole of the Company's operations and programme output . . . the job will be unique in British broadcasting' and a Director of Finance, 'responsible for all the financial aspects of the Company's operations . . . and oversight of a budget amounting to possibly some £70 million initially.'[10]

Although it was assumed that one or two senior BBC and ITV people, such as Brian Wenham, the Controller of BBC-2, would apply for the Chief Executive post, Jeremy Isaacs was generally regarded as the clear front-runner. Edmund Dell said later that he received so many letters and read so many newspaper articles telling him that Isaacs was the best-qualified person for the job that he started to become resistant to the idea of appointing him. Dell was not alone. Michael Jackson recalls a widely held feeling among the campaigners that 'Everyone was reluctant to give it to Jeremy Isaacs because he was the person who was going to get it.'[11] Dell, who knew no programme makers, had to ask who Isaacs was. Told of his record as a programme maker and as Director of Programmes at Thames Television, Dell was directed to the speech Isaacs had made at Edinburgh. Dell found the speech 'dissuasive not persuasive'. He might not know much about television 'but what I did know was that there wasn't much on television that I actually liked, and I therefore wanted it to be different'. Jeremy Isaacs had described his vision for Channel Four as 'different but not too different, and ITV-2 not Channel Four'.[12]

Isaacs was widely admired by programme makers and seen by many as a friend, yet they, like Dell, had been dissuaded rather than persuaded by his speech in Edinburgh. His lukewarm attitude towards independents, together with his cautious approach to the distinctive character of the channel, worried many campaigners and would-be independent producers. Was he perhaps too cautious? Had he spent so long in the senior executive echelons of ITV, and been so bruised by his fights with people like Bryan 'Ginger' Cowgill, that he was no longer capable of the real vision needed? His other weaknesses were remembered – a kind of aggressive impetuousness which was the obverse side of his instinctive creative impulse, what one future Channel Four board member and friend describes as his 'fatal flaw – a compulsion to fight with the establishment and the people who are his bosses' (a quality which often endeared him to like-minded fellow programme makers like me) and his perceived weakness as an administrator (a weakness he had

previously been able to make up for at Thames, by appointing brilliant administrators to work with him). Members of the Channel Four Group started to float
other names. What about Charles Denton of ATV?

Denton, after his time at the BBC and his work as an independent when he
and John Pilger had made their controversial Vietnam programme for *World in
Action*, had ably taken over from Bob Heller at ATV. He had run the features
and documentary department with every bit as much élan as Bob, while still
providing a safe haven and an opportunity for many of the most controversial
and adventurous spirits in television. He had defended as many good brave
programmes from the wrath of government ministers, self-appointed censors
and the IBA as Isaacs at Thames or Forman at Granada; in fact, considering that
ATV had no regular network current affairs programme, probably rather more
– programmes such *Death of an Informer* (a dramatised account of one man's
experiences as a Special Branch informer on the IRA), numerous programmes
by John Pilger and, only that April, *Death of a Princess*, Anthony Thomas's
reconstruction of the beheading of a Saudi princess and her lover for adultery.
In the very week that it had been publicly announced that Dell and
Attenborough were to head the board of the new channel, it had been
announced that two American-based Saudi lawyers were suing Denton and ATV
for no less than $20 billion on behalf of 600 million Muslims, claiming that *Death
of a Princess* was 'part of an international conspiracy to insult, ridicule, discredit
and abuse followers of Islam throughout the world'.[13] Denton was also defending
a Ken Loach documentary about steel workers from cuts demanded by the IBA.
Denton had been Director of Programmes at ATV since 1977 and so had almost
the same level of executive experience as Jeremy Isaacs. He was quieter, more
diplomatic and, with his track record, almost, if not quite, Isaacs' equal.

Iain Bruce and I invited Denton down from Birmingham to meet members of
the Channel Four Group committee. Denton explained to the committee that
a substantial proportion of the productions for which he had been responsible
at ATV had been 'independent production under another name'. The ITV
companies, he said, 'were hag-ridden by the hold that the unions had on them'.
He saw the importance of having a pool of freelance labour, always available, and
not just in the producer and director area, but of technicians as well. This had
been particularly important for ATV as it specialised in one-off programmes.
From the campaigners' point of view this was his great strength above Isaacs – as
a central plank of his policy at ATV Denton had worked with and commissioned

programmes from a great range of freelance producers, directors and technicians, engaging them to work for ATV in many ways as if they were already independents. Unlike Isaacs, he had no problem with the concept of independent producers and would not be repeatedly telling Chris Rowley at the IBA that there were no such things as independent producers. In advertisements for the post, the Fourth Channel Company's 'Consultants' had said that they would 'be glad to receive nominations or suggestions for their consideration'. It was decided to put Denton's name forward.

Dell has suggested that because Isaacs was such a strongly favoured candidate some other qualified people did not bother to apply. But, interestingly, Isaacs himself hesitated over applying: 'Bemused by the too-good-to-be-true attraction of it (the Chief Executive's job), I did nothing. A message was conveyed; did I mean to apply? If so, would I please write?' So Isaacs wrote. He did not mention where the programmes were to come from, nor what proportion might come from the independents. Nor did he mention how different his channel might be from ITV. Instead he listed his priorities:

- To encourage innovation across the whole range of programmes;
- To find audiences for the channel and for all its programmes;
- To make programmes of special appeal to particular audiences;
- To develop the channel's educational potential to the full;
- To provide platforms for the widest possible range of opinions in utterance, discussion and debate;
- To maintain as flexible a schedule as practicable to enable a quick response to changing needs;
- To make an opening in the channel for criticism of its own output;
- To accord a high priority to the arts;
- If funds allow, to make, or help make, films of feature length for television here, for the cinema abroad.[14]

Charles Denton had not applied either but, not long after meeting members of the Channel Four Group, he got a phone call asking him to come and meet Dell, Attenborough and another member of the Fourth Channel consultative board. This he did. Among the things discussed were what the job might entail and when it would be necessary for him to start if he were appointed. When Denton returned to Birmingham he wrote to Dell, telling him that he had thoroughly enjoyed the discussion, but that he would be totally committed to ATV and the retention of its ITV franchise until at least the end of 1980. Whoever was appointed would need to be able to devote his time to Channel Four from the autumn of 1980 onwards. Applications for new ITV contracts, due to come into force from the beginning of 1982, had closed on 9 May 1980. ATV was in serious danger of not having its franchise renewed. The process of applicant interviews by the IBA and submission of supplementary evidence was already in full swing and was likely to continue without respite until almost the end of the year. As a result, Denton ruled himself out of the running.

Wenham did not apply either. The Fourth Channel board considered inviting him to apply but concluded that he must have decided that his career lay with the BBC. (Years later Dell reflected that if Wenham had applied he might well have been appointed and, as a result, gone on thereafter to become Director-General of the BBC.) However, twenty-nine people did apply and three were considered by the board to be worthy of final interview. They were Jeremy Isaacs, Paul Bonner, Head of BBC Science and Features, who had been central to the internal BBC debates over the creation of self-managing production units which could operate in much the same way as independents inside the BBC, and John Birt, the Director of Programmes at LWT. On paper at least, Birt had held many of the right appointments – joint editor with Gus Macdonald of *World in Action*, producer with Germaine Greer in the 1960s of the zany (in this author's view wet) Granada comedy show, *Nice Time*, featuring Jonathan Routh and Kenny Everett, and the man behind LWT's current affairs show, *Weekend World*. His credits, with the exception of *World in Action*, looked better on paper than many of the programmes had looked on the screen. He had seemed in recent years to be prepared to pontificate about a whole range of issues in television. Michael Grade has described how Birt, in characteristic style, set out 'his master plan for the channel's future' in 'a document ten inches thick' (an equally characteristic story-enhancing Grade exaggeration, but one gets the point), stuffed with so-called 'analytical data'.[15]

There have been a number of accounts of the selection process gone through by Edmund Dell and his colleagues before they decided on who was to be the first Chief Executive of the Fourth Channel Company. The sharpest comes from Isaacs himself in his 1989 book, *Storm Over 4*: 'Eventually I was summoned to an interview in Brompton Road. "Thank you, Mr Isaacs, that will be all." Silence. Rumours that others were favoured – John Birt, Brian Wenham (but had he applied?). There was a dark horse; but who? Another summons, another interview. Tamara [Isaacs' wife] drove me on a Friday morning in late September to the IBA. "How do you find and put together a schedule of programmes? How can you ensure they are of any interest?" "You say yes to good ideas; no to bad ones." "Last question" (from Dell): "How should a chief executive relate to a chairman?" "He should keep him informed of anything of moment, consult him and seek to carry him with him in any major matter." "Thank you." And out.'[16] Dell, it seems, continued to harbour serious doubts about Isaacs, who he described as giving at both interviews 'the laid back performance of a man who knew . . . that the job was already in his pocket. The outstanding candidate,' in Dell's view, 'both at the first and second interviews, was John Birt. He had been recommended to me by John Freeman, chairman of LWT. He had worked hard at his application. He had very clear ideas for the future of Channel Four which he had developed in a 50-page submission.'[17] However, other Consultants disagreed. This is how one of them, who had better remain anonymous, describes Birt's interview: 'One of the most spooky things I've ever heard.' The 'dark horse' mentioned by Isaacs was Bonner. All the Consultants were impressed. But Bonner, as he had told the panel, did not feel that he yet had sufficient experience to qualify for the job. So it came down to Birt or Isaacs. Dell later said that his colleagues on the panel told him that under Birt the channel would be too serious and pointed out that Birt had at that stage never yet held an appointment as senior as Programme Controller and that to appoint him Chief Executive of the new channel would be too great a risk.[18] On Dell's account, therefore, Isaacs was appointed by default. The panel felt, according to Dell, that with Isaacs there were other risks and therefore decided to put it to Isaacs that Bonner should be appointed to a senior post, amounting to being Isaacs' deputy on the programme side.

Dell's assessment of the considerations behind Isaacs' appointment seems unduly negative, coloured by later disagreements between them. Fifteen years later, by which time he had read Birt's fifty-page Fourth Channel application document, Isaacs commented that the fact that Dell, unlike the rest of his board, thought Birt the outstanding candidate said as much about Dell as it did about the candidates.[19] The fact remains that Isaacs was the outstanding candidate, whether or not Dell liked his performance at interview or was impressed by Birt's studious analysis of the readership of every major newspaper in the country, and even if one takes into account those who in the end did not apply such as Denton and Wenham. There were possibly only two people who could be said to have an equal claim – Alasdair Milne and David Attenborough. Both had ruled themselves out.

At half past three the telephone rang. It was Edmund Dell. 'We have resolved unanimously to offer you the job. Congratulations. Can you come and see me now in my office.'[20] Isaacs went over immediately to Dell's office in the City and they agreed a contract for five years, starting on 1 January 1981 at a salary of £35,000 a year – the IBA had authorised a salary of £30,000, Isaacs had asked for £35,000 and Dell had agreed. Dell has suggested that the appointment of Bonner led to resentment by Isaacs arising from his discovery that 'his chairman had had strong doubts about his appointment' and 'the fact that Bonner had been imposed on him'.[21] Isaacs has repeatedly denied both resentments. He knew and admired Bonner and regarded his strengths and experience as likely to complement his own. It was, after all, Bonner who, as Chair of the Edinburgh International Television Festival, had invited Isaacs to give the 1979 McTaggart Lecture. Ill-feeling did grow up between Dell and Isaacs, but that was later and by then there was ill-feeling not just between Dell and Isaacs (here one recalls the anonymous board member's description of Isaacs' 'fatal flaw'), but between Dell and other members of the board. 'Dell was the worst chairman I've ever had,' recalls one. 'He was like the King in Petite France – a former king bouncing around on a small island. It was the only way he knew how to behave.'

But that is to run ahead of our story. At a press conference held at the IBA on Tuesday 30 September, Dell, sitting behind a desk, with an empty chair beside him which should have been occupied by the unavoidably absent Bonner, introduced Isaacs somewhat ruefully, saying that he was 'delighted to announce what has been extensively forecast in every paper'. By this time the press was rife with speculation about others who had not been appointed. The fact that Bonner was missing from the press conference provoked further speculative comment. It centred on the empty chair where Bonner should have been. Was Isaacs anxious to be seen to be 'putting a certain amount of distance between himself and Bonner from the outset?' The real gulf, that between Dell and Isaacs, went unremarked.

Answering questions, Isaacs told journalists that neither the independents nor the ITV companies would be awarded a fixed quota of programmes on the Fourth Channel. He was opposed to the whole notion of quotas and no one would have their programmes accepted 'as of right and willy-nilly'. Everyone was welcome to bring their ideas to the channel for acceptance or rejection. He challenged the ITV companies to extend and improve the service they already provided, the independents to demonstrate the quality of their work and the innovators and newcomers 'to speak to television audiences in language they will understand'. The channel would represent a broad spectrum of opinion from extreme left to extreme right: 'But there must be a selection. There will be no room for everybody and there will not be room for loonies.' Asked about his oft-repeated Edinburgh description of the channel as 'different, but not that different', Isaacs confessed to being 'not altogether happy' with it. It was the penalty for attempting to sum up something very complex in too few words. The campaigners detected that a year on from his Edinburgh speech, Isaacs' ideas about the channel and his attitude towards independents were shifting.

Jeremy Isaacs and Edmund Dell with an empty chair beside them at the press conference to announce Isaacs' appointment as first Chief Executive of Channel Four on 30 September 1980.

Courtesy of *Broadcast*

On past form Isaacs would be no diplomat and might antagonise a lot of the people that the channel would need as allies. The channel's output was likely to be idiosyncratic and uneven, unpredictable but probably exciting and some-times dangerous. With Bonner at his side to watch over the administration of the channel and a powerful Director of Finance – who was still to be appointed – Jeremy would be free to get on with what he did best – inspire programme makers.

*　　*　　*

In the meantime there had been a succession of reminders of just how big a task Isaacs, the new channel and the independents were taking on. At the end of July the Law Lords had handed down a judgement ordering Granada Television to reveal the source of documents used in a *World in Action* programme which alleged that a strike at British Steel had been largely engineered against the wishes of both the management and the unions by Mrs Thatcher's government. Sir Denis Forman and David Plowright, the two senior Granada executives most closely involved, stood firm, risking imprisonment and possibly an unlimited fine. They were urged on by the press to defend press freedom: 'Prison should be preferred to paralysis,' said the *Daily Mirror*.[22] In the end compromise was reached, albeit one that cost Granada some £200,000. Nevertheless, it posed a serious question for the campaigners: would an independent ever be able to take on the kind of current affairs reporting undertaken by the regular ITV current affairs departments when the financial risks were so great?

The BBC, meanwhile, was also suffering a series of public humiliations at the hands of the Musicians' Union. These started one morning when a scratch band, made up of striking union members calling themselves 'Aubrey's Nemesis', turned up outside the BBC's central London headquarters at Broadcasting House to serenade senior executives as they arrived for work with *Colonel Bogey*. A total of 172 BBC staff musicians had been sacked by Aubrey Singer, now the Managing Director of BBC Radio, in a cost-cutting exercise (itself an oblique throw-back to the ill-fated McKinsey report *Broadcasting in the '70s*). That season's Promenade Concerts were cancelled and, when the House of Commons debated the issue, striking musicians hired a boat and drifted down the Thames past the Houses of Parliament playing Handel's *Water Music*. In late July, after the Musicians' Union had scored a series of public relations triumphs, the BBC and the Musicians' Union (with Singer excluded from negotiations) reached a compromise.

These events raised a nagging question – could independents and an under-funded channel which did not even employ its own staff of programme makers survive in this kind of league? Did the independent programme makers *really* want to become embroiled in such time- and energy-sapping issues as union/management relations, rates of pay, High Court hearings, government and broadcaster relations and editorial control?

In his speech in the House of Lords welcoming the government's proposals for the fourth channel, Lord Annan had highlighted the important role he expected the independents to play in bringing down programme costs: 'Channel

Four, through the independent producers, has a chance to break not just the monopoly of the companies, but also the monopoly of power which the ACTT enjoys and ruthlessly exploits.'[23] Real and escalating programme costs were addressed specifically by a Royal Television Society conference held at Southern Television's studio centre in Southampton early in November 1980, under the general title 'The Production Explosion'. In a star turn at the start of the conference entitled 'Harsh Realities of Production', Michael Checkland, Controller of Planning and Resources at the BBC, spelled out the 'realities' which managements as much as unions, and many traditional programme makers, seemed unwilling to face. Taking as his starting point that an additional 5,000 hours of programmes would be needed (2,500 for Channel Four and the rest as a result of extended transmission hours on the BBC and ITV), Checkland calculated that only 4% – or 200 hours – out of this total could be drama. Assuming a continuing television production cost inflation rate of 10% (an optimistic assumption as inflation in the country as a whole was currently running at over 15%), 200 hours of drama would in only five years' time cost £40 million, equal to more than half of Channel Four's entire £70 million budget. Checkland said that the BBC had calculated that an hour of BBC drama currently cost £112,000 – averaged out between costly filmed and costume drama and cheap studio-produced serials. This included the cost of staff and equipment, but still excluded the BBC's central overheads. On the same basis, Light Entertainment programmes cost £85,000 an hour for comedy and £45,000 an hour for variety, documentaries cost almost £50,000 and purchased programmes just £9,000. Only £3 in every £10 were spent on actors, sets, writers, film stock and so on. Of the remaining £7, a massive £6 was spent on BBC staff, and £1 on buildings and new equipment. (A number of outside analysts and interested independents subsequently went into these cost calculations in detail and estimated that Checkland's figures were over-optimistic and that true total costs of programmes were substantially higher.) On Checkland's figures the lesson for Channel Four, and for the other broadcasters, was obvious. Costs were going to have to come down. This, of course, was precisely what many of the campaigners had been saying since the 1960s. The outlook, particularly for people who wanted to make expensive drama on film, was stark. New, cheaper ways of working would have to come in or the days of copious amounts of original one-off and short series drama were numbered. In theory, of course, new technology should make it possible to cut back on the number of staff needed. But, as Checkland showed, in practice this was not what happened. New technology widened producers' creative horizons; creatively ambitious programme makers wanted to stretch the possible. The result was not fewer staff or reduced costs, but more staff and enlarged costs. Checkland then turned his attention to those other sacred cows of television – manning levels, the grading systems which created demarcation problems and multi-layered management. Equipment that was simpler to use would have to start to produce lower manning levels and less use of over- – or inappropriately – skilled people. These things were going to require co-operation from the unions. Checkland concluded that the production explosion came down to numbers; to grappling with the true costs of programmes rather than hiding behind notional cost systems of the kind with which most of the executives present at the RTS had worked throughout their television careers. Yet many of these executives, particularly those in ITV, refused to see the value of the exercise undertaken by Checkland. Astonishingly, companies such as Yorkshire argued that as they were required under the terms of their IBA franchises to equip themselves with a particular amount of studio space, a specific number of cameras and quantities of other equipment and with the permanent staff to operate it, putting an itemised cash cost on each of these items was pointless. They had the resources anyway, so they had the incentive to make as much use of them as possible. To others Checkland's paper was an eye-opener. He was reportedly offered jobs by three ITV companies more or less on the spot.

If the true *total* costs of entertainment and current affairs programmes (the kind of programmes most independents aspired to make for Channel Four) averaged, as many of us believed they did, about £100,000 an hour and drama cost between three and four times that, the position facing Channel Four and independent producers, who would be working in real money and total costs only, seemed bleak. With an annual budget of £70 million and fifty hours to fill each week it was going to have less than £30,000 for each hour of programming. How would it fill the screen? Presumably the ITV companies, able to bury their true costs, would have nothing to fear from the independents? True, the IPPA Steering Committee had called for a common system of accounting between their own members and the ITV companies when they made programmes for the Fourth Channel, but so far the IBA had not responded to this call and the Fourth Channel Company still did not exist.

However, in the aftermath of the previous year's ITV strike and with a serious economic downturn still affecting advertising income, most of the ITV companies were not in any particular hurry to start supplying the Fourth Channel with programmes. So they simply made airy promises in their applications for the new ITV franchises starting in 1982 about the range of programmes they expected to supply to the new channel and then waited for the Broadcasting Bill to complete its passage through Parliament and for the IBA to announce its decisions over their franchise applications. LWT said that it would be 'disappointed' if it did not supply 130 hours to the new channel each year, while Yorkshire claimed that it would be 'necessary' for it to provide more than 100 hours. Southern presumed to offer up to 156 hours plus 'much of the bedrock', adding that 'the success of the Fourth Channel will depend on the ability of companies such as Southern to produce a broad range of programmes consistently over many years rather than the ability of independent producers contributing from time to time'. Granada claimed to have 'pressed the case that independent producers should have a proper place in the scheme of things by right' (a claim which certainly came as news to the campaigners!) and proffered a selection of weighty series, including a history of Western music and *The End of Empire*. Both series seemed designed for their ongoing international sales potential rather than to meet any obligation to innovate. Thames likewise, having made a lot of money from the overseas sales of *The World at War*, proposed a range of long shelf-life part histories, including the Twentieth Century and the Renaissance. The companies also promised to extend their facilities so as to meet the needs of the new channel, but added the proviso that they needed guarantees that this additional productive capacity would be fully utilised. An article about the companies' plans, headed *Tickets for ITV-2? – Companies Ready to Take on the Beeb*, in the October/November edition of *AIP & Co* concluded ruefully that the companies appeared to be preparing to crush the independents on the one hand and blackmail the IBA on the other.

Jeremy Isaacs had been at the RTS Southampton conference and had been asked how he hoped to achieve programmes good enough to attract a new audience with his small budget. He had contented himself with saying that he would get by. 'Channel Four will only be as good as the programmes people make for it, and those programmes will only be as good as the ideas from which they come.'[24] Of course, Isaacs knew perfectly well that with £70 million many of his programmes could not be newly commissioned or fully funded by the Fourth Channel. 'Much of what we would broadcast I knew, but was not yet saying, would be acquired material, foraged from the bazaars of the world. And some would be repeated material, picked up at a mere fraction of its total original cost, and still likely to find new audiences . . . And some would be provided below full cost by ITV companies who retained rights in their material while allowing us the two UK transmissions we needed.'[25] Although he ducked answering questions about money at Southampton, one question which he did answer was what the new channel would be called – 'The Fourth Channel, Channel 4 Television, or what?' 'Channel 4,' he said, 'and, ultimately, 4.' Channel 4 it was.

The attitude of the unions to manning on programmes for the new channel continued to concern the IPPA Steering Committee. In September I prepared a paper for the ACTT Television Freelance Shop which was due to discuss union policy on productions by independents for the channel. I reminded members of the history of changing union attitudes towards the channel and then went on to quote a leading independent producer with extensive experience of both the BBC and ITV who had recently said that the money available meant that a typical Channel Four programme 'certainly isn't drama, it certainly isn't documentary with any prolonged shooting schedule or involving any ambitious travel, it's probably a quiz game which can be syndicated in several languages across the world'. I commented that that 'certainly isn't programme making as most of us know it or would want it to become'. So what was the answer for us as freelance union members, I asked? To give up our belief in a new channel dependent on new sources of production and support ACTT members in ITV who had always maintained that only the ITV companies could afford to make the programmes for the channel, cashing in as best we could from any new work created? That would be disastrous, not only for ourselves as freelance union members but for the quality of British television as a whole. That would kill all possibility of an extension in its variety and range. The growth of a wide-ranging and financially stable independent sector, under the protected conditions offered by the Fourth Channel, was our best hope in a world of proliferating channels and new technology. Only in this way could we ensure 'the survival of a body of high quality and varied indigenous production which will remain independent of a shrinking number of ever-larger giant multi-national production conglomerates, concerned increasingly with maximising corporate profits through the production of mid-Atlantic or mid-Pacific entertainment, at the expense of the quality of our own television. The story of the British film industry provides a disheartening precedent.' We had to recognise that the accusations levelled at our industry of incipient 'Fleet Street disease' were not all groundless. There was already a new industry springing up in the independent facilities house businesses which embraced new technology and was, as a result, servicing everything from American networks to educational video production. New equipment was getting smaller and easier to use all the time and as a result we would need to develop working practices and crewing arrangements to match these changes. 'Because we are not dealing with a monolith, hard-arteried through twenty years plus of working practices and scarred by the injuries of old battles, we can develop new arrangements . . . We do not want to create a flea market in place of a well-founded industry; a happy harem for rip-off merchants to profit at the expense of the technicians and creative workers who make the product . . . but the fourth channel, by the accident which has led to its creation at this moment in history, provides an opportunity to encourage the creation of a responsible, well-founded and . . . regulated independent sector which can, in time, along with the large multinational companies, provide the bulk of the programme material which will be needed in future.' I said that it seemed unlikely that either the IBA or the Fourth Channel Company would wish to enter into direct negotiations with the unions over production agreements. It therefore behoved the union and the Freelance Television Shop to start discussions with the newly formed independent producers' association, IPPA. I then suggested, without referring to Iain Bruce's and my conversation with Sapper and Lockett, that the union's Short Film Agreement, with its built-in flexibility, could provide the starting point from which to develop agreements to cover production for the Fourth Channel. 'For too long our union has vacillated over the Fourth Channel, taking a negative, or at best half-hearted attitude . . . It is in the interests of all of us to reap the benefits of the Fourth Channel. To do so we have to adopt a positive stance to what we want from it, informed by a realistic attitude to what we can reasonably expect to get.'[26]

Inevitably not all freelance members of the ACTT agreed. There were those who unsurprisingly suspected that, as I was a member of the Council of the Channel Four Group, of AIP and the IPPA Steering Committee as well of the ACTT's Fourth Channel Committee, I had an axe to grind. 'A cynical view of the Paper', two of my critics wrote, 'could suggest that it is a cleverly disguised argument for the TV Freelance Shop to act unilaterally in sanctioning the introduction of short crews, new equipment and untried participation deals.' As an alternative it was suggested that the Freelance Shop should adopt a policy which stipulated that 'pay and conditions' on productions made by independents for the Fourth Channel should be 'no less favourable than those which obtain within the ITCA companies'.[27] Argument banged back and forth over the next few weeks. Those who saw things as I did suggesting that, however unpalatable it might be to some union members, a 'tide of financial and technological change' was rising around the world which would not be prevented from engulfing us 'because we sit on the beach in the attitude of King Canute'. We had a unique opportunity to harness that tide to our ends and we should take it. Slowly IPPA and the union moved towards each other and to an acceptance of the ideas discussed by Iain Bruce, Sapper, Lockett and me six months earlier.

*   *   *

The Broadcasting Bill received the Royal Assent on 13 November 1980.[28] The Channel Four Company was incorporated as a company limited by shares wholly owned by the IBA on 10 December 1980 and the Board of Directors of the Company, comprising the Consultants together with Jeremy Isaacs,[29] held its inaugural meeting on 17 December when Terms of Reference were presented to it by the IBA.

The following day Jeremy Isaacs announced plans to meet independent producers for the first time at an open meeting. 'At the moment,' he said, 'there is a great deal of ignorance and uncertainty among many of the independents as to what the procedures are going to be when the time comes for them to offer us their programmes or programme ideas. The preliminary purpose of this meeting is to clear up any misconceptions on that score and to answer whatever questions have occurred to them since Channel Four was first announced.'[30]

Frustrated hopes and pent-up creativity dating back, in some cases, to 1968, the Hatton BFI revolt and the birth of the Free Communications Group, now helped to carry events along. Since his appointment Isaacs had, in his own words, become 'enthralled by being given the job of my dreams . . . I was being buoyed up by waves of enthusiasm from programme makers . . . I was a different person by the beginning of '81, and even more different by the beginning of '82 and '83.'[31]

Working to the publisher model originally prescribed by Anthony Smith and now enshrined in the Act, Isaacs had been looking for a number of commissioning editors to acquire and commission programmes in much the same way as editors in a publishing house. On 5 January 1981 he announced the names of his first three senior commissioning editors – David Rose for 'Fiction' (what in other broadcasters would have been called drama), Naomi McIntosh for the 15% of the channel's airtime that was to be devoted to education, and Liz Forgan for Actuality (the programmes others called News and Current Affairs). Isaacs, it seemed, was determined that from the outset his channel would be different.

The people chosen for these crucial roles seemed to say something about Isaacs' developing vision for the channel. David Rose, with twenty-five years in BBC Television, which included being one of the original team which had created the BBC's long-running breakthrough police series *Z Cars* back in 1960, and most recently as the Head of English Regions Drama based in Birmingham, was the most experienced. In recent years Rose had commissioned a range of new writing, including scripts from members of ethnic minorities. Isaacs had originally wanted Christopher Morahan but Morahan had turned him down owing to his other commitments. He had suggested Rose. In his letter of application for the post of Chief Executive Isaacs had mentioned commissioning films of feature length. With limited funds, Rose and Isaacs had decided to make their first priority putting up to £300,000 into each of twenty original films per year to be shown on television in Britain and in cinemas elsewhere in the world. As Isaacs later described it, they were to be 'the sort of films which a healthy British cinema would be supplying if there were one'.[32] As we shall see later, the effects of this decision were to be both extremely positive and decidedly negative.

Although she had little experience of conventional television production outside the specialist education field, Isaacs' choice of Naomi McIntosh, the Professor of Applied Research and Pro-Vice-Chancellor at the Open University, and former chair of a government Advisory Committee on Adult and Continuing Education, could be seen as sound and reassuring. However, the third of his appointments, Liz Forgan, to head Actuality, was much bolder – exciting or dangerous depending on the viewpoint of the person commenting. Forgan, the Women's Editor of the *Guardian*, had no previous television production experience. During his 1979 McTaggart Lecture in Edinburgh Isaacs had said that in the 1980s he hoped to see 'more programmes made by women for women which men will watch'. Women's groups had been lobbying throughout the 1970s against discriminatory employment and promotion practices in the media, in particular in broadcasting. The Women's Fourth Channel Lobby (later re-named the Women's Broadcasting and Film Lobby) had been active since 1979. During an extremely effective session at the Edinburgh International Television Festival in 1980, entitled 'Women's Reality', Mary Holland had given a paper *Out of the Bedroom and on to the Board*, in which she had produced figures showing that of 157 producers in the BBC only 25 were women, and that in ITV of the 74 producers/directors working on the three regular current affairs programmes only 10 were women. Following this, Forgan, working on a series of articles for the *Guardian* entitled *Women and the Media Men*, had written to Isaacs asking for an interview and saying that she hoped he was aware that he was 'the great white hope of 51 per cent of the population who feel themselves completely traduced by television'.[33] While she was interviewing him Isaacs had impressed Forgan by saying that he would like to get women to make the channel's weekly current affairs programme which should depend for its success 'on its ability to interest viewers, not to promote a cause, but which had the added bonus that it comes from people who are standing at a different angle to the universe from the male sex. It may therefore come up with a different set of attitudes, a different mix, a different set of priorities.'[34] At the end of the interview, after she had turned off her tape recorder, Isaacs had asked Forgan if she would be interested in taking charge of all Channel Four's News and Current Affairs output. She had replied: 'Do you realise that I never watch television? I'm a print journalist, I hate television, I loathe and despise it, it's a poisonous medium about which I know and care nothing.' 'Perfect,' he replied, 'just what I want.'

*   *   *

On 16 January 1981 Isaacs held his first formal set-piece general meeting with independents. Once again, the level of interest from independents, would-be independents and others had been underestimated. The steeply raked semi-circular bowl of the lecture theatre of the Royal Institution, constructed like an intimate indoor Greek amphitheatre, will seat 430. Channel Four had asked those who wanted to attend to apply for tickets in advance; 500 applied for tickets and as a result some of the audience had to be accommodated in an over-spill room with sound relayed to them via a public address system. Even then some ticket holders were unable to get in. Many of those unable to get in were genuine independents while many who did get in were not. In the words of *Broadcast* – 'One quick glance around the room showed that the place was packed with company faces and salesmen.'[35] Despite such frustrations the independents who were at the meeting gave Isaacs a genuinely warm greeting, even though some of the things he had to say to them were a disappointment. Isaacs, with Dell and Paul Bonner sitting beside and behind him at the desk at the amphitheatre's focal point, addressed the audience and answered questions for a total of two and a half hours without once turning to Bonner or Dell for assistance, clarification or support. 'The Ayatollah Isaacs' was how one independent unkindly described his performance afterwards.

Listing the type of programmes he was looking for in order of priority after the fixed 15% quota of educational material, he highlighted programming for 16–25 years olds – a group largely overlooked by the BBC and ITV – including the kind of music they wanted to hear, programmes that showed women as they are rather than as men desired them to be, programmes reflecting that Britain is a multi-racial society, debates stretching across the spectrum from far right to far left, and entertainment. The channel's programmes had to reach a large audience at least some of the time and, as the Act dictated, to be innovative and cater for audiences not adequately catered for elsewhere on television. On budgets, the average figure of slightly less than £30,000 per hour was wheeled out, but with the proviso that a few programmes might get five times that amount and a lot a great deal less. Inexpensive television need not be bad television, witness *Mastermind* or *Snooker*. No one would make a fortune from Channel Four, but there would be scales of profit margin, the percentage varying in inverse proportion to the scale of a programme's total cost – so a programme or series with a small budget would receive a proportionately larger percentage margin than one costing more. The independents, Isaacs said, would provide a minimum of ten hours of programmes a week, equal to about 20%. 'You call that *substantial?*' asked one independent and was told firmly, 'Yes.' Isaacs told independents that they should do what they could do very well, identify a need that is not being satisfied elsewhere and then persuade Channel Four that you are the best person to meet that need. 'Do not', he said, 'make a programme without a commission from us, and do not leave steady jobs, mortgage the house and send the family out to work unless you've had your programme commissioned.'[36] Independents would need to satisfy the channel that they could pay union members' wages and, he announced, negotiations were already going on about the possibility of IPPA becoming the independent producers' negotiating body. However, Channel Four would not exclude independents because they were not members of IPPA. Turning back to the unions, Isaacs said that he realised that they feared the possible destabilising effect that the arrival of the independents might have on the industry and that it might suit them if he were only to commission programmes from six independents. That might suit them, but it would be unfair. The channel would be open for business as far as producers with major project proposals were concerned from 1 April. After the meeting Alan Sapper, General Secretary of the ACTT, pronounced himself 'sanguinely encouraged'.

What followed was a period, lasting until late 1982, of frantic gearing up, negotiation and refinement all round in preparation for Channel Four to go on air. Now each day seemed to produce an announcement about the appointment of a new member of staff by the channel. On the day after Isaacs addressed independents, the *Guardian* reported the appointment of Derek Hill as the channel's programme buyer, along with Leslie Halliwell, who was to combine his job of buying major feature films for ITV with buying and scheduling them for the Fourth Channel. Hill had founded the Short Film Service back in the 1960s and had more recently been programming two London film clubs – The Essential Cinema and the ICA. Hill was a long-time friend and supporter of the aspirations of the campaigners. A few months after his appointment he made public his commitment to independent film suppliers in a sensational open letter to Isaacs. 'Parliament has instructed Channel Four to support the independents, not to milk them,'[37] he wrote. Traditional film-buying practice in television must be abandoned in favour of a policy which paid much more regard to the needs of struggling independents. Isaacs rebuked Hill – the channel did not want to screw anybody, but such a line of argument carried to its logical conclusion could cost the under-funded channel dear. The channel had been instructed by Parliament to foster television production by British independents rather than to prop up foreign film makers.

Nevertheless the essential difference between attitudes at Channel Four and elsewhere in television was becoming steadily more marked. As more commissioning editors were taken on, Hill was not the only one who was a known friend and ally of the independents and campaigners. Paul Madden, the television officer at the BFI, was taken on to look after archive programmes, with responsibility for single documentaries. Alan Fountain, a member of the IFA and of the BFI Production Board, was taken on to look after independent film and video makers. He was to be responsible for £250,000 that would be set aside for the work of small film workshops and collectives like the London Film Makers' Co-op and the people organised by the IFA.

Sue Woodford of *World in Action* was to nurture work by and for the ethnic minorities, even more scandalously excluded and under-represented than women both in and on British television. These were good people. They were joined by more from outside television – the man who ran the most interesting music radio station in Britain – Andy Park of Clyde Radio – and Walter Donohue, who had worked with new writers including Hanif Kureishi and Michael Wilcox at the Royal Court, to work with David Rose. The unpredictable Michael Kustow who had run and, in Isaacs' phrase, 'been run out of', the ICA, before moving on to work at the RSC and the National Theatre with Peter Hall came in to look after arts programmes. Most were taken on on three-year contracts. Isaacs made it clear that as television lived off new ideas and especially as Channel Four had been charged with a duty to innovate, it would require a regular supply of new blood to commission its programmes. He therefore intended, as a principle, to change his commissioning team on a regular basis. This was becoming unlike any television company any of us had ever seen before, and it was certainly a long way from the safe, refined and advertiser-catered colour supplement world conjured up repeatedly during the 1970s by Howard Thomas and successive committees or apologists for the ITCA and the IBA.

The new channel was steadily gaining mass and personality. It was exciting. It was also haphazard and chaotic. After his address to the independents at the Royal Institution Isaacs had been approached by 'a sallow, dark, hollow-eyed fellow in a T-shirt, jeans and dirty sneakers',[38] who had asked him if it was true that he was prepared to allow, in the interests of realism, dialogue that other broadcasters would not countenance. Isaacs told him that it was and his interlocutor, who it turned out was Phil Redmond, the author of the BBC's controversial new early-evening drama series set in an inner city secondary school, *Grange Hill*, told Isaacs that he had something for him. It turned out to be *Brookside*, the Channel Four soap that was to run for more than twenty years. Stories multiplied of Isaacs being cornered by enterprising and impetuous programme makers in restaurants, bars, after meetings and even in gents' lavatories and of him agreeing or rejecting ideas on the spur of the moment. Isaacs has told of being accosted twice by producers on the short walk between Warren Street and Tottenham Court Road. Meanwhile those who were less courageous, more shy or without the opportunity to corner Isaacs in person, wrote in with their ideas. They often waited months in vain for a reply.

Independents continued to worry about how many programmes they would be allowed to make and the terms under which they would be commissioned. The ITV companies continued to whinge that they would be 'subsidising' Channel Four and in return expected to supply the lion's share of its programmes. Anthony Smith and the other 'independent' members of the Channel Four Board eventually got fed up with this repeated refrain and started to speak out against it. In the spring of 1981 the Channel Four Group again attacked the ITV companies' claims. They would not be subsidising Channel Four, they would be paying a subscription in return for the right to sell airtime to advertisers on the new channel. If advertising did not exceed the subscriptions paid by the companies in the early years, most of the shortfall would be covered by the resulting reduction in the Exchequer Levy paid by the companies to the government. This riposte to the complaints of the ITV companies turned out to be almost the Channel Four Group's last act. By now most of the day-to-day work on behalf of independents was being done by IPPA. Increasing amounts of the programme makers' time was being taken up trying to win and then make programme commissions.[39]

Notes

1. Colin Young, interviewed by the author in November 2000.
2. John Gau, interviewed by the author in October 2000.
3. Michael Peacock, interviewed by the author in November 2000.
4. Five days after the Hyde Park Hotel meeting, after two hostages had been killed, the SAS did storm the Iranian embassy.
5. From the first draft version of the original 'Aims and Objectives' of the Independent Programme Producers' Association.
6. *Aims and Objectives of the Association*, IPPA statement, June 1980.
7. *Controversies in the Early History of Channel Four* by Edmund Dell, included in Catterall, *op. cit.*
8. *Ibid.*
9. Quotations taken from a transcript of *A Consultation. The Fourth Channel: Production Facilities*, held on 20 May 1980, produced by the Independent Broadcasting Authority and issued to participants.
10. Advertisement placed in television industry trade publications and elsewhere by the IBA in the week commencing Monday 21 July 1980.
11. Michael Jackson, interviewed by the author in October 2000.
12. Dell, quoted in Catterall, *op. cit.*, and Docherty, *op. cit.*
13. See *Broadcast*, 2 June 1980. Later the Edinburgh International Television Festival was threatened with closure because it had decided to organise a showing of the programme to allow delegates who had missed it on transmission to see for themselves what all the fuss was about. The threat was successfully resisted by the Festival's organisers.
14. *Storm Over 4: A Personal Account* by Jeremy Isaacs, George Weidenfeld & Nicolson Ltd, London, 1989.
15. See Grade, *op. cit.* and Catterall, *op. cit.*
16. Isaacs, *op. cit.*
17. Catterall, *op. cit.*
18. See *ibid.*
19. See *ibid.*
20. Isaacs, *op. cit.*

21. Catterall, *op. cit.*
22. Quoted by Forman, *op. cit.* Some of the newspaper executives who in August 1980 were so vociferous in urging an adherence to principle at whatever cost turned out to be a good deal less courageous than Forman, Plowright and Granada a few years later when a row over the leaking of a Department of Defence document placed them in a similarly exposed position.
23. *Hansard*, 24 July 1980.
24. Quoted in an internal Channel Four Group paper, entitled *The Story So Far*, March 1981.
25. Isaacs, *op. cit.*
26. *The Freelance and the Fourth Channel*, paper by the author prepared for the ACTT Television Freelance Shop meeting of 16 September 1980.
27. *The Freelance and the Fourth Channel Service: A Critique of the Michael Darlow Paper*, Richard Key and Peter Farrell, ACTT Television Freelance Shop, undated.
28. All the legislation in the Broadcasting Act 1980 was consolidated on 30 October 1981 in the Broadcasting Act 1981, Chapter 68, with the provisions creating Channel Four in sections 10 to 13, 32 to 36 and 43 of that Act.
29. Isaacs was later joined on the Board by the Managing Director and Deputy Chief Executive Justin Dukes and Paul Bonner.
30. Quoted in *The Story So Far*, an internal paper produced by the Channel Four Group in March 1981.
31. Sir Jeremy Isaacs, interviewed by the author in October 2000.
32. Quoted in *Channel Four: Television with a Difference?* by Stephen Lambert, BFI Publishing, London 1982, from an unpublished transcript of a speech entitled *Channel Four – A Different Sort of Television?* given by Jeremy Isaacs at the National Film Theatre on 19 January 1982.
33. Liz Forgan, interviewed in Catterall, *op. cit.*
34. *Guardian*, 'Sticking Pins into Wax Dolls', 1 December 1980.
35. *Broadcast*, 26 January 1981.
36. *Ibid.*
37. Derek Hill, open letter to Jeremy Isaacs, 17 July 1981.
38. Isaacs, *op. cit.*
39. In 1980 *Time Out* had put up £500, largely at the instigation of the magazine's young television editor, John Wyvver, to continue the Channel Four Group's work into 1981. In 1982 it was replaced by a Channel Four Users' Group, intended to hold the Channel to its remit and defend it when it came under attack. This group, like others before it, ran out of steam.

9

Storms over 4! – 1981 to 1983

Channel Four was not coming to birth in a political vacuum. The historian Arthur Marwick describes the spring and summer of 1981 as a key moment in the rise of Thatcherism. The previous autumn Thatcher had told the Conservative Party conference that 'the lady was not for turning' and in March 1981, despite a threatened revolt by some members of her cabinet, her Chancellor Geoffrey Howe brought in a swingeing budget. He slashed public sector borrowing, cut a further £3,500 million from public expenditure and increased taxation. It was the most deflationary budget in modern history. Unemployment rose to over three million and the recession deepened, becoming worse even than in the 1930s. The post-war assumptions, the context in which the ideas and aspirations of the film-maker rebels and programme-producer campaigners had been born and nurtured – full employment, powerful trade unions and the public service ethos – were each being overturned. In April rioting broke out in Brixton. Shops, homes and cars were smashed up or torched, 143 policemen were taken to hospital, many civilians were injured and almost 200 arrests made. As summer progressed the riots spread to other deprived areas – to Finsbury Park, Wood Green, Southall, Toxteth in Liverpool, Bristol, Manchester, Leicester, Birmingham, Hull, Wolverhampton and Preston. The Thatcher government's reputation as inflexible and devoid of compassion grew. But Thatcher and her two staunchest cabinet lieutenants, Howe and Joseph, were not to be deflected. Ministers who objected to her policies, 'Wets' as she called them, were simply removed and replaced with hard men. Out went Conservatives of the old school – Soames, Gilmour, Prior (some removed from the cabinet altogether, others moved to posts where they could do less 'harm'). In came others who were 'dry', Nicholas Ridley, John Nott, Nigel Lawson, Cecil Parkinson and Norman Tebbit. As if all this were not enough, in Ireland members of the IRA held in custody by the British had gone on hunger strike. In May the first of them, Bobby Sands, died. His death was followed in succeeding months by the deaths of nine more hunger strikers. There was a new wave of IRA bomb attacks in mainland Britain. But Thatcher still refused to bow to their demand to be treated as prisoners of war rather than as convicted criminals. By late 1981 opinion surveys showed the Thatcher government was one of the most unpopular ever to hold office. Experts inside her government and out, believed the government could not survive beyond the next election.

The Labour Party, now led by Michael Foot, was also in disarray. The deepening split between Left and Right drove moderates Shirley Williams, David Owen, William Rodgers and former Labour Chancellor Roy Jenkins (dubbed the 'Gang of Four' in echo of the four senior Maoist leaders arrested after Mao Tse Tung's death in China in 1976), to issue the Limehouse Declaration and form a new party, the SDP (Social Democratic Party). The new party rapidly gained support among both Labour and Conservative voters and MPs. As a result, in November 1981 Shirley Williams won the first of a series of stunning SDP by-election victories, overturning a Conservative majority of 19,000 in Cosby, Liverpool.

As well as greater economic turmoil and political volatility than at any time since 1945, there was also an air of unreality. In July, while skinheads and Asians fought in Southall and Toxteth went up in flames, the country prepared for Lady Diana Spencer to marry Prince Charles in St Paul's Cathedral. What seemed the consummation of a perfect fairy-tale romance was watched by the largest worldwide television audience in history. That autumn the British film industry underwent yet another of its miraculous re-births. A film called *Chariots of Fire*, produced by former commercials' producer David Puttnam, directed by a commercials' director Hugh Hudson and written by television writer and former *Z Cars* actor, Colin Welland, was wowing them in Hollywood and London alike. We had said that 'the British film industry is alive and well and living in television' – if you counted commercials perhaps it was true. In March the following year the film won four Oscars (it had been nominated for seven), including Best Picture. In an outburst of unbridled exuberance Colin Welland, on being presented with his Oscar for Best Original Screenplay, announced exultantly to the assembled Hollywood tuxedos: 'The British are coming!'

The McTaggart Lecture, which opened the 1981 Edinburgh International Television Festival, was given by Peter Jay, Chairman of the new TV-am which had been awarded the ITV breakfast television franchise and was due to start broadcasting early in 1983. Jay was a top person's top person. The son of a

Labour Cabinet minister, Douglas Jay, he had been educated at Winchester and Oxford. He had married Labour Prime Minister Callaghan's daughter Margaret. An economist and journalist, he had been the presenter of John Birt's LWT current affairs show *Weekend World*, the co-author with Birt of influential articles about the inherent weaknesses of television news and current affairs and the British Ambassador in Washington when father-in-law Callaghan was prime minister. In 1974 he had been named by *Time* magazine as one of the 150 people most likely to achieve leadership in Europe and dubbed by the *Sunday Times* 'The Cleverest Man in England?'. In his McTaggart Lecture Jay gave his vision of television in the year 2000, when the proliferation of outlets – video, satellites and fibre optic cable – would result in almost total deregulation of broadcasting. No one, he said, should be 'disposed to ask with feigned astonishment how it is that the chairman of a company holding a franchise under the existing system is to be found advocating the eventual liquidation of that system'. He looked forward with enthusiasm to the time when television companies were like publishers, providing consumer–viewers with any kind of programme that they cared to pay for. Some special laws might be necessary to deal with copyright and obscenity, but apart from that: 'The only necessary function of the State is to lay a duty on British Telecom to provide and operate the technology of the system, to accept all programmes which conform to the law, to collect charges from the viewing public and, after deducting its own costs and any other approved taxes or charges, to pass what remains over to the publisher of each item.' He concluded that 'there need be literally no limit to what can be published electronically, other than the general law and what the public (and others) will pay for'.[1]

Writing in 1980 about an earlier occasion on which Peter Jay had produced much the same thesis, Michael Jackson had written that the Jay equation seemed to add up to this: 'More and different broadcasting outlets = more diversity of ownership and control = more choice of programming. But could it be that a different equation might be more appropriate: more and different broadcasting outlets = greater monopoly = less choice?'[2] During Jay's Edinburgh lecture Phillip Whitehead, who was sitting next to me, whispered in my ear, 'Get up and ask him why it is that the invention of the photocopier didn't liberate publishing?' As soon as the lecture was over Whitehead crept out of the hall. Among my notes on Jay's lecture I recently found this: 'Recognising that there was no point in telling a traveller staggering into Damascus that what he had seen was not what he believed it was but the onset of a particularly severe attack of migraine, I too tiptoed silently away.'

Six months after Jay's lecture the government announced the setting-up of an inquiry under Lord Hunt of Tamworth to look into the issues and in particular at how to 'secure the benefits' of cable technology and direct broadcasting by satellite 'in a way consistent with the wider public interest, in particular the safeguarding of public service broadcasting'. The Hunt Inquiry Report, when it came out a year after Jay's Edinburgh lecture, paid rather more attention than Jay had to the inherently much higher costs of producing a television programme than of writing and printing a book. The Hunt Report also recognised the danger of 'the bad driving out the good' and the need to protect public service broadcasting.[3]

Peter Jay delivering 1981 McTaggart Memorial Lecture at the Edinburgh International Television Festival. Damascene vision or onset of a particularly severe attack of migraine?

Courtesy of *Broadcast*

*   *   *

In September 1981 Channel Four announced its first twenty-four programme commissions – all of them going to independents. Isaacs had said that he intended to commission initially only those projects which required long lead and production times or could only be made if they were shot immediately. Accordingly, major drama projects, Channel Four-financed feature films and programmes with a strong topical element featured heavily. The documentaries included one about the National Youth Jazz Orchestra going on tour in Turkey, *Playing Turkey*, produced by Sophie Balhetchet. One of the producers working on another, *The Sixties*, a major series commissioned from the Robert Stigwood Organisation, was Michael Jackson. The list included the first five *Film on Four* low-budget feature films, a music series from Chris Nupen, the brilliant maker of music films whose dedication, at whatever financial cost to himself, had made such a strong impression at the presentation of independents' work at BAFTA in the summer of 1979. More curious was an arrangement to record for television the whole of the Royal Shakespeare Company's hit stage adaptation of *Nicholas Nickleby*.

Michael Grade had been to see the show with Melvyn Bragg and become convinced that LWT must televise it. 'We began to negotiate the usual minefield laid by the unions and, as we feared, the provisional budget had almost as many noughts in it as the National Debt. Layers of over-manning, Spanish practices, penalty payments for trivial infringements of the union agreement and grossly inflated wages sank the project without trace.'[4] So Grade approached the man responsible for the overseas sales and distribution of LWT's programmes Richard Price (it was Price who had organised the ADP soirée for Conservative MPs attended by Leon Brittan in 1979). Grade suggested that Price should set up an independent production company and do the show through that. In turn, Price approached the BBC and other ITV companies but they could not agree satisfactory terms with the cast and Equity either. So he and his business partner, Colin Callander, went to see Isaacs in his office above the IBA in Brompton Road. Isaacs said he would commission it. But, of course, Channel Four had no union agreements either. So Price went direct to the senior official in Equity with responsibility for television. By now so much time had elapsed that it looked as if the recording would not happen, as the show was due to transfer to Broadway. With time running out Price and a senior Equity official met on a Sunday evening. At the eleventh hour they hammered out a deal. The recording could go ahead provided that all the members of the cast agreed and were each made shareholder–partners in the recording so that they would have a share in any profits that were made from it.[5]

The drama behind setting up the recording of *Nicholas Nickleby* and the protracted negotiations Sophie Balhetchet had had to go through with Channel Four's embryo staff over her programme both served to highlight the by now pressing need for standard terms of trade and agreements between the new channel, the producers' trade association, IPPA and the unions. Although the deals agreed by Price and Balhetchet had in practice set many of the parameters for future deals, independent producers urgently needed an ongoing formal template upon which to base their financial calculations when putting forward projects. Artists, technicians, producers and the channel needed agreements that both regulated and regularised the way they worked for and dealt with each other. In the background, and unknown to the independents, the ITV companies continued to try to cause trouble by bringing pressure on Channel Four to adopt the ITV union agreements. If they succeeded the ITV companies would not only make their own lives easier, they would wipe out much of the advantage the independents hoped to have in programme costs.

By the autumn of 1981 IPPA had over 200 members. Isaacs had repeatedly gone out of his way to caution people employed in the BBC and ITV against rushing out and setting up their own production companies in expectation of commissions and possible wealth from Channel Four. But increasingly it looked as if some people, perhaps not in the expectation of wealth but in the hope of an opportunity to make long-cherished programmes and find a freer way of working, had not heeded Isaacs' warnings. Even those who had founded IPPA were surprised by the rapidity with which its membership had grown. In the process it had developed into a curious hybrid, between a campaign, a lobby group and a producers' trade association. Most of the money initially needed to get the association formally incorporated and functioning had been put up in the form of two cheques written out shortly after that first exploratory meeting at the Hyde Park Hotel by Peacock and Mike Luckwell. Until IPPA could afford offices of its own the Steering Committee had usually met in Mike Luckwell's office in the Moving Picture Company in Soho or just across Oxford Street in Michael Peacock's office at Video Arts. To those of us who had been involved in successive campaigns over the fourth channel and the reform of broadcasting since the 1960s there was a strange excitement about those early steering group meetings and the formative months of IPPA. As independent producers we were coming of age back in the Soho streets where so many of us had begun dreaming and plotting ten or fifteen years earlier. Since January 1981 IPPA had been headed by an elected twenty-member council, made up of some of the original campaigners, new young producers like Sophie Balhetchet, a few well-known producers who had recently left the broadcasters and representatives of the older established independent companies, like Mike Luckwell and Michael Peacock. It was governed by a set of rules cobbled together by me during a rain-sodden weekend in a caravan by the river Thames. The rules, as Michael Peacock later described them, were 'a heady mixture of democratic process and paranoia about ITV'.[6]

In June 1981 representatives of IPPA, led by Peacock, the treasurer Mark Shelmardine, Denise O'Donoghue, the association's young first administrator recruited from a large firm of city accountants and Graham Benson (Benson was married to the Free Communications Group's first organiser, Christine Fox. In the 1970s he had been a shop steward in the BBC and later, as a producer, one of those involved in trying to get the BBC to experiment with smaller self-contained production units), began a series of sometimes bruising and often frustrating negotiations with Channel Four's newly appointed senior administrative officers Justin Dukes, David Scott and Frank McGettigan. The negotiations covered how programmes were to be commissioned and the financial and legal terms that would govern them. The frustration of the meetings arose from the fact that while the producers had no real clout other than the vague promises of politicians, the Channel Four negotiators had no real understanding of television or how show-business deals worked and the needs of the producers. They had been recruited from outside television. Justin Dukes, the Channel's recently recruited Managing Director, and Frank McGettigan, Head of Administration and Industrial Relations, had both come from the *Financial Times*. David Scott, the Finance Director, from the accountants Peat Marwick. Later they were joined by Colin Leventhal as Head of the Channel's Programme Acquisition Department, who had been Head of Copyright at the BBC. Unfortunately, while the BBC's interests as a broadcaster might be the same as those of Channel Four, the interests of its producers were substantially different.

The areas of agreement and disagreement became apparent at their very first meeting. The areas of disagreement were essentially the same then, in the summer of 1981, as they were to remain between independent producers and broadcasters for the next twenty years. They centred on the purpose and definition of profits and programme rights. Although the issues would be discussed many times they would never be really satisfactorily resolved. One element in the disagreement was the so-called 'Production Fee', the margin of profit to be retained by the independent production company, calculated as a percentage of the total budgeted costs of a production. 'Justin Dukes didn't come out of broadcasting,' recalls Michael Peacock. 'I could not get him to see sense. If the Production Fee is too low there will nothing to show for the producer. I told him, "You will have a lot of *dependent* producers, and a few very big *independent* ones." Which is more or less what happened. The negotiations were all about rights and Production Fees.'[7]

Channel Four's first 'discussion draft' of the standard terms of trade accepted that the Channel should meet all the overheads, such as office and secretarial costs, that were directly attributable to a production, together with any agreed development costs. The draft suggested that the all-important 'basic Production Fee' should be 'up to 15%, subject to the scale of the production'. As an incentive to producers to save money, it also proposed that the producer should receive 50% of any savings achieved on the agreed budget during production. Conversely, profligacy would be punished – the producer would have to find the money to meet overspends except where they resulted from circumstances beyond his control. The Channel intended to introduce a system of detailed budget scrutiny prior to the authorisation of a production, backed by a system of cost reporting and cash-flow financing, similar to that used in film production. The Channel hoped in this way to maintain control of programme costs. The nightmare scenarios painted by Michael Checkland at the RTS's Southampton conference the previous autumn, the horror stories about union malpractices and Spanish customs, together with Isaacs' own experience of working in ITV, added to the already generally accepted view of producers as spoiled children who were uninterested in and/or incapable of controlling their own costs. Senior executives at Channel Four were extremely fearful that their meagre programme budget would be seriously overspent. Although a contingency element was built into some budgets, Isaacs later admitted that he had assumed privately that there would be a 10% overrun on the Channel's budget in the first year and had feared it might substantially exceed this.[8]

Crucially, Channel Four proposed to take ownership, both copyright and physical ownership of the master tape, of each programme which it commissioned. Professional advisers had told the Channel that it was important for tax purposes to be able to demonstrate to the Inland Revenue that the channel owned the programmes it had paid for. IPPA was seriously worried by this because of the adverse effect it was likely to have on independents' ability to build up the asset base of their businesses. IPPA therefore sought its own expert advice. This flatly contradicted the Channel Four interpretation of the tax rules. However, Channel Four remained immovable. On top of this Channel Four proposed that 75% of all income arising from overseas sales and other exploitations, such as book publication or records of the music, from any programme which the channel had commissioned and 100% financed should go to the Channel.

'What I objected to at the time was that most independent producers were going to be dependent',[9] says Michael Peacock. Inevitably, as Chief Executive of the new channel, Isaacs saw things differently: 'We saw independent producers as a source of diversity, as a help towards the fulfilment of our pluralist purpose rather than primarily as businesses . . . We were charged to provide a distinctive service first and foremost, not principally to sustain a viable business sector.'[10] Isaacs' corporate view was informed by his background in the television of the 1960s and 1970s, a background shared by many of the independents: 'The socio-political beliefs that I had about Channel Four hindered the growth of the independent sector. I wanted the individual voice. I felt I was doing them a favour by allowing them to make programmes that they had proposed to us, not that we proposed to them. Through my attitude and the cost-plus basis of commissioning I was not allowing businesses to develop.'[11]

Channel Four remained adamant over the principles that would underpin the determination of profits and the entitlement to rights in the programmes. In the final analysis, the Channel had all the weapons and the independents had virtually none. It says a lot for the hard-nosed negotiating skills and gravitas of Michael Peacock, and the combination of bluster and bluff with which he and his team carried on the negotiations, that IPPA gained as much from Channel Four as it did. The negotiations laid down the basis on which the independent sector has been built ever since. The 'basic Production Fee of up to 15 %, subject to the scale of production' became a sliding scale of between 10% and 25%, based on the size of the budget – the smaller the budget, the higher the Production Fee, with 25% attaching to budgets of £50,000 or below and 10% to those of over £1 million. The producer's entitlement to a share of the net profits from overseas sales and further exploitation of his programme was raised from 25% to 30%, with a provision for this to be 40% in some instances. IPPA had argued for 50%.

At their first negotiating meeting, IPPA told the Channel Four representatives that it hoped to set up a joint industrial relations committee with the film producers' association, the BFPA, and to employ the BFPA's industrial relations officer jointly. IPPA's decision to combine its industrial relations operation with the BFPA's had been made in full knowledge of the risks – past disagreements between the established film producers and the campaigners (in particular with members of AIP), film producers' working practices and the profligacy of their methods, the high fees they paid to technicians and actors and the poor manning agreements they had with the unions. IPPA had explored the idea of setting up its own industrial relations service but had eventually decided, in spite of the severe doubts of some members of IPPA's Council, that working with the BFPA would simultaneously avoid costly duplication and reassure suspicious trade unions. But what really decided IPPA was that industrial relations officers with experience of the film and television industries were very thin on the ground. The BFPA had one of the few, John Walton, who was respected by unions and employers alike. IPPA had no chance of finding anyone else who was half as good.

At that first IPPA/Channel Four negotiation the IPPA team had told the Channel Four representatives that the Channel would have to pay the market price to people employed on its programmes; it would not be possible to make programmes for Channel Four 'at a special reduced rate'. The Channel Four representatives responded that they did 'not seek to use cheap labour or to underpay people, but were concerned to see a proper relationship between skill and reward and not to pay for excessive crewing/overtime/expenses/resources'. IPPA said it shared these aims and that the Channel was welcome to be involved in its negotiations with the unions. Channel Four replied that while they wished to take 'an intelligent and active interest' they had no desire to become 'a mini-industrial relations industry'.[12] At last the road lay open for us to conclude a set of agreements with the unions along the lines first discussed between Sapper, Lockett, Bruce and me more than a year earlier.

* * *

Most of the independents who by late 1981 and early 1982 were scurrying to create companies, or in more idealistic cases to set up co-operatives, were not business-men and many did not want to be. Their interest was in making programmes, programmes that *they* wanted to make, preferably in the way they wanted to make them. Channel Four offered the opportunity to do that. Channel Four had said that it could only enter into production contracts with businesses, not with individuals. Michael Peacock realised that in order to achieve their dreams, whatever their politics or philosophies, independents would have to survive as businesses. To this end, relying largely on the resources and expertise of his own company, Video Arts, Peacock set up a series of training sessions in the basics of running and surviving as a company. Using brilliant Video Arts instructional films starring the likes of John Cleese, the accompanying back-up training books written by Antony Jay and lectures which Peacock and his colleagues had developed to go with them, Peacock set about tutoring a whole new breed of broadcast producers. Programme makers new and old, well-known or just starting out, crowded into lectures and film shows with titles such *Cost, Profit & Break-even* or *The Balance Sheet Barrier*. It was exciting and frightening at the same time. One could almost hear the tinkle of scales falling from eyes as the mysteries of balance sheets and asset values were explained to people who had previously only seen themselves as programme makers. The new independent producers were getting a free course in business management for which their counterparts outside in industry would have been willing to pay thousands of pounds. Those sessions organised by Peacock and his colleagues probably did as much to ensure the success of the independent production sector in the first vital years of Channel Four as any other single thing.

The number of independent producers being offered commissions by Channel Four was growing all the time. The issues which, by now, were most exercising producers offered commissions were not so much the level of Production Fee or profit share as more immediate matters – the channel's budgeting procedures and the way in which commissioning editors played their roles. At IPPA's second Annual General Meeting, on 28 January 1982, held this time in Kensington and Chelsea Town Hall to accommodate the growing membership, there was what Michael Peacock later described to Jeremy Isaacs as a 'vigorous and instructive debate'. Peacock was instructed by the members to convey to Isaacs their 'deep concern' over a number of key issues, among which was 'the apparent change in the way in which Channel Four staff perceived their role; as financiers and executive producers rather than publishers'.[13] Writing to Isaacs the next day, Peacock told him that independents felt that the Standard Terms of Trade were 'over-protective and legalistic and, in particular, that the rights of approval, intervention, control and ownership required by Channel Four amount to a negation of the generally accepted meaning of independent production. Members pointed out that Channel Four's present interpretation of independent production was totally different from that of the government and Parliament when the Act was passed or in earlier announcements from the IBA'.[14] Peacock spelled out the resentment felt by experienced independent producers about the way in which

Channel Four commissioning editors, often with no television experience, exercised their right to intervene at all stages of production. He complained that they seemed unable to evaluate or respond to programme ideas in 'a timely and professional manner', seemed only interested in commissioning what they called 'their sort of programmes' and in some cases acted as de facto executive producers. Independents complained that the commissioning and budgeting staff at Channel Four seemed 'insulated' from each other, with the result that producers' budgets were being cut long after the broad outline of a programme had been agreed between the commissioning editor and the independent producer. The cuts appeared to be made on an arbitrary basis rather than out of any knowledge of market rates or the realities of programme production.

Isaacs, who was due to face the members of IPPA a few days later, responded with characteristic vigour. He told Peacock that while he could understand IPPA members' feelings about Channel Four's Terms of Trade being protective and legalistic, he could not accept that they amounted to a negation of independent production: 'Some would-be independent producers have a highly romanticised notion of what constitutes independent production . . . The fact is that the only independent producer who has total control over his programme is one wealthy enough to make the programme without pre-sale having been arranged. Anyone else has to take account of the needs of the purchaser. Channel Four's Terms of Trade seek to ensure simply that we get what we pay for.' His commissioning editors had to have the right to view programmes as they went through production in order to ensure that Channel Four was indeed obtaining what it was paying for. His commissioning editors commissioned what the Channel wanted and needed. Isaacs did agree, however, with IPPA members that, 'Commissioning Editors should act as such, and not as executive producers. That is my instruction to them.' As to the rate of commissioning and the length of time being taken to reach decisions over whether to commission or not, Channel Four was proceeding in accordance with the timetable laid out by Isaacs when he met independents at the Royal Institution. He was aware that the Channel was 'cutting budgets as tight as possible', but fatter budgets meant fewer commissions for others. In fact both the independents and Isaacs were overstating their cases. Isaacs and his team were a lot less rigid in their demands than those running the existing broadcasters. More than once Isaacs repeated to independents the story of a reprimand delivered by Bill Ward, Lew Grade's Programme Controller at ATV, to a luckless producer who had shown him the rough cut of a programme: 'I asked for a pound of apples and you have bought me back a pound of pears. Go away and get me a pound of apples!' Isaacs told independents that he would not mind too much if a producer bought him a pound of pears, as long as they were good pears.

On 3 February 1982 Isaacs, with eight of his commissioning editors and members of the Channel's business affairs team, faced a packed meeting of independents in the Chelsea Town Hall for what was billed as a 'State of the Nation' session. Producer after producer asked why was it taking so long to get answers from the commissioning editors to the programme proposals they sent in? David Rose explained that for every one hundred ideas sent to him only about two could result in a commission. The channel had been simply bombarded with proposals. Another suspicion, voiced by Michael Peacock and taken up by others, was that the channel was not dealing even-handedly between independents and the ITV companies. Peacock instanced reports of Channel Four agreeing 'bulk supply arrangements' with some ITV companies which covered a slate of programmes for a fixed overall price as against the Channel's 'alleged policy not to commission drama or situation comedies [for] more than £30,000 per half hour from independents'.[15] Justin Dukes replied that ITV's production costs were higher than could be accepted by Channel Four and that this meant that as a result more programmes were being commissioned from independents than originally envisaged. This was true, but it was not the full story.

It had begun to be noticed that the regular reports in the trade press of new Channel Four commissions included very few from ITV companies. Rumour, supported by conversations with colleagues working in the ITV companies, fuelled the suspicion that the ITV contractors were deliberately holding back from supplying programmes to the new channel. It appeared that they were doing this in order eventually to gain control over the Channel. Still convinced that the independents would fail as a reliable and economic source of the programmes, they seemed to be working on the assumption that, at the eleventh hour, the Channel would have to turn to them, allowing them to ride to the rescue with a plentiful supply of programmes at a time when the Channel would be in no position to argue about the prices or conditions they attached. Thus, with control of the sale of the Channel's advertising airtime already in their hands, with four out of the ten members of the board, and finally with a stranglehold over the Channel's programme supply, the control of the Channel which they had always sought would be theirs.

The truth was rather more complex. Following the announcement of the new

ITV contracts which were to operate from January 1982, the ITV companies had spent much of 1981 negotiating the detail of their franchises with the IBA – detail, which included the subscription which each company was to pay in return for the right to sell the advertising in their regions on Channel Four. Although there had not been the wholesale change in the franchises that had occurred in 1968, the companies had a lot of work to do replacing executives who had left during the franchise round and negotiating new inter-company deals inside ITV. Channel Four had pointed out to the ITV companies that, while it wanted programmes from them, it did not want them at whatever price the companies might care to ask. The companies had long argued that they could make programmes for the fourth channel out of spare capacity at marginal cost, using under-utilised staff and uncommitted studio time. However, when Isaacs had taken them up on this they had not been so keen.

Even those ITV companies that did have the spare capacity to make programmes for Channel Four held back. 'It was that old Granada arrogance and fear of loss of control', is the way David Plowright, by 1982 Managing Director of Granada, describes his own company's tardiness in supplying programmes to Channel Four in the run-up to it going on air. 'We knew how our programmes should be made, how much they should cost and where they should be placed – the time, date and network.' There was also an element of hurt pride: 'They didn't court us – that Granada arrogance again. We didn't want our programmes placed against our prize blooms. We had a promotion document made with photos of all our heads of department and sent it to Channel Four. And we wanted to know, in turn, about their commissioning editors. It was a case of "We'll show you ours if you'll show us yours." '[16] Ray Fitzwalter, who became Editor of *World in Action* in 1982, puts Granada's attitude rather differently: 'They were paying for it through the subscription so to them Channel Four was a kind of colony.'[17] However, Anthony Smith, a member of the Channel Four Board, entertained the same suspicions as the independents: 'By holding back their programmes, refusing Channel Four's terms for acquiring them, the ITV companies were assuming that the independents would fail as programme suppliers and then the channel would have to call on them to come to the rescue. As a result they would be able to dictate the terms and take effective control of the channel.'[18]

On arriving at the IBA as its new Director-General in April 1982, John Whitney, who kept a diary, noted the expectation among the ITV companies that the independents wouldn't deliver. The companies seemed to regard the independents as 'an irritation rather than anything else'. The companies were, Whitney noted, 'generally grumpy'. They were supported in their expectations by the members of the Authority who, Whitney observed, were 'generally on the companies' side', regarding them 'as our children' who they wanted to prosper. Sometimes, when these children didn't get their own way, as Whitney put it, they 'got a bit unruly and banged on the table with their spoons'.[19] Colin Shaw is also in little doubt that the ITV companies still believed that they would take control of Channel Four. But, he says, the IBA's officials were equally determined that they should not. 'If the ITV companies had established a supply position (re. Channel Four and programmes) they would have been thanked by a grateful government, as the government also doubted whether the independents could supply programmes and some people in the government were fearful that it [the channel] would fail.'[20] Shaw sums up the ITV companies' attitude to supplying programmes to Channel Four as being one of 'Sod off!' exacerbated by the fact that the IBA was, for the first time, asserting itself, insisting that the ITV companies would not dominate the Channel's board or control its output. As Paul Fox of Yorkshire, puts it, the ITV companies were told to 'Back off'. They would not be allowed to flood Channel Four with their programmes.[21]

For his part, Jeremy Isaacs, although he wanted programmes from the companies, was 'pretty choosy' about what he was prepared to take from them. 'We wanted our commissioning editors to deal directly with programme producers, not through directors of programmes or even heads of department, and so on down hierarchically, but face to face. Some managing directors did not want to trust their company's fortunes to the persuasive powers or business acumen of their subordinates. Did a commissioning editor, perhaps new to television, really know enough about it to deal with a programme producer direct? Surely Managing Director should deal with Chief Executive?' As a result, according to Isaacs, the companies 'decided that until terms were agreed formally between themselves, and then between the Independent Television Companies Association and us, no one ITV company was to enter into a contract with Channel 4'.[22]

Of course, many of the programme makers inside the ITV companies wanted to make programmes for Channel Four, which they saw as an outlet for the programmes they could not make for ITV. The smaller ITV regional companies, which some ITV executives like David Plowright will today admit had always been treated appallingly by the big five ITV Network companies, saw Channel

Four as a potential godsend. It offered an outlet for the ideas of their programme makers who for years had been frustrated by being able to make only a limited diet of small-scale programmes for broadcast in their local regions. Yet they too were prevented by the ITCA embargo from entering into contracts with Channel Four. When James Graham arrived at tiny cash-strapped Border Television in the autumn of 1982 as Managing Director, he found a proposal, *Land of the Lakes*, which had been approved by Channel Four, had lain on the desk of his predecessor unsigned for a year because of the ITCA embargo and difficulties with his company's union shop. Graham, who had gone to Border from the BBC for freedom and the chance to work in the mainstream, immediately ordered his subordinates to get the contract signed and get on with the programmes. Jim Graham was not going to be stopped by the large companies and the ITCA. He called together the union leaders and staff at Border. He told them that he could deal with their problems, 'but they should get on with it and seize the opportunity'.[23] They did.

LWT and Thames also eventually broke ranks with the other ITV companies and signed contracts with Channel Four. As Brian Tesler, who as well as being a director of Channel Four was the Managing Director of LWT, says, 'Our programme departments jumped at the chance to do programmes we couldn't get on the network.' Tesler set up a separate LWT Channel Four Department headed by John Birt. 'It was a chance to sell programmes to Channel Four, all the programmes that there wasn't airtime for, particularly the less popular programmes and the ethnic programmes.' But, as Tesler soon discovered, ITV had a problem. 'Our "cheap" was actually expensive until we got on top of it. No one in ITV was prepared to loss-lead to sell programmes to Channel Four.'[24] Even so, Tesler was repeatedly surprised when the programme commission lists came to the Channel Four Board by how few there were from the big ITV companies. They were finding that they could not lean on Isaacs and his team. The only thing, according to Tesler, which the companies found the independents could not do as effectively as themselves was large-scale light entertainment shows.

Jeremy Isaacs sums up what happened in the crucial months between his announcement that the Channel was open for ideas and the ITV companies starting to submit them: 'The ITV companies shot themselves in the foot. They were suspicious of the new channel, not really sure it would succeed. John Freeman (Chairman of LWT) had repeatedly drawn attention to the strain on ITV of supporting Channel Four's finances and seemed to cast doubts on the companies future relationship with it. For a whole year ITV held back from making programmes and barred members of the ITCA from doing separate deals . . . They created a vacuum into which the independents raced. It was like taking a cork out of a fizzy bottle. The energy of the independent sector gushed out. It almost swept us away. By the time the ITV companies woke up the opportunity had gone.'[25]

The result was that the independents wound up making as many of the Channel's programmes as all the ITV companies put together. By the end of May 1982, after commissioning 400 hours of programmes from independent producers, Channel Four had to cry halt. The Channel had commissioned 'more than we dreamed possible', announced Isaacs. The Channel wanted no further submissions until January 1983 so that they could clear the backlog. A report in *Broadcast* estimated that in its first year on the air 30% of the channel's material would come from independents, 30% would be new material from ITV and ITN (ITN had been contracted by the Channel to provide its news), 10% would be ITV repeats and 30% would be material acquired from elsewhere.

Not only was there a backlog of unanswered programme submissions from independents, there was a logjam in Channel Four's commissioning process. In July *Broadcast* carried this short joke item: 'Well-attended IPPA meeting. Chairperson: "Will everyone with a Channel 4 commission put up their hands." A sea of hands wave around. Chairperson: "Will everyone with a contract from Channel 4 please put up their hands." No movement.'[26] On the eve of Channel Four's first transmission *Broadcast* ran a cartoon strip re-telling the history of the Channel's creation under the heading 'Your contract's in the post.' In the same edition of *Broadcast* Michael Peacock wrote, 'When C4 got underway, nearly a year ago, at least one ITV managing director fell into the habit of demanding to know the names of five independent production companies capable of making worthwhile films for the channel. Channel Four is going on air with the work of no less than 150 independent companies which have made 180 projects.'[27] None of them, Peacock pointed out, had gone over budget.

*   *   *

ITV companies which had held aloof, like Granada, might in 1982 have claimed with some reason that their attitude was the product not so much of arrogance as of a justified pride in their own achievements. The autumn of 1981 had seen the first transmission on ITV of Granada's *Brideshead Revisited*, arguably the greatest television drama series ever made. Spaciously adapted from Evelyn Waugh's novel by John Mortimer in thirteen commercial television one-hour episodes, superbly crafted and with a cast which included many of the greatest British actors of the twentieth century – Laurence Olivier and John Gielgud among them – it stands the test of time as a fitting monument to the old, closed BBC–ITV public service broadcasting system before the advent of Channel Four. *Brideshead Revisited* also stands as a monument to some of the reasons why the old system could not survive. That such an ambitious project could be undertaken by a single company without massive overseas finance, the price of which might have been to compromise the integrity of the adaptation, casting or perfectly measured style of the direction, was a measure of the financial might and unquestioned right of Granada as a Big Five ITV Network company to have its output transmitted in a prime spot on ITV.

The series had gone into production before the 1979 technicians' strike and had had to be completed after it was over. As a result an already very expensive series went massively over budget, making each fifty-minute episode more than four times as expensive as an average hour of BBC drama as costed by Michael Checkland in his 1980 Royal Television Society lecture. These costs and the overspend were a direct result of the outdated and impractical agreements operated by the ITV companies and the unions. Having by now concluded satisfactory agreements with the trade unions, independent producers embarking on their first programmes for Channel Four appeared to have avoided being drawn into the same trap. After eighteen months of formal existence IPPA, its industrial relations service financed by means of a small fee amounting to 1% of the budget of each programme commissioned by Channel Four, now had a membership of 245 and was financially secure.

By early 1982 Channel Four had found a permanent home in an office block in Charlotte Street on the spot once occupied by the Scala Theatre, home for years of the annual Christmas production of *Peter Pan*. Isaacs wrote later that he liked the idea of the spirit of J. M. Barrie's *Peter Pan* helping the Channel on. He was also attracted to Charlotte Street because it was one of the first places where he had seen Londoners eating out of doors. Young film makers and campaigners, who did not know of J. M. Barrie's play, or perhaps might not care to admit to being influenced by the spirit of anything so politically incorrect as *Peter Pan*, could find satisfaction in the fact that it had also once housed a cinema of the kind which many believed that a British film industry founded on proper social and cultural priorities would have fostered. Altogether the sense of excitement surrounding the Channel, despite the remaining frustrations, was rising all the time. Jeremy Isaacs, and with him his Channel, clearly was 'a different person' from the Isaacs who had given that cautious McTaggart Lecture at Edinburgh in September 1979. Perhaps all those years of campaigning might prove to have been worth it after all.

*   *   *

On 2 April Argentina invaded the Falklands. The invasion was the product of British military intelligence failure and Thatcher government cock-up. That Britain had retaken the islands by 14 June was the result Admiral Sir Henry Leech's unflinching clear-sightedness, Mrs Thatcher's determination and the bravery of the British sailors, soldiers and airmen of the Task Force. The upshot was the fall of the Argentine Junta, a transformation in Mrs Thatcher's political fortunes and the casting of a very long shadow over the whole of British broadcasting.

The weeks between the Argentinian seizure of the Falklands and the islands' recapture by the British were, according to the BBC's new Director-General Designate, Alasdair Milne, weeks when 'feeling about the BBC sowed seeds of enmity in the minds of newspapers and politicians which would come to fruition at a later date'.[28] Reporting the Falklands presented the broadcasters, and the BBC in particular as 'the state broadcaster', with essentially the same problem which had faced them at the time of Suez in 1956. Margaret Thatcher and her Conservatives, like Eden and his Conservatives in 1956, regarded Britain as being at war even though no war had been declared between Britain and Argentina. With our servicemen at risk, Mrs Thatcher regarded the broadcasters' duty as being to raise morale and promote Britain's side in the argument. The broadcasters, on the other hand, saw it as their duty to remain, as the BBC Charter and the Broadcasting Act required, politically impartial, to report the facts even when they were uncomfortable, and to explore the political divisions in the country. Opinion polls showed that the majority of the population opposed the military action but supported the Task Force. Mrs Thatcher and her henchmen such as Norman Tebbit regarded the broadcasters' stance as incomprehensible. Unlike during Suez in 1956, when the Conservative government faced a coherent and powerful Labour opposition, this time the Labour opposition, which was led by Michael Foot and reluctantly supported military action, was an incoherent and divided shambles. In such a situation trouble for the broadcasters was inevitable.

The scene was set and the temperature raised to a level of jingoist hysteria by the leading tabloids, the *Sun*, the *Daily Mirror* and the *News of the World*, each vying to outdo the other in headlines that proclaimed their patriotic fervour in a way which would not have disgraced an editor working under some latter-day Goebbels. 'STICK IT UP YOUR JUNTA!' to put down talk of a negotiated peace settlement; 'BRITAIN 6, ARGENTINA 0' as the air war began; 'GOTCHA!' on the sinking of the Argentine cruiser *General Belgrano*. On the BBC's *Newsnight*, presenter Peter Snow, reflecting on the fact that the first casualty in war is the truth, explained why it was that so far he was more inclined to believe the British version of events in the war than the Argentinian – 'We cannot demonstrate that the British have lied to us but the Argentinians clearly have.' Government anger grew when, after the sinking of the *Belgrano* with heavy loss of life, both the BBC and ITN showed footage from Argentina of the grieving relatives of Argentinian sailors. The temperature was raised still further when HMS *Sheffield* was hit by an Exocet missile and twenty seamen were killed. Finally, prompted by a suitably provocative question from one of her own backbenchers, Mrs Thatcher lashed out at the broadcasters: ' "Many people are very, very concerned indeed that our case is not being put over fully and effectively . . . it would seem that we and the Argentines are almost being treated as equal and on a neutral basis . . . If this is so, it gives great offence and causes great emotion among many people." (Conservative cheers)'[29] Two days after that the *Sun* launched an even more outspoken and specific attack. Its front page that day, under the giant headline 'BURIAL AT SEA', was devoted to emotional coverage of the committal to the sea of the bodies of the dead British seamen from HMS *Sheffield*. Elsewhere in the same edition the *Sun* launched its own fund for 'dependants of our lost men' with a donation of £1,000. And on page 4 it carried a story headed 'TV Men Treating Argies as Equals'. It reported that 'a major target of Mrs Thatcher's anger is BBC TV's Peter Snow – although she did not name him'. The paper ran a fiery leader headed 'Dare call it treason' followed by a sub-heading 'There are traitors in our midst'. 'The Prime Minister did not speak of treason. The *Sun* does not hesitate to use the word,' it said. 'What is it but treason to talk on TV, as Peter Snow talked, questioning whether the government's version of sea battles was to be believed? . . . A British citizen is either on his country's side – or he is an enemy.'[30] The *Guardian* also came in for the *Sun*'s censure for a cartoon it had published featuring a torpedoed British seaman under the words 'The price of sovereignty has been increased – official'. Three days later a *Panorama* programme explored the views of those who opposed the war (a recent survey had shown that public support for Mrs Thatcher's handling of the Falklands had fallen from 75% to 71% in a week). The programme balanced interviews with opponents of the war against extracts from an earlier interview with Mrs Thatcher and other material. The programme left viewers in no doubt that it was Argentina which had started the war by its illegal and unprovoked seizure of the Falklands nor that the majority of opinion in Britain was behind Mrs Thatcher's policy. Nevertheless, as Robert Kee explained when he introduced the programme, there were still reservations about launching an actual war and it seemed worth exploring what weight those who harboured such reservations carried. 'Perhaps,' Milne reflected later on his decision to sanction the programme, 'I should have known better.'[31]

Three days later Alasdair Milne and George Howard, the Chairman of the BBC, were due to meet the Conservative Backbench Media Committee in a committee room of the House of Commons. An event that might normally have attracted a dozen or so MPs was now packed with well over one hundred. A few days earlier George Howard, himself a Tory grandee if ever there was one (the owner of Castle Howard, the grand stately home where much of *Brideshead Revisited* had been filmed), had said in a speech that the difference between Argentina and Britain was that Britain was a democracy and that our people liked and expected to be told the truth. Howard opened his address to the Conservative backbenchers by saying that, while he understood the feeling among Conservative MPs, he did not believe that the *Panorama* programme had been a mistake and so he would not apologise for it. The ranks of Tory MPs growled in disapproval. By the time Milne came to speak, the Tory pack's blood was up. 'Speak up,' they barked. When he spoke up they howled 'Stand up!' As Milne reflected later, 'We were clearly in for a very special form of Star Chamber.' The meeting had been supposed to be private, but the next morning the press carried lurid accounts of how Howard and Milne had been 'roasted', describing it as an 'ox-roasting' with George Howard as the ox. The BBC's defence that it had tried to live up to its wartime reputation for truthful reporting had been jeered at. Winston Churchill, grandson of the wartime leader, sneered that during the war equal time had not been given to the propaganda machine of Joseph Goebbels. As the meeting ended and Milne and Howard were getting up to leave, one young MP approached Howard and said

'You, sir, are a traitor.' Howard jabbed a finger back at him, 'Stuff you!' Later, as Howard and Milne sat in William Whitelaw's office having a much needed drink, Whitelaw made it clear that he was personally disgusted by the behaviour of his colleagues. While he thought the meeting had provided a useful chance to let off a head of steam, he understood and sympathised with the broadcasters' dilemma. Sadly for broadcasting, Thatcher, Tebbit and others did not share such a measured perspective – and Whitelaw was not going to be there for ever.

*   *   *

Greeted by Mrs Thatcher at a reception at Number 10 in the summer of 1982, Jeremy Isaacs was moving away when she called after him, 'Stand up for free enterprise, Mr Isaacs, won't you?' Returning to answer her, Isaacs responded, 'The channel will not stand up for free enterprise. But some of our programmes will.'[32] With so many different people's expectations riding on it, built up over so many years, Channel Four could not hope to fulfil all of those expectations all of the time and Isaacs was wise enough to know it. He had also been wise enough not to have promised that it would. But with luck the channel might match some of the expectations of each of the people some of the time.

Channel Four went on air for the first time on Tuesday 2 November 1982. It had been agreed that S4C in Wales should make its debut first and so it had started broadcasting the day before. Eschewing the temptations of a pompous opening ceremony (memories of the disastrous first night of BBC-2 and the anti-climax surrounding the first weekend of LWT must have suggested that to launch with an overblown fanfare was to tempt fate), Isaacs started as he intended the Channel to go on.

At 4.45 p.m. the Channel 4 test card vanished and the screen went to black. Then out of the black came the Channel's call sign, an announcer's voice and a montage of promotional images with music. Sitting in his office glass in hand, Jeremy Isaacs reached over and shook Edmund Dell by the hand. It turned out to be one gesture of amity before a long descent into disagreement. The first programme proper was *Countdown*, a word game which encouraged viewers to join in at home, presented by Richard Whiteley from Yorkshire Television. This was followed by *The Body Show*, billed as the first in a half-hour series on 'dance exercise with a difference', made by an all-women company, Fifty One Percent Productions. A bought-in American series *People's Court* came next, followed by an LWT series on books produced by Melvyn Bragg. *Channel 4*

News at 7 p.m. was followed by the soap, *Brookside*, with the strong language promised by Phil Redmond when he button holed Isaacs after his first presentation to independents back in January 1981. After that *The Paul Hogan Show*, bought in from Australia. At 9 p.m. the first *Film on Four*, *Walter*, starring Ian McKellen, directed by Stephen Frears and photographed by Chris Menges. It was the realisation of a long-cherished project by independent producer Nigel Evans. It aimed to bring home the brutal realities of institutional care for many mentally and physically handicapped young people. Next came a spoof on Enid Blyton, *Five Go Mad in Dorset*. Finally a feminist review, *In the Pink*. All in all, as Isaacs intended, pretty typical Channel Four.

Even on day one Channel Four attracted a mixture of bouquets and brickbats. *Countdown* was judged 1950s BBC rather than cutting-edge 1980s. *Channel 4 News*, at an hour in length, as a valuable addition to coverage in depth and analysis, but badly presented in a jarring set – needs work. *Brookside*, which still had to find its feet, soon found that its vocabulary was unacceptable to the likes of Mary Whitehouse. *Walter* had been hailed as 'A Shocker!' by the press even before it was transmitted. But once seen, it was rightly praised. 'The Cosy Days of TV are Over for Ever', proclaimed Herbert Kretzmer in the *Daily Mail*. *Five Go Mad in Dorset*, even at 10.15 p.m., produced predictably angry viewers' phone calls. 'Absolutely Disgusted' was one comment recorded in the duty logbook. A comment that would prove a harbinger of things to come.

As its first week of transmissions progressed, there were further programmes to attract fire and excite praise. Day three provided perhaps the most notorious. *The Animals Film*, screened at 9.45 p.m. on Thursday, was an opinionated documentary narrated by Julie Christie and billed as showing 'the way in which humanity exploits and abuses animals'. The IBA had insisted on cutting the last twelve minutes which had included footage of a raid by the Animal Liberation Front. Isaacs himself had found some of the things being done to animals in the film so horrible that he had been unable to view parts of it except by running it on fast-forward. Yet he had deliberately scheduled it on the Channel's third evening 'because I knew many would want to watch it, partly to cause a stir, and partly because I thought it right to confront the IBA at the word go with the channel's intention to broadcast provoking opinion'.[33] Knowing the programme would excite controversy, Isaacs had commissioned an *Animals Film Follow-Up* for 9 p.m. the following evening. Opinions about the programme were predictably polarised. *The Animals Film* was criticised for allowing the views of the Animal

Liberation Front a hearing. But allowing a hearing to people whose views were considered by many people to be unacceptable was an important part of the Channel's *raison d'être*. It was one of the things the campaigners had fought for.

Another controversy in Channel Four's first week was over a lecture given by the left-leaning historian E. P. Thompson, author of the seminal *History of the English Working Class*. Thompson had been invited by the BBC to give their prestigious Richard Dimbleby Lecture in 1981 and had accepted the invitation. Then the BBC hierarchy had panicked and cancelled his lecture. The story had come out and the BBC was made to look as if it had chickened out for fear of offending the Thatcher government. This was too good an opportunity for Isaacs and Channel Four to pass up and Isaacs had written to *The Times* saying that had the Channel been on the air it would have been happy to offer Professor Thompson a platform, as it would to all shades of opinion. The upshot was that Thompson was booked to give the first in a series of half-hour scripted to-camera lectures in Channel Four's *Opinions* slot. That night's duty log reflected viewers horror and also delight: 'This programme has completely cut the bullshit . . . May I say, madam, your programme has balls.' ' . . . bowled over by the programme and thought Channel 4 has earned its place in heaven.' 'Thank you – it's great to be treated as adults at last.' Others, including some in the IBA and on the Channel Four Board, were less delighted. Overlooking the fact that later programmes would feature polemics from right-wingers such as Paul Johnson, a general accusation began to be heard – the Channel was biased in favour of the Left.

Earlier on the first Friday evening, before the *Animals Film Follow-Up*, there was the first edition in a series which was to prove perhaps the most contentious and controversial of all the programmes in the early months of Channel Four. The original campaigners for the Channel had always argued that there must be a place for news and current affairs programmes which openly declared their political stance rather than having to contort themselves to fit the conventions of 'balanced reporting'. *The Friday Alternative*, produced by a former *Panorama* producer called David Graham, aimed to fulfil that campaigners' ambition. David Graham had caused a stir inside the BBC a few years earlier when he had made programmes about *The Real Unemployed*, people who signed on as unemployed, but who, caught in the poverty trap, worked in the Black Economy. Although many trade unionists had supported Graham for describing the world as it really was, his programmes had upset colleagues in the BBC, colleagues whom Graham described as 'the educated intelligentsia'. 'The educated left said in effect "Don't tell the truth as it denigrates the unemployed." [34] But Graham reasoned 'if these people haven't got proper jobs, or jobs that support them, isn't it better that they worked in the Black Economy than that they just sit back drawing benefit? Who was to blame them?' His editor in the BBC at the time, Roger Bolton, had supported him: 'I was not concerned whether David's politics were left, right or anything else, only that his journalism was honest, factual and as objective as possible. It was, and he was a remarkable producer. I understood why he moved over to polemical journalism on Channel 4.' [35] In the minds of his BBC detractors Graham became identified with Keith Joseph and came to be regarded as, in his words, 'the house Thatcherite'. It was unsurprising therefore that Graham should have got out of the BBC or that he should have become steadily more convinced by the arguments of the New Right, of economists like Hayek and the Thatcherites. He was also fascinated by the possibilities of new video technology, particularly for graphics and picture manipulation. With a video artist called Peter Donebauer who, when Graham met him, was living in a squat in Brixton, Graham had set up a small independent studio. In 1979 Graham had become a member of the Channel Four Group. From his more right-wing perspective he had just as great a distrust of the idea of the state exerting control over broadcasting as had the majority of his fellow campaigners who belonged to the political left.

Graham had written to Jeremy Isaacs and Paul Bonner with three programme ideas, one of which was a money/consumer programme for blue-collar workers. Isaacs had invited him to meet him. 'You're interested in C2s are you, David?' he had asked and then suggested he 'fix up something' with Liz Forgan. Forgan had invited him out to lunch and *The Friday Alternative* had been the result. Graham describes the starting point for the series as 'the kind of divergence between the "respectable" political view and what most people think. For instance, on capital punishment and Britain getting out of Northern Ireland. Members of the public are in favour of capital punishment. So the programme took someone who was in favour of capital punishment to meet a murderer who had been let out of prison.' [36] Instead of relying on conventional voice-over narration or presenters linking the programme from the studio, Graham and Donebauer relied heavily on new, often quirky, video graphics. Graham recruited his production team and consultants from among 'people from ordinary backgrounds rather than people from the elite universities and the traditional intelligentsia'. Graham deliberately chose consultants from right across the political spectrum. He had been asked by

Forgan and Isaacs, in Isaacs' words, to 'provide a commentary on the media, showing how events had been covered; and second, to involve people who had been on the receiving end of political decisions that made the news, who had in their own lives been subject to the pressure of events, so as to give their perspective, not the commentators' and not Whitehall's, of the pit closure, the change in EEC agricultural policy, the IRA explosion, the reduction in child benefit or whatever. The worm's eye view. There would also be journalistic reports which offered views in sharp contrast to others more widely disseminated.'[37] *The Friday Alternative* was to fill the final half-hour of the slot allotted to the *Channel 4 News* on Friday evenings. 'Nothing prepared me for the sheer élan of *The Friday Alternative* on our first Friday on the air. It had spark, it had sparkle. It was presented not by men or women, but by graphics . . . It had visual wit. It caught the attention.' Of course the programme had faults. Items were sometimes overly dismissive or glib. Both Edmund Dell and Lord Thomson, the new chairman of the IBA, quickly took against the series. In Graham's view it was seen as 'Too modern, quirky graphically and not serious enough'. But, as Graham admits, in choosing his team he had inadvertently hired too many people with left-leaning sympathies. The charges of left-wing bias and lack of due impartiality in the whole of Channel Four's output, and in *The Friday Alternative* in particular, grew. Isaacs and Forgan tried gallantly to defend the programme. 'The staff of *The Friday Alternative* . . . could take the line that all news had a bias; theirs had a different bias. Surely, at half an hour a week only, that need present no problem.' Isaacs himself accepted the argument put by the 1960s and 1970s campaigners of the FCG and the academics in SCOB and the Glasgow Media Group: 'There *is* a subtle centrist, conformist bias in much television output, fact and fiction, whose coded messages convey a reassuring view of the world. A complete broadcasting service ought to carry in itself also regular antidotes to complacency, a touch of vinegar, or anyway of different vinegars, on the chips.' But, as Isaacs and Forgan soon discovered, even this fairly modest proposal proved 'a hard argument to maintain in a mainstream, peak time, current affairs programme'.[38] It was an argument that became untenable when it could be shown that *The Friday Alternative*'s 'alternative bias' was more often a bias to the left than to the right.

Rumours of growing tension between Isaacs and his chairman, Dell, and the IBA over the Channel's alleged left-wing bias grew, fuelled by off-the-record comments from influential politicians. Norman Tebbit approached Isaacs at a

German Embassy party a few weeks after Channel Four's debut and told him 'You've got it all wrong, you know, doing all these programmes about homosexuals and such.' (Isaacs comments in his account 'We'd only done one, actually.') 'Parliament never meant that sort of thing. The different interests you are supposed to cater for are not like that at all. Golf and sailing and fishing. Hobbies. That's what we intended.'[39] Such remarks, eagerly passed around and enlarged by television's rumour factory, heightened a growing unease and dismay among commissioning editors inside the channel and independent producers outside it. In the winter of 1982–3 I and many another independent producers not infrequently found ourselves taking out shaken and inexperienced Channel Four commissioning editors for morale-boosting drinks. Although Dell and Members of the governing body of the IBA were becoming concerned about the new Channel's perceived left-wing bias, the IBA's senior officials, Whitney and Shaw, were not unduly worried. Shaw recalls that 'Unlike George (Lord) Thomson, I had lived through *The Wednesday Play* nonsense at the BBC and Mary Whitehouse at her worst'. To Shaw the early days of Channel Four were 'extraordinarily exciting – a renewal of one's youth almost'.[40] Whitney was also less worried than his Chairman about charges of political bias. Whitney's concern was the amount of apparently gratuitous bad language in the programmes. Channel Four's films, its soap opera *Brookside*, its comedy shows and even the Channel's sports programmes included a generous quota of bad language. Isaacs records that, not having had time to see all the bought-in programmes and films, sitting at home when *Semi-Tough* was transmitted at 9 p.m. on the Channel's second Tuesday on the air, 'I nearly fell out of my armchair.'[41]

The Channel was not helped by the fact that, owing to a dispute between the actors' union Equity and the Institute of Practitioners in Advertising (IPA) over the rates to be paid to performers in commercials aired on Channel Four, there were very few adverts. In the breaks where there should have been commercials there were disfiguring, audience-losing holes, plugged with the Channel 4 ident, music and the message 'Next Programme Follows Shortly'.

By Christmas 1982 it had become open season on Channel Four. The press, led by the *Daily Mail* and the *Sun*, dubbed it 'Channel Swore', 'Channel Bore' or 'Channel Four Letter Word'. The *Sun* started to keep a swear-word tally. In one week the count reached 173. Every time Mary Whitehouse complained about a programme, which was often, the papers emblazoned her words of condemnation across their pages. Before the channel had gone on the air, sections of the press had dubbed it 'Egg-head' television. Now Anne Leslie in the *Daily Mail* let her hair down, accusing it of being too politically correct. 'Channel 4 is the home of . . . an Islington co-operative of *Guardian*-reading-feminist-single-parent-social-workers who wear sandals hand-crafted by Guatemalan freedom fighters, and who'd die rather than let a racist South African orange pass their lips.'[42] When Channel Four announced its Christmas schedule early in December 1982, which included a Jonathan Miller production of *Rigoletto*, the comedy drama series *The Irish R.M.*, a series on the Spanish Civil War, the first of a contestants' gameshow featuring a pretty presenter in a helicopter, *Treasure Hunt*, and a charming cartoon adaptation of Raymond Brigg's *The Snowman*, the *Daily Telegraph* and the *Daily Mail* picked out just one programme, scheduled for 11 p.m. on New Year's Day, called *One in Five*, for headline treatment. It dealt with homosexual lifestyles – surely a reasonable alternative for the Channel supposed under the Act to offer an alternative to the kilts, Hogmanay sing-songs and old films of the other channels? Nevertheless the *Daily Mail* ran a front-page story: 'Party for gays starts new row', followed by 'BAN TV4 DEMANDS ANGRY MP'. Inevitably the MP quoted was a Tory. Because of the regularity of such stories Isaacs came to call them 'Stormovers'.

The storm of criticism might be ridden out. Far more worrying was the fact that the Channel's respectable 6% of audience share in its first week had collapsed to a nadir of 2.8% by the last week of 1982. A few weeks after that an IBA projection forecast that instead of earning an anticipated £80 million in its first year from the sale of advertising airtime, the Channel would earn only £20 million. It was lucky, perhaps, that Mrs Thatcher could hardly disown the Channel so soon after she had created it. Even so she was reported to be very angry. It seemed that, belatedly, she was grasping the full implications of the way in which Channel Four was funded – by allowing the ITV companies to deduct the value of their Channel Four subscriptions from their income before calculating Exchequer Levy, the Treasury was in effect subsidising the Channel out of lost tax revenue.[43]

A couple of days after Christmas, the *Star* ran: 'Secret shake-up to save Channel 4. TV CHIEF FACES SACK.' The story claimed that ITV chiefs had met over Christmas and decided that Isaacs must go, the minority programmes must be cut back, that *Brookside* and its four-letter words was to be dropped and that a new schedule featuring hit shows and old favourites was to replace the audience-losing, highbrow fare. Reading this and other similar stories, the campaigners feared that the long-expected ITV attack on the Channel had come at last. The ITV companies had certainly been complaining vociferously about how much money they were supposedly losing because of Channel Four's poor ratings and their inability to sell its airtime to advertisers. In their laments they had tended to play down the effect of the continuing IPA–Equity dispute on advertising income and omit the fact that in compensation they were being allowed by the IBA to sell an extra minute of airtime in each hour on ITV. They also ignored the fact that they could offset their Channel Four costs against their liability to Exchequer Levy. Anthony Smith and those on the Channel Four Board who supported Isaacs' programme policy tried to correct the exaggerated impression of the losses the ITV companies were suffering. There were angry exchanges at board meetings. Anthony Smith remembers that at one meeting when the ITV representatives criticised him for speaking out in public on the issue, he turned to Brian Tesler and said, 'You stop telling lies about us, and we will stop telling the truth about you.' But the real issue was Isaacs' schedule. Tesler was a realist and knew that in practice there was no way that the IBA would let him 'lean on Channel Four either as an ITV company or as a member of the board'. Tesler wanted Channel Four to be popular both for the Channel's own sake and for ITV. At a board meeting in January 1983 Tesler, a brilliant ITV scheduler himself, launched into Isaacs' method of constructing his schedule. To him what Isaacs was doing was incomprehensible. This, he believed was 'The Last Chance Saloon'. There were not enough entertaining programmes, the Channel was too heavy and serious, particularly at the weekends (the point in the schedule that particularly concerned Tesler's company LWT). What was needed was complementary scheduling with ITV against the BBC. Channel Four needed alternative programmes, but not the sort of alternative being offered by Isaacs' schedule. The alternative to ITV entertainment was alternative kinds of entertainment, not serious programmes. Those, and the small audiences that could be expected to go with them, could be left to the BBC. Instead of constructing his schedule in such a way as to build the audience from one programme to the next, Isaacs was scheduling a succession of different kinds of programmes, appealing first to one kind of audience and next to another, thus inviting audiences to stay for one Channel Four programme only rather than encouraging them, as was done in ITV, to stay tuned to his station all evening. Isaacs understood Tesler's point and LWT's need for Channel Four to maximise audiences and, with them, revenue across the weekend. However, he knew that his duty and the purpose of Channel Four was different. LWT's revenue was

Tesler's problem. His was Channel Four's remit. In the end the argument that won the day was practical. It was simply not possible to change the Channel's schedule at short notice. The Channel already had contracts with programme suppliers that would take them into 1984.

Happily relief was at hand in the unwilling form of Peter Jay and TV-am.

Notes

1. From the James McTaggart Memorial Lecture given by Peter Jay at the 1981 Edinburgh International Television Festival and reproduced in part in *Broadcast*, 7 September 1981.
2. Michael Jackson, *Independence for Producers on the Fourth Channel* in the Royal Television Society Journal, Vol. 18, No. 2, March–April 1980, commenting on *Access to Grind* by Peter Jay in *Radio Times*, 25 September–1 October 1976.
3. *Report of the Inquiry into Cable Expansion and Broadcasting Policy*, Chairman: Lord Hunt of Tamworth, Cmnd. 8679, October 1982.
4. Grade, *op. cit.*
5. I am grateful to Richard Price and Michael Grade, whom I interviewed in September and November 2000 respectively, for their accounts of these events.
6. Chairman's Report, Minutes of IPPA AGM, 10 February 1982.
7. Michael Peacock, interviewed by the author in November 2000.
8. Isaacs made this admission when addressing independents a few years after the channel had gone on the air, although he does not mention it in his book *Storm Over 4*. Confidential Board papers reveal that in fact the contingency built into the Channel Four budget at the beginning of 1982, the year when the channel was due to go on air, was only £3 million, less than 4%.
9. Michael Peacock, interviewed by the author in November 2000.
10. Isaacs, *op. cit.*
11. Sir Jeremy Isaacs, interviewed by the author in November 2000.
12. *Report of First C4/IPPA Working Party Meeting*, held on Wednesday 10 June 1981, at the Capital Hotel, Basil Street.
13. *Minutes of IPPA Annual General Meeting*, 2.30 p.m., Thursday 28 January 1982.
14. Letter from Michael Peacock, Chairman of IPPA on behalf of IPPA Council to Jeremy Isaacs, Chief Executive, Channel Four Television Co. Ltd, 29 January 1982.
15. IPPA Report on *Channel Four and the Independent Sector: Terms of Trade and Prospects for the Future*, 3 February 1982, held in Chelsea and Kensington Town Hall.
16. David Plowright, interviewed by the author in October 2000.
17. Ray Fitzwalter, interviewed by the author in December 2000.
18. Anthony Smith, interviewed by the author in September 2000.

19. John Whitney, interviewed by the author in January 2001 and quoting passages from his private diary.
20. Colin Shaw, interviewed by the author in November 2000.
21. Sir Paul Fox, interviewed by the author in November 2000.
22. Isaacs, *op. cit.*
23. James Graham, interviewed by the author in October 2000.
24. Brian Tesler, interviewed by the author in November 2000.
25. Sir Jeremy Isaacs, interviewed by the author in October 2000.
26. *Broadcast*, 5 July 1982.
27. *Broadcast*, 1 November 1982.
28. Alasdair Milne, *DG: Memoirs of a British Broadcaster*, Hodder & Stoughton, London 1988.
29. *Hansard*, 5 May 1982.
30. *Sun*, 7 May 1982.
31. Milne, *op. cit.*
32. Isaacs, *op. cit.*
33. Isaacs, *op. cit.*
34. David Graham, interviewed by the author in November 2000.
35. Bolton, *op. cit.*
36. David Graham, interviewed by the author in November 2000.
37. Isaacs, *op. cit.*
38. *Ibid.*
39. *Ibid.*
40. Colin Shaw, interviewed by the author in November 2000.
41. Isaacs, *op. cit.*
42. *Daily Mail*, 10 February 1983.
43. The story that Mrs Thatcher had not grasped the full implications of the Channel Four funding mechanism, while amusing and much repeated at the time, never seemed to me to be entirely plausible. Thatcher was legendary for her grasp of detail and would hardly have either overlooked or misunderstood what was intended, even if Whitelaw and the Home Office had minimised the likely effect. She may have underestimated the length of time it would take for Channel Four's income to increase sufficiently to offset the effect on the ITV Levy. If so, she was not alone.

10

Half of Four to 25% of All – 1983 to 1986

TV-am, the ITV breakfast-time company, began transmissions on Tuesday 1 February 1983. 1 April might have been more appropriate!

TV-am was an almost exact repeat of the LWT fiasco in 1968. In fifteen years the IBA, it seemed, had learned nothing. Like the LWT contract fifteen years earlier, the breakfast-time franchise had been awarded to a consortium put together by David Frost. Like LWT the consortium consisted of an all-star cast of television names, backed by solid-looking money. This time the stars that dazzled the IBA were presenters rather than programme makers (although there were some reputable programme makers among them). In addition to Frost himself, the line-up included Michael Parkinson, Robert Kee, Anna Ford and Angela Rippon (a BBC newsreader famed for showing a shapely pair of legs as a guest on *The Morecambe and Wise Show* and for her enunciation of the word 'guerrilla' in news bulletins so as to distinguish it from 'gorilla'). The line-up was headed by golden boy and TV pundit, Peter Jay.

In addition to his Edinburgh International Television Festival McTaggart Lecture, Jay had been the author, with John Birt, of a series of articles in *The Times* in 1975 about the shortcomings of television journalism. These, starting with an article by Birt in February 1975 and followed up by Birt and Jay together in September and October, had come to be collectively referred to as the 'Bias Against Understanding' debate. Birt's premise had been set out in the opening words of his first article: 'There is a bias in television journalism. It is not against any particular party or point of view. It is a bias against understanding.'[1] The root of the problem, Birt had argued, lay in television news' brevity, its need to hold the attention of the mass audience and in its reliance on powerful pictures. The result was a failure to contextualise, to analyse or to explain in such a way as to allow people to understand. As so often in this story, Robin Day, Anthony Smith and others had each produced similar and rather better argued theses a few years earlier,[2] but Birt and Jay, smarter publicists, had made headlines and provoked an ongoing debate. In a joint article, having diagnosed the problem, they had proposed the cure – the BBC (Birt worked for ITV and presumably it would have been unreasonable to expect ITV to do it) should overhaul and revamp its whole news operation, introducing a range of regular news and analysis programmes of different lengths aimed at providing viewers with 'the maximum feasible understanding of the important (and diverting) events which happen in the world about them'.[3] No one seemed to take any notice of the fact that the Birt–Jay analysis stated what was already the obvious to most thoughtful programme makers or that their proposed cure both undervalued the positive virtues of the medium and underestimated its financial and practical realities. Likewise, the fact that Birt and Jay's own weekly current affairs series, *Weekend World*, was watched by tiny audiences, and was praised primarily by politicians and opinion formers who liked to see themselves and their opinions taken seriously on the box. This was due not simply to its being transmitted on Sunday mornings, it was due to the fact that it was often unbearably tedious television. Nevertheless, the BBC Governors had been so impressed by the Birt–Jay arguments that, after the publication of the Annan Committee's withering criticism of the BBC, they had summoned Birt and Jay to meet them (apparently without telling the Director-General Charles Curran). They even considered inviting the pair to administer their medicine across the gamut of BBC news and current affairs output. Happily, Curran was having none of it.

When Frost's team, headed by Jay, had applied for the TV-am franchise, Lady Plowden and her fellow IBA Members had, like Lord Hill and his colleagues faced with the Frost–Peacock team in 1967, been dazzled. In their submission, the 'bias against understanding' had been developed into 'The Mission to Explain'. To anybody who remembered the detail of the original Birt–Jay analysis rather than just the headlines, it seemed odd that, although in their analysis they had said that part of the problem lay in the fact that television reporters and news readers had to be personalities and in the requirement on news to be entertainment, the TV-am pitch was based largely on well-known personalities and highlighted a 'mission to entertain' in addition to a 'Mission to Explain'. However, this had deterred neither the IBA nor TV-am's financial backers. Before the station went on the air Jay addressed his staff. He told them that TV-am was:

1.   About making television at a new time of day;
2.   About making a new and different kind of television;

3.   About making a new and different kind of television journalism;

4.   About putting into practice a new and different kind of management style and philosophy; and

5.   About a new and different kind of ITV company.

But, he continued, 'We have of course an equal mission to entertain – not by traditional light entertainment but by entertaining, informing and diverting our audience.' They were to be the pioneers of a 'new frontier of television journalism'.[4] It sounded like guff. And so it quickly proved.

TV-am was nothing if not optimistic. It was also, like LWT before it, extravagant. Its building beside Regent's Canal in a run-down part of Camden Town, crowned with giant eggcups on its roof, was fitted out in a style that would have done justice to the imagination of a latter-day Orson Welles contemplating a re-make of *Citizen Kane*. When Jeremy Isaacs was invited to go round it he was struck by such items as the atrium with 'arbours in the Cambodian style', by Greek colonnades and 'a Mexican Indian temple, with spiky cactus on ochre sand'.[5] The whole TV-am operation stood in stark contrast to Channel Four's economy. Isaacs could not help noticing the huge numbers of people employed by TV-am to get a rather limited range of programming onto the air for only a few hours each day.

The station was also undermined by the same Equity–IPA dispute over fees for performers in commercials that had hit Channel Four. The killer blow, however, was dealt by the BBC. Learning of TV-am's heavily publicised plans, the BBC had launched its own downmarket cuddly 'BBC Breakfast Time' and started transmitting it exactly two weeks before TV-am went on the air. The BBC's programme, a deliberate spoiler, was presented by Frank Bough, known and loved by audiences as the host of BBC Saturday afternoon sports coverage, dressed in a deliberately informal woolly sweater. His co-presenter was a beautiful fair-haired girl called Selina Scott, with a way of fluffing her lines that made all the mums want to put their arms around her and the men . . . In homage to the tabloid newspapers which were its model, the programme featured its own fortune teller who provided a daily horoscope.

TV-am's start was promising enough. 'TV-am Looks a Winner'; 'My Money Goes on the Jay All Stars', said the *Daily Mirror* and the *Daily Mail*, highlighting the rivalry between the two services on the day after TV-am began. But as the television critic of the *Daily Telegraph*, Sean Day-Lewis, pointed out, TV-am's news effort was not 'a patch on the BBC's'. The popular papers noted that TV-am was 'unexpectedly up-market' and that its schedule was all over the place. Crucially the BBC, with its two weeks' start, attracted twice as many viewers as TV-am – 1.6 million to 800,000. Over the next four weeks TV-am's audience fell still further. By the end of February it was getting only 300,000. The amount TV-am could charge for a thirty second advertising slot fell with the audience – from £2,000 to £600. The press, which had been having such fun at the expense of Channel Four, now turned its attention to TV-am and to rows and ructions among the staff and between Jay and his board.

By a dramatic twist in news timing that must have appealed to its editors, it was *Channel 4 News* which on 17 March broke the story that Peter Jay was to resign. His management style and the company's mounting losses had turned some of the programme staff and the company's financial backers against him. He was replaced by Jonathan Aitken. Once again the IBA had been driven to go back on its own rules. Active politicians were barred under the IBA's rules from becoming the bosses of TV companies, but Aitken, an MP (later a minister[6]), was allowed by the IBA to become chief executive of TV-am. Expediency, as in the case of LWT, was once more allowed to override principles and invalidate promises. More sackings followed. In May Greg Dyke, poached appropriately perhaps from LWT, was put in to take charge of all TV-am's programmes. Out went the last of the station's pretensions and in came a cheery glove puppet – Roland Rat. TV-am and BBC Breakfast Time chased each other happily downmarket.[7]

The drama at TV-am took the press spotlight off Channel Four and provided a vital respite. But, beyond that, the lasting significance of what happened at TV-am was not the loss of TV-am's ideals, the removal of Jay and some of the star presenters, nor the *schadenfreude* of other less exalted programme makers at seeing pretensions brought to earth. It was that the ignominious collapse of an over-hyped TV-am once again brought the whole ITV system of governance and regulation into discredit. 'THE IBA's DOG'S BREAKFAST' ran the headline above the *Observer*'s leader on the Sunday after Jay's resignation. The method by which the IBA awarded contracts had produced another high-profile failure. The Authority's power and willingness to regulate had once more been found wanting. Once again the costs of the traditional methods of running television and making programmes for it, the overmanning, high wages and overtime rates, coupled with the extravagance of those in charge, had led to a high-profile ITV collapse. The causes for this now stood out even more clearly because they could be compared to the frugality and budgetary control of Channel Four and the independents.

* * *

'I found the early years of Channel Four absolutely delightful.' While the hopes of the founders of TV-am were being crushed, programme makers new to television and old hands who had left ITV and BBC were experiencing a completely new sense of release in making programmes for Channel Four. 'It was because of the atmosphere that Jeremy Isaacs created. It was a good thing that not all the commissioning editors were experienced programme makers, that they hadn't made any programmes – it meant they had open minds to what could be done . . . It was wonderful. They valued what you brought them.' That is how Phillip Whitehead, who by 1983 had twenty years of experience of working in television, remembers the early years of Channel Four. 'It was really like a publishing house. They didn't see it as their job to tell you what programmes they wanted made. It was because of the role reversal. The creative people, the programme makers, were valued. Programme makers were in the ascendant and accountants were not. Everywhere else you had to make your case – you were presumed guilty until you were proved innocent.'[8]

Whitehead's contemporary, that other great champion of the publisher–broadcaster idea, Anthony Smith, also felt that once Channel Four got into its stride it was able to realise 90% of his original aspirations for it. In his 1973 book *The Shadow in the Cave* he had argued that the real question of access to the medium ultimately came down to opening up the minds, working practices and personal outlooks of the broadcasting professionals who mediate the entire process. That, he believed, was now beginning to be achieved 'in the fact that people from outside television, new people or professionals trying things that they hadn't been allowed to try previously were making programmes'.[9]

To those programme makers who had fallen foul of the existing broadcasters Channel Four offered a lifeline. Colin Thomas, after his very public resignation from the BBC in 1978 over the censorship of his Irish programmes, had got six months' work with the Irish broadcaster RTE. But once that had ended he had had to survive on odd bits of teaching. Once the Fourth Channel started he and a group of like-minded producers and technicians had set up a co-operative, Teliesyn, to make programmes for Channel Four and S4C in Wales. Thomas and his colleagues were determined to avoid what he saw as 'the production line/

continuous process factory' and the hierarchical structures they had experienced in organisations such as the BBC. The aim was that all would contribute to their programmes as equals. 'The whole thing of being an independent is, or was, that you could do things you cared about.'[10]

In April 1983 the second season of *Film on Four* included a film commissioned from Maurice Hatton, *Nelly's Version*. Previously, when Hatton's work had been shown in a retrospective season at the National Film Theatre, Hatton had quipped ruefully but with justification, 'My films went from production to retrospection without distribution or exhibition intervening.' The sense of release experienced by long-time campaigners like Hatton and Whitehead was also felt by new programme makers. John Wyvver who, after leaving Oxford in 1977, had become television editor of *Time Out*, had tried to get into television a number of times but, like others before him, had found it impossible. Despite the fact that his serious critical writing about television in *Time Out* had made him well known and widely respected, in the five years between his leaving Oxford in 1977 and 1982, there had been only two advertisements for posts in the production side of television for which he could apply with any hope of being considered. One had been for a researcher on LWT's *South Bank Show*. 2,000 people applied for that. Wyvver attended three interviews for the job but still didn't get it. Early in 1982 he had sent some programme ideas to Jeremy Isaacs at Brompton Road. Isaacs had interviewed him and given him £2,000 with which to develop three of his ideas. Eventually two of them were commissioned – one was a dance piece and the other a discussion programme. He got together a company with another producer and set up in a single office belonging to one of the pre-existing small independent film companies. Wyvver later joined forces with Michael Jackson. Apart from his body of writing and critical work on the medium, Wyvver was typical of new producers coming into television for the first time to work for Channel Four. 'I broadly thought this is wonderful. It suddenly seemed to open up such a range of possibilities . . . The sense of it being an enormously broadening and deepening force lasted right through the '80s.' Wyvver had been involved in the campaign for Channel Four. Like other campaigners he felt he had a special relationship with it: 'When Channel Four came on we had such an extraordinary sense of ownership of the channel.'

An important source of the feeling of liberation among more experienced programme makers was that, for the first time, they were in control of their own budgets and resources. Whitehead cites the fact that programme makers rather than accountants were in the ascendant in dealings with Channel Four. 'Here you were asked how much money you needed to make the programme – of course you couldn't be silly and there were people to check. But everywhere else the managers didn't trust you. You had to justify wanting to use their equipment or to have any money.' Michael Peacock and producers with experience of independent production before the arrival of Channel Four wanted even more freedom and were unhappy about the Channel's insistence on its staff exercising detailed budget scrutiny. However, for producers new to independent production, even if they had a lot of experience as programme makers working inside traditional broadcasting institutions, being put in charge of their own budgets, taking responsibility for employing their own crews and hiring their own equipment could be simultaneously liberating and daunting. Even John Gau, who before he set up as an independent had been a senior executive in the BBC, found embarking on his first independent production 'nerve wracking'. For all his experience as a programme maker, Gau was entering new territory. 'I had never had to do it all myself before – doing budgets, finding cameramen. I remember sitting upstairs trying to deal with budgets and VAT, VAT in particular. It was quite exhilarating, but it wasn't very creative. I used to argue (in the BBC) that you need to know the price of everything otherwise you become self-indulgent.'[11] Now Gau had to put what he had preached into practice. Gau, like Wyvver and producers who were completely new to programme making, found the Channel's finance staff and standard budget forms were a positive asset. Wyvver in particular singles out 'the very sympathetic way in which the Channel set up a framework through which we could get into it. The budget form was very, very important. In the way the Channel made it possible for us to work. It was a step-by-step guide to a completely inexperienced producer.' As a result few people went over budget. Isaacs later paid tribute to the independents for being scrupulous about not overspending. Revealingly, those who did overspend were often the most experienced producers, those for whom controlling their own budgets was supposedly not a new experience. Among the worst were those from the film industry. Offenders included Goldcrest (the company led by those responsible for the big-screen successes *Chariots of Fire* and *Gandhi*).

I had complained more than once in articles in the 1970s that being a producer inside the BBC or ITV, where you were continuously admonished to control your programme costs but not allowed to exercise actual control over your own budget or who worked on your programmes, was like being a guard dog with your teeth pulled. I, like others, found making my first programmes for Channel Four in the autumn of 1982 a liberating experience. I was part of a company made up of producers, directors, writers, composers, designers, cameramen, sound men and editors in which we were all equals. The programmes I made with those colleagues in that company were not necessarily the best I ever worked on but they were undoubtedly the happiest. To the pleasure of making an early *Film on Four* entirely on location with a designer, production manager, cameraman, sound recordist, editor, composer, producer and executive producer who, as equal shareholders in the company, each had an equal share in the production and a mutual wish to work together, was added pride in scheduling and budgeting it ourselves and shooting it exactly as we wanted to shoot it, topped off by bringing it in on time and substantially under its modest budget. This simply added to our sense of achievement. It was nice that it received favourable reviews and was popular with television audiences, disappointing that it never made it into cinemas. But these things were unimportant compared with our sense of fulfilment in having done something in the way we wanted to do it, with people we wanted to work with. It was liberation indeed. Not that the work that I had done, and continued to do, inside the conventional broadcasting institutions was unhappy, unfulfilling or uncreative. It was just that there was an extra dimension to this. Making programmes for Channel Four had started to live up to what we had dreamed of and talked about more than a decade earlier.

*   *   *

Euphoria does not last forever. On 9 June 1983 Mrs Thatcher won her second general election. She now had a majority of 144 seats, the largest since Labour's victory in 1945. The Liberal–SDP Alliance had received almost as many votes as Labour, but because of the electoral system only a fraction of the seats. Michael Foot immediately resigned as leader of the Labour Party and was replaced by Neil Kinnock. For the previous fifteen years the thinking and tactics of the broadcasting campaigners had been framed by the expectation that the party in government would change every few years. Since the Falklands War it had looked as if that calculation would have to change. The result of the 1983 election sealed it. Mrs Thatcher was likely to be around for a long time – probably until the end of the decade. It was she, and her hard-line policies, that would determine the future of both the BBC and ITV and set the course of broadcasting into the next millennium. William Whitelaw, creator of Channel

Four and chief protector of broadcasting from the worst extremes of the Tory Right, was replaced as Home Secretary by Leon Brittan. From here on any initiatives taken by programme makers would have to take account of a new political reality.

Senior management at the BBC had been left in no doubt about Mrs Thatcher's continuing displeasure at the way in which the Corporation had reported the Falklands. At a dinner with the governors in the BBC Television Centre a few months before the 1983 election she, according to Bill Cotton who was there, had ranted on for about twenty minutes about the BBC's coverage of the Falklands. 'When she drew breath for long enough to get a word in I asked, "Are you saying the BBC are traitors, Prime Minister?" Thatcher replied, "I have said what I have to say." Milne chipped in, "Yes, the Prime Minister has said what she has to say." "But it is not good enough for me," I said and asked for an answer. There was a stunned silence for a moment before someone moved the conversation to another topic.'[12] During the election campaign itself matters had got worse. During a live early evening programme, *Nationwide*, a Bristol geography teacher, Mrs Diana Gould, had ambushed Mrs Thatcher with a question about the sinking of the Argentinian battleship, the *General Belgrano*. Mrs Thatcher had wriggled and blustered but Diana Gould had kept pressing her. Denis Thatcher, who had been watching the programme in a BBC hospitality room, had been livid. Roger Bolton, the programme's editor, later recorded that Denis Thatcher seemed to believe his prejudices about the BBC confirmed. It was 'a nest of long-haired Trots and wooftahs'.[13]

Over at Channel Four, with still no end in sight to the IPA–Equity dispute, advertisers had started to make do without actors for their adverts. The likes of Freddie Laker and Bernard Matthews (of the 'bootiful' turkeys) seemed to revel in the added fame that resulted from appearing in their own commercials – could any self-respecting actor have been induced to give such an over-the-top performance as the real-life Bernard Matthews? As a result, its audience and the income that the companies received from selling its advertising airtime picked up a little. City editors were beginning to describe Channel Four as a commercial success. In May Miles Kington in *The Times* said that Channel Four jokes were becoming out of date 'because people are now beginning to say nice things about Channel 4. How varied it is, how good the film and book items are, what wonderful repeats and films they have, how refreshing the pop music programmes are, how unusually interesting their news coverage is.'[14] Nevertheless, rows and problems both internal and external persisted. On the day after the general election, and with IBA Director-General Whitney's agreement, it transmitted *Scum* at 11.30 at night. Even at that hour it was watched by 2.3 million people. *Scum* depicted life in a borstal institution, included a homosexual rape and culminated in an inmate being beaten to a pulp with two billiard balls in a sock. It had originally been produced by Margaret Matheson for the BBC's *Play for Today* in 1978. But Bill Cotton, then Controller of BBC-1, had banned it. Cotton's ban had been supported by Alasdair Milne, who had not only thought the violence too concentrated and extreme for the domestic audience but that people might be persuaded that all borstals were as bad as this. *Scum* had subsequently been made into a film, again directed by Alan Clarke, and shown with an X certificate. Isaacs, who had seen a tape of the original BBC production, viewed the film, which he found coarser, but possessed of 'a steely beauty. The moral seemed to be: treat people like scum, and they will behave like scum.'[15] Isaacs agreed to show the film, but with two cuts – one in the homosexual rape scene, the other of a lingering shot of blood seeping through a sheet covering a suicide. He had then submitted it to the IBA for transmission. Colin Shaw, the Director of Television, recommended that *Scum* should not be shown. But Whitney, the Director-General who was a prison visitor, viewed it himself at home with his wife and decided that Channel Four should be allowed to transmit it. After viewing it he recorded in his diary, 'I wonder how many will rally to the cause.' He reckoned *Scum* 'a right and proper thing for Channel Four to show', based on his experience as a voluntary worker for Recidivists Anonymous. 'This was a good example', he believed, 'of how Channel Four should be standing on its values.'[16] This was one of the first of many occasions on which Whitney would stand out for what he believed to be the right values but feel unsupported internally.

Whitney had been a surprise appointment when he took over from Sir Brian Young as Director-General of the IBA in November 1982. He had made a fortune, first by acquiring the UK patent on the American Autocue system (a device that enabled presenters and newsreaders to read from a script while appearing to address the camera), subsequently from commercial radio and by operating as one of the early independents which packaged popular upmarket drama series such as *Upstairs, Downstairs* and *The Flame Trees of Thika* to LWT and Thames. A Quaker, with a strong sense of moral purpose and the importance of 'putting something back in the community', Whitney had taken the job, at considerable personal financial cost, out of a sense of duty and in appreciation of the honour of being asked. Whitney was not the only newcomer in the IBA. In addition to Lord (George) Thomson, a former Labour cabinet member, who had taken over from Lady Plowden at the beginning of 1981, no fewer than eight other new Members had joined the Authority's ruling body. As Whitney noted in his diary when he joined the IBA, the combination of himself, the new Members of the IBA and Lord Thomson was a potential 'recipe for turbulent waters'.

Mary Whitehouse was outraged by the transmission of *Scum* and appealed to the High Court for a legal declaration that by permitting the transmission the IBA had breached its statutory duty. It was a crucial case. If Mary Whitehouse won, Whitney and the IBA would be much less likely to stick their necks out again and Channel Four's ability to transmit controversial programmes would be seriously curtailed. Two court cases and two years later, the High Court upheld Whitney's decision. As Isaacs commented, the High Court had found that, 'The two million who watched the film on our screen had rights also, and these were vindicated.'[17] Although the IBA won, the case was a significant token of the increasingly censorious climate that was developing by the start of Thatcher's second term.

To offset against this one victory there were equally serious defeats. In July 1983 the board of Channel Four, overruling the advice of Jeremy Isaacs and Liz Forgan and the advocacy of its own non-ITV members, cancelled *The Friday Alternative*. The programme had got itself into particular trouble by attacking the way in which the other media reported events. It had looked at ITN's reporting of the views of the rising miners' leader Arthur Scargill and found it had misrepresented him. It had given the media a taste of their own medicine by doorstepping the BBC Director-General Alasdair Milne outside his home. It had questioned television's coverage of the Falklands War. It had shown that when reporters were telling viewers in Britain that the runway at Port Stanley was full of bomb craters it was not true, and showed pictures to prove it. Dell took particular exception to the Falklands programme because it had failed to offer Mrs Thatcher an immediate right of reply. Criticising ITN might have seemed a legitimate and laudable undertaking for any programme with *The Friday Alternative*'s brief, but it was trailing its coat a little too ostentatiously. After all, ITN provided the *Channel 4 News* and its ratings were already dreadful without attacks from an upstart independent. At Isaacs' insistence, David Graham and his company Diverse Productions were given another current affairs series, *Diverse Reports*. For this David Graham engaged programme makers with contrasting political views and outlooks to present and produce a range of openly opinionated reports on current topics. However, conventional broadcasters argued that any broadcast service which allowed opinionated journalism to coexist alongside 'objective' news and current affairs would 'poison the wells of truth' for the whole service. Isaacs countered that opinion co-existed alongside 'objective' news in any decent newspaper and why should broadcasting be any different? *Diverse Reports*, by general consent, worked much better than *The Friday Alternative*, balancing opinion left and right over time rather than in each programme. However, Isaac's Chairman, Edmund Dell, remained unconvinced: 'The idea that there were a lot of people with particular views around who had never had an opportunity to express them, therefore the channel had to give them an unbalanced opportunity so to do, is in my innocent view absolute nonsense.'[18]

Arguments between Dell and Isaacs, between Members of the Channel Four Board, with the IBA, with politicians and with members of the public, increased, extending to programmes other than *The Friday Alternative* and *Diverse Reports*. They enveloped programmes on Third World aid made by the International Broadcasting Trust (a company set up by aid organisations), programmes as disparate as the brilliantly realised poem '*V*' by Tony Harrison, directed by Richard Eyre, a historical series about the civil war in Greece between Communists and the military in the aftermath of the Second World War and many more, some very good, some quite a lot less good, but nearly all the sort of thing that would not have found a place on television before Channel Four. John Ranelagh, who had worked for the Conservative Research Department in the run-up to Thatcher's first election victory, and then became Secretary of the Channel Four Board between 1981 and 1983, has summed these arguments in this way: 'This was a deeply serious disagreement that spread beyond personalities. At its core was a question: was the channel an opportunity lost or taken? Was it doing all that it could to break new ground, illuminate new issues, establish fact and reflect the country as it was changing so rapidly in the 1980s? Or was the Channel resurrecting dated (1960s) concerns, catering to interest groups, accepting of simple opinion, content with chattering class blessing, presenting polish as innovation?'[19] There is, now as then, no clear answer to Ranelagh's question. Any answer will depend on the view of the person giving it. In his introduction to the examination of Channel Four in which the passage by John Ranelagh occurs, Anthony Smith wrote that Channel Four 'constituted, at least in the world of British television, a radical experiment which allowed new and sometimes very discordant voices onto the screen. Strong personalities such as Dell and Isaacs had firmly-held and to some extent opposed visions of how the new channel would develop. The very creation of a channel which was primarily a publisher of other people's material, and therefore an outlet which had not previously existed, was itself bound to create diverse expectations.'[20]

Isaacs says that by April, May, June and July 1983, the principal matter of concern to those who attended the Channel Four Board meetings was not high-flown intellectual arguments about the station's purpose and performance, nor the political bias of its programmes, but the behaviour of its Chairman: 'Edmund Dell conducted those meetings in the manner of a Grand Inquisitor consigning heretics to the flames.' Isaacs says he was struck by the expressions of incredulity on Board Members' faces during Dell's long and passionate harangues. 'Is he always like this, they seemed to ask . . . If he is so violently . . . opposed to some of what we are doing, even if he's right on a particular issue, how long can he and Jeremy work together?'[21] Isaacs began to harbour the suspicion that Dell hoped by these tactics to provoke his resignation. Dell always denied any such intention. Talking to members of the Board today, one has to accept that the problems between Dell and Isaacs were exacerbated by their personalities, by Dell's imperious manner and by Isaacs' predisposition to get into fights with those in authority. It was this predisposition and his adherence to his own view of the Channel's purpose which, as reports of the rows between Dell and Isaacs leaked out, helped to make him into such a hero to independent producers from 1982 onwards.

By late July 1983 the news that *The Friday Alternative* was to be dropped seemed to confirm mounting evidence that Isaacs and his supporters were losing the argument. Channel Four seemed to be heading downmarket and into the arms of ITV. On top of all this one of the all-women current affairs teams, Broadside, had self-destructed amid internal wrangles. At the end of August a major *Sunday Times Insight* investigation appeared under a cartoon showing an hourglass in which the sands of Channel Four in the top globe were running out into ITV-2 in the lower globe. Harking back to the Channel's formal launch a year earlier, the *Insight* team suggested that the promises of a new generation of news programmes more akin to 'the inside of a quality newspaper than the front page of the *Sun*' now looked pretty hollow. Alongside the loss of nerve over the Channel's current affairs coverage, *Insight* highlighted a parallel increase in the light entertainment budget and the promotion of Cecil Korer, the man responsible for it. Korer's promotion, the article suggested, 'marked a deliberate shift in policy' following a 'turbulent meeting' at which Isaacs and his team had been put under pressure to increase the Channel's ratings. Michael Peacock's Video Arts, commissioned to provide the station with 'a monthly State of the Nation series – a serious examination of how organisations such as nationalised industries serve the community' had been 'abruptly told by commissioning editor Forgan it was coming to an end. "She made no bones about why the decision had been made," Peacock says. "Channel 4 needs ratings; light entertainment, not current affairs gets ratings." So State of the Nations has gone, and Peacock is now working on a comedy series for Channel 4.' As the *Sunday Times* article pointed out, the quest for ratings and the Channel's remit were fundamentally incompatible: 'The question remains,' the article concluded, 'who runs Channel 4.'[22]

Of even more immediate concern to the majority of producers than who was running Channel Four was the issue of the number of independents who might in future expect to be commissioned by it. Ever more people were leaving the BBC and ITV, setting up as independents and endeavouring to win commissions. But Channel Four increasingly talked of commissioning from fewer independents, reminding those who had already won a commission that because they had won one it did not follow that they would win another.

Speaking to AIP members in October 1983 Isaacs said that Channel Four 'would like to see the number of independents they are dealing with reduced'.[23] In February 1984 Isaacs told IPPA that Channel Four had been spending and would continue through 1985 to spend more than 60% – £52 million – of its programme budget on programmes made by independents. However, 'The ITV companies are coming on horrendously strong at the moment and arguing that we ought to be spending much more of our funds with them.' Isaacs told the independents that the Channel was resisting this pressure, but the ITV companies had recently started to bring down the prices they quoted to Channel Four for programmes to below their total actual costs. As a result ITV companies were now quoting prices on a par with the costs of independents. It was by now becoming all too clear that the huge expansion in the independent sector that had occurred in the previous three years was at an end unless, as Isaacs said, 'the sector can find other markets to trade in'. Channel Four currently had contracts with 150 companies and yet some commissioning editors continued to receive 100 new programme proposals each week. 'We're not going to arbitrarily determine either that we always wish to trade with 200/250 companies, or that we want to bring down the number of

companies that we trade with to some much more manageable smaller total. I think that the problem that an independent producer is faced with is, "Am I earning enough from any commission I get from Channel 4 to keep me and my company in business?" That is a question that we have to have some regard to in some of the commissioning decisions that we take. But we don't intend to say to people, "The only way you can keep going is if you go and amalgamate with somebody else." '
That might be a sensible thing to do, Isaacs said, but that sort of question and how many independent companies survived was an issue for the independent sector to decide, not for the Channel. His basic philosophy in this matter remained that the Channel must commission on the basis of the appropriateness of programmes to the Channel's needs, their quality and their price, adding, 'We have a philosophical bias always to keep the door open to newcomers and to people who've got one particular programme or series of programmes that they are particularly keen to make for us.'[24]

Growing debate over the future shape of the independent sector was sharpened by the fact that the nature and composition of the independent sector was changing. IPPA now had a corporate membership approaching 150 companies, plus a similar number of individuals. Its twice monthly newsletter had a circulation of 1,000. The independent television production sector, although it still had less than one tenth the annual production spend of ITV or the BBC, was now a substantial industry. Yet the number of independent or would-be independent producers seemed to be growing ever faster. Isaacs' figures in his address to the IPPA 1984 AGM – 150 companies with commissions but up to 100 proposals submitted each week to a single commissioning editor – revealed the degree of hidden frustration and insecurity behind the success story. Isaacs' speech confirmed that, as many leading independents had suspected, Channel Four was paying on average lower Production Fees than it had anticipated in return for ceding to independents a slightly greater proportion of the rights in their finished programmes. This might suit the larger established companies which had sales arms and international contacts but it was bad news for small companies existing between one specifically Channel Four commission and the next, or companies specialising in current affairs. In order to function effectively they required relatively large staffs and overheads but, because of the nature of the programmes they made, could hope to earn only modest amounts of additional income from selling them abroad. Even the ITV companies only earned 3% of their total income from overseas sales. The vast majority of independents were, therefore, going to continue to be dependent for survival on the money they could amass through Production Fees.

Some producers were already turning to the BBC as an alternative source of work. But most of the few commissions that could be won from the BBC were not really independent commissions in the sense that a Channel Four commission was. They were usually service and packaging agreements under which the independent supplied an idea or a script. In return the BBC took on some key personnel from the company to make it – usually the producer, a director, a writer or performer – leaving the producer with a substantial proportion of the overseas or other rights to exploit. For the vast majority of independents, concentrating on programmes suitable for British audiences and reared in the British tradition of public service broadcasting, this was not a viable way forward. The fact was, as Michael Peacock had forecast, that most independent producers were 'dependent' producers – dependent on Channel Four.

With so many 'dependent producers' now all scrambling after a limited pot of Channel Four money and commissions, it was almost inevitable that divisions would open up between them. Latent divisions had been apparent even before the birth of IPPA; between the large companies that held aloof from the battles for the creation of Channel Four and the individual campaigners and idealists; between the companies who saw themselves primarily as businesses in production for the long term in order to grow and make profits, and the individual producers, or groups of programme makers, who viewed the fact that they were corporate entities merely as a necessary means to an end; between companies with substantial ongoing overheads and permanently employed staffs, and companies working essentially from kitchen tables and small rented offices, taking on staff and hiring equipment in accordance with the needs of a particular programme or series. The needs and aspirations of these producers were essentially different. The pressures on Channel Four from the government to 'justify itself commercially', from ITV companies to become more popular and to take a greater proportion of its programmes from them, coupled with the end of the expansion that had fuelled the rapid growth of the independent sector, served to deepen such latent divisions.

As these problems grew a young graduate, Cheryl Miller-Houser, compiled a report into the obstacles to further expansion of the independent sector. She conducted in-depth interviews with twenty independents chosen as a representative cross-section of the sector. Her report provides an accurate picture of the hopes and fears of independents at this pivotal moment in the sector's history. Almost all those who Miller-Houser questioned were pessimistic about prospects. They felt that the proportion of programmes which Channel Four commissioned from independents was likely diminish as the ITV companies continued to press for an ever larger proportion of their own programmes to be shown, backing their pressure by selling programmes to the channel at less than their actual cost. Independents did not believe that growth in independent commissions from the BBC and ITV would ever be enough to accommodate all the talent that wanted to work in the independent sector, or even to sustain those who were already in it. One or two saw hope in diversifying into other areas such as the production of industrial and corporate films, instructional material, commercials or pop videos, in concentrating on programmes which could be sold overseas, in the expansion of cable or direct broadcast satellite. All agreed that the central problem for independents was the lack of outlets for their work. Short of fundamental changes in the industry or a major government initiative, both of which were thought unlikely, independents were likely to remain over-dependent on Channel Four. Producers recognised that no one could 'expect to have stability along with independence and autonomy; that if people want security they should work for the BBC or ITV; that if one is not willing to take risks or entrepreneurial initiatives, he/she should leave the field'. A majority, while not believing that Channel Four should give guarantees of future work to specific companies, did believe that the Channel ought to make a commitment to commission a certain amount from the independent sector each year. Miller-Houser concluded that while some people were optimistic about breaking into the BBC and ITV, and others did not know where they would be or what they would be doing in six months' time; almost all 'predicted a growing gulf between large, stable, diversified independent companies and those dependent on Channel Four. Some thought that in a few years' time 20 to 25 large independent companies would dominate the field. Everyone felt that if this did occur, it would mean less broadcast "innovation" and a lowering of overall quality.'[25]

Some of the bigger independents, those with larger staffs and overheads, now started to press for guarantees of continuity of work. They argued that not only did the Channel have a responsibility towards sustaining the companies which it had 'created', it was in the interests of the Channel itself and of independent production as a whole for there to be a group of 'core' companies which could be relied upon to provide a substantial proportion of the programming the Channel needed year in and year out. In the spring of 1985 David Elstein, who ran a company specialising mainly in current affairs, put forward specific proposals to the Channel for a small group of 'core companies'. Elstein wanted these companies sustained by guarantees of a specific volume of work over a given period of years. A paper outlining Elstein's proposals was submitted for discussion by the Channel Four Board.

Reacting to news of Elstein's proposal, I wrote an article in the *IPPA Bulletin* voicing the concerns of smaller independents. Headed *Down on the Farm – or, Questions to Elstein*, I wrote that I was disappointed that Elstein, who had been such a doughty champion of the independents' cause, should put forward such a proposal. Was he really arguing for the re-creation in the independent sector of cumbersome and inefficient companies such as Thames, which he had so recently escaped? Channel Four did not provide the basis from which to build a large corporation. Nor should it. 'Scrambling about, we independents do, however, comfortably undercut and out-think the corporations.' The necessary price of remaining adventurous and inventive was the loss of a little bit of security.[26] Responding, David Graham showed up the limitations of my argument. In an article called *The Hazards of Clientism*,[27] he countered that the health of the sector and its ability to innovate across a range of programmes required more than one type of company. Small companies, while well suited to one-off, relatively high-cost specialist programmes such as drama or documentaries, were not capable of handling political and topical current affairs programmes, nor things that required a fast response. These required organisation in depth and an ongoing team. Graham said that by being concentrated in small, insecure companies the independent sector was denying itself the ability to benefit from economies of scale.

In the end Jeremy Isaacs came down against 'core' companies. They were, he decided, 'an example to be avoided at all costs. Core suppliers was the notion of American independent producers', such as he had met on programme-buying trips while he was Director of Programmes at Thames, 'who were proud to tell you that they were huge and profitable. They boasted of their independence, but they didn't seem to me in the least independent as they were wholly dependent on networks buying new series.' He refused to extend limited guarantees except to ITN (which supplied the Channel's news) and perhaps *Brookside*.[28] When Elstein received news of Channel Four's refusal to give his company any long-term commitment he announced that he intended to close it, and seven months later returned to Thames, taking Isaacs' old job, Director of Programmes.

Since coming to power Mrs Thatcher had had little success in her avowed intent of curbing union wage demands, industrial unrest or trade union militancy. Cumulative national inflation since she came to power amounted to almost 50%, unemployment remained at 12.5%, more than double what it had been at any time in the 1970s. In television ITV remained a byword for restrictive practices and inflationary wage settlements. Broadcasters and broadcasting, with its high profile, inflationary costs, bad industrial relations and, as Mrs Thatcher saw it, recalcitrant attitude to reporting, were an affront to many of her most cherished beliefs and policies. The BBC licence fee, set in December 1981 at £46, was expected to remain fixed for three years, while in the same period the BBC's costs had almost doubled. By 1983 it had become clear that the BBC was going to have to seek a substantial increase in the licence fee or cut back heavily on its costs. Herein, perhaps, lay the independents opportunity? Perhaps the government might be persuaded that, before agreeing to any licence fee increase, both the BBC and ITV should be subjected to a dose of the kind of market competition and cost-efficient programme making offered by independent producers.

In 1983 Michael Peacock stepped down as chairman of IPPA and John Gau took over from him. Having joined the BBC from university in 1963 as an assistant film editor, Gau had risen rapidly through its ranks, gaining a reputation for standing up for his programme makers and supporting their controversial programmes. He had been tipped for the very top. But his career had been blighted by the row over the *Panorama* filming at Carrickmore in 1979. In 1981, in spite of backing from the out-going Director-General Ian Trethowan, his designated successor Alasdair Milne and the previous Controller of BBC-1 Bill Cotton, Gau had been passed over by the BBC Governors for the post of Controller BBC-1. To Gau it seemed clear that the BBC's management could no longer stand up to the governors: 'So one said "Fuck off." Channel Four was starting up, so I could go. One knew a new world was being created. I felt the BBC was no longer a place I wanted to be.'[29] When Peacock had announced his decision to stand down as IPPA chairman, Gau had seemed the natural successor.

On becoming chairman of IPPA, Gau was convinced that his task was to take the independents 'on to the next stage', to open up a wider market for their programmes. This, rather than reducing the number of independents to a core of more prosperous and stable large producers, Gau believed, was the answer to the sector's frustrations and problems. With his good connections inside the senior ranks of the BBC and with people in influential positions in ITV, he seemed the ideal person for the task. From the start of his chairmanship he urged producers to start looking beyond Channel Four: 'Until we got into the BBC and ITV we would still be like country cousins.'

For the original campaigners, as for Gau, the reasons for wanting to be free to make programmes for the BBC and ITV as well as for Channel Four went beyond financial self-interest to fundamental principle. Any medium, but particularly one as influential as television, ought to be open to the full range of creative voices, ideas and opinions. Closed institutions such as the BBC and ITV were simply incompatible with that ideal. However, on their own such arguments were unlikely to appeal to the institutions themselves or to the Thatcher government. In order to succeed in any campaign for a right of access to the BBC and ITV, the campaigners arguments were going to have to be couched in the stridently commercial and 'Market' terms employed by the leaders of the Channel 4 Group when they re-launched their campaign after the Conservative election victory in the summer of 1979.

On becoming chairman of IPPA, John Gau stepped up the organisation's lobbying effort, himself making the rounds of the BBC, the ITV companies, IBA and MPs. Gau is an affable man, who sometimes has a useful ability to hide his sharp intelligence behind his large frame, round face and comfortable features. He referred to his lobbying efforts as – 'Eating lunch for IPPA'. For a year or so Gau's efforts appeared to make no appreciable difference. But by 1984 broad-casting and its costs were moving up the political agenda. In January ITV had started transmitting Granada's *Jewel in the Crown*, Ken Taylor's fourteen-part adaptation of Paul Scott's *Raj Quartet* novels about the last days of the British Empire in India. The whole enterprise, made at enormous expense, had been supervised by Sir Denis Forman. It was widely regarded as one of ITV's finest achievements. It would turn out to be almost the last of its kind. Against this BBC-1 was playing *The Thorn Birds*, a seven-part American import based on a romantic best-seller larded with a reverential attitude to the church. It featured a priest who discards his vows for a romantic screw, summed up by the television critic Philip Purser as: 'Kiss, Kiss, ugh, ugh.' *The Thorn Birds* played at 7.45 p.m. on Sundays while *The Jewel in the Crown* transmitted on Tuesdays. *The Thorn Birds* duly made it into the audience ratings top ten, getting 15 million viewers, while *Jewel in the Crown*, with 9 million viewers, got nowhere. Unflattering comparisons were made between 'the public service commitment' of ITV and the crass commercialism of the BBC.

In mid-February 1984, halfway through the run of *The Jewel in the Crown*, the ITV companies invited Mrs Thatcher to lunch. Basking in critical acclaim, it seemed an extremely opportune moment. They were in for a shock. Waiting to greet the Prime Minister outside the ITCA's nondescript office block head-quarters in Mortimer Street, the centre of London's fashion garment workshops district, Paul Fox, the Chairman of the ITCA, found that word of her arrival had got out and a small crowd of seamstresses, machinists, messengers and secretaries had formed. As her Jaguar drew up they started to cheer and clap. Buoyed up and at the height of her powers, she swept in to confront the assembled ITV bosses. 'David Plowright and Bill Brown opened for ITV and we played it extremely badly . . . we shouldn't have invited her.' Crammed round the long table of the ITCA's narrow, neon-lit, upstairs conference room were representatives of all fifteen companies, too many to fit in comfort along the two sides of the table. Jammed elbow to elbow, 'in a disgusting place' and, according to Sir Paul Fox, eating 'a second rate meal'[30] it quickly degenerated into an event all those present came to regret. The ITV executives listened as Mrs Thatcher told them that the only night that she ever watched television was Saturday ' . . . and Saturday night television is appalling. There is nothing to watch. Why don't you do some decent concerts or operas on a Saturday night?' Bill Brown, the Managing Director of Scottish Television, made the mistake of trying a joke in response: 'Well, you could always watch *Union World* on Channel Four, Prime Minister.' Mrs Thatcher responded with what Brown later described as 'the treatment, the full laser treatment for about half a minute on the iniquities of ITV's labour relations'.[31]

Meanwhile Gau set up a six-man IPPA Lobby Sub-Committee of its Council (often referred to as 'The Political Group') under his own chairmanship. Its primary purpose was to gain access for independents to broadcasters other than Channel Four. An obvious first target was ITV. Gau approached Paul Fox, whom he knew well from the time when both had worked for the BBC. They met for lunch, with Martin Tempia, IPPA's Administrator, in attendance. It turned out to be an unhappy occasion: 'Fox was incredibly hostile and kept putting Martin down. Fox rubbished us both.'[32] Gau went away feeling that it would be a very long time before he or his company did any work for Paul Fox or Yorkshire Television.

Repulsed, the committee looked at other ways of getting independents' pro-grammes into ITV. That summer, 1984, the Cable and Broadcasting Bill (arising from the 1982 Hunt Inquiry into the expansion of cable services) was passing through Parliament. It would set up the Cable Authority, impose controls on ITV franchise holders' financial interests in cable companies and establish a revised system of vetting for advertisements. Might it not be possible to use the Bill as a means of getting the government to impose a quota of independent productions on ITV? The independents approached Roger Gale, the Conservative MP for Thanet North, who had himself been a producer at Thames and so knew a thing or two about the realities of working in ITV. He was persuaded to introduce an amendment to the Cable and Broadcasting Bill requiring the ITV contractors to include in their schedules 'a proper proportion of programmes by companies and persons resident in the United Kingdom other than' ITV companies, their subsidiaries or the BBC. Gale told the Commons that his aim was to extend 'the genuine independent programme-making market into markets which are closed to it at the moment'. Attacking the 'unholy alliance between the ACTT, NATTKE[33] and the ITCA', he cited an article by Paul Fox about how ITV companies were forced to give way to unreasonable union demands rather than be taken off the air by strike action. At that moment the government was hyper-sensitive over such issues as it was locked in a life-and-death struggle with the miners, led by Arthur Scargill, over the National Coal Board's plans to close pits. With flying pickets and thousands of strikers fighting pitched battles with hundreds of policemen at coal depots, coking plants and pit-heads, the government was scornful of managements which opted for 'a peaceful life' rather than take on militant trade unions. 'We know', Gale thundered, 'industrial problems have been solved by huge pay settlements and gross over-manning levels.' The differences between the industrial relations records of ITV and of the independent sector were abundantly clear. As expected, Douglas Hurd, the Home Office Minister responsible for piloting the Bill through the Commons, rejected Gale's amendment. But in doing so he said, 'My honourable friend . . . is anxious to encourage independent production. So am I, so are the government, and so we have proved.' But imposing a quota of independent production on ITV was 'an idea which would need a good deal of further thought and consultation'. For the moment the route to greater access for independent production in ITV was closed. However, Hurd's words seemed to offer encouragement for the future.

*   *   *

The Cable and Broadcasting Bill had dealt principally with the emerging technologies of broadcasting. Perhaps these technologies might themselves offer an alternative means by which the independents could broaden the market for their programmes? By 1984 transmission of television services direct to the home from satellites – Direct Broadcasting by Satellite or DBS – was the subject of even more excited debate within the industry than the possibilities of fibre-optic cable. Ever since the first satellite transmissions from the USA via Telstar in 1962 there had been talk of starting DBS television services. The BBC had planned to launch their own services but in the summer of 1983 had pulled out, defeated by the technical difficulties and enormous expense, estimated at £400 million. However, the government remained enthusiastic. Its interest was less in what the technology might do for the quality of television services or the viewing public and more in satellite technology and what its development, fuelled by a presumed public appetite for more television, might do for British hi-tech aerospace and electronics companies. So by the summer of 1984 a new joint DBS venture, between ITV and the BBC, was being planned. The services were to be transmitted via a satellite built, on government insistence, by British Aerospace. In addition to the BBC and ITV, the consortium providing the DBS service would include a 'third force'.

This, Gau's IPPA Council Lobby Sub-Committee decided, was the independents' most immediate opportunity of finding a new outlet. The Sub-Committee included Phil Redmond, the Liverpool-based producer of Channel Four's ongoing soap *Brookside*, Simon Olswang, IPPA's Treasurer, a media lawyer whose clients included many of the largest and most commercially successful independent production companies, and Jeremy Wallington, who had been Controller of Programmes at Southern Television until the company was deprived of its ITV contract in the 1982 franchise round (a decision with which, three years on, Wallington had still not really come to terms). Wallington now headed Limehouse, a large independent with a spectacularly situated studio complex in the old Limehouse West India Docks. As well as being used for Limehouse's own productions, this studio complex was rented out to other producers. Wallington, therefore, had a strong interest in the opportunities for high-volume, low-cost programming which satellite seemed likely to offer.

The BBC was expected to take 50% of the DBS venture and ITV 30%. The IBA had invited companies interested in the remaining 20% to send in applications. Seventeen of the largest British corporations with interests in entertainment and television – including Thorn-EMI, Virgin and Granada TV Rental had applied. In June 1984 the IBA had interviewed these applicants and passed on its recommendations to the Home Office. On 31 July the Home

Secretary, Leon Brittan, announced the names of the five companies which had been selected as the potential candidates for the remaining 20% stake in the DBS consortium. One of the companies named by Brittan was Consolidated Satellite Broadcasting, in which Radio Tele Luxembourg held a controlling interest. Independent producers, and particularly IPPA Council members, reading reports of Brittan's announcement the next morning in the newspapers were astonished to learn that the successful Consolidated Satellite Broadcasting bid included a group of prominent independent producers, among them John Gau, their Chairman, and Jeremy Wallington. (Others were Andrew Brown and John Hawkesworth, both producers of glossy drama, and John Pringle.) Another name mentioned was 'media lawyer' Simon Olswang. Three out of the six members of IPPA's Lobby Sub-Committee, it appeared, were in some way directly involved in the successful Consolidated bid for a slice of DBS. The bid's success, according to the *Financial Times*, rested in part on its inclusion of 'a group of independent producers such as Mr John Gau and Mr Jeremy Wallington'. Mr Wallington, readers learned, had 'agreed to serve as a director'.[34] The astonishment of IPPA Council members reading the press reports arose from the fact that this was the first they had heard about any members of the Lobby Sub-Committee being directly involved in Consolidated's satellite bid themselves. So far as IPPA Council knew, the Association's policy was to win access to DBS for all independents. Press reports suggested that much play had been made with the fact that the whole independent sector would gain access to DBS through this small group of named independents.

But how? What was going on? Why had it not been discussed in the IPPA Council? Within hours my phone was ringing. Anxious IPPA members now looked to me, as one of the founders of IPPA and still a serving member of its Council with known sympathies for the 'culture' of the 'programme maker producer' rather than the 'businessman producer', to find out what was behind the announcement. Martin Tempia, IPPA's administrator, was also receiving calls. Council members pointed out that there had been IPPA Council meetings in June and July, and also a Lobby Sub-Committee meeting, attended in each case by at least some of the people reported to be involved in the Consolidated bid. Yet nothing had been said about it. The story appeared to raise a range of fundamental issues. What precisely was IPPA's involvement? The Association's rules specifically excluded from membership anyone with an interest in a broadcaster. A broadcaster by satellite would still be a broadcaster and, in any case, Radio Tele Luxembourg was a European broadcaster and had a controlling interest in the consortium. If the three named Council members were acting for IPPA, why didn't the Association know about it? If they were not acting for IPPA, had they or had they not used their association with IPPA in furtherance of their own interests?

Gau was out of the country on holiday. Unable to contact Gau, Tempia wrote to Wallington: 'At the risk of sounding a little tetchy, I would have appreciated some indication from either John Gau or yourself that John Gau Productions and Limehouse were bidding for a share of the DBS enterprise. Whilst I recognise that on one level it is absolutely none of IPPA's business what transactions and commercial arrangements its members individually enter into, I feel that I should have been informed of the interests of certain members of the Political Group prior to the Home Office announcement. We have all invested a lot of time and effort into our lobbying campaign over recent months. It would be wrong for the bulk of IPPA members to conclude that the Association's efforts were influenced by considerations other than wishing to promote the interests of the independent sector as a whole.'[35]

Wallington replied immediately. He was worse than a little tetchy. He told Tempia that he had become aware that his actions were 'capable of misrepresentation', but Tempia's comments about the 'feelings of the bulk of IPPA members' were 'not appropriate and frankly, I find it a little bit offensive'. He continued, 'Part of the reason why neither I nor John had been able to keep you up-to-date . . . is that we have not met for weeks and weeks. Had we met, both of us I know would have informed you and the others in the political group fully, how it had come about and what we are doing for the independent sector through our activities.' He had been asked by Consolidated to become a member 'just a few days before we appeared before the Authority'. At the meeting with the IBA he and Gau had 'underlined . . . that we were there not simply to get a slice of the cake for our own companies but so that the independent sector as a whole could have a voice, as roughly represented by us, in the setting up of DBS and eventually, one hopes, in the supply of programmes to it.' Those involved were eventually going to have to contribute a very substantial sum of money to the venture. 'A trade body such as IPPA is in no position to do this, nor are most independent producers.'[36]

On his return from holiday Gau also wrote to Tempia. Gau inferred from what Tempia had said that some members of the Lobby Sub-Committee were implying that he had been using the activities of the committee to further his own interests. This he denied absolutely. He recognised that in acting for IPPA any Council member might inadvertently further his or her own interests through the very act of being the person who negotiated on behalf of the Association with representatives of a broadcaster. But just as often a Council member might damage his own interests, for instance when he or she had to take a tough line with a broadcaster on IPPA's behalf. He had been approached 'out of the blue' by Consolidated for the first time on 6 June, after the announcement of the government's decision that there would be 'a third force' in the DBS initiative, and after discussions in the Lobby Sub-Committee had moved on from consideration of outlets for independent production on DBS to the issue of access to ITV. 'My main reason for agreeing to take part in the bid . . . was a simple one. Given that we had been making a lot of noise about independents being involved in other markets than Channel Four, I could hardly say no when offered an opportunity to put my name forward.' Gau added that had he 'felt for one moment that there was a conflict of interest, I would either have declared it, or not taken up the offer'.[37]

Speculation and adverse comment in the trade press about the involvement of IPPA Council members in the successful Consolidated DBS bid increased as August progressed. Yet IPPA remained silent. With no IPPA Council meeting scheduled for August because of the summer holidays, there was no chance to clear the air.

When IPPA's Council did meet in September, with Gau and Olswang present, but not Wallington, it was an understandably charged occasion. Wallington had exacerbated the situation by telling *Televisual* magazine that, as far as he was concerned, the IPPA Lobby 'doesn't exist. It hasn't met for months.' Explaining their role, Gau told the council that he and Olswang had originally been approached by John Whitney and asked to put in an application 'to represent independents in the DBS scheme'. Gau felt that this initiative was important and that he, Olswang and Consolidated 'saw their role as representing the independent sector as a whole'. Olswang, pointing out that he had originally been 'co-opted onto the Lobby Sub-Committee to provide advice particularly on legislative matters', said that he 'did not feel that he was subject to conflict of interest'. He shared Gau's view that it was important that the interests of independents were represented. A lengthy and sometimes heated debate followed, during which it was pointed out that the three people concerned with the Consolidated DBS bid had been remiss in informing neither their colleagues on the Lobby Sub-Committee nor the Association's Administrator, Tempia. Gau offered to resign but was asked not to. His actions seemed beyond reproach. However, Wallington's seemed deeply questionable and it was decided that he must be pressed to clarify his ideas about how the Consolidated DBS bid was to further the interests of the independent sector as a whole. It was also agreed to draw up specific guidelines for Council members on Declarations of Interest.

It quickly became clear that Wallington had very little real idea how Consolidated's involvement in DBS was going to benefit the IPPA membership as a whole. He had, he said, 'kicked around the idea of a Trust Fund which could be based on a percentage of profit when it is achieved, to be used to help independent companies in trouble or individual members of our Association' but had decided that this was 'a bit old-fashioned and rather a long way off'. The best that he could offer was the vague possibility that 'people like ourselves' might act as the 'vehicle or conduit for independent programmes being arranged with the DBS company'.[38]

As the months passed and the DBS venture failed to get off the ground, interest in the Consolidated DBS bid and any IPPA involvement in it faded. However, the rift between the cultures of the two types of independent producer, and the latent distrust between people who had been long-time campaigners for the independent cause and those who had come into independent production more recently and saw it primarily as a business opportunity, had been deepened. The guidelines on Conflicts of Interest, drawn up by a committee consisting of Sophie Balhetchet, Tim Fell and me, based on rules relating to publicly elected bodies and the guidelines for company directors issued by the Institute of Directors, were adopted by the Council. These were to lie largely forgotten, only to be recalled years later during another, even bigger crisis in the independent sector. Looking back at the row today, Gau says that he was naïve to have gone along with the Consolidated DBS bid. His lasting impression is of how divisive it was.

*   *   *

The other possible outlet for independents' productions was the BBC. It claimed it was already doing more than one hundred hours of independent production, although the figures appeared deeply suspect and had never been quantified to the independents' satisfaction. In any case most of the programmes involved were not independent commissions in the Channel Four sense, but the kind of packaging deals put together by producers like John Whitney before he joined the IBA.

However, by 1984, with the BBC turning its collective mind increasingly to how to win a licence fee increase from a reluctant government, a government that looked kindly on the new breed of independent producers, IPPA saw a possible opportunity. It was an opportunity which Gau, with his good contacts inside the upper echelons of the BBC, seemed ideally placed to exploit.

Shortly after the announcement of his appointment as the next Director-General of the BBC in 1982, Alasdair Milne had been invited round to Number 10 for a drink. In the relaxed atmosphere, in so far as it was possible for any BBC Director-General Designate to be relaxed with Mrs Thatcher, drinks in hand, Mrs Thatcher had asked:

'Mr Milne, you will take advertising, won't you?'

Milne had immediately replied, 'No, Prime Minister.'

'Why not?'

'Because if we did we would destroy ITV.'

'No, I don't mean that. I mean you will take a bit, just to pay for some of the things that can't be paid for.'

'No, Prime Minister, I don't think so. We won't do that.'[39]

Since that conversation the BBC's relations with the government had deteriorated steadily. In addition to the rows over reporting from the Falklands, two Conservative MPs were now pursuing a libel case following allegations in a *Panorama* programme, entitled *Maggie's Militant Tendency* (Militant Tendency was a far-left group bringing great division and discredit to Labour Party), about their connections with extreme right-wing neo-fascist groups such as the National Front. On top of this the miners' strike, now widely seen as an open struggle to the death between the government and the trade union movement, presented the BBC with a reporting problem almost as great as during the General Strike in 1926. Mrs Thatcher, like Churchill in 1926, believed that the BBC should be firmly on the side of the government. Milne, unlike Reith in 1926, believed that the duty of the BBC was to report both sides fairly. Early in his director-generalship, in the aftermath of the Falklands War, Milne had made a speech in which he had recommitted the BBC to its primary duty to telling the truth, come what may: 'Our country takes the BBC's dedication to truth-telling wholly for granted. You have only to look at the highly organised lying in the service of an ideology or a creed or a state which afflicts entire continents, to see how rare truth-telling is in broadcasting or, for that matter, what extraordinary efforts are being made by totalitarian régimes to prevent our undoctored broadcasts from reaching their own citizens.'[40] Milne was a committed broadcaster, a fighter rather than a diplomat.

Against such a background the BBC was all too aware that in asking for a licence fee increase it risked losing the licence fee system altogether. As recently as May 1984 Douglas Hurd had told the House of Commons that it would be 'foolish to stand here and say that the licence system would never be modified'. So as a first step in preparing the ground for its licence fee increase application, the BBC had called in the international accountancy firm Peat Marwick Mitchell to prepare a 'Value for Money' report. The heart of the BBC's case was to be that the licence fee, at roughly the cost of a broadsheet newspaper each day, represented one of 'the best bargains in Britain'.

As Peat Marwick got down to picking their way around the BBC, the Corporation's executives started to up the ante, making speeches in which they pointed out that unless the licence fee was increased to £60 there would have to be cuts in the BBC's services. In November 1984 the whole issue of broadcasting costs was given a thorough airing at an RTS convention in HTV's gleaming new Cardiff studio complex, itself a fresh monument to methods of production and IBA franchise requirements which were already obsolete. In one session, *The Price Is Wrong*, Michael Checkland provided an updated analysis of the BBC's costs, stressing what a good buy the BBC was for the public. He pointed out that the BBC spent just £4.80 per year per household on drama, less than it would cost a man and his wife to visit the theatre in the cheapest seats once a year or to eat an after-theatre dinner at McDonald's. The amount the BBC spent on news and current affairs would buy one copy of the *Sun* every fortnight. The BBC's award-winning drama, *An Englishman Abroad*, cost only 75% of one of Goldcrest's *First Love* films for Channel Four. But now, unlike at the RTS session in Southampton in 1980, representatives of Channel Four and the independents were present to give the argument a different slant. Janet Walker, one of Channel Four's original Programme Cost Controllers, who had subsequently headed the finance department of an ITV company and now worked for an independent, told the broadcasters that they ought to be grateful to the independents for making them more cost conscious: 'In my experience there is no doubt that the independents do produce more cheaply than the institutional broadcasters.'

One week after the formal launch of the BBC's bid for a licence fee increase to £65, I wrote to the Home Secretary, Leon Brittan. Explaining that I was a freelance director and producer who still worked fairly regularly for the BBC as well as for my own company, I asked him to learn the lessons of his government's creation of Channel Four. Technicians and programme makers from the BBC and ITV, together with new talent which had been clamouring in vain to get into the industry for years, had created well over one hundred new businesses which together supplied approximately 50% of Channel Four's programmes. 'No one doubts that the quality of these programmes matches those made by the ITV companies or the BBC.' But the significant fact, I told him, was that 'the "independents" have made their programmes considerably more cost effectively than the older institutions'. The best estimates available to the industry, supported by examination of the operating costs of the BBC, ITV and Channel Four, suggested that '"independents" produce 25% more economically than the BBC and 40% more economically than ITV'. Independents had achieved these results 'without the industrial relations problems that so frequently beset the rest of the industry. They are the result of dispensing with unnecessary elements of ineffective and non-productive bureaucracy and administration.' Away from the large institutions independents had been 'able to give free rein to both their creativity and their entrepreneurial enterprise, while being able to take advantage of ongoing advances in technology'. People like me were 'uneasily aware that when we work for the BBC or an ITV company we are unable to produce as efficiently' as we would were we making an identical programme for our own independent companies. I was not advocating the dismemberment of the BBC nor the withholding of a substantial licence fee increase, I assured him. Nor was I championing the introduction of advertising on BBC television as a supplement to the licence fee – like the BBC and the ITV companies I believed that it would prove the thin edge of a wedge leading inexorably to the lowering of standards on both services. 'However, I would suggest that as a condition of an adequate increase in the licence fee and in return for leaving ITV's monopoly of television advertising intact, both systems should be obliged to accept programmes specifically commissioned from independents.'[41]

The following February Peat Marwick Mitchell handed over their 'Value for Money' report to the BBC. According to the gloss put on their findings by the BBC it cleared the Corporation of anything other than minor organisational and financial slackness. In truth, however, it was damning. While it admired the dedication and commitment of the BBC's staff and the senior management's resolve to identify and achieve savings and greater efficiency, it was 'not confident that there is sufficient pressure or that adequate mechanisms exist . . .

to ensure that best value is obtained'.[42] Management skills were lacking and accountability poor.

As part of its campaign for an increased licence fee the BBC wanted to appear as open as possible. So, when Gau approached Milne about meeting a small delegation of IPPA Council members, they were invited round to lunch. Gau provided IPPA's five-person delegation with a set of confidential briefing notes. 'Alasdair Milne is a highly intelligent, slightly prickly chap. He can be very charming and agreeable. But like all old Wykehamists he can also seem abrupt, arrogant and aggressively dismissive. In the circumstances, therefore, our best approach must be supportive of the BBC's standards and goals.' The line Gau suggested that the independents should take was one of 'what's good for the independent sector . . . happens also [to be] good for the BBC.' Because the independents make programmes more cheaply, the independents could help the BBC to save money. Gau pointed out that there were senior people in the BBC (he was unsure if Milne was one of them) 'who feel the BBC is a great organisation because it makes the programmes itself. Being a production house is part of the BBC's indefinable essence.' IPPA should therefore accept that the BBC must remain a great production house, but that the independent sector should be allowed to help out. He concluded: 'What we must say is that we are offering a way out of the BBC's financial dilemma – which allows them to retain their comprehensive and dominant role as a public service broadcaster without jeopardising their programme standards or editorial integrity.' Working with independents was 'surely a small price to pay for retaining their role as the national instrument of broadcasting'.[43]

During the lunch, at which Alasdair Milne was accompanied by a small group of his senior executives, it soon became clear that the BBC had a philosophical problem with the whole concept of working with independents and still doubted that the quality of the programmes made by independents matched their own. The fact that the programme makers responsible for the programmes were often the same in both cases seemed not to affect the BBC's attitude. Nor was the BBC convinced that independents made their programmes more cheaply – the BBC believed that like was not being compared to like. Milne was totally opposed to the idea of quotas – the idea floated by me and others to the Home Secretary. On the other hand the BBC did seem to recognise the political advantage that might be gained from being seen to be open to independent production. Milne accepted that new programmes and talent had been generated through Channel

Four and its use of independents. However, when Gau suggested that IPPA representatives and the BBC should hold more meetings, Milne remained non-committal.

A month later the government announced its decision over the licence fee. It was to be £58 not the £65 that the BBC had asked for. But it was to last for only two years not the three that the BBC had expected. And there was a sting in the tail – the government intended to set up a committee to inquire into possible ways of financing the BBC. The chairman of the committee was to be an economist, Professor Alan Peacock.

Professor Peacock himself wrote later: 'It was widely assumed that the Committee members were hired guns instructed to conclude that the BBC should cease to be publicly funded and should rely on advertising income, a view particularly associated with Mrs Thatcher.'[44] But, as he told reporters at the time, he 'wouldn't have taken the job if I was to be regarded as a hired gun'.[45] The truth, as that best-informed and most perceptive of media correspondents, Ray Snoddy, pointed out in the *Financial Times* a couple of days after the Home Secretary's announcement, was that Professor Peacock was 'a man who sees himself as a classic liberal economist in the tradition of Adam Smith, sympathetic to some of the ideas of monetarism, but not to its more rigid exponents'.

Peacock had previously chaired an Arts Council committee on orchestral funding, been the Chief Economic Adviser to the Department of Trade and Industry in Heath's time and was kept on by Harold Wilson. However, the press and most of the broadcasters concentrated on the fact that after leaving the DTI in 1976 Peacock had done work for the Thatcher government on education vouchers and had run the privately financed Buckingham University, which was held up by fervent Thatcherites in support of their case for the privatisation of the public services. Peacock was also understood to be an admirer of Peter Jay's views on broadcasting.

The widely held impression that Peacock had been appointed to do a Thatcherite hatchet job on the BBC was strengthened in May when the names of the other members of the committee were announced. They included Samuel Brittan, brother of Home Secretary Leon Brittan, Assistant Editor and principal economic commentator on the *Financial Times*, who was another economic liberal and a fan of the Jay nostrums – broadcasters should act like publishers, providing consumers with whatever programmes they felt inclined to pay for. Institutions such as the BBC would shortly be obsolete, rendered unnecessary by the universal availability of fibre-optic cable. The proper job of the Committee was to recognise this and hasten their abolition. However, there were others who might act as counterweights – a Keynesian economist, Jeremy Hardie, and Alastair Hetherington, former Editor of the *Guardian* and Controller of BBC Scotland, who was now a professor of media studies, director of a small independent production company and an IPPA member. Unlike others in broadcasting, the independents recognised from the start that this was not such an unbalanced committee as the commentators presumed, nor would it be as easy to sway as the conspiracy theorists believed.

In fact, although Professor Peacock had been able to put forward names for membership of his committee, the selection of members had ultimately been dictated by the Home Office. Professor Peacock had been given no instructions by either Mrs Thatcher or the Home Office as to what conclusions his committee should reach. In the event neither the Prime Minister nor her office gave the committee any evidence and although the Home Office provided a survey of the current organisation of broadcasting, it made no recommendations. Other government departments proved even more reluctant to give assistance, let alone their views. 'We almost pleaded with some Departments, such as the Treasury, to give us their views, but they were not to be drawn.'[46] Presumably Mrs Thatcher assumed that having appointed a good liberal economist to head the committee and a team of intelligent people to support him, they must reach the same conclusion as herself. Professor Peacock was not even provided with an official letter of appointment. He merely received a phone call from Leon Brittan who asked if he would be willing to chair such a committee. Once he had given his agreement in principle, he settled down to negotiating with the Home Office over what resources were to be available to the committee.

There was much criticism that the terms of reference given to the committee were so narrow as to limit the scope of its enquiries and predispose it to reach the result required by the government. However, in addition to being required to assess the effects across all the broadcast media of the introduction of advertising or sponsorship as a means replacing or supplementing the BBC licence fee, the final paragraph of the committee's terms of reference charged it with considering 'any proposals for securing income from the consumer other than through the licence fee'. This gave the committee licence to look well beyond the narrow issue of deciding for or against the BBC taking advertising. One of the first things that Professor Peacock did was to inquire as to how widely the committee could interpret these terms of reference. He was told that this was up to the committee itself.

The Committee aimed to report within one year. Its first move was to send out invitations to a large number of bodies and groups with an interest in broadcasting to submit evidence and to issue a press statement inviting submissions from anyone else who felt that they had something to contribute. The committee said that it would like to receive submissions by 31 August. During the next twelve months the committee held twenty meetings and received evidence from no fewer than 843 individuals and organisations.

On the night that the setting-up of the Committee had been announced, John Whitney, the Director General of the IBA, had written in his diary: 'Thundercloud hanging over the BBC and we ain't going to get the rain!' So secure did the IBA feel that it did not submit its evidence to the Peacock Committee until after the deadline. In its submission the Authority rejected advertising on the BBC, stressing that the main issue was not the size of the advertising cake, but the range and choice of broadcasting available in Britain. Any change in the system should show that it would result in an improvement.

The ITV companies individually, and through their trade association the ITCA, put forward much the same set of arguments as the IBA. To them the prospect of advertising on the BBC was a threat. It would break their monopoly and almost certainly reduce their income. However, when members of the ITCA appeared before it in person, the Committee set them what David Plowright describes as an 'Examination Paper'. The questions covered tendering for ITV franchises, the use of 'unoccupied' hours (those hours when ITV was not on the air) and the possibility of a new transmission authority. The questions set for ITV by the Committee ought to have started alarm bells ringing, but the companies remained supremely confident. They believed that they had the Home Office in their pockets. As Sir Denis Forman (the Chairman of Granada Television) explains, he was 'not frightened of Tebbit and Thatcher moving in on broadcasting. [I knew] the Home Office wouldn't allow Mrs Thatcher to wreck it. I was never alarmed. They were a very good department. They were on our side. Hurd was a zombie as far as television was concerned, but Whitelaw and Brittan and the top three or four civil servants were good. Dominating the Home Office was the most important thing as far as I was concerned. They were sensible, civilised, biddable people.'[47] However, less than six months into the Peacock Committee's deliberations, Mrs Thatcher reshuffled her cabinet, moving Leon Brittan out of the Home Office and promoting Douglas Hurd to take his place as Home Secretary. At the same time she made Norman Tebbit Chairman of the Conservative Party.

As was to be expected, the advertising industry supported the introduction of advertising on the BBC. But even they were cautious, advocating that it should be done a little at a time, allowing the amount earned by the BBC to increase with time as the BBC's financial needs increased. In this way, they said, there would continue to be enough advertising revenue to meet both the needs of ITV and the increasing needs of the BBC.

The possibility of introducing advertising to the BBC represented a threat to its fundamental character. Ever since the Sykes Committee in 1923 had rejected advertising as a means of funding the BBC, the BBC and the British concept of public service broadcasting had rested on twin pillars – a strict separation between the broadcasters and the government, and not allowing commercial imperatives to determine programme choice or content. The difficulties inherent in maintaining these twin separations had increased massively since the introduction of ITV and lay at the root of many of the battles and upheavals in broadcasting since the 1950s. In countries which had modelled their broadcasting systems on Britain where in recent years advertising had been introduced into the main public service broadcast systems, such as in CBC in Canada and the ABC in Australia, the result had been the steady degradation and increasing marginalisation of their public service broadcasters. The BBC was determined to resist the introduction of any advertising. To many of the campaigners in groups such as the FCG, the BBC's programmes had already become dangerously dependent on outside finance through such things as co-production money, overseas sales and hidden forms of sponsorship. Those campaigners, many of them now independent producers, were as appalled by the prospect of advertising on the BBC as the BBC was itself.

The BBC prepared its evidence for the Peacock Committee, backed by specially commissioned research reports, with great care and in considerable detail. Those appearing before the Committee in person went through rehearsals in advance in order to iron out any weak points in their presentation. They were greatly helped by the fact that their Chairman, Stuart Young, who had come from a commercial background and had initially favoured a commercial solution to the problem of the BBC's funding, could tell the Committee with absolute conviction that he had changed his mind and had come to realise how essential the system of funding was to the BBC's fundamental character. The BBC's battery of research showed how damaging advertising would be to the BBC and its programmes. The first and only concern of the BBC was the provision of programmes of appeal to the nation as a whole, and to all of the minorities within it. The introduction of advertising would alter that essential priority. New, more efficient ways could be devised for the collection of the licence fee, separate licences could be introduced for such things as car radios, more money could be realised from overseas programme sales, further economies could be achieved in the BBC's operations. The BBC was already working on many of these things and was willing to explore others.

Despite all of this the BBC made a number of serious errors. It had been agreed that more progress would be made if the meetings between the BBC team and the Committee were informal and confidential. Yet after the first meeting the BBC leaked details of what had been said to *The Times*. As a result, in Peacock's phrase, 'The BBC started one down with us.' At that first meeting the BBC had told the Committee that it was prepared to do all the Committee's research. Sir Alan Peacock recalls that the BBC team told the Committee: ' "We will be preparing evidence. When do you want it by?" "The end of August", I replied. "Oh, we can't do that!" ' said the BBC team. Peacock pointed out that his committee's report had to be in in one year's time. 'They never did do adequate evidence,' Sir Alan says. After this bad start, the BBC and the Committee held a series of meetings, which Sir Alan later described with characteristic wit: 'Once the BBC had realised that we knew what questions to ask, they seemed only too willing to act as our guide, philosopher and friend through the labyrinthine structure of broadcasting, even to the extent of arranging our visits abroad. This offer had to be politely refused. It would have been wrong to have proceeded on the assumption that the BBC knew all that was to be known about broadcasting even if it were true. Indeed some of us suspected, and it turned out to be the case, that they were unfamiliar with the economic analysis of broadcasting for the simple reason that they had never had to concern themselves with major economic issues . . . The BBC missed a crucial opportunity to display its command of broadcasting issues in its presentations. Instead of taking the lead in a full discussion of the financing options available and how these might relate to criteria for policy, the BBC brushed aside any suggestion that change was necessary, other than some minor adjustments in the methods of raising the licence fee which might make the fee more acceptable to the public. It relied on the weight of its authority and its past experience and not on properly structured economic analysis which considered how far past experience would remain relevant.'[48] One of the first bits of evidence which it provided for the Committee dealt with the way in which the licence fee should rise to meet the Corporation's rising costs. When Peacock queried some of this evidence and raised questions about the control of costs the BBC seemed surprised. 'They didn't seem to have got hold of the idea that their costs might be questioned.'

The BBC and ITV had barely mentioned the independents in their submissions to the Peacock Committee. However, the BBC, having commissioned the Peat Marwick Mitchell 'Value for Money' investigation, was sensitive about claims that the independents' production costs were substantially lower than its own, even though senior BBC executives doubted the truth of such claims. These sensitivities were heightened by a the *News of the World* story saying that the BBC's costs were higher than independents'. A few weeks after the Committee got down to work the BBC made a heavily publicised announcement of staff cuts totalling 4,000 and the introduction of 'efficiency measures'. One of these, much trumpeted by the BBC while the Peacock Committee was sitting, was to be a 'New Deal for Independents'. In practice this amounted to setting aside what the BBC described as a 'handsome six figure sum' with which to increase the number of 'independent' productions it 'commissioned' from 80 or 90 hours a year to 150. Just what the BBC meant by either 'independent' or 'commission' was unclear. As one IPPA member put it, if it meant 'independents being encouraged to introduce funds to programmes which the BBC itself will make', then it was not independent production. If it meant that the BBC would 'acquire' more programmes made by independents then the meaning of the word 'commission' would depend on how much the BBC was prepared to pay. Until such time as the BBC was prepared to pay the full cost of a production made by an independent, plus a margin for overheads, as Channel Four did, it would not be 'commissioning' programmes as understood by independents.

From the moment that the Committee had been announced, the IPPA Council had recognised that it presented them with an unparalleled opportunity. The master-minding and presentation of IPPA's evidence to the Peacock Committee would prove John Gau's finest hour in the service of the independent production community. He organised the preparation of expert research, wrote most of the first draft of the submission himself, championed and cajoled it through a sometimes doubtful and reluctant Council and led the delegation which appeared before the Committee in person. Happily, one of the members of the IPPA Council already knew Peacock. Robin Crichton owned a small studio and facility company outside Edinburgh (Peacock held a post at Heriot-Watt University, Edinburgh). Within days of the announcement of Peacock's appointment, Crichton had arranged for Gau, Roxanna Knight (IPPA's new administrator) and two other members of the Council to fly up to Edinburgh and have lunch with Peacock at the studio. The man that Gau met was not the hard-faced Thatcherite monetarist being portrayed by much of the industry and press, but an extremely cultured, considerate and quiet-voiced Scot. At that first informal meeting Gau did not press the cultural side of the independents' case but the small business side. He found Peacock extremely supportive. What Gau wanted IPPA to propose was bold – that no less than half of the new programmes transmitted by both the BBC and ITV should be made by independent producers. When Gau first put this idea to the IPPA Council many of its members believed that he was being hopelessly unrealistic. 'They'll never give that,' they said. He retorted, 'If you don't ask you won't get anything.' Eventually Gau won them over.

The submission that IPPA finally put in ran to just twelve pages, each section leavened by an apposite quotation from a variety of sources which ranged from Art Buchwald to Rabindranath Tagore. It opened by quoting Publilius Syrus, writing two thousand years ago: 'No pleasure endures, unseasoned by variety' and continued 'Britain offers a uniquely wide range of choice in its television programmes'. It was, IPPA argued, one of the triumphs of the British system that as broadcasting had expanded the diversity of the programmes on offer had increased. It could easily have been otherwise: 'Most pressures in broadcasting, whether technical, ideological or commercial, tend to reduce what is distinctive, encourage uniformity and narrow the range of choice. In television the centre always holds – it is on the wings that the retreat begins.' Calling Milton Friedman, the guru of the Thatcherite free marketeers and monetarists, in aid of its argument, the submission urged the Committee, whatever it decided, 'to recommend nothing that reduces the audience's real range of choice'. IPPA's solution to the problem of financing the BBC was designed to preserve the essentials of the system while altering certain elements within it radically enough to provide a solution. IPPA reminded the Committee that there was nothing inherent in television broadcasting that required the broadcasters to be the producers of the programmes shown. Channel Four had now shown that the old system was not only no longer necessarily the only system, it was no longer even the best or most appropriate system for the future: 'Like the battle ships of the Second World War, which, after a lifetime's service to their country, suddenly found themselves the wrong design for the struggle ahead, so the present structure of the BBC is unsuitable for the competitive pressures of the future.'

'What profiteth a man to gain an Emmy, if he lose his market share?' IPPA continued, quoting Art Buchwald. The introduction of advertising onto the BBC was not the answer, as it would not only threaten the income of ITV and Channel Four, it would tend to make all the services the same. The *raison d'être* of the BBC and ITV systems was different. 'For ITV, programme-making is in the final analysis a means to other ends; for the BBC it is an end in itself. It is the public service function that lies at the heart of the BBC, and it shapes its programme output.' But such considerations went beyond the philosophical to the practical: 'We believe that if ITV and the BBC had to compete for advertising, both, in a sensible precautionary measure against losing too much of their share of audience, would tend to transmit similar programmes against each other.' The solution, IPPA believed, lay in the BBC adopting 'in significant measure' the Channel Four model. The BBC should not give up all its programme making, but it should divest itself of many of its in-house activities and reduce the number of its in-house producers. In this way it would substantially reduce its costs. 'Just as it proved possible to slim down British Airways without in any way losing its essential character or effectiveness, so we think it could and should be done with the BBC.' IPPA had sought expert outside advice in trying to quantify the level of savings that could be achieved. The BBC's own published accounts were so opaque as to make a reliable calculation of its real programme costs impossible, but every indication suggested that substantial savings could be made in this way. The BBC had recently, and rapidly, managed to make savings of £30 million by divesting itself of certain 'back-up services and the deferment of what had hitherto been considered essential commitments . . . surely there is scope for equally large savings from a similar treatment of programme services? Given the enormous disparity in capital expenditure between BBC Television and Channel Four (approximately £70 million against £3 million in 1983/1984) are there not opportunities here for appreciable savings if the BBC was to rethink its traditional requirement for creating all its own capital facilities?' There was much to be learned from the 25% disparity between the programme-related costs of BBC-2 and Channel Four, particularly when one considered that BBC-2 enjoyed all the advantages of economies of scale and of being part of a jointly operated two-channel system. It would, IPPA realised, take time to introduce such a change to the BBC system, but it could produce savings that would allow the BBC to survive on a licence fee tied in some way to the Retail Price Index, thus taking the setting of the BBC Licence Fee out of the political arena. But the introduction of the Channel Four model to the BBC would do more than this: 'It would forge a partnership that linked the BBC's traditional programme strengths with the entrepreneurial skills of the independent sector. It would bring much needed competition into a cosy and protected market place. It would introduce greater financial rigour and accountability into an industry that is not as efficient or cost effective as it could be. The BBC itself would be able to absorb some of the spirit of enterprise, the intellectual excitement and the refreshing innovation that characterises independent production.'[49]

The IPPA submission went down well with the Peacock Committee. Sir Alan Peacock remembers that it was well presented and 'appreciated both the economics and the economic context of what was likely to happen. It took in the wider picture and slotted in very well with the whole perspective of the Committee's thinking. The independents offered competition and freedom of entry into broadcasting . . . It was unlike the BBC's evidence, which took a BBC only view.'[50] The fact that the independents were offering a market for ideas as much as the discipline of the commercial market in the production of pro- grammes appealed to the committee.

The independents were helped by their sheer numbers. Unlike the BBC and the ITV companies, the independents, as well as making submissions through their trade association, were free to make submissions and lobby the Committee individually. IPPA could call on independent producers who between them knew every one of the members of the committee. So, when IPPA appeared before the Committee to give evidence in person, Gau was able to ensure that David Graham was a member of the delegation. Graham already knew Professor Peacock. While he was at the BBC he had interviewed him for a *Panorama* programme on the public funding of the arts and so knew the most effective line to take.

After its first appearance before the Committee IPPA was asked to provide supplementary evidence and to appear in front of the Committee a second time. The Committee seemed particularly anxious to know more about how the independents had arrived at their estimate that their programme production costs were 25% lower than those of the BBC and about how independents managed to keep control of these costs. By this time IPPA had obtained a copy of the BBC Peat Marwick Mitchell 'Value for Money' report and were able to use it to highlight the shortcomings found by Peat Marwick Mitchell in the BBC's cost and resource management and the greater ability and motivation of independent producers to control their costs. After IPPA's second appearance before the Peacock Committee in March 1986, John Gau felt able to report to the Association's Council that their second appearance had 'been an interesting one . . . JG said that he felt that the Committee's attitude was encouraging to us and that it seemed likely that the use of independents would appear in some form in the final recommendations.'[51]

When news of IPPA's evidence to the Peacock Committee reached the industry trade press they headlined the fact that it called for massive cuts in BBC staff. Responding, the BBC made it absolutely plain that it would fight the IPPA proposals by every means at its disposal.

Quite the strangest event in the whole year-long Peacock saga was a so-called public conference staged by the Peacock Committee at Church House, Westminster on 28 November 1985. Only those who had been invited to speak were permitted to express a point of view or ask questions of other speakers. Only if these speakers ran out of questions would others in the audience be allowed to ask a question. The small number of invited speakers included representatives from the ITCA, but not from the IBA, from the Incorporated Society of British Advertisers, the Cable Television Association, the Association of Independent Radio Contractors, the National Consumer Council, the BBC and Peter Jay, speaking for Peter Jay. It was chaired by the former Liberal Party leader, Jo Grimond, who freely admitted at the outset that he was deaf. It was notable for one minor event and some acid published descriptions afterwards. The noteworthy minor event was described by Brenda Maddox in the following week's edition of *The Listener*. Describing Jo Grimond's chairing and his lack of knowledge of who was who in British television, Maddox wrote: 'Clearly unable to tell his John Birt from his elbow, he curtly ordered the controller of London Weekend Television, because he was "a member of the public", to confine his remarks to 30 seconds. Mr Birt was thus classified because he had been required to sit towards the back in the benches reserved for the supposed public and which included among their sparse occupants such faces from the Clapham omnibus as Paul Fox and Michael Grade. Mr Birt wisely declined the opportunity.'[52] (One can only wish that Jo Grimond had been chairing the BBC Governors a couple of years later when they came to consider appointing Birt to the BBC.)

Few independents bothered to attend, but one who did was Phillip Whitehead. 'As a forum for debate', he wrote, it was 'about as stimulating as a mogadon cocktail.' His enduring memory was of two former Head Boys of Winchester, Peter Jay and Alasdair Milne, arguing loftily in Church House about the people's medium, television. For Whitehead there was something utterly and depressingly unreformedly English about the scene, even in 1985 at the height of Thatcherism and in an arena which should itself have been the epitome of Thatcherism. 'The tall Jay, fluent to the point of arrogance, pouring out his vision of the "free" world of electronic publishing, which will be upon us before you can say Bob's your Maxwell . . . Milne, a slight figure padded out by an old-fashioned suit read out that curious mix of BBC programme gongs and political grovels which the Secretariat still think is their best case.'[53]

The BBC at this time had plenty to be proud about. Its programmes in 1985 and 1986 were not only winning back audiences, they revealed a renewed creative vigour and boldness, stimulated perhaps by the impact of Channel Four, comparable to the best of the 1970s. *Edge of Darkness* (Troy Kennedy Martin's nightmare drama series starring Bob Peck about an international conspiracy to convert nuclear waste into weapons-grade plutonium), Denis Potter's *The Singing Detective* (with an incomparable performance from Michael Gambon as the detective lying in hospital racked by a skin disease and trying to come to terms with a childhood in which he watched his mother commit adultery with his father's best friend), *Tumbledown* (Charles Wood's searing indictment of the human cost of recapturing the Falklands, brilliantly directed by Richard Eyre[54]) and *The Fishing Party*, Paul Watson's brilliantly savage *40 Minutes* documentary indictment of the selfishness, greed and callousness of the Thatcher era, in which, against a soundtrack of news reports of industrial unrest, inner city violence and mounting unemployment, a group of wealthy City futures traders spoil their ghastly children, go to Scotland for a weekend to try to break a fishing record and end up shooting at seagulls, revealing themselves as incompetent fishermen and as being abusive to the waitresses and others who serve them. Milne even authorised the showing of Peter Watkins' *The War Game*, banned since 1965. However, such programmes, although a proper part of the fare provided by a public service broadcaster, did not appeal to the Conservative government or to the organised prudes in groups such as Mrs Whitehouse's National Viewers and Listeners Association.

The attacks on the BBC by Conservative politicians had been more or less continuous ever since Mrs Thatcher came to power, but particularly since William Whitelaw had been moved from the Home Office. From mid-1985 onwards they seemed to be ratcheted up still further. Despite the fact that Mrs Thatcher had finally beaten the miners that spring and seemed impregnable inside her own party, the government was afflicted by a bout of insecurity. In May the Conservatives suffered a string of defeats in the local elections at the hands of the SDP/Liberal Alliance and in July lost a by-election in Brecon and Radnor on a 16% swing to the Alliance. When governments are having difficulties it is always easier for them to blame the messenger and not the message. And so it seemed in the summer of 1985. One of the Government's ongoing difficulties was Irish terrorism. Thatcher was at that time wrestling to secure some kind of agreement with the Irish Government over joint security measures. (The IRA had come close to assassinating Mrs Thatcher when they had exploded a bomb in the Grand Hotel in Brighton during the Conservative Party conference a year earlier.) At the same time, Arab terrorists had hijacked an American airliner and held it at Beirut Airport, providing the American television networks with days of dramatic news coverage. In July, Mrs Thatcher, keen to reduce American support for the IRA and enlist the USA in her fight against the terrorists, told the American Bar Association's convention in London that ways must be found to starve terrorists of 'the oxygen of publicity on which they depend'. The effect was much like that produced by Henry II when, referring to Archbishop Thomas Becket, he asked the knights around him, 'Who will rid me of this turbulent priest?' The priest in this case was clearly broadcasting, and in particular the BBC. the *Sunday Times*, now owned by Rupert Murdoch and edited by Andrew Neil, led the way. The paper picked up the fact that the BBC was preparing to transmit a documentary called *Real Lives, At the Edge of the Union* featuring two locally elected Ulster politicians, one an extreme nationalist, Martin McGuinness, the other an extreme Protestant, Gregory Campbell. Both had been interviewed for the programme about their political beliefs and been filmed going about their daily lives. Both were seen either handling arms or at events where arms were openly carried. The Home Secretary, having been alerted to the programme's existence by the *Sunday Times*, wrote to the Chairman of the BBC and released a press statement saying that, while he was not instructing the BBC not to transmit the programme, he would be failing in his duty if he did not let the BBC know that he believed that the programme 'should not be broadcast' on account of the harm and offence that it would give. At the same time at a press conference during a visit to America, Mrs Thatcher was asked by a *Sunday Times* reporter, who did not name any particular programme, what she would think if a British TV company were to show a film which included an interview with a prominent IRA terrorist. As was to be expected, and no doubt as the *Sunday Times* had hoped, Mrs Thatcher, unaware of the precise context of the question, went off the deep end. She would 'condemn them utterly', she said. 'We have lost between 2,000 and 2,500 people in the past 16 years. I feel very strongly about it and so would many other people.' The next day the *Evening Standard* ran a lead story headed 'BBC TOLD: BAN IRA FILM'.

An already alarming situation for the BBC was made infinitely worse by the fact that Milne was at that moment on holiday in Scandinavia and, as the crisis unfolded, could not be reached. Worse still, owing to a series of accidents and oversights, he had not seen the film. The Home Secretary had the reserve power to order the BBC not to show the programme but had deliberately held back from using it; to do so would be to undermine the BBC's essential independence from government, the foundation on which the British system of broadcasting had always supposedly depended. From the point of view of any government bent on cowing the BBC, as Wilson had demonstrated during his premiership, Eden during the Suez crisis in 1956, and Baldwin and Churchill during the 1926 General Strike, the goal was to get the BBC to accede to government wishes without directly forcing it to do so. A. J. P. Taylor's acid comment in relation to the General Strike held (and holds) good: 'the vaunted independence of the BBC was secure so long as it was not exercised.'[55]

Stuart Young, the Chairman of the BBC, decided, against established practice, to arrange a joint viewing of the film by the Board of Governors and the Board of Management, without waiting for Milne's return. This was extremely unusual. Normal practice required that the management of the BBC made the day-to-day decisions about programme content and what was transmitted. The BBC Governors only commented after the event and provided general guidance, leaving the Director-General to exercise his function as the BBC's editor-in-chief. The last programme the Governors had viewed in advance of transmission had been *Yesterday's Men*. After viewing *Real Lives*, the management team (headed by Michael Checkland, who had recently been promoted to Deputy-Director-General and Bill Cotton) and the Governors were bitterly divided. The management team, which had already seen the film and passed it for transmission, saw no reason to change their minds. The Governors, dominated by Thatcher appointees, ordered that the film be banned.

On his return from Scandinavia Milne saw the film immediately and, like his management colleagues, believed that the film was transmittable. If the BBC's reputation for independence was to be maintained the Governors' decision had to be reversed. Young, too, understood the serious implications of the Governors' decision. Eventually, after strikes by BBC journalists, supported by their colleagues at ITN, the decision to ban the film was reversed and the programme was transmitted, albeit more than two months late. The reaction of most who saw it was to wonder what all the fuss had been about. However, the fall-out from the *Real Lives* affair was profound. Relations between the BBC's Governors and the Board of Management and, above all, the confidence that the Governors had in Alasdair Milne (who was almost entirely innocent in the whole affair) never really recovered.

This kind of incident, the first of a succession, represented a threat to the cherished freedom of programme makers to make programmes unfettered by unwarranted censorship and to report all shades of opinion. It concerned all those of us who had campaigned for greater freedom of expression in broadcasting ever since the 1960s, whether we were inside the BBC or outside it. In the midst of all this, the *Observer* ran a story finally revealing the MI5 vetting of BBC employees, the existence in Room 105 of Broadcasting House of a shadowy figure, Brigadier Ronnie Stonham, with the title 'Special Assistant to the Director of Personnel' and the upside-down 'fir-tree' symbols attached to the confidential personnel files of those deemed 'unreliable'. Those of us who worked regularly for the BBC, particularly those who had taken part in the various broadcasting campaigns down the years or had 'unsuitable' political allegiances, had known about all this for years, as had the programme executives who had had to devote valuable time to outwitting the system in order to employ some of the most talented programme makers around. The BBC, of course, had always steadfastly denied the existence of any such system. After the *Observer* story, one prominent programme maker suggested that all those who knew for sure that they had had security fir-tree symbols attached to their BBC personnel files should hold a public wake during which they would ceremonially burn fir trees. It sounded like a potentially jolly occasion, but as far as I know never happened.

In December 1985 and January 1986 the government was caught up in a complex crisis over defence contracts for the ailing Westland Helicopter

Company. As a result on 9 January Michael Heseltine literally walked out of the Cabinet and was filmed as he made his way out of Number 10 by newsreel cameramen waiting in Downing Street. Leon Brittan, by then in charge of the DTI, followed him less publicly two weeks later. In the following days it looked just possible that Thatcher herself could be toppled. Labour called an emergency debate for 27 January and as she left for it, Thatcher actually said to one colleague, 'I may not be Prime Minister by 6 o'clock tonight.' However, Neil Kinnock, the leader of the Labour Party, muffed his opportunity and instead of nailing Mrs Thatcher indulged in a load of his worst long-winded Welsh rhetoric. Thatcher survived.

The next major attack by the government on the BBC began just a couple of months later in the wake of a United States bombing raid on Libya in April 1986. Libya was accused of giving shelter and support to terrorists including the IRA. Some of the US planes that took part in the bombing had flown from British bases. The BBC's offence was that their correspondent Kate Adie had vividly described the raids from a vantage point in Libya itself, and reported the deaths and injuries of innocent women and children. I remember that on that morning I was due to record the chorus *The Heavens are Telling the Glory of God* from Haydn's *The Creation* for a Granada series on the history of music. After listening to Kate Adie on the BBC I drove to the hall where we were to record it. As the choir and orchestra launched into Haydn's soaring joyous music celebrating the beauty of the creation I found that I was crying. I was not alone – we had all heard Kate Adie and knew what had been done in our names. That is what public service broadcasting is about, whether governments like it or not. The raid failed to topple Qaddafi, although it did damage some military installations and training camps. It has since emerged that Thatcher herself privately had severe misgivings about the raid. But on that beautiful April morning she turned her fury on the BBC for, as she saw it, whipping up public sympathy for the Libyans and inflaming public opinion against her government's support of the US foreign policy. Tebbit, Chairman of the Conservative Party, instigated what he described as a Conservative Central Office investigation into the BBC's 'uncritical carriage of Libyan propaganda'.

There was trouble elsewhere in broadcasting as well. Following further horrific riots in run-down inner-city areas which had become virtual ghettos for ill-used British black and Asian minorities in Handsworth, Birmingham, in Brixton, in Toxteth and on the Broadwater Farm housing estate in Tottenham, during the course of which PC Blakelock was brutally murdered, Ceddo, a black video workshop, had made a programme *Down on the Farm*, which attempted to articulate the deep anger and sense of frustration felt by many black people over their treatment at the hands of the police. The film amounted a tirade against the police, social conditions and the government, and Mrs Thatcher in particular for her reception in Britain of the South African apartheid regime's president, P. W. Botha. When I saw it, it seemed to me a clear, if overwrought, first-hand expression of the true depth of anger, amounting to hatred, felt by many black, and especially young, people. I knew some of the young film makers who had been involved in its making and so I may have been prejudiced in their favour, but it seemed to me that it was important that the film was seen by a wider audience in the hope that we all might eventually come to understand how others in our community felt and why. Unfortunately Ceddo could not agree with Channel Four, nor Channel Four with the IBA, on a version that could be transmitted even on Channel Four. As a result the film was not transmitted.

The reverse side of the climate of violence engendered in deprived areas under Thatcherism was a renewal of a particularly British kind of public puritanism. As a result, in 1985 and 1986 the platoons of prudes and censors were active in the field of broadcasting in a way they had not been since the 1960s and the advent of Mary Whitehouse. Winston Churchill MP (grandson of the wartime leader) attempted to bring in a Private Member's Bill that would bring broadcasting within the scope of the Obscene Publications Act. The effect of this move, if it succeeded, would be to provide those who wished to 'Clean Up TV' with enhanced opportunities to bring private prosecutions against broadcasters. Although prosecutions under the Obscene Publications Act would be unlikely to succeed, the executive time and legal expense of defending them was potentially immense, with the result that the broadcasting authorities would be even more cautious over programmes that might cause offence on grounds of taste and decency. Michael Grade, newly returned from three less than glorious years in Hollywood, to be Controller of BBC-1, made most of the public running in opposing the Churchill Bill and was ably backed by others, notably David Attenborough, who pointed out that, if passed, the Bill would result in a number of specific acts appearing on a list of things that could not be shown on the screen. He continued: 'I have to tell Mr Churchill that the praying mantis does four of these things at the same time!' In the end Churchill did not succeed in getting his measure onto the statute book, although Mrs Thatcher herself voted in support of it.

In ITV the confederate character of the system itself was under threat as a result of company takeovers and consolidations between contractors. In October 1985 the IBA blocked a proposed takeover of Thames Television by Michael Green's Carlton Communications and only weeks later had to use its powers again to prevent Granada falling prey to a hostile takeover bid by Rank. As Thatcherism approached its zenith the pressure to consolidate, to censor, to follow the imperatives of business and the City at the expense of good or bold programmes and the spirit of the public service broadcasting, grew with it.

*   *   *

It was against such a profoundly depressing background that in 1985 a group of programme makers associated with the birth of Channel Four and IPPA started to meet informally in the early evening in each other's offices or a private room in the Groucho Club in Soho. The initiative for starting these meetings had been Sophie Balhetchet's. Balhetchet had been a member of the IPPA Council from soon after the Association came into being. Her feeling that there was a need for meetings in another forum was, in her words, 'fed by dismay at the quality of the debate'. This she believed applied both to the debate inside the IPPA Council and in the wider broadcasting world. 'Everything seemed so reductive and so much about the bottom line. There was never a wider debate.' She felt a need 'to think out of the box'.[56] The first person she approached was David Graham. Although she did not necessarily agree with his ideas she liked the quality of his mind. She found that he too felt frustrated. Graham remembers the chief objective of the group was the pooling of knowledge. When she contacted other independents she found that they too shared many of the same frustrations.

Over time the get-togethers of this small group came to be held roughly once a month. Meetings were invariably in the evenings, though not on a regular day of the week or week in the month. It was more a matter of when people were around. The discussions, held over a few glasses of wine, were entirely informal. There were no minutes (although Balhetchet jotted down some short notes after each meeting for her own use). There was no formal membership or organisation. What was said was in strict confidence. Among those who attended fairly regularly other than Balhetchet and David Graham, were Iain Bruce, Michael Jackson, John Wyvver, Lavinia Warner, Jane Wellesley, Paul Madden and myself. There were others who attended on a more occasional basis when they could or when we were likely to be discussing something that particularly interested them. Five of the regular attendees were members of the IPPA

Council. A feeling of alienation from the IPPA Council and a sense, particularly since the row inside IPPA over the Consolidated DBS bid, that the some of the spirit of the independent sector and of the ideals that had been a central part of the battle to create it had been lost, helped to feed our feeling of a need for such a group, for somewhere one could talk freely and float ideas among a small circle of like-minded people. That, and a sense of some shared history, served to strengthen a sense of identity between those within what came to be referred to as 'Sophie's Group'. There were never more than a dozen people present. Occasionally someone from outside the group was invited to lead the discussion or provide views on a topic people felt they ought to know more about.

By the end of May 1986 the ITV companies thought that they had a good idea what the Peacock Committee was going to say and in June the ITCA issued a strictly confidential briefing paper, the aim of which was to assist the ITV companies in maintaining a unified front and stay on message when dealing with the press in the immediate aftermath of publication of the Peacock Report. The ITCA also copied the document to senior officers in the IBA. The covering letter to members of the ITCA's Council said: 'Our latest, provisional information is that the report is likely to be published on about 8 July.' The briefing document's purpose, the ITV company executives were told, was 'to ask the right questions and to suggest the appropriate ITCA replies. We will need to offer a confident and united front for, following the expected rejection of advertising on the BBC, we are bound to come under intense pressure from a range of individuals and organisations determined to make us suffer.' In reacting to the Peacock Report as a whole, the companies were advised to welcome the rejection of advertising on the BBC because of the damage that this would do to the stability of the system as a whole. The document's authors forecast that the Report would recommend that in future ITV contracts should run for ten years. This should be welcomed, but with the qualification that they would prefer rolling contracts. However, any proposal to put ITV contracts out to tender should be dismissed out of hand: 'This does not deserve serious consideration. The disadvantages are all too apparent. It is attractive only to those who believe that broadcasting is to be regarded primarily as an instrument of profit-making. It is a prescription for squeezing the orange dry . . . delivering the greatest numbers to advertisers – the curse of the US networks – would be a natural response . . . the real losers, therefore would be the viewers.' In reacting to any 'call for more independent productions to be shown on ITV and BBC' the ITCA recommended the response: 'This presupposes not only that ITV currently fails to do enough in this field, but also that "independent production" can be precisely defined and measured.' ITV's 'two-channel system certainly has nothing to be ashamed of, but the same cannot be said of the BBC. Were the BBC to match our commitment to the independent sector there would be no need to ask this question.' ITV spokesmen were then advised to stress the amount and value of the independent production commissioned by Channel Four. 'The independents depend upon the ITV companies for the provision of crucial elements in the system: transmission system, training facilities, revenue gathering arrangements, rental payments, etc. The programming record of ITV and the BBC is built on the fact that they operate their own production teams, supported by integrated operations and considerable back-up resources.' They were also recommended to point out that the ITV companies 'employ large numbers of freelance people who are representative of the independent sector'. ITV spokesmen were to reject forcefully proposals for Channel Four to sell its own advertising as it would 'result in the same damaging competition for revenue that made the idea of advertising on BBC Television unacceptable'.[57]

The source of the ITCA's advance information about the contents of the Peacock Committee's report seems likely to have been those 'civilised, biddable' people in the Home Office. If not them it must have come from the IBA, which remained as the Pilkington Committee had described the ITA twenty-five years earlier, the companies' friend and partner rather than their 'master'.

Unlike the ITV companies, the independents were not privy to detailed information about what had been going on inside the Peacock Committee. On the evening of Friday 30 May (unknown to the group, the Peacock Committee had held its last meeting the previous day), Sophie Balhetchet's Group met in Lavinia Warner and Jane Wellesley's first-floor office in Covent Garden. There seems to be no record of exactly who was there that evening but Sophie Balhetchet certainly was, as were Lavinia Warner and Jane Wellesley, Michael Jackson, David Graham, John Wyvver, Roger Graef and me. Jane Balfour, the head of a small independent programme distribution company, had been invited as our guest speaker. Her assessment of the prospects for independent producers in the world's programme markets was depressing. Taken together with the domestic situation, the outlook that evening looked more gloomy for independents than at any time since the birth of Channel Four. The Channel seemed to be demanding tougher and tougher contracts, while commissioning fewer programmes.

When Jane Balfour left the meeting of Sophie's Group that evening most of those who had been present stayed behind discussing possible solutions to the independents' problems. John Wyvver remembers people sitting around disconsolately 'considering whether we could reconstruct the Channel Four Campaign'. After about an hour we had come to the conclusion that the only real solution was to campaign in earnest for the rapid introduction of a proper quota of independent productions on both the BBC and ITV. But what constituted a 'proper' quota? Like the broadcasters, we assumed that Gau's call for 50% was impossibly high and would be rejected. Wyvver thinks that the people sitting about in Lavinia Warner's small Covent Garden office that evening were thinking in terms of between 5% and 10% until I said that it needed to be much more, say 25%. To have any chance of success we had to come up with a figure sufficiently high to convince the government that such a quota would introduce genuine competition into the BBC and ITV systems, but not so high as to appear impractical or risk wrecking the BBC's and ITV's own in-house production operations. The higher the quota the more the broadcasters and trade unions would resist it. We had seen the reaction to the IPPA submission to the Peacock Committee for a 50% quota. On the other hand, if the quota was not high enough the broadcasters would simply be able to reverse it at a later date, once the political climate had changed. These considerations pointed to needing a figure of at least 15%, but no more than 30%, of all BBC and ITV original programmes. Whatever figure we campaigned for, we were unlikely to get all that we asked for, so it had to be above 15%. 30% seemed too high and might risk undermining the in-house production basis on which the broadcasters claimed public service broadcasting rested. The appropriate target figure for any campaign therefore appeared to be 20% or 25%. In view of the worsening prospects of the independent sector it seemed vital to launch such a campaign immediately, before the Peacock Committee reported and while broadcasting was still high on the government's agenda.

After little more than an hour's discussion a decision had been all but reached. After our experience with the Channel Four Campaign six years earlier and the accumulated experience gained in earlier campaigns, the people in the room had a pretty good idea of how to go about it, and of who and what support they were likely to need. Upon examination the choice between campaigning for 20% or 25% was easy – 25% allowed for a greater margin to be conceded in negotiation and simply sounded a better rallying call than 20%. Decisively, 25% was a figure that lent itself much more easily to making a good logo for campaign literature and notepaper. All that now remained was to decide on a name for the campaign. The '25% Now Campaign' had a good dynamic ring, while 'The 25% Campaign' was easier on the ear and offered less of a hostage to fortune if the campaign was protracted. So 'The 25% Campaign' it was.

*   *   *

The following Monday, 2 June, Jeremy Isaacs was due to brief independent producers at the Royal Institution on Channel Four's forthcoming programme requirements. It was a warm summer morning as members of Sophie Balhetchet's Group moved among the producers waiting to go in. We were seeking out people who could be relied on to help in the coming campaign. Later, during coffee breaks and over a buffet lunch given by Channel Four in a function room at the Cafe Royal,[58] Sophie's team continued to spread the word and enlist campaigners.

Later that afternoon Sophie Balhetchet and I met in her office to start planning a detailed strategy. More planning meetings with other members of the group, and a few outsiders who we knew could be trusted not to talk, followed throughout June. One of those I enlisted was Greg Smith, a successful film producer and member of the BFTPA Council, who was not attached to either an American studio major or an ITV subsidiary. We met in a restaurant off Edgware Road. He remembers, 'It was all very Guy Fawkes – we're going to blow up the Houses of Parliament and we don't want anyone to know.' He remembers me warning, 'It may make us all very unpopular.'[59] Undeterred, Greg agreed to join The 25% Campaign steering committee.

Within days a fourteen-strong steering committee had been put together. It consisted of Iain Bruce, Sophie Balhetchet, John Ellis, Michael Jackson, Phillip Whitehead and me, all of whom had experience from the Channel Four Campaign, plus Roxanna Knight, David Graham, Paul Madden, Lavinia Warner and John Wyvver who had been regular participants in the discussions in Sophie Balhetchet's Group. There was Greg Smith from the BFTPA and two people from AIP. No one could be said formally to represent the organisations to which they were affiliated, but all would be able to bring influence to bear inside those organisations.

One of the Campaign's first tasks was to get IPPA to back it. Six members of The 25% Campaign steering group were also members of the fifteen-strong IPPA council. However, lobbying of IPPA had to be done in ways that would not provoke disagreement or lead to the group's plans leaking out before preparations were complete. Already this campaign was taking on even more of the qualities of a military operation than the battle for Channel Four. The June Council of IPPA was scheduled to discuss ways of advancing IPPA's objective of increasing the access for independent productions to the BBC and, in particular, ITV. It was still too early to risk announcing the formation of The 25% Campaign to the full Council. If we did, news of what we were planning would be bound to leak out. However, independents in Scotland had recently succeeded in persuading STV to engage in meaningful talks about increasing the number of hours of independent production on ITV in Scotland. So we persuaded the IPPA Council that it should investigate ways in which their initial success could be repeated with other ITV companies to the benefit of independents all over the UK. I was detailed to formulate ideas and report to the next IPPA Council meeting.

By the end of June enough key members of IPPA Council and from all over the independent sector had been won over. Enough money and support had been pledged to begin the 'active phase' and announce the campaign's launch. The 25% Campaign was formally launched on 1 July 1986, based at the address of my own independent production company just north of Oxford Street, between the traditional home of the film industry in Soho and of Channel Four in Fitzrovia. The signal that the new campaign had begun was the release of a statement to the press, drafted and signed by Michael Jackson and John Wyvver. The announcement began by saying that 'The 25% Campaign' is being launched out of 'concern for the health and quality of our television system'. Its aim, to get a commitment from the BBC and ITV that '25% of the programme material produced for them will come from independent producers'. 'The regulated introduction' of this level of independent production would, it went on, enhance the whole television system and protect the ideals on which public service broadcasting was founded by improving 'the variety, quality and range of programmes while sustaining those elements of our broadcasting system which have created the standards of excellence, integrity and originality upon which its fame has rested'. Detailed arguments stressed the potential of independent producers to stimulate more cost-efficient production within the broadcasters' own in-house production operations. Independents would bring new blood and fresh energy, while expanding employment opportunities for freelance personnel within the framework of sound industrial relations enjoyed by independents working for Channel Four. 'THE 25% CAMPAIGN is founded with a commitment to the best of public service broadcasting . . . THE 25% CAMPAIGN starts with a concern for the quality of television and the protection of the public interest. It is already supported by a broad range of companies and individuals, and it expects to involve all those concerned with access, accountability and the health of public service broadcasting. THE 25% CAMPAIGN believes that the way is open through independent production to more and better television, not more and worse.'

Just two days later, on Thursday 3 July, the Peacock Committee published its report.

Notes

1. *The Times*, 28 February 1975.
2. Robin Day, 'Troubled Reflections of a TV Journalist', *Encounter*, May 1970 and Smith, *op. cit.*
3. *The Times*, 1 October 1975.
4. Peter Jay's address to new members of TV-am staff quoted in *Treachery? The Power Struggle at TV-am* by Michael Leapman, George Allen & Unwin Ltd, London, 1984.
5. Isaacs, *op. cit.*
6. The same Jonathan Aitken would years later take up his 'Sword of Truth' to fight the *Guardian* over allegations about his 'improper' dealings with a Saudi arms dealer and be sent to prison for perjury.
7. Roland Rat was already a feature of TV-am, but with Dyke's arrival its role became more prominent.
8. Phillip Whitehead, interviewed by the author in November 2000.
9. Anthony Smith, interviewed by the author in September 2000.
10. Colin Thomas, interviewed by the author in October 2000. Teliesyn would flourish for twenty years.
11. John Gau, interviewed by the author in October 2000.
12. Bill Cotton, interviewed by the author in October 2000. Cotton gives a similar account, although with slightly different dialogue, in his book, *Double Bill: 80 Years of Entertainment*, Fourth Estate Limited, London, 2000.
13. Bolton, *op. cit.*
14. Miles Kington in *The Times*, 2 May 1983.
15. Isaacs, *op. cit.* In my account of the *Scum* incident I have also drawn on Bill Cotton's accounts in his book, *op. cit.*, the interviews which I conducted with him, Alasdair Milne, John Whitney and Sir Jeremy Isaacs.
16. John Whitney, interviewed by the author in January 2001.
17. Isaacs, *op. cit.*
18. Quoted in Catterall, *op. cit.*

19. John Ranelagh, *Channel 4: A View from Within*, in Catterall, *op. cit.*

20. *Ibid.*

21. Isaacs, *op. cit.*

22. *Sunday Times*, 28 August 1983.

23. *Jeremy Isaacs Reports Back* in *AIP &Co*, No. 48, November 1983.

24. Minutes of IPPA AGM and Address by Jeremy Isaacs, 15 February 1984.

25. *The Way Forward: A Compilation of Independent Producers' Attitudes about Obstacles Facing the UK Independent* by Cheryl Miller-Houser, January 1985.

26. *Down on the Farm – or, Questions to Elstein, IPPA Bulletin*, October 1985.

27. David Graham, *The Hazards of Clientism, IPPA Bulletin*, December 1985.

28. Sir Jeremy Isaacs, interviewed by the author in November 2000.

29. John Gau, interviewed by the author in October 2000.

30. Sir Paul Fox, interviewed by the author in November 2000.

31. Interview with Bill Brown, quoted in Bonner, *op. cit.*

32. John Gau, interviewed by the author in October 2000.

33. NATTKE – National Association of Theatrical, Television and Kine Employees – the union representing technicians such as stage hands, drivers, some make-up and wardrobe workers.

34. *Financial Times*, 1 August 1984.

35. Letter from Martin Tempia to Jeremy Wallington 7 August 1984.

36. Letter from Jeremy Wallington to Martin Tempia, Administrator of IPPA, copied to John Gau, 8 August 1984.

37. Letter from John Gau to Martin Tempia, Administrator of IPPA 16 August 1984.

38. Letter from Jeremy Wallington to John Gau 19 October 1984.

39. Alasdair Milne, interviewed by the author in October 2000.

40. Speech made in Glasgow in January 1983 by Alasdair Milne and quoted in his *DG: Memoirs of a British Broadcaster*, Hodder & Stoughton, London 1988.

41. Letter from the author to the Home Secretary, Leon Brittan, 18 December 1984.

42. Peat Marwick Mitchell, *Value for Money*, report for the BBC, quoted in *Beyond the BBC: Broadcasters and the Public in the 1980s*, Tim Madge, Macmillan Press Ltd, London, 1989.

43. Briefing notes by John Gau for members of IPPA delegation to meet Alasdair Milne, 26 February 1985.

44. *The 'Politics' of Investigating Broadcasting Finance*, an article by Professor Sir Alan Peacock, reprinted in *Political Economy of Economic Freedom* in 1997. It in turn was based on a Robbins Lecture given by Professor Peacock at the University of Stirling on 9 October 1986. I am particularly grateful to Sir Alan for drawing my attention to this article and supplying me with a copy.

45. *Sunday Times*, 26 May 1985.

46. *Ibid.* In my account of the inner workings of the Peacock Committee, in addition to drawing heavily on Professor Sir Alan Peacock's account in his *'Politics' of Investigating Broadcasting Finance*, I have relied to a large extent on the interview I conducted with Sir Alan in November 2000.

47. Sir Denis Forman, interviewed by the author in October 2000.

48. Peacock, *op. cit.*

49. *Independent Producers' Association's Submission to the Peacock Committee on Financing the BBC*, August 1985.

50. Professor Sir Alan Peacock, interviewed by the author in November 2000.

51. IPPA Council Minutes, 9 April 1986.

52. *The Listener*, 5 December 1985.

53. *New Statesman*, 6 December 1985 and Phillip Whitehead, interviewed by the author in November 2000. After his exit from TV-am, Peter Jay had gone to work for Robert Maxwell as his 'Chief of Staff'.

54. Despite the limited amount of work he has done for television, Richard Eyre, by his superb direction of material as varied as his wonderful studio production of *The Cherry Orchard* with Judi Dench, Ian MacEwan's *Imitation Game*, *Tumbledown* and his interpretation of Tony Harrison's long poem '*V*' for Channel 4 in 1987, must stand out as one of the greatest television directors ever, even if he never directs anything else for the small screen.

55. A. J. P. Taylor, *English History 1914–1945*, Oxford University Press, 1965.

56. Sophie Balhetchet, interviewed by the author in December 2000.

57. Confidential paper, *Reactions to Peacock*, circulated by the ITCA to members of its Council in June 1986.

58. It was exceptional for Channel Four to give the independents lunch in such exalted premises.

59. Greg Smith, interviewed by the author in February 2001.

11

'The most audacious political lobbying campaign . . .' – Autumn 1986

Evening Standard, 3 July 1986

'BBC Television should not be obliged to finance its operations by advertising' but the Corporation 'should have the option to privatise Radios 1, 2 and local radio in whole or in part'. Five out of the seven members of the Committee went further, recommending 'Radio 1 and Radio 2 should be privatised and financed by advertising'. The Committee had accepted that the introduction of advertising to BBC Television would, for the time being, reduce the range of choice available to viewers. The BBC licence fee should be index-linked to the annual rate of general inflation and more efficient means of collecting it introduced. The ITV franchises should be put out to competitive tender and awarded on a rolling review basis, consideration being given to extending the franchise periods to ten years. Channel

Four should be given the option of selling its own advertising rather than being funded by ITV company subscriptions.

The Committee said that if they had to sum up their report in one slogan it would be 'direct consumer choice' rather than continuation of the licence fee. To this end the Committee majored on the introduction of arrangements designed in the longer term to facilitate the replacement of existing public service broadcasting structures with a subscription system of 'Pay-per-programme or pay-per-channel' services delivered by fibre-optic cables or direct-broadcast-to-the-home – DBS – satellites and the creation of what the report called a 'full broadcasting market'. 'Well before the end of the century' the licence fee should start to be phased out. Eventually, the Committee hoped 'to reach a position where the mystique is taken out of broadcasting and it becomes no more special than publishing became once the world became used to living with the printing press.' Broadcasting regulation would be phased out, too, to leave only the laws covering such things as obscenity, defamation, blasphemy and sedition, together with the laws of the marketplace to determine what was or was not seen. In short, the Committee had, as expected from the beginning and with a few insignificant reservations, bought the full Peter Jay vision. However, the Committee could not dismiss entirely the arguments of those, like Milne, who had said that in the real world as opposed to Jay's utopian vision of market perfection, the phasing out of the licence fee, of all but the most basic regulation and of all the existing public service broadcasting structures, would result in the disappearance of some socially or culturally desirable programmes. To make good the possibility of such 'market failure' the Committee proposed the creation of what it christened a Public Service Broadcasting Council, financed either out of taxation, the money paid over by the ITV companies under the proposed new tender system or the continuation of some kind of licence fee. This body would hand out money for the transmission of desirable programmes by any service rather than just the BBC, in much the same way as the Arts Council.

Phillip Whitehead summed up the Peacock Committee Report thus: 'Most reports look at ways of winning the last war; this one examines how we can surrender in the next.'[1] The philosophical engine supplying the drive to the whole report worried the majority of the members of The 25% Campaign profoundly. While a few, most notably David Graham, shared the Peacock Committee's faith in the beneficial powers of the market, most viewed the committee's planned replacement of public service broadcasting regulation with the discipline of the market not as a scheme to improve broadcasting but as a proposal to replace a rational philosophy with an irrational theology. Past experience had shown time and again that whenever broadcasting had been left to the market the quality and range in the totality of programmes had deteriorated. The market had been demonstrated to be the enemy of public service broadcasting rather than its friend. The reason that British broadcasting was generally better than American, and that the BBC was admired and envied around the world, was that when radio broadcasting began in the 1920s it had been decided to regulate broadcasting for virtue and the public good, whereas in America it had been decided to leave its development to commerce. Whatever the arguments over the years about what constituted 'virtue and the public good', whenever regulation in any sector of broadcasting had been appreciably relaxed the result had been loss of quality in the whole. Competition from ITV had, eventually, improved the service offered by the BBC, and Channel Four had improved both ITV and the BBC, but only because of strong regulation of programme quality and diversity. The BBC had so far shown that, provided that it was not driven by a commercial imperative, it could generally be left to regulate itself within the terms of its Charter. ITV was different, as had been shown in the aftermath to its disastrous start and during the LWT affair. Of course ITV bosses liked to receive praise and the approval of their peers when they made good programmes, but on its own (as the Peacock Committee appeared partially to acknowledge) that was not enough. The ITV bosses and their shareholders liked profits even more than praise. It was only through firm regulation and incentives, both big carrot and strong stick, that ITV had been made as good as it was. Ever since programme makers had started campaigning in the 1960s, we had been motivated by a desire to make broadcasting better, more open, all-inclusive and responsive. We had campaigned repeatedly for firmer regulation and more appropriate incentives. We wanted more access and more appropriate regulation, not a commercial market and weaker regulation. So while the findings of the Peacock Committee seemed to offer us the most immediate thing which we wanted, it also presented us with serious problems.

The Committee's 'call for more independent productions to be shown on ITV and BBC' turned out to be a good deal louder and more specific than even the authors of the ITV briefing document had feared. Recommendation 8 of the Peacock Report said: 'The BBC and ITV should be required over a ten year period to increase to not less than 40% the proportion of programmes supplied by independent producers.'² David Glencross, the Director of Television at the IBA, says that the Peacock recommendation on independent production genuinely surprised them. The Committee had spelled out what it meant by an 'independent producer', insisting that they must not be subject either directly or indirectly to the influence or control of a broadcaster. To the question: 'Why 40% and 10 years?' the Committee's answer was that the 'gradualism and limited nature' of its proposal was intended both to recognise the existing investment of the BBC and ITV contractors in programme-making capacity and to give the independents time to adjust to their new, enlarged role. The IBA's reaction was that by setting the figure so high they threatened to destabilise the whole in-house production system which, its officials believed, was why the idea had appealed to the Conservative free marketeers on the committee. Professor Sir Alan Peacock admits that the 40% over ten years figure was a 'cockshy', intended by the committee to 'raise the debate'.

Presenting the Committee's report to Parliament, Douglas Hurd it gave what was widely interpreted as a lukewarm reception. The Committee, he said, had 'put forward a number of interesting and constructive proposals' which would receive 'careful study'. The government would only reach final views in the light of public and Parliamentary reaction. The Report, he concluded, was 'a challenging piece of work'. On the issue of increasing the proportion of programmes supplied by independent producers, he would say only that he 'saw merit in it' but that it would 'need careful consideration'.³ For the opposition, Gerald Kaufman said simply that the Report 'should be put in the waste paper basket'. Peacock had heard that Bernard Ingham had said that the Report would be 'kicked into the long grass'. So when he appeared in front of a press conference Peacock told journalists that the 'Report cannot be shelved because it raises issues that go far beyond the immediate interests of the government'. Nevertheless, the press was generally scathing. Newspapers forecast that, having not given Mrs Thatcher what she wanted, the Report would simply disappear. 'The first Peacock to end up in a pigeon hole' and 'a dead duck' were *Broadcast*'s assessments of its chances. The ITV companies responded exactly as advised in the ITCA's briefing paper, Yorkshire Television being the most outspoken: 'Leave well alone – that's the message from Yorkshire TV to the Peacock Report.'

Reactions to the recommendation that both the BBC and ITV should take 40% of their programmes from independents were predictably hostile. Alan Sapper of the ACTT described it as 'a poisonous pie which threatens up to 50,000 jobs in the BBC and ITV', while David Plowright on behalf of the ITCA simply dismissed it as 'unrealistic' and 'impossible'. Although privately Alasdair Milne thought it was 'a fantasy', the BBC was rather more circumspect in public – the percentage was unrealistically high but the independent sector would 'grow with our support'. Having got off the worst of the advertising hook, at least for the time being, the BBC did not want to risk antagonising Thatcher unnecessarily. The independent quota was a distant prospect and with time, and a few well-timed gestures, could be allowed gently to wither on the vine. That, at least to people like me, appeared to be the BBC's thinking.

On the evening before the Peacock Committee Report was to be made public, with rumours and leaks rife, the IPPA Council had considered the paper which I had been asked to prepare into ways of increasing the volume of programmes taken from independents by broadcasters other than Channel Four. I reminded the Council that it had identified two main long-term objectives for the Association – reducing the divisions between the different independent producers' organisations while increasing IPPA's influence, and substantially increasing the value and volume of independent productions commissioned by the BBC and ITV. I argued that the most immediate way of furthering both objectives was by backing The 25% Campaign. I suggested that on its own IPPA was neither powerful enough, nor representative of a wide enough constituency to achieve 'such a major change in the whole "ecology of television" '. By being the prime sponsor of The 25% Campaign, it could simultaneously achieve its objective of increasing the volume of independent production on the BBC and ITV while reducing the tensions between the organisations which would become involved in the Campaign. The effect would be to increase IPPA's influence with them. Because The 25% Campaign would be a separate entity, rather than a tripartite body working through a liaison committee answerable to IPPA, the BFTPA and AIP, the organisation would function more effectively and be able to react more rapidly to outside events. This was one of the lessons of the success of the Channel Four Group. By not being too closely associated with any one producer's group, The 25% Campaign would be better able to lay claim to be acting in the public interest, drawing in support from the wider community and from those with an interest in the health of public service broadcasting.

Having studied The 25% Campaign's detailed Policy Statement, the IPPA Council decided to back it and suggested that I should front any campaign. Paul Styles, IPPA's new Director, who was attending his first full Council meeting, remembers thinking 'The 25% Campaign could act as a gadfly. 25% could be IPPA's "Provisional Wing". It didn't matter if The 25% Campaign lost, IPPA would still be able to bring in other troops and other associations.'[4]

On the morning of the Peacock Report's publication, a small team – consisting of Sophie Balhetchet, David Graham, Paul Styles, Nicholas Fraser (the editor of the *IPPA Bulletin*) and I – sat in IPPA's small office above Berwick Street Market in Soho and broke it down clause by clause. Digesting the 40% independent production quota over ten years, we asked ourselves whether in launching The 25% Campaign two days earlier and getting IPPA to back it, we had jumped the gun and set the target too low. On reflection we decided that we hadn't. Peacock's 40% recommendation gave us an opportunity. 25% suddenly looked very reasonable. The campaigners could now argue for '25% in five years' rather than 40% in ten – offering more immediate action to satisfy Mrs Thatcher and a less damaging total to comfort the broadcasters.

Later, The 25% Campaign would be called 'the most successful political lobby of the Thatcher years' and 'one of the most audacious political lobbying campaigns of the post-war era'. But to those involved at the outset it did not seem it. That weekend I wrote a confidential strategy paper which I circulated to all the members of The 25% Campaign steering committee. It suggested that, in spite of the fillip given to the Campaign by the Peacock Committee's Report, it was still likely to take at least a year to get the 25% quota adopted by the government as a condition of both the new ITV franchises and any increase in the BBC licence fee. 'The most striking feature of the present situation is that the Peacock recommendation on independents has not so much been attacked as sidelined – i.e., it has received scant attention in reporting of the Peacock findings and has been received by the BBC and ITV alike with low-key dismissiveness. The most likely course for BBC and ITV will be to use the absence of headlines to make the odd token gesture and then allow the idea to slip off the agenda.' The 25% Campaign's first goal had, therefore, to be to get the Peacock recommendations on independents back on to the public and political agenda. This, I said, had to be done in such a way as to make the BBC and ITV recognise that attempting to fob off the independents or the government with token gestures would 'be insufficient to meet the political reality'. At the same time, we must 'raise the awareness of independents so that they will not be seduced by token gestures'.

I reminded the steering committee that divisions between the different ITV companies had made our lives easier throughout the years of the Channel Four campaign. We should reckon on exploiting those differences again. We ought to start talking quietly to the IBA, initially with Chris Rowley but probably with Glencross as well (Colin Shaw had left the IBA to join the ITCA in 1983). We should also work on our many contacts with senior producers and programme heads in the BBC. Were there perhaps individual BBC Governors whom we might approach and hope to win over? IPPA would be writing to Milne asking for negotiations in the light of the Peacock Report recommendations. We needed a membership, staff, resources and cash. In the background to our calculations was an awareness of the approach of the next general election, probably sometime between May 1987 and May 1988. It was vital to secure a firm commitment to an independent quota before that got too close and moved broadcasting off the political agenda.[5]

Faced with the combined financial muscle of ITV and the BBC, a lukewarm Home Secretary, hostile unions and a dismissive press, The 25% Campaign had cash pledges amounting to about £2,000. IPPA, which the Campaign expected to be its principal ally, was itself short of cash and could not offer much beyond in-kind assistance. My strategy paper estimated that the Campaign would need some £5,000 almost immediately and about £20,000 over the coming year. Alerted by the independents' success in the Channel Four Campaign, the broadcasters were unlikely to underestimate the campaigners' ability again. We anticipated that ITV and the BBC would work in collusion with each other against us. In spite of the Peacock recommendations we seemed a long way from achieving our goal.

*　　*　　*

If The 25% Campaigners still had any doubts about how difficult the task we had set ourselves was they were quickly dispelled. Five days after the Peacock Report's publication the BBC held a long-scheduled seminar for independents at BAFTA. This now took on a wholly new significance and 800 people clamoured for admission to the 200-seat BAFTA auditorium. Instead of one lone co-production executive, the BBC now fielded a team of six, headed by Bill Cotton and including the Controllers of BBC-1 and BBC-2; 'All men, they couldn't find any women to bring along', as the AIP journal noted acidly. The 'handsome six figure sum', which the BBC had made so much hoop-la about 'setting aside for independent production' while the Peacock Committee was deliberating, now jumped from about £600,000 for 150 hours of programmes to a headline-grabbing

£1.5 million. Although examination quickly revealed that this was not so generous as it looked – £1.5 million for 150 hours of programmes represented about £10,000 per programme hour whereas the BBC's in-house figure was £40,000 per programme hour – it was still a headline grabbing two times what it had been before. Enough, we wondered uneasily, of a token to seduce unwary independents? Persistent questioning of the BBC team during the BAFTA seminar revealed £1.5 million in fact amounted to only about £500,000 a year for the next two years and was to be used as 'top-up funding for independently-made programmes with other funds already in place'. Cotton begged independents: 'Please don't call it tokenism, we're trying to break the mould gently. We accept that there is now a decent-sized independent sector and that the BBC must come to terms with where the talent wants to go.' Michael Grade said that cost comparisons were not the issue: 'The arguments will be about flair, imagination and originality.'

The following day the IPPA Council decided to press for immediate negotiations with the Director-General. Gau stressed that as 'the Peacock Report had let the BBC off the hook, IPPA must fight against their complacency'.[6] However, as the very next item of business Gau announced that he was stepping down from the IPPA Council and from the chairmanship. He was to be the next Chairman of the Royal Television Society, a role in which he might do much to raise the standing of the independent sector, but he could not very well be chairman of both organisations at the same time.

Gau's sudden departure from the IPPA chairmanship in mid-term presented a new dilemma. The 25% Campaign strategy had been based in part on the calculation that in order to achieve our goals it would be more effective to mount a campaign that was not too directly linked to any one of the programme-producer organisations. Of the people who were members of The 25% Campaign Steering Committee only Phillip Whitehead and I had inside experience of the campaigns going back before the Channel Four Group and a wide range of professional and personal contacts inside the both BBC and the ITV companies. Phillip suffered from the disadvantage, from the point of view of winning over the Conservative government, that he had been a Labour MP. At the same time, since the rows inside IPPA over 'core companies', and particularly the Consolidated DBS bid, the members of Sophie Balhetchet's Group distrusted those members of the IPPA Council who came from the bigger, business-orientated companies. It was important that one of them was not appointed to serve in Gau's place. There was already speculation among IPPA members, The 25% Campaign Steering Committee and in even the trade press that I would take over from Gau as Chairman of IPPA. However, it seemed to me that attaining a 25% quota of independent productions on ITV and the BBC was at that moment of more significance for our original goals for the independent sector than the future of IPPA. On top of which I relished a battle for The 25% Campaign more than I looked forward to the possibility of becoming chairman of IPPA. I thought that Sophie Balhetchet would make a very good chairman of IPPA; she was young, bright and immensely able, on top of which, by appointing a woman we would provide a valuable and pointed contrast to the male-dominated BBC and ITV. Sophie was 'up' for running to be IPPA chairman and others in The 25% Campaign and Sophie's Group favoured the idea. The members of IPPA's Council were also happy for Sophie to take over. So she stood unopposed in a specially organised ballot of IPPA members and took over in October 1986.

So in a space of weeks, IPPA had got a new Chairman, Sophie Balhetchet, and, in Paul Styles, a new Director. In the meantime The 25% Campaign had begun looking for a full-time paid organiser – someone to take on the role filled by Michael Jackson in the Channel Four Group. As a result, a day after the Peacock Report was published, a short story headed 'Indie Lobby' had appeared at the bottom right-hand corner of page 3 of *Broadcast*. The story said that a new lobby group had been formed 'demanding that the BBC and ITV companies should commission 25 per cent of programming from independents'. It named two members of the new group, Michael Jackson and John Wyvver. By chance Helen Baehr, a lecturer in Nick Garnham's Department of Communications at the Polytechnic of Central London, read the story and passed it over to her partner, a former student at the Polytechnic, called John Woodward. When Woodward read it he got the impression that five or six producers had met in a pub the previous week and decided to campaign for a 25% quota. Woodward had left the Central Polytechnic three years earlier hoping to find work as a television writer and director, but had found himself caught in the old ACTT-created catch-22 which had so frustrated would-be film makers in the 1960s – 'I couldn't direct a film or TV programme until I had got a union ticket, but I couldn't get a union ticket until I had directed a film or TV programme.' Woodward had found that the only work he could get was writing scripts for corporate films. At the time when Baehr handed the copy of *Broadcast* over to him, Woodward was working on a script for a company specialising in high-risk motor insurance in Guildford.

Woodward had never heard of Michael Jackson or John Wyvver and asked Baehr if she knew anything about them. She told him that Jackson had been at the Central Polytechnic and had left a year before Woodward went there. She went on: 'He is very bright. He was involved in The Channel Four Campaign.'

Hoping that becoming involved in the campaign might make him some useful contacts with producers, Woodward phoned Jackson and volunteered to help. 'I thought it would be like the Labour Party – hours of stuffing envelopes and then down to the pub together, where I would have the opportunity to talk to these producers and put myself forward if there was any work going.' Wyvver had been given the job of going through the CVs of people who applied to the Campaign and Jackson passed Woodward's name over to him. Wyvver arranged for them to meet for a cup of coffee in Soho. Having decided that he sounded promising, Wyvver passed Woodward's CV over to other members of the steering group. I rang Nick Garnham and asked him whether he remembered Woodward. He did. Moreover, he thought he might be a good candidate for the job. Not as precocious as Jackson, he said, but hard-working and thorough. So Woodward was invited to meet Iain Bruce, Lavinia Warner and John Wyvver in a Japanese restaurant in Brewer Street. 'I wasn't sure if it was a social test or what it was. Could I eat with chop-sticks, perhaps?'

Having survived the meal and impressed his three interrogators, Woodward was told he could have the job of organising The 25% Campaign, and that the pay would be £900 per month. Not bad, but there was one snag. First he had to raise the money to pay his salary by approaching producers and television facilities companies. Woodward set to work at once and quickly proved a very effective fundraiser. 'Among the places I got good cheques were Trillion (a large facilities company), Cheerleader (a company of which Iain Bruce was a director, which specialised in televising sports events) and David Graham. 'I was given a 25% Campaign office with Iain Bruce in the offices of Cheerleader, which paid all the overheads – such as they were – phone calls, bikes and taxis.'[7]

Woodward, Styles, Balhetchet and myself would, over the next five years, form the ongoing central core of the campaign to achieve a 25% independent production quota. Others, including David Graham, Iain Bruce and John Wyvver remained crucially involved throughout, but were unable to be active on quite the same day-to-day basis. Still others came and went, depending on their work commitments. Michael Jackson became a BBC producer in 1989. The campaign itself would change its name more than once, yet the same four people remained at its core throughout. It seems, therefore, worth briefly examining who each of these people was and what their motives may have been. Later a variety of motives would be ascribed to them collectively, most far wide of the mark. Woodward was a quiet, soberly dressed 25-year-old. After a 'gap year' spent travelling, he had gone to the Central Polytechnic for three years to do a degree in media and communications, where Nicholas Garnham was his Head of Department. Garnham had not had a particularly strong influence on Woodward's ideas, but in Woodward's time the Media and Communications Department of the Polytechnic in Riding House Street, off Regent Street, 'was full of Marxists. It was known outside as "Little *Red* Riding House Street".' Woodward had left in 1983 with his degree but, as we know, had found getting the kind of work he wanted difficult. By the time he became the organiser of The 25% Campaign he seemed generally dispirited. However, his spirits soon revived. He was not only as hard-working and conscientious as Garnham had forecast, he quickly developed into a first-class tactician and strategist. He could be witty, inventive, quietly mischievous or accommodating and diplomatic as circumstance demanded. Above all he had stamina. As things turned out, he was going to need it.

Styles, at 36 years of age, was far more experienced than Woodward. He had been a member of the Vietnam Solidarity Campaign in the 1960s and President of the Student Union at the Oxford Polytechnic in 1969. On leaving he had started a co-operative (it survives to this day). He had gone into the charity movement, working for among others Age Concern – 'In earlier days I would have been a trade unionist, I guess.' He had moved on into local government, working in Leeds on schemes to help people who had been made redundant and school leavers with low expectations. When IPPA decided to start an industry training scheme for people working in the independent sector – Jobfit (later Skillset) – Styles had been brought in to set it up and run it. His first task had been to win over the ACTT membership. Older members of the ACTT were very suspicious, as they had always been of anything that threatened to let new, young technicians into their already insecure and overcrowded industry. Addressing one ACTT shop meeting Styles had been booed off the platform. On another occasion, wanting to get Jobfit trainees taken on to the Bond films, he had arranged to see the producer Cubby Broccoli at Pinewood Studios. But he had been kept waiting all day. Then, 'Broccoli and entourage came down the corridor. An aide came over to me and said "Mr Broccoli says 'No!' " ' But Styles was not the kind of person to be intimidated or fobbed off. So he simply sat down on a chair outside Broccoli's office and waited. 'Half an hour later the aide reappeared and I was asked in. I got trainees on to the Bond pictures. On another occasion I had to meet the ACTT Sound Shop (the sound technicians). It was in a blue smoke-filled room. Under Standing Orders one guy stood up and said, "I move we throw this cunt out before he steals all our jobs." I was thrown out while they debated the motion. I sat outside again and then I was called back in. I got a standing ovation. They said it was for my courage. Anyway I got the scheme approved.' Balhetchet had spotted Styles' potential early on and had lobbied hard to get him the Jobfit position and later to get him appointed as Director of IPPA. He would take some hard knocks during his time at IPPA and after, but always remained remarkably unaffected by bitterness. This he puts down to his radical background. 'The marriage between me and the IPPA ideals was perfect. I was terribly enthused by the people I met when I got there.' He accepts that he was, in his words, 'very combative, in a public way. But once you've stood up in front of hundreds of trade unionists baying for your blood, being bullied by a TV executive is nothing. At Jobfit I cried in private, but I never did in my time at IPPA.'[8] Styles turned out to have an unexpected flair for publicity and getting the Campaign (and with it often himself) press coverage. This would be a huge asset, and occasionally an embarrassment.

Sophie Balhetchet was coming up to 30. She had progressed rapidly in the eight years since joining AIP as an organiser almost straight from Oxford. After winning one of the first Channel Four commissions she had gone on to produce a string of original documentary and arts programmes, plus a low-budget film for the Channel. She had recently set up her own independent production company and, when she became Chair of IPPA, was in the throes of producing her first drama series, *The Manageress*, starring Cherie Lunghi, about a woman who becomes the manager of a professional football team. Around the industry she was known for her formidable intellect and chic clothes. Her judgements were informed by a strong moral sense and driving determination to correct what she saw as injustice.

At 52, I was much the oldest of the four. By now I had almost twenty years' experience of campaigning in television, starting as an apprentice to masters such as Phillip Whitehead, Gus Macdonald, Anthony Smith, Nicholas Garnham and David Elstein. Because I had been in television the longest I had not only the highest profile as a programme maker but access to a wide range of senior people in the BBC and ITV. To the hunger and energy of the other three I might, therefore, be able to bring experience. In my work I had interviewed all kinds of people, from heads of state to prisoners on death row, and worked with temperamental stars of all kinds, so I was not easily going to be intimidated by politicians or thrown by temperaments. At the start of my career I had been an actor and had even worked briefly as the straight man to a top comedian, so I knew roughly how to work an audience and speak in public without undue panic. However, unlike the other three, I was a television director rather than a producer or a full-time organiser. As a result, although I could organise my time to a certain extent, there were inevitably whole days – sometimes weeks or months – when I was away on location or shooting in a studio, when I was simply unavailable, no matter how vital or urgent anything else might be.

In a sense, the four of us complemented each other. Although there were a few blazing rows (the other three were extremely tolerant of my occasional outbursts), on the whole we managed to maintain a remarkable tolerance of each other's foibles and to work together exceptionally harmoniously. But, unlike the broadcasters and the politicians we were up against, Sophie Balhetchet and I had to do our campaigning in time we could make in full, and sometimes stressful, careers.

*   *   *

Less than a month after the publication of the Peacock Report the Royal Television Society staged a major seminar at the Barbican Conference Centre. Senior representatives of all the broadcasters, together with civil servants from the Broadcasting Department of the Home Office, the IBA, other interest groups, and Professor Peacock were all due to be there, so it was going to be vital for The 25% Campaign to make a good showing. It would also provide an opportunity to assess the strength and tactics of our opponents.

I had thought that I was unlikely easily to be intimidated, but as I entered the pine, glass and indoor palm-tree crowded assembly area that late July morning and took in the full range of milling, be-suited director-generals, programme controllers, academics, economists, civil servants, trade unionists and representatives of organisations with vested interests in the outcome of the struggle to come, I surreptitiously clutched the neatly folded typescript of the short speech I had prepared which was nestling in my inside pocket.

Paul Fox, President of the Royal Television Society, introducing the chairman of the seminar, Lord Swann, to the two hundred or so participants, quoted the previous day's *Guardian*: 'It is time to cut the Peacock cackle and get on with the real issues.' Not disguising the fact that he believed that British broadcasting was entering a fight which could see it knocked out of its acknowledged position as the best in the world, Fox then quoted the announcer who had introduced a recent world heavyweight boxing title fight with the words: 'Here's how Frank Bruno

Lord Swann, former Chairman of the BBC, with Professor Peacock standing opposite him, at the start of the Royal Television Society seminar on the Peacock Committee Report in the Barbican Conference Centre on 29 July 1986.

Courtesy of the Royal Television Society

lost the heavyweight championship of the world.' Fox said that he was not looking to give a repeat performance.[9]

Opening the proceedings, Lord Swann reminded the assembled broadcasters and broadcasting regulators that: 'Politicians are not interested in programmes. They don't really watch the programmes, as a matter of fact; they are much more concerned about politics and how much exposure they get on the BBC and, by definition, they never get enough.' But in the current debate over the Peacock Report, Lord Swann warned: 'There is an enormous political dimension which I believe to be profoundly important and profoundly difficult.' That underlying political dimension became manifest in the most immediate way a few minutes later when Sam Brittan, who had been a member of the Peacock Committee, intervened to complain angrily about what he called the deliberate 'campaign of denigration by the Home Office of the Report before it was published.' It was, Brittan declared, 'very serious indeed'. Hurd's half-hearted welcome for the Report when introducing it to the House of Commons would, Brittan claimed, have been even more dismissive if others in government had not found out what he was planning and intervened. An internal Home Office analysis alleging that the Report 'lacked intellectual coherence' had, he said, been leaked to selected correspondents. 'Somehow I don't think we need lectures on intellectual coherence by the Broadcasting Unit of the Home Office', Brittan sneered. Quentin Thomas, the Assistant Under-Secretary at the Home Office in charge of the Broadcasting Department, responded at once. In a classic Civil Service utterance, he flatly denied any Home Office campaign of denigration. There had, Thomas said, been nothing other than 'an attempt to allow the Report to find its proper level in the market-place of debate' – a form of words which deserved rather more careful examination than could be given to it in the heat of debate that morning. Mark Bonham Carter told Sam Brittan that 'anybody who is shocked by the Home Office is a very young fella'. Others, including Lord Swann and Professor Peacock, joined in to defend the Home Office. Yet they did so in ways that, while absolving the Home Office of dishonourable behaviour, implied that they did not believe that other offices of government had been quite so innocent. The effect of these denials was to deepen my own already considerable suspicion of the Home Office and add to my belief that it was likely to remain on the side of the broadcasters over any introduction of independent production into the BBC and ITV. As the correspondent of the Royal Television Society Journal concluded in his report of the seminar: 'There is evidently a dirty tricks department in the Home Office.'

Milne presented the BBC's official reaction to the report. As was to be expected, he welcomed the Committee's recommendation that 'advertising for the BBC should be taken off the agenda'. But he complained about the proposed tying of the level of the licence fee to the Retail Price Index, particularly because RPI was so heavily affected by mortgage lending rates.

Milne then turned the full force of his rapid, clipped and dismissive delivery on the independent production sector. The proposal that over a ten-year period 40% of programmes should come from the sector was 'wholly unrealistic'; 40% of BBC output would be 3,500 hours, he said. 'A year ago I announced that we intended to move towards 150 hours a year of independent production – and we are already discussing with independents how we might achieve that.' (So that is what the display of tokenism at BAFTA three weeks earlier had been, I reflected – 'discussion'.) 'I don't see', Milne went on, 'how any group of independents could take on two weeks of Wimbledon, a week of the Open Golf Championship and, on consecutive days, the Royal Wedding (Prince Andrew had married Sarah Ferguson in June) and then 10 days of the Commonwealth Games.'

John Whitney followed for the IBA. We must not, he said, prematurely dismantle or destroy the 'packaged' terrestrial broadcasting services that give such good value. David Plowright, for the ITV companies, condemned the proposed cash auction for ITV franchises. Turning to Sam Brittan to take the mickey out of him, Plowright said: 'There is an elusive factor in the broadcasting equation; it is called quality and some economists – er [looking hard at Brittan] have difficulty with it because of its subjective nature . . . Economists in television companies as well as on government Committees get impatient with its use; they regard it as an excuse for indiscipline by people who are spoilt, arrogant, and should be subjected to the test of whether audiences really want what they offer. Instead of being indulged by monopolist managements they should face up to the commercialism of the market which they have so far avoided in common with the Universities and, I suppose, the Falklands invasion.' Plowright simply dismissed the 40% independent quota without even wasting the number of words expended on it by Milne. It seemed, as the correspondent of the Royal Television Society Journal observed, 'Almost a case of "What Curzon has let Curzon hold." '

David Elstein, who had recently left the independent sector to return to Thames as Director of Programmes, reminding people that he had fought the independents' corner for a long time, said he had once gone to Lady Plowden to ask for a 2% quota. But now he damned the proposed 40% quota. 'I've *never* deluded myself into thinking that you can do more with the independent sector than make it operate as a discipline on the margin of the large broadcasters. This I think applies to the BBC and ITV. There is a substantial merit in large-scale production. It means you can plan. You can plan drama output, you can plan current affairs output, you can plan sports output. You can do a large amount of cost saving by knowing where you are going to be in 3, 4, 5, 6 or 7 years' time. That is simply impossible if the degree of independent production that is suggested by Peacock were to come about.' Arguing that the introduction of a quota of 40% of independent programmes, even on a gradual basis, would 'reduce every ITV company to the status of an American network company, i.e., producing news, sport and nothing else', Elstein said that while it might be good for viewers, costs and creativity for independents to have access to the BBC and ITV, by proposing 40% Peacock was 'casually throwing away the entire existing system'. Perhaps, I wondered as I listened to Elstein, he felt it necessary to convince his colleagues in ITV that he really was one of them now. If so, he had certainly said enough, and more than enough to persuade them. Over the years, as Elstein's migrations from executive post to executive post around the different parts of the broadcasting system continued, I would come to refer to him among my close colleagues as Broadcasting's Vicar of Bray.

Elstein was followed by Alan Sapper of the ACTT, providing a demonstration, if demonstration was needed, of the 'unholy alliance' between the unions and the ITV companies. Independent producers, Sapper said, were not 'independent' at all. They were 'dependent' on ITV and the BBC for the distribution to the public of their programmes. Without the BBC and ITV they would not exist. A 40% quota would destabilise and destroy the BBC, ITV and with them the whole public service broadcasting system. 'The independents are shooting themselves in the foot when they support 40% in ten years' time.' It was OK on Channel Four, but if it spread to ITV and the BBC, 'I think we will be in a disaster situation.' (I remembered that Sapper had come out with similar prophesies of doom about the effects of independent production at the time of the debates over Channel Four.)

Towards the end of the afternoon I got my chance to speak. It turned out that I had been selected as the lone voice from the independent sector.[10] Lone, it certainly felt, after being hammered all day. I was extremely nervous as I went to the front clutching the text to which I had been making hasty adjustments all day as speaker after speaker had attacked us. I reasoned that, although in the few minutes I had, it was necessary to lay out the main points of our case and to counter the objections in a way that would be understood and accepted by the government, attack was the best form of defence. 'Speaking to *Broadcast Magazine* recently of Channel Four's achievement in taking work from film and video makers who would previously not have got on television, Jeremy Isaacs said, "The British independent film maker has been treated very snottily by the BBC and ITV over the years and now we have an absolute triumph of their work." The same snotty attitude characterised the reception accorded by the BBC and ITV to Recommendation 8 (the 40% independent quota) of the Peacock Report, a recommendation singled out for commendation by the Home Secretary. The same snotty attitude', I said, looking pointedly at the broadcasters while trying to make sure that I had the attention of the civil servants and politicians, 'was in evidence again this morning in the remarks of Alasdair Milne in particular and Alan Sapper . . . Unlike many of the other recommendations in the Peacock Report which look to speculative futures and are based on remedies that are untried and uncertain, the benefits of independent production are already apparent on the air and in the balance sheets of Channel Four. I would suggest that Recommendation 8 is the most practical in the Report and the one that it behoves all who care about the quality and future of our television to take on board and start working at immediately . . . It is sometimes suggested that the introduction of a significant proportion of independent production into the BBC and ITV threatens public service broadcasting. Provided that regulation is kept, the reverse is surely true: the prime responsibility of the controllers of public service television channels – BBC, ITV and C4 alike – is to determine what programmes they want to broadcast and then with, in the case of the BBC in particular, less money than they would ideally like, by use of the editorial and entrepreneurial skills available to them, to seek the best means of getting those programmes supplied. Today the structures, vast establishments and huge sums of money tied up in both the BBC and ITV . . . restricts that vital freedom. The Peacock Committee takes this matter further – "It is extremely unhealthy, for reasons of freedom of speech and expression, that independent producers should face what is virtually a monopoly buyer in Channel Four",' I reminded the assembled politicians and civil servants that Peacock had found that the broadcasters, who his Committee had dubbed 'the comfortable duopoly', were unlikely to put cost minimisation uppermost in their considerations and that the BBC's budgeting and monitoring of its use of funds seemed to be 'of the crudest kind'. Over the previous three years Channel Four had reported costs of between 13% and 38% less per hour broadcast than BBC-2. Extrapolation suggested that the difference between Channel Four and BBC-1 and ITV was as much as 50%.

Representatives of the 'comfortable duopoly' had raised doubts about how good the independent producers' programmes really were. To that, I said, 'I merely point out that 75% of the listed award winning programmes in the Channel Four Report this year were made by independent producers.' Independents, I went on, had also proved themselves good businessmen: 'The *Televisual* annual survey of the industry published in June shows that "the fastest growth rates in turnover have been made among independent producers who are on course to outstrip the ITV companies." The independents also showed the greatest rates of profitability. The same survey also revealed that "the independents took on a higher rate of staff than ITV and above the national average".' Independents also attracted much higher percentages of overseas co-production money to their productions than either the BBC or the ITV companies. Relative to the amount of money invested in production the independents were already outselling the BBC in programmes sold abroad and fast catching up with ITV. I then turned to the failure in recent years of the BBC and ITV to recruit new young programme-making talent, and compared that with the success of the independent sector in this area, adding: 'Television needs new blood – it also needs different blood.'

Concluding, I said that the 'snotty attitude' which had greeted the Peacock Committee's recommendation of a 40% independent quota 'looked suspiciously like the attitude of people with a vested interest. Could their fears be not so much for the health of television as for the continuance of their unhealthily comfortable duopoly? It is a wise industry which looks ahead, adapts and reforms itself while there is still expansion in the pipeline. In this country we have witnessed too many examples of industries that failed to grasp the opportunity to reform while times were still comparatively good.' The ship-building industry provided an appropriate warning: 'Once the nation's pride, it did not use the opportunity of full order books after the war to modernise its methods. Television could well go the same way. However, the vanguard of the modern, young and cost-effective builders are, in the case of our industry, here in this country, not in the Far East . . . we are not interested in hiving off bits of the BBC. We seek stable institutions, stable working practices and a multiplicity of sources to ensure editorial freedom. Let me close with words from the Policy Statement of The 25% Campaign – "Television stands at a crossroads. The way is open through independent production to more and better television, rather than more and worse." I stand, as I hope we all do, for building up systems that will maintain regulation but also encourage creative diversity.'

That evening John Whitney, the Director-General of the IBA, recorded his impressions of the Barbican seminar in his diary: 'A dampish affair. A bit like trying to make yourself sick by sticking two fingers down your throat.'

*   *   *

With the battle lines now clearly drawn, over the next four months leading members of The 25% Campaign made much the same points repeatedly. But the more we tried to push the independent production quota up the political and broadcasting industry agenda, the more outspoken became the broadcasters' attacks on us. We hoped that by repeating that we shared the broadcasters' concerns over maintaining public service broadcasting, and reiterating that we had no interest in dismantling regulation, we could prepare the ground for reaching a negotiated settlement over independent access. Then, we hoped, we could combine with them to defeat any government attack on public service broadcasting. But the more we strove, the greater became the broadcasters' hostility. They seemed to think that the threat of an independent quota outweighed any help we might be able to offer in a joint campaign to defend public service broadcasting.

At the International Television Festival in Edinburgh at the end of August, the independents took an even worse hammering than they had at the RTS Barbican seminar. A session entitled *Are Independents Working?* lined up Bill Cotton and Paul Fox, formidable representatives of the BBC and ITV, with trade union representatives, Tony Hearn, the General Secretary of BETA, and Roy Lockett, the Deputy General Secretary of the ACTT, against the chairman of IPPA's industrial relations committee, Tim Fell (a former trade union official) and an inexperienced AIP administrator, Sally Davies. I had been drafted in at the last minute as chairman. Paul Fox, opening the debate in his toughest ex-Second World War para 'Don't try messing with the big boys' style, roundly condemned the Peacock 40% independent quota. The ITV companies were not prepared simply to be 'jostled out of the way', he thundered. He accused independents of wanting to make 'all the fun programmes while leaving other companies with the factory stuff'. Today Fox explains the ferocity of his attack that day on the fact that 'I had always thought that Edinburgh was for children and the RTS Convention at Cambridge was for the grown-ups.'[11] He had worked hard to get good programme makers to join the staff at Yorkshire Television and he did not want ITV Network programmes which he had fought for taken away by independents. Without the backing of financially strong and courageous companies like his own, he feared that difficult, challenging investigative programmes like Yorkshire's exposé of the maltreatment of patients in Rampton Mental Hospital would not get made. 'Bravery in television does require considerable backing by the board, of resources, of money and the will to say we will trust the programme makers . . . Over Rampton, Yorkshire Television stood in the dock at the Old Bailey accused of criminal libel. At no stage did Ward Thomas (Yorkshire's Managing Director) say, "Bloody programmes, look at what they cost us!" '

Sitting next-but-one to Fox on the platform, Bill Cotton was surprised at the vehemence of Fox's assault. He thought it bad tactics if nothing else. But no matter what his private doubts, Cotton pitched in too, repeating that 40% would spell doom for the whole system. Comparing the BBC to a large house, he accused the independents of wanting to burn it down before decamping into separate pre-fab bungalows. To independents listening to the debate, what was being said was bad enough, but the way in which it was being said was even worse. The combative, even contemptuous tone adopted by Fox and Cotton each time they mentioned the words 'independent' or 'quota' seemed to send its own clear message – independents were not wanted in ITV at any price and in the BBC only on sufferance and at the furthest margin. The union representatives were little better. Tony Hearn attacked the whole free-market drive of the Peacock Report, saying that if Peacock's 40% recommendation was enacted in full it would result in nothing but 'pain, grief and suffering'. However, 'if the independents can guarantee stable and reasonable terms and conditions then we will deal with them'. Lockett reminded everyone that the ACTT already worked harmoniously with the independent sector on programmes for Channel Four. So, while he was prepared to countenance further development of the independent sector, the film industry served as a dire warning against the evils of wholesale deregulation of television along the lines envisaged by Peacock. The core and base of British television must not be eroded or destroyed. He was not prepared to watch 'the heart being ripped out of the permanent employment system'. Later, a journalist, describing the session in *The Listener*, said that he now understood what the Nuremberg rallies must have felt like.

The two independents on the platform were no match for this quartet. Although they tried valiantly to reassure unions and broadcasters that they did not want to destroy the structure of broadcasting or take away jobs, they did not convince. They seemed unable to explain how job losses and fragmentation were to be avoided. Inexplicably, perhaps disastrously, The 25% Campaign had failed to get any of its most experienced speakers to the session. Chairing it was agony. As chairman I could not join in to support Davies and Fell. The audience, which in fact contained a lot of independents, was becoming audibly frustrated by the combined onslaught of the broadcasters and unions and at their own representatives' inability to articulate an adequate response. John Woodward, whose first public outing as the organiser of The 25% Campaign this was, was sitting in the hall about three rows back. He stuck his hand up to indicate that he wanted to speak. I called him, hoping that he could stem the tide. But no. New to the job and uncertain, John was not yet up to taking on Fox, Cotton, Hearn and Lockett in full cry. Fortunately, towards the end of the session, Paul Styles, speaking from near the back of the hall, managed to introduce a note of urgency to the independents' case. He warned the industry as a whole that, given the forces massing outside it, especially DBS, it had to change or die. If it did nothing, he warned, it would die just as surely as British ship-building or textile manufacturing had died when faced by the combined weight of unfettered foreign competition and a refusal to change traditional ways of doing things. Belatedly, another independent, Geof Perks, joined in to support Styles – unless the industry changed before the full effects of competition from DBS were felt everyone, unions, management, independents, freelances and staff alike would suffer.

On this showing, and in spite of Styles' and Perks' late interventions, The 25% Campaign was not only unfit to act as the 'Provisional Wing' in an IPPA campaign to 'liberate' the independent sector, it was not going to be capable, as the boys used to say in the playground when I was about eight, of 'knocking the skin off a rice pudding'. Outside the hall afterwards, Georgina Henry, the *Guardian*'s Media Correspondent, cornered me. How did I feel about the independents receiving such a public mauling? Surely, after this the independents' campaign for a quota was as good as dead? On the contrary, I told her, sounding a good deal more confident than I felt, the more the broadcasters showed themselves to be 'haughty and intransigent about new talent and competition', the more they helped to make our case for us and hasten government intervention. I cannot say that I believed it as I said it, but thinking about it later, I began to believe that there might just be something in what I had said. We might be able to use the broadcasters' and unions' intransigence as a reason for seeking government assistance to get an independent quota brought in through legislation. Although they appeared to have won on the day, it seems that the broadcasters were none too happy about what had happened either. When I interviewed Sir Paul Fox for this book he told me: 'At the end of it I knew it had been a bloody day.'

In fact, the broadcasters' and unions' Pavlovian reaction every time the subject of a mandatory quota of independent productions was raised drew attention to the issue. Unwittingly, they pushed the issue up the political agenda for us. On top of which, not all of the independents' advocacy was a disaster. Series of articles by Phillip Whitehead and John Wyvver in August and September made a deep impact, both with undecided programme makers and journalists, and among civil servants and senior broadcast executives. Whitehead, writing article after article in *Broadcast*, the AIP and IPPA magazines, and in the journals of news and opinion of the left, mocked the entrenched attitudes of the broadcasting mandarins, reminding readers that a decade earlier the same attitudes towards new talent had been repeatedly paraded before his fellow members of the Annan and Parliamentary Committees responsible for the 1981 Broadcasting Act: 'I was told the same old story by the duopolists . . . There isn't the talent, old boy. They're all innumerate. You need accountants and managers like ours.' Pointing out that independents' costs had been shown to be as much as a third lower than the BBC's and more than 60% lower than ITV's, Whitehead asked, 'So who needs cost accountants most?' But this was not the half of it, he went on: 'There is no way of quantifying on the balance sheet the sheer satisfaction of working in the independent sector, in smaller production units which see themselves as that, rather than as real life soap operas of corporate intrigue, obfuscation and delay. No one in the independent sector spends time worrying about hierarchy, or believes that if only he keeps his nose clean he may grow up to be the next Billy Cotton but three. One of my researchers who recently returned from a project in Channel Four to his more lucrative post in an ITV company said: 'It's like walking through glue in there.'[12] In other articles Whitehead stressed that no one who had witnessed the 'Paul Fox/Bill Cotton double act at Edinburgh' could be left in any doubt that, whatever one thought of rigid quotas, 'no concession worth the name is likely to be wrested from those who control the real estate of broadcasting without them'.[13] Whitehead mocked broadcast managements and unions alike. '[They] circle round each other looking for the football of a precedent conceded, a practice changed. If you puzzle over the theology of it, these are the last adults to be believe in the Tooth Fairy; the belief that if you wrench out a fang there will be money automatically under the pillow. And all the time the world is changing. The technology is on the move. So is the competition.' But, Whitehead emphasised, 'the independents share the public service ethic, to a far greater degree than the schedulers who adulterate our peak time viewing. The real threat is the multinational competition, outside British ownership and control, wholly unconcerned with public service values, and destructive of them.'[14]

Wyvver argued similarly that if the independents based their case solely on the economic arguments they led themselves into a trap. There was 'no reason whatsoever why more independent production should "tear the heart out of the system" as the ACTT Deputy General Secretary Roy Lockett has claimed.

External forces, from Europe and elsewhere, threaten to do that unless changes are introduced. And those forces will have far less regard for the quality of our system and the traditions of public service broadcasting than do domestic independents. That is a present reality which neither David Elstein, nor the unions, nor independents, nor anyone else who cares about television can afford to ignore.'[15] (Later Wyvver heard that this article had helped to persuade officials in the Home Office that the argument for an independent quota should not be judged in commercial terms alone.)

Once more, as during the Channel Four Group's campaign seven years earlier, we set about taking civil servants and MPs from all parties out of the dusty corridors, echoey vaulting and gloom of their rooms in Westminster to the superficial glamour of studios and high-tech facility houses. Visits to Limehouse Studios proved particularly popular, especially when they were taken to the workshop where they could see the puppet caricatures of their political masters being prepared for *Spitting Image*. In a twist on the normal studio visits procedure, Phillip Whitehead and I invited three of his former Parliamentary Labour Party colleagues (Phillip had ceased to be an MP in 1983) to lunch at Thames's factual and current affairs base in the company's unprepossessing office complex in Euston Road. Thames was a convenient journey from Parliament, enabling us to invite the MPs to lunch and get them back to the House in time for Question Time. Phillip and I could both get into Thames without any difficulty because we had both worked there as freelances over many years. We thought that Thames might be a suitable venue in which to demonstrate the profligacy of so much of ITV. Apart from the mass of people who were likely to be in evidence in the canteens and dining rooms at lunch time, the Euston Road site was only one of three fully staffed sites operated by Thames, the others being their main drama and entertainment studios beside the Thames at Teddington and an Outside Broadcast base in West London. As things turned out our point was made more quickly and effectively than we could have expected. Wanting to be able to talk to the three MPs without being too readily overheard, we had booked a table in the waitress-service staff restaurant next to the company's canteen. When we sat down the waitress brought the menus. As the MPs started to scan them we explained that the restaurant did rather good steaks. Finding the steaks on the menu the MPs let out gasps of surprise. They had seen the price. 'Is that correct?' 'Is that all?' 'Good God!' The price, which I cannot now remember precisely, was incredibly low; less than a third of what it would have been in even a fairly modestly priced restaurant. 'All right. You don't need to convince us any further. If Thames can afford to subsidise the food of its already well paid staff to this extent there must be something fundamentally wrong with the system.'

Every bit as effective as our own lobbying was the help inadvertently given by the ITV companies and unions. Each time a Government Minister or a Conservative MP was interviewed on some issue of the day, they could not fail to note that, while the independent producer's crew consisted of two or three people, the BBC's team often consisted of four, while the ITV company would often turn up with as many as six or seven people and three or more vehicles. The press continued to revel in stories of over manning and BBC profligacy. The most notorious incident occurred in March 1987, when a cross-Channel ferry, The Herald of Free Enterprise, sank with the loss of 188 lives as it sailed from Zeebrugge. Lurid stories of the fantastic sums in overtime claimed by ITV cameramen covering the tragedy adorned the tabloids and broadsheet newspapers alike.

Shortly after the Peacock Report had been published, IPPA had approached the Home Office to ask for a meeting with David Mellor, the Minister of State. He agreed to meet a delegation from the IPPA Council at the end of October. Mellor, who when he first entered the government in 1981 had been its youngest minister, was now almost mid-way through what Nigel Lawson in his memoirs calls 'a somewhat erratic progress through a number of middle-ranking ministerial posts.' Round-faced, round spectacled and even somewhat round-bodied, Mellor, who Lawson describes as 'a brash, self-confident, ambitious and not over-sensitive lawyer . . . eager, hard-working and keen to impress',[16] was to play a large part in our affairs for the next six years. Led by Sophie Balhetchet (it was exactly three weeks after she had officially taken over from John Gau as Chair of IPPA), we entered Mellor's office in the ugly new Home Office tower in Queen's Gate. He immediately struck one as simultaneously bumptious and eager to make an impression, especially on women. As a result the meeting almost came to grief before it began. Sophie, small, attractive, formidably intelligent but unsure of herself in her new role as Chairperson of IPPA, was still inclined to be stilted when nervous. She began the IPPA side of the introductions by describing herself as 'Chair of IPPA'. Mellor, who seemed for a moment to have decided on presenting a picture of languid bonhomie, suddenly perked up. He flashed back challengingly, 'How very Hackney Council!' We all tensed; if he spread that idea among his ministerial colleagues, or worse, mentioned it to Mrs Thatcher, the independents case was doomed. But Balhetchet was on her mettle at once. She quickly laughed it off and hastily got on with introducing the members of her delegation. Although the independents' rapport with Mellor later improved, their relationship with him would never be genuinely easy. Not only did some of us believe that the officials in the Home Office were more open to the arguments of the broadcasters than to those of the independents, I, at least (and I think others too), got the feeling that from the start Mellor was more attracted by the glamour and power of the big broadcasters than by anything that we independents might represent. There was even a suspicion in the minds of some that he might have half an eye on what he perhaps perceived could be 'the main chance' if he were ever to leave politics. At that first meeting Mellor made it clear that whilst the government was very sympathetic to the independents and that he was happy to 'broker' their 'case', the government had no wish to legislate for access to ITV and the BBC.

As an alternative to talking to the Home Office, one of the inner circle of The 25% Campaign, David Graham, had suggested that we consider lobbying the DTI. He believed that Lord Young and his civil servants at the DTI would be more inclined than the mandarins of the Home Office to listen to arguments based on economic efficiency and competition. The DTI already had responsibilities in the fields of exports, broadcasting transmission equipment and film production. Graham believed the DTI was interested in finding means of extending its influence in broadcasting. To me, Graham's approach seemed fraught with risks because of its possible knock-on effects. Encouraging a government department principally interested in commerce to assume too much influence in an area of policy which was primarily cultural and social might lead to an undermining of the very foundations on which British broadcasting had been built ever since Lord Reith had established the BBC. For all its faults, the Home Office seemed likely to be a better guardian of public service broadcasting than the DTI. Nevertheless, a joint party from IPPA, AIP and the BFTPA went to the DTI for an informal meeting with officials in the film and competition departments. During the meeting the officials revealed that a joint Home Office/DTI working party, chaired by the Prime Minister, was about to start work reviewing broadcasting policy in the light of the Peacock Report.[17] So, our meeting with Mellor having confirmed our suspicion that the Home Office was not going to be the best government department through which to press our case and with our apprehensions about the effects of becoming too closely associated with the DTI, it became clear that we needed some other way of ensuring that the independents had a powerful advocate inside the Prime Minister's committee. Preferably, direct through Downing Street. But how? For the moment we did not know.

* * *

As well as pursuing our first priorities, increasing our political influence and promoting our case with the wider industry and public, we continued less publicly to try to overcome union opposition and lessen resistance within the BBC and ITV. I had a private, off-the-record lunch with Alan Sapper of the ACTT in the recently reopened and refurbished Criterion Brasserie and a similarly confidential meeting with the senior television officer of BETA in the BBC. It was clear that both anticipated considerable difficulties with their own memberships inside the BBC and the ITV companies if they were seen to be over-enthusiastic about more independent work. At the same time it was clear that both recognised that change was coming and that the controlled introduction of independent production would be preferable to the wholesale dismantling of the industry, implemented by the likes of Rupert Murdoch. As a result of these meetings it seemed to me that, so long as we acted with care and in our public utterances did not antagonise the unions unnecessarily, a basis could be worked out for introducing increased independent production into the schedules of the BBC and ITV without a major clash with the unions.

Meanwhile the ITV companies had been taking steps to see off the triple threat of a franchise auction, allowing Channel Four to sell its own advertising and an independent production quota. In mid-September the ITCA's Peacock Report Committee had sought an urgent meeting with the Home Office. In contrast to the three months it had taken Mellor and the Home Office to get round to agreeing to meet the independents, it agreed to meet the ITV companies' representatives later in the same week. The ITCA's two senior officials, David Shaw and Ivor Stolliday, told Quentin Thomas and the other senior civil servants present that the ITV companies needed 'broad guidance' over which areas of the Peacock Report 'were likely to be decided rapidly, and which would be postponed into the longer term'. Thomas warned them that the fact that the Prime Minister herself was chairing the Ministerial Group dealing with the Report underlined the political seriousness attached to the issues. Contrary to press speculation, the Report 'was not dead'. However, legislation on major change was 'most unlikely before the General Election', although legislation to extend the existing ITV contracts, which were due to expire at the end of 1989, might be necessary earlier 'to allow the government to keep all options open for the longer term'. Summing up the conclusions he drew from what Thomas had told them, Shaw wrote to his masters in the ITV companies that:

1. The contract extension will be for three years.
2. Tendering will be rejected.
3. Positive and early initiatives are needed on our part if we are to have any hope of not having a quota for independent production thrust upon us.[18]

Unknown to us, therefore, the ITV companies now knew that they had every incentive to appear ready to enter into an agreement with the independent sector while in fact playing for time. Their contracts were likely to run without serious amendment until 1 January 1993.

Although the members of The 25% Campaign's committee knew that Hurd and Mellor might be more inclined to accept the independents' case if it was couched in cultural and creative terms – freedom of expression, 'the market for ideas' and opportunities for new talent – we knew that the majority of the members of the Prime Minister's committee were likely to see the argument mainly in economic terms. This seemed to be confirmed when John Woodward and Iain Bruce were among a group of people who escorted Professor Brian Griffiths, the new Head of the Prime Minister's Policy Unit, on a tour of the *Spitting Image* workshops at Limehouse Studios. At lunch on the Limehouse boat anchored in the old dock which surrounded the studio, one of the independents raised the issue of news values and the alternative perspectives that could be brought to them by an infusion from the independent sector. Griffiths responded to the effect, 'Don't you people realise why I'm here? That's not the sort of thing we are after at all. We don't want any more communists in the BBC.' (Griffiths denies that he used these words, but the sense he conveyed, albeit possibly intended as a joke, seemed clear to those who heard him.) Whatever Griffiths' precise words, for Woodward it was a crucial moment. 'It became clear to me that day that the campaign was no longer about "the market-place of ideas" or cultural expression. From now on it was going to be about market-forces and competition. I saw the scales lifted off Iain Bruce and the other person who was with me's eyes.'[19]

The first indication that the campaigners' efforts were beginning to pay off, that the broadcasters' total rejection of the Peacock proposals and public bullying of the independents were proving counter-productive came in early November. Speaking at an RTS event to mark the fiftieth anniversary of the start of the BBC's first television service, Douglas Hurd warned that, far from having buried Peacock, the government was studying the Committee's report and the 'agenda' set out in it 'with great care'. Rather than simply deciding how the new channels now being created by the new technologies were to be allocated 'between the two wings of the existing duopoly', Hurd told the RTS, 'There is talent elsewhere with its own claim to a place in the sun.'[20]

The first real breakthrough came two weeks later, on 20 November. During a House of Commons debate on the Peacock Report, Hurd announced that, 'Many sensible people, inside and outside the broadcasting world, consider that it is desirable to encourage the independent sector for reasons of diversity, freshness and efficiency. We agree with that view and believe that the independents, too, deserve a place in the sun . . . We believe that independent productions should form a substantial proportion of ITV and BBC television programmes. We would like to see a major shift – a shift more substantial than that so far contemplated by the broadcasters. Peacock recommended an increase of at least 40 per cent of programmes to be supplied by independent producers over a period of ten years. We have been in touch with the independent producers, who campaigned for a figure of 25%. Perhaps that is a more realistic goal. We look for somewhat faster progress than that envisaged by the Peacock Committee. However, important issues are involved – such as how one defines independence – which must be considered quickly. I have, therefore, arranged to meet the directors general of the BBC and IBA soon to discuss the means of achieving the broad targets that we have in mind'.[21]

On the face of it, The 25% Campaign had achieved its first goal and registered all the main points in its case in less than half the time that I had forecast.

Notes

1. Phillip Whitehead, summing up from the chair in a debate entitled *The Third Age of Broadcasting* at the Edinburgh International Television Festival, August 1986.
2. *Report of the Committee on Financing the BBC*, Chairman: Professor Alan Peacock, DSC, FBA, July 1986, Cmnd. 9824.
3. Text of *Home Secretary's Statement on Publication of Peacock Report*, Home Office, 3 July 1986.

4. Paul Styles, interviewed by the author November 2000. Styles' predecessor, Roxana Knight, had decided to become an independent producer.

5. Confidential 25% Campaign document, *Notes Towards a Policy Strategy and Timetable*, 5 July 1986.

6. IPPA Council Minutes, 9 July 1986.

7. John Woodward, interviewed by the author in October 2000.

8. Paul Styles, interviewed by the author in November 2000.

9. Quotations from the Royal Television Society Seminar on the *Report of the Peacock Committee Inquiry into the Financing of the BBC* on 26 July 1986 are taken from an audio recording made by the Society.

10. Phillip Whitehead had spoken in the debate but, as a former MP and member of the Annan Committee, had confined himself to the indexation of the BBC licence fee.

11. Sir Paul Fox, interviewed by the author in November 2000.

12. Phillip Whitehead, *What Price the Prof's 40 per cent Solution?*, *Broadcast Magazine*, 22 August 1986.

13. Phillip Whitehead, *Supping with the Devil*, *IPPA Bulletin*, October 1986.

14. Phillip Whitehead, *What Price the Prof's 40 per cent Solution?*, *Broadcast Magazine*, 22 August 1986.

15. John Wyvver, *March of the Indies*, the *Guardian*, 22 September 1986.

16. *The View from No. 11: Memoirs of a Tory Radical* by Nigel Lawson, Bantam Press, Transworld Publishers Ltd, London, 1992.

17. The committee, named 'Miscellaneous 128', met for the first time in October 1986.

18. Minute of an informal meeting held between Home Office officials and representatives of the ITCA on 19 September 1986. In 1987 a short Broadcasting Bill did extend the ITV contracts until the end of 1992.

19. John Woodward, interviewed by the author in October 2000. When I asked Lord Griffiths about the alleged remark about Communists and the BBC he denied that he had said it: 'I never thought the BBC was that left-wing. It was about the same as a university . . . What I was getting at was that ITN had the edge on BBC News. The question that interested me was how can you free up the system to allow the Head of BBC News to have the same freedom (from bureaucracy) as the Head of ITN. It would have been easier if the BBC had been full of Communists, then it would have been clear. I am not especially anti-Communist, although I am a Christian.' My own knowledge of Griffiths also suggests that the words ascribed to him by Woodward are not his style.

20. Home Secretary's address, by Douglas Hurd, to an RTS symposium dinner in the Royal Hotel, Nottingham, Saturday 8 November 1986, published in the Royal Television Society Journal, January–February 1987.

21. *Hansard*, 20 November 1986.

12

Showdown at Number Ten –
January to September 1987

'The independent producers, for perhaps only a brief moment, could do no wrong because they represented, at one and the same time, the attractions of the alternative society, wearing interesting shirts and so on and being at the forefront of artistic creativity, as well as being prototypes for the Conservative dream of the entrepreneur starting a new business in his garage. And they combined both these things; they could do absolutely no wrong and when they said 25 per cent, of course, it was given to them on the instant . . . ' Quentin Thomas, the senior civil servant in charge of the broadcasting department at the Home Office at the time of Douglas Hurd's House of Commons announcement on independent production in November 1986, interviewed a decade later by Paul Bonner.[1]

The independents' apparent victory may have seemed that easy to disappointed mandarins in the Home Office, but it certainly did not seem so to us in The 25% Campaign. Nor were most of us under any illusion that one victory meant that we had won the war. Hurd's statement had indicated that he was looking for voluntary co-operation from the broadcasters to achieve the 25% quota. We, however, were convinced that the broadcasters would continue to do everything in their power to evade implementing the quota unless it was made a legal requirement. In his statement Hurd had said that, in order to allow time for consideration of the longer term future, the government intended to bring in a short bill extending the life of the existing ITV contracts until the end of 1992. It seemed to us, therefore, that unless we seized the opportunity presented by this short bill to get the 25% made binding on the broadcasters, full implementation of the 25% would be delayed until a comprehensive broadcasting bill could be enacted, which would probably not be before 1990. By that time the political climate might have changed and realisation of the independents' quota might be put off indefinitely. We therefore started to lobby for a clause making the achievement of the 25% quota mandatory to be added to the short bill. As we had anticipated, the BBC, the ITV companies and the broadcasting unions began to use all their influence to prevent this.

On 5 December Hurd summoned the chairmen of the BBC and the IBA, the Directors-General and an aide apiece to meet him, David Mellor and the senior civil servants in the broadcasting department at the Home Office. In the event, Hurd was summoned to a meeting in Downing Street and Mellor was left to conduct the meeting. Mellor made it clear to the broadcasters that they were going to have to do something which, as David Glencross of the IBA, later put it in a note of the meeting, 'would satisfy ministers – and by implication the Prime Minister herself' – about the independents' 25%. 'Home Office officials', Glencross noted, 'were aware of the practical difficulties faced by the broadcast-ers'.[2] Lord Thomson, for the IBA, put in a stout defence of ITV, saying that the companies were already making a major contribution to the independent sector through the Fourth Channel Subscription; ITV was fundamentally a system made up of regional contractors, while the great majority of the independents were based in London; the ITV companies were five years into eight-year contracts which had required them to spend an enormous amount on new regional facilities and staff. But Mellor, under pressure no doubt from Mrs Thatcher and Lord Young at the DTI, was not to be so easily put off. A week later, on 11 December, Hurd wrote to Thomson telling him that, while it might take some time to build up to a share of 25%, he hoped that an early 'start' could be made and that 'we can look forward to a target of this kind being achieved in four years'.

The IBA turned to their lawyers for help. They sent copies of Glencross's note of the Home Office meeting, together with the follow-up letter from Hurd, to their solicitors with a request for advice. The solicitors replied the following day, helpfully pointing out that in the absence of any statutory powers under the 1981 Broadcasting Act, legal difficulties would arise if the Authority were to try to force the ITV companies to accept a specified proportion of programmes from independent producers or to make them devote any specific percentage of their programme budgets to acquiring such programmes. The lawyers then went on to list a set of alternatives. All were contentious. They ranged from reducing the amount of network production demanded from the ITV companies so as to allow space for independents, to making some independents into programme contractors, thus entitling them to supply programmes to ITV. The common factor in all the solicitor's suggestions was that each offered scope for obfuscation, delay and litigation, and thus strengthened the IBA's case to the government for delay. The lawyer concluded that no changes of 'any magnitude would seem appropriate before 1990'. He was not even sure 'on what basis' the Authority could 'usefully consult with independent producers' unless it was simply to gain more information about their 'capabilities'. Even a voluntary agreement might lead to action under the Restrictive Trade Practices Act.

Throughout December and into January the ITV companies secretly continued to devise ways to thwart, dilute or delay imposition of a quota. On 5 January the IBA's David Glencross and Chris Rowley went round to the ITCA's headquarters in Mortimer Street to discuss tactics with the two top bureaucrats in the ITCA, Colin Shaw and David Shaw, plus three ITV managing directors, David McCall of Anglia, Brian Tesler of LWT and Bill Brown of Scottish Television. The notes of the meeting reveal that they discussed two alternative strategies for dealing with 'the government's apparent determination to award the independents their "place in the sun" '. They could 'publicly oppose such a move', or 'appear to go along with the philosophy while spelling out the problems'. David McCall of Anglia noted that the points about difficulties with quotas and ITV's regional system had 'registered with the Home Secretary'. To him this indicated that the 'gradualist approach' might be most effective. David Shaw reminded his colleagues that their information indicated that the Home Secretary was 'in a difficult position. He had to deliver something to the PM.' More and more of the Peacock proposals seemed to be failing to stand up and as a result the Home Secretary's 'main cards had to be indexing the licence fee and a role for the independents. The message coming through from the Home Office', David Shaw told the company bosses, 'was that failure to impress the PM with the latter part of this package could result in ITV being brought to heel by means of contract tendering – a process which held little attraction for Home Office ministers. The onus [so the message ran] was on ITV to give the Home Secretary evidence of positive thinking and actions with regard to independents. The companies and the IBA thus had to decide on their stance; were such messages to be taken seriously, or ignored – maybe at our peril?'

Colin Shaw, demonstrating that, as so often before, he was the wiliest and most forward-looking tactician in the room, suggested that they might do best to agree an action plan with the independents and then approach the Home Secretary together. But the others raised objections. They pointed out that there were splits inside the independents' own ranks. ITV should spin matters out, and refuse to deal in concrete numbers or definitions. They must avoid being too specific about either time scales or the volume of production. To this end, the seven men agreed that the IBA should take the lead in making further approaches to the independents. It should then provide feedback to the companies before they made their next move. There should be 'no frontal attack on government policy because such action will not succeed'. Quotas and targets would be 'held in abeyance' for the next two to three years.[3] The note of the meeting suggests that the IBA officials acquiesced in this approach, or at least failed to oppose it. The decisions taken that day were to have a massive effect on all that followed.

Of course that meeting, and the strategy devised during it, remained a closely guarded secret. To the outside world the companies continued to present an image of themselves as open-minded and co-operative. On 12 December they had announced a scheme under which ITV would put up £15 million over three years to encourage investment in British films. The companies were careful to add that they would 'have no interest in establishing such a fund *except* [author's emphasis] as a recognised and very substantial contribution to meeting the government policy objectives in relation to independent production'.

Determined not to be fobbed off with this kind of token gesture, I wrote to David Mellor on behalf of the independents suggesting that the forthcoming short Broadcasting Bill extending the life of the ITV franchises should include a simple clause requiring the IBA to include 'a substantial proportion' of programmes made by independent producers in the schedules of ITV by the end of the three-year franchise extension period.

Ever since it had become apparent that Mrs Thatcher herself was taking a direct interest in broadcasting policy and was chairing the relevant cabinet committee, we had been casting about for some way of gaining influence inside Downing Street itself. It turned out that two members of Sophie Balhetchet's original meeting group, both now members of The 25% Campaign steering committee, knew Professor Brian Griffiths, the new head of the Prime Minister's Number 10 Policy Unit. They were Roxanna Knight, who had met Griffiths a number times at social occasions and got on well with him, and David Graham, who had used him in programmes while he was a producer on *Panorama*, and had a family connection with Griffiths. Graham's father had been the Bursar of Capetown University and Griffiths had stayed with the family when visiting Capetown to give lectures at the University. Thinking about it, Sophie Balhetchet and I decided that the best route to Griffiths might be to ask Roxanna to try to arrange an informal meeting with him for us. Roxanna approached Griffiths and we duly received an invitation to go round to Number 10 to have tea with him. The information we had about Griffiths told us that he had been an economics lecturer at the LSE, Professor of Banking and International Finance at the City University, Professor of Ethics at Gresham College and a Director of the Bank of England, in addition to holding various visiting professorships and being the author of a number of works on monetarism. We also knew that he was an evangelical Christian.

That afternoon his small office seemed to be an awfully long way up in the building, off the main staircase to the left, almost in Number 11 Downing Street. Griffiths himself turned out to be charming, courteous, quietly spoken and rather obviously Welsh. It was also immediately apparent that he inspired affection among his small staff. We had deliberately decided not to go with 'an agenda'. We wanted, as far as possible, this to be an exploratory, almost a social meeting, a chance to get to know him. For his part, Griffiths asked us quite a lot of searching questions about the independent sector, its potential and what progress we were making with the BBC and ITV. We responded by plugging our now familiar line, while trying to gauge him. He was clearly a strong free-market liberal, but it was also clear that he had considerable respect for the BBC and a concern for many of the ideals of public service broadcasting. Equally clear, however, was that his interpretation of public service ideals and how best to achieve them was likely to be substantially different from ours. As we were leaving, I asked him if he would mind if I wrote to him from time to time to update him on events in television and the independents' progress towards gaining access to ITV and the BBC. Griffiths said that he would welcome any information that I cared to send him.

* * *

The following week, on 29 January 1987, an event occurred which, in the long run, would have as much bearing on what happened as anything that The 25% Campaigners might do. On that day the Governors of the BBC unceremoniously dumped the Director-General, Alasdair Milne. Milne, although an outspoken opponent of the independents, had in some ways been of help to them. Because of the very outspokenness of his attacks, he had made it easier for us to paint the BBC as unreasonable and arrogant, closed to fresh blood and new ideas. Yet the removal of Milne set alarm bells screeching among all thoughtful independents, indeed with anyone who cared about public service broadcasting and the independence of the BBC.

Although the story of Milne's removal has been told many times before it is worth reminding ourselves of the circumstances in which it occurred. In August 1986 Stuart Young, the Chairman of the BBC, had died of cancer and a few weeks later Marmaduke Hussey had been appointed to succeed him. At his appointment, few people inside broadcasting had heard of Hussey, a big, shambling man who, as a result of losing a leg in the battle of Anzio, walked with the aid of a stick. He seemed on first meeting bluff, amiable, harmless. But that belied the reality. After the war he had joined the Thomson newspaper organisation and risen to be Chief Executive and Managing Director of Times Newspapers. In 1978 he had taken on the print unions, locking them out when they refused to accept new printing technology and new terms and conditions. Unfortunately for the Thomson Organisation, Hussey, in the words of his group chairman, turned out to have 'only a plan of attack, not of campaign'. As a result, when the dispute was finally over, the print workers had made only a few unimportant concessions while Times Newspapers had lost £39 million and a lot of circulation. Both *The Times* and the *Sunday Times* were sold to Rupert Murdoch. To the surprise of many, Hussey, although 'put out to grass like a tired and useless old war-horse', had been retained by Murdoch as a consultant and subsequently as a director of Times Newspapers – the reason, it was widely assumed, being Hussey's useful connections with other newspaper proprietors, trade union bosses and, possibly most importantly, because his wife was a lady-in-waiting to the Queen and the sister of a rising Conservative minister William Waldegrave. Hussey's translation from a more or less passive role in Murdoch's empire to the Chairmanship of the BBC was seen as overtly political. It had come as much as a surprise to him as to the outside world. Shortly after Stuart Young's death, Hussey had told a friend that he had no idea who would be appointed Chairman of the BBC, adding for good measure, 'but the BBC is in a terrible state, obviously out of control, with some unreliable characters there too. They'll be hard pushed to persuade some idiot to take it on.' Four days later, as Hussey records in his memoirs, 'The telephone rang at about 9.30 in the evening. "Oh, Dukie, it's Douglas Hurd here, with a very odd question to ask you. Would you like to be Chairman of the BBC?" ' Hussey had said no, but Hurd (who had originally approached someone else, but then been overruled) had repeated the request and given him a couple of days to think it over. Hussey records that he had gone to bed 'in a state of shock', where his wife found him 'lying motionless in bed, as white as a sheet. She thought I might have had a heart attack.' Recovering from his surprise Hussey had decided that it would 'be wet just to turn it down because it was a challenge'. Pressed by his brother-in-law, Waldegrave, and encouraged by the information that 'the whole Cabinet wished me to accept it', he had agreed. When he asked Hurd for a briefing about what he was expected to do in the BBC, Hurd had said 'Don't worry about that. You'll find out what's necessary when you get there.'[4] However, in the *Sunday Times* on the Sunday after the announcement of Hussey's appointment, Norman Tebbit, the Chairman of the Conservative Party, who had never made any secret of his dislike for the BBC and what he regarded as its left-wing bias, stated bluntly that Hussey's appointment was intended to make it 'bloody clear' that change was demanded inside the BBC and his job was 'to get in there and sort the place out'. A story spread around the industry that (although Hussey doesn't mention it in his memoirs) Denis Thatcher had told Hussey during a conversation in a London club that the BBC was a 'nest of vipers. A lot of bloody reds' and that he had to 'do something about it'. Hussey records that shortly after his appointment he had consulted Lord Victor Rothschild, a former head of the Downing Street think tank. Hussey had asked, 'Now what about the BBC, Victor?' Rothschild had replied, 'How much power have you got?' 'I'm not sure.' 'Can you fire the Director-General?' Hussey had said that he thought he could. 'Well, that's all that needs to be said, isn't it?'

That autumn, as Hussey was taking over as chairman, the BBC came under fire from the Conservative government as never before. The libel row over the 1984 *Panorama* programme about extreme right-wing influence in the Conservative Party, *Maggie's Militant Tendency*, had finally been settled out of court before the BBC had even started its defence. Two Conservative MPs, Gerald Howarth and Neil Hamilton (who was later disgraced in the 'cash for questions' scandal and unseated in the May 1997 general election by ex-BBC reporter Martin Bell) each received £20,000 in damages and had their costs of £500,000 paid by the BBC.

Worse followed. Two weeks after the settlement in the *Maggie's Militant Tendency* case, a document prepared under the aegis of Norman Tebbit by the Conservative Party Central Office arrived, which purported to prove anti-Tory bias in BBC news. It harked back to Kate Adie and the BBC's reporting of the bombing raids on Libya the previous April (interestingly, the document did not name Adie – perhaps someone feared that she might sue?), claiming that a comparison of the BBC's news with ITN's *News at Ten* on the evening of 15 April

1986 revealed that while '*News at Ten* was able to preserve an impartial editorial stance . . . editorial and journalistic decisions' taken by the BBC on the same evening had had an effect which was to 'enlist the sympathy of the audience for the Libyans and to antagonise them towards the Americans'. In response, Milne and his senior management colleagues issued a statement saying that Tebbit's complaint 'could suggest that the Conservative Party is attempting to intimidate the BBC'.

Shortly after that still more 'grim wolves' emerged from what Milne would later describe as 'the foul contagion'. Tebbit, seemingly determined to hound Milne, launched an attack over a statement made by the BBC's Head of News, Alan Protheroe, in which he had said that the BBC was against apartheid. Tebbit demanded a public correction. Such a statement, he claimed, was contrary to the BBC's policy of having no editorial opinions (the fact that Tebbit claimed that he too was against apartheid was apparently beside the point). No, responded Milne robustly, although the BBC had no editorial opinion, Hugh Carleton Greene, while he was Director-General, had said that the BBC was against racism, which was no more than saying that it was against evil. There was no need for any public correction.

Equally perverse, days before Hussey's appointment in September, sections of the right-wing press had fallen on a BBC four-part drama series called *The Monocled Mutineer*, about a mutiny in the British army in France in 1917, based on a book published seven years earlier by William Allison and John Fairley.[5] Until Allison and Fairley had unearthed it, the story had been hushed up by successive governments. Although the drama was based squarely on fact, the BBC had made the mistake of promoting it as 'a real life story' when, as interpreted for the screen, it had been a piece of admirably crafted drama. Using this error of judgement as a pretext, sections of the press castigated the BBC for glorifying desertion and belittling patriotism – further evidence, they claimed, that the BBC was in the hands of the Left.

Further fuel had been added to the same fire in October when Ian Curteis, author of well-received BBC plays about Churchill's wartime relationship with his generals and Eden at the time of the 1956 Suez crisis, had gone to the press with a story that the BBC was delaying production of a play he had written, with encouragement from Milne, about Thatcher during the Falklands crisis. The BBC was accused of a monstrous left-wing plot to block production of a pro-Thatcher play. The fact that the BBC had decided to go ahead with Charles Wood's very different Falklands play, *Tumbledown*, was cited as further evidence of a BBC anti-Tory plot.

By late 1986, despite the fact that he had all the qualifications to count as one of their own, the entire British establishment seems to have had it in for Milne. After only two to three weeks as Chairman of the BBC Hussey had decided that he was not up to the job of Director-General. In part the fault they found with Milne and other BBC top executives was that they did not move around 'in society'. In his memoirs Hussey comments that it was 'a measure of how little they moved around London that [when he took over as Chairman] I had only met one, Alasdair Milne, once, at a dinner party'. When Hussey informed Lord Goodman that he was contemplating firing Milne, he had responded that it would 'be a merciful release to us all'. Milne had steadfastly encouraged the BBC to stick to its duty, to report the truth and provide a balanced account of all sides in an increasingly polarised society. As a result by the end of 1986 he had rocked various establishment boats rather too often.

The final and most damaging cloud of contagion, the one that was in a sense the last straw, emanated from a series of investigative programmes undertaken by the reporter Duncan Campbell, who was best-known for his investigative reports in the *New Statesman*. At a press conference on BBC-2's 1986 autumn programme line-up, mention had been made of a series called *Secret Society*, which would 'disclose restricted information on government emergency plans in case there is another war'. One of the programmes was to deal with 'communications with particular reference to satellites'. This, it transpired, was a reference to a British secret spy satellite code-named Zircon, and why £500 million of government expenditure on the satellite had not been passed for approval through the Public Accounts Committee. Shortly before Christmas Milne had learned that the Zircon programme might cause serious problems with national security in the USA. So he viewed rough cuts of all six programmes in the series and decided that while five, with further work, were OK for transmission, the Zircon programme must be held back, perhaps to be transmitted at a later date in a different format. Milne informed the Governors of his decision on 15 January. But three days later the *Observer* carried the headline 'BBC GAG ON £500 MILLION DEFENCE SECRET'. The next day, the programme's reporter, Duncan Campbell, announced that he would being showing the film to MPs in the House of Commons. Milne instructed BBC solicitors to slap an injunction on Campbell and remind BBC staff of the terms of their contracts. Nevertheless, to the BBC

Governors it looked ominously like another embarrassing BBC cock-up. Hussey and his Deputy Chairman, Lord Barnett, had by now had time to lay their plans. So on 19 January, after a routine Governors' meeting at which Milne was present, he was summoned into the Chairman's office and told by Hussey and Barnett that the Governors had unanimously decided that he must leave the BBC immediately. Milne was taken aback. Totally unprepared and without time to think, he told them that for the sake of the BBC, which he had loved all his life, he would resign. Milne then returned to Bill Cotton's office, where he had been when summoned by the Chairman. Ashen-faced, he briefly told Cotton what had happened, adding, 'But I haven't given them the pleasure of firing me, I've resigned, and I'm off home.'

Cotton briefly considered resigning in protest himself, but decided against. He had only a year left at the BBC before retirement and concluded that his resignation would be a futile gesture. No one else resigned either. Cotton later wondered if it would have been better if Milne had refused to resign and insisted on a confrontation with the full Board of Governors. Perhaps some of these unwise and spineless people might have flinched from looking Milne, a man who had devoted his whole life to the institution of which they were supposed to be the guardians, in the eye and telling him to go. Perhaps others who cared about broadcasting, inside the BBC and out, would have stood up and protested. Perhaps.

Whatever his faults, and a lack of diplomacy and political nous were among them, Milne was a great broadcaster, the best-qualified programme man ever appointed to the director-generalship of the BBC – a statement which begs the question whether fine programme makers are the best people to appoint as Directors-General. When Stuart Young was appointed Chairman in 1983 Bill Cotton had reflected that with Young keeping an eye on the finances and Milne looking after the programmes the BBC would be in safe hands. And, although there had been rows and mistakes, so the BBC had been. Michael Grade states an obvious but essential truth when he says that the BBC exists to make programmes and that everything else is housekeeping. Yet, he says, when he joined the BBC in 1984 he found that inside its upper reaches 'the whole hierarchical system operated on the unspoken assumption that policy made programmes'. Good programmes, Grade points out, rarely originate from the Board of Governors or the Board of Management, they come from producers and programme makers. 'I have always believed that programmes should make policy and not the other way round.' In his time, says Grade, 'in spite of saying all the right things in the BBC's annual reports, the Governors acted more to curb creative risk-taking than to encourage it'.[6] Measured in programme terms, Milne's achievement as Director-General was formidable. History shows that it takes time for BBC Directors-General to get into their stride and make a mark. Milne's tenure was the same. In 1982 and 1983, immediately after he took over, the BBC's programmes were repeatedly eclipsed for their originality and freshness by those from the newly launched Channel Four, while ITV embarrassed it by transmitting work such as *The Jewel in the Crown* while the BBC was putting out *The Thorn Birds*. The courage of Granada's investigations for *World in Action* into such things as cover-ups in the Department of Defence and the secrets of British Steel, at least matched anything undertaken by the BBC. Yet, by 1985 and 1986, BBC-2 had been freshened up and was producing work as original as anything on Channel Four. Under Milne the BBC had not only at last transmitted *The War Game*, in 1986 it had commissioned and transmitted the definitive documentary evocation of Britain under the spell of Thatcherism, Paul Watson's *The Fishing Party*, a documentary essay as enduring and precise as Humphrey Jennings' *Listen to Britain* or *Diary for Timothy* forty years earlier. In Milne's last two years, the BBC was commissioning drama to eclipse both Channel Four and ITV – *Edge of Darkness*, *She Devil*, *The Singing Detective* and, even if Norman Tebbit and some readers of the *Daily Mail* did not like them, *Tumbledown* and *The Monocled Mutineer*. The public's need for a BBC dedicated to the provision of a complete range of high-quality programmes had never been greater. That year British public expenditure on the arts had fallen to the lowest in Europe. If Grade is right, and anyone who cares about good broadcasting can hardly believe anything else, if 'the BBC existed to make programmes, (and) everything else was house-keeping', then, only four years into Milne's term, the BBC Governors should have been defending him, while at the same time perhaps trying to sharpen up some of the housekeeping. They should certainly not have been conspiring to fire him. It had taken Hill the best part of a year after being appointed Chairman by Wilson to 'put the BBC in its place', to ease out Hugh Carleton Greene. Then Greene, who had been in the post for more than eight years, had been more or less willing to leave anyway. It had taken Hussey, encouraged by Thatcher's obedient 'knight' Tebbit 'to get in there and sort the place out', less than three months to turf out Milne.

A few months later, Cotton and other senior managers gave a farewell party in the sixth floor suite at the Television Centre for Milne to celebrate his thirty years of work for the BBC. At the end the lights were dimmed and the curtains opened. High on the balcony opposite a line of Scots pipers played a lament. That era of BBC history, of which Milne had been an integral part, ushered in by Greene twenty-five years earlier, was over.

* * *

As I have said, the removal of Milne set alarms jangling among broadcasters everywhere. If Thatcher's government could move their place-men and women onto the BBC Board of Governors and then have the Chairman of the BBC get rid of the Director-General because BBC programmes gave the government offence, was the position of British broadcasting really so different from the position in France in 1968? Was the Thatcher government's treatment of the BBC so different from the de Gaulle government's treatment of ORTF, treatment which had so exercised those who had joined the embryo FCG? As though to underline the point, two days after Milne's dismissal, the police raided the BBC's offices in Glasgow and seized the *Secret Society* series tapes and files. The government's handling of the BBC served at the same time as a clear warning to ITV, to Channel Four and to programme makers wherever they worked. Our whole drive as campaigners had been to open up broadcasting, to lessen the controls over what was made, to broaden the range of views, people and ideas included in broadcasting; to challenge, expose and explore. On the evidence of what had happened in the last few years, and in the BBC since the autumn of 1986 in particular, Tebbit, Hussey, the government and the Governors did not want any of those things. What they appeared to want was tighter control, a narrowing of what was seen and discussed.

In these circumstances could the independents go on pressing their case, and in seeking their 25% quota of programmes risk adding to the attacks already being made on the BBC? Should we just drop all that and join in a common defence by all programme makers of public service broadcasting and of genuinely independent broadcasting institutions? On 29 January 1987, as news of what had happened to Milne began to spread, it was a profoundly troubling question. Later, in their important book *The Battle for the BBC – A British Broadcasting Conspiracy*, Steven Barnett and Andrew Curry summed up the role of the independents in Thatcher's campaign to curb the BBC, as giving her attack 'cultural credibility'. The idea that we might, no matter what our real intentions, be assisting in an attack on those things in broadcasting which we held most dear, worried us greatly. At about this time, shortly after Hurd's Commons announcement on the 25% quota, Roy Lockett of the ACTT (referring principally to our potential effect on permanent employment, but implying a wider relevance as well) accused the independents of being 'Thatcher's Trojan ponies'. That really stung. We feared it might be true.

We had always tried to couch our arguments in terms that were actively supportive of the ideals of public service broadcasting. Phillip Whitehead, John Wyvver and John Ellis had written articles repeatedly since the start of The 25% Campaign which stressed the cultural importance of independent access. In this, our campaign was no more than the logical extension of the campaigns that had preceded it. In my speech at the RTS Barbican Seminar the previous summer I had said that 'independent production should be the friend of public service broadcasting rather than the instrument of its destruction'. We believed that by embracing the independent production sector the broadcasters would both prepare themselves to face the multi-channel future, and at the same time go a long way towards satisfying government demands for greater efficiency. With the 25% independent quota we had hoped to forge a creative alliance with the BBC and ITV sufficiently outward-looking to persuade the government to defer attempts to dismember the institutions of broadcasting; an alliance sufficiently inclusive to deflect threats to their independence, and sufficiently formidable by virtue of its unity to see off threats to public service broadcasting. But our overtures to the broadcasters had been met with hostility or at best tokenism. When I interviewed Milne for this book, he agreed that it might have been better if we had talked more, sooner, and have united to defend the BBC.

With Milne gone, the BBC Governors set about finding a new Director-General, Michael Checkland having agreed to stand in until one was found. There were a couple of credible inside candidates and two realistic outsiders – Paul Fox and Jeremy Isaacs, who, in accordance with his own dictum that no one should stay in any creative post in Channel Four for more than about seven years, was ready to move on. Grade and Cotton went to see Hussey and pressed the case for appointing Fox. But it is hard to see how Cotton or Grade can have imagined that the Governors would ever agree to appointing Fox. They had found Milne too tough and insufficiently suggestible, so there was really no chance that they would appoint a bruiser as loyal to the ideals of the BBC as Fox. He would certainly have put up with no nonsense from them. Hussey implies in his book that Barnett and he would have been happy to appoint Fox, but one feels that it would have been as a last resort. In any case, at sixty-two Fox could plausibly be said to be too old. Whatever the truth, Cotton and Grade had left Hussey's London flat realising that Fox was unlikely to get the job. Which left Isaacs, if the Governors cared about the BBC and broadcasting, as unquestionably the outstanding candidate. He had been a senior producer at the BBC, Director of Programmes during an outstanding period at Thames and made a triumph of the Conservative government's own creation, Channel Four. He inspired extraordinary loyalty in those who worked for him and would undoubtedly be able to raise the morale of the BBC's demoralised staff.

Once the news was out that Isaacs was a candidate, the press started to tout his candidacy and bookmakers quoted short odds. Triumph might yet come from disaster. But at the interview with the Governors, as he records in his book, Isaacs found that almost their sole concern seemed to be the prevention of future programme rows and cock-ups. Isaacs' reputation for controversial programmes had preceded him and his chances were probably not helped by the vociferous support he was attracting inside the BBC and out. One Governor said to him, 'Mr Isaacs, you do not seem to me like a man who takes kindly to discipline. Now I see by your smile that you take that as a compliment. But I can assure you that some of us here see it as a criticism.'[7] It was precisely Isaacs' positive qualities in the eyes of programme makers which counted against him with the majority of the BBC's Governors. Hussey records that Barnett believed that Isaacs should be appointed but, to Hussey, Isaacs was 'Alasdair writ large, the producers' pet'.[8] Hussey wanted David Dimbleby, a presenter rather than a programme maker or administrator, who Hussey felt 'had the prestige, the political nous but was unpopular'.

Needless to say, Isaacs did not get the job. Michael Checkland, the only candidate without a programme background, did. From the Governors' point of view a safe pair of hands, who would take care of the housekeeping without causing waves. A nice enough man, bright and well-liked among his colleagues, but not the choice that would have been made by a set of Governors who wanted the BBC to strike out boldly, claiming its place as the nation's leading cultural institution in the face of a philistine government bent on reining in its independence, nor of a Board mindful of the Corporation's justified reputation as the most respected public service broadcaster in the world. A pity: they could have had Jeremy Isaacs. People have questioned whether Isaacs could have worked with Mrs Thatcher. My superficial impression, based on a day in Downing Street when I was able to observe them together, is that he could have done. When I put the same question to

Isaacs during my interview with him for this book he told me that he also believed that he could have worked with her because he believes in being forthright and so did she. But, he added, 'The Governors' prime concern was to keep the BBC out of trouble. I was not the DG to do that.'[9]

Checkland had been appointed, as Hussey would later put it, 'on condition that he brought in a deputy who could successfully undertake the much needed overhaul of news and current affairs'.[10] So a few weeks later John Birt, his name put forward by Michael Grade and a previous Deputy Chairman of the BBC, William Rees-Mogg, was brought over from LWT to be Deputy-Director-General. Although it was publicly understood that his specific task was 'to do something' about the BBC's journalism, it quickly became evident that Birt was intended to 'do something' about a lot more than just that. Within weeks of his arrival at the BBC, Cotton felt driven to go to Checkland and tell him that he would have to stop Birt interfering with the television service. 'Mike told me he was powerless to do that.'[11]

*   *   *

With the BBC unprepared to defend itself except in the narrowest possible sense and with no revolt inside its senior ranks against the removal of Milne, there seemed no reason to halt our campaign for the 25% quota. So we persuaded the Liberal MPs Clement Freud and David Steel to sponsor an amendment to the short Broadcasting Bill extending the ITV franchises until the end of 1992, that would require ITV to include 'a substantial proportion' of independent programmes – wording taken from the 1981 Broadcasting Act covering independent production for Channel Four.

When the Broadcasting Bill came up for discussion in the relevant Commons Committee in March 1987 our amendment was carried, against the advice of the government, by one vote, every opposition member of the Committee, together with two Conservatives, supporting it. Although the government made no secret of the fact that once the Bill returned for consideration by the whole of the Commons it would use its large majority to get the amendment thrown out, it now had to be seen to make some progress towards introducing independent production into ITV. So Mellor wrote an open letter to Lord Thomson, the Chairman of the IBA, telling him that he was eager to hear 'the progress that you have made in developing proposals in the light of discussions with the ITV companies and representatives of the independent producers' towards achieving the broad target of 25% over a four-year period. He added that although the government did not think it 'sensible at least at this stage to consider embedding the government's target in statutory form', it did 'not rule out the possibility of legislation in due course . . . should it prove to be needed'.

We had put down a powerful marker. Under pressure to be seen to be taking action, in mid-March the IBA convened a face-to-face meeting between the ITV companies and the independents. At the head of the long boardroom table in the IBA sat Whitney (who, it will be remembered, had once himself been an independent producer, albeit of a rather less bare-footed kind than most of those of us who now lined the table on his right). He was flanked by four of his senior Authority colleagues, including Glencross and Rowley, the two IBA representatives who had been present at the secret strategy meeting with the companies a couple of months earlier. The independents' side comprised four representatives of IPPA, headed by Sophie Balhetchet and Paul Styles, two representatives of AIP, two from the BFTPA, the Head of the joint IPPA-BFTPA industrial relations service and David Graham and me from The 25% Campaign. The independents had met the previous evening to work out an agreed line and arrived at the IBA in good time for the scheduled ten o'clock start. Arriving last, the ITV representatives hurried in – six of them in all. They included the Secretary of the ITCA David Shaw, David Plowright, Brian Tesler and David Elstein. Watching them file somewhat breathlessly along the narrow space between the wall and the back of the chairs to squeeze into the gaps at the table opposite us – was it our imaginations or were some of them squirming? – Phil Redmond whispered hoarsely, a whisper loud enough for some of the ITV bosses who were by then hastily unpacking sheaves of papers from their briefcases to hear, 'I'd have paid good money to see this!'

Whitney started proceedings by saying that the IBA was opposed to rigid quotas, but nevertheless supported the government's wish to 'widen the role within ITV of independent programme makers'. He now wanted 'to make progress on implementation of the 25%'. What was needed, he said, was 'a flexible approach, but one that is focused'. The IBA was therefore looking for 175 to 225 hours of network programmes and from 200 to 400 hours of regional programmes to be made each year by independents by the end of 1989. Although at first sight this looked to be a considerable step forward, it did not take many seconds to see that it was a good deal less generous than it appeared. By 1989, because of the planned extension of broadcasting hours, it was estimated that ITV would be producing more than 4,000 hours of new network programmes each year. So the IBA was proposing that by halfway through the government's four-year period for the introduction of a 25% independent quota the independents would be contributing just 5%. For regional programmes the figures were no better – by 1989 the ITV companies would be making more than 5,500 hours of new regional programmes, of which independents were to get between 3.5% and 7%. On the subject of how much money ITV would devote to independent productions the IBA's officials were even more vague, saying only that the programmes should be spread across the range of programme types.

When discussion moved on to defining who would qualify as an independent, Plowright immediately raised the issue of ITV companies owning shares in independents. ITV knew that this was likely to divide the independents and Sophie Balhetchet tried to stamp on the idea immediately, saying that any shareholding by an ITV company must bar a company from being defined as an independent for the purposes of the government initiative. Glencross, however, pressed the point – 'partial ITV shareholding might encourage more out of London production companies'.[12] When the discussion turned to where the productions were to be made and whether independents would be expected to use ITV companies' facilities, the ITV companies made it clear that they were very keen to have their facilities used. The independents were equally determined not to find themselves being forced to use ITV facilities or union agreements. On regional programmes ITV representatives from the smaller companies – Bill Brown from Scottish and David McCall from Anglia – insisted that a 25% quota would be very damaging to the quality of their local output and would increase costs. There was almost no mention of the contractual terms under which these independent productions were to be made. This was a vital issue for the independents. At the original meeting of Sophie Balhetchet's Group at which The 25% Campaign had been born, it had been agreed that any quota of independent productions on ITV and BBC must stipulate terms as least as good as, and preferably rather better than, the terms currently in use with Channel Four – the crucial points being ongoing rights in programmes and the profit margin or Production Fee.

Further separate meetings between the IBA and the companies and between the IBA and the independents followed. Then, on 8 April, there was a second three-way meeting, at the end of which John Whitney announced that the ground had been sufficiently prepared for the independents and the ITCA to start meeting bilaterally to thrash out the remaining issues – the definition of an independent, rules about the use by independents of ITV companies' facilities, arrangements for regional production and Terms of Trade. He hoped 'that these bilateral meetings would be completed within about four weeks and that the whole debate should be over by the summer'.[13] In his diary after that meeting, which Whitney noted had lasted about two hours, he reflected on the state of mind of the ITV companies and the significance of these events for British broadcasting:

> The companies see the advancing hordes and are uncertain how to respond. They are in a difficult and complex situation. If they appear too welcoming they will lose the confidence of their staff, too unaccommodating and they will be confronted by a wholly hostile government (and public opinion) [Whitney's parenthesis] as well as the IBA. They have few friends. This is dangerous in itself, for who do they turn to for help and security? Other opportunities beckon them across the English Channel, unregulated expansion alluring both in wider market terms and greater freedom. Who would turn their backs on that!
>
> The government is accomplishing its aims of bringing about the fragmentation of independent and BBC public service broadcasting without even firing a shot.
>
> ... The exodus from public service constraints will gather momentum as the grip on audiences by ITV weakens through competition. Thus it is that these meetings between the independents and the ITV Companies mark a seminal moment in the history of British broadcasting. I believe the sense of history and change has not escaped those around the table on Tuesday.
>
> David [Glencross] and I will be seeing David Mellor to report progress in about five weeks time.[14]

*   *   *

Meanwhile things were stirring again over on the BBC front. The new BBC Director-General, Michael Checkland, in talking to BBC managers had signalled that he intended to alter the government's perception of the BBC. He emphasised that the Corporation was 'a thousand-million pound business' and had to change as other organisations in the country had changed. These changes, Checkland told his managers, would include introducing more independent production. Accordingly, on 31 March he called a meeting of independent producers at BAFTA. It would be his first public appearance since becoming Director-General. Strangely, although she had been chairing IPPA since the previous autumn, it was also to be Sophie Balhetchet's first public speech in her new role. She was to respond to Checkland as soon as he had finished speaking. The BBC had promised that she would receive a copy of Checkland's speech the night before so that she could prepare what to say. She was keenly aware that for the first time she would be 'speaking as a politician, the representative of a constituency'. But the BBC, 'duplicitous to the end', she says, held Checkland's speech back so that she was only handed it immediately before she and Checkland stepped onto the BAFTA stage together. Waiting in the wings, Checkland turned to her and asked 'Are you nervous?'

'Yes.'

'So am I.'

Checkland presented what he called a '12 point action plan' outlining how the BBC intended to open its doors to independent producers. By the summer of 1990 the BBC would 'allocate from the licence fee sufficient funds to increase the present 100 hours of independent production' commissioned by the BBC by 500 hours, making 600 in all, of which 400 would be network programmes. The programmes would be across the entire range, excluding news. 'At least £20 million will be set aside for these additional 500 hours.' Co-production packages produced by the BBC with independents would be additional to these hours. To make way for these independent productions there would be cuts in BBC in-house operations and Lime Grove studios would be closed. New costing procedures would be introduced 'to allow clear and unarguable comparability between the costs of BBC and independent productions. Too much time has been spent by all of us on proclaiming the economic virtue of our production methods. We now need the facts . . . ' He understood that 'the BBC's commitment will be judged by its actions in the next few months and not by its words'. He was therefore allocating a further £4 million 'to commission an additional 100 hours of independent production in the year which begins tomorrow'. If the IBA's proposals were also implemented, Checkland said, the two initiatives together would 'double the independent production sector in three years'. Once the programmes had been made and transmitted the BBC would 'review this broad-casting policy in terms of cost and quality . . . If the criteria of quality and cost can be met, independent production can perhaps move forward to another phase of development . . . The door really is open to you.'[15]

This really did seem like a bit of a breakthrough. Although Checkland's 600 hours still fell far short of the 4,000 hours which Milne had estimated was 25% of

BBC programmes or the roughly 1,500 hours of BBC network and 1,000 hours of BBC regional programmes which we reckoned represented 25% of BBC new production each year, it seemed a big step forward, not least because it appeared that the BBC might be prepared to commission these hours on a proper cash basis rather than through the weasel-worded combination of cash-and-resources which ITV appeared to have in mind. Sophie Balhetchet welcomed Checkland's initiative and IPPA called for an early start to negotiations to fill out the details.

It had been clear for some weeks that we needed a small centralised team embracing all the independents' organisations to co-ordinate our policies and conduct negotiations. The informal arrangement under which leading members of IPPA and The 25% Campaign sorted out who did what between them privately was unlikely to work for much longer. The other associations, the BFTPA and AIP, were demanding to be part of the action and although the BBC continued to look mainly to IPPA, the IBA had been summoning representatives from all three organisations. We certainly did not want to give the broadcasters any opportunity to exploit the deep-seated differences between the organisations going back to before Channel Four and the creation of IPPA. Some leading AIP members had still not forgiven the fact that, back in 1980, having accepted support from AIP in the late 1970s, members of the Channel Four Group had set up IPPA as a trade association separate from AIP – one AIP chairman regularly referred to the creation of IPPA as 'the greatest betrayal since Judas'. Some older members of the BFTPA's Council had gone so far as to try to get Greg Smith expelled from the BFTPA simply because he had joined The 25% Campaign.

As a result in May 1987 AIP, the BFTPA and IPPA set up a joint steering committee, The Independent Access Steering Committee – or IASC. It was made up of members of the ruling bodies of its three constituent organisations and run by a secretariat made up of John Woodward as its salaried Co-ordinator and me as the unpaid Head of Negotiations. The funds were to be provided by IPPA and the BFTPA. For ease of operation John moved into an office in the same building as me and an already close working relationship became still closer. As well as covering John's salary and office overheads, the new arrangement enabled us to draw on the expert advice that already existed in the associations which made up the IASC. The negotiations themselves would be conducted by teams drawn from amongst the ranks of the membership of the IASC's constituent associations, chosen by me on a 'best team for the match' basis.

*   *   *

The BBC now seemed eager to reach agreement and for the next few weeks negotiations appeared to advance quickly. The BBC had no desire to force independents to use its facilities and agreed that, wherever possible, independents should make their programmes outside BBC studios and use existing BFTPA/IPPA trade union agreements. The BBC was also clear that its definition of an independent producer would exclude any company which was even partially owned by another broadcaster. Although worries remained about the number of hours to be commissioned and whether the BBC's target of 600 hours by 1990 was sufficient to meet the target of 25% in four years, by the end of May it was possible to believe that since Checkland had taken over from Milne as Director-General a transformation had occurred in the BBC's relationship with independents. Even on the all-important issue of the Terms of Trade to cover independent productions made for the BBC, the BBC promised that it would present terms by early June.

However, only a few days after the BBC negotiators had made this promise, notes were leaked to us from inside the BBC of an internal meeting that had taken place some weeks earlier. These recorded a discussion about independent production between Checkland, Grade and other senior BBC managers and BBC union leaders. Checkland, it seemed, had told the union leaders that he and Hussey had met Mellor on 30 April and had 'successfully argued for the acceptance of 500 hours and a 12 point plan' over the next three years, rather than the 25% of all new output over four years which had been promised by Hurd. He had apparently reported that 'IPPA had accepted this as a reasonable deal'. Nevertheless, Checkland told the unions, 'political pressure to achieve 25% in four years was still strong. If this could be delayed until at least 1994 then [he] believed the BBC would have achieved a sensible way forward.'[16]

In contrast to the IASC's meetings with the BBC, which had generally been friendly and conducted with good humour, face-to-face meetings with the ITCA immediately degenerated into ill-tempered squabbling. At the beginning of April Whitney had said that he hoped that the bi-lateral negotiations on Terms of Trade between the independents and the ITV companies could be completed in about four weeks and that the whole debate would be over 'by the summer'. But a whole month elapsed before the ITV companies got round to talking to the independents at all. An indication of their attitude came during the very first bi-lateral meeting, on 7 May. It had been suggested at the beginning of the meeting that at the end the two sides should have a drink together in the ITCA's hospitality room to celebrate making a start. But as the meeting broke up, little more having been agreed than a list of issues that required further discussion, the ITV negotiators, who included Fox, Tesler and Elstein, hurried out to an adjoining room. James Graham, the managing director of one of the smallest ITV companies – Border Television – had not noticed his colleagues' abrupt exit and remained behind packing his papers into his overnight bag for his journey back to Carlisle. Graham, as the head of a small company, was suspected by his colleagues of being sympathetic to the independents' cause – 'I was a fellow-traveller, if you like.' He believed that the introduction of independents into the system would give small ITV companies like his own the same opportunity to pitch programme ideas to the network as the independents or the bigger ITV companies. He assumed, therefore, that he had been asked to join the ITV negotiating team 'as an oil-can'.[17] Graham, unaware of his colleagues' sudden exit, was somewhat startled when suddenly one of his big company colleagues banged back into the room and briskly commanded him to come into the next room. A few moments later David Shaw re-appeared and announced that the drinks were off.

At that first meeting the ITV bosses had repeated all the familiar objections to working with independents which they had been trotting out ever since publication of the Peacock Report. Such a level of independent production would decimate their profits, undermine the health of the whole production industry, throw thousands of able technicians out of work, lower programme standards. How were the percentages to be counted? What constituted a bona fide independent? Would ITV companies be allowed to invest in target independents to ensure a strong and financially stable sector? Even the apparently straightforward issue of independents' use of ITV companies' facilities had led to an extraordinary and, to us sitting on the independents' side of the negotiating table, amazing spat between the ITV companies themselves. The BBC had already said that there would be no compulsory use of BBC facilities or staff, although independents would be free to use and pay for BBC facilities on a normal market basis if they were available and if they so chose. We expected a similar arrangement to be accepted by ITV. But not a bit of it. We told them that all we sought was that 'the market' should determine whether an independent used an ITV company's facilities or not. But David McCall, who was chairing the ITCA team, said that such a stipulation was meaningless – 'the ITV companies could always undercut any independent facilities house. ITV was in a position to offer facilities at no charge if it so wished.'[18] McCall's argument was then repeated with greatly added force by Paul Fox. When, with admittedly deliberately pointed gentleness, I responded that if the companies started charging nothing for their facilities it seemed likely that the companies' finance directors, shareholders and, presumably, the tax authorities and the Treasury, might start to ask questions about how it was that ITV companies' facilities could be marketed at zero cost to independents when the costs the companies incurred in creating and operating these facilities still figured so large in those same companies' annual accounts, Paul Fox blew up. He told me that it had nothing whatsoever to do with shareholders or the Treasury. I should mind my own business. Whereupon, Brian Tesler, who was sitting next to Fox, turned to him and said mildly that he thought I might have a point. The companies did not want the IBA looking into the way the companies charged the costs of their facilities. Artificially low pricing of their facilities might have serious implications for the way that the Exchequer Levy paid by the ITV companies was calculated. Fox now turned angrily on Tesler – the Levy did not have anything to do with discussions with the independents. After which he pointedly turned his back on Tesler, and faced away from him for the rest of the meeting.[19]

So frequent did these spats between the ITV representatives become that the independent negotiators started to lay bets with each other about which of them would be the first to cause a blow-up at the next meeting – the person who achieved this feat being stood free drinks by his colleagues in the pub afterwards. During our pre-meeting briefings the members of the independent team would predict how the ITV side would behave, acting out what each member of the ITV team would do, imitating how each would react to whatever idea or point we put forward. Paul Styles recalls that 'We had nicknames for the ITV team. Tesler was "The Herbivore", Fox something like "The Ox", "The Bully" or "The Bull".' Styles remembers that during one meeting Fox did not utter one word, but spent the whole time slowly tearing the agenda into very small pieces – 'Our team slowly became mesmerised by this, and people started to falter in what they were saying. When we tabled a short paper on how to get to the [25% of] hours Fox screwed it up, threw it on the table and said, "That's what I think of your paper." ' Styles says of some of the ITV representatives' antics at the meetings that, 'If it had been an Arnold Schwarzenegger movie it would have provoked the phrase "Now it's getting personal".' The effect was to galvanise and bond the campaigners. We could go back to the IASC Committee and regale them with these stories. 'We would say "You wouldn't script that and get away with it." '

John Woodward says that Fox 'seemed to be saying to us that he thought this was a complete waste of time and that he simply did not want to be here with us in the room'.[20]

Fox more or less confirms this impression: 'In the ITV/IASC negotiations I was protecting our own [Yorkshire Television's] interests . . . We made good programmes and had good people in ITV, provided that the talent was refreshed. That was my interest. I wasn't very keen on bringing in people I didn't know. You have to remember that there was still an ITV carve-up.' (That is to say programmes for the network were still divided up and shared between the five major ITV companies on the basis of haggling and to the virtual exclusion of the smaller ITV companies.) 'Yorkshire Television was vulnerable . . . [so] I wasn't going to take any nonsense from the independents.' He also confirms the depth of the splits on the ITV side: 'The companies loathed each other more than they loathed the BBC, and had a contempt for the IBA. You could play one company off against another.'[21] In contrast to Fox, Tesler says that he viewed the independents as a potential means of cutting back the exorbitant costs and appalling labour practices in ITV. James Graham, coming from tiny Border Television, was able to view the members of his own side with a certain detachment: 'The intellectual power on our side was Brian Tesler, whereas Paul (Fox), the paratrooper still in him, was still the ultimate public service broadcaster. Tesler was a shrewd, highly intellectual figure – [at LWT he was] heading a BBC with commercials. The BBC were very good politicians. When I had moved over to ITV I had found that they were very good businessmen but had a contempt for politics.'

By early June, by which time a fresh general election campaign was in full swing, three bilateral meetings with ITV had taken place. The only substantial issue that had come even close to resolution was the use by independents of ITV companies' facilities, the ITV companies having accepted the principle that programme commissions could not be made conditional upon independents agreeing to use ITV facilities. On all the other issues which were crucial to the independents – the definition of what constituted an independent, ownership and ongoing exploitation of rights in their programmes and profit margins (production fees), no agreement had been reached. Indeed, on the last two there had been almost no discussion. The companies had repeatedly promised that they would come forward with proposals, but at successive meetings had failed to do so. Having promised to produce minutes of the meetings, the ITV companies had thus far failed to do even this. Over what constituted an independent for the purposes of the 25% quota, the ITV companies had repeated that they wanted the right to invest in independent producers' companies without the companies being disqualified as independents. Some of the independents' negotiators saw attractions in this, but the majority of us were fearful that in practice it would lead to a proliferation of 'sweetheart deals', to unfair competition rather than to a genuine opening-up of the market and an erosion of the distinction between genuine independents and broadcasters.

With no progress being made, the broadcasters started busily spreading the idea that the independents were being 'bloody-minded' over the issue of ITV companies taking shares in independents. So in mid-June I wrote to Whitney in an attempt to dispel this idea. Far from being 'stubborn and unreasonable', we were doing no more than follow the logic of what had been said during our earlier tri-partite meetings at the IBA. Drawing his attention to the minutes of those meetings, I reminded him that a clear understanding had been reached 'that what was needed was independent producers who were genuinely independent, i.e., not under the control, direct or indirect, of ITV companies'. Holding shares in independent producers must 'by its nature be in conflict with the government policy objective of fostering a third force to compete in the supply of programmes which is genuinely independent of the existing broadcasters'.[22] Whitney's reply arrived ten days later. The IBA was 'not impressed', he said, 'with arguments which could sometimes seem based upon the spiritual or cultural purity of ITV companies'. The IBA had 'always seen the quality of production and the costs of production in this new development as more important than detailed rules. All parties', he averred, were 'agreed on the basic principles of the real independence of the independent producer and the need for fair, unbiased decision making'. Insisting that the 'flexible approach' advocated by the IBA would not be 'misused', Whitney assured me that the Authority would 'not hesitate to take strong remedial action if it is thought necessary'.[23]

Unfortunately, over the years we had seen too many instances of what happened when the chips were down. Despite numerous promises of 'strong remedial action' and similar ringing phrases, the IBA had repeatedly caved in before the commercial demands of the companies. So we simply did not believe the IBA and suspected that it was up to its old tricks, acting as the ITV companies' advocate rather than their regulator. We remembered the Authority's 'fearless stand' over LWT, its sponsorship of the companies' plans for ITV-2, its patronisingly dismissive attitude towards the capacity of independents in the run-up to the start of Channel Four and its failure to hold TV-am to its programme commitments. When word got round the independent sector about the stand we were making we received numerous messages of support from independent producers big and small.

IBA officials, however, seemed unperturbed. Four days after my letter to Whitney, Chris Rowley rang John Woodward with a 'timetable for the ITV negotiations to be concluded'. Within a week, he said, Whitney was to 'OK a draft IBA statement/policy document on the negotiations/results so far'. This should be 'fairly straightforward, with the exception of the ITV shareholding question'. The fact that still nothing had been resolved over the number and value of programmes which constituted 25%, nor on the essential details of any 'Terms of Trade' between ITV and the independent sector seemed not to matter. After receiving the IBA draft the ITCA and the IASC were, Rowley told Woodward, to be given about a week in which to comment or raise issues, after which Authority Members would 'review' the document before sending it off to the Home Office. The IBA intended 'go public' with their policy statement before the end of July.[24]

Now the ITV companies tabled their long-awaited draft Terms of Trade. It was quickly apparent that they contained nothing beyond a collection of general clauses lifted, when not watered down, more or less verbatim from the Terms of Trade employed by Channel Four for commissioning programmes from independents. On all the important material issues – the level of Production Fees, rights in programmes and entitlement to a share of income from the overseas sales or other uses of independents' programmes – the document was silent. These matters were to be swept into an absent 'Business Checklist'. Unknown to us David Shaw, the General Secretary of the ITCA, had sent a separate private note with the proposals to his ITV member companies, assuring them that 'there is no intention of defining business matters in such a way as to interfere in, or inhibit, the way in which each company will carry out its negotiations'.[25] In other words, the ITCA's real intention remained what it had always been, not to reach any meaningful agreement with the IASC at all.

The repeated delays in ITV forwarding proposals, coupled with the by turns aggressive or dismissive deflection of all discussion of the material business issues, had made us deeply suspicious. When discussions with ITV had begun the 1987 general election had been in full swing. Now, with the election over and Thatcher re-elected for an unprecedented third successive term, the prospect of broadcasting legislation seemed to have receded. The Queen's Speech contained no reference to a Broadcasting Bill or legislation on the 25% quota. In the post-election government reshuffle David Mellor had been moved from the Home Office and a new minister, Timothy Renton, appointed to replace him. Renton was also to have responsibility for immigration, traditionally one of the most time-consuming portfolios in government. In his first press interview Renton made no secret of the fact that broadcasting would come a poor second in his list of priorities. As the *Sunday Times* reported, the government's promise to introduce comprehensive broadcasting legislation 'early in the new parliament must be taken flexibly'. Home Office officials told reporters that the earliest any broadcasting bill could be put before Parliament would be in the autumn of 1988 'and even that target looks ambitious'. At the start of its third successive term, the Thatcher government was entering its most unheeding and radically extreme period – the Poll Tax was in the pipe line, education was to be put through the fire and the Health Service subjected to market discipline. Broadcasting was clearly no longer uppermost in the government's mind and the broadcasters no longer had any obvious incentive to press ahead towards an agreement with the independents.

Confirmation of these suspicions came at the end of June at a meeting between ITCA and IASC specialist teams dealing with detailed Terms of Trade. Pressed by the independents to begin negotiations on the substantive business items, the ITV team announced that it was 'not empowered to negotiate'. The independents responded that in that case they would themselves prepare and table a set of comprehensive proposals. Later the same week, at a meeting of the full negotiating teams, the ITV companies repeated their refusal to negotiate on the central issue of Terms of Trade. When I listed ten essential items which had to be agreed, Elstein responded, in shocked tones, that in spelling out the items in this direct way I had 'gone far beyond the original brief of the Terms of Trade Working Group'. He found 'the quest for minimum Production Fees quite extraordinary'. We were inviting the ITCA to 'act as a cartel. Competition would, in fact,' he said, 'be better achieved without terms of trade.'[26] A statement which should have been breathtaking from anyone who had so recently himself been an independent but for the fact that we were by now accustomed to the idea that in changing his job Elstein seemed to lose both his memory and his beliefs – 'The Vicar of Bray' indeed.

Shortly before the election the government had publicly reminded the IBA that it expected progress, so I pointed out that if we failed to agree, an agreement was likely to be 'forced' on us. That would 'not be helpful to either the ITCA or the IASC'. We repeated that we remained ready to conclude a deal within the timetable set by the IBA. That, the ITV companies responded, was impossible. They would never be able to get the agreement of all fifteen of their member companies within the time. Really? we responded. We represented hundreds of companies in three different associations, yet we could achieve it in the time. Why, if they were serious, couldn't they?

Just two days later David Norris, the IASC's resident legal mind (Norris was one of the best lawyers in the business and had helped many independents to set up their companies and negotiate contracts in the early days of Channel Four) produced our proposed Terms of Trade. These were immediately sent to the ITCA.

*   *   *

By this time there were serious areas of disagreement in our discussions with the BBC as well. The number of hours and sum of money 'on offer' to the independents following Checkland's announcement at BAFTA at the end of March still remained too low to convince us that it was a serious incremental step towards achieving 25% of the BBC's original production in four years' time. As with ITV, the levels of Production Fee and shares in ongoing rights and income from overseas sales remained unresolved. Although the BBC accepted the principle of a Production Fee, they remained reluctant to put any figures on it. So we put forward figures. These were modelled closely on those applied by Channel Four. We reasoned that, as the BBC, like Channel Four, was a public service broadcaster, the same terms ought to apply.

Our negotiations with the BBC had by now taken on what we increasingly came to see as a deliberately disconcerting pattern. For the meetings, which were chaired by Michael Grade, the independents would be summoned to the Television Centre in White City early in the morning. The room in which the meetings were held was invariably some windowless basement deep in the bowels of the Television Centre. Somehow the air conditioning never seemed to be in proper working order (perhaps it was no more than the earliness of the hour?). Although the early start time suited most of us as we were often working on productions during the day, having trailed into the Television Centre at the appointed hour from homes all over London, we would wait in whatever airless basement Grade had chosen. Tea and coffee were never provided. After waiting for ten to fifteen minutes Grade would sweep in with his small team, dressed in shirt, bright tie and trademark red braces. He would then plunge briskly into the business of the meeting, employing a mixture of humour and thinly veiled intimidation. A number of the members of our team still depended for much of their own freelance professional work on the BBC. (During that summer I, for instance, was directing a large-scale production of Ibsen's *The Master Builder* for the BBC with Leo McKern and Miranda Richardson.) A key member of our small BBC team was Paul Jackson, who had started out years previously as a studio call-boy at the BBC before rising to become one of the country's most distinguished light entertainment producers. Grade's own specialist field was light entertainment and Jackson (and through him his own independent production company) was potentially vulnerable if he took on Grade over issues affecting light entertainment programmes, issues where Grade often appeared at his most intimidating. However, this never seemed to deter Jackson. No matter how insistent or bulky Grade managed to contrive to make himself seem at the head of the table; Jackson, usually positioned quite well up the table so as to be near Grade, would always chip in. He was reasoned, good-humoured but could never be deflected, except by sound argument. Since then I have questioned Michael Grade about his tactics during these sessions – the airless rooms, the early hour, the lack of coffee, his late appearances and his 'carry-the-battle-to-the-enemy' style. He response was to smile in what I took to be acknowledgement of the tactics, adding 'If I'd had a free hand we would have reached agreement. But I had a constituency. The only thing that interested me was – where can I get the best programmes. I knew that parts of the BBC were creatively bankrupt.' Of the whole battle between the independents and the BBC he said, 'It was silly.' The BBC, he says, is like the Civil Service: 'The BBC has only one agenda – to defend their territory.' Like civil servants 'the imperative is to make territorial gains for the department. A good year in the Civil Service or the BBC is one when at the end of it you can say, "We got more territory this year." The independents were threatening their territory. Therefore the independents had to be seen off. You try to take territory off the BBC, they'll fight like stuck pigs. Civil servants are good at defending their turf.' He added that once the independents had acquired sufficient political clout, he could not blame them when they used it against the BBC and ITV: 'The greatest sin of Hollywood is to have clout and not to use it.'[27]

By July meetings of the full negotiating teams of the IASC or of sub-groups dealing with specific issues, were taking place with the BBC and ITV once and sometimes twice each week. Yet still no progress was being made. The BBC had even started to go back on some items which had been agreed. Woodward and I began to suspect that the BBC, realising that since the election immediate pressure from the government was off, was, like ITV, playing for time. It was at this moment that we got evidence that seemed to confirm that the ITV companies were filibustering. One of the excuses used by the companies for refusing to negotiate on Terms of Trade since the election had been that first they needed to see the draft of the IBA's proposed statement in order to be sure that anything that they might propose conformed to Authority policy. Now we discovered that at the very time when the companies were telling us this they had already been in possession of a draft of the IBA's proposed policy document. Some of the proposals in the IBA paper were, it emerged, more favourable to the independents' case than the ITV companies had expected.

I decided that the time had now come to make use of the access I had gained earlier in the year to Professor Brian Griffiths at Number 10. Until then, knowing that as Head of the Number 10 Policy Unit Griffiths must have a huge workload, I had decided not to take up his time unless or until it became really important. Now I drafted a long letter to him. I needed to draw the Government back into play over achieving the full 25% quota rather than some token number of hours of programmes made by possibly dubiously defined independent producers. I was by now certain that we required legislation, as I was convinced that without it the broadcasters would engage in repeated attempts to evade any quota. I also needed to begin the process of inducing the government to come in on the independents' side if we failed to reach an acceptable agreement with the broadcasters on minimum Terms of Trade. The bulk of my letter to Griffiths dealt with a research paper which we had commissioned from an outside consultant, Jonathan Davies, on the total number of hours and costs of programmes produced by the BBC and ITV. To date, I reminded Griffiths, the BBC had been talking about achieving a full independent quota of 25% of original programmes over a period of 6 years, while the IBA had been talking to the government about achieving 25% in 4 years. To this end the BBC and ITV had made 'offers' to the independents of 500 hours, to be achieved in the case of ITV by the end of 1989 and by the BBC in 1991–2. Davies's paper, I told Griffiths, showed that by 1989 25% of ITV original output would amount to 2,430 hours,[28] while by 1991–2 25% of BBC output would amount to 2,569 hours.[29] The BBC, I reminded him, had added the proviso that before moving on to accepting that level of programmes from the independents, it would carry out a review of 'cost and quality' based on the programmes already supplied by independents. As increments towards achieving 25% of independent productions within the time scales the broadcasters themselves had set, these 'offers' of 500 hours from each were simply unconvincing. 'The money the BBC has earmarked for Independent production', I told Griffiths, 'is more derisory still – £20m against the £113m that the BBC would itself spend on the programmes.' ITV's 'indicative figures' had no specific sum of money earmarked at all. Davies's paper, I told him, commissioned by the IASC 'to give us an objective assessment of the viability of these "offers" as a means of progressing to the full implementation of the government's objectives' had been checked by 'two of the best known firms of City accountants with intimate working knowledge of ITV and BBC'. Both had found Davies's conclusions 'stark'. Using the BBC's own accounting methods, they had compared independent producers' costs with those of the BBC and found that while, on average, an hour of Network programming produced by the BBC cost £63,000, it cost independents only £44–46,000. The BBC, therefore, appeared to be expecting the independents to find some 40% of the money required to make the BBC's programmes. I enclosed a copy of the full Davies paper, telling Griffiths that we were planning to release it during the coming week to 'selected journalists'.

I then turned to Terms of Trade. On a number of matters 'crucial if the independents are ever to become a third genuinely competitive force in broadcasting', we remained far from agreement. It looked, I told him, as if the 'offers' from both the BBC and ITV, although 'ostensibly aimed at making the government's policy work' would in practice not do so. 'I am afraid', I told him, 'that there appear to be only two interpretations that can be placed on the BBC and ITV proposals – either they are not really trying to grapple with implementation of government policy or they have skilfully devised a ploy which is aimed at frustrating the government policy because it is calculated to fail – and when it does fail will give the appearance that that failure is due to the independents.' Not only were the hours too few to act as a first step towards smooth implementation of a 25% quota, the money on offer was too little to allow the independent sector to grow sufficiently to become a genuine competitive force. On top of which, the broadcasters' refusal to agree on fundamental matters governing Terms of Trade threatened the breakdown of the talks. 'A series of vital negotiations are scheduled during the next ten days and I will let you know their outcome. At the moment failure to agree on a range of fundamental matters is decidedly on the cards.'[30] I sent similarly, though marginally less starkly worded letters to the officials in the Broadcasting Unit of the Home Office and the DTI.

Sophie Balhetchet, John Woodward, Paul Styles and I were now convinced that the strategy of the ITV companies, probably with a degree of collusion on the part of the IBA, was to play for time until after Parliament rose at the end of July for the long summer recess, after which it would be difficult for us to raise an effective political hue and cry. They appeared to hope that by the time Parliament reassembled in the autumn, heat and interest would have gone out of the issue of the independents' 25% quota. The IBA clearly remained anxious to provide the government with 'evidence of progress' and Whitney had continued to stress that the IBA was determined to issue a policy statement 'by the end of the month' even if 'all aspects of the agreement' had not been agreed. Re-reading the minutes of our meetings with ITV today (there had now been no fewer than eleven), it is almost comic how, at each one, the independents patiently try to bring up each of the material issues in turn – programme rights, profit margins, budgets, funding, number of hours, definition of an independent – only to have the ITV companies refuse to discuss each of them. Today it is hard to understand why busy men – the only women who ever participated were Sophie Balhetchet and Janet Walker – should have been prepared to waste so much of their valuable time in such a seemingly futile exercise (meetings rarely lasted less than two hours). When I interviewed Sir Paul Fox for this book I told him that we assumed that once the 1987 general election was safely out of the way and the threat of immediate legislation to introduce a 25% quota had been postponed, he and his colleagues had simply decided to play for time rather than seriously try to reach a deal. This he confirmed. He had been 'stalling, playing for time to see out the ITV contracts before the 25% was introduced'.

A week after my first letter I wrote to Professor Griffiths again. 'I have to report that things have not gone well, especially in the case of ITV. While there are still a few more days to go before any breakdown could become formal I am anxious that once Parliament rises it may be difficult to institute action to counter what looks increasingly like a policy of deliberate prevarication, coupled with the aim of inhibiting the economic growth of the independent sector, on the part of the ITV companies in particular.' I told him that I would be 'advising' the IASC that the three independent producer associations 'must consider publicly dissociating [themselves] from any statements in the next few weeks from the IBA or the BBC suggesting that a basis for a voluntary agreement between the broadcasters and the independents has been arrived at . . . The reasons for this advice are that the BBC and ITV companies are unwilling to offer guidelines as to the principles that should underlie the business terms applied to individual contracts between independent producers and broadcasters which hold out any hope of the independent sector being able to develop as a genuine "third force" in the supply of television programmes. They are unwilling to agree even to the minimum guarantees of profit for the independent producer promulgated by Channel Four.' By denying the independent producers any ongoing rights in their programmes, the broadcasters were seeking to use 'their public asset – the right to transmit (and in the case of ITV make a profit from selling advertising) to take over the most valuable asset of the independent – the right to exploit and build a proper asset and capital base from his intellectual and creative property'. While negotiations with the BBC had not yet 'reached quite the degree of disagreement reached with ITV, a similar chasm has opened between us over the question of principles to underlie deals'. In concluding, I told Griffiths, 'I am sorry to have to report to you in such gloomy terms,' but I thought that 'you would rather be advised in advance about the way things appear to be moving'.[31]

In the months since detailed negotiations with the broadcasters had begun, both sides had been interested in keeping stories about their progress out of the press in order to reduce the pressure on the negotiators and give them a better chance of reaching agreement. But now, faced with what looked like a plot by the broadcasters to bury the 25% quota, we urgently needed to bring the issue back into the public arena in a way that would make it impossible for them to bury it. Accordingly, in addition to our lobbying inside government, we started lobbying MPs – telling them what we suspected the broadcasters were up to. We also talked to journalists in ways that would generate stories. Using the Jonathan Davies research paper as a starting point, we argued that the number of hours which the broadcasters had 'offered' to the independents amounted to no more than a token, a sop which went almost nowhere towards meeting the government's 25% target of independent productions within four years. On top of which, the IBA was preparing to extend the ITV companies' contracts for an additional three years without placing any formal obligation on them to meet the 25% target. The ITV companies were simply refusing to discuss equitable business terms. It was now that Paul Styles began to prove himself a brilliant manipulator of the press – so much so that I had to intervene to cool down members of AIP and the BFTPA who complained that the press coverage Styles got made it look as if The 25% Campaign was an IPPA initiative rather than a joint effort.

On 19 July the *Sunday Times* ran a story under the headline 'Walk out by independents in ITV talks' which quoted me as fearing that the IBA was about to put out a policy statement which failed to meet the needs of either the independents or government policy: 'If the IBA and the ITV companies go ahead with their unreasonable plans, we will have no option but to disassociate ourselves from the discussions.' The *Sunday Times* article continued, 'An IBA spokesman denied that the Authority or the ITV companies were being obstructive. "There's no question of the companies digging their heels in . . . Our intention is to submit a document to the Home Office which is acceptable to all parties." ' The article concluded, 'The prospect of a collapse in negotiations is sure to be discussed tomorrow when the Prime Minister chairs a Cabinet sub-committee on broadcasting policy. The independents hope the Prime Minister will intervene to force ITV into line.'

A couple days after the appearance of the *Sunday Times* article the Secretary of State at the Home Office, Tim Renton, reiterated in a Commons written answer that government policy remained 'to ensure that at least 25 per cent of programmes broadcast on both ITV and BBC television are supplied by independent producers as soon as possible. We have asked the IBA and BBC to come forward with firm plans for the achievement of this target.'[32]

That looked like a small victory. The broadcasters would now not be able to simply bury the issue. However, once again getting reiterations of government policy was to prove easier than getting the broadcasters to actually move forward. Two days after Renton's Commons statement, the ITCA sent a letter to John Woodward saying that they would not now be able to produce an amended draft of proposed Terms of Trade until the second half of August.

Then at the end of July the BBC, which had maintained a silence for the previous four weeks, burst back into the news with what bore all the hallmarks of a carefully constructed Michael Grade press coup. Unfortunately for Grade, it went spectacularly wrong. Just after 7.30 on the evening of Tuesday 28 July, a fax from the BBC press office spewed out of the fax machine in the IPPA office. Addressed to Sophie Balhetchet, it contained a BBC press release, embargoed until 12 noon the next day, when, the BBC announced, it would be holding a press conference. The headline on the release trumpeted 'BBC COMMISSIONS OVER 200 HOURS FROM INDEPENDENT PRODUCERS.' It detailed 'a £4.8 million package of 128 hours of new programmes being commissioned from British independent producers during 1987–8'. Quoting an evidently ebullient Grade on how far the BBC had moved since Checkland's BAFTA speech in March: 'We have come a very long way in four months. Today BBC Television is demonstrating its commitment to the healthy growth of British independent production.' It announced 'some 44 new commissions' from 30 different production companies over a spectrum including drama, entertainment and documentaries. 'In the meantime,' Grade continued, 'our negotiations to establish detailed terms of trade with the independents are making good progress'. But this was only the beginning, said Grade. 'We will reach our target of 600 hours of independent production by 1990.' The BBC press officer who had sent the release was not to know that there would still be anyone in the IPPA office that evening. However, there was and they rang Sophie Balhetchet and other members of the IASC at home to tell them about a 'very interesting BBC press release' which had turned up in the office. Early next morning a group of us went into the IPPA office and started to tear the BBC release apart item by item, phoning the individual producers on the list and asking them for details of their programmes. What rapidly emerged was that no more than half a dozen of the BBC's so-called 'commissions' were genuine. They were co-productions, package and development deals. Some were even buy-ins from Australia. We quickly cobbled together our own press release, debunking the BBC announcement and spelling out the truth behind each of the BBC's independent 'commissions'.

Meanwhile, John Woodward had called the BBC press office, 'all innocence', and asked if he could come along to the press conference at midday. The press officer agreed. When he got to White City, Woodward found that the press conference was being staged in a hospitality suite in formal style with food and drink laid on. At the appointed hour Grade swept in – this was clearly intended to be a big show event. 'Grade and his team were at a table at the far end. Grade was very confident. He laid out his news and press releases were handed out. The press were then invited to ask questions. I stuck my hand up and Grade, not knowing who I was – why should he? – called me. I said, "Can I give an alternative view?" I then proceeded to outline how the programmes on the BBC's list were not genuine independent programmes at all, and offered the IASC alternative press release to journalists, giving the real provenance of the programmes on Grade's list. Afterwards most of the press gathered round me asking questions, and took our press release.' Grade and the BBC men were furious, but they could hardly physically throw Woodward out in full view of the press. So they quietly seethed, more or less bundling him out as soon as they decently could. John then got back on the tube and returned to the IPPA office where many of us were waiting to hear what had happened. The next day the press had a field day. A couple days after that John received what he describes as 'foul letter' from Grade saying that 'from henceforward you are forbidden to set foot on BBC property'. Woodward was very worried: 'I had joined The 25% Campaign in the hope of finding work and now I seemed to have got myself ruled out with the BBC for ever. I think Grade was particularly put out because we had beaten him at what he particularly prided himself on, PR. To me it is a very good example of the difference between the two groups. On the one side us, kind of guerrillas on bicycles and on the other the broadcasters, with big conventional PR, press conferences, food and drink.'[33]

Grade had claimed during his press conference that the BBC had 'more than a head start on ITV' in commissioning productions from the independents. Clearly smarting, a few days later ITV responded: 'ITV and Channel Four are the "lifeblood" of Britain's independent producers . . . Irrespective of the outcome of negotiations about greater access, we will remain the independents' biggest customers. Our track record speaks for itself.' £20 million pounds worth of independent productions were now 'in the pipeline', on top of the '£50 million plus commissioned by Channel Four. It is absolute nonsense to suggest that the £4 million the BBC is spending on commissions from independents is leaving ITV behind.'[34] Once again, examination of these claims suggested that they were largely bogus. ITV had not repeated Grade's mistake of issuing a list of actual programmes but, as far as we could ascertain, only six of the ITV programmes, which together had a running time of just 9 hours, were genuine independent commissions. The rest were purchases of old programmes or straightforward ITV productions with some key personnel hired on freelance contracts. We reacted by accusing ITV of another piece of crude PR aimed at getting the government off its back and, as a result, the press had almost as much fun with ITV as it had had with the BBC.

A couple of days after that, on 6 August, the IBA released its long-promised Policy Statement. It bore all the signs of being a craftily worded attempt to offend no one while claiming that the IBA was implementing government policy. Although it included no increase in the initial target tranche of 500 hours of independent productions, it did say that the IBA would 'reserve the right to include requirements for independent production' in the contracts extending ITV companies' franchises until the end of 1992 and did refer to independents needing to be separate 'in ownership, management and control' from ITV companies and their subsidiaries. After prodding from the independents, the IBA statement had also included a reference to a 'Production Fee' being included in programme budgets. It added that neither independents nor ITV companies were 'as a principle . . . to be excluded automatically from a share in the rights for further exploitation' of their programmes.

After careful scrutiny, and despite its apparent cynicism, the independents decided to try to make use of the IBA statement as a lever with which finally to force the ITV companies into meaningful negotiations or compel them to openly refuse to negotiate. If they refused to negotiate we believed we would be able to call in the government. With this in mind, we issued a press release headed: 'INDEPENDENT PRODUCERS GIVE QUALIFIED WELCOME TO IBA POLICY STATEMENT.' It went on to quote Sophie Balhetchet: 'We have discussed the content of the IBA's cleverly worded statement. On the face of it there is just enough here to set the agenda for future talks on Terms of Trade.' For good measure, we added that the IBA's statement 'should leave the ITCA with no option but to negotiate'.[35]

How wrong we were! After yet more prevarication the ITCA told us that there would be a further delay in coming forward with the ITV companies' response to our proposed Terms of Trade. At the same time the independents began to come under fire in the press. Articles in *The Listener* by that admirable critic Sean Day-Lewis and by William Phillips in *Broadcast* suggested that independent production was likely to do nothing for viewers or the quality of BBC and ITV programmes. Because independents would have an even greater incentive than their in-house colleagues to pander to the caution of already cautious BBC and ITV managers, independent production was likely to make ITV and BBC schedules even more dull and predictable. Phillips said that, 'by a brilliant political lobbying campaign', independent producers had made themselves 'into television's little tin gods'.[36]

When the ITCA did finally come forward with the companies' revised Terms of Trade at the beginning of September they marked no advance. Ten of the essential clauses put forward in the proposals drafted for the independents by David Norris two months earlier had simply been deleted. None of the business issues which, as we had repeatedly told them since May, were the 'lifeblood' of the independent sector, had been addressed at all. As I told the members of the IASC in a Strictly Confidential briefing note on 4 September: 'The ITCA document amounts to a list of obligations on the independent producer, omitting all reward.'

I was now seriously worried. If the broadcasters really were not going to negotiate on minimum terms of trade, we were going to have no option but to call in the government. But this risked opening the door to goodness knew what other kinds of free-market-driven government meddling. We had aimed to protect what was best in the British broadcasting system and at the same time give the established broadcasters access to new talent and a proven means of controlling their costs. Already more and more cases were being reported to us of ITV companies using their positions of market power to force independents into accepting deals on terms far worse than those that pertained for programmes commissioned by Channel Four. It was now more clear than ever that if we accepted terms of trade with the BBC and ITV which were not at least as good as those with Channel Four, the already fragile economic viability of the vast majority of the independents would be seriously undermined. All but the most nakedly commercial independents might be forced out of business or back onto the staff of the BBC and ITV companies, returning programme making to a kind of closed-shop, closed-minded world worse than had existed before the creation of Channel Four.

Privately I remained convinced that at root we and the broadcasters wanted many of the same things. They wanted full-scale government intervention even less than we did. They had no more desire than we had to see the end of public service broadcasting or the unleashing of uncontrolled market-forces. Therefore, I reasoned, no matter how tough the negotiations between us might become, both sides had a vested interest in reaching a deal. I recognised that their negotiators had a constituency to satisfy as much as I had. While, in reaching any compromise, I had to satisfy both the large independents and the small programme maker independents, the BBC negotiators had both to reassure their own staff that they were not going to be thrown out of work and at the same time get terms with the independents which would enable the BBC to bring down its programme costs. The ITV companies had an even greater interest in using the independents as a means of cutting their costs. But, at the same time, the ITCA negotiators had to satisfy the competing needs of both the smaller regional ITV companies and the big five network companies. I recognised that ITV companies also might fear the emergence of the independent sector as a source of programme supply powerful enough to threaten them commercially in UK and overseas markets. I was now so convinced that we were heading for a major collision of a kind which might result in the sort of active intervention by the government which would damage all of us and British broadcasting as a whole that, without telling my colleagues, I approached Michael Grade and David McCall and asked for private meetings with each of them.

On 9 September I met McCall for lunch in his Anglia Television London headquarters overlooking Park Lane. I did not know McCall particularly well, as I had never worked for Anglia and had only met him across the table in negotiations. I put it to him that it was in the interests of both sides that we reached an agreement. I told him that I recognised that he had a constituency to satisfy, but that he must recognise that so had I. McCall agreed that both sides did, indeed, have a shared interest in coming to an agreement and a strong incentive to get on with doing so. We then moved on to explore, in general terms, what was needed in order to reach a compromise satisfactory to our two constituencies. I explained why we could not settle for business terms that were less good than the terms already on offer from Channel Four and reminded him that in dealing with the ITV companies as opposed to the BBC or Channel Four, we were dealing with commercial organisations who would be using programmes made by independents in furtherance of commercial objectives. I hinted that while we had campaigned for a 25% quota and that that was the government's target, we might be prepared to take a fairly easy-going view of how it was interpreted so long as the result was not to reduce the figure too drastically or to narrow the range of programmes which independents were allowed to make. Although I did not say so, what I had in mind was the figure – 'at least 15% ' – which we had originally come up with during the meeting of Sophie Balhetchet's Group at which The 25% Campaign had been born. At the same time I pointed out to McCall that, while we cared as much about public service broadcasting as ITV, we would have no option but to attack ITV with every means at our disposal if the ITV companies continued to be intransigent. There were already those on my side calling for just such an all-out public assault.

By the end of our lunch I thought that we understood each other's positions and I went away expecting to see evidence of greater flexibility at forthcoming meetings. The next day I had a private meeting with Whitney, reiterating that, after the optimism engendered by the IBA's policy statement at the beginning of August, it was particularly disillusioning to find that a month later the ITV companies' proposals appeared to completely ignore what the IBA had said. I got the impression that he was as worried about the lack of movement as I was.

My illusions were quickly shattered. Six days later, on 15 September, as I journeyed in on the tube to White City for a private meeting with Michael Grade similar to the one I had had with David McCall, I saw that the *Financial Times* was running a story headlined: 'ITV ultimatum to independent producers.' It quoted David Shaw, General Secretary of the ITCA, saying that negotiation of terms of trade covering all the ITV companies 'is not on, never has been on and never can be on'. The document that the companies had sent us at the beginning of the month was their final offer and independent producers would have to negotiate separate deals with each of the fifteen ITV companies. I was incredulous. I could not believe that the ITV companies would do such a stupid thing, particularly after my conversation with David McCall.

After digesting the news and checking with Sophie Balhetchet, John Woodward and Paul Styles that what ITV was reported to have done was true, I sent a note round to John Whitney at the IBA. Referring to the press stories, I said, 'It looks awfully as if the ITCA have put the fat in the fire.' If David Shaw had really said that Terms of Trade were not on, had never been on and never can be on, 'then all I can say is why did the ITCA not say this at the outset and save you, the Government and ourselves a great deal of time and frustration. However, if prevarication was the name of the game all along then I suppose that to waste six months of everyone's time must be counted a success from their point of view.' Which raised the question – what was the role of the IBA in all this, and in particular of John Whitney? We know now, as the independents did not know then, that back in January the ITV companies had agreed between themselves on precisely the strategy of prevarication which we had now seen played out. We know, too, that the two ITV officials who had been present at that meeting had appeared to acquiesce in the companies' strategy. Did Whitney know about that meeting or had his two officials simply not told him everything that had been decided? In early July Whitney had confided to his diary that, after the government had again chased up the IBA about progress on the independent quota and the IBA had in turn told the companies that it intended to issue its policy statement on independent production whether they had reached a voluntary agreement with the independents or not, the companies had been 'mightily displeased with the resolute course we are taking'.

Unfortunately Whitney's diary seems to contain no mention of what had been decided by the companies and his officials back in January. However, David Glencross, who had been present at the private meeting with the companies in January at which the policy of prevarication had been agreed, says now that as 1987 had progressed he and his colleagues in the IBA had simply come to 'assume that the companies would come to the same conclusion as we had and would come to a voluntary agreement with the independents'.[37] What seems to have happened, therefore, is that, whether Whitney knew about the agreement between the companies to prevaricate or not, he and his colleagues in the IBA had subsequently come to the conclusion that a voluntary agreement of some kind would have to be reached with the independents, and had simply assumed that the ITV companies must come to the same conclusion.

As well as writing to Whitney about the ITCA ultimatum, I wrote in a similar vein to civil servants in the Home Office, the DTI and to Professor Griffiths. Again I deplored the way in which the ITV companies appeared to have been wasting the government's time, as well as ours, all along. I ended my letter to Professor Griffiths: 'I fear that in their statement yesterday the ITV companies have shown that they have been engaged all along in a deliberate policy of prevarication on this crucial issue aimed at deferring the onset of real competition.' It now seemed to me that my private approach to McCall had been counterproductive. It appeared to have been interpreted as a sign of weakness on the independent side. If so, that impression would have to be corrected.

A few days after my letters to Professor Griffiths and the officials in the Home Office and DTI, Douglas Hurd repeated, this time in a speech to the Royal Television Society's Biennial Convention in Cambridge, that the 'possibility of legislation' over the independents' 25% quota remained 'open if it is needed'. But by then the arena had shifted to the Prime Minister's Seminar on the Future of Broadcasting, due to be held inside Number 10 on Monday 21 September.

*   *   *

I think I had been asked to attend Mrs Thatcher's 'Seminar on Broadcasting' largely because of my contact with Professor Griffiths. By the time the day of the seminar arrived I knew that about twenty people from broadcasting and related fields such as advertising and facility services had been invited to take part. These people were broadly the great and good, or at least the powerful, in broadcasting – John Birt and Michael Grade from the BBC, the chairman and deputy chairman

443

of the ITV contractors' association, the chief executive of ITN (David Nicholas) and Sir Ian Trethowan, a former Director-General of the BBC and since 1982 the chairman of Thames Television, John Whitney and Jeremy Isaacs, Michael Green of Carlton (then still no more than a large facilities company in spite of unsuccessful bids in recent years to buy into various ITV companies), and the bosses of some of the satellite and cable companies. In addition to Margaret Thatcher, there were to be three other Cabinet Ministers – the Chancellor of the Exchequer, Nigel Lawson, the Home Secretary, Douglas Hurd, together with his junior Minister responsible for broadcasting, Tim Renton, and Lord Young of the DTI. Professor Alan Peacock and a posse of officials from Number 10 were to be in attendance, along with Home Office and DTI officials, the government's Chief Scientific Officer and Bernard Ingham, Mrs Thatcher's Press Secretary. Three other independents had been asked to attend – Richard Price, largely because of his knowledge of overseas programme sales, Tim Bevan, a young film producer who had come to prominence following the success of his Channel Four-funded film *My Beautiful Laundrette*, and David Graham, who was due to give a brief introductory talk before the section of the seminar to be devoted to exploring measures 'to introduce more competition and cost consciousness' into the existing broadcasting duopoly.

Because of the way in which each of us had been invited and because we had no clear idea of how proceedings were intended to pan out, we four independents had had no real opportunity to plan how we were going to handle the day. We could do no more than agree that we would each use whatever opportunities might present themselves to push the independents' case. But, since the ITV companies had so obviously thrown down the gauntlet with their 'ultimatum', I had a strong hunch that for the independents the Prime Minister's seminar might be make or break. If we failed to make a good case in this company our cause might be harmed irreparably. At the same time, we were all too aware that the broadcasters would be likely to be gunning for us at every opportunity, eager to show up any perceived weakness in our arguments. I had been given one piece of invaluable advice by Professor Griffiths and a civil servant in the DTI about how to deal with Mrs Thatcher. No matter what you want to say, say it clearly, firmly and succinctly and then shut up. If challenged, hold your ground and don't be intimidated. If she sees what she thinks betrays doubt in your own mind she will go for you. On the other hand, she will respect you for stating your case logically and then sticking to it, even if she disagrees with you.

Unable to prepare whatever I might get a chance to say, I had thought a good deal about how to handle the day. It seemed to me that apart from the actual discussion itself, the seminar and the breaks between the sessions would provide an unrepeatable opportunity to establish some sort of contact with people who would be there whom I did not already know but who might be useful to us. The most obvious of these, apart from Mrs Thatcher herself, was the Chancellor of the Exchequer, Nigel Lawson. At the same time, the breaks during the sessions might provide an excellent opportunity to observe who among the broadcasters seemed to have the best relationships with which officials and Ministers. We were pretty sure, for instance, that the broadcasters had particularly good relations with the Home Office, but we were not so sure whether they were on quite such friendly terms with officials in the DTI, the Treasury or Downing Street. At the same time, it seemed important to me not to let anyone spot that over the months I had got to know Professor Griffiths and a couple of the civil servants in the DTI quite well. Talking in recent years to the broadcasters with whom we struggled, it is clear that they never became fully aware of how important our contact with Downing Street was for us.

We four independents were not alone in feeling nervous. At my private meetings with them in the previous couple of weeks, John Whitney, David McCall and Michael Grade had each confessed to much the same private terror as myself. On the morning itself I arrived in good time, having strolled gently in the September sunshine from the underground at Green Park, stopping to admire the ducks on the lake in St James's Park. I turned the corner into Whitehall just as the reverberations of Big Ben striking quarter to ten died away. As I walked up Downing Street after having my name checked on the policeman's list at the barrier at the entrance to the street, I became aware of an array of reporters and newsreel cameras waiting for the guests. Gone were any lingering vestiges of the idea that this was to be purely a confidential exchange of views or a learning exercise – until then I had kept pretty quiet about the fact that I had been invited in the hope of avoiding having journalists pestering for quotes or individual independents asking me to plead their particular gripes. But it was now clear that this was intended to be a news event as much as anything else. At that moment one of the broadcasting executive's chauffeur-driven cars swept past me. Looking towards the door of Number 10 I noticed that a vast stretch Rolls, belonging to Michael Green, the boss of Carlton, was already occupying a huge acreage at the top of Downing Street.

Inside the entrance hall of Number 10, friendly officials – familiar because, by then, I had been there a couple of times to visit Professor Brian Griffiths – took my printed invitation card and ushered me with others through to the Chief Whip's office. In the large light panelled room, its big sash windows overlooking St James's Park and Horse Guards Parade, were some twenty people, mostly broadcasters and civil servants, chatting expectantly. Ministers started to arrive – Tim Renton, then Lord Young and Douglas Hurd. A minute or so before ten o'clock Mrs Thatcher entered with a small clutch of officials in her wake. While she shook hands with those nearest the door, officials moved among us asking everyone to take their seats. There were three rows of green upholstered chairs in an arc facing a table in a corner close to the windows. I found a place in the centre of the second row. There was an empty space in front of me, so I was in an ideal spot from which to catch the eye of the Prime Minister if I wanted to speak. At the same time, I retained quite a good view of the other participants. Immediately behind me were grouped the combined contingents of ITV and ITN – Bill Brown, David McCall, Sir Ian Trethowan and David Nicholas. Jeremy Isaacs of Channel Four and John Whitney of the IBA were in front of me to the left and John Birt and Michael Grade representing the BBC on the end of the row behind me to the right.

Mrs Thatcher took her place at the table facing us, with Douglas Hurd and Lord Young on either side of her and a civil servant at one end taking notes. Sir Alan Peacock recalls that 'the Number 10 seminar is when I realised that Mrs T hadn't got a sense of humour. Seeing me hovering somewhere near the back of the room, she said, "Come and sit down here, Alan." I said, "I take it this is the stool of repentance, Prime Minister?" She just glared at me.'[38] At 10 a.m. sharp Mrs Thatcher started the seminar by standing to welcome everyone and outline the timetable. She explained that anyone who wished to say anything should raise their hand so that she could see it and, when called, stand so that others could see and hear, and give their name. Just as proceedings were getting under way, Nigel Lawson hurried in to take his place at the end of the table beside Lord Young. Pausing for a moment, Mrs Thatcher remarked that it was always those who had least far to come who turned up last. Later the press would make much of this remark, suggesting it was a calculated put-down which revealed the extent of the growing rift between the Prime Minister and her Chancellor, but at the time it seemed to me, and I think to most of those present, no more than a jocular comment. It certainly appeared to be taken in that spirit by Lawson, who simply got out his papers as if to signal that he was ready for business.

After Mrs Thatcher's introduction, Sir Alan Peacock, seeming nervous and reading from notes, reviewed events in the fifteen months since his committee had reported. Richard Hooper, the boss of Super Channel, followed Peacock with a witty paper which he had entitled 'The Three Ts – Television, Technology and Thatcherism'. He dealt with the delivery of additional television services. He argued that the issues to be decided were political, social, commercial and regulatory, but not technological. The technology with which to deliver as many additional services as might be wanted was already available. In the discussion that followed two things emerged immediately – Mrs Thatcher was formidably well-briefed both technologically and legally and she had a strong interest in anything likely to make a rapid impact on opening up broadcasting to the market. It also seemed evident that the ITV lobby had cooled a great deal about their previous enthusiasm for a fifth advertiser-funded service. I interpreted their apparent change of heart as an indication that, having got control of the revenue from the fourth channel, they did not now want a fifth channel which would compete with them for income. By now the strains of the band of the Household Cavalry changing the guard on Horse Guards Parade were drifting faintly in through the closed windows.

During discussion of Hooper's paper, David Nicholas of ITN seized what he saw as his chance to impress on Thatcher the excellent work that he believed that ITN was doing – as well as providing news services for ITV, it was selling its services to Super Channel and others. Sir Ian Trethowan joined in to support him. Warming to the theme, Bill Brown, the Chairman of Scottish Television, rose to remind the Prime Minister of what 'a splendid and unique' public duty the regional ITV companies were fulfilling with their output of regional programmes. Such a bout of ITV PR from behind me was altogether too much and could not, I felt, go unchallenged. I raised my hand slightly and caught Mrs Thatcher's eye. Asked to speak, I reminded her, and the Chancellor, that the ITV companies operated under a tax regime which gave them every incentive to make programmes but no incentive to operate more efficiently. Both the BBC and ITV, I reminded her, were united in actively shutting out independents. Yet independents, many of whom were based in the regions, were at least as committed to regional programmes as the ITV companies. I suggested that, if the ITV companies were really so committed to the regions, she might like to ask Mr Brown why it was that the ITV companies found that it cost them four times as much to make regional programmes as it did the BBC or the independents.

The ITV people behind me fumed darkly about the figures being open to question but dared not rise to challenge them. As I sat down Mrs Thatcher joined in. We all knew the reason for the disparity in costs, she said, it was because 'ITV is the last bastion of restrictive practices'. Later that remark, although, interestingly, it was omitted from the official record of the seminar which was circulated afterwards, became Mrs Thatcher's most widely reported contribution to the entire proceedings. Made much of in the press, it would haunt the ITV companies for the rest of the decade.

Shortly after making this comment, Mrs Thatcher called a coffee break. From the independents' point of view, I reflected, while heading for the back of the room in search of a cup of coffee, the morning seemed to be going pretty well. Then I noticed Bill Brown and the other ITV people standing with their coffee cups huddled in earnest conversation with the Home Office Minister responsible for broadcasting, Tim Renton. I moved over to hear what they were saying. They were re-running the argument about comparative costs. Bill Brown was describing, in glowing terms, new cost-saving working arrangements that his company had recently negotiated with the unions. A few moments later, unseen by Brown, Mrs Thatcher walked over with her coffee and stood behind him listening. As Bill Brown drew breath at the end of his explanation, Mrs Thatcher startled him by joining in from behind – 'Nonsense. Don't give me that, Mr Brown.' Nonplussed by this unexpected intervention, Brown took a moment to respond. But by the time he had started his reply Mrs Thatcher had turned away and was talking to someone else. I had never found Bill Brown a particularly easy person for whom to feel sympathy, but at that moment I actually found myself feeling quite sorry for him. It did not last.

After the coffee break, Charles Jonscher talked enthusiastically about the possibilities of new subscription services and then it was Michael Grade's turn to speak about the future of the existing services. Grade had prepared his three-minute speech carefully. 'I knew the vital thing was not to screw up. I told my colleagues we are not on the radar. The trick is to get on and get off without drawing her fire; to sound as if we are embracing change; to take more of a Grade tone than a mandarin tone. That wouldn't go down at all well.'[39] He succeeded admirably. The BBC, he told Thatcher, was not frightened of competition from independent producers or new channels. He saw the need for more quality programmes of all kinds. Then David Graham gave his short paper on introducing competition into the current system. He supported the Peacock Committee recommendation on auctioning off ITV franchises to the highest bidder and giving Channel Four the right to sell its own advertising, provided that there were safeguards to prevent it from going downmarket in head-to-head competition with ITV. He favoured a general reduction in regulation of programme content on all channels and urged the rapid introduction of competition in the supply programmes – giving independent producers the right to supply programmes to each of the existing channels. He advocated pushing on beyond a 25% quota to a day when broadcasters no longer both produced and transmitted their own programmes, but all operated as publisher–broadcasters like Channel Four. Above all, independents needed to be given the right to retain ownership of the intellectual property bound up in their own programmes. The current struggle between the independents and the broadcasters over access was 'the future colliding with the present'.

Looking at me, Mrs Thatcher asked if the independents were having difficulties in their negotiations with ITV. Yes, I responded. We were having difficulty getting them to negotiate properly at all. We were faced with the demand from ITV that an independent making a programme for an ITV company should hand over the entire copyright in the programme. This amounted to the ITV company seizing the independent's intellectual property and with it his most valuable asset. Britain, I said, had a golden opportunity; worldwide demand for programmes was growing, we spoke English and already enjoyed an international reputation for the quality of our programmes. If British television could get its costs under control we could supply much of that new demand. All the independents needed, I said, was 'a runway of opportunity long enough to get airborne in competition on equal terms with the BBC and ITV'. It was in this context that we needed the protection of guideline terms of trade. 'Once airborne any special protection of the independent sector can be removed and competition in programme supply can be allowed to flourish.' The current offer to the independents from the BBC and ITV, I told Mrs Thatcher, fell way short of the government's target of 25% of all programmes, while the financial terms on which we were being invited to supply even this paltry number of programmes were simply unrealistic – far short of the terms under which independents supplied programmes to Channel Four.

Douglas Hurd intervened to ask if I could give any assurance that the implementation of the 25% quota would not result in a loss of production jobs in the regions to 'fat cats' in London. I responded that already half of the turnover in the independent sector was accounted for by companies based outside

London. Experience from Channel Four showed that production had sprung up wherever there was demand. As long as the commitment to regional diversity in programmes was maintained, work would grow in the regions as the demand for independent production grew. In informal discussion with Tim Renton and Lord Young at the end of that session of the seminar I promised to get further research done on independent production in the regions and on the experience in other countries, such as the USA, where independent production thrived.

Richard Price, drawing on his knowledge as a programme distributor in the world's markets, stressed the importance of independent producers as potential makers of programmes for export, underlining the advantage they enjoyed over the BBC and ITV on account of their more flexible agreements with the talent unions. He stressed the need to build the independent sector as an industry rather than as a group of freelances who had to live from hand to mouth. Unfortunately, Tim Bevan, the independent film producer who might usefully have added to what Price said, seemed too overawed to say anything.[40]

Jeremy Isaacs had the potentially tricky task, given Mrs Thatcher's known views, of defending public service broadcasting. This he accomplished with wit and confidence. Whatever the BBC Board of Governors' views on Isaacs as a potential Director-General of the BBC, it was clear that Mrs Thatcher admired his plain speaking. Next, John Whitney, the Director-General of the IBA, had the unenviable duty of introducing a discussion on control of programme content. Just four weeks earlier, a deranged gunman had run amok in a small Berkshire town called Hungerford, killing sixteen people. The press had played up an assumed connection between violence on television and this act of madness. Not a charismatic speaker, Whitney was in trouble even before the start – crossing Whitehall on the way to the seminar he had had to leap for his life in order to avoid being run over by a cyclist. Facing the semicircles of participants but with Thatcher behind him, butting in when she felt like it, Whitney was too honest to offer some windy panacea to a near impossible problem – how to control material that could now be beamed into the country from satellites by unregulated commercial operators based in other parts of the world. The IBA itself was deeply divided about the issue of regulation in the new circumstances created by technological change and had been unable to provide Whitney with any guidance. When Whitney turned to the regulation of material from UK broadcasters he was caught between the mutually exclusive tenets of Mrs Thatcher's brand of free market capitalism and her stern moralism. In the febrile atmosphere that had gripped public debate in the weeks since Hungerford, no politician, and certainly not Mrs Thatcher, was willing to sit by patiently and listen while a senior broadcasting regulator spelled out the difficulties of the problem and the contradictions in the politicians' philosophy. What Mrs Thatcher, like any politician, wanted at that moment from those responsible for broadcasting was not the honest expression of genuine doubts, but confident pronouncements that offered readily achievable and moral-sounding solutions. As Whitney spoke, Thatcher, her expression plainly visible to his listeners, became steadily more irritated. By the time he had finished, Whitney's career in the public service, which until then had been distinguished and honourable, lay in ruins. Later one of his colleagues is reported to have asked, 'Will he get a knighthood?' To which another, who had been at the seminar, is said to have replied, 'He'll be lucky if she lets him remain a mister.' It is to Jeremy Isaacs' credit that, alone amongst the broadcasters present, he spoke up on Whitney's behalf during the seminar, telling Mrs Thatcher that he was glad that there was no way of stopping satellite broadcasters from other countries getting into people's homes, even if that did mean people in Britain might receive stuff put out by Colonel Qaddafi. He never again wanted the situation where the Soviet authorities could prevent its citizens from receiving the BBC. In the years since the Number 10 seminar, senior executives in ITV have blamed Whitney, and his performance at the seminar, for many of the misfortunes visited on ITV by the Thatcher government. That is unfair – he faced an impossible task; it also overlooks these people's own even greater responsibility for much of what happened.

With that, it was time to break off from the formal part of the seminar and to mingle with the civil servants and Cabinet Ministers over drinks in the reception room next to the state dining room of Number 10, prior to lunch. Two hours later it was all over. Leaving the dining room, Mrs Thatcher shook hands with each person and we filed down the famous staircase lined with portraits of former Prime Ministers into the lobby of Number 10 and out into Downing Street. Camera bulbs flashed and news crews cornered people for interview. On the news bulletins that night and next day in the papers, Mrs Thatcher's comment that ITV was the last bastion of restrictive practices made the headlines. Later, Nigel Lawson recalled that his memory of the day was that it 'generated neither heat nor light, merely the deafening sound of axes being ground'.[41] Mrs Thatcher's memory was of a strengthening in her resolve that there should be greater choice and competition in broadcasting, and that independent producers were a vital element in that. Richard Price concluded from a remark made to him by a Cabinet Minister after the formal part of the seminar was over, that what the independents had said had sunk in.

Notes

1. Bonner, *op. cit.*
2. IBA notes of meeting at the Home Office, Friday 5 December 1986, quoted in *ibid*.
3. Notes of a meeting held at Knighton House (the ITCA's headquarters) on 5 January 1987. Although I and my colleagues soon guessed that some such plan had been cooked up between the IBA and the ITV companies, I did not know about it for sure until I started research for this book and an ITV source provided me with a copy of the ITCA/IBA note.
4. Conversation recorded by Marmaduke Hussey in his memoirs, *Chance Governs All*, Macmillan, London 2001. To anybody wishing to understand the operation of the establishment and the way in which power is wielded in Britain, Hussey's book is required reading. The other person approached by Hurd has asked me not to reveal his name.
5. *The Monocled Mutineer* by William Allison and John Fairley, Quartet Books, London, 1978.
6. Grade, *op. cit.*
7. Isaacs, *op. cit.*
8. Hussey, *op. cit.*
9. Sir Jeremy Isaacs, interviewed by the author in November 2000.
10. Hussey, *op. cit.*
11. Bill Cotton, interviewed by the author in October 2000.
12. Minutes of meeting between the IBA, ITCA and the independent sector on Tuesday, 10 March 1987.
13. Minutes of meeting between the IBA, ITCA and the independent sector on 8 April 1987.
14. Private diary of John Whitney, entry for week ending Sunday 12 April 1987. Reading this entry in Whitney's diary raises the question of how much Glencross and Rowley had told Whitney about what had transpired at their private meeting with the companies on 5 January. As we will see, the companies had certainly not decided on any change in their tactics between 5 January and 12 April.
15. Michael Checkland's address to IPPA's Independents' Day on 31 March 1987.
16. Notes of meeting headed 'Special Meeting of the NJC(N) to discuss independent production held on Wednesday 6 May 1987 in the Council Chamber at 3 p.m.' leaked to IPPA and the IASC.
17. James Graham, interviewed by the author in October 2000.
18. Minutes of a meeting between the ITCA and IASC, 7 May 1987.

19. Rereading the minutes of these meetings today they seem almost surreal. The dry-as-dust recording of the substantive points in the debates conveys no hint of the vehemence of many of the discussions or outbreaks of bickering between members of the ITV team.

20. Paul Stykes and John Woodward, interviewed by the author in October and November 2000.

21. Sir Paul Fox, interviewed by the author in November 2000.

22. Letter dated 15 June 1987 from Michael Darlow, Head of Negotiations, IASC, to John Whitney, Director-General, IBA.

23. Letter dated 25 June 1987 from John Whitney, Director General, IBA, to Michael Darlow.

24. Note of phone call from Chris Rowley, prepared by John Woodward.

25. Memo from David Shaw, General Secretary, ITCA to ITCA Council, *General Terms of Agreement for Independent Commissions* 16 June 1987.

26. Minutes of meeting between the ITCA and the IASC, held on 2 July 1987.

27. Michael Grade, interviewed by the author in November 2000.

28. 25% of ITV original programme output was made up of 1,024 hours of Network production and 1,406 hours of Regional production. In the negotiations the ITV companies were arguing that hours supplied by independents to Channel Four should be included in assessing the achievement of the ITV Network 25% quota. An argument which the independents angrily rejected as a transparent ploy aimed at halving the number of hours independents supplied to ITV.

29. 25% of BBC original programme output – made up of 1,512 hours Network and 1,057 Regional.

30. Letter dated 7 July from Michael Darlow, Head of Negotiations, IASC, to Professor Brian Griffiths, Head of Policy Unit, 10 Downing Street.

31. Letter dated 15 July 1987 from Michael Darlow, Head of Negotiations, IASC to Professor Brian Griffiths, Head of Policy Unit, 10 Downing Street.

32. *Hansard*, 22 July 1987.

33. John Woodward, interviewed by the author in October 2000.

34. ITCA press release, 4 August 1987.

35. IASC Press Release, 6 August 1987.

36. *Broadcast*, 21 August 1987.

37. David Glencross, interviewed by the author in October 2000.

38. Professor Sir Alan Peacock, interviewed by the author in November 2000.

39. Michael Grade, interviewed by the author in November 2000.

40. Although my notes, written shortly afterwards, do not record Bevan saying anything and I do not remember him speaking during the formal sessions, I am sure that he more than made up for any silence by pressing the independents' arguments in the breaks between the sessions.

41. Lawson, *op. cit.*

13

All or Nothing – September to December 1987

Another meeting between the independents and ITV was scheduled for the day after the Prime Minister's seminar. Would the pressure brought on ITV in Downing Street and my private meetings with Whitney and David McCall have persuaded them to bend a little and reach agreement? Or would they still stick doggedly to their unacceptable position? The meeting seemed set to be a watershed.

When we assembled once again on either side of the by now tiresomely familiar table in the Independent Television Association's headquarters in Mortimer Street – this was the twelfth such bi-lateral meeting – McCall announced that the companies now awaited the independents' response to ITV's latest proposals. From the independents' point of view, of course, the ITV companies had still not put forward any meaningful proposals. All that they had put forward was a set of standard contractual clauses deliberately crafted to exclude any numbers for such things as Production Fees or percentage shares of ongoing income from further exploitation of independent producers' programmes. They had, as one of the independents' negotiators put it, excluded all the 'real meat'. After some minutes of the usual fencing and semantic hair-splitting, McCall spelled out that, as far as the ITV companies were concerned, the actual financial issues had always been beyond the scope of inter-trade association negotiations. These issues would have to be dealt with on a case-by-case basis with each of the ITV companies separately, or possibly with groups of ITV companies of a similar size. The ITV negotiators had no mandate to agree business details.

Apparently unaffected by the mauling they had got from Thatcher at the Downing Street seminar the day before and unmoved by my private conversations with McCall and Whitney, the ITV companies were, it seemed, throwing down the gauntlet and challenging the independents to walk out of the negotiations. If we did so, the companies would doubtless make a great public fuss and complain to the Home Office, Number 10 and the press, accusing the independents of

454

being unreasonable; they would claim that the ITV companies had sent the independents proposals designed as the basis on which to implement government policy and that the independents had refused to so much as discuss them. So breaking off negotiations at this point did not seem an option.

Instead we carried on talking, engaging in yet another tautologous discussion lasting all morning. Pressed by the independents, the ITV companies said that, while they could not discuss minimum Production Fees, shares of profits from programme sales and the like, they could, subject to ratification by their member companies, negotiate maxima because these, as McCall put it, 'would leave room for negotiation'. So that was it – the companies were empowered to negotiate figures so long as the independents accepted in advance that these were figures that they would rarely, if ever, receive. The companies, operating in a strong buyer's market, would not agree to any basic protective minimum fees or percentages, even if we were to agree to these being phased out once competition in the supply of programmes had been established – that is to say, after what at the Prime Minister's seminar I had called the 'runway' period was over. David Norris suggested that the ITV companies' document and the IASC's set of proposals sent to the companies in July could be combined and reworked into a set of 'Guidelines' or 'aids as to how you behave in business', thus avoiding the over-prescriptive designation 'Terms of Trade'. This should meet the criteria set out by the IBA in its August policy statement and circumnavigate the objections of both the ITV companies and the independent sector. At the end of a long morning all that had been agreed on was a patently empty form of words with which to fob off press enquiries. Both sides were now intent, it said, on 'moving ahead quickly'.

It was common knowledge throughout the industry that the government was already thinking about the contents of a new broadcasting White Paper which was likely to be published some time in 1988. For the next few weeks, while we prepared David Norris' proposed 'guidelines' document, both sides endeavoured to strengthen their own respective hands with the government and in the press. The ITV companies played up the importance of the network's regional structure, stressing to anyone who would listen how it gave a voice to each of the regions in the British Isles while bringing much needed employment. The independents, they argued, would damage it, and take work away from the regions to London. The companies also tried to paint the independents as a 'cartel', determined to fix prices for programmes. In the first of these objectives the companies seemed to have found a ready audience in the Home Office. Following Douglas Hurd's question to me during the Prime Minister's seminar about a possible loss of jobs in the regions to 'fat cats' in London, the companies played up the issue at every opportunity. We attempted to counter this with research showing that there were already a thousand independent facility and production companies outside London employing 6,000 people.

The other charge, that the independents were a cartel, seemed too far-fetched to be taken seriously. Nevertheless, we felt that we must counter it, pointing out that the ITV companies' trade association, the ITVA (it had recently changed its name from the ITCA – the Independent Television Companies Association – to the ITVA – the Independent Television Association) represented sixteen companies which operated the ITV network through a set of closed agreements. On the other hand, the IASC brought together three separate trade associations which between them represented more than 600 companies who were in fierce competition with each other for survival in a broadcast market in which there was just one real buyer – Channel Four. At the same time, we stressed the independents' greater cost efficiency, sending out research which showed that, on average, for every £100 of costs incurred by an independent, the BBC incurred £120 and a typical ITV company £170.

Four weeks later, on 19 October, following both a hurricane in Britain which had ripped up oak trees and left 300,000 homes across southern Britain without electricity and the worst fall on the Wall Street stock market since 1929 (in London 10 per cent was wiped off share values and £50 billion removed from the value of British public companies), the independents sent off their revised 'Guidelines' document to the ITVA. Our document had been carefully crafted so as to conform to the IBA's August policy statement, while at the same time borrowing words and paragraphs wherever possible from the last document put forward by the ITV companies. The actual figures, no longer expressed as minima but as guideline figures, were, in spite of our serious misgivings, now as close as realistically possible to those in the Channel Four standard Terms of Trade.[1] We had come down a long way in our demands, but were determined to give the ITV companies as little excuse as possible to reject our new proposals out of hand. We knew that if ITV did simply reject the proposals out of hand the document was likely to become a 'political weapon', in which case we would want to be able to demonstrate how unreasonable the ITV companies were being.

With the proposals went a lengthy letter, spelling out each of the places where we had made a major concession. We stressed that, in the areas where there had been ongoing disagreements between the two sides, the IBA's policy statement provided 'a sensible lead', a lead which we had endeavoured to 'interpret and follow'. We also sent a copy to the IBA. At the same time I wrote to Professor Brian Griffiths outlining the nature of the new proposals. They had, I told him, 'been compiled in a spirit of bending over backwards to try to make it possible for them [the ITV companies] to enter into serious discussion. However, I remain less than optimistic about ITV agreeing to wholehearted implementation of government policy short of very great pressure, which may well have to be backed by legislation.'[2]

We knew that ten days later all the ITV managing directors and programme controllers were due to meet over two full days in Jersey for a 'Programme Strategy Conference'. We assumed that they would discuss our new proposals during their conference. However, just before their meeting began, we heard that our paper was not even on their agenda. So I wrote urging them to consider the new proposals while they were all together. So often they had used the fact that they had to get all sixteen of their member companies to agree as an excuse for not agreeing to anything at all. All I got back was a rather shirty hand-delivered letter from David McCall saying that they had made no change to their agenda because their working party was due to consider our document on 2 November and that if our 'drafters' had 'interpreted' their views accurately 'we should have little difficulty agreeing the Guidelines'.[3]

*　　*　　*

In mid-November it was announced that, following widely rumoured rows with John Birt, Michael Grade was leaving the BBC and would succeed Jeremy Isaacs as Chief Executive of Channel Four. During the summer Isaacs had announced that, in line with his own dictum that no one on the programme side of Channel Four should stay for more than a few years, he would be standing down from the beginning of 1988. By then Isaacs had been in the job for seven years and in the five years that the Channel had been on the air he had overcome most of its initial problems. As a result of the increase in its advertising revenue, the Channel was no longer a drain on the ITV companies and the quality of its programmes had become more consistent. At the same time, some of the initial zip and excitement surrounding it had evaporated. It was time for someone else to take over. But

Michael Grade? The independents and campaigners who had fought for the Channel were horrified. The very thought of Michael Grade, the king of competitive scheduling and PR-driven glitz, the scourge of the independents, stepping into the shoes of Jeremy Isaacs filled most of them with foreboding. Grade had publicly attacked the Channel for showing Derek Jarman's frankly homoerotic film *Sebastiane* and only two months earlier had made a speech at the Royal Television Society's biennial convention in Cambridge in which he had advocated the privatisation of Channel Four. We were not alone in our reaction to Grade's appointment. When Grade went into Channel Four to meet the press after the news of his appointment had leaked out, Isaacs met him outside his office. They shook hands and Isaacs wished him well, but then added: 'I am handing on to you a sacred trust. If you screw it up, if you betray it, I'll come back and throttle you!' Others had overheard the exchange and news of what Isaacs had said went round the industry like lightning.

Yet, in spite of Grade's often bombastic manner during our meetings, negotiations with the BBC over the 25% quota had continued to make slow but steady progress. However, in November, with the announcement of Grade's appointment to Channel Four, the talks began to become bogged down. Although most of the terms of trade had been agreed, on the two lifeblood issues for independents, Production Fees and programme rights, we were still far apart. Now suddenly the BBC started to throw up new obstacles. They went back to suggesting that the level of Production Fee an independent received should be reduced if individuals with a financial interest in the production company worked on the production. This would hit not only the mass of small companies owned and run by individual programme makers or small groups of programme makers, but the many idealistic companies set up when Channel Four started, in which a range of technicians and programme makers had come together to form a company so that they could work jointly. Worse, the BBC having already announced that it intended to exclude all news and news-related current affairs programmes from the total number of hours of original programmes on which the 25% quota would be calculated, now came out with a set of very broadly drawn definitions of which types of programmes were to fall within this exclusion. These included many more categories of programmes than we had originally expected, taking in a whole lot of regional programmes and network current affairs strands, including many where independents could realistically have expected to add to the BBC's own coverage. The BBC had previously received Government approval for the idea that the quota should exclude news programmes and directly news related current affairs, but the BBC now seemed to be using government acquiescence as a means of excluding independents from an extremely wide swathe of programming. Independents had regularly supplied current affairs programmes to Channel Four and had even contributed stories to Channel Four News. We calculated that the BBC's new, wider definition of the news exclusion would result in a reduction in the government's proposed 25% quota to a mere 14%. This was below the vital 15% of total output which the original members of Sophie Balhetchet's Group had calculated was the essential minimum if we were to effect the kind of fundamental change in broadcast production which we were looking for. I wrote to the Home Office and the DTI, alerting them to this new difficulty. I closed my letter to the Assistant Under-Secretary of State in the Broadcasting Department at the Home Office with a reference to the popularly understood reasons for Grade's defection from the BBC to Channel Four: 'Michael Grade reportedly feared that John Birt was enlarging his remit at his expense. I have a sense that once the independent sector hears about the new definition [of news and current affairs] they are going to feel much the same.'[4] The Home Office responded that they did not believe that the BBC was drawing the definition of News and News-related Programming any more widely. Based on conversations they had had with the BBC, they believed that the Corporation intended 'to take a genuinely narrow view' of the definition. However, shortly after the BBC's announcement, ITV announced a similar exclusion.

The issue of how the 25% was to be calculated extended beyond the total number of hours to be commissioned from independents to the value of the programmes commissioned. The independents continued to argue that logic demanded that the 25% should be calculated on a basis of both hours and money. The 25% should mean not just 25% of the broadcasters' total hours but also 25% of the broadcasters' total programme budget (what independents termed 'the taxi-meter model'). If the 25% total applied to the number of hours alone there would be nothing to stop the broadcasters from only commissioning low-cost programmes from independents. Thus they would meet the letter of the quota, while conferring the minimum benefit on the independent sector and incurring only minimum impact on their own production operations. Conversely, the broadcasters might choose to meet the quota by commissioning just a small number of high-cost drama or entertainment programmes, leaving most of their own production unaffected. The BBC and ITV refused to be tied down on the issue, saying that it would have to be decided by the Government or, in ITV's case, the IBA.

We were becoming increasingly suspicious that the broadcasters were acting in concert, that in negotiating with one broadcaster, we were at the same time negotiating with all of them, even with Channel Four. Chance remarks made during meetings revealed that letters or papers sent by the independents to one of the broadcasters, or things said during a particular meeting, had been passed to the other broadcasters. Either the broadcasters must be passing information to each other, or someone was acting as a go-between. This suspicion became much stronger when a Channel Four executive congratulated Janet Walker on the excellence of the drafting in a document recently sent to the BBC. An alternative possibility was that officials in the Broadcasting Department of Home Office were acting as go-betweens. We had little doubt that the Home Office still regarded itself as the patron of the broadcasters or that Home Office officials remained antipathetic to the aspirations of independent producers, particularly since we had enlisted the help of the DTI. When John Woodward and I started discretely asking around about our suspicions of collusion we drew a blank. Everyone we approached denied it – but then, as Mandy Rice Davies famously remarked at the time of the Profumo scandal, they would, wouldn't they?

Today there seems little doubt that there was some measure of collusion between the broadcasters in their dealings with the independents in the autumn of 1987. However, its extent remains in doubt. David Glencross, the Director of Television at the IBA at that time, says that there was no formal collusion or agreement to share information between the broadcasters about their negotiations with the independents, but that the IBA had been in touch with Channel Four. Beyond that, Glencross says, there were 'anecdotal exchanges of news only'. David Plowright, then Chairman of Granada Television, also says that the contacts between the broadcasters had remained informal, although he did hazard a guess that if there was a go-between the most likely candidate was one of the officials in the ITV Association. What Professor Brian Griffiths (now Lord Griffiths of Fforestfach) told me, on the other hand, tends to point the finger of suspicion at officials in the Home Office. 'It had been totally captured by the broadcasters. It was a classic example of capture.' Whatever the truth of our suspicions or whoever was the real conduit between the broadcasters, John Woodward and I concluded at the time that if the broadcasters were acting in concert it would be necessary to find some means of opening a split between them.

Our distrust of the Home Office was further fuelled in November when Tim Renton, the Minister with responsibility for broadcasting, told us during a meeting that the Home Office wished to move slowly over independent access to the BBC and ITV. Only days earlier Hurd had said in yet another speech that the government still held in reserve the possibility of legislation over the independents' 25% – 'should discussions [with the broadcasters] fail to produce the right results'. However, at the same time he had gone out of his way to say how 'heartened' he was, 'by the progress which has been made in opening the airwaves to independent producers . . .' The broadcasting authorities would 'be keeping a sharp eye out for programme quality and to discourage any tendency for independent production companies to adopt some of the less acceptable working practices of their better established partners'.[5]

By late November the independents were becoming tired and increasingly demoralised. It was now a year since Hurd had made his speech in the House of Commons holding out the promise of independents gaining their 'place in the sun'. It was more than six months since Checkland had announced the 'opening of the BBC's doors to independents' at BAFTA and Whitney had summoned the ITV companies and independents to joint talks which were to have been 'all over by the summer'. But here we were in November and nothing definite had been decided. Disappointment fuels discontent more surely than never having one's hopes raised at all.

Furthermore, after six months of campaigning the IASC's resources were depleted and the energy of our negotiators was becoming exhausted. Each negotiator had not only to find the hours needed in busy careers for the negotiations themselves but also for the long hours of preparation – studying documents, attending team briefings, taking part in strategy meetings and briefing members of their own producers' organisations. The fragile unity that the producers had achieved so tortuously during the spring and summer was now in danger of breaking down. The volume of fractious comments and suggestions about better ways of conducting the negotiations, proposals for superior tactics and more successful strategies coming from those not directly involved in the negotiations was growing. Old enmities were resurfacing. Some of the larger producers who at the start of negotiations had threatened to set up a breakaway group to establish their own agreements with the broadcasters were becoming openly critical of the lack of progress, while members of AIP were becoming steadily more vocal in their resentment of what they perceived as the dominant role of IPPA. Late in November it was decided that the IASC would have to be reorganised from the beginning of 1988. I knew decisive action was needed, soon.

It was perhaps apposite that, as the independents' negotiations with the broadcasters staggered towards a crisis in late November 1987, I was rehearsing a BBC Television production (which I was directing as a freelance rather than as an independent) of a play about an industrial dispute, Galsworthy's *Strife*, with Timothy West in the role of the strike leader – the story of a titanic struggle between two sides who, through their stubbornness, destroy themselves.

It was now two months since our last meeting with ITV and more than five weeks since we had submitted our revised proposals to them. A week after sending off our proposals to ITV, I had written privately to Professor Griffiths at Number 10. I had told him that I feared that the ITV companies would continue to put off meaningful negotiations. I shared with him my suspicion that they aimed to hold off real negotiations until well into 1988, by which time they would be able to take on board whatever might be included in the forthcoming government White Paper on broadcasting.

At last, on 26 November, a letter arrived from David Shaw of the ITVA. Shaw informed me that, although the ITVA had discussed the independents' proposals more than three weeks earlier, he had only now got round to writing to me. Even now he still needed further time for consultations with his sixteen member companies. Only after that would the ITVA be in a position to come up with a definitive response. He said that the companies' considered views would be conveyed to us at a meeting scheduled for 2 December. However, he was able to give me the companies' initial reactions to our proposals. These amounted to a total rejection of each one of the material proposals that we had put forward. The ITV companies absolutely refused to accept any scale of Production Fees. The furthest they would go was the inclusion of the general statement that 'a reasonable Production Fee' would be negotiated between each ITV company and each independent producer on a production-by-production basis. They remained similarly intransigent over the issue of division of income from the onward exploitation of programmes. Not only did they refuse to stipulate any guideline percentages, they would not even set out principles that might govern the division of income between the producer and the ITV company.

This looked suspiciously like a ploy intended either to waste yet more time or to provoke us into precipitate action. I wrote back to Shaw at once, deliberately keeping my letter short and neutral. Without making any comment on the contents of his letter, I said simply that 'with the best will in the world' I could not possibly canvass the views of the three constituent organisations which made up the IASC in the four working days left before our 2 December meeting. I therefore asked to postpone the meeting. However, I said, I would be grateful if he could let me have the detailed comments of his sixteen member ITV companies in writing by the scheduled 2 December date, so that we could reschedule the meeting for before the end of December.

Rumours of ITV's rejection of the independents' proposals quickly began to spread around the industry, probably as a result of the ITV companies themselves disclosing the contents of Shaw's letter. On 1 December 1987, a couple of days after David Shaw would have received my non-committal letter, John Whitney telephoned David Norris in what Norris later described as 'something of a lather'. He had heard that the independents had postponed the next scheduled meeting with ITV. He had heard rumours that the independents 'were on the verge of declaring "foul" and walking off the pitch'. Norris had calmed what he called the 'immediate panic', telling Whitney that it was true we had received a letter from the ITVA and that it was 'fair to say that we were very unhappy with some of the statements made in that letter'.[6] However, he had stressed that we had only postponed the meeting, not cancelled it. The ITVA, Norris explained to Whitney, had said that they were still waiting for comments from their sixteen member companies. To meet before those comments had been received would be to waste everyone's time. Whitney had been reassured but, he told Norris, he would 'be horrified' if things did reach an impasse and the independents declared a complete breakdown in talks before first giving the IBA an opportunity to mediate.

On the evening when our IASC negotiating team should have been meeting the ITVA we met privately to consider the ITVA's letter. It was clear to everyone that we could not accept the ITVA's terms. But it was also obvious that many on our side now thought that we should settle for what we had already got from the BBC rather than continuing to hold out for terms on a par with those that pertained with Channel Four. They feared that by continuing to hold out, we risked encouraging the BBC to take a leaf out of the ITVA's book and go back on what they had already conceded. With Michael Grade about to take over as Chief Executive from Jeremy Isaacs, many independents feared that Channel Four was going to become much tougher over contracts. Similar views had been expressed at an IPPA Council meeting the previous evening.

I was deeply depressed and worried by these developments. Thinking back eighteen months to the meeting of Sophie Balhetchet's Group at which we had decided to go for access to the BBC and ITV, I was as convinced as ever that to settle on terms with either the BBC or ITV which were worse than those that were the norm with Channel Four would be disastrous. To do so would not only spell defeat, it risked undermining the financial viability of the whole independent production community. I did not sleep that night.

By morning I had formulated a plan but for the moment kept it to myself. As a first step I got up early and, before setting off for my rehearsals for the BBC production of *Strife*, I drafted a letter to Michael Checkland, the Director-General of the BBC. I explained that previously when 'specific major problems' had arisen in our detailed negotiations with the BBC I had been able to go informally to Michael Grade 'as a higher authority' to find a way around the problem. Now we found ourselves confronted with just such a 'specific major problem' in our negotiations with the BBC over the division of income from programme sales and levels of Production Fees. Because of Michael Grade's impending departure to Channel Four I now found myself in 'something of a vacuum' without a 'higher authority' to turn to in order to prevent 'reaching a deadlock'. Reiterating my long-held belief that the independents and the BBC had much to gain from each other, I asked him to intervene to help in finding a mutually satisfactory way of resolving the impasse.

The following day there was a dramatic new development on the ITV front. The ITV companies issued a press release announcing that the independents had postponed their scheduled meeting with ITV companies. Nevertheless, the ITV companies claimed, they had been getting on with commissioning independent programmes. Their latest unofficial survey, the press release said, revealed that 'some £42 million of independent commissions are in the pipeline. This compares with a figure of £20 million during the first half of August.' It went on to quote David Shaw as saying that, 'given the complexity of the issues . . . we have made considerable progress since talks began in May'.[7] No details of the £42 million's worth of programmes were given. The next day a *Financial Times* headline read: 'ITV says independents to get £42m commissions', and Paul Styles was quoted as saying, 'If we accept ITV guidelines there will be no independent sector in two years. We will all have gone bust.'[8]

The ITV announcement was clearly designed to convince the government that ITV was getting on with implementing government policy, while the independents were still 'being difficult' about terms of trade. The announcement seemed calculated to increase the frustration of independent producers who, earlier in the year, had had their hopes raised that by the end of the year they would be getting commissions from the BBC and ITV.

Over the months of working together John Woodward and I had developed a kind of war-game technique for testing any strategy before we actually adopted it. One of us would play the role of the IASC deploying the strategy, the other the role of our opponents in reacting to it. In this way we would play out, as in a game of chess, all the possible moves that each side might make. I had warned John Woodward that I had formulated a plan for breaking out of the impasse that the independents now found themselves in and wanted to play it out in our 'war game'. So at the end of the day on which the ITVA issued its press release, I returned from my rehearsals of *Strife* to meet John in the office. I had come to the conclusion that we must act decisively and at once. I told John that the IASC should immediately, and without further prior warning, publicly break off its negotiations with ITV. I knew it was a risky strategy that would lay the independents open to the charge that they were behaving unreasonably and that the ITV companies would complain vociferously. Nevertheless, we played through the various possible scenarios for what might happen after such an announcement. After playing through each sequence of reactions and responses, John agreed that we seemed to have nothing to lose. I believed that by unilaterally breaking off our negotiations with ITV we could seize the initiative and, following my letter to Checkland, might drive the BBC into coming to an agreement on terms acceptable to the independents. Once that had happened, ITV would have no option but to follow suit. If, on the other hand, the broadcasters ganged up together and both refused to negotiate any further, we would in effect be no worse off than we were now. The government would then be forced to intervene.

We agreed that John would call the inner circle of our IASC team to a meeting the following evening, Friday 4 December. Speed and secrecy were essential for the plan to work and for both the BBC and ITV to be thrown off-guard. We agreed, therefore, that it would be wiser not to involve all the representatives from each of the independent producers' organisations. We realised that later some of them would be very angry that they had not been consulted, but we dared not risk either a leak of what we were planning or a delay.

On the Friday evening, at the end of my day of *Strife* rehearsals, seven of us met in David Norris's office. John had told Sophie Balhetchet and Paul Styles about what we had in mind and knew that they would back us. Greg Smith, who now led the AIP/BFTPA element in the IASC, was unable to come that evening, but John had run our plan through with him and he had agreed to back it. The others John had got together were David Norris, our lawyer, Janet Walker and Charles Denton (no longer Controller of Programmes at Central Television, but a member of the council of the BFTPA and in charge of a large independent). The proposal to be discussed was that the IASC immediately break off negotiations with the ITV companies, citing the fact that there had not been a negotiating meeting since September, that ITV had rejected all our conciliatory proposals for breaking the deadlock, and that in their most recent letter the ITV companies had even gone back on some of the proposals put forward by the IBA in its statement in August. The IASC would announce publicly that further meetings with ITV could serve no purpose as the companies had demonstrated that they had no intention of conducting serious negotiations and were intent on frustrating government policy.

John and I emphasised that the risk in adopting my proposed course of action was that ITV would respond by claiming publicly that the independents were being intransigent and use what we had done as a further excuse not to negotiate. But as this was pretty much their position already it did not seem a serious risk. More serious, was that the BBC might use the IASC's action as a pretext to renege on what they had already agreed and break off discussions. But the more John and I had tested this possibility, the more irrational and self-defeating for the BBC it had seemed. It was far more likely, we reasoned, that the BBC would recognise the new development as both a threat and as an opportunity: the threat being that if they did not improve their offer the independents might break off their negotiations with them as well and go back to the government to ask it to intervene; the opportunity being that the BBC could seize the initiative and impress the government by coming to a swift agreement with the independents, thus deflecting government pressure from itself onto the ITV companies – a strategy which the BBC had deployed successfully in their dealings with the Peacock Committee. After about an hour of discussion everyone was won round to the plan. It was agreed that the IASC would make its announcement the following Tuesday. This gave the team the weekend and one working day, Monday, in which to prepare letters for delivery by courier to Mrs Thatcher,

Professor Griffiths, Lord Young and Douglas Hurd, and to post formal letters breaking off negotiations to the ITV Association and the IBA.

Over the weekend, between preparations for the shooting of my production of *Strife*, with John Woodward's help, I drafted letters to Mrs Thatcher, Professor Brian Griffiths, Douglas Hurd, Lord Young, the IBA and the ITVA. During the Monday the ITVA's comprehensive response incorporating the comments of all sixteen member ITV companies to our October proposals arrived. It simply confirmed in detail all the things that David Shaw had said in his earlier letter. It changed nothing. So while I was out at the final rehearsals for *Strife*, John Woodward, Paul Styles, Sophie Balhetchet and David Norris finalised the letters to the government and made arrangements for a press conference to be held on the Wednesday. At the small inner circle meeting on Friday it had been decided that we could not go ahead with such a momentous step without having obtained the formal consent of the full IASC steering committee. It had therefore been decided to call a meeting of the full committee at short notice. This was the last potential stumbling block. We already knew that a majority of the members of the committee would back the plan, but what if the rest raised really strong objections? Some, I was certain, would be worried by such precipitate action. On top of which, they would probably be angered by the fact that they had not been taken into our confidence earlier. As predicted, one of the AIP members and the chairman of the BFTPA expressed deep misgivings. Negotiations with the BBC, they argued, were at a delicate stage and the consequences of breaking off negotiations with the ITVA were utterly unpredictable. They wanted a postponement of action so that they could report back to their full parent bodies and get instructions. That, we explained, was simply impracticable and would jeopardise the whole plan. They were irritated still further by the story in the previous Friday's *Financial Times* about ITV's £42 million's worth of independent commissions and the quotation from Paul Styles, which they thought implied that we had already been considering breaking off negotiations. However, in the end, realising that they were in a minority, they agreed to go along with the plan.

The next morning, Tuesday, while I went into a BBC studio to start shooting the Galsworthy play about the strike – a battle between two sides who, through their stubbornness, destroy themselves – John, Sophie, David and Paul continued to put the final touches to our arrangements, preparing a complete timetable for the press which listed all the failed meetings and prevarications employed by the ITV companies since meetings had started under the aegis of the IBA back in

March, booking couriers to deliver the letters to the government early the next morning and posting the letters to the ITVA and the IBA. By the time I came out of the studio at ten o'clock that night, John was able to report that everything was in hand. In my letter to Professor Brian Griffiths I had told him that, while we might 'go through the form of giving the IBA a chance to see if they can intervene to ensure what John Whitney has called "a level playing field", I fear, on the evidence of the IBA's past record, that they will prove ineffective. The only course then would be legislation. If I am right in my conclusions then the sooner legislation is enacted the better.' I concluded: 'I and my colleagues are very aware at the moment of the extent to which we are some kind of David, deprived of much in the way of stone, fighting a Goliath in ITV. They have been using their wealth extensively to promote their cause in recent months – and we do not have anything like the resources to match them. However, you may rest assured we shall not give up – the future of television is too important to us.'[9]

The next morning, Wednesday 9 December, at eleven o'clock, just as John, Sophie and Paul were starting the press conference announcing that the IASC was breaking off negotiations with ITV, I was going down a ladder from the director's gallery on to the floor in Studio 4 at the BBC Television Centre to resume shooting *Strife*. As I reached the bottom, the floor manager, Alan, rushed up to me – I was to go straight back up to the director's gallery – 10 Downing Street was on the phone. When I got to the phone Professor Griffiths was on the line demanding to know more details of what was happening. Were we expecting press coverage? What did we expect to happen next? The Prime Minister would want to know. When Alan, the studio floor manager, wrote up the studio log at the end of the day, he wrote 'Director late on to the floor. Taking a phone call from 10 Downing Street.' So far as he knew, it was the first time that such an entry had ever been made in a drama studio log.

The following day, the ITVA told a hastily convened press conference that the independents' action was a further example of 'playing politics' with the issue – the independents were 'behaving in the manner of the worst sort of trade union leaders'. The ITV companies had previously tried to depict the independent producers as a dangerous cartel. That had not stuck and it seemed unlikely that their depiction of us trade union leaders would stick either. Unfortunately for the ITV companies, at the very moment when they were holding their press conference, the IBA was phoning John Woodward. The IBA had decided that it was time for the Authority to intervene. Would the IASC come to an urgent meeting convened by the IBA with the ITV companies? John agreed with alacrity and a meeting was arranged for breakfast time the next morning. The IBA then issued a press statement announcing that the Authority was stepping into the negotiations.

But the sweetest call of all that day was the one that John took from the BBC. They had taken the bait exactly as we had forecast they would – they were eager to reach speedy agreement. Over the next few days there was an intensive series of meetings between a small team of BBC executives and four members of the IASC team led by Sophie Balhetchet and David Norris. Just five days after the press announcement that we were pulling out of talks with ITV, the BBC and the IASC reached agreement. The BBC team went off and produced a bottle of champagne. Later that evening Janet Walker and John Woodward were due to address a meeting of AIP members. Dashing out of Broadcasting House, late for the AIP meeting with heads full of champagne and exhilaration, they searched in vain for a taxi. Running along Oxford Street they realised that they had promised the BBC that they would not mention what had happened so that the BBC could issue its own press statement on the agreement the next day. Racing into the back of the hall where the meeting was already in progress they apologised for being late and then faced a barrage of searching questions from anxious producers who wanted to know how things were progressing. It was only with great difficulty and self-control that they managed to get through the next two hours of often difficult and sometimes hostile questions without giving themselves or the agreement away.

The following day the BBC issued a 'Joint Press Release from BBC Television and the IASC' announcing 'a historic agreement' on Terms of Trade for productions made by independent producers under the aegis of the government's independent producers' policy initiative for the BBC. That evening, on the sixth floor of Television Centre, the Managing Director of BBC Television, Bill Cotton, threw a party, attended by the Director-General, Michael Checkland, for members of the IASC and senior BBC executives to celebrate the agreement. I was by then working on location on *Strife* at Ironbridge in Shropshire, but I dashed down the motorway after the day's shooting to join the party. It meant getting up at four the next morning to drive back to the location for the next day's shooting, but it did not matter.

There would be other victories for the independents in the years to come, but that evening remains the high point in the memories of most of the members of the inner circle of the IASC. Both sides had got what they wanted from the agreement and I don't think that either we or the BBC thought that we had harmed the BBC; rather the reverse, we had helped to keep the Thatcher government's hands off it. By that time, many of our small team had worked together for many years, some of us since the late 1960s. We would never be so effective again.

Notes

1. The proposed scale of Production Fees now matched those of Channel Four. It was proposed that income from the further exploitation of programmes should be 'shared equally'.
2. Letter from Michael Darlow to Professor Brian Griffiths, Head of Policy Unit, 10 Downing Street, 22 October 1987.
3. Letter from David McCall, Chairman of Council, ITVA, to Michael Darlow, IASC, 30 October 1987.
4. Letter from Michael Darlow, Head of Negotiations, IASC, to the Assistant Under Secretary of State, Home Office, 25 November 1987.
5. Speech entitled 'Images of the Future' given by the Rt. Hon. Douglas Hurd, Home Secretary, to the Television and Radio Industries Club Conference on 5 November 1987.
6. Confidential note of conversation with John Whitney, dictated on 1 December 1987 by David Norris.
7. ITV Association press release, 3 December 1987.
8. *Financial Times*, 4 December 1987.
9. Letter dated 7 December 1987 (delivered by courier on 9 December) from Michael Darlow, Head of Negotiations, IASC, to Professor Brian Griffiths, Head of Policy Unit, 10 Downing Street.

14

Conspiracies of Mandarins –
December 1987 to the fall of Mrs Thatcher

'My ministerial group agreed that we should set a target of 25 per cent of BBC and ITV programmes to be provided by independent producers. But there was a sharp division between those of us like Nigel Lawson and David Young who believed that the BBC and ITV would use every opportunity to resist this and Douglas Hurd and Willie Whitelaw who believed that they could be persuaded without legislation.'

Margaret Thatcher, *The Downing Street Years*

By 1988 television was changing. The technological changes, which for ten years pundits had been predicting would transform the whole nature of the medium and the relationship between programme makers and their audiences, were at last beginning to take effect. Not so much in the ways predicted by people like Peter Jay or the cable relay operators in the early 1980s, but in ways that real businessmen like Rupert Murdoch had understood and been investing for. Channel Four's arrival in 1982, although it had introduced additional choice, had not really affected the essential nature of television or its ecology. It and the other three terrestrial channels had remained tightly regulated, while the additional element of competition had been restricted to extending the range of programmes available and the breadth of tastes catered for, rather than opening the field to naked commercial competition for audiences or in the sale of advertising time. But in 1988 that started to change. New operators were emerging who would provide real competition, who offered new styles of service, stripped by genre, rather than the existing mixed programme channels. Channel 5, and probably Channel 6, were expected to arrive by 1992, following a new broadcasting act. At Mrs Thatcher's Downing Street seminar in September 1987 there had been expectant talk about the arrival of micro-stations which would offer highly targeted city and local community services.

In the spring of 1988 Murdoch did a deal that would get his Sky television service onto the Astra satellite beaming down advertiser-supported services, free of public service broadcasting regulation, into the closed British broadcasting market. This was relatively cheap and cheerful television. It was free of the expense and technological complications imposed on the rival BSB service which would, because of the government's earlier decision to use it to bolster the British aerospace and electronics industries, be lumbered with the costly untried, although technologically superior, D-MAC system. Murdoch got in first, stealing a march on the worthy and well-intended BSB.

The independent producers were changing too. The entrepreneurial and business rhetoric they had adopted after Thatcher's election victory in 1979 in order to salvage Channel Four from the Conservative pre-election commitment to ITV-2, was now fast becoming the reality. Until the summer of 1979 most programme makers had not been really interested in becoming businesses. After the birth of Channel Four they had set up as businesses as a means of being able to make programmes, not as a means of making money, satisfying shareholders or building assets. The fact that many of these businesses were collectives, co-operatives or companies limited by guarantee rather than by shares, had reflected the idealism that had been one of the dominant characteristics of the independent sector in Channel Four's early years. During the next five years, while they were working primarily for Channel Four, and in the process demonstrating that as small operations they could make programmes for appreciably less than the BBC or ITV, the primary motives of the vast majority of the 500 or 600 producers who supplied programmes to the Channel had remained essentially unchanged. But in the mid-1980s, as these producers had found that they could not depend on just one outlet for their work, they had had to diversify, seeking opportunities to sell their wares to other broadcasters or make films for corporate clients. In order to make their programmes many had had to raise co-production money from abroad. As a result, their attitudes and priorities had started to change. It was significant that it had been a talk by an overseas programme distributor that had been the spur to the members of Sophie Balhetchet's Group in the spring of 1986 that had prompted them to launch The 25% Campaign. The government, with its championship of business values and determination to open up broadcasting to market competition, had added impetus to this change. On top of which, every year new producers, who did not share the history or ideals of the early independents who had campaigned for the creation of Channel Four, had joined the sector. This new breed of independent producer did not view programme production through the rose-tinted spectacles of the pioneers. Many of them viewed independent programme production as a business little different from any other.

By 1988 there were as many producers outside IPPA vying to make television programmes as there were inside it. The old film producers' association had long since added a 'T', for Television, to its name, to become the BFTPA. It increasingly represented those television producers who did not fit within the membership profile of IPPA, companies in which an ITV company had a financial stake, the UK subsidiaries of foreign companies and producers whose primary interest was the cinema, commercials production or sponsored films. Of course AIP, which had spawned IPPA in the first place, had continued to exist. It had been revitalised by Channel Four's successful policy of funding low-budget British films for the cinema as well as for television. As its members had become real rather than aspirant film producers it had drawn closer to the BFTPA. The traditional British film industry had, despite yet another of its false dawns in the early 1980s after the Oscar success of *Chariots of Fire* and Colin Welland's premature boast that 'the British are coming', gone down as so often before in a welter of extravagance and bad management.

There had always been divisions between independent producers who came from different backgrounds and traditions. The decision of the small inner circle in the IASC, predominantly people from within the IPPA Council, to take all-or-nothing action by breaking off talks with ITV without telling the other members of the committee had been, in part, an acknowledgement of these divisions. Fortunately the IASC's action had been successful. If it had not, the cloak of unity that had been thrown over the independent sector would have been fatally torn away. Even so, the producers who had been excluded from the decision, primarily people from the BFTPA and AIP, were extremely angry. The tide of anger was only stemmed when Greg Smith, who was chairing the AIP/BFTPA side, threatened to resign unless the protestors withdrew a letter of censure. From the beginning of 1988 the IASC committee was reconstituted in a way intended to soothe damaged egos and give more transparent equality of representation between the different groups within it. Even so, there was no escaping the fact that underlying competitive antagonisms between different kinds of independent producers were growing.

*   *   *

473

The breakfast meeting called by the IBA in response to the IASC breaking off talks with ITV (held so early in the day because I had been due back in the BBC studio to continue shooting *Strife*) had only served to emphasise the gulf between the two sides. Chaired by Whitney, flanked by David Glencross and Chris Rowley, David Shaw and I had faced each other unsupported by either representatives of the ITV companies or of the three independent producers' trade associations. After the usual civilities Whitney had explained that he wanted to explore ways in which a scale of Production Fees and independents' shares in income from programme sales might be agreed which would cover a 'runway period of say two or three years'. Shaw responded that 'the ITVA could not agree to any numbers on a scale for exploitation or Production Fees through ITVA federal machinery'.[1] These could only be agreed by the ITV companies individually or in small groups. Whitney had pressed him to be more flexible, but Shaw had repeated that he could not move on the issue. I had responded that, in that case, there was nothing to discuss. The IASC would not be willing to have further talks with the ITVA unless there were acceptable terms of reference. Afterwards Whitney noted that it had been a difficult meeting, recording that after I left to return to shooting the Galsworthy play for the BBC, he and David Shaw had continued their discussion alone. Shaw had suggested that the ITV companies could each publish a set of guidelines on minimum Production Fees and shares in income from programme sales. Whitney had told Shaw that he thought that he could get the independents to accept this, but went on to record in his diary that if the independents refused this and still stuck to their demand for a national agreement, 'The IBA will declare its hand and announce that the independents are behaving unreasonably and in a manner calculated to lead to a breakdown in talks.'[2]

However, once it was announced that the independents had reached agreement with the BBC, the IBA's attitude, as John Woodward and I had forecast, shifted. As David Glencross confirms, 'The IBA's attitude and policy did change by an order of magnitude after the BBC's deal with the indies was announced. The companies' position was increasingly untenable. Why should they hold out when everyone else had resolved the issue?'[3] On 11 January, in what he described in his diary as 'a major test for the IBA and the companies', Whitney met the ITV companies and told them that the IBA would publish 'indicative figures on Production Fees and rights'.

While the IBA struggled to bring the two sides back to the negotiating table we continued to work at other ways of bringing pressure on ITV. I wrote to Nigel Lawson urging him to introduce fiscal measures in his next budget which would give ITV companies positive incentives to commission programmes from independents. All three independent producers' associations appeared in person before an all-party House of Commons Home Affairs Committee inquiry to stress the cost effectiveness of independent production, independents' greater success in export markets and the benefit of extending the publisher–broadcaster model beyond Channel Four into the BBC and ITV.

Almost a year earlier David Norris had persuaded us to get a legal opinion on the competition aspects of the ITV companies' network programme agreement. This was the legal agreement by which the companies bought and sold programmes from each other for transmission over the whole ITV network. Back in April we had received our QC's opinion – the ITV networking agreement 'is probably a breach of the Restrictive Practices Act'. This had seemed potential dynamite and represented a real threat to the ITV companies. If our QC was correct, the restrictive practices court might be used to force the ITV companies to buy and transmit independent producers' programmes across the ITV network on the same terms as they transmitted their own. However, like a terrorist's bomb, it might also blow up the independents who planted it. Not only might the application of competition law to the scheduling of television programmes limit still further the already restricted access to the network of smaller ITV companies such as Border, it might undermine the whole edifice of public service broadcasting. It might lead to the introduction of naked commercial competition across the whole spectrum of broadcasting and result in the banishing of serious, less popular programmes from protected slots in peak-viewing hours. It might end protection for high-cost, high-quality programmes and might make it even more difficult to persuade the ITVA to negotiate Terms of Trade with us on behalf of all the ITV companies. For these reasons I had persuaded my colleagues to sit on the information, keeping it in reserve as a weapon to use as a last resort. However, in the state of all-out war we had now reached with ITV we were ready to use it.

As a result, in mid-February 1988 we met with Lord Young and urged the DTI to refer the ITV networking agreement to the Office of Fair Trading on the grounds that it was anti-competitive. Still suspicious of how the BBC and ITV would count the number of hours which would make up the 25%, we also suggested that the OFT should act as an impartial monitor of the number of hours and value of independent programmes commissioned under the quota.

Despite our decision to try to draw in the Office of Fair Trading, we remained convinced that the only way in which either the BBC or ITV would be induced to meet the government's target of 25% in full was through legislation. As 1988 progressed the press was reporting ever more 'sweetheart deals', arrangements where the BBC and ITV companies encouraged members of staff to leave to become independents by offering them lucrative contracts to make programmes for them. Often the programmes made by these new independents were the same programmes they had made while they had been on the broadcaster's staff. In some cases these new 'independents' even hired the same studios and technicians from their former employers. To some extent, of course, this was understandable. The broadcasters could reasonably argue that if they were no longer going to make so many programmes themselves they would have to shed staff. It was only reasonable, therefore, to offer people who they were forcing out some of the work that they would in future be commissioning from outside. What alarmed us was that the broadcasters appeared to be ready to use this as a device with which to sabotage the intentions behind the 25% quota. Taken together with the broadcasters' decision to exclude all news and current affairs programmes from the total from which the 25% was calculated, the broadcasters seemed set to reduce the impact of the government's 'independent production initiative' to virtually zero. Our aim, therefore, in the period leading up to the publication of a broadcasting White Paper and eventually to a new broadcasting bill, had to be not only to persuade the government to include a clause making the 25% quota (expressed as both a percentage of original hours of output and as a percentage of the broadcasters' total programme budgets) binding, but to get it to define who qualified as an independent producer, the categories of programmes that counted towards the total and the range of permissible contractual and financial arrangements that would govern independent commissions.

Agreement to restart face-to-face negotiations between ITV and the independents was finally reached in late April after the IBA had come up with a formula on Production Fees and shares of income from programme sales similar to those already agreed with the BBC and Channel Four. The figures put forward by the IBA were still not as much of an improvement on those secured from Channel Four and the BBC as many of us had hoped, especially when account was taken of the fact that ITV companies were highly profitable commercial organisations. However, the IBA's proposed terms were as good as we were likely to get without delaying the whole process of introducing independent production into ITV still further. Even after negotiations had restarted they progressed extremely slowly and a final agreement was not reached until late in October 1988.

For much of the first half of 1988 I had been working abroad on large-scale documentary series for my own independent production company and on a BBC production of a play by David Mercer. Because I still had overall responsibility for the independents' negotiations with the government and the broadcasters, this led to some pretty strange telephone calls and faxes to government offices from airports and hotels around the world. On one occasion, responding to a tannoy announcement as I made my way across from the check-in to the departure gate at Heathrow, I took a phone call from Professor Griffiths at Number 10. Could I get a story about some new twist in negotiations into the next morning's *Times* or *Telegraph*, so that he could bring it up during a meeting of the Prime Minister's Cabinet Sub-Committee the next morning? I immediately called a correspondent I knew on *The Times*, luckily finding him at his desk, gave him a spin on the new development so that he had a story, and dashed for my plane. I heard later that the story had made the paper and that Griffiths had raised it with the Prime Minister next day. On another occasion, as my flight was called, I handed a hand-written note addressed to 10 Downing Street to the somewhat startled girl on the desk of the executive class lounge, telling her that it was vital that it was got to the addressee as quickly as possible. That, too, reached its destination. Years later, when I interviewed him for this book, Lord Griffiths[4] explained that as Head of the Number 10 Policy Unit it was important always 'to have a few campaigns going. It's great to have people saying things like they're cheaper, or to have a piece in the newspaper. It gave you ball all the time.'

By now I was having fairly frequent private meetings with Brian Griffiths at Number 10. Although Griffiths knew that I and most of my independent colleagues in the IASC were politically and philosophically opposed to Thatcherism and the free market, I found Griffiths very easy to deal with. As a result, a considerable measure of mutual trust grew up between us. Without overstating the closeness of the working relationship, we both wanted something from each other and it suited us to collaborate.

More than once at our meetings Griffiths advised me that the independents must keep pressing for the full and timely implementation of the 25% quota and not let up over the exclusion of news and current affairs from qualifying programmes. It became clear to me that Downing Street was having trouble with the Home Office over broadcasting policy and that Mrs Thatcher wanted to build up the role of the DTI in broadcasting. When I interviewed Lord Griffiths for this book I asked about the relationship between Number 10 and the Home Office over broadcasting policy and he confirmed my impression. He also confirmed that both the BBC and ITV had continued to campaign to dilute or reverse government broadcasting policies: 'The BBC and ITV were back-tracking all the time, trying to emaciate the whole policy. You had to watch them like hawks.'

My meetings with Brian Griffiths in his office in Number 10 usually took place at tea time. Alternatively, if I had something urgent, I knew that if I telephoned him on his direct line between 6.30 and 7 p.m. I was very likely to find him at his desk. During the small talk of our meetings we used frequently to discuss wider issues to do with broadcasting, particular programmes or broadcasting personalities. He once asked me who in television I particularly looked up to and admired. The first two people that came to mind were Denis Forman and Huw Wheldon. He seemed not to know about Forman but was fulsome in his praise of Wheldon, who had encouraged him when he was a young man trying to make his way in his own discipline. Always aware of our fears about what Thatcherite policies might do to the BBC and public service broadcasting in general, I tried to impress upon Griffiths the folly of damaging or dismembering the BBC, stressing the long-term damage that this would do to the government's reputation both in Britain and abroad. On one occasion I told him that for Mrs Thatcher's government to be seen by posterity as having been responsible for damaging the BBC would be the same as if it had defaced a respected British public monument. Did I make any difference? I very much doubt it. Griffiths told me later that, contrary what some people have suggested, he had never wanted to privatise the BBC. 'I had seen in the university world that it helped to have more freedom, but it had to be incremental change. The cost advantage was not the major concern. The major reason was to solve the question – how do you free up the major companies when the BBC has such an archaic culture to it?' He told me that he personally had a great regard for British broadcasting and had always seen himself as a Reithian. He said that Mrs Thatcher once said to him, 'The BBC is a great national institution,' but that it needed 'an injection from the private sector'.

Since those days Griffiths and his role in the formation of broadcasting policy has often been portrayed as some kind of malevolent hidden force. It seems to have remained something of a mystery to many senior people in the broadcasting institutions of the time. But his ideas always seemed fairly clear if you were lucky enough to get to know him. He has written since: 'The world of business is an open market place and the world in which business values are discussed should be just as open. It should be a forum of debate whose symbol is not the pulpit but the agora of ancient Greece.'[5] In his writings and in his conversations with me both at the time and since, he claimed to attach the same importance to a marketplace of ideas as to a business marketplace: 'I didn't see this [the policy of encouraging independent production] as in anyway a right-wing thing. It was not that, at the end of this, Norman Tebbit would be much happier. You could see it as a small business initiative, small people having a chance to challenge big business.'[6] I believe that in the impetus behind the Conservative government's backing for the independent producers, for Griffiths the attractions of both the commercial and the intellectual and imaginative markets weighed equally.

*　　*　　*

In the spring of 1988, shortly after agreement had been reached to restart talks with ITV, I had stepped down from my role as the IASC's Head of Negotiations. Originally I had only agreed to head the IASC negotiations for three months and I had now been doing it for a year. Both my own work and the kind of lead I could give in the negotiations with the broadcasters were suffering. Because of my absences abroad there had been misunderstandings and cross words between my long-suffering IASC colleagues back in England and me, stuck somewhere on a telephone in a different time zone. It was time to step back and let others, better qualified and with more time than me, bring the negotiations with the broadcasters to a conclusion.

By 1988 the wider threat to broadcasting from the combination of technological change and the doctrines of Thatcherism seemed to loom ever larger and more immediate. In its third term, the Thatcher government had become even more radical in its drive to dismantle or open up to unfettered market competition all the old instruments and institutions of the post-war state. British Petroleum, British Aerospace, the ports, the airports, Jaguar, British Telecom, British Gas, British Airways and even Rolls-Royce had already been privatised. British Steel, the water and electricity supply industries were due to follow. Increasingly, it appeared that ideology was of more concern to Mrs Thatcher than public benefit. Local authorities had their money cut and their powers drastically curtailed. Student grants were to be replaced with student loans. Even the National Health Service was coming under attack. In February nurses had marched on Parliament to demand better wages, yet in the budget the following month Lawson slashed taxes on the rich. The government persisted in trying to maintain a ban on the memoirs of a former MI5 man, Peter Wright, even after the book, *Spycatcher*, had become widely available in almost every English-speaking country except Britain. It was only after Mrs Thatcher's senior civil servant, Sir Robert Armstrong, had admitted to an Australian court that he had been 'economical with the truth' in his dealings with the book that the House of Lords ruled against the government and permitted the book's publication in Britain. In this climate what chance was there that public service broadcasting could be saved from the long arm of the government? Not much, most programme makers concluded gloomily.

As 1988 progressed, leading independents repeatedly sought to raise issues concerned with programme quality and to warn of the danger of the networks becoming dominated by a handful of tycoons. Rupert Murdoch was the person we had most in mind, but we also saw the coming dangers of the domination of ITV by just one or two large companies. Independents had always argued that a vigorous independent sector could be a major factor in ensuring the ongoing availability of fresh, innovative, high-quality television. It had been one of the most important motivations of the original campaigners of the 1960s. The success of Channel Four had seemed to give the argument credibility.

In a speech which Sophie Balhetchet made to the Royal Television Society in March 1988 – 'The Free Market – A Fatal Attraction?' – (things had moved on since 1979. Independents now not only went to RTS gatherings, they were invited to address them), she had warned of 'the tilt towards market forces' and – Thatcherite buzzword – 'deregulation'. Discussing proposals for deregulation in television, Balhetchet said, 'I would prefer to call it the introduction of so-called "light touch" or poor regulation. Whatever we do call it, it has not been conspicuously successful in sustaining quality. Already in the US, in Italy, we can experience a foretaste of this new world – and they are not systems which inspire confidence even amongst some of the more fervently de-regulationist of MPs.' In the face of this threat she discerned what she described as 'a growing fatalism among broadcasters'. Their reaction was to say 'more will mean worse' but then to seek means of reducing their costs in order simply to maintain their profits when the floodgates of competition opened. She continued, 'We independents have an interest in resisting that fatalism. It will not benefit us to have spent much energy in creating our companies if we can have no respect for the product we create.' Independents, Balhetchet explained, made a distinction 'between the introduction of measures which would maintain quality within the system while increasing competitiveness, and those which would merely increase competitiveness'. In the face of increased competition from new broadcasters, the established broadcasters seemed likely to seek to shed their public service obligations – namely those programmes which Richard Dunn of Thames Television, appearing before a House of Commons committee, had recently called 'the more tedious aspects of public service broadcasting'. Balhetchet argued that in the coming multi-channel world the proper response was 'strong but flexible regulatory systems' which would ensure the continuance of public service broadcasting. 'But,' she continued, 'regulation is not a popular word in the 1980s. Unbridled and unabashed greed under the guise of the efficiency-inducing free-market has been in vogue. And in our business, the prospects of Regulation have not been helped by the inept way in which her still less marketable sister, "Public Service Broadcasting", has been defended.' The defence of public service broadcasting in the current hostile climate required the industry as a whole, rather than the competing sector lobbies within it – ITV, BBC and independents – to present 'a coherent and stalwart defence' of the regulatory and structural features of British broadcasting that had ensured programme quality. 'Mrs Thatcher has said she wishes to preserve the quality of British television.' Balhetchet hoped that Mrs Thatcher would recognise that 'matching budgets to audience figures and calculating value according to cost per person' did not result in quality programmes. For Balhetchet such a system, the system that the deregulators seemed to favour, was 'the antithesis of my understanding of the term "Public Service Broadcasting" '.[7]

Just four weeks after Sophie Balhetchet's speech to the RTS, Thames Television's regular current affairs programme, *This Week*, in spite of strong pressure from the government on the IBA to delay or ban it, transmitted a specially extended and heavily promoted programme entitled *Death on the Rock*. The *This Week* team had investigated the truth behind government versions of what had happened during the shooting in Gibraltar on 6 March of three members of an IRA 'active service unit' by British security forces. The initial horrific event had been made still worse when, during the funeral of the three IRA people at Milltown Cemetery in Belfast, gunmen had opened fire on the thousands of mourners, killing three and injuring sixty-eight of them. Later, during the funeral of two of these dead mourners, members of a predominantly Republican mob, watched by television cameras, had pulled two British soldiers from their car and lynched them. Government accounts of precisely what had happened during the initial shooting of the three members of the IRA active service unit in Gibraltar, which had given rise to this whole gruesome sequence of events, did not, in the words of *This Week*'s editor, Roger Bolton, 'quite add up'. This was clearly an important story of great public interest. Bolton had been the editor of the BBC's *Panorama* who had survived an attempt to sack him in the wake of another controversial Irish story, the Carrickmore affair. He had later incurred Mrs Thatcher's wrath when, as editor of the BBC's *Nationwide*, Mrs Diana Gould had cornered Thatcher live on air with questions about inconsistencies in her defence of the sinking of the Argentine cruiser *General Belgrano* during the Falklands War. The Director of Programmes at Thames, who sanctioned the making of *Death on the Rock*, was David Elstein. He, like Bolton, had experience of the kind of trouble that programme makers could expect if they made programmes which revealed facts that were unpalatable to the government.

New witnesses to the Gibraltar shootings found by the *This Week* team gave rise to the conclusion that rather than, as the government had indicated, shooting the IRA unit in self-defence or in order to prevent the immediate detonation of a car bomb in the vicinity of a nearby parade ground, the shooting had either been the result of some kind of cock-up or of a deliberate, premeditated plan by the security forces to assassinate the two men and one woman of the IRA unit. In spite of pressure on both Thames and the IBA by the Foreign Secretary, Sir Geoffrey Howe, the programme was transmitted on 28 April 1988. Mrs Thatcher described her reaction to it as 'deeper than fury'. The programme, she told a group of Japanese journalists, amounted to 'trial by television'. The next day pro-government newspapers were vitriolic in their condemnation of the programme. Other newspapers praised it as an important piece of journalism. Later, an inquiry conducted for Thames Television by Lord Windlesham and Richard Rampton QC, found that, contrary to what Sir Geoffrey Howe had argued in his requests to the IBA to stop the programme's transmission, the programme had not prejudiced the forthcoming inquest in Gibraltar. Carmen Proetta, one of the main witnesses to the shooting who had appeared in the programme, and Roger Bolton won damages, a settlement and a full retraction from the newspapers that had attacked them for their roles in the making of the programme.

The lesson that was to be drawn by all programme makers, inside the broadcasting institutions and outside in the independent sector, from the *Death on the Rock* incident was the absolute necessity of making sure that there continued to be a robust and independent system of public service broadcasting legislation, together with broadcasters and regulators who were sufficiently strong, confident and politically independent to stand up to even the most severe pressure from government or vested interests.

That autumn saw the birth of a new lobby group called the Campaign for Quality Television. Apparently the spontaneous response of programme makers alarmed at the direction in which broadcasting policy was moving, it was largely the brainchild of David Plowright, the Chairman of Granada. Ray Fitzwalter,[8] a senior Granada current affairs producer, had already discussed establishing some sort of organisation through which programme makers could voice their concerns about the increasing pressures on the freedom to report on controversial matters, but the catalyst had been a discussion in the Granada Programme Committee about the threats to broadcasting posed by Mrs Thatcher and her government. Plowright had sounded off at his assembled senior producers: 'You ought to be bloody well ashamed of yourselves, the lot of you. You've been castrated by her. In my day Isaacs, Fox and myself, we'd have been writing to *The Times*. We'd have been demonstrating that the people in the industry, not just hacks like Chairmen, Managing Directors and Finance Directors, cared about it.'[9] The Granada producers had responded by proposing the creation of a new organisation – the Campaign for Quality Television. Plowright had promised some Granada cash and to second a Granada person to run it. But, he said, the Campaign must not be seen to be Granada. As a result the Campaign was widened to include people from other ITV companies, the BBC and the independent sector, an HQ was established in the office of an independent producer and Simon Albury, a Granada producer, was made the Campaign's organiser. The Campaign for Quality Television issued a statement saying it had been established 'to express the concern of programme makers' about shortcomings in recent government broadcasting policy. Its principal aim was to promote 'public service television, choice and quality for all viewers in the United Kingdom'.[10] The new Campaign quickly gained the support of a number of well-known names and faces. Following the example of earlier programme makers' campaigns, it took a quarter-page advert in the *Independent* and published an open letter to Mrs Thatcher expressing its concerns.

One would have expected the independent sector to give such a campaign its full-hearted backing. Yet in the event, although some individual independents and members of the IPPA Council became enthusiastic members of the Campaign, the sector gave it, at best, half-hearted support. The truth was that the Campaign for Quality Television presented the independents with a dilemma. Some independents argued, with considerable justification, that the issues being pursued by the Campaign for Quality Television were of more importance than whether the independents got their 25% and Terms of Trade, that the battle being fought by the Campaign was the one that we should throw all our effort into. But others were doubtful, realising that, in fact, the independents had still not got their 25% and might never get it unless they kept the pressure up. For all David Plowright's concern to banish the connection between Granada and the Campaign, few people with any inside knowledge of what went on in the industry were unaware of the connection. The Campaign, for all its noble aims, smacked too much of being an instrument fashioned by Granada in order to create the impression that the ITV companies were the true guardians of programme quality. As Alex Graham, the editor of the *IPPA Bulletin*, and himself an outstanding independent programme maker, wrote, 'The Campaign has too often been seen as an ITV pressure group, rather than as one embracing all broadcasters.' He dubbed it 'Save the World in Action'.[11] The suspicion remained that, although the Campaign for Quality Television's members were completely sincere in their commitment to broadcasting values which the vast majority of independents strongly supported, its real purpose was as a weapon intended to help see off government plans to introduce competition in the sale of advertising airtime, weaken the case for a highest bid auction for the ITV franchises *and* to undermine the case for the independents' 25% quota.

In many ways the Campaign for Quality Television can be interpreted as much the smartest move the ITV companies made in their campaign for self-preservation. The independents certainly did not want to attack the general sentiments which the Campaign promoted. On the other hand, whole-hearted support for the Campaign carried with it the implication of endorsement of the status quo in ITV. As a result the independents wavered, giving some rather half-hearted support but not full-hearted backing. The BBC, and most of its programme makers, also maintained a low profile. The result satisfied no one. Once again Public Service Broadcasting was left inadequately defended by the very people who should have been its most committed champions, the vast bulk of programme makers themselves.

As though to underline the urgent need for a vigorous and articulate campaign on behalf of programme makers, on 19 October 1988 the Home Secretary announced new restrictions on broadcasters reporting on terrorism in Northern Ireland. They were forbidden from broadcasting interviews which included direct statements by members of proscribed organisations, such as Sinn Fein, or their supporters. Mrs Thatcher believed that by this measure the terrorists would be deprived of 'the oxygen of publicity'. Broadcasters and programme makers were united in seeing this new restriction as censorship. Rather than pursue a policy of opposition to it, they exposed the restriction to ridicule, hiring actors to read the words of interviewees in synchronisation with the speakers' lips. The result was not to curb the inclusion in programmes of the views of Irish republicans, but to render the ban ineffective and make the government look silly. When John Major succeeded Mrs Thatcher he rescinded the ban at the first decent opportunity.

*   *   *

In November the government published its long-awaited White Paper *Broadcasting in the '90s: Competition, Choice and Quality*. For all the emphasis placed by Douglas Hurd in the Home Office press release which accompanied its publication on his faith in increased consumer choice bringing with it more quality, to most programme makers it seemed that, in the form envisaged in the White Paper, programme 'Quality' would come off a bad third to both 'Competition' and so-called 'Choice'.

Fellow cabinet minister Kenneth Baker would later say of Douglas Hurd's performance as Home Secretary that 'he is reactive rather than proactive. As Home Secretary measures were either pressed on him by the flow of events . . . or by Mrs Thatcher, who bullied him into the Broadcasting Bill'.[12] The White Paper, which was that Bill's precursor, certainly seemed to bear more of the stamp of Mrs Thatcher than of Douglas Hurd. The White Paper said it aimed to open the doors to forthcoming 'technological, international and other developments . . . so that individuals can choose for themselves from a much wider range of programmes and types of broadcasting', while at the same time overhauling the means of safeguarding 'them and their families from shoddy wares and exploitation'. The government professed to believe that 'with the right enabling framework, a more open and competitive broadcasting market can be attained without detriment to programme standards and quality'.[13] The proposals, which Hurd said were 'necessarily radical to enable broadcasters to make the most of the opportunities opened up by new technology', promised the start of a fifth national commercial television channel 'with different companies providing services at different times of day' and a sixth if 'technical studies show this to be feasible'. There was to be 'a new flexible regime' for the development of local services through cable and microwave transmission. ITV was to become Channel 3, with 'positive programming obligations but also greater freedom to match its programming to market conditions'. Crucially, these 'programming obligations' were to be limited to the provision of regional programmes, of a news service and current affairs programmes during peak hours and to offering 'a diverse programme service calculated to appeal to a variety of tastes'. The IBA was to be replaced by a licensing body, to be called the Independent Television Commission, or ITC, which would no longer be empowered to exercise detailed prior approval of the ITV schedule or of particular programmes, nor to block the takeover of ITV contractors. The ITV franchises were to run for ten years with an opportunity to apply for a further ten. Instead of the much criticised and complex secretive system of programme promises under which ITV franchises had previously been awarded, there was to be a two-stage procedure under which applicants for Channel 3 licences would first have to pass a so-called 'quality threshold' – i.e., be able to show that they could meet the not very demanding programme standards required by the White Paper – and would then take part in a straightforward, sealed-bid financial auction.

The White Paper said that Channel Four had been 'a striking success' and that its remit was to remain in force. However, the Channel was to be separated from ITV and would stand on its own feet financially, selling advertising airtime in competition to Channel 3. The precise corporate form of the Channel was left open and suggestions invited. The IBA was to advertise for operators for two additional DBS channels in addition to the three already due to be provided by BSB. The BBC was to continue its two-channel service but the night hours on one of its two networks were to be handed over to the ITC, while on the other the BBC was to be encouraged to develop subscription services. The BBC was also to be encouraged to raise finance through sponsorship. The government accepted that the licence fee would have to remain as the principal means of funding the BBC but, at the same time, it looked forward to its 'eventual replacement'. The Corporation was therefore to be encouraged not only to increase the role of subscription but to develop still further its commercial activities.

The White Paper confirmed that the independents were to get their 25% quota and advocated that this should come about 'as quickly as possible'. However, the

White Paper said nothing about who would qualify as an independent, it was mute as to how the 25% of programmes was to be measured and which programmes were to be excluded from the 25% quota.

The industry's responses to the White Paper were predictable. No one had the courage to challenge it publicly, whatever their misgivings in private. However, in a valedictory speech at the Banqueting Hall in Whitehall a fortnight after the White Paper's publication, Lord Thomson, who was due to step down as chairman of the Authority and be replaced by a businessman George Russell (who had also been named as first Chairman Designate of the new ITC), expressed his own feelings, and those of many others, about not just the White Paper but about the government's whole attitude to broadcasting policy. His more cautious colleagues in the IBA who had seen a copy of Thomson's speech in advance had tried to persuade him to tone it down, fearing that it ignored the realities of political power and gave the impression that the IBA was unwilling to change. But Thomson had refused to be deflected. As a result he delivered one of the most powerful and eloquent defences of public service broadcasting made by any senior figure in broadcasting during the Thatcher years. The government's proposed system of auctioning ITV franchises to the highest bidder, he told his audience, ran the risk of damaging 'the quality of programmes for viewers'. The government stood in danger of being seen as, in Oscar Wilde's words, 'knowing the price of everything and the value of nothing'. Broadcasting, Thomson said, was more than an economic or business activity, it was 'a creative activity' and 'perhaps the major influence on our society's capacity to be informed, to provide enhancing ways for increasing leisure, to nurture a sense of identity, to preserve and enhance the rich diversity of its cultural life'. Public service broadcasting, he concluded, was 'more likely to be damaged by zealots in Whitehall than by satellites from outer space'.[14] Unfortunately in the weeks that followed other broadcasters of equal seniority failed to speak up in support of what Thomson had said. Former colleagues of his in the IBA set about dissociating themselves from his words.

The IBA's formal response to the White Paper, master-minded by its Deputy Chairman Sir Donald Maitland, a former diplomat who had deep personal misgivings about the government's policy, went no further than to question whether, in the form in which they had been put forward, the proposals would really deliver the results that the government desired. The IBA then went on to advocate that in deciding the outcome of the competitive tendering process for franchises, weight should be placed on both the quality of the applicants' money and the quality of their programmes. At the press conference at which the IBA unveiled its response, Ray Snoddy of the *Financial Times* asked George Russell what his reaction would be if the government decided to ignore the IBA's advice and limit the franchise-tendering process to acceptance of the highest money bid. To most people's surprise Russell replied, 'If I am faced with a straight envelope tender, which I cannot believe in, if that actually happens, I do not think I could continue the job.'

Suddenly, and unexpectedly, this was fighting talk and amounted to an ultimatum. The next day what Russell had said was well-received in the press. The Home Office hastily called a press briefing at which Tim Renton went out of his way to banish the impression of a breach between the IBA and the government. The IBA's submission was praised as 'ingenious' and 'extremely constructive'. The Conservative chairman of the Home Affairs Committee also went out of his way to praise Russell, saying that he had done 'a first class job' and had 'cracked' the problem of how to conduct the tendering for new ITV franchises.

What Russell had belatedly done was to demonstrate that the government could be made to hesitate if only the opposition was both forceful and resolute. Would others learn from his example?

*   *   *

By this time, the spring of 1989, the signs that an era was ending were unmistakable, in the outside world even more clearly than in Britain. In the Soviet Union Mikhail Gorbachev had declared a policy of *glasnost* – openness – and *perestroika* – restructuring. Massive demonstrations and strikes in East Germany, Poland, Hungary and Czechoslovakia which, at the start of the year, had been put down with customary brutality, were succeeded a few months later by elections in which candidates other than Communists were allowed to stand. Everyone waited to see if Soviet troops would intervene as they had in Hungary in 1956 and Czechoslovakia in 1968, but they did not. The 'Brezhnev Doctrine' was clearly dead. The countries of eastern Europe were in future to be allowed to determine their own political systems. In May, the Hungarian government began to dismantle that hated physical embodiment of the Iron Curtain, the security fence which ran along the border between Hungary and Austria. Refugees from East Germany and other Communist countries started to stream in their thousands into the West. However, it soon became clear that this was not to be the start of a new era of peace and personal freedom everywhere. In China, on 3–4 June a mass demonstration started by students and young people who demanded greater democratic freedom was put down by force; 2,000 of the demonstrators in Tiananmen Square in Beijing were mowed down by troops, police and tanks. Meanwhile, in February Iran's Islamic fundamentalist leader Ayatollah Khomeini had declared a *fatwa* calling for the death of the British writer Salman Rushdie for his book *The Satanic Verses*. In America former CIA man George Bush had replaced Ronald Reagan as President, while in Britain Margaret Thatcher privatised the ten regional water boards and imposed the Poll Tax on the protesting Scots. Splits inside her government became steadily more apparent.

By June 1989 Sophie Balhetchet had chaired IPPA for three years and felt that she had had enough. I was elected to succeed her. It was exactly three years since the launch of The 25% Campaign. At its first meeting with me as its chairman the IPPA Council set two major goals to be achieved in the next two years – to see the 25% quota enshrined in legislation and to bring the independent producers together into one organisation. By creating one unified body in place of the three existing mainstream independent producers' organisations – AIP, the BFTPA and IPPA – we believed that the whole independent sector would become more effective in fighting its own corner. To my mind the only uncertainty was whether one amalgamated association, representing a bigger and more diverse community of producers, could really meet the needs and aspirations of both the institutional and film-based producers of the BFTPA and AIP, and of the smaller, free-spirited programme makers who still made up the core of IPPA's membership. On balance, I believed that the benefits of creating one more powerful association were likely to outweigh the disadvantages.

As we have seen, IPPA was already changing. There were increasing tensions within it because of the different interests of the mass of small producers and of the few, but growing, number in larger companies, between the independents who were happy to remain small and those whose aim was to grow as businesses. A new report commissioned jointly by IPPA, the BFTPA, the BBC, ITV and Channel Four into manpower and employment patterns in the television indus- try showed that now, seven years after the start of Channel Four, 50% of independent production companies turned over £500,000 or less per year, that still only 40% of that income came from making programmes for television, that 50% of independent producers still employed five or fewer people, while only 4% employed fifty or more. Broadcasting remained a predominantly white and male field; less than 1 per cent of the people who worked in it came from the ethnic minorities. Most of the industry's training was still provided by the BBC and ITV.

Unknown to me, on the day of the IPPA Council meeting Mrs Thatcher was writing to tell me that the government had now made a firm decision to include the 25% independent quota as a statutory requirement in the forthcoming Broadcasting Bill. In her letter she confirmed that she understood and shared the independents' concern lest the exclusion of 'news and news-related' programmes should be used 'to obfuscate progress towards the 25% target . . . we are determined to see that the initiative is implemented, both as to the letter and as to the spirit'. The government was consulting over issuing 'clear guidelines as to what is original television output, when a producer is independent . . . what sort of programmes should be counted . . . and how co-productions should be dealt with'. She closed with the words: 'I entirely share your concern that this initiative should be a success.'[15]

That might look like game, set and match, but experience had taught us that the broadcasters and Home Office civil servants would not abandon their attempts to block, water down or evade the independents' quota.

In the meantime grim portents of what the future had in store for broadcasting as a whole continued to multiply. At the Edinburgh International Television Festival that year, Rupert Murdoch, whose Sky Television had recently started broadcasting on its medium-powered satellite, gave the prestigious opening McTaggart Lecture. Was Murdoch a worthy successor to James McTaggart himself, or to Jeremy Isaacs, John Mortimer, Jonathan Miller, Denis Forman or Phillip Whitehead? Or just a sign of the times? Some old festival hands shook their heads and asked: 'With Janet Street-Porter as Festival Chair rather than people of the calibre of Gus Macdonald or Melvyn Bragg, what do you expect?' The Festival's organisers would no doubt have retorted that they were simply facing reality.

Murdoch's lecture seemed to contain all his bottled-up frustration and fury with British broadcasting, dating back to his IBA-blocked attempt to take control of LWT twenty years earlier. He dismissed all the programme obligations placed on ITV – quality, diversity and regional programmes – as 'subordinating commerce to so-called public service'. Such obligations, Murdoch said, were part of a paternalistic and anti-democratic conspiracy foisted on the public by the British establishment. The market, Murdoch believed, was the best safeguard of democracy and plurality. He started, he said, from 'a simple principle: in every area of economic activity in which competition is attainable, it is to be much preferred to monopoly. The reasons are set forth in every elementary economics textbook, but the argument is best proved by experience rather than theory . . . Why should television be exempt from these laws of supply and demand, any more than newspapers, journals, magazines or books? I can see no reason, which is why I believe that a largely market-led television system, with viewers choosing from a wide variety of channels financed in various ways, will produce a television system better than today's.' He broadened his attack to include the BBC and Channel Four: 'Much of what is claimed to be quality television here is no more than the parading of the prejudices and interests of the like-minded people who currently control British television.' British television is 'obsessed by class, dominated by anti-commercial attitudes and with a tendency to hark back to the past'. In contrast to this, he told his audience, American television was wonderful. PBS in America 'had helped to enrich the American TV scene'. In saying this, of course, Murdoch (no doubt deliberately) overlooked the fact that PBS was perennially strapped for cash and in recent years had repeatedly been found by expert US academic commissions to provide an inadequate service. That it kept going as well as it did was largely due to it being able to acquire high-quality British material at minimum cost. Murdoch then reeled off what he saw as the glories of American cable channels, ignoring completely their considerable cost to those who viewed them. Next he attacked what he characterised as the 'less than independent, neutered journalism' of British broadcasting, suggesting that British television was unlikely ever to reveal a Watergate. This was rich indeed, considering that earlier that year it was Thames that had broadcast *Death on the Rock* and it was Murdoch's *Sunday Times*, whose editor Andrew Neil was also chairman of Sky Television (Neil sat next to Murdoch throughout the speech), which had been unsuccessfully hounding Thames ever since. The audience, which included many of British television's great and good, sat mute throughout. Afterwards, although there was much private muttering, barely a dog barked.

By that autumn rumblings of coming political change were growing louder. On 26 October Nigel Lawson, the Chancellor of the Exchequer, resigned, following mounting disagreement with Mrs Thatcher and her refusal to get rid of her financial adviser Sir Alan Walters. Having presided over a boom timed to coincide with the 1987 general election, Lawson resigned as Britain started to enter an equally spectacular bust. In the wake of the resignation, a-little-known backbench MP, Sir Anthony Meyer, stood against Mrs Thatcher in a leadership election and to everyone's surprise took the votes of 60 Conservative MPs. Now Mrs Thatcher really did look vulnerable.

Lawson's resignation triggered a major cabinet reshuffle. David Waddington, an unwavering Thatcher loyalist, became Home Secretary and Douglas Hurd was moved to the Foreign Office. Waddington, although he had had a spell as a junior minister in the Home Office, had had little to do with broadcasting policy. However, there was little doubt about his attitude to public service broadcasting and to many of the things which programme makers in all sections of the industry held dear. While he had been Chief Whip some members of the Campaign for Quality Television had tried to talk to him about the forthcoming Broadcasting Bill during a dinner organised by Granada at the Conservative Party Conference in Blackpool. After only five minutes he had dismissed all that they had to say with the words, 'Look, you people, you have no influence in the Conservative Party, you have no support in the country. This Bill is going through.'[16] There was some relief, therefore, that the reshuffle brought David Mellor back to the Home Office as Waddington's number two. It would be Mellor's task to pilot the Broadcasting Bill through Parliament.

The Broadcasting Bill was finally published on 7 December 1989. It contained many of the things which the independents had lobbied for over the previous three and half years. Channel Four was to keep its remit but, while continuing to be financially underpinned by a minimum income guarantee based on total ITV advertising revenue, be cut loose from the ITV companies to sell its own advertising airtime. It was to become a public, non-profit-making corporation. The BBC was to be left largely untouched until the next Charter renewal, due in 1996. The emphasis on moving to subscription funding, which had been a feature of both the Peacock Report and the White Paper, was absent. However, the proposals covering ITV were even worse than we had feared. The ITV franchises and new the fifth channel contract were to be decided by a highest money bid auction. The quality provision, dubbed by David Mellor 'a Bechers Brook', over which George Russell had taken such a firm stand, was reduced to just two brief references. The independents' 25% quota was duly included in the Bill, but was stated simply as a percentage of hours broadcast rather than as a combination of both hours and money. As in the White Paper, there was no indication of which programmes would qualify for inclusion within the 25% total, nothing about programme ownership, nor any indication of who would qualify as an independent. These issues were to be left to the discretion of the Secretary of State through the laying of a statutory instrument before Parliament.

That evening a small group met in the IPPA office to discuss what to put into our press release in reaction to the Bill. As we sat scratching our collective heads, trying to avoid the boringly anodyne, Georgina Henry, the media correspondent of the *Guardian*, who had phoned to ask for our reaction to a statement just released by the ITV companies. She said that they had announced that they intended to fight against just two of the Bill's main provisions – the blind-bid cash auction for new Channel 3 (ITV) franchises and the 25% independent quota. We scratched our heads no longer. Sophie Balhetchet was first off the mark, rapidly drafting a very tough statement saying that the ITV companies' announcement confirmed what we had been saying all along – the ITV companies had never had any intention of granting the independents their 25%. I told Georgina that ITV now had 'a real fight on their hands'. We were now 'really angry'.

However, we knew that we could not afford to underestimate the ITV companies. Despite what Mrs Thatcher had said, ITV still had formidable allies in the Conservative Party and supporters among the opposition. As a result of the cabinet reshuffle we faced a new ministerial team at the Home Office. Although Mellor was a known quantity, we still suspected that he was more inclined to be dazzled by the show-business big names associated with ITV than impressed by the more down-at-heel, earnest image of the independents. What David Waddington's attitude would be was unclear. But with a new ministerial team it seemed likely that detailed legislative guidelines on the matters that were vital to the independents would be even more firmly in the hands of the Home Office civil servants.

Next day I wrote a Christmas letter to all 700 members of IPPA. I told them that because of the ITV companies reaction to the Bill the season of peace 'will be a bit late this year! . . . Make no mistake, the ITV companies have been expending a great deal of money and energy lobbying government, wining and dining MPs and influencing journalists and opinion formers. We cannot match them for money. But what we lack in cash we can make up in numbers. I ask you therefore, as a matter of urgency, to write or talk to your MP, your Councillor, your Trade Union, your Chamber of Commerce, your radio station, your newspaper, your friends in consumer groups and among journalists.' I said they should remind people that in recent years it was independents rather than the broadcasters that had been behind the programmes which had been winning a disproportionate number of the international awards for British television. 'Point out where the real concern with quality and ability to deliver good programmes rests. Explain the independent's proven ability to bring not only efficiency to programme making, but to create employment and generate investment in all regions of the country, not just London.' I concluded, 'We are now back in a fight.'[17]

The renewed mood of confrontation between ITV and the independents was quickly registered by the press – 'Rapprochement will have to wait' was a typical broadsheet comment. Numerous individual independents across the country began to lobby MPs, journalists and trade union branches. A week after our angry press announcement, David Mellor warned the ITV companies that if they tried to 'back out of the independent 25% quota' the government might increase it. That evening I wrote in my diary: 'Round One to us!'

*   *   *

Some months earlier John Woodward had received a bulky, but mysterious document in a brown envelope. There was no covering letter and no indication of who had sent it (although John had said that he could hazard a guess, he had not been prepared to[18]). Upon examination we had found that the document, which ran to sixty pages of dense figures, was a confidential management copy of the BBC management's current five-year plan. John and I had poured over it, studying the on-going expenditure projections for wages and materials, and the detailed provisions for future capital expenditure on items such as equipment and studios, for exceptional items such as redundancies or early retirement. However, we had been unable to see how to make the most effective immediate use of the information. So we had locked the document away without saying anything about it until a day came when it would be useful.

On the morning of 21 December, Professor Griffiths telephoned out of the blue: 'How would you react if the BBC were given until 1994 to reach the 25% target?' I replied that I would be disappointed, although I recognised that they might have difficulty in reaching the target. Did I think that it was actually possible for the BBC to reach the 25% target by 1991–2? Yes, I think so. The real problem is that the BBC management hasn't made up its mind to take the difficult decisions necessary to reach the target. Did I have any evidence for that? Yes! I deduced it from having seen BBC management's current five-year plan.

I then told Griffiths about the mysterious confidential document that had turned up in the brown paper envelope and the figures and projections that it contained. Could I fax it over to him immediately, as he wanted to put the information in front of the Prime Minister in ten minutes' time? I explained that, as the document was some sixty pages long and densely packed with detailed figures, it would take a bit longer than that to extract the relevant material from it. I promised to phone him back in half an hour's time.

In fact I did not have the document. Since the reorganisation of the IASC John had become the Deputy Director of IPPA, and so he no longer worked in the same building as me. He was working from IPPA's offices half a mile away in Soho. The brown envelope and the document were locked in an IPPA safe. Desperately I phoned John. Luckily I found him at his desk. I told him to get over to my office with the document as fast as he could.

He arrived, breathless, about ten minutes later and we set to work extracting the evidence. The five-year plan took no account in its projections of staff numbers and wages for a reduction in programme production commensurate with independent producers supplying 25% of the BBC's programmes. The BBC's planners had clearly largely discounted this as a possibility. As far as we could see, the estimates for capital expenditure on such items as studios and new equipment forecast no reduction. Twenty minutes later, while John parcelled the precious document up and ordered a motorbike to take it round to Number 10, I phoned Griffiths and gave him the figures. He questioned me on the details and then concluded that the evidence did indeed seem to point to the conclusion about the BBC's intentions which we had drawn. Next Griffiths asked me a series of questions about the effect of the news exclusion. I explained that the BBC's five-year plan specifically referred to taking 600 hours of independent productions by 1991–2, not the 2,300 hours which we calculated represented 25% of the BBC's total output if news programmes were included, or of the 1,600 hours that the BBC's own figures showed if news and news-related current affairs programmes were excluded. Griffiths thanked us for our help, apologised for asking for the information at such 'ludicrously short notice', promised to keep his source for the BBC's internal figures confidential and to return the document to us. He wished us a Merry Christmas and rang off. Describing what had happened in my diary afterwards, for comment I wrote the one word 'Wow!'

Later that day John, Paul Styles and I discussed the meaning of what had happened. It seemed likely that the statutory instrument which would extend the 25% quota to the BBC was being drafted on that day, and that the BBC probably expected to meet the Prime Minister or her officials that day or the next, as part of a concerted lobbying campaign to get the implementation of the 25% quota postponed until at least 1994 – by which time another election would have taken place and there might no longer be a Conservative government. Styles said that at a BBC party two nights earlier a senior BBC resources manager he knew had more or less admitted in his cups that this was indeed what the BBC was playing for. Later Professor Griffiths told me that as a result of what had happened we would get our 25%. In his memoirs Marmaduke Hussey says of Michael Checkland's attempts at that time to cut BBC costs and reduce over-staffing: 'I was beginning to suspect he wasn't making much progress because he really didn't want to. The 1 per cent savings per annum that he had been achieving were just not enough, but try as I might I couldn't push him further. He flinched from the difficult decisions.' Elsewhere Hussey says that one of his colleagues used to refer to Checkland as ' "the staff representative", with the implication that he saw his job as being to protect the status quo for BBC employees'.[19]

*   *   *

The year 1989 ended with what amounted to the final collapse of the Soviet bloc and the end of the Cold War. On Christmas Eve a Romanian friend rang us from Poland and said that he had just been on the phone to relatives in Bucharest who had told him that Romania's hated Ceausescu regime, after two days of civil war, had been overthrown. The next day, Christmas Day, brought the news that Ceausescu and his wife had been summarily tried and shot. On 29 December, Václav Havel became President of Czechoslovakia. Meanwhile, in Britain, ambulance crews who had been taking industrial action over their pay and working conditions since the previous September showed no signs of backing down in the face of government pressure and increasing hardship.

With the coming of the New Year the independents started to concentrate all their efforts on the Broadcasting Bill. They aimed to secure amendments to it during its passage through Parliament which would close each of the loopholes that might allow the broadcasters to prevent them from reaping the full benefits of the 25% quota – the way in which hours of programmes were counted, the definition of who qualified as an independent and programme ownership. Late in January I met Richard Dunn, the Managing Director of Thames Television and Chairman of the ITVA, privately over lunch in a Soho restaurant. He assured me that the ITV companies would not now push their opposition to the independents'

25% quota during the passage of the Broadcasting Bill through Parliament. With that out of the way, we moved on to discuss areas where the independents and ITV might co-operate in the future.

In spite of this helpful development and some equally useful contacts between me and Paul Fox who, after Milne's dismissal and Bill Cotton's retirement, had returned to the BBC to be Managing Director, Television (Fox always seemed somehow more relaxed and at home in the BBC than in ITV), we independents remained convinced that we could no longer leave anything to chance or promises of goodwill. After all that had happened we needed things guaranteed in legislation. Accordingly, we went to work on each of the issues where we were vulnerable. I had discovered that a friend of mine, the writer Robin Chapman, and his wife, knew David Waddington, the new Home Secretary. (In the mid-1970s I had directed a BBC *Play for Today* of Robin's which had satirised the political antics of Vanessa Redgrave and the Trotskyite members of the actors' trade union Equity.) Robin agreed to write to Waddington personally, explaining that, for as long as the broadcasters had the right to own programmes made for them by independents, the independents would remain 'on a commercial hiding to nothing' and be unable to grow into a truly competitive force in programme supply. Robin explained to Waddington that Anti-Trust legislation in the USA prevented broadcasters there from both making and broadcasting programmes because it was recognised that without such a measure broadcasters retained 'a dangerous monopoly of power over a vital creative and cultural commodity'.

At the same time we persuaded a former vice-chairman of the Conservative Party, Emma Nicholson, who had recently appeared in a series made by my company and was to be a member of the House of Commons Committee which would scrutinise the Broadcasting Bill, to move amendments to the Bill for us.

When the time came and Emma Nicholson put forward the first of our amendments, aimed at ensuring that the 25% quota was measured in money as well as hours, David Mellor responded by telling her that the government fully accepted the aim of her amendment and would introduce an amendment of its own, worded in a way which he believed would produce the desired effect more efficiently. Next a Labour member Robin Corbett moved an amendment which sought to limit the holding that any broadcaster could have in an independent producer. Again Mellor quickly intervened to assure Corbett that the government intended to introduce an order that would 'stop any company owned, or partly owned by a Channel 3 licensee from being counted as an independent for the purposes of the quota'. However, when Emma Nicholson moved an amendment on programme ownership, Mellor told her that he could not think why the independents would accept terms with broadcasters which they did not like and that, in any case, the issue of programme ownership was outside the remit of the Home Office. It was a matter that should be taken up with the DTI.

John Woodward, who had been in Parliament to listen to the debate, knew that Emma Nicholson had succeeded in getting all the Conservative MPs on the committee to agree in advance to support her programme ownership amendment. However, late in the day the ITV companies had got wind of what we were trying to achieve and had mounted an effective lobby of Mellor and persuaded him to reject Emma Nicholson's amendment. Watching the debate, Woodward had got the impression that Mellor had been 'very inadequately briefed' on the programme ownership issue. John Woodward, Paul Styles and I had suspected for some time that letters we had written to Mellor about the ownership issue were going unnoticed, or perhaps were not reaching his desk at all. It seemed preposterous, but our suspicions were now strengthened. We agreed that I should contact Professor Griffiths and outline our concerns, while the IASC would contact Nicholas Ridley who, following the cabinet reshuffle, had succeeded Lord Young at the DTI.

When I talked to Professor Griffiths on the phone the next evening, he doubted whether programme ownership could be tackled through the Bill but advised me to talk to a Mr Smith in the DTI. Neither I nor any of my colleagues had ever heard of this 'Mr Smith', but Griffiths gave me to understand that he was very influential and had already been active behind the scenes on the independents' behalf. Griffiths gave me 'Mr Smith's' direct number at the DTI and advised me to call him. He would, he said, be expecting my call and knew all about me and our efforts. Accordingly, fifteen minutes later, I phoned 'Mr Smith' who, although it was a Friday evening, immediately answered his own phone. He said, rather ominously I thought, 'I know all about you. We have been keeping an eye on you.' He also knew all about our attempted amendment to the Broadcasting Bill and told me that he thought that the amendment was in line with new copyright legislation which had recently come into force. There was therefore no practical reason why what we were attempting could not be achieved. He said that he would call me on Monday, after he had 'talked to one or two colleagues'. That evening in my diary I commented, 'The ways of government are very strange.' That weekend the South African government released Nelson Mandela from prison after twenty-seven years. It was almost exactly thirty years since I had been in a crowd of thousands in Trafalgar Square protesting outside South Africa House over the Sharpville Massacre. Against such events the struggles of the independent sector suddenly looked very puny.

When 'Mr Smith' called me the following week he had depressing news. His colleagues did not think that independents' rights to ownership of their own programmes could be brought within the scope of the recently enacted copyright legislation, nor did they think that the government would be willing to amend this legislation so as to accommodate the independents' needs so soon after it had come into force. However, he said he would convene a meeting between representatives of the IASC, the DTI, the Home Office and the Office of Fair Trading.

In the meantime we tried other means of bringing influence to bear. Iain Bruce managed, through an intermediary, to arrange a private lunch with David Mellor. He discovered that Mellor was becoming steadily more disillusioned at the stance of the ITV companies. More tellingly, Mellor had told Iain that he had not received any of our letters on programme ownership. If true, and it still seemed hard to believe, this would tend to confirm our suspicion that civil servants somewhere in the Broadcasting Department of the Home Office were still actively working against us, even preventing some of our letters and other communications from reaching the Minister. It would also explain why Mellor had seemed so ill-briefed on the programme ownership issue during the debate on Emma Nicholson's amendment. Mellor asked Iain to get a paper to him on programme ownership as soon as possible. He also provided him with a means of making contact with him without going through his civil servants.

When the meeting arranged by 'Mr Smith' between the DTI, the Home Office, the Office of Fair Trading and ourselves took place some three weeks later, it became clear that the surest way of achieving our aims over programme ownership remained via an amendment to the Broadcasting Bill, backed by an early and clear commitment from the appropriate government minister. It seemed that all the broadcasters, including Channel Four, had been lobbying hard to prevent the independents being given ownership of their own programmes. 'Mr Smith' advised me to continue to pursue the issue through Brian Griffiths at Number 10 and simultaneously with Nicholas Ridley at the DTI and David Waddington at the Home Office. As one of 'Mr Smith's' DTI colleagues put it afterwards, Mellor and his Home Office officials were 'possibly too close' to the broadcasters.

In mid-March, on the last day of the Commons Committee stage of the Broadcasting Bill, the government introduced a new amendment giving the Office of Fair Trading the task of monitoring the BBC's achievement of the 25% quota. A similar duty was placed on the ITC (the authority replacing the IBA) in respect of ITV. The Government's action appeared to be a result of Brian Griffiths' dramatic intervention immediately before Christmas. The same government amendment gave the OFT the task of reporting on the continuation of a fair and competitive market in programme supply. While this might go some way towards meeting the independents' concerns over ITV companies taking shares in independents and over programme ownership, it fell far short of giving independents the guarantees they needed.

The next day a new facet of the labyrinthine and devious ways in which the Home Office had of getting its own way against opponents inside government and out, began to emerge. Chris Rowley from the IBA called me. He said that he wanted 'a chat about the matter of independents owning their own programmes'. I was immediately suspicious and asked him if, by any chance, he had been 'talked to' recently by the Home Office. Oh no, he assured me. I was unconvinced, but said nothing, curious to see what would come next. He then launched into a lengthy and circumlocuitous speech which amounted, in sum, to suggesting that very little needed changing in the trading guidelines already negotiated between the IASC and the ITV companies. I pointed out that unless the issue of programme ownership was tackled while legislation was still under consideration, the balance of power in the negotiation of programme contracts between the broadcasters and independents would remain unfairly weighted in favour of the broadcasters. This, of course, cut no ice and he rang off.

It would hardly have defeated an Inspector Clouseau to detect that the IBA and the Home Office Broadcasting Department were up to something, presumably to pass off the previous day's announcement of the OFT's role in reporting on the 'continuation of a fair and competitive market in programme supply' as having dealt with the programme rights issue. John Woodward and I assumed that since Lady Littler, who had replaced John Whitney as Director General of the IBA, had, before she joined the IBA, headed the Home Office's Broadcasting Department, the Home Office and the IBA were working more hand-in-glove than ever. John rang the Home Office civil servant who had been at the joint meeting with the DTI and the OFT to try to find out what was going on. The official view, John was told, was that the programme ownership issue 'could probably be put off' until the Home Office presented its statutory instrument defining which programmes would qualify towards fulfilment of the 25% quota. Home Office officials, John was told, were 'not convinced' that the measures we had been suggesting would be effective.

This was all beginning to seem a bit too horribly neat. So next I called 'Mr Smith' on his direct line. He told me, in confidence, that the letter I had written to Mrs Thatcher on programme ownership had now been passed over by Downing Street to the Home Office for an answer. Once the Home Office had worked out its response, he said, the letter would pass to the DTI for its input and then it would go back to Downing Street, where Professor Griffiths would get a chance to influence matters. The Home Office, 'Mr Smith' told me, believed that there were two options – 'The Big Stick', by which they meant putting retention of ownership to programmes by independents into the legislation either in the Bill itself or through the statutory instrument, or what they called 'the more flexible approach'. This would entail renegotiation of the Trading Guidelines between the ITV companies and the independents. I told him that legislation would be the more effective. Next, I called Brian Griffiths at Number 10 and told him that I detected all the signs of a concerted effort by the IBA and the Home Office to kick the ownership issue far enough into the long grass to allow them time first to deflect and then to defeat it. He said that he too didn't trust 'the blighters'. He said that he would 'keep his eye on it'.

The battle over programme rights continued through the ensuing months with meetings with Ministers and civil servants, private discussions with Professor Griffiths and 'Mr Smith' and contacts between Robin Chapman and David Waddington. The issue was eventually passed to the OFT, where the independents, led and guided by David Norris and John Woodward, appeared a number of times to give evidence and face gruelling and meticulous cross-examination. It was not resolved until 1993 when the OFT ruled that independents must have equal rights with the ITV companies to offer programmes to the ITV Network Centre and that ITV must demonstrate even-handedness as between programmes offered by independents and ITV companies. ITV's ability to acquire rights in programmes made by independents was to be limited to the UK broadcasting rights only. Only after that could John Woodward, who was by then the Chief Executive of the combined IPPA and BFTPA trade association PACT, say that the independents had won a considerable victory. But that is to run ahead of our story.

* * *

In June 1990, three months after the start of the brouhaha over programme rights, during the course of a meeting at the IBA we caught sight of a letter from a senior Home Office official to the Secretary of the BBC and his opposite number in the IBA. Although we could not study it properly, the letter appeared to show that Home Office civil servants had been working hand-in-glove with the IBA and the BBC over a whole range of issues vital to the independent sector for at least a year. A few minutes after spotting the letter John Woodward left the room to photocopy some documents that were under discussion. As soon as we got back from the meeting to the IPPA office Paul Styles said to John, 'Well, where is it?' Smiling, John produced a photocopy of the Home Office official's letter from his briefcase. A reading of the full letter revealed that the Broadcasting Department of the Home Office had already reached an agreement with the IBA and the BBC on almost every element of the secondary legislation which was to be included in the Statutory Instrument to be issued after the Broadcasting Bill had completed its passage through Parliament – the definition of an independent producer and the wording for the operation of the news exclusion. This, it appeared, had been done without so much as a mention by the Home Office to the independents apart from one brief and inconclusive discussion during a meeting on other topics a year earlier. All our representations on the news exclusion and categories of qualifying programmes appeared to have been ignored completely. As Sophie Balhetchet commented, we seemed all along to have been dogged by 'a bizarre conspiracy of Mandarins'.

Talking to Professor Griffiths at Number 10 a few days later, I told him that 'the only construction my colleagues and I can put on this sorry epic (the affair of the news exclusion) is that the BBC and a group of Home Office officials, together with some of their colleagues in the IBA, have colluded in fobbing us off while selling the government the news exclusion on the grounds of practicality', even though they knew all along that the effect of the exclusion would be to take 'the guts out of the 25% initiative'.[20] I added that I suspected a similar degree of connivance over other issues affecting the 25% quota. At about the same time David Graham wrote a letter to Brian Griffiths saying that he believed that the whole independent production initiative was 'slipping away'. Having worked ourselves to near exhaustion trying to win a 25% independent quota while at the same time holding down full-time jobs running companies or making pro-grammes, was it at the last all going to prove to be for nothing, or at least for a great deal less than we had been led to expect?

It seemed that we were not alone in thinking that the Broadcasting Bill was not going to produce the results that had been expected. Over the next few days I heard reports from three separate sources high in government that Mrs Thatcher herself had become so disenchanted with David Mellor and the Home Office's handling of the Broadcasting Bill and, as she saw it, its watering down, that she had flown into a great rage and threatened to scrap the whole Bill.[21] She had, I was told, only been talked out of this by senior colleagues who had pointed out to her that it would be completely impractical to introduce another Bill and get it through Parliament before the next election.

*   *   *

As the Broadcasting Bill continued to work its way slowly through Parliament during the spring and summer of 1990 there were issues other than the essentially parochial matter of programme rights, the definition of who would qualify as an independent producer and the news exclusion that concerned independents. First, there was the unresolved question of the Fifth Channel which, although it was in the Broadcasting Bill, seemed to have no defined purpose nor role beyond the fact that, because it was to be funded by advertising, it would offer competition to ITV. Writing about the Fifth Channel in the *Guardian* in May 1990, Phillip Whitehead pointed out that 'No terrestrial channel has ever been the product of a double negative – the hostility of both the government and the advertising lobby to ITV's profits . . . We know the negative reasons why C5 has been invented, but what are the positive ones? . . . Strengthening all the national terrestrial channels will seem a bigger priority than crudely deconstructing them as in recent years.'[22] He asked that 'at the very least' the new fifth channel 'increase the common store of good broadcasting in the UK'. In the same series of *Guardian* articles Sophie Balhetchet, Phil Redmond, the former Controller of BBC-2 Brian Wenham, and I all raised similar concerns over the purpose of Channel 5. But, although the Broadcasting Bill continued to edge closer to becoming law, the government remained mute.

More important still to independents, as to other programme makers, were the futures of the BBC and ITV. The independent sector continued to urge a strengthening in the quality provisions which were to govern the outcome of the franchise bidding process and an increase in the powers of the ITC over the Channel 3 schedule. IPPA came up with a slogan to encapsulate its attitude: 'Re-regulation not deregulation!' In mid-April 1990, David Mellor put more flesh on the government's statement of a year earlier about the 'exceptional circumstances' under which the ITC could award a Channel 3 franchise to an applicant who had not entered the highest money bid in the auction. The circumstances were to include instances where the quality of programmes being offered was 'exceptionally' higher than those being offered by the highest bidder. John Woodward formed the impression from his meetings with Mellor at this time that 'Mellor personally did not want to associate himself with the cultural philistinism of the Tories.' There is no doubt either that the Campaign for Quality Television had made a significant impression on Mellor – much greater than anything achieved by the ITV bosses themselves who, whatever they said, were suspected of special pleading. Barry Cox of LWT summed up the impact of the Campaign for Quality Television and its ability to enlist stars such as Michael Palin, Rowan Atkinson and Terry Jones to go along to meetings with Mellor. The Campaign, he believed, had 'a very important symbolic value. I think Mellor was a star fucker and loved all that stuff.' Mellor himself has since said that they were 'very influential' and 'provided the pressure that gave me the ability to tell my elders and betters that changes had to be made, because these people were in a position to cause the government severe embarrassment.'[23] Nevertheless, it must be doubted that Mellor would have been allowed to introduce such a potentially significant change to the Channel 3 highest bid auction process without Mrs Thatcher's express agreement. But even with this change the Broadcasting Bill seemed certain to drive ITV downmarket into an even more single-minded pursuit of ratings and profits, and would almost certainly drag BBC-1 downmarket with it.

Another issue of particular concern to the independent sector was the future character of Channel Four. Since Michael Grade had replaced Jeremy Isaacs as Chief Executive, relations between Channel Four and the independents had become noticeably more edgy. Although Grade had not driven Channel Four downmarket in the way that Jeremy Isaacs and most independents had feared, he had instituted a number of changes which had materially altered the creative and constructive relationship between the channel and the independents. In addition to giving more prominence in the schedule to audience-pulling, notably American, on-going series, he had reorganised the programme-commissioning structure in a way that created an additional layer of management bureaucracy between the individual commissioning editor and the programme maker. He had also encouraged commissioning editors to take a much more interventionist role during the actual production of programmes. Some had started to dictate which directors or senior technicians an independent producer could engage to work on a programme. Commissioning editors now spent more time in the cutting room dictating how programmes were put together. In some ways, of course, this was more efficient and made for more consistent quality control of programmes. Although the threat of privatisation had been lifted, thanks largely to Michael Grade who had, with his Chairman Richard Attenborough, put up a brilliant, unwavering and ultimately successful public fight against privatisation, Channel Four was now perceptively more 'flash' and less quirky, more stranded and less surprising; more concerned with big names and less inclined to take risks. We feared that once it had to depend entirely on the sale of its own advertising these tendencies would grow.

Asked by Anthony Smith during a public interview at the National Film Theatre to describe his vision for Channel Four, Michael Grade had appeared flummoxed. Increased professionalism, which seemed to be Grade's main goal at the channel, while worthwhile, was no substitute for idealism or vision. For the many programme makers, both inside the National Film Theatre and beyond it, who were hanging on his words at that moment it had been a glum moment. Worse, the Director-General of the BBC, Michael Checkland, still seemed unable to come up with anything more inspiring as a vision for the BBC than that it was 'a billion pound business'. Older independent producers, rooted in programme making, their sector born out of campaigning for greater freedom and improved opportunities to make challenging programmes and give expression to ideas beyond the safe broadcasting consensus, increasingly asked, as Sophie Balhetchet had asked in her Royal Television Society speech in 1988, what would be the point of being an independent if one could have no respect for the programmes that one could make?

In the summer of 1990 a new and even more fundamental worry confronted the whole industry when Lord Wyatt of Weeford (formerly Woodrow Wyatt, Labour MP, who by that time had travelled so far to the right of the Conservative Party that he seemed almost off the scale) tabled an amendment to the Broadcasting Bill in the House of Lords which, if passed, would have the effect of forcing each individual programme to satisfy rigid rules of absolutely strict political balance. The amendment would mean that it would no longer be sufficient to offer a fair, impartial and balanced account of an issue, nor to satisfy the requirements of balance over a run of programmes or a reasonable period of time. As a result, programme makers would be condemned to following a strict 'on one hand, on the other' routine throughout each programme, no matter what the subject or how inappropriate such an approach might be. The Wyatt amendment would render current affairs programme making anodyne, if not impossible. Not only would programmes such as *World in Action* disappear, most current affairs output would be rendered impotent. 112 Conservative MPs had signed an Early Day Motion backing the Wyatt proposals and Mrs Thatcher, apparently without informing either the Home Secretary David Waddington or David Mellor, was reported to be giving Wyatt and the amendment's sponsors her support.

Late in June Michael Grade rang me up. Pointing out that the independents enjoyed 'a fair political wind' with the government, he asked if the independents could 'use your influence' against the Wyatt amendment. I agreed at once. In a curious way the independents, because they were disliked at that moment by both the BBC and ITV with almost equal fervour, were in a good position to act as go-betweens to bring them together to fight the amendment. At its next meeting the IPPA Council voted to put up £10,000 towards a fighting fund.

In September, Mellor told the Royal Television Society that it was going to be necessary to make concessions to Lord Wyatt and his supporters. Following this, and renewed efforts by Grade and Channel Four's Director of Programmes, Liz Forgan, Mellor agreed to meet a deputation. Although senior people I had approached in the BBC had at first seemed reluctant for fear of offending the government, John Birt for the BBC, Michael Grade from Channel Four, Steve Morrison and Stuart Prebble of Granada, the Editor of ITN, representatives of the two satellite broadcasters Sky and BSB and I all trooped into Mellor's office. Our aim was to demonstrate to the government the united strength of feeling across the industry. Mellor candidly admitted that he was under pressure from the right wing of the Conservative Party and some members of the government. He said that he was going 'to have to go some way towards meeting them'. He showed us, in confidence, a government amendment which he and his officials had drafted, claiming that this gave the amendment's supporters 'the shadow but not the substance'. When he said this my instinctive alarm bells rang. John Birt now took up the running for the broadcasters, arguing cogently and persuasively, spelling out the difficulties and dangers of accepting the Wyatt amendment, drawing Mellor's attention to the rules that already existed. It was an extremely effective performance and clearly got through to Mellor. By the time we left Mellor's office we all felt somewhat reassured. I had known John Birt since my time at Granada in the 1960s, but until that afternoon I had never really understood what people saw in him, beyond a rather well-honed ability to ingratiate himself with those in positions of influence.

When the Broadcasting Bill was debated again in the Commons late in October, Mellor went out of his way to stress the strength of the impartiality provisions that already existed. It was Parliament's right, and had been so for forty years, to insist on due impartiality on matters of 'current political or industrial controversy'. However, he said, 'it is not for us to usurp the function of the regulators and state exactly what the detailed rules should be'.[24] The Wyatt amendment was defeated. Once more it had been shown that resolute and united action by broadcasting's leaders did work.

Outside events now removed the spotlight from the Broadcasting Bill. That autumn, while the recession gathered pace, John Major, who had succeeded Lawson as Chancellor of the Exchequer, took Sterling into the European Exchange Rate Mechanism at the dangerously high rate of 2.95 Deutschmarks to the pound and cut 1 per cent off the interest rate. In the Middle East, following Saddam Hussein's invasion of Kuwait in August, the threat of war deepened. In late October a Russian peace mission returned from Baghdad empty handed. Meanwhile Mrs Thatcher, who had already humiliated Sir Geoffrey Howe, the loyal Chancellor of her early years in government, by shunting him off into the meaningless post of Deputy Prime Minister, made an outspoken attack on the European Union. Thatcher's outburst was widely read as an open affront to Howe's known pro-European views.

On 1 November, Howe, until then seemingly the most docile, placid and loyal of Thatcher's senior Ministers, decided he had taken enough, and resigned. Denis Healey had once memorably remarked that being attacked by Howe was like being savaged by a dead sheep. It was therefore an even bigger sensation, not least in the Conservative Party, when twelve days later Howe used his resignation speech in the Commons to deliver a devastating attack on Mrs Thatcher. In his careful, measured tones, he spelled out the 'tragic conflict of loyalties' with which he had wrestled for so long – loyalty to the Prime Minister, maintained over many years, and loyalty to his party and his country. In resigning now, he said, he had chosen loyalty to his party and his country. The time had come, he concluded, 'for others to consider their own response to the tragic conflict of loyalties with which I have myself wrestled for too long'.[25]

A Conservative Party leadership election was certain to follow and the next day Michael Heseltine announced that he would stand against Mrs Thatcher. A week later, having failed to win an outright majority in the first round of the Conservative leadership election, Mrs Thatcher resigned. On 1 November (the day on which Sir Geoffrey Howe delivered his devastating resignation speech in the House of Commons), unremarked and unremembered, the Broadcasting Bill finally received the Royal Assent, becoming in the process the 1990 Broadcasting Act.

Notes

1. From a confidential note made by the author of a meeting held at the IBA at 9 a.m. on 11 December 1987.
2. Entry in John Whitney's dairy for 10 December 1987.
3. David Glencross, interviewed by the author in October 2000.
4. Professor Brian Griffiths was created Lord Griffiths of Fforestfach in 1991.
5. *The Business of Values* by Lord Griffiths of Fforestfach, The Hansen-Wassener Memorial Lecture, Service Master Corporation, USA, 1996.
6. Lord Griffiths of Fforestfach, interviewed by the author in October 2000.
7. Speech given by Sophie Balhetchet to the Royal Television Society on 29 March 1988.
8. Fitzwalter had been the young researcher who fifteen years earlier had unearthed the material on which Granada's controversial programme about the corrupt architect John Poulson had been based.
9. Interview with David Plowright, quoted in Bonner, *op. cit.*
10. Statement of aims of *The Campaign for Quality Television*, 1988.
11. *Save the World in Action* by Alex Graham, *IPPA Bulletin*, Winter 1989–90.
12. *The Turbulent Years: My Life in Politics* by Kenneth Baker, Faber & Faber Ltd, London, 1993.
13. *Broadcasting in the '90s: Competition, Choice and Quality*, Cmnd. 517, HMSO, London, 1988.
14. Lord Thomson of Monifieth, *Robert Fraser Lecture*, 24 November 1988.
15. Letter from The Prime Minister to Michael Darlow, 10 July 1989.
16. Told by Ray Fitzwalter, one of the founders of the Campaign for Quality Television and a member of the delegation, to the author in December 2000.
17. Letter from Chairman of IPPA to all members, 11 December 1989.
18. I had assumed that John Woodward knew who had sent the mysterious package but had thought it wiser not to say. However, when I interviewed him for this book and asked who the sender was he said that he genuinely did not know.
19. Hussey, *op. cit.*
20. Quoted from a confidential letter from the author to Professor Brian Griffiths, Head of the Prime Minister's Policy Unit, 27 July 1990, written for the purpose of confirming what had been said during our conversation.

21. It may be worth noting that David Mellor does not get so much as a mention in Lady Thatcher's memoirs, although she gives quite extensive coverage to broadcasting and the Broadcasting Bill.

22. Phillip Whitehead, *On to a Fifth Dimension*, *Guardian*, 14 May 1990.

23. Barry Cox and David Mellor, interviewed in *Independent Television in Britain, Vol. 5*.

24. *Hansard*, 25 October 1990.

25. *Hansard*, 13 November 1990.

15

Victories and Self-inflicted Defeats –
November 1990 to October 1991

In the immediate aftermath of Mrs Thatcher's fall we independents could take satisfaction from the fact that our 25% quota was now safely enshrined in legislation, even though it was still likely that in practice it would amount to a lot less than a genuine 25% of all original programmes transmitted by the BBC and ITV. Even on some of the gloomier forecasts it still looked as if we would get something like the 15% of all original programming that the members of Sophie Balhetchet's Group had calculated three and a half years earlier was the minimum necessary to effect the kind of change which we had sought in broadcasting and to secure the future of the independent sector. The independents could also hope, that while they might now weaken the grip of the old broadcasting establishment to which they had so objected in the 1960s and 1970s, with Mrs Thatcher gone the best of public service broadcasting might at the same time survive. The independents could take comfort from the fact that at the end of Mrs Thatcher's reign the worst of the trade union restrictive practices in television were out, or on the way out, and that their own sector still enjoyed good industrial relations.

The announcement of Mrs Thatcher's resignation came through on the morning of Thursday 22 November during a meeting of a joint working party to discuss the amalgamation of the independent producers' trade associations. Someone came in and announced what had happened. The discussion stopped and we all started to watch television. There were smiles everywhere. Afterwards, walking back to my own production company office across the district of Soho where many of the film and small television production offices were still concentrated, everyone suddenly seemed cheerful. As I noted in my diary that evening: 'It is not only the end of an era, it feels like the end of some awful dictatorial enemy occupation. As a public moment it feels like D-Day in 1944, the end of the war in 1945 and the collapse of Macmillan's government in 1963.'

This may seem an odd reaction considering that when Mrs Thatcher came to power in 1979 there had been no independent television production sector to speak of, that the creation of Channel Four and the rise of independent producers to their current comparative affluence and security had all come about under her premiership. Surely, the independents had much to thank her for and should have been apprehensive rather than relieved at her going? Of course, my perception of independents' reactions may be coloured by my own political sympathies. But this on its own is not an adequate explanation. Others also noted the pleasure and relief among independents. To be baffled by the independents' reaction to Mrs Thatcher's departure is not only to overlook the continued, although in many cases reduced, personal allegiance of most independents to the political left. It is also to forget that when Mrs Thatcher came to power in 1979, most of the programme makers who had been campaigning for a fourth channel and against ITV-2 had assumed that Thatcher would be a short-lived phenomenon. In 1979 they had thought in terms of a salvage operation as an alternative to capitulation to the commercial television barons' apparently unstoppable drive to get ITV-2. That Channel Four had been salvaged from what had looked like the wreck, and that it turned out as well as it had, was largely thanks to Willie Whitelaw, to the skilful translation of long-nurtured ideas and ideals into new language acceptable to the new government by seasoned campaigners like Anthony Smith, Phillip Whitehead, Iain Bruce and David Elstein, to the energy and new-learned political skills of new recruits to the campaigners' ranks such as Sophie Balhetchet and Michael Jackson and, finally, to Jeremy Isaacs for his unflinching commitment to challenging programmes and new ideas.

Until the Falklands War the opinion polls had shown Mrs Thatcher as one of the most unpopular Prime Ministers ever. Until halfway through 1982 the independent producers had assumed, like others, that after four or five years Mrs Thatcher and her extreme brand of market Conservatism would simply go away. Thanks to the adventurism of General Galtieri and the death wish of the Labour Party, that had not happened. As a result from 1983 onwards the independents and campaigners like myself had had to accept a new reality. A little like a Frenchman or a Dutchman in 1942, we had had to accept that the Second Front was going to be a long time coming. Under the continued 'occupation' the independent sector started to change, not least because after 1982 new people who had not taken part in the earlier campaigns had started to come into it. The creed of competition, market forces and wealth creation became more widely accepted. However, that did not mean that even those who were content to live with 'the philosophy of the market' accepted the moral and political intolerance associated with the Thatcherite wing of the Conservative Party, particularly as it affected broadcasting. Norman Tebbit's attempts to bully the BBC over its coverage of controversial issues, the attacks on Kate Adie for her reporting of the Libya bombing, the Conservatives' courting of Mrs Whitehouse and her followers, the allegations of bias promoted against plays like *Tumbledown* or docu-dramas such as *The Monocled Mutineer*, were not acceptable to most programme makers whatever their political or economic views. No thoughtful programme maker could be happy about the politically manufactured fusses over programmes which raised important questions about law enforcement and the operation of the judicial system in the face of terrorism, like *Who Bombed Birmingham?* or *Death on the Rock*, nor about the whole 'oxygen of publicity' episode and the ludicrous ban on the direct broadcasting of statements by supporters of the IRA and Sinn Fein which had led to the idiocy of actors being engaged to read interviewees' words for them in sync. No one who cared about the health of British broadcasting and its independence from the state could be happy about the blatant packing of broadcasting authorities and boards with people such as Marmaduke Hussey or Lord Chalfont (Chalfont had replaced Sir Donald Maitland as Deputy Chairman of the IBA in 1989). Programme makers were generally liberal-minded even when they were not lefties. Mrs Thatcher and her acolytes were seen as threatening the impartiality of factual broadcasting and, from her second term onwards, the open-mindedness and creative breadth of the entire output. To most of us, therefore, her going seemed to herald a 'liberation'.

*   *   *

Producers expected wholesale changes to the industry once the new Broadcasting Act came into effect in 1993. That the news of Mrs Thatcher's resignation came through during a discussion about the creation of a single trade association to represent all producers could be seen as symptomatic of the likely scale of those changes. An older organisation, representing the smaller, more radical producers, the IFVPA, had already been wound up. They had been an important element in the coalition of campaigners which had emerged in the 1960s and developed into the independent producers' movement of the 1970s. But, as Margaret Dickinson puts it in her study of oppositional film making, *Rogue Reels*, by the end of the 1980s the main thrust of the advice being given to these politically and culturally motivated small companies and co-operatives was 'to cultivate a more businesslike approach' and to seek 'more training in finance, management and marketing'. Such advice, coupled with the thrust of government cultural funding policies, which tended to value the arts according to their potential to bring in commercial revenue, had made it almost inevitable that sooner or later these film and video makers would be driven to seek survival inside the institutional mainstream.

Early in 1991 Jonathan Davis undertook an analysis of programme producers and production trends in the UK. He concluded that, while Channel Four had from the beginning encouraged a large number of small independent producers, the major independents who were now starting to make programmes for the BBC and ITV were 'a new breed'. While Davis found that some 'have been set up by the broadcasters' former employees to handle a single commission. Others are specialising in producing low-cost, high volume programming which the 25% access quota is doing a great deal to encourage . . . To a degree, the independent sector is changing from being driven by the desire to make programmes to being driven by the desire to survive. The alternatives faced are to expand the company or to adopt a virtual hibernation mode, awakening to make the single commission. As profit margins become slimmer, forced down by hard-pressed broadcasters and the fierceness of the competition between so many companies, the ability to fund growth internally or to attract outside investment is probably declining.' Davis forecast that between 1991 and 1995 the market for independent producers 'new originated general (i.e., not news) programming' was likely to grow by almost 50% in terms of hours but by only half that in value.[1] So while it appeared that the independents had got much of what they had campaigned for, they had not got it all. They now faced a production landscape very different from the landscape from which they had set out.

IPPA still represented the overwhelming majority of independent producers, but the IPPA Council that had been elected in the summer before Mrs Thatcher's resignation was very different in composition from those that had preceded it. IPPA was now ten years old and many of the longest serving and most experienced members of its Council, those who had been involved in the early struggles and had helped to establish the Association's underlying principles, had withdrawn to concentrate on their own work. People with wide experience and track records as doughty fighters had gone. Barely a third of its twenty members had been members of IPPA's Council or of IPPA's various working bodies for more than a year or two. With a greatly increased and scattered membership, those who got elected, if they were not those who were already on the Council, tended to be those who already had high-profile professional reputations in the industry. In practice this had increasingly come to mean those who ran the bigger and more successful companies or made high-profile programmes. That, in turn, increasingly meant the narrow segment of programme suppliers described by Jonathan Davis as 'a new breed'. Among older hands there was a growing suspicion that in standing for the Council some of these people had more of an eye on advancing the fortunes of their own companies than on protecting the interests of the majority of IPPA's members, the small producers.

By the time John Major was elected by the Conservative Party as its leader and Prime Minister, those leading the independent sector were already squaring up to the problem of what would be in the all-important Statutory Instrument which the Home Secretary was to issue on detailed implementation of the 25% independent production quota. Although the IASC had tried to get definitions of 'qualifying programmes' and 'independent productions' included in the Act itself, we had failed. Mellor had announced that these matters were to be left to an Order in Council. This meant that these rules could be changed or updated as circumstances demanded. With the 'news exclusion' already accepted in principle and the matter of programme ownership at least on the way to partial resolution as a result of the reference to the Office of Fair Trading, the outstanding issues really boiled down to just one – who, for the purposes of the quota, was to be counted as an independent producer. This was a crucial issue for the future character of the independent sector.

Arguments over who should qualify as an independent producer for the purposes of the 25% quota went back to 1987. The ITV companies had argued that they should be allowed to hold shares in any independent production company from which they commissioned a programme. The independents had rejected this – there was no point in the independents gaining the right to make productions for the BBC and ITV if in return the broadcasters were to be allowed to gain control over them. The 25% Campaign had been started because the independents wanted to become genuinely 'independent' rather than having to remain solely 'dependent' on Channel Four. Even if the ITV companies were prevented from holding 50% or more of the shares in an independent, even if they were restricted to owning only a small minority share, once they were allowed to own any shares in an independent, they were likely to acquire a measure of influence over it which would in practice far outweigh whatever percentage of the shares they did own. Almost any shareholding seemed likely to amount to control. As both a vital customer and probably the wealthiest investor, the ITV company would almost certainly call the tune in a company. Allowing broadcasters to invest in independent production companies was also likely to distort competition in programme supply – the government's stated reason for introducing the independent quota in the first place. Any ITV company which had an investment in an independent would be much more inclined to take programmes from that company than from one in which it had no investment. Allowing broadcasters to take shares in independent producers would give a further sharp twist to the tendencies in the independent sector spelled out by Jonathan Davis.

During the lead up to the publication of the Broadcasting Bill in December 1989, the ITV companies had returned to pressing their case for being permitted to invest in target independent producers. They had argued that, in order to become a viable third force in programme supply, the independent production sector was in need of outside investment. Who better to supply that investment than ITV companies? They already had expertise in the industry and could provide the producers with continuity of work. It was a seductive argument. It was true that, denied the ownership of their own programmes by Channel Four, independent producers had had no asset base with which to attract outside investment. It was a familiar lament among independents that they could never plan for the future or invest properly in new projects or equipment because they never knew where their next commission was coming from. Quite a lot of Conservative MPs had been won over by the ITV companies' arguments.

Shortly before the issue had been debated during the Committee Stage of the Broadcasting Bill, in February 1990, David Mellor had put it to us that if we wanted the government to limit the stake that a broadcaster was allowed to take in an independent producer whose programmes were to count towards the 25% independent quota, then equity demanded that independents accept a corresponding limit on the percentage of shares an independent producer could hold in a broadcaster. We assumed, almost certainly correctly, that this proposition was the product of special pleading by the ITV companies or another piece of devious quasi-legal argument by the independents' opponents among the mandarins of the IBA and the Home Office Broadcasting Department. We had responded by pointing out to Mellor that, whereas in most instances the effect of allowing an independent to hold a few shares in a broadcaster would be negligible, the effect of allowing a broadcaster even a small holding in an independent was likely, because of the influence that the broadcaster would be able to exert, to be out of all proportion to the size of that holding. Many individual producers, particularly those who had once worked for an ITV company, already owned a few shares in ITV companies. A number of ITV companies had encouraged employees to acquire shares in the company which employed them. ITV shares had generally done well over the years and had represented a prudent investment. Other programme makers, among them independent campaigners, had sometimes bought a few shares in ITV companies in order to be able to go to shareholders meetings and ask awkward questions. However, we had told Mellor that, if forced to chose between allowing broadcasters to own some shares in independents in return for independents being allowed to hold a reciprocal number of shares in a broadcaster, or to give up independents' right to hold any shares in a broadcaster, we would choose the zero-zero option. Shortly after this exchange Mellor had made his announcement that the matter of cross-ownership for the purposes of the quota would be dealt with by the government in secondary legislation in the form of Orders in Council. In answer to a question from the Labour MP Robin Corbett, Mellor had said that the government would 'stop any company owned, or partly owned' by an ITV company from being counted as an independent for the purposes of the quota. There the matter had rested pending the completion of the Broadcasting Bill's passage through Parliament.

Five months later, in July 1990, the letter from the Home Office which John Woodward had managed to photocopy and smuggle out of the IBA, had revealed that the IBA had, no doubt prompted by the companies, reintroduced the matter of the ITV companies owning shares in independent producers from which they commissioned programmes. The Home Office's response, evidently composed in early July 1990, had been included in the 'smuggled' letter. The letter had contained a complete draft of the guidelines (already conveniently post-dated 'August') covering all of the matters to be covered by the forthcoming Order in Council. The Home Office civil servant had informed his opposite number in the IBA that the crucial paragraph in the guidelines dealing with broadcasters' right to own shares in independent producers had been left 'as originally drafted *for the present*' [author's emphasis]. The original draft, which appeared to have been seen by the broadcasters and discussed with them as long ago as the previous autumn, had stuck more or less precisely to what Mellor had said in his statement during the Committee Stage of the Broadcasting Bill, i.e., that the government intended to 'stop any company owned, or partly owned' by a broadcaster qualifying as an independent producer for the purposes of the 25% quota. However, the use of the words 'for the present' in the civil servant's letter was ominous, particularly as he added that he and his colleagues intended to 'invite comments' when the guidelines were 'circulated more widely'. A week before we had spotted the Home Office letter in the IBA, I had raised the issue of the definition of an independent producer in a letter to Mellor. I had told him that we had heard rumours and been picking up odd hints of 'something going on' between officials in the Home Office and the broadcasters over the cross-ownership issue. Rumours 'on the industry grapevine' had indicated that the Home Office was seeking the views of broadcasters on the issue. I pointed out to Mellor that we, too, had 'views'.

Once I had studied the 'smuggled' Home Office letter in detail I had asked Robin Chapman to raise the issue with David Waddington. I had also raised the matter in a confidential letter to Professor Griffiths and again when I went to see him in Downing Street three days later. I pointed out that, while the Home Office civil servants appeared to have been discussing the issue with the broadcasters for the best part of a year, they had not consulted us.

On 2 August 1990 I had received a reply to my letter to Mellor from his new Junior Minister, Peter Lloyd. He told me that consultations on the definition of an independent were 'not a new exercise', adding that I would no doubt recall having had 'discussions with my officials last year'. That was news to me. We had no record of any such specific discussion, let alone 'discussions' beyond one unspecific and inconclusive exchange with Home Office officials during a discussion of a whole range of topics more than a year before. None of us remembered 'discussions' on the matter of cross-ownership. In any case, since then Mellor had made his clear statement in Parliament saying that the government intended to bring in an Order preventing 'any company owned or partly owned' by a broadcaster from qualifying towards the quota.

Just two weeks after Lloyd's letter, another arrived from the Home Office 'inviting comments' from IPPA on the 'scope and contents' of the Order to be made later in the year which would set out 'definitions for the statutory quota' under the 25% Independent Production Initiative. We noticed at once that this letter was somewhat changed from the 'smuggled' draft which we had seen a few weeks earlier. Apart from taking account of the government's decision to refer the issue of programme rights to the Office of Fair Trading, most of the changes appeared to have been made to meet the concerns of the broadcasters.

On the crucial issue of who was to qualify as an independent and cross-ownership in companies between broadcasters and independents, the wording remained unchanged from the draft we had already seen. Nevertheless it was evident that the broadcasters had been hard at work bending the ears of their friends in the Home Office. It also began to look as if they had been receiving 'assistance' from some of the 'new breed' of independents. In the 'explanatory notes' which were included with the Home Office's letter there was a new heading *Cross-ownership*. It opened: 'Hitherto we have taken the view that a producer should be treated as an independent only if no shares in the company . . . are held by a broadcaster. This stemmed from our wish to ensure genuine competition, and the need to avoid suspicion of backdoor influence or collusion. However,' the Home Office mandarin continued, 'there is a contrary argument. Broadcasters will already be quite tightly regulated . . . [so] a complete ban may no longer be necessary or appropriate. Some independent producers might, for example, benefit from financial backing from their regional broadcasters. And should an independent best suited for a job lose a commission because its parent company held some shares in a different broadcaster?' This last point was palpable nonsense, as the civil servant must have known. As we had pointed out when the ITV companies had first put this idea forward three years earlier – there was still the remaining 75% of airtime unaffected by the 25% quota in which the programmes of these 'excellent' programme makers could be transmitted. These 'contrary' arguments, as outlined by the civil servant, sounded remarkably like the views which had been put forward by David Plowright and David McCall during our very first discussion with the companies at the IBA more than three years earlier. The Home Office official concluded his letter by saying that we had five weeks in which to submit our 'views'.

It was at this point that the changes in the IPPA Council really began to show. Despite repeated warnings from me as the Chairman to members of the Council about their duty to represent the interests of all the members of IPPA and drawing their attention to the guidelines on conflicts of interest drawn up at the time of the row over the Consolidated DBS bid six years earlier, some of the newer members of the Council increasingly seemed to be pursuing their own interests to the exclusion of all else. Two in particular by now spoke regularly at Council meetings on all manner of issues in ways that seemed blatantly to put the interests of their own companies ahead of those of the wider membership. I had repeatedly to check them, but my warnings appeared to be of little avail. I noted in my diary after one meeting, 'the rats really are starting to emerge from the woodwork'.

When IPPA came to discuss its response to the Home Office letter in mid-September 1990, the debate quickly became more acrimonious than anything I could recall in ten years of IPPA Council meetings. Four members in particular argued very strongly in favour of allowing some level of cross-holding between broadcasters and independents. They argued pretty much along the lines outlined in the Home Office's 'counter argument', but they also suggested that IPPA's membership rules in this area were out of date, that by continuing to prevent broadcasters from investing in independents we might prejudice the whole sector's future ability to grow. Others, generally those who had been members of the IPPA Council for longer or had been involved in earlier independents' campaigns, argued with equal fervour against them. They said that to allow cross-holdings by broadcasters would advantage a few companies to the disadvantage of the many, that for IPPA to support such a change would fly in the face of the fundamental principle of opening up broadcasting and providing equal access for all. I reminded Council that IPPA and the IASC, which included the BFTPA and AIP, had consistently campaigned for what, following Mellor's announcement during the Committee Stage of the Broadcasting Bill, was thus far the government's own publicly stated position, i.e., no cross-ownership. We had adopted our position because we understood that it accorded with the wishes of the wider membership. I feared that any change of policy at this moment would provoke a major split in IPPA. Allowing cross-ownership between broadcasters and independents was likely to distort competition in programme supply. On top of which, to change tack now would be bad tactics and was likely to lead to a perpetuation of broadcasters' market dominance. I was in no doubt that if the question was put to the IPPA membership as a whole they would back IPPA's existing policy. In view of the position which, as the lead negotiator for the whole independent sector I had taken for the last four years, to change our policy at this point would place me in an impossible position and I would have no alternative but to resign.

Sophie Balhetchet had been absent for the first half-hour of the discussion because she had been taking part in a similar argument in a meeting of one of the other industry bodies whose views were being sought by the Home Office, the British Screen Advisory Council. At that meeting she had succeeded in persuading those involved to hold to the existing producers associations' line. So she was visibly astonished when she walked into the meeting of the IPPA Council to find that it, of all bodies, was engaged in angry argument over the issue. Having got her breath back and received a whispered explanation of what was going on from Paul Styles, she joined in the debate with considerable vigour. Bringing to bear all her authority as IPPA's previous chairman and one of the original organisers of the Channel Four Campaign, she reiterated IPPA's long-standing policies and the reasons for them. After her intervention the debate restarted, and was conducted with better reasoned arguments and in more civilised tones on all sides. Eventually I was able to construct a consensus from the chair: the wording of the current government draft should remain unchanged – that an 'independent production' is 'a programme made by a producer who is . . . not a subsidiary of a broadcaster (UK or foreign), or a fellow subsidiary in a larger group, or partly owned by or in common ownership with them. In these contexts any shareholding will normally disqualify.' However, in our discussions with the Home Office we would acknowledge that with the passage of time and after independent producers had had a chance to establish themselves as suppliers to broadcasters other than Channel Four, this position might become inappropriate. For the moment everyone seemed satisfied.[2]

A reply along these lines was sent off to the Home Office and in subsequent discussions with officials we duly made the point about the possibility of some easing in IPPA's position perhaps becoming appropriate over the course of time. A period of five to ten years had been mentioned during the IPPA Council debate. Sophie Balhetchet, Paul Styles, John Woodward and I feared that if news of a split within IPPA on the issue reached the ears of the ITV companies or of the Home Office officials who were supporting them, it might provide them with a sufficient pretext to persuade Ministers to change the government's position. At the same time we knew perfectly well that the IPPA Council debate would not be the end of the matter. Neither the broadcasters nor the opportunist producers in the independents' own ranks, who came to be referred to among some of the longer serving IPPA Council members as 'the enemy within', were likely to give up that easily.

From late 1990, with the Broadcasting Act on the statute book, the incumbent ITV companies and would-be bidders for the new Channel 3 franchises had a new inducement available with which to seduce ambitious independent producers into dropping their support for existing IPPA policy on cross-ownership. They began to approach influential independents and those with representatives on the IPPA and TPA councils (the BFTPA had merged with AIP to form a single trade association TPA – The Producers Association) with offers of investment and attractive programme output deals, guaranteeing them continuity of work in return for letting them take a stake in their companies. In December 1990 news reached us that, during a meeting with Simon Albury, formerly the organiser of the Campaign for Quality Television and now one of the front men for a group bidding for the Channel 3 franchise in the south of England, the Junior Minister responsible for broadcasting had said that the government intended to define an independent as a producer not owned more than 20% by a broadcaster or as a producer holding not more than 5% of the total shares of a broadcaster. This was a major retreat from the government's position as announced by Mellor less than a year earlier. It now looked as if the independents had suffered a major behind-the-scenes defeat.

As it happened, Charles Denton (who was now the Chairman of TPA), John Woodward and I were due to meet the Minister concerned, Peter Lloyd, the next day. We determined to leave him in no doubt that we regarded the Home Office's recent actions as hostile to the independent sector and that we deplored the fact that he had told a bidder for a Channel 3 licence about the government's decision on the cross-holdings question before making a public announcement or informing the independent sector. As a result, we had learned of a change in government policy affecting the vital interests of our members through rumour.

The following day the meeting with Lloyd, a little-known Minister to the right of the Conservative Party who, I noted in my diary, was 'very much a grey man, and faded, but quite jolly and affable' although 'a political non-entity', lasted well over an hour. He was flanked by two Home Office civil servants. The Minister was clearly very embarrassed that we knew about what had been said during his meeting with Albury and that we were taking a tough line on it. In response he and his officials gave us to understand that the figure of 20% was 'very much too high' and was the result of a 'wrong construction' put on something said by a civil servant. No decision had been taken on cross-holdings and no formal announcement would be made 'until Easter'. However, Lloyd said, a Parliamentary Question would 'flush out' some indication of government thinking before then.

The meeting then turned to other issues which concerned independents. Charles Denton, with all his previous experience as a senior ITV executive, was proving an enormous asset. First he effectively demolished a recent comparative costing exercise undertaken by the BBC which suggested that some independents' programme production costs were as high as the BBC's own. The BBC had been attempting publicly to deduce from this that the introduction of an independent quota would not save it money. Denton showed, based on his own experience of running a broadcast company, that the methodology employed for the charging of costs in the BBC's study, and particularly for charging BBC overheads, was seriously flawed. He also delivered a devastating attack on recent 'sweetheart deals' between broadcasters and so-called independents, presenting the Minister with a paper giving precise details of a notorious recent BBC deal under which one BBC in-house producer, having been encouraged to set up as an independent, now accounted for almost half of the independent quota for a whole BBC region. I noted afterwards that whenever we hit upon what we knew the Home Office civil servants regarded as a 'difficult' issue the Minister 'as politicians will, tried to slide off the subject. But we bullied him somewhat and got through all our points.' Yet, although by the end of the meeting we were in little doubt that we had made a strong case and got each of our points across, I still had an uneasy feeling that we were wasting our time, that we were playing against 'a stacked deck'.

By the New Year of 1991, with Mrs Thatcher gone, Brian Griffiths had left Downing Street (receiving a peerage in Mrs Thatcher's resignation honours list). Kenneth Baker had replaced David Waddington as Home Secretary and Peter Lloyd had been moved up to replace Mellor. Mellor, despite our continued distrust of his motives, had been bright and generally well-briefed – as I noted in my diary more than once, the brightest and best-briefed Minister apart from Thatcher that I had ever met in any government. Meetings with him, although they could be testing and he could be rather full of himself, holding forth for long stretches, were often good humoured and punctuated with genuine laughter on both sides. I noted that near the start of his last spell in the Home Office he had introduced comfortable, brightly covered chairs and a sofa into his office and had started to wear smartly cut suits and fashionably expensive ties. Peter Lloyd, therefore, could hardly have been a greater contrast. However, as Prime Ministers, Ministers and ministerial advisers came and went, most of the civil servants in the Broadcasting Department of the Home Office remained in place. As a result, after Mrs Thatcher's departure the broadcasters could once more realistically hope, as Sir Denis Forman put it, to 'dominate the Home Office', confident in the expectation that its Ministers and civil servants would remain 'sensible, civilised, biddable people'. We no longer had Brian Griffiths or Lord Young through whom to counteract this.

At the same time, with the country as a whole moving deeper into recession, rising unemployment and the start of the first Gulf War against Iraq, the independent sector was going through a recession of its own greater than at any time since the start of Channel Four. The result, despite the overall expansion in programme hours, was a sense among independent producers of uncertainty and of being beleaguered. The division between the small number of companies making a lot of programmes and all the rest became more marked than ever. At the end of January 1991, as the preparations for putting in bids for the new ITV/Channel 3 franchises moved into higher gear, John Woodward alerted me to fresh moves by some of the larger independents to get the government to allow cross-holdings of up to 20% by broadcasters in independent producers. Over the next two to three weeks, these reports and rumours multiplied. Early in February a Home Office civil servant, whom I knew was the person likely to do much of the legal drafting, asked me about the definition of 'an independent producer' for the purposes of the government's vital Statutory Instrument. What level of cross-holding by broadcasters in independents did IPPA think was appropriate, if any? I repeated all the familiar arguments. However, he pressed the point. What would IPPA accept? From the way in which he was talking I got the clear impression that the government had now definitely decided that some level of cross-holding would be allowed. So the question appeared no longer to be whether we would swallow this, but how much would we swallow. I told him that, while I could not be certain before further consultation with my Council and possibly with the wider member-ship, I thought that in practice and if pushed, while we might complain, we would probably accept up to 5% ownership by broadcasters in independents. I said that I thought anything above that would be impractical as it would have the effect of damaging the competitive intention behind the government's Independent Initia-tive. He said that he understood and indicated to me that '5% was probably in line with Home Office thinking'. He also added that 'certain independents with broadcasting franchise aspirations' had been 'making all kinds of approaches', suggesting higher limits in order to make their franchise bids credible. He told me that Ministers were 'well aware of these people's vested interests'.

Bids for the Channel 3 franchises had to be in by 15 May and the government had to make an announcement on the cross-ownership rules sufficiently far ahead of that date to allow potential bidders to finalise their applications. During February civil servants repeatedly quizzed me about the cross-ownership issue. They seemed to be looking for any hint of a change or softening in opinion among the IPPA membership. I had recently toured the country and heard the views of hundreds of independents in regional centres in Bristol, Birmingham,

Manchester and Edinburgh as well as London. So each time the civil servants asked for IPPA's views I tried to tell them as honestly as I could how I thought opinion stood.

It was now evident that the energy of those with a vested interest in getting the policy changed was being concentrated on IPPA rather than on TPA. It was also becoming clear that most of the fire and heat was actually being generated by a very few of the bigger and more nakedly commercial IPPA companies. As a consequence, the bulk of small producers in IPPA were becoming alarmed that they might be disadvantaged if cross-holdings were allowed. If the issue were put to a referendum of the entire membership of IPPA it was clear that the smaller companies who wanted to stick to the 'zero-zero option' would win hands down. However, it was also clear that if the question were to be put to a referendum it would lead to an open split in the membership. Enough companies would vote in favour of some measure of cross-ownership (my estimate was at least 50 and possibly as many as 100 – including many of the biggest and most financially successful, out of a total membership of 700) to enable the ITV companies and their supporters to argue there was a difference of opinion in the independents' own ranks. That, they would argue, was sufficient reason for the government to allow it.

As the days passed it became evident that two companies, both of which had representatives sitting on the IPPA Council, had been urging both the OFT and the Home Office to allow them to own up to 20% of a broadcaster. They seemed to be arguing along not dissimilar lines to those we had used in our arguments with Mellor a year earlier, that for them to have a 20% shareholding in a broadcaster did not pose the same threat as allowing a broadcaster to own 20% of an independent. The waters were getting increasingly muddy. We were now back to what Mellor had described as the 'equity' problem. Maintaining the current clarity of the 'zero-zero option', under which no cross-holdings whatsoever either way were allowed, at least until the new franchises had come into operation and everyone had enjoyed an equal opportunity for at least two or three years under the new set-up, seemed ever more attractive. By now, however, it was also clear that the ITV companies and other consortia bidding for Channel 3 franchises had made seductive promises of work and investment to most of the biggest and most ambitious independents with representatives on the IPPA Council.

Charles Denton was encountering similar problems in TPA. Because of the composition of TPA's membership it had always seemed more likely that it would be the first to change its policy in favour of allowing some level of cross-ownership with ITV companies. Many TPA members were subsidiaries of ITV companies or of international corporations with substantial TV interests. Nevertheless, privately Charles was as convinced as I was that for the next few years the interests of the independent sector would be best served by preventing broadcasters from taking shareholdings in independents which qualified under the 25% quota.

In mid-February Charles Denton told me that he feared that the next meeting of the TPA executive might result in its members taking up completely irreconcilable positions. I told Charles that I proposed to put the whole issue on the agenda for the next IPPA Council meeting, which was due take place on the same day as the meeting of TPA's executive. I had asked Jonathan Davis to prepare a paper for the IPPA meeting, setting out the whole position for Council as objectively as possible, stating the pros and cons in both arguments. I had also made sure that each member of the Council had a copy of the 'Conflicts of Interest' paper prepared for IPPA and adopted by its Council as a 'guide to good practice' at the time of the row over the Consolidated DBS bid in 1984. I told Charles that I thought that the IPPA Council would be unable to take any definite decision on the issue that was safe because of the degree of conflict of interest among the members of its Council. I intended, therefore, to try to ensure that there was a rational airing of all views. I told him that I thought that in order to reach any clear decision it would be necessary to consult the IPPA membership as a whole, perhaps by means of a referendum coupled with a general meeting. Charles suggested that, with the prospect of an amalgamation between the two associations in the near future, we might have a joint IPPA/TPA members meeting.

By now the clash over cross-ownership was taking on a symbolic significance even greater than its practical importance. It was, in a sense, a conflict between two different concepts of what it meant to be an independent producer. On the one hand, there was an older, more idealistic view which saw being an independent as essentially about creativity, freedom and opportunities for all kinds of voices. On the other, there was a more pragmatic, modern view, which looked upon being an independent primarily in business and commercial terms. According to this view the opportunity that mattered was the commercial opportunity and all else flowed from that.

By mid-February big independents who were pressing to be allowed to have significant holdings in ITV companies were giving headline-grabbing stories to the trade press attacking IPPA's policy and me personally. So far none of these producers had approached me or IPPA to inform us of their intentions or worries, nor had they asked for more information about IPPA's current position. It appeared that this was now an undisguised political campaign, nothing more and nothing less, and was aimed at achieving one simple legislative result. One company in particular, which had a representative on the IPPA Council, announced publicly that it was withdrawing from IPPA in protest at its policy on cross-ownership. The boss of this company gave a quote to a journalist in which he described me as 'a Luddite'. I suspected that he had made a serious tactical error as this would alert the mass of IPPA members to what was really going on and that they would rally to the support of IPPA's existing policy. Within hours members were calling in, urging us to stick to the 'zero-zero option'.

Asked by a journalist to respond to this particular company's attack, I had said simply that, while I regretted any company's withdrawal from IPPA, if that company or others intended their actions as some sort of threat to IPPA, or to me, they were in for a disappointment. I did not react very well to threats and, I said, I did not think that IPPA's members would either. Independent producers, I told the journalist, had been threatened by a lot of people, particularly broadcasters and trade unions, over the previous ten years and they had stood up to those threats. I suspected that this would be no different. The day after the companies' press attacks started there was a joint meeting of the IPPA and TPA merger teams. Everyone present on both sides expressed their anger at what they saw as the 'antics' of a few companies which they were convinced were acting purely out of self-interest.

By the time of IPPA's February Council meeting, so much heat had been generated over the broadcaster/independent cross-ownership issue that it was widely anticipated that there would be an cataclysmic bust-up and an irreparable split in the independent sector. It was also evident that a government announce-ment on the detailed rules to govern the independent quota was imminent. It was widely understood that the government had already decided to depart from the 'zero-zero' position without waiting for any formal statement on its position from IPPA. So it seemed that whatever IPPA decided, it would be unlikely to affect the government's decision. The result, coupled with Jonathan Davis's well-reasoned paper and the copy of the Conflicts of Interest paper which I had had issued to everyone taking part, was to considerably diffuse the tension. Nevertheless, it was clear that those members of the IPPA Council who had the greatest interest in changing its policy, believed that they now had a majority and wanted a show-down which would force the matter to a decision that evening. They did not want to wait for the wider IPPA membership to be consulted, as they knew very well that a referendum of the entire membership was likely to see them heavily defeated.

The parameters of the IPPA Council's debate had been largely set by Jonathan Davis's paper. He spelled out the advantages for the sector of allowing a degree of cross-ownership in all its permutations and the disadvantages. He concluded that producers would 'be making judgements in their own best interests when it comes to links with broadcasters'. The sector, he wrote, 'will definitely survive if there is no cross-ownership but it may not prosper. It may find itself the recipient of a grudging 25% (which is in reality far less than 25%), without the muscle to win a greater share of the TV programme supply business. On the other hand, a sector which accepts cross-ownership will become a sector dominated by cross-ownership. Its character will be irreversibly changed, both for better and worse. Some of the aspirations and achievements of the sector would undoubtedly be lost, but some of the sector's profound structural limita-tions would be overcome. At issue, therefore, is a choice of future . . . The key is the independence of independents.'[3] Although I knew that some of those who wanted the policy changed were seething, the actual discussion which followed, although vigorous, remained logical and well-ordered. Trade press journalists, who I knew were hoping to be told afterwards that there had been a violent bust-up, were disappointed. At the end of the discussion the IPPA Council agreed that no firm decision could be taken at that moment. Any policy outlined by the government would have to be judged by the extent to which it was likely to further open competition and increase opportunities for all independents. It was recognised that, historically, IPPA had always campaigned on a strongly 'anti-Trust' line and that the Association should not depart from that now.

The end result, therefore, was a fudge. An honourable and well-reasoned fudge, but a fudge nevertheless. By contrast, at its meeting on the same day, the Executive of TPA, the producers' organisation which because of its membership was widely thought likely to back a relaxation of the 'zero-zero' rule, made a clear decision. Despite considerable division of opinion, it decided to stick firmly to the 'zero-zero option', the position which had until then always been associated with IPPA. At the meeting Charles Denton, John Woodward and David Norris had made it clear that they believed that, for the benefit of the whole independent sector, TPA should continue to reject the idea of allowing broadcasters to take shares in independents. The rest of the executive had accepted their judgement. When John Woodward phoned IPPA to ask what decision it had reached, he was, in his words, 'nonplussed' to be told that IPPA had, in effect, softened its strict 'zero-zero' position.

The joint meeting of members of TPA and IPPA which took place a couple of weeks later was equally reasoned but indecisive. By then it was known that a government announcement would be made later in that week. When that announcement came, in the form of a Written Answer to a parliamentary question on 14 March 1991, the Minister said that he was 'minded to make one important change to the current arrangements' under which an independent producer was defined as one 'in which no broadcaster has any shareholding'. Although the Minister still accepted 'the need to limit the scope for undue influence which may arise through cross-holdings of this kind', he now believed that 'the present requirement is too restrictive and is not in the best interests of the independent sector itself. I therefore propose to permit a broadcaster to have up to a limit of a 15% shareholding in an independent producer, and to apply a similar limit on investment by an independent producer in a broadcaster.'[4]

That basically was the end of it. It no longer mattered what the independent sector thought or how individual members might vote in a referendum, the government had decided. The large independents and consortia bidding for the new Channel 3 franchises had won. On the day that the government announcement came through I was away in North Wales hunting for locations for a drama series. I did not even note the announcement in my diary. I already knew that the independent sector had suffered what I regarded as a major defeat. The defeat had happened weeks earlier. It had occurred at the point at which it had become inevitable that the government's zero-zero policy would change.

Discussing the whole cross-ownership saga with Sophie Balhetchet and John Woodward in the days immediately after the government announcement, I told them that I feared that we were witnessing the beginnings of what amounted to a form of corporate reintegration in programme production which might ultimately lead to the disappearance of the independent sector as a distinctive cultural, social and political force for good in British television. The end result might mean that all we had achieved through all our years of effort was the replacement of one kind of monopoly by another. New kinds of large cross-holding production houses, broadcasters and talent agencies, which sold their wares across all of the broadcast channels in Britain and overseas, with outlets and links into other media as well, could be much more pernicious than the kind of thing that had been operated by the Grade brothers or Granada and the Bernsteins twenty years earlier. The new monopolies were potentially much more malign than the kind of thing which we had so happily lampooned in *Open Secret* in the days of the Free Communications Group. I told Sophie and John that these monopolies were likely to be a lot harder to break than the old. They told me that I was wrong, things were not as bad as I feared. I suggested that in the new world 'the true producers, those who combine creative vision, independence of mind, a sense of the cultural, social and political importance of the media with entrepreneurial flair',[5] would be placed at a disadvantage. John reminded me that four years earlier, when we had embarked on The 25% Campaign, independents were confined solely to working for Channel Four and were, as a result, at its mercy. Now they had a much wider field of choice and variety of outlets for their work.

John and Sophie were right of course, at least in the short term. The consequences of the government's new policy of allowing cross-ownership between broadcasters and independents turned out, for reasons that will become apparent in the next chapter, to be far less than anticipated and were negligible for the great mass of independent producers. Nevertheless, a few companies were, as Jonathan Davis had predicted, enabled to grow as a result. By the time the kind of corporate reintegration which I had feared started to be really apparent, in the second half of the 1990s, the issue of the 25% quota itself was largely irrelevant, superseded by much bigger and more fundamental problems that went far beyond the scope of a simple protective quota designed to allow one sector of the industry to grow, compete and survive.

I have dwelt on the cross-ownership issue at some length not so much because of its practical importance but because I believe it marked a decisive break with the independent sector's past. When I came to discuss the writing of this book with Sophie Balhetchet and we turned to this issue, she described the cross-ownership debate within IPPA as 'a watershed – although its symbolic impact was greater than its actual impact'. Even at the time we both sensed that something had changed. Looking back, I realise that it was the first time in IPPA's ten-year history that a policy based clearly on principle (fairness, equality of opportunity for all) as opposed to practical expediency, had been defeated; defeated not by outsiders – broadcasters or politicians – but by a small group from within the independent sector itself. I felt then and still believe that something intangible had been lost for ever. That something was, if you like, the independent sector's innocence.

The idea that the independent sector had embodied a higher principle, an idealism which did not exist elsewhere, was probably always a delusion. Yet that delusion had contained an element of the truth, at least in the early years and for many of those who had founded the sector, had spoken for it, fought for it and led it in the years before the birth of Channel Four. These are the people who I have called throughout much of this book 'the campaigners'. The delusion, if delusion it was, persisted into The 25% Campaign and helped to motivate many of those of us who launched it and carried it forward. With the cross-ownership debate the delusion was finally shattered. The independent sector had finally become no different from any other part of the television industry, a complex amalgam of forces, driven by commercial competition, self-interest, money, greed, individuality and creative energy.

Notes

1. *TV, UK Special Report* by Jonathan Davis, Knowledge Research, Peterborough, 1991.
2. My account of what occurred at this IPPA Council meeting, and others during my chairmanship, is taken from the *Minutes of IPPA Council* (12 September 1990), relevant entries in my own diary, personal correspondence and the personal recollections of some of those who took part.
3. Jonathan Davis, *Cross-Ownership – A Briefing Paper Prepared on Behalf of the Independent Programme Producers' Association*, by Knowledge Research, February 1991.
4. *Hansard*, 14 March 1991.
5. Private letter from the author to Sophie Balhetchet, dated 10 March 1991.

16

Muddied Transparencies –
November 1991 to May 1997

In her memoirs Lady Thatcher regretted that compromises forced on her as a result of the political process had 'muddied the transparency' which she had wanted to achieve in broadcasting. Nevertheless she took satisfaction from the fact that, as she saw it, the combination of the appointments of Marmaduke Hussey and John Birt at the BBC, the auction system for awarding ITV franchises, 'the 25% target for independent producers, the arrival of the new satellite channels, and a successful assault on union restrictive practices – went some way towards weakening the monopolistic grip of the broadcasting establishment. They did not break it.'[1]

By the time Lady Thatcher's memoirs appeared in 1993 and people had started to see the effects of the changes that she had wrought in television, only the most die-hard disciples of market theory could any longer claim that her changes had produced any visible improvements. Richard Dunn, the former Managing Director of Thames Television and Chairman of the ITV companies' Council, spoke for many, especially in ITV, when he said in a Royal Society of Arts lecture in 1994 that the 1990 Broadcasting Act, the centrepiece of Mrs Thatcher's broadcasting legislation, had produced just one 'great benefit . . . it has taught us how not to do it, ever again'.[2]

Damning evidence in support of Dunn's assertion had been provided by the announcement by the ITC (the licensing body which had replaced the IBA) of the winners of the Channel 3 franchises on 16 October 1991. In all, 37 bids had been received for the 16 franchises. In three of the franchise areas, one of the smallest, Border, and two of the most profitable, Scottish and Central, there had been only one bidder, the incumbent. As a result, those three incumbent ITV companies had been re-appointed unopposed, Central and Scottish each bidding just £2,000 and tiny Border, having heard a rumour that someone else was planning to bid, with a bid of £52,000. None of these bids, with the possible exception of Border's, in any way reflected the true market value of the public asset which the companies had acquired. This result on its own, therefore, completely invalidated the one possible justification for the whole cash bid system. The other licence awards produced results which were equally absurd. Worse still, they stored up trouble for the future. In the remaining thirteen regions, nine incumbent ITV contractors retained their franchises and four lost them. The contractors who retained their franchises included Granada and LWT, both of which had made substantially lower bids than their challengers. These companies retained their franchises as a result of the programme quality 'threshold' which had been forced on the government by the new ITC chairman George Russell. Granada bid £9 million, not much more than a quarter of the amount bid by its rival, North West TV Ltd, a consortium led by the independent producer Phil Redmond. Perhaps as a result of its predecessor the IBA's experience with LWT and TV-am, the ITC was less inclined to accept at face value the glowing promises of consortia headed by programme makers. Redmond's consortium was judged by the ITC not to have satisfied the programme quality requirements and so its bid was ruled out. Whatever Phil Redmond's qualities as a producer, it was hard to believe that the team he had mustered could match the talent and proven record of Granada. Superficially, this looked like a vindication of the government's decision to give way to Russell on the quality threshold.

However, that was to overlook the changes that, by the time the ITC's decisions were announced, were already taking place in Granada, changes that would render it unrecognisable as the 'bread and circuses' institution of the old days when its reputation had been built. The 'circuses' would remain, in the form of cheap and popular programmes and soap operas like *Coronation Street*, but the 'bread' – courageous investigative journalism from the *World in Action* stable, documentary series and expensive dramas of the calibre of *Brideshead Revisited* and *The Jewel in the Crown* – were soon to disappear. On 21 October, just five days after the ITC announced the franchise winners, it was announced that Gerry Robinson had been appointed Chief Executive of the Granada Group. This, the City pages said, was in response to shareholder discontent and a falling share price. Robinson was a businessman, formerly the Finance Director of Coca-Cola and Chief Executive of a large catering company, Compass plc. He had no experience in television, show business or the media and confessed to knowing nothing about Granada, beyond having seen *Coronation Street* and having 'a vague feeling that they ran motorway service stations'.[3] Robinson's appointment exemplified changes that were about to sweep the ITV system. He was one of a small group of businessmen who moved into television in the wake of the franchise bidding process who, according to Paul Bonner in the official history of ITV, shared a common belief in seeing 'money as the most effective determinant of any business, including television'.

Ray Fitzwalter, one of the leading spirits in the Campaign for Quality Television, for eleven years Editor of *World in Action* and by 1991 Head of Granada's Current Affairs and Documentary Departments, was told that, shortly after his appointment, Robinson had warned an internal meeting of senior managers that, 'Anybody in the new Granada who doesn't put profits first, second and third has no place.' Fitzwalter recalls, 'It was a horrible time.' Not long afterwards Fitzwalter saw himself described in an internal management note as 'an internal structural limitation'. Shortly after that he decided to leave and became an independent – 'It was a matter of no choice.'[4]

To those who knew what was going on inside Granada it came as little surprise when, early in 1992, three months after Robinson's arrival, David Plowright, the Chairman of Granada Television and last survivor in the company's top management from Granada's golden era as the home of fearless, high-quality ITV programme-making, resigned, citing 'fundamental disagreement' with the Granada Group board. Few in the industry were surprised to be told that the 'fundamental disagreement' was over Robinson's escalating demands for cost cutting and for Plowright to squeeze more and more profits out of the television operation. Plowright had been seen by many, not least by the ITC when it rejected the Redmond consortium's far higher cash bid for the north west Channel 3 franchise, as one of the chief guarantors of the continuing quality of Granada's programmes. Following the announcement of Plowright's departure, the industry was up in arms, the press publishing angry denunciations of Robinson by well-known television personalities as a 'bean counter in every way'. The most publicised attack came in the form of a fax sent to Robinson by John Cleese in which he was reported to have said, 'Fuck off out of it, you ignorant, upstart caterer.' Sir Paul Fox, who knew more than most about the realities of ITV, told a *Times* reporter that 'All pretension of good programme making in ITV now falls by the wayside.'[5] Faced with the first real test of Thatcher's new 'light touch' regulatory regime, the ITC wrung its hands and, as its far more powerfully equipped predecessor the IBA had done when faced with ITV companies reneging on their franchise promises, summoned company executives Gerry Robinson and the Chairman of the Granada Group, Alex Bernstein, to its headquarters. Having demanded ritual promises that the undertakings given in Granada's successful franchise application would be honoured (did the ITC imagine that the Granada Group's two bosses would not give such assurances?), the ITC put out a limp-wristed statement, outdoing in its feebleness even the statements that had been issued on similar occasions by its predecessor the IBA. It quoted Russell as saying: 'I acknowledge the widespread concern caused by the resignation of David Plowright but I am confident that Granada Group will give Granada Television the wholehearted backing it needs to fulfil the terms of its licence.'[6] So that was all right then! A few months later Granada moved in another young executive to run its television operation, a close colleague of Robinson's at Compass catering, Charles Allen. Allen cheerfully admitted that he knew nothing about television either. But he too enjoyed *Coronation Street*. So that was it. From now on not even limited experience in television or show business was regarded by those in charge as a necessary qualification for those running ITV.

One franchise contest did appear to offer some reassurance for the future. LWT had put in an even lower cash bid, relative to its rivals, than had Granada. The highest bid for their London weekend franchise, amounting to almost five times that of its highest bidding rival, had come from LIB (London Independent Broadcasting). This group included Tom Gutteridge and other producers who had been amongst those who had argued most vociferously for allowing share cross-ownership between broadcasters and independents. Gutteridge and his chums' bid was ruled out because, like Redmond's, it was judged by the ITC not to have passed the 'quality threshold'. In view of the vehemence of the attacks made by Gutteridge and his colleagues on those of us like Sophie Balhetchet, Alex Graham, Charles Denton and myself who had opposed cross-ownership (we were accused of being Luddites who did not understand modern needs), there was a certain *schadenfreude* in learning that the ITC had had 'serious reservations about LIB's proposals for using independents', that it had judged LIB's franchise application inconsistent and regarded only one of its key post holders as having adequate 'programme-making or commissioning experience'.[7]

Other ITV companies who retained their franchises, Anglia, HTV, Tyne Tees and Yorkshire, were all widely judged to have bid too much. As a result, they risked not only weakening themselves as commercial entities but endangered the quality of the programmes in ITV as a whole. There were four new franchise winners. These included Meridian, which took the south of England contract from TVS. Meridian was headed by Lord Hollick, a tycoon who had been part of a failed application for the TV-am franchise in 1982. Hollick, who already had interests in cinemas and outdoor advertising, had recruited Simon Albury and others who had been heavily involved in the Campaign for Quality Television to help to map out his bid. The company intended not to own its own production facilities but to be a publisher–broadcaster, commissioning programmes from independents. Meridian had signed up an impressive array of independent producers, including some of those who had been most strident in support of easing the cross-ownership rules. But unlike LIB's or Redmond's bids, the ITC had been impressed by the quality of Meridian's plans and by the personnel it had lined up. In order to beat off the challenge from Meridian, the incumbent contractor, TVS, had bid almost £60 million, which the ITC judged unrealistic. A third bidder failed to pass the quality threshold. As a result Meridian was yet another company that won on a substantially lower bid than its only real rival.

The new contract which caused the most consternation was the award of the London weekday franchise to Michael Green's Carlton. The outcry was mainly on account of the fact that the company defeated by Carlton was Thames. Dark suspicions were voiced that the reason for Thames's defeat, despite its record for high-quality programmes and strong application, was *Death on the Rock*. Although the decision was probably welcome to the government and to some members of the ITC, the suspicion was almost certainly groundless. The fact is that Carlton had put in a substantially higher cash bid than Thames (£43 million as opposed to less than £33 million from Thames) and had met the requirements of the 'quality threshold'. Nevertheless, there seems little doubt that if it had been free to chose on the basis of the likely quality of the bidders' programmes, the ITC would have appointed Thames rather than Carlton. Carlton's application had been judged by the ITC's staff 'clear and lucid' rather than of 'exceptionally high standard'. Unlike Thames's application, the ITC staff found the 'overall feel' of the Carlton application 'competent, well-reasoned but unimaginative . . . put together by a facilities house rather than a broadcaster with a commitment to original creative ideas'. Carlton, like Meridian, intended to be a publisher–contractor and had signed up a number of leading independents to make its programmes. At the end of the day the difference in the quality of the programme plans of the two applicants had not been judged by the ITC to be sufficient to justify rejecting the Carlton application and, as Carlton had put in the higher cash bid, Carlton won the contract. The Thames v Carlton franchise contest exemplified the effect of the new auction system brought in by Mrs Thatcher – the 'competent, well-reasoned but unimaginative' would tend to drive out the bold, imaginative and committed broadcaster.

The ITC announces the franchise winners on 16 October 1991. (David Glencross, nearest camera, looks grim and George Russell, next to him, has his head in his hands.) Do they realise what they have done, but feel they were powerless to stop it?

Courtesy of *Broadcast*

The franchise auction had one other shock to deliver, this time to the person behind the whole thing, Mrs Thatcher. The winner of the breakfast-time franchise was Sunrise Television (later renamed GMTV). It outbid two others, including the incumbent TV-am. TV-am's boss, a colourful Australian, Bruce Gyngell, had, following a successful showdown between TV-am and the unions in 1987–8 in which 200 technicians were sacked, reputedly become Margaret Thatcher's favourite broadcaster. The morning after the announcement of TV-am's defeat Gyngell received a hand-written note from Margaret Thatcher in which she said, 'When I see how some of the licences have been awarded, I am mystified that you did not receive yours and heartbroken. You of all people have done so much for the whole of television.' She added, 'I am only too painfully aware that I am responsible for the legislation.' Later that day Gyngell read out Thatcher's hand-written note to assembled journalists at a TV-am journalism awards lunch at Claridge's. It caused a sensation. Mrs Thatcher, who had always proclaimed that 'you-can't-buck-the-market', had introduced this new system because it was supposedly more 'transparent'. Now she had admitted that it had not yielded the results which she had wanted. Nor had it realised for the Treasury cash bids commensurate with the monetary value of the public assets acquired by the successful franchise applicants. As a result of the auction some would be paying too much, some a lot too little. At the same time it seemed bound to lead to lower quality and less varied programmes all round. As Richard Dunn said, the 1990 Broadcasting Act should teach us 'how not to do it, ever again'. Would it? Either way, the viewers and we in television were stuck with it.

*   *   *

One of the changes which she had brought about which Lady Thatcher was happy with was 'the 25% target for independent producers'. But whether even this was such an unalloyed benefit to broadcasting as a whole or to those who made the programmes was to become steadily more open to question. With the cross-ownership rules relaxed and the new Channel 3 contractors looking increasingly for long runs of safe, popular, tightly budgeted programming, the polarisation forecast by Jonathan Davis between the large independents able to win such ongoing slates of work and the mass of smaller producers who lived from one production to the next grew rapidly more marked. Even in the first year or two after the Broadcasting Act came into effect, when it was bestowing its most obvious benefits on the independents in the form of rapidly increasing volumes of independent production on the BBC and ITV, the transparency of the measure, to which Lady Thatcher attached so much importance, was already decidedly muddied. The relaxation in the cross-ownership rules meant that it was now often far from clear how 'independent' some of the largest independent producers really were. Thames, having lost its franchise, shed 90 per cent of its staff but kept its main studio complex to become the largest independent producer, supplying the same popular hits, such as *The Bill*, to the ITV network that it had while it was an ITV contractor. Thames was part of a complex group of companies with interests in three UK broadcasters as well as in a lot of other related media. It had ambitions to extend its financial interests in broadcasting still further. As well as Thames, there were now a significant number of independents in which broadcasters had some sort of financial interest, blurring beyond recall the old clear distinction between independents and broadcasters. On top of which a whole range of other hybrids began to emerge, such as talent agencies which were also independents and overseas media corporations which already controlled broadcasters in their own countries and now bought into UK independents.

Old transparencies were becoming muddied in other areas too. In the autumn of 1991 IPPA and the TPA had finally merged to form one united producers' association, the Producers' Alliance for Cinema and Television – PACT. Charles Denton became its first Chairman and John Woodward its Chief Executive. Paul Styles, who would, with his courage, tenacity and clear-sightedness in pursuit of the independents' cause, in the more self-confident and less mean-spirited 1960s or '70s, have been offered a string of important posts by leading broadcasters, had instead been lured into the City to take up a senior position in media consulting with a highly regarded firm of financial advisers. I, having achieved the two goals set when I became Chairman of IPPA in 1989 – getting the 25% quota enshrined in legislation and creating a single producers' trade association – had been relieved to step aside from the day-to-day politics of the independent sector so that I could concentrate more single-mindedly on my own work.

Denton and Woodward's task at PACT would be by no means easy. The two associations from which PACT had been created had, by the end, been in a parlous state. As John Woodward, who knew IPPA as well as anyone, puts it: 'By the end IPPA was in severe danger of being driven by short-term issues and being burst apart by them.' Charles Denton, the last chairman of TPA, says that by 1991 it too was 'a moribund organisation, held up by its union agreements'. From the moment that PACT came into being, Woodward and Denton knew that the new organisation would have to be primarily a trade association in the way that TPA had been rather than the kind of hybrid between a campaign and a trade body which IPPA had been. Woodward says: 'From the moment when PACT began I always tried to turn it into a trade association rather than having it driven by cultural issues. By then it wouldn't work as anything else than a trade association because of the differences between its members. It is no good kicking the dog because you wish it was a cat.'[8] Denton and Woodward quickly succeeded, so much so that by the time Graham Benson became PACT's Chairman in 1995 he, like the majority of his Council and probably most of the association's members, no longer believed that it had any business campaigning over such things as public service broadcasting unless these could be shown to directly impact on PACT members' interests as businesses: 'I thought it was wrong for producers' trade association representatives to argue what was, in effect, an editorial point of view.'[9]

One of the first actions of the new association was to commission a paper called *The Business of Independence*. The headings of its subsections made clear the new emphasis: 'Towards a More Competitive Market', 'Anticipating a New Age of Independent Supply', 'Financing Growth', 'Inward Investment', 'Diversification'. From 1993 onwards, after the OFT had finally ruled in PACT's favour over the issue of rights in programmes made by independents for ITV, it became possible for independents who made popular programmes to negotiate contractual terms with ITV which were far in advance of anything they had previously been able to win with Channel Four. As a result a small number of producers of popular series, particularly those with an appeal to overseas audiences, now possessed valuable assets. By taking advantage of these they were enabled to grow and become wealthy. However, while this enabled some companies to grow, the OFT's ruling also acted like the uncorking of a genie's bottle. It ushered in many of the less attractive aspects of financing which had been commonplace in the film industry for decades. It encouraged an increasing number of independents to concentrate on the kind of safe and culturally non-specific programme making which had been one of the main causes of alarm to the original campaigners in the 1960s and early 1970s. The effect was to widen still further the gap between the few wealthy independents with the financial resources and assets to enable them to take advantage of the most profitable co-financing and programme rights deals and the rest of the smaller independents, who often made programmes of great interest or importance for British television audiences, but which had little or no international sales potential or exploitable format rights. Nevertheless, despite these potential downsides to the new dispensation, but in line with its new prime focus on its members' business rather cultural interests, PACT now renewed its efforts to gain the same access and programme ownership rights as it now enjoyed with the ITV companies from the BBC and Channel Four. To most people inside PACT this was a straightforward matter of fairness, and in direct line of succession to the arguments put forward by IPPA ever since its earliest negotiations over Terms of Trade with Channel Four in 1981. Even those who were now beginning to have doubts over the real long-term benefits to the majority of independents of winning the argument about programme rights recognised that for them to attempt to introduce a new agenda into the debate at this stage, so soon after the new Broadcasting Act had come into effect, would be futile and probably counterproductive.

The whole issue of independents as businesses rather than as primarily creative people who were businesses only incidentally or as no more than a matter of legal necessity was thrust even more firmly into the spotlight in 1993 when the Edinburgh International Television Festival decided to commission Sir John Harvey Jones to do a special *Trouble Shooter* video for one of its sessions. The idea was for Sir John, a former boss of ICI, who had become well-known on television for a series of popular programmes which analysed the problems of businesses, to examine a selection of independent production companies. Robert Thirkell, the organiser of the session, approached Sophie Balhetchet and asked her to chair it and help him choose independents to be subjected to Sir John's scrutiny. While the video was likely to highlight the difficulties under which most independents still laboured, the risk was that it might also show some of them up as unworldly or as simply bad businessmen. At the same time, if the independents were seen by Sir John as too effective or efficient it might lead to renewed calls for the early removal of their protective 25% quota. Aware that the video and the whole Edinburgh International Television Festival session was a 'potentially a double-edged sword', Balhetchet proposed that three independent production companies, companies that could be regarded as a representative cross-section of the independent production sector, be subjected to Sir John's scrutiny. She nominated one of the biggest, one that was middle-sized and one which, although small, produced highly respected programmes. Having carried out his investigation into these companies, Sir John concluded that most independent production companies were not really businesses at all; they were, in his phrase, 'lifestyle companies'. Balhetchet had anticipated just some such result and now set about persuading PACT to turn Sir John's 'finding' to its own use in its campaign to get the terms under which independents traded with Channel Four and the BBC improved. PACT could now convincingly argue that 'If three of the most successful and critically acclaimed independent producers are not businesses because of the constraints under which they operate, then no independent can be a business.'[10] It therefore followed, Balhetchet concluded, that the rules under which independents were forced to trade with Channel Four and the BBC must be changed. Unfortunately for Balhetchet and PACT, neither the BBC nor Channel Four was moved by Sir John's 'finding'. Both remained impervious to the new argument.

However, reaction among the body of independent producers themselves to the Harvey Jones' *Trouble Shooters* video provided a striking demonstration, if further demonstration were still needed, of the extent to which the sector and the picture which independent producers had of themselves had by now changed. In the early days of Channel Four the vast majority of independent producers would have hailed Sir John's description of themselves and their companies as 'lifestyle companies' as a vindication, recognition that, in establishing themselves as small but viable 'lifestyle' businesses, they had achieved what they had set out to achieve. But ten years on, in 1993, the majority of independent producers saw Sir John's analysis as a damning indictment, a diagnosis of failure. Watching this reaction, I said sadly to a colleague, 'In 1982 or '83 they would have been rejoicing, throwing their bonnets into the air. Now they go around rending their clothes, wailing and wearing sackcloth and ashes.' By 1993 most independent producers, as much as broadcasters, saw themselves as businesses which made programmes, not as they had a decade earlier, as programme makers who also ran businesses.

From the moment the effects of the new Broadcasting Act had started to bite, what had once seemed fixed points in the broadcasting landscape had started to shift, sometimes in ways that could seem disorientating. This was as true among independent companies, even where there were no legal doubts about the true nature of the company's independence, as for the broadcasters. So in 1991, even as the battles over the character of the independent production sector were being played out inside IPPA and the TPA, I had found myself directing a children's drama series for the BBC, being produced by a big independent company created by executives from a leading talent agency, the managing director of which was Paul Jackson (who in the 1980s had been so fearless during our early-morning confrontations with Michael Grade in airless BBC basements), which was chaired by Bill Cotton, who five years previously had been such a scourge of the independents during the infamous Edinburgh International Television Festival debate on The 25% Campaign but was now retired from the BBC, and produced by Shaun Sutton, formerly the BBC's longest serving Head of Drama. A year later, I hired Sir Denis Forman, once my boss at Granada Television, to produce two series of programmes made by my own independent company for Channel Four – one putting organised religion on trial and the other examining moral choices.

* * *

Similarly seismic shifts in attitudes and priorities were taking place among broadcasters. As Greg Dyke, who had become the Chairman of the ITV Council in 1991, put it: 'The 1990 Broadcasting Act told the ITV companies that being a business was more important than being a broadcaster.'[11] The galloping prioritisation of financial interests over everything else in broadcasting now seemed unstoppable. In November 1993 the government announced that the moratorium on takeovers in ITV would be lifted from 1 January 1994. Over the next year ITV companies began to swallow each other in quick succession. Michael Green's Carlton took over Central, Gerry Robinson masterminded a Granada takeover of LWT and Lord Hollick's MAI Group, which owned the south of England franchise, Meridian, absorbed Anglia. In the process, various senior executives in the companies that were taken over, who, during the ITC franchise bidding race had been provided with generous share options – 'golden handcuffs' – to induce them to stay loyal to their companies, were made millionaires. As a result of all these takeovers, by the end of the 1990s the three men who headed Carlton, Granada and MAI, the men who, as Paul Bonner put it, saw 'money as the most effective determinant of any business, including television', would exercise a domination over ITV more absolute than anything achieved by Lew Grade, Sidney Bernstein, Howard Thomas and Captain Brownrigg in the 1960s.

With takeover fever at its height in ITV, there were calls for further relaxations in other cross-ownership rules. In his lecture to the Royal Society of Arts in which he said that the 1990 Broadcasting Act had 'taught us how not to do it, ever again', Richard Dunn, the Chief Executive of Thames Television, the ousted London weekday contractor, called for a further substantial relaxation in the rules governing cross-ownership between broadcasters and independents, between newspaper publishers and broadcasters and between broadcaster and broadcaster. He said that Thames's parent company Pearson should be allowed to own not only the *Financial Times*, 15% of the new Channel 5 and 15% of the ITV company Yorkshire Tyne Tees, it, or any other newspaper owner, should be permitted to own up to 49% of an ITV company or of Channel 5, and in addition a broadcaster should be permitted to own up to 25% of an independent or vice versa. All this, Dunn argued, should be done in the name of allowing Pearson, 'the kind of champion the Government should be doing everything to back', to compete more successfully on the international commercial stage. Thereafter, Dunn opined, broadcasting (and broadcasters) should be left alone by politicians, so that it could 'reform itself with the minimum of legislative interference'.[12]

There were to be many more refrains in a similar vein. They all overlooked or, more often, chose to ignore the one consistent lesson that was clear from even a fairly cursory knowledge of British broadcasting and its legislative and regulatory history – left to themselves commercial imperatives had, with very few exceptions, always tended to produce worse broadcasting, less real range and variety, and poorer quality programmes for the public. The single factor that had made British broadcasting the most admired in the world was its regulatory framework and the hindrances put in the way of naked commercialism. I, and a dwindling band of former campaigners who still thought as I did, might continue to believe that the lesson of the 1990 Broadcasting Act was not that we should abandon broadcasting regulation and leave broadcasting and the broadcasters to reform themselves, but that what was needed was better and more appropriate broadcasting legislation, backed by genuinely independent regulators with the powers and will to enforce rules in the interest of the public and community at large. However, as the 1990s advanced, such ideas were increasingly regarded by politicians of all colours, by broadcasters, by independents and even by growing numbers of ordinary programme makers, both inside the broadcasting institutions and out, as heretical and out of date. When we spoke out it was in vain.

Perversely, as commercialism was given ever greater licence to run riot across television, the volume of restrictive regulation and the number of bodies empowered to operate various forms of programme censorship, had reached an all-time high. I had willingly stepped aside from the day-to-day politics of the independent sector, but in 1992 I seized the invitation to speak out at a European Union conference on Strategy for the Audio-Visual Industries. Urging delegates to push for more positive broadcasting regulation across the

European Union, regulation aimed at getting more challenging programmes made, I said: 'Mrs Thatcher, the great freedom fighter and believer in unfettered competition, did not believe in the competition of ideas. The result is that [in Britain], on top of commercial caution by the channel operators, we now have a plethora of regulators – the ITC, BBC, BCC, BSC, OFT, MMC, DTI, Oftel, Obscene Publications Act, Anti-Terrorism Act, impartiality rules. All we need now is Ofgas, the regulator responsible for gas supplies in the UK, to regulate the amount of hot air talked and we shall have the complete package. Of all those regulators only the BBC and ITC are positive regulators – that is to say, regulators charged with making sure that things get on to the screen that might not if the field were left to commerce on its own. Almost all the rest are aimed at making sure that things don't happen – that programmes don't offend or provoke.'[13]

By this time a pretty good idea of what broadcasting might look like without positive regulatory constraints could be seen in BSkyB and Rupert Murdoch's other media operations around the world. Murdoch's Sky and his other services offered news, comprehensive coverage of selected sporting events and newer movies than the free-to-air channels. But these services came at a price. Otherwise Sky offered a bland mix of low-cost programming, much of it acquired cheaply in the international market, plus a few specialist services. These services too came at a cost to the viewer. To anyone brought up in the British public service broadcasting tradition the fare offered by Murdoch was far from exciting television. It therefore seemed astonishing when, in December 1992 just as Thames's ITV licence finally ran out, David Elstein joined Sky to become its Head of Programmes. The move certainly boosted my image of him as television's Vicar of Bray. But why, we asked, had such a distinguished public service broadcasting executive, the person who at Thames had sanctioned the making of *Death on the Rock*, former leading independent campaigner and programme maker joined the 'unacceptable face of commercial broadcasting'? It seemed inconceivable that one of Rupert Murdoch's channels would have sanctioned *Death on the Rock*, given the knowledge that it was likely to give mighty offence to the regime in which it was broadcast. A few years after his move to Sky Elstein told Mathew Horsman, 'It looked to me very interesting to move to a company which had a much more strategic approach to broadcasting and which absolutely believed in what I had long believed: multi-channel subscription TV, a direct relationship with the consumer.'[14]

Once at Sky Elstein's public persona underwent a rapid transformation (I am tempted to write 'transfiguration') – from high-principled champion of public service broadcasting and erstwhile fearless Channel Four campaigner to indispensable public face of the Murdoch public relations effort – 'the acceptable face of Sky' or, as I dubbed him, 'Murdoch's representative on earth'. With this transformation Elstein appeared to don the vestments of the smile-on-your-face nuncio of cheapo-cheapo television by the yard. Shortly after he joined Sky my company tried out on him an idea for a low-cost ongoing interview series featuring a well-known agony aunt. He expressed some interest, but when we started to discuss terms Elstein told me that the most that Sky could pay was $3,000 per hour. Discussions got no further.

*   *   *

Former IPPA Chairman John Gau, who had returned to the independent sector in 1991 after two years as Director of Programmes at the ill-fated British Satellite Broadcasting, had been appalled to discover how *dirigiste* (his word) Channel Four had become in the three years since Michael Grade had taken over as Chief Executive. Under Jeremy Isaacs' leadership the Channel had seen it as part of its *raison d'etre* to be open-minded and to welcome fresh approaches, new subject matter or ways of doing things. This new *dirigisme* applied in particular to the way in which it now treated its programme makers: 'I found it quite tricky, as the commissioning editors said, "I want this sort of thing." They, and the BBC commissioners, [now] behaved just like in-house executive producers.'[15]

By 1991 Channel Four had become a serious cause for concern to many of Gau's fellow independent producers. Although initially they had been pleasantly surprised by Michael Grade's handling of Channel Four it had quickly become clear that, in Jeremy Isaacs' words, 'Some of the things I stood for were among the first things to go under Michael Grade.' Among the changes that Isaacs and the independents were least happy about was the way in which Grade had re-organised the programme commissioning structure. 'The idea that all Commissioning Editors reported to Jeremy Isaacs was impossible as far as Michael Grade was concerned . . . That was the biggest thing Michael Grade did to change the tone of the channel.' Another was to abandon Isaacs' rule under which the entire commissioning body got turned over at least every ten years so as to ensure that no commissioning editor got too settled and that fresh minds were always being brought to bear on what programmes the channel commissioned. To Grade that was 'completely mad'. If once you had got a good executive, you held on to him; you did not fire him.

Isaacs had boasted, with reason, that he had been attempting to do things that neither the BBC nor ITV would do. Summing up his time at Channel Four shortly after he left, Isaacs had written: 'We broadcast our fair share of junk, and our fair share of quality. We bought and commissioned from as many as we could for the sake of as rich a variety as we could encompass. We encouraged programme-makers to do their thing, rating diversity of judgement as important as quality as product.'[16] Grade, on the other hand, was not so much concerned to do different things as to do things better. Facing Channel Four's commissioning editors for the first time, he had told them that, while he admired the Channel's great achievements, there was 'too much mediocre material, badly executed, which the BBC would never have transmitted'. He told them that his aim was 'to ensure that Channel Four lost its amateur status'. The quality control of its programmes was not rigorous enough. Could they imagine, he asked, 'Marks and Spencer ordering a number of jumpers from a factory and putting them straight on the shelves without satisfying themselves about colour, size and quality?' He wanted the consistent performance which, in his view, marked out the professional from the amateur: 'The heady early days when ratings counted for nothing and no programme idea was too far-fetched were gone.'[17]

Grade knew perfectly well that in eliminating the amateur work he risked throwing out the original work as well, but he believed his approach was justified. British television was entering a period of unprecedented competition and Channel Four would be no less affected than any other broadcaster. 'Rupert Murdoch doesn't mess about,' he said. Yet one could not escape the fact that Marks and Spencer's virtues were to be safe and dependable rather than dangerous or exciting.

In 1992 John Wyvver, who had been one of the most thoughtful and articulate independents, was invited to deliver a paper addressed to the Channel's commissioning editors on Channel Four and the independent sector a decade on from its founding. He wrote: 'Combining commercial success with innovation and a distinctive character, especially in the television environment of the early 1990s, might seem impossibly schizophrenic. I would argue, however, that such a combination is precisely the key to its success.' Addressing what he saw as the Channel's current inadequacies, he suggested that the strengths derived from Grade's programme policy – more stranding, more consistent programme quality and a more predictable schedule – were also among its weaknesses. 'The schedule, for example, for all that it helps viewers to actually find the programmes, can also act as a straitjacket, restricting the possibilities for the kind of surprising and successful "event" programming that BBC-2 has been doing so well.' The Channel's main strands, such as the single documentary slot *Cutting Edge* and the current affairs strand *Dispatches*, 'can constrain makers by a kind of formula, and so result in predictability. And just precisely because there are so few programmes to which one reacts with surprise or incredulity, the Channel seems to have lost its provocative and challenging edge. Channel 4 has become simply bland.'[18] Invited to speak to Channel Four's commissioning editors one evening after dinner while they were gathered in a hotel outside London to discuss the Channel's future, Wyvver told them that Channel Four had gone fundamentally wrong. It had 'lost any interest in developing innovative form and content, and betrayed the Statutory Instrument' under which it operated. One Commissioning Editor, who had been appointed since Isaacs' time, reacted by yelling out, 'You're talking through your fucking arse, Wyvver!' Afterwards, David Scott, who had been with the Channel since the start and was by then its Director of Finance, approached Wyvver to offer his sympathy. Commenting on the commissioning editor's outburst, Scott said, 'Now you are seen as a reactionary, taking us backwards.'[19]

Grade terminated the Independent Workshops Initiative (chief product of the successive campaigns by groups like the IFA before Channel Four's founding). Although the programmes that had been produced as a result of the Independent Workshops Initiative had been uneven and drawn only small audiences, they had provided an essential window for the work of alternative film makers, video artists, co-operatives and black film makers. It had brought the work of major artists like Isaac Julien to a wider audience.

Mounting discontent among Channel Four's programme makers and even some of its commissioning editors came to a head when, in February 1991, as peace talks in the Gulf War collapsed, Saddam Hussein set fire to Kuwaiti oil-fields and recession deepened in Britain, the Channel announced programme budget cuts of £14 million, 8 per cent of the total. At the same moment, with a timing that could have been calculated to inflame its relations with independents, it announced that it was going to move out of its familiar but cramped offices on the site of the theatre in Charlotte Street which had once been home to the annual production of *Peter Pan* into state-of-the-art new premises, to be built specially for the Channel to a design by the fashionable architect Richard Rogers, at a cost of £80 million. These new offices were not to be in a part of London associated with the film or television industries, or anything so bohemian as the sight of people eating out of doors which had originally helped to attract Jeremy Isaacs to Charlotte Street, but in one of the most faceless and impersonal areas imaginable – Horseferry Road, Victoria, close to Whitehall and the seat of government.

That autumn at the Edinburgh TV Festival Roger Graef, one of the few independents who still had the courage to voice in public what others were thinking in private, attacked Michael Grade to his face during a session on the future of Channel Four. Graef told Grade that he feared that in saving the Channel from outright privatisation, and getting the government to agree to it becoming a free-standing public corporation selling its own advertising, he had lost the war to preserve Channel Four's unique place in British broadcasting. Channel Four was not a business, Graef told Grade, but 'a cultural public service', made possible through a unique piece of social and financial engineering. Graef warned former campaigners among his audience that they might 'have to fight to save Channel Four once again'.

Through the early months of 1991, as new consortia had been forming up to bid for the new Channel 3 franchises, a brief story had appeared in *Private Eye* about Michael Grade accepting a 'golden handcuffs' deal to stay loyal to Channel Four. Amid the welter of other stories that spring about which television executives had signed to what consortium, the 'transfer' and pay packages they were being offered, the *Private Eye* story about Grade's 'golden handcuffs' had got lost. But, in mid-September 1991, after the Channel 3 bids closed, the *Independent* broke a story on its front page saying that Michael Grade had accepted a payment of £500,000 not to defect to any of the consortia which had lodged Channel 3 bids. Seven other Channel Four executives, the *Independent* reported, had accepted smaller 'golden handcuff' payments, together totalling a further half a million pounds. Picking up the story in an editorial, the *Sun* asked with a fine show of moral outrage, 'How can Michael Grade look himself in the eye when he is shaving?' Channel Four was a public institution and supposed to be dedicated to the values of public service broadcasting. It was not a commercial station where all of those involved were in it for as much as they could get out of it.

IPPA fired off furious letters to Channel Four's Chairman, Sir Richard Atten-borough, and the IBA: 'At a time when the country as a whole is experiencing the industrial and social consequences of a prolonged recession, and a time when the television industry is particularly enfeebled by the collapse of advertising revenues, cash inducements to the tune of a million pounds appear nothing less than obscene.' IPPA's Director continued, 'I have tried and failed to identify the moral and managerial high ground the channel occupies while doling out a million pounds to its executives. If the channel depends so exclusively on a few individuals, then its managerial problems are severe. If it can keep them only through cash, then probably those problems are insurmountable. If it expects any kind of continued respect or sympathy from its suppliers, it is desperately out of touch.'[20] In almost my last act as IPPA Chairman, I had dashed up to Cambridge to speak from the floor in an emergency session at the Royal Television Society's Biennial Convention entitled 'Has Channel Four Lost Its Way?'

Michael Grade confronting his critics at the RTS Cambridge
Convention on 20 September 1991
Courtesy of the Royal Television Society

The session, intended to provide an opportunity for Grade to answer questions, opened with him giving a spirited defence of his programme policies. Some searching questions from journalists about the 'golden handcuffs' payments followed. Called to speak on behalf of independent producers I said that ultimately this was a moral issue. Channel Four was supposed to be something special in public service broadcasting – what Jeremy Isaacs had called 'a sacred trust'. If those running the Channel regarded the making and receiving of such exorbitant payments as acceptable, particularly at a time of recession and high unemployment, then the ethos at the top of the Channel was wrong. The Channel had not simply 'lost its way', it had lost the map.

Afterwards reaction to what I had said was mixed. Some believed that I had got to the heart of the matter, others that I had dragged in a moral element where none belonged. Later, as I strolled across the grass outside King's College Chapel, John Birt, who it had recently been confirmed was to be the next Director-General of the BBC, hove into sight accompanied by a small entourage. Spotting me, he detached himself and came over. He wanted, he said, to congratulate me – I had said something that had needed saying. Thanking him, I congratulated him on his forthcoming appointment and we parted. Eighteen months later the *Independent on Sunday* carried another headline: 'The BBC helps its chief to avoid tax.' Birt, by then Director-General of the BBC, the story said, was still claiming tax relief through his own private company for items such as his much derided Armani suits and payments to his wife.[21]

*   *   *

As the 1990s progressed Channel 5 continued to remain, in Phillip Whitehead's apt formulation, no more than 'the product of a double negative'. When the contract to run it was finally awarded, in October 1995, it went to a consortium headed by Lord Hollick's MAI group, owners of the south of England ITV contract, and Pearson, the parent company of Thames, the ITV contractor that had been deprived of its franchise by the ITC in 1992. Some months after the announcement of the Channel 5 contract award David Elstein defected from BSkyB to become the new channel's Chief Executive. To mere bystanders and his former colleagues, Elstein's succession of appointments was by this time becoming somewhat dizzying. Gone, it now seemed, was his 'long-held' belief in multi-channel subscription television and the 'direct relationship with the consumer'. Channel 5 was to be an old-fashioned, free-to-air, terrestrial broadcaster. Still confused, while I was preparing this book I asked David Elstein about his peregrinations around the various broadcasting institutions and whether there had been any consistent thread to his broadcasting beliefs. He told me that Channel Four, and his involvement in the Channel Four Group, had been important 'because it was the last opportunity for the foreseeable future to change television'. His attitude to BSkyB and Channel 5 had been based on his experience of the BBC and ITV as a programme maker. 'In the BBC and ITV those who controlled them were the elite, the only people who mattered. Programme makers were only tolerated. The owners, with the unions, had their hands on the throats of broadcasting at the expense of the programme makers.' Going to Channel 5, he knew that compared to ITV, the BBC or Channel Four, it would have little money to spend on programmes. But this was not necessarily a bad thing, he said: 'One of the weaknesses of British broadcasting was that it was locked into a very high cost basis. There had to be the opportunity for high-volume, low-cost programming. This was an opportunity for the independent sector to really become self-sustaining and take off.'[22]

Richard Dunn, in his lecture to the Royal Society of Arts late in 1994, had provided a unique insight into what such new 'opportunities' really amounted to in money and jobs. He explained how his company, Thames, the largest ITV contractor until the end of 1992 when it lost its franchise, had changed to become the largest independent, producing mainly high-volume, low-cost programmes for a multi-channel, deregulated market. In 1990, as an ITV contractor, Thames had produced 400 hours of original programmes for the ITV network and sold it a further 100 hours of repeats. In addition, Thames had made 500 hours of original programmes for transmission inside its London region only. In total 900 hours of original programmes. To do this it had employed a staff of 1,500 and its turnover had been £350 million, netting the company a profit of £21 million after payment of Exchequer Levy. By 1993, as an independent, Thames was making 2,300 hours of original programmes, but only 150 hours of them for ITV, the BBC or Channel Four. It now employed only 150 people. Thames also sold 1,000 hours of repeats in 1993, many of which were programmes made while it was still an ITV contractor. Taken together, sales of new productions and repeats netted Thames £80 million in 1993, leaving it with a profit of £16 million. If one strips out that 1,000 hours of repeat sales, one is left with a pretty stark picture of what a future of making 'high-volume, low-cost' programming would really amount to for even the most successful independent. The early independents and campaigners had originally thought in terms of perhaps halving the costs of making high-quality programmes. But by the mid-1990s it seemed clear that the reality of making programming that could be sold to the new markets meant dividing costs and manpower by ten or more. This was not better, freer programme making nor more varied viewing for the audience, it was factory production, even broiler-house production, one of the things that the early campaigners had been most vehemently against.

At the same time even single programmes commissioned by the most open-minded and free-spirited of the broadcasters, Channel Four and the BBC, were becoming subject to much more rigid and all-embracing editorial control. So whereas in the 1980s I had occasionally been called in by Channel Four to act as an executive producer or some kind of guiding hand for a totally inexperienced programme maker who was learning the ropes, by the mid-1990s I found myself being called upon to act as the executive producer on all kinds of programmes. This might be understandable when Channel Four commissioned a film from a young film maker whom I had met when he was an applicant for the documentary directing course at the National Film and Television School, making a film exploring the beliefs and actions of members of the Animal Liberation Front. The young film maker's flat had been raided by the police twice before the production contract for the film had even been issued and this was followed by a concerted attempt by elements of the scientific establishment to get the film banned before it had started shooting. In the event, when the film was eventually shot much of it had been done clandestinely.[23] However, such close supervision hardly seemed necessary in the cases of a young film maker producing a film about the leading university for African-Americans in the USA, an established international award-winning Swedish film maker making a film about a former Stasi informer, a seasoned Anglo-French company making a film about Mozambique, an experienced producer making a film about Emeric Pressberger or another doing a personal account of his own struggle to reconcile his family and his Christian faith with the fact that he was gay. Although I might be able to relieve a bit of the bureaucratic burden placed on these young film makers or act as an additional sympathetic pair of eyes and ears, while in a few cases wringing rather less onerous contractual terms out of the Channel on the film makers' behalf, the imposition of an executive producer seemed largely unnecessary and a long way from the spirit of the Channel Four of Jeremy Isaacs' days when 'diversity of judgement was as important as quality of product'.

The lesson of my experiences as an executive producer for Channel Four during the mid-1990s seemed obvious: if this degree of supervision was now deemed necessary by the channel in dealing with one-off programmes likely to be of interest to a minority audience, how much greater would be the degree of detailed supervision deemed essential when it came to the dealing with the 'high-volume, low-cost' programmes that were forecast as the independent sector's future? And how much greater would be the loss of creative expression and freedom to experiment in both form and content? Things might not yet quite have reached the point warned of by Sophie Balhetchet in her 1988 address to the Royal Television Society where 'having spent much energy in creating our companies we can have no respect for the product we create', but the writing seemed ever more clearly to be on the wall.

*　　*　　*

The BBC, Mrs Thatcher's principal target when she had set up the Peacock Committee in 1985, seemed to have escaped the effects of the 1990 Broadcasting Act largely unscathed. By the end of 1990, with Mrs Thatcher gone, the worst of the threat to the BBC had appeared to be over. However, by the mid-1990s some of the BBC's most dangerous enemies appeared to be senior people inside it. Margaret Thatcher had written in her memoirs that the appointments of Marmaduke Hussey as Chairman and John Birt as Deputy Director-General and then Director-General had 'represented an improvement in every respect'. When the public row over John Birt's contract and tax status had blown up in 1993, Hussey had dismissed criticism of Birt and of his own failure to act earlier. In his memoirs he describes the whole affair as 'a huge, unnecessary, malicious fuss about nothing', got up by the press and malcontents inside the BBC. Even while the row was at its height he had concluded that it was nothing to worry about. The people who he believed were behind it had, he said, 'failed to enlist anybody who mattered. There were no ministers, no MPs, nothing from anyone of any substance or importance, just journalists and BBC staff.'[24] Nevertheless, he had belatedly got Birt to accept changes to his contract of employment. However, when the BBC's General Advisory Council, a consultative body intended to convey the views of the BBC's audiences to the Board, passed a vote of no confidence in Hussey and the Board over their handling of the affair, Hussey had ignored it and encouraged moves to have the Council, in his phrase, 'put down'.

It had been noticeable working as a freelance for the BBC through the first half of the 1990s and, as a result, being in and out of it at regular intervals, how rapidly staff morale had been falling off. This was because of continuing staff cuts and insecurity, but also because of a perceived loss of courage in the BBC's programmes. Above all, it could be attributed to John Birt. At the time of the Gulf War, in early 1991, John Birt had been accused, in his role as overseer of all BBC news and current affairs output, of postponing a *Panorama* exposé which revealed how British machine-tool manufacturers had been exporting equipment

553

to Iraq for a sensational long-range gun, the 'supergun', in contravention of government export guidelines. Birt's defence, according to witnesses quoted in Steve Barnett and Andrew Curry's *The Battle for the BBC*,[25] was that the British public would not tolerate such a programme at a time when British troops were going into battle against the Iraqis. But had that been a sufficient reason to postpone a sensational and soundly researched story of national importance at a moment when it was both relevant and a cause of legitimate public concern? Was not the real reason for the postponement that if the programme had been broadcast Tory backbenchers would have been up in arms against the BBC?

In March 1992, during the run-up to the general election fought largely on the economy, Peter Jay, the BBC's Economics Editor and in the 1970s co-author with Birt of the 'Bias against understanding' articles, had been due to present a *Panorama* programme – *Sliding into Slump*. The programme would analyse the roots of the nation's economic problems. This again was a programme that was clearly about a matter of relevant public concern and was planned for transmission at a time when it could properly be regarded as a prime example of the BBC fulfilling its obligations as a public service broadcaster. This programme was also pulled – put back until after the election. It seemed that, with people such as those who were now running the Corporation, John Major's government no longer had any need to lean on the Corporation in the way that had been done in Thatcher's time. The BBC could by the 1990s be trusted to 'lean' on itself.

In his McTaggart Lecture, which had opened the 1992 Edinburgh International Television Festival, Michael Grade launched an attack on the way in which the BBC's management style stifled the creative process. He had described the outgoing Director-General, Michael Checkland, and John Birt, then shortly to step into Checkland's shoes, as 'the lame duck and the Trappist monk'. An even more damaging assault had come in October 1992 when, in his last months as Director-General, Michael Checkland, addressing the Royal Television Society, had attacked Marmaduke Hussey and the BBC Governors. Checkland suggested that Hussey was too old to lead the BBC. During a radio festival the following July, the respected, long-serving BBC journalist Mark Tully had launched a further attack on the BBC's management. However, the most damaging attack of all had come from Dennis Potter in his McTaggart Lecture at the start of the 1993 Edinburgh International Television Festival. He attacked what he saw in the BBC as a new 'culture of fear and loathing'. Describing Birt and Hussey, he had said, 'You cannot make a pair of croak-voiced Daleks appear benevolent even if you dress one in Armani suits and call the other Marmaduke. The world', Potter said, 'had been turned upside down. The BBC is under Governors who seem incapable of performing the public trust that is invested in them, under a chairman who seems to believe he is heading a private fiefdom, and under a Chief Executive who must somehow or other have swallowed whole and unsalted the kind of humbug punctuated pre-privatisation manual that is being forced on British Rail or British Coal.' If public service broadcasting was no longer safe with the BBC, Potter had said, it should be broken up and its heritage entrusted to other trustees. A month later, Liz Forgan, who in 1993 became Managing Director of BBC Network Radio, attacked the BBC's new internal budgeting and cost control system championed by Birt, Producer Choice. She called it 'a shambles'. Even Hussey was eventually forced to admit to friends that Birt lacked judgement. He later recorded that Lord Carrington once said to him of Birt: 'Odd sort of fellow, he seems to me. Very good at drawing straight lines I should imagine.' Elsewhere Hussey described Birt as 'a very good guided missile, on autopilot he is just as likely to hit his own troops as the enemy'. Yet, as Hussey also recorded, Birt was apparently making such a favourable impression on the government that he had been invited by Virginia Bottomley, the Secretary of State for Health, to conduct a teach-in for top NHS managers.[26]

And that surely had been the point all along as far as Hussey were concerned – to make a good impression on the government. In 1995 the government's broadcasting White Paper confirmed an extension of the BBC Charter for a further ten years until 2006. The licence fee would be retained and all of the BBC's services would survive. But, and it was potentially a big but, the BBC was to expand its commercial activities still further and develop itself into an 'international multi-media enterprise'. In rescuing the BBC from advertising, had those who had saved it damaged it beyond repair?

According to Hussey, when he retired from the BBC in March 1996 Denis Thatcher pronounced that he had 'done a superb job' and 'changed the BBC'. When Hussey had started, in 1986, Denis Thatcher had been reported as telling Hussey that the BBC was 'a nest of vipers' and that his job was to 'do something about it'. That, a decade on, he had apparently discharged that duty to Denis Thatcher's entire satisfaction surely needs no further comment?

A year later, on 1 May 1997, New Labour won the general election with a landslide. Addressing celebrating party workers, Tony Blair said, 'A new dawn has broken,' and then, after a fractional pause added, 'has it not?'

Notes

1. Margaret Thatcher, *The Downing Street Years*, HarperCollins Publishers, London, 1993.
2. Richard Dunn, *The Broadcasting Act: A Benefit or a Disaster?*, Peter Le Neve Foster Lecture, delivered on 16 November 1994 and reproduced in *The Journal of the Royal Society of Arts*, London, March 1995.
3. *The Times*, 26 February 1994.
4. Ray Fitzwalter, interviewed by the author in December 2000.
5. *The Times*, 4 February 1992.
6. ITC news release, 11 February 1992, quoted in *Independent Television in Britain, Vol. 5, op. cit.*
7. ITC assessment, quoted in *Independent Television in Britain, Vol. 5, op. cit.*
8. John Woodward, interviewed by the author in December 2000.
9. Graham Benson, interviewed by the author in October 2000.
10. Sophie Balhetchet, interviewed by the author in November 2000.
11. Greg Dyke, quoted by Dunn, *op. cit.*
12. Dunn, *op. cit.*
13. *Address to Euro-Aim* in San Sebastian, delivered by the author, 1 June 1992.
14. David Elstein, quoted in Horsman, *op. cit.*
15. John Gau, interviewed by the author in October 2000.
16. Isaacs, *op. cit.*
17. Grade, *op. cit.*
18. *A Decade of Independents, The Experience of, and the Prospects for, Independent Television Producers in Britain* by John Wyvver, Illuminations Television Ltd, London, 1992.
19. John Wyvver, interviewed by the author in October 2000.
20. Letter from Margaret Windham Heffernan, Director of IPPA, to Sir Richard Attenborough, Chairman, Channel Four Television, 11 September 1991.
21. Grade would later claim in his memoirs, *op. cit.*, that his Director of Programmes, Liz Forgan, who had also been 'golden handcuffed', had sat through the entire RTS session and said nothing in his defence. Grade's hurt at the attacks on him perhaps explains his claim. Unfortunately, his memory was false. Liz Forgan did speak up for Grade towards the end of the debate, defending not only Grade but the Channel's output. The RTS possesses a video tape of the entire proceedings which I have seen and there is no doubt that this is what actually happened.
22. David Elstein, interviewed by the author in November 2000.
23. The young film maker concerned has since gone on to win awards around the world and have one of his short films selected as an official British entry at Cannes.
24. Hussey, *op. cit.*
25. *The Battle for the BBC*, Steve Barnett, Aurum Press, 1994.
26. Hussey, *op. cit.*

17

Lost – 1997 to 2003

'The creatures outside looked from pig to man, and from man to pig, and from pig to man again; but already it was impossible to say which was which.'

The end of *Animal Farm* by George Orwell

In the summer of 2000, when I was starting my research for this book, I received a phone call from Sir Paul Fox, formerly a tough adversary during the IASC's negotiations with ITV. 'Well,' he said, 'you won.'

'No,' I replied, 'we both lost.'

We discussed the television landscape of 2000 for a few moments and agreed. Neither the independents nor the broadcasters had won. Both lost.

Why did we reach this apparently paradoxical conclusion? On the face of it by the summer of 2000 it did indeed look as if the independents had won. In place of the few discontented film and television programme makers of 1968, discontented with the elitism and unaccountability of the BFI, the cowardice, bureaucracy and lack of openness of the BBC and ITV, by 2000 independent producers made up a vital sector of Britain's audio-visual production industry. Every year independent producers were making and selling almost one thousand million pounds worth of programmes. They made three times as many of Channel Four's programmes as the ITV companies, they supplied almost 30% of the ITV network's non-news programmes and 25% of the BBC's. Independents were making more than 20% of all the programmes shown on all the channels available in Britain, including satellite channels such as Sky. This amounted in total to more than 10,000 hours of programmes sold to UK TV every year. In addition, British independent producers continued to win awards for programme excellence at home and overseas. In 1999 British independents had won 40% of the American International Emmys, the television world's Oscars. PACT, the independent film and television producers' unified trade association, had over 1,000 members, of whom more than 900 were producers, an annual administrative budget of more than

£2 million, a staff of 15 and a wages bill of more than half a million. In proportion to its size the independent sector was paying more towards new-entrant and in-career freelance training in the film and television industries than the BBC or ITV and all the other sectors of the industry combined.

That summer, when Sir Paul Fox and I spoke, it certainly did not seem that being involved in our campaigns had harmed the careers of most of the individuals concerned. Gus Macdonald was by then Lord Macdonald, a senior Minister in the Blair government (having previously been Chief Executive and Chairman of Scottish Television), Steve Morrison was Chief Executive of Granada Media, Phillip Whitehead was a Euro-MP, Anthony Smith was the President of Magdalen College, Oxford, having previously been the Director of the BFI, John Woodward had recently been made the Chief Executive of the newly established Film Council after a spell as the Director of the BFI, Roger Graef was firmly established as one of the country's leading documentary film makers and Sophie Balhetchet was the Head of Drama at Tony Garnett's World Productions. Among the programmes made by independents were many of the most popular – *Who Wants To Be a Millionaire*, *Changing Rooms*, *They Think It's All Over*, *Hall of Fame*, *Have I Got News for You*, *Men Behaving Badly*, *Brookside*, *Bad Girls*, *This Life*, *The Big Breakfast*, *Tellytubbies*, *Time Team*, *Big Brother*, *Clocking Off*, *Footballers Wives*, *Pop Idol*, *Survivor* – and on, and on, new ones being added all the time. Many individual independent producers had become rich. A continuing stream of them were successfully floating their companies on the stock exchange, expanding overseas or being bought out by international media conglomerates and UK broadcasters, becoming millionaires in the process. Independent producers regularly topped the industry's annual 'Rich List', accounting for more than half of the top 100. Even after the fall in value of media companies following the dot-com companies' crash the following year, Anne Wood of Ragdoll, makers of *Teletubbies*, was number three in the *Broadcast* Rich List, reported to be worth £130 million. Mike Luckwell was listed as worth £120 million, Phil Redmond – £40 million, Denise O'Donoghue – £35 million, Tom Gutteridge – £16 million, Alex Graham – £10 million.

A month before Sir Paul's and my phone conversation, in May 2000, Michael Jackson had given the Royal Television Society's annual Fleming Lecture. Referring to the independents he had said, 'What was once a radical idea on the margin is today the mainstream.' After Jackson's speech the RTS had presented silver medals in recognition of their services to television, citing their part in the rise of the independent sector, to Sophie Balhetchet, David Graham, Phil

Redmond, John Wyvver and me. The evening was presided over by the Society's president Sir Jeremy Isaacs.

'Service or disservice?' Sophie Balhetchet, the author, John Wyvver and Phil Redmond after being presented with Silver Medals by the Royal Television Society (David Graham was unavoidably absent).

Courtesy of the Royal Television Society

Yet even during that evening of celebration at the RTS a nagging question remained. Had the rise of the independent sector and the translation of that 'radical idea on the margin' to the mainstream, really been such a 'service to television'? If the real aim of the leading protagonists on the independents' side had been to advance their own careers, to make themselves and other independent producers rich, many must have succeeded beyond their wildest dreams. If so Sir Paul's initial assessment of the outcome of the programme makers' war with the broadcasters was correct. But had that been their aim? It certainly was not what they claimed at the time. Their aim, and I believe that the majority were sincere in that aim, had been to bring freer television to Britain; to provide themselves and others with the opportunity to make more adventurous programmes, using the means they thought were most appropriate; to open up television to the expression of a range of ideas, tastes and styles which were excluded; to make entry into the medium open to people from all backgrounds; it was to free the television organisations from a combination of stifling bureaucracy, trade union restrictive practices, pompous self-aggrandisement and rampant greed.

Measured against these aims, the independents' success had to be judged as at best partial and at worst counterproductive. In 2000 did we really have better television than in 1968? Was it any less driven by self-aggrandisement and greed? It was undeniable that along the way the campaigners had had real successes and could claim some lasting achievements. They had played a vital part in freeing up the way in which programmes were made, in ridding the production process of overmanning and restrictive practices and in opening up television to new entrants. Those new entrants, who themselves became independent producers, had been the bringers of new ideas, styles, tastes and perspectives – political, social and aesthetic. The independent campaigners had played a vital role in wresting the second commercial channel from ITV and bringing about a publisher–broadcaster Channel Four. All of these things were real advances and most of them had endured. In its first five years Channel Four did more to enliven and reinvigorate television creatively and intellectually than anything in the previous twenty years. That by the summer of 2000 it did not seem quite so ground-breaking or courageous as in its early days was not really so surprising. It was, after all, getting on for twenty years old.

So why were Sir Paul and I both so gloomy?

To find the answer one had to look at all that had happened to television since the passing of the 1990 Broadcasting Act and, in particular, at events since New Labour had won its landslide general election victory on 1 May 1997. Tony Blair had taken office with the biggest majority since the Second World War, bigger even than Attlee's in 1945. After eighteen years of Tory rule the electorate had seemed to be looking for something more than an end to the sleaze and party in-fighting that had characterised the last years of John Major's government. 'New Labour. New Britain!' Blair had proclaimed repeatedly during the election campaign.

The mood among most people in television had been little different to the mood in the wider electorate. After years of Tory rule, which had to many in television often felt like an enemy occupation, they had breathed a sigh of relief. Government threats to broadcasting had, they now hoped, been lifted. Yet even then nagging doubts remained. Those of us who remembered the 1960s and 1970s reflected uneasily on the record of past Labour administrations. Harold

Wilson's tenure of Number 10 had been generally bad-to-disastrous for broad-casting. Much of the impetus which had led to the campaign for Channel Four and the creation of the independent sector had been born out of the frustrations of programme makers under Labour governments. It was Wilson who had started the practice of packing the BBC Board of Governors and the IBA with his cronies and placemen. It was he who, in an act of spite at least the equal of anything done by Thatcher, had translated Lord Hill from the Independent Television Authority to the BBC, provoking the BBC's Vice-Chairman to say that 'It was the end of the BBC as I knew it.' Yes, it was the Wilson government that had appointed the Annan Committee and then resurrected it after Heath had stood it down. But it was Wilson who had barred people he did not approve of like Anthony Smith from sitting on it. It was Callaghan's government that had failed to act on Annan's recommendations and which intensified the pressure on broadcasters not to report uncomfortable truths about what was happening in Northern Ireland. Labour governments had done the groundwork for many of the most illiberal interventions into broadcasting of the Thatcher regime.

New Labour's 1997 election manifesto had promised the early establishment of a new broadcasting regulator, but by the summer of 2000 when Sir Paul and I talked, it had done nothing about it. Instead, the new government had put out a Green Paper which told us that it was not yet clear which way communications markets were moving and that, in any case, the current regulatory system was flexible enough to deal with anticipated developments. This had been followed by further papers, 'consultations', seminars and reports which together served to tell us that, pending a White Paper, the government would continue with its present 'evolutionary' approach of adapting communications regulations as circumstances required. Although back in 1991, while in opposition, the Labour Party had said it would prevent takeovers between ITV companies, once in office it had done nothing to halt the onward march of the companies towards 'a single ITV' and their 'evolution' into one giant company. It had become all too evident that the emphasis on 'markets' rather than good broadcasting that had characterised Tory broadcasting policy remained in place under New Labour. On the night of his election victory Tony Blair had said, 'A new dawn has broken,' and then, as though facing a moment of doubt, had quickly turned it into a question, 'has it not?' Three years on, for many of those in broadcasting who cared about programmes, the answer to Blair's tentative question now seemed to be 'No'.

With a timing that had seemed auspicious, on 2nd May 1997, just hours after

Tony Blair had hesitantly hailed a new dawn, Michael Jackson, one-time organiser of the Channel Four Group, after eight years at the BBC in which he had been promoted first to Controller of BBC-2 and then to Controller of BBC-1 and Director of Television, had been appointed Chief Executive of Channel Four. That had looked like a genuine liberation. Now one of the campaigners' own would be in charge of what was still widely regarded by independents as *their* channel. Two months earlier Channel 5 had started transmissions with another former campaigner at its head, David Elstein.

Shortly after Michael Jackson had taken over at Channel Four Sophie Balhetchet was approached about joining the Channel Four board. Unfortunately Tony Garnett and Balhetchet's colleagues at World Productions felt that for her to accept would create an unacceptable conflict of interest and, even though the invitation was repeated, Balhetchet was forced to decline. I say 'unfortunately' because, with her relationship with Jackson going back to the idealistic days of the Channel Four Group, she might have been in a position to exert the kind of influence on him that might have averted some of the disasters to come.

A year before becoming Channel Four's chief executive, Michael Jackson had made a speech at a Royal Television Society dinner. In it he had warned that Channel Four, of all the established channels, was the one losing the most credibility: 'Am I alone in thinking that the pursuit of demographics – in particular, young, lager-drinking, upwardly mobile men – has led to a sapping of Channel 4's originality?' Giving the implied answer, 'No', Jackson had continued: 'Treating the audience simply as categories of consumers is the worm in the bud of any television channel that wants to be taken seriously.'[1] But, four years on in March 2000, after Jackson himself had been in charge of the Channel for almost three years, the *Guardian* had run a three-page feature headed *What Is Channel 4 for?* and subtitled ' . . . the end of Britain's great broadcasting experiment'. Reminding Jackson of his speech four years earlier, the *Guardian* had accused Jackson of an even deeper betrayal of the Channel's values. Channel Four's offerings, the *Guardian* said, were characterised by being loud and sensational, designed to produce tabloid headlines whatever the subject – 'Sensation is always the selling point. Good looks seem obligatory . . . You can watch *Ibiza Uncovered*, a fly-on-the-wall series about roistering Britons abroad, or *Caribbean Uncovered*, which is another, or *Greece Uncovered*, which repeats the formula. You can see *TFI Friday* or *The Priory*, which are talk-shows for trendy celebrities and studio crowds of students in low-cut dresses. You can snigger at *Something for the Weekend*, as Denise Van Outen quizzes blushing lads about their sex lives. You can stay up for *The 11 O'Clock Show*, and hear undergraduate jokes about Gary Glitter. You can follow *Friends*, for which Channel 4 recently paid £120 million for exclusive broadcast rights, along with *ER*, and stare at more young dimples and firm jaws.' An anonymous independent was quoted as saying of the Channel, 'They're very safe. They say they're radical, but it's all tits and willies, not anything difficult.'[2]

A month before the *Guardian* article appeared, Jackson himself had asked one of his closest friends and colleagues from his Channel Four Group days to prepare some confidential notes on the Channel's problems and future strategy. Jackson's friend had written that Channel Four's key problem was that its brand values and commercial success were grounded in qualities such as boldness, daring, distinctiveness, that better characterised the Channel Four of five or seven years earlier than the Channel Four of 2000. The Channel was, he told Jackson, living on its reputation. Innovation was now almost exclusively focused, fetish-like, on new technology. As a result of over-concentrating on retaining its audience share the Channel was coming to feel more homogenous and bland than it ever had before, with the result that it was in danger of heading for a niche somewhere between Sky One and Channel 5. He told Jackson bluntly that he was underestimating his audience. Since he had been in charge commissioning editors had come to understand their jobs exclusively in terms of delivering audience numbers. Discussions of cultural, social, aesthetic and even moral values were seen as unimportant and often derided. Alternative traditions and bodies of work were dismissed as irrelevant and the world in which the Channel lived seemed only to have one foreign country – the USA.[3]

By 2000 Channel Four seemed personified by the forbidding aura of its expensive Richard Rogers-designed building. Sitting in the reception area one winter evening in 2000 waiting to see Michael Jackson, it came to me where I had encountered this atmosphere before: 'It feels like the interior of a modern American penitentiary. The semicircle of glass and steel, with the twelve TV monitors facing out showing repeated images of C4's output like security camera monitors; the galleries above the void which is the reception area, even the wire bracing struts give the illusion of the anti-suicide nets stretched between the galleries in the open well of a prison to break the fall of prisoners who throw themselves off. The galleries only need equipping with bars and grilles and one would be in a prison hall. All that is missing are the caged prisoners, their hands and arms poking out through the grilles, faces pressed against them, calling out to each other, voices reverberating across the void to produce the imitable sound of echoing desperation that typifies a modern prison.'⁴ Channel Four, in aura and spirit, was by now a far cry indeed from the slightly chaotic, tatty but somehow friendly confusion of people and motor-bike messengers, benignly haunted by the optimistic shade of Peter Pan, and overseen by the ebullient figure of Jeremy Isaacs and his team of young, enthusiastic commissioning editors that had characterised the Channel's premises in its Charlotte Street days.

In September 2000 Jackson and Channel Four came under fresh attack, this time from one of the Channel's own most staunch and respected creative guardians, Anthony Smith. In an article in the London *Evening Standard* Smith declared, 'Channel 4 is floundering.' Reminding readers that Channel Four was unique in the world because it was charged with being 'utterly different' from its competitors and was required to encourage innovation and experiment, Smith challenged, 'Look at the schedules and find me one programme that contributes towards a "distinctive" character. Of course there is a scattering of good stuff but where are the programmes for uncatered "tastes and interests"? *Big Brother* is the only innovation, dubious and unoriginal though that project was in its purposes and values.' Smith damned the Channel Four schedule beside the programmes of fifteen years earlier. 'All one hears nowadays from young would-be producers is a tale of endless stonewalling from commissioning editors whose eyes are trans-fixed not even by the BBC's programmes but by those of Channel 5, which has become Channel 4's most serious rival, apparently.' Smith reported a telling phrase recently used by a documentaries' commissioning editor about the kind of programmes he wanted – he was 'looking for intelligent tabloid stuff'. Commis-sioning editors, Smith said, were no longer 'the receivers of ideas', they were now solely intent on finding 'people to carry out their own low-rent whims'. Under Jackson the channel had ceased to be a 'common room' seething with ideas for how to re-build the world and become instead 'a Vatican of commissioning editors serving a Pope-like chief executive mesmerised by the arcana of tele-vision'. Surely, Smith lamented, 'there are people around who still believe in Channel 4's real purposes, rather than in the pursuit of television for its own sake'. That very week one able and successful independent had told Smith that 'Working for Channel 4 has just become a job – I came into this as a vocation.'⁵

Although Jackson tried to defend the Channel's output, dismissing Smith's attack as rose-tinted nostalgia for a past which had not been as wonderful as hindsight made it seem, the attacks continued. They came now not just from the

Channel's founding fathers and disillusioned programme makers, but from its commercial competitors and the prophets of the free market. They accused Channel Four of pouring large sums of money, earned from operating a public asset free of charge, into setting up and subsidising commercial ventures, such as the pay services FilmFour and E4. They accused the Channel of using its protected position not to benefit public service broadcasting or in furtherance of its remit, but to fund its own commercial expansion. Jackson responded that while some of his new services, such as a schools' homework service, would perform a public service and were unlikely ever to make a profit, his new commercial services represented a prudent investment in the Channel's future. With the coming proliferation of television channels, Channel Four could not expect its single terrestrial advertiser-funded Channel to continue to provide it indefinitely with enough income from which to fund the full range of programmes required by its remit. By 'sweating the public assets' now and using surplus funds to support new ventures until they were successful, he was acting to guarantee the future of the Channel and the survival of the ideal which it embodied.

However, Jackson's new ventures continued to lose prodigious amounts of money and on 23 July 2001, Jackson announced that he was leaving his half a million pounds a year job at Channel Four to take up what was described as 'the lucrative post' of President and Chief Executive Officer of a major American media corporation.

*　　*　　*

By the summer of 2000 Channel 5 provided an even more glaring demonstration than Channel Four that having a former campaigner at the helm of a channel and getting as many as 85% of its programmes from independent producers was no guarantee of either quality or idealism.

In the 1988 broadcasting White Paper, Channel 5's purpose had been described as to 'enlarge choice and introduce competition in the advertising market'. After winning the franchise, Lord Hollick, Blairite boss of UBM, had described Channel 5's purpose as to be the Channel that 'helps people cope with life'. By 2000, after three years on air under David Elstein's leadership, it had become all too clear exactly what that gnomic statement meant. As Dawn Airey, Channel 5's Director of Programmes had jauntily told a Royal Television Society dinner in the autumn of 1999, she was 'in the commercial broadcast business. Channel 5 is there to make money for shareholders, to return value on their investment . . . I am not a traditional public service broadcaster and I am not aiming above people's heads – a little lower is more my style.'[6] More bluntly, Channel 5 was 'the films, football and fucking channel'. An unambitious enough goal. But Channel 5 wasn't very good at even that. Too often on Channel 5 the films were old and lousy, the football was the games that no one else wanted and the fucking, well, that wasn't much good either. Neither I, nor I suspect most other programme makers, had any objection to any of these things *per se*, but surely even if the presentation of films, football and fucking was the purpose of Channel 5, and assuming that the licensing authority, the ITC, was indeed happy with those aims, someone still ought at least to have been trying to ensure that each was good of its kind? In August 2000 Channel 5's Controller of Special Events tried pushing the Channel's luck even further. He called for British television channels to be allowed to show hardcore pornography. The ITC, however, was only spurred into action when, following a string of complaints about shows like *Naked Jungle* (a nude game show introduced by a naked Keith Chegwin), the Secretary of State for Culture, Media and Sport (DCMS), Chris Smith, gave vent to concern in Parliament about the amount of 'smut' on television. Now, in a move that seemed perverse after its previous lack of action, the ITC announced that it would be holding 'early discussions' with Channel 5 executives. Then, in September 2000, David Elstein resigned (industry rumour having it that he had jumped before he was pushed). As a result the forthright Dawn Airey was left to get on with running the Channel alone. Shortly after this, much started to be made of the fact that Channel 5 had begun to transmit a few 'serious' programmes – a development which provoked in many programme makers much the same response as that provoked in Samuel Johnson when he compared women preachers to a dog walking on its hind legs: 'It is not done well; but one is surprised to find it done at all.' In January 2003 Dawn Airey moved on to become Director of Rupert Murdoch's Sky networks. A match made in heaven, to be consummated by direct signal from the ionosphere, perhaps?

*   *   *

For all Channel Four and Five's shortcomings, it was in ITV (also with a number of former campaigners in very senior posts) that the most dramatic impact of the new 'light' or, as Sophie Balhetchet had called it, 'poor' regulation brought in by the 1990 Broadcasting Act could be seen. By 2000 independents supplied some

30% of ITV's non-news programmes, roughly 900 hours, worth more than £150 million. Yet the quality and range of programmes on ITV had deteriorated so much since the 1980s that even its enfeebled regulator, the ITC, had repeatedly to condemn its schedule. In its annual report in that year the ITC had damned even ITV's entertainment shows. They had, the ITC said, 'begun to look all the same'. Where in 1968, when the campaigners started, and even in 1988, after Channel Four had been on the air for six years, there had still been two major current affairs series, *World in Action* and *This Week*, on air on ITV in peak time each week, plus *Weekend World* on Sunday mornings and a regular succession of major documentaries in a 10.30 p.m. weekday slot, by 2000 there was only *Tonight*, a current affairs magazine which the ITC condemned repeatedly: 'Too great a concentration of lighter treatments and the focus on celebrity interviews tended to provide insufficient depth.' ITV's once-proud documentary tradition had been reduced to 'cheap and easy television' with 'caught on camera' (docusoaps and security camera footage) and ' . . . from hell' series predominating. ITV's arts output was by 2000 so inadequate that the ITC called on ITV to overhaul it 'so as to meet fully the definition of arts programming'. ITC research showed a narrowing of diversity in peak-time programmes on all the main terrestrial channels, together with a drop in the volume of arts and current affairs in peak time of 40% and 50% respectively. The ITC's programme department head called arts and current affairs programmes a 'threatened species'. ITV's drama, which had once boasted *Armchair Theatre*, *Brideshead Revisited* and *The Jewel in the Crown*, was now almost completely restricted to soap operas, thrillers, doctors and the emergency services. On the rare occasions when it did produce a lush costume series, such as *Dr Zhivago* in 2002, it was skewed towards the romantic, possible international sales and, in the case of *Dr Zhivago*, graced by a string of performances in leading roles so inept that they would not have been countenanced by the producers of series such as *Brideshead* or *Jewel in the Crown*.

The overall decline in ITV, which until the beginning of 1993 had been regarded in both the quality of its programmes and the variety of its schedule, as being at least the equal of BBC-1, was perhaps most clearly illustrated by the ITC's comment that without the game show *Who Wants To Be a Millionaire?* its schedule would 'look thin indeed'. ITV's retreat from its once proud traditions was perhaps best exemplified by the fact that Granada's factual department, which had once been the home of series like *World in Action* and *Disappearing World*, was now the home of ITV's latest hit reality show *I'm a Celebrity, Get Me Out of Here!* Yet despite its downmarket skelter ITV was still failing to stem the desertion to other channels of its audience. By July 2002 ITV's share had fallen to a nadir of 22.8%.

* * *

In 1977 the Annan Committee described the BBC as the most important cultural institution in the country. In his autobiography, published in 1999, *It Seemed Like a Good Idea at the Time*, Michael Grade says that when he joined it as Controller of BBC-1, in 1984, it was 'a community of highly creative programme makers'. But, he goes on to say, 'At least, it *was* a community until my erstwhile friend John Birt ... took a spanner to it, then reassembled the resulting pieces to make a factory, all system and no soul.'[7] The original dissidents and *samizdat* writers in the BBC of 1968, from among whose ranks many of the leading independents later came, had complained even then that the BBC was too much like a factory, and that its management lacked soul and courage. By the year 2000 a combination of the continued Director-Generalship of John Birt and the operation of the 25% independent production quota had, far from improving morale in the BBC or reinvigorating its creative management, only served to add to the deterioration in staff morale and increase professional insecurity among the Corporation's programme makers.

Where once the BBC had produced more than 400 hours of television drama per year, most of it original single plays or series and no soap operas, by 2000, although the total number of hours of drama had not decreased, the proportion of single, original plays had fallen dramatically. In 2002 BBC Television's output of single dramas and films fell to just fourteen single dramas in all – eight feature films and six TV films. Even as late as 1983 the BBC had been producing 113 single dramas (if one added in ITV and Channel Four the total number of single dramas transmitted was 215 – 330 hours in all). By 2000 the BBC's drama output was mainly soaps, or formulaic hospital and police series. These were spiced up with some two-part thrillers, generally featuring a popular television star, plus a few lavish classic series. The BBC's films were now made with an eye on cinema release, the classic series deliberately pitched so as to maximise overseas sales and co-production finance. In the 1960s television had helped to discover and nurture many of the finest dramatic writers of the age – Harold Pinter, Alun Owen, Peter Nicholls, Dennis Potter, David Mercer, Alan Bleasdale, Alan Bennett, Alan Plater, Jack Rosenthal, John McGrath, Jim Allen – while other, already established,

writers had been happy to work for it – John Osborne, John Mortimer, Terence
Rattigan, C. P. Taylor, Tom Stoppard. By the end of the 1990s openings that
might once have attracted the best writers had become limited to the occasional
high-profile series, such as Peter Flannery's *Our Friends from the North* and
Stephen Poliakoff's absorbing, multi-layered *Perfect Strangers*, or adapting a
literary classic. Writers of real creative ambition soon tire of writing episodes for
soap operas or formulaic thrillers. They go elsewhere. This is graphically brought
home in Dominic Dromgoole's book *The Full Room*, published in 2000, where he
inspected the work of over one hundred contemporary playwrights, many young
and most of them writing for the British theatre. Although some of them had
written for television in the past almost none did so by 2000. Dromgoole wrote
that we were living 'in the middle of a carnival, a free revel, a fête, flower show, a
harvest home . . . a grand glorious tender burst of new plays'. We were, he said,
living in 'golden age' of playwriting.[8] Had Dromgoole been writing a similar book
in the 1960s or 1970s, many of these writers would have been creating original
work for television and the claim to be living in a 'golden age', carnival or 'harvest
home' of writing would have applied every bit as much to television as to the
theatre. It was in the 1960s that John Hopkins' quartet *Talking to a Stranger* was
hailed as 'television's first authentic masterpiece' (a judgement amply confirmed
by its re-showing on BBC-4 in 2003. Although clearly the product of its period,
its four ninety-minute plays encompass more ideas and truth about family relationships and society's interaction with the family than a whole year's output from
all today's television drama departments combined). It was in the late 1960s that
the single play was first recognised as television's one original art form. By 2000
the one-off television play as a work of art worthy of consideration alongside a new
work for the theatre, cinema or dance theatre, barely existed.

Of course, a few bold and beautifully executed examples of drama did still
somehow continue to emerge through the prevailing mediocrity – Dominic
Savage's brilliant and savagely perceptive *When I Was Twelve* in 2001 on BBC-2
and his *Out of Control* on BBC-1 in 2002, a bold, modern reworking of *Othello* on
ITV, the superb, relevant and lavishly produced adaptation of Trollope's *The Way
We Live Now* starring David Suchet, on the BBC and, less happily, in 2001 the
superb and flawlessly directed series *From a Land of Plenty* on BBC-2 which, when
it did not get the size of audience the BBC had hoped for it, was allowed to play
out its remaining segments without adequate promotion.

Part of the blame for the virtual extinction of the original play for television lay in the success of Jeremy Isaacs' decision at the start of Channel Four to accede to the repeated demands of struggling British film makers and concentrate most of his limited drama budget on making low-budget films designed also to have a potential life in the cinema. Unfortunately when the BBC and ITV had seen the critical and box-office success of Channel Four films such as *Angel*, *Dance with a Stranger* and *My Beautiful Laundrette*, and realised that it was possible to get both critical acclaim, good publicity and sometimes even some useful income from a comparatively modest outlay on drama, they had followed suit, although not always with quite such striking results or cinematic courage. The result of Jeremy Isaacs' and David Rose's original decision, although welcomed at the time by the campaigners, had over time done a massive disservice to television drama as a whole.

Twenty years on, when justly celebrated films like *The Full Monty*, *Brassed Off* or *Bend It Like Beckham*, usually made with the assistance of television money and which would once have been made solely for television, finally arrived on television after successful runs in the cinema, they still drew large audiences (larger than they might without the cinema exposure). However, by the time they were shown on television their showing no longer made the same social or critical impact that they would once have made. By allowing what should have been its most politically and culturally significant work to be produced in the first instance for another medium, television had shot itself in the foot. It had bolstered the reputation of the British cinema while blunting its own relevance and reducing the social, political and cultural immediacy of what was once widely seen as the apex of its own creative achievement. When Ken Loach's *The Navigators*, set among a gang of track maintenance men on Britain's failing railways, was shown on Channel Four in December 2001, it went out at 10 o'clock at night and passed largely unheralded and unsung. Loach, more than anyone, epitomises that generation of directors nurtured by the BBC's *Wednesday Play* in the 1960s. At any time until the birth of Channel Four, *The Navigators* would have been made as a television play and almost certainly would, and should, have caused a major stir and an outcry, as his and Jeremy Sandford's *Cathy Come Home* had when it was transmitted in 1966. These films, which would once have been television plays, were still efficient consumer products. They drew audiences and, if they were successful in the cinema, their revenue-earning potential was enhanced. However, they were now increasingly regarded by television as just that – consumer products. They were a prime example of the 'commodification' of television. The result, as David Hare put it in 2002, had been to rob us of 'the most important new indigenous art form of the 20th century'.[9]

It was the latent tendency to treat their work simply as a species of consumer product, measured and valued by its capacity to draw audiences and sell advertising space, that had been one of the chief concerns of the original campaigners. By 2000, the people who owned and ran independent production companies, just as much as those who owned and operated commercial television channels, were increasingly forced to value their own work in just that way – as a species of consumer product. In perhaps a final ironic twist to the tendency of things to come full circle in this story, and in the baleful history of the British cinema, in the summer of 2002 Channel Four announced that its film arm, FilmFour, had lost so much money as a result of extravagance and unwise investments in high-budget, supposedly commercial projects, as opposed to the low-budget specialist films upon which its reputation had been built, that it was to be brought back under the direct control of Channel Four's drama department and made to concentrate on providing the kind of films for the channel which Jeremy Isaacs and David Rose had in mind when they set up Film on Four in the early 1980s.

A similar 'commodification' had been evident in factual programming of all kinds. In 1999 Steven Barnett and Emily Seymour's research for the Campaign for Quality Television in *A Shrinking Iceberg Travelling South. . .* had quantified the resulting narrowing of content. On all channels there was a relentless burgeoning of so-called 'reality shows' like *Big Brother, Survivor, Pop Idol* and *I'm a Celebrity, Get Me Out of Here!* Coverage of foreign stories had almost disappeared from current affairs on ITV, while on the BBC it had largely migrated from BBC-1 to BBC-2. Although there were still admirable overseas current affairs reports in BBC-2's *Correspondent*,[10] *Panorama*, mostly shorn of foreign stories, was being bounced around all over the BBC-1 schedule and out of the best peak hours until by 2002 it seemed likely to wind up on BBC-2. One could still sometimes find excellent factual series, such as Laurence Rees's *The Nazis – A Warning from History* from the BBC in 1999 and Adam Curtis's *Century of the Self* on BBC-2 in 2002, which easily matched the celebrated series of thirty years earlier like *Civilisation* and *The Ascent of Man*. However, the single creative documentary in the tradition of Humphrey Jennings, which had largely been saved from extinction and then nurtured to new heights in television between the late 1950s and the 1980s by director–auteurs like Denis Mitchell, Philip Donnellan and Paul Watson, was by the end of the 1990s once more an endangered species (Watson's brilliant study of the effects of Alzheimer's Disease in *Malcolm and Barbara, a Love Story* in 1997 from Granada was merely the exception to prove the rule). First the creative documentary had been corralled into series such as *Modern Times* (BBC) and *Cutting Edge* (Channel Four) and from March 2002 onwards had been pretty much banished to the outer space of BBC-4 (where individual films were seen by only a few thousand viewers). In order to get documentaries made at all they had become ever more dependent on international co-production money, thus further undermining the documentary as a mode of creative interpretation of Britain and British society for British audiences.

The cumulative result of all these pressures was that television as a whole had lost much of its creative ambition. Instead of offering its programme makers creative challenges, it more than ever sought to channel their energies into attention seeking and 'easy viewing'. BBC-1 increasingly resembled ITV, while BBC-2, which after the advent of Channel Four had seemed spurred into a new energy and originality, was crammed with consumer and lifestyle programmes. While it eschewed the kind of 'every-night is Friday night' laddishness of Jackson's Channel Four, its schedule too often seemed drawn from the index page of some supermarket or DIY customer magazine. The hours from 7 p.m. to 9 p.m. each weekday were crammed with make-over shows, cooking programmes or what appeared to be versions of 'What Car?' and 'Gardening Magazine'. The cooks and gardeners who appeared on the BBC were allowed to lend their names to the promotion of commercial brands and retail outlets. The line between public service detachment and commercial promotion was becoming ever more blurred – this blurring not helped by the BBC's insistent on-air promotion of its own products, additional services, spin-offs, up-coming programmes and brands. The overall tone and effect of these often seemed designed as much to make BBC channels appear and sound like commercial channels as to sell the programmes and services being promoted. The distinction between commercial and public service values was being further undermined by the growing list of BBC joint ventures with Murdoch's BSkyB (of which their successful bid in 2002 to operate the spectrum vacated by the defunct ITV Digital was to be but the most spectacular). In short, television had become almost indistinguishable from any other branch of consumerism. The audience on all channels was increasingly treated in the first instance as consumers and only secondly as citizens.

Even some of those who had been among the main architects of the 1990 Broadcasting Act were by this time beginning to have doubts about the wisdom of what they had done. When I interviewed Lord Griffiths of Fforestfach (who as Professor Brian Griffiths had been the Head of Mrs Thatcher's Number 10 Policy Unit in the 1980s and one of the godparents of the legislation) for this book in the autumn of 2000 he said: 'If you ask me – is television today better than it was in the 1980s? I have to say – no.' He and his colleagues, he believed, had been 'too optimistic about how the broadcasters would behave if given greater freedom in the Broadcasting Act'.[11]

*   *   *

After a decade of independents supplying a major proportion of the programmes on all five terrestrial channels, far from improving, the quality of the programmes offered by these channels had declined to a level not seen since the early days of ITV. Of course responsibility for this could not be laid entirely at the independents' door. They had, after all, only been supplying the programmes that the broadcasters had wanted from them. The main responsibility lay with Mrs Thatcher's legislative reforms and the increased emphasis on competition and commercial goals which these had brought with them. Yet the independents could not escape responsibility altogether.

When he left PACT to take up the post of Director of the British Film Institute in February 1998, John Woodward had written two articles.[12] In one, written for PACT's members and published in the PACT Magazine, he told of how, while clearing out his desk, he had found a copy of The 25% Campaign manifesto. It made, he said, 'for extraordinary and surreal reading. It was produced in 1986 yet the document reeks of post hippie, pre-Thatcherite liberal consensus. I had forgotten that the underlying purpose of the campaign was to open up the BBC "to new or unheard voices" and "to broaden the range and diversity of ITV's output." ' In the other article he repeated the story of how a group of independents had had lunch with Professor Griffiths on the Limehouse Studios boat after a tour of the *Spitting Image* workshops and of their blinding realisation that the Thatcher government's aim was greater efficiency in the BBC, not 'more communism'. Woodward described how the campaigners' reaction had been to adopt wholesale the language of Thatcherism. 'Suddenly being an independent meant being part of a new entrepreneurial business sector . . . independents who had been lifelong union members stopped paying their ACTT subs and started buying double-breasted suits with ridiculously large lapels.' Woodward asked, 'Did we grow up or did we sell out?'

The answer to Woodward's rhetorical question was not straightforward. It lay in the independents' history and successive campaigns. The original campaigners for the fourth channel had never had any real doubt about their aims. They had been founded on concepts of creative freedom, ideals about cultural and political diversity and a commitment to plurality in broadcasting. But in order to achieve their cultural goals they had had to act in the political arena. As a result, and particularly after the election of Mrs Thatcher, they had been forced increasingly to adopt the rhetoric of the time. While adopting the language of Thatcherism most of the original campaigners, the people who had gone on to become the first leaders of the independent sector, had never lost sight of the fact that this new language was just words, words chosen for their political expediency and as a cover with which to win over the government. For them the real aim had remained what it had always been. However, from the mid-1980s onwards, and particularly after the start of The 25% Campaign, for many of the new breed of independents who had joined the sector after the start of Channel Four, and for older ones who had undergone a change in priorities, the language of the enterprise culture increasingly came to reflect their new, more corporate goals. For them increasing their market share, opening up new financial opportunities, building their businesses and their profits, had become the number one objective. Because many of the independents had been seasoned campaigners, better at presenting their arguments than the broadcasters, they had eventually won their case. However, in the process, and because they counted among their number a lot of the most talented programme makers in the business and brought with them a whiff of idealism, they had at the same time played a significant role in making the goals of profit, audience maximisation and flash respectable in broadcasting. They had, as Roy Lockett put it, acted as 'Thatcher's Trojan ponies', and, in the words of Steven Barnett and Andrew Curry in *The Battle for the BBC*, clothed Thatcher's free-market policies in cultural respectability. As time had passed many independents had lost sight of why they were doing what they were doing. For these reasons, and because their struggle was so long drawn out, winning the battle for the implementation of the 25% quota had become almost an end in itself.

It may be argued that technological advance and the multiplication of channels since 1990 had made what had happened inevitable. Perhaps so. Nevertheless, it surely remained unarguable that, even if we campaigners had not 'sold out', by concentrating too exclusively on winning our war with the broadcasters we had made matters worse. We had, in short, lost the plot. Independents had failed to speak up with sufficient conviction for programme quality. Although they had spoken out against the more draconian of the Conservative ideas for bringing broadcasting under control – such as the Woodrow Wyatt 'balance' amendment to the 1990 Broadcasting Bill – they had not done so often enough. Because they spent so much of their time and energy at loggerheads with the broadcasters, they had weakened what should have been a united front within broadcasting to resist the most fundamental of Thatcher's 'reforms'.

So by the end of the 1990s the ideals of the campaigners who had founded the independent sector seemed to those within it 'surreal' and their principles 'extraordinary'. PACT, the unified independent producers' organisation, and its most influential members, now saw themselves, as much as broadcasters, as businesses which made programmes, not as they had in the 1980s, as programme makers who also ran businesses. Shaun Williams, who succeeded John Woodward as PACT's Chief Executive, told me when I interviewed him in November 2000, that new people joining the Association no longer 'see themselves as artists in the romantic sense of wanting to express themselves or affect society through making a piece of art'. As a result, although PACT still paid lip service to the aim of improving the quality of broadcasting which had been built into the original Articles of Association of its predecessor IPPA, those aims now rarely figured strongly in the Association's initiatives. At a meeting of independent producers in Bristol in 2000 when PACT members questioned one of the association's senior executives about what representations the Association had made to government during the run-up to a new broadcasting White Paper about the role of public service broadcasting, they were told: 'PACT finds it difficult to enter the Public Service Broadcasting debate.'

The polarisation between large and small independents had continued apace. A decade earlier, at the time of the original dispute inside IPPA about whether broadcasters should be allowed to own shares in independent producers, just 3% of independent companies had turned over more than £500,000 per year. Most of the remaining 97% had been turning over far less than this, each making just three or fewer programmes a year. Since that time the distance between the large and small independents had become steadily more marked, with the result that now the largest twenty or so companies between them made as many programmes as all the rest combined. This was pointed up by the way in which the two groups regarded the programmes which they produced. For the small producers the programmes were still the point and purpose of what they did – as Colin Thomas told me: 'The whole thing of being an independent is, or was, that you could do the things you cared about.' But for the large companies producing programmes had become simply a means to an end – the end being rights ownership and the opportunity to exploit them. As David Frank, the managing director of RDF, an independent formerly associated with high-quality documentaries such as *Century of the Self* but more recently better known for reality shows such as *Wife Swap* and *Faking It*, put it: 'We are like a large rights factory. Our production side creates products that we can sell. How and where we vend them is driven by what the markets are like at any time.'[13] In the words of RDF's Director of Programmes, Stephen Lambert: 'We are trying to create a company of value . . . one that will either float or be bought.'[14]

As the differences in priorities between large and small independents had increased, PACT, the organisation which represented all producers, had been led into a number of positions which would have horrified the original programme maker campaigners. Under EC legislation introduced in the 1990s, programme makers – directors and director–producers – had been granted rights, similar to those of authors, in their work. As a result they had become entitled to royalty payments each time that one of their programmes was shown on a channel or in a medium other than the one for which they had made the programme in the first place. This went a long way towards meeting one of the programme makers' original demands – that those who make programmes should have an ongoing interest in what happens to their work after its initial transmission.[15] But in 1999, at the same time as it had been mounting a renewed campaign to force the broadcasters to recognise independent producers' right to ongoing ownership of rights in programmes they had made, PACT had refused to recognise the new rights granted by the EC to directors and director–producers. PACT's representatives argued, in an echo of the arguments that had been used by the broadcasters' against the independents a decade earlier, that if an individual director or producer was unwilling to sign a contract which did not include rights to royalty payments, he or she was always 'free to walk away'. Therefore, PACT argued, 'a free market' existed. PACT feared that to recognise the programme makers' rights would reduce broadcasters' willingness to do business with independents. Yet many of PACT's member companies were still small producers, people who produced and directed the programmes they made and who therefore stood to benefit from the implementation of the new European legislation.

Since stepping down as Chairman of IPPA when it amalgamated with the TPA to form PACT in 1991 I had deliberately kept out of the Association's day-to-day affairs, believing that ex-chairmen should not try to tell their successors how to do things. But by now deeply dismayed at the way in which the independent sector had been moving, and incensed by this latest turn in PACT's policy, I contacted the trade union BECTU and the Directors' Guild to offer my services to try to change PACT's attitude. As a result another former campaigner, Mike Dibb, who like me ran a small independent production company, and I staged an ambush at PACT's 1999 Annual General Meeting. Turning up separately, we took up places in adjacent rows near the middle of the room – PACT AGMs were no longer the packed, often emotional affairs involving more than a hundred people staged in public halls because of the numbers who wanted to attend them that IPPA's had been in the 1980s. Held in the association's anonymous modern West End offices opposite the Middlesex Hospital, PACT's 1999 AGM was attended by about fifty people, most them members of PACT's Council, committees or staff members. When the Chair turned to the end of year accounts, normally a formality, I interjected with an objection. Consternation. Astonishment. I explained, I was moving for one pound to be deducted from the amount, more than a quarter of a million pounds, paid during the year by PACT to the Industrial Relations Service. I was objecting on the grounds that in its handling of the directors' rights issue it had acted against the interests of many of PACT's smaller company members. I added, for good measure, that if no change of heart was forthcoming I would resign from PACT as publicly as possible. The Chief Executive of the Industrial Relations Service was hastily summoned from the back of the room to defend PACT's actions. Reiterating the Association's arguments, he said that the only way in which the nature of a director's contribution to any particular programme could be properly reflected was by means of separate individual negotiation between director and company over each programme. Mike Dibb promptly countered that this was rubbish – experience showed that individual negotiations simply did not work. After some more discussion, and two Council members who had been colleagues in our campaigning days had deplored the tactics that Dibb and I had employed, it was agreed that PACT would re-open the issue and invited us to discussions with the people who were handling the negotiations. Almost a year later, and after united action by members of the Directors' Guild and BECTU, PACT backed down and reached an agreement with the directors.

As the gulf between big and small independents had widened it had placed the smaller or newer producers at an ever greater disadvantage, stifling the opportunities for new voices, people and ideas which once had been an essential element in the independent sector's *raison d'être*. By May 2002 Peter Bazalgette, the boss of Endemol, one of the biggest producers, could say: 'It is true that there is no point in a small company pitching for, say, *Big Breakfast* on its own. It's not credible that they could deliver it.'[16] If this had been the case in the early days of Channel Four Phil Redmond and his company would never have got to make *Brookside*, David Graham would have remained a frustrated current affairs producer dabbling in video graphics and in the late 1980s Tom Gutteridge would never have landed the long-running listings series upon which he had built the future wealth of his company, Mentorn.

Over the previous decade broadcasters had increasingly adopted policies under which they would only deal with a limited number of the bigger 'core' independent suppliers. Channel Four now held special briefings for small numbers of their most prolific suppliers, while staging more impersonal, less frequent meetings for the rest of the programme making hoi polloi.

It was no more than a logical next step, therefore, when, in October 2001, Channel Four announced that it was planning to buy stakes, through a wholly owned commercial subsidiary, in some of its largest independent suppliers. Prohibited under the terms of the Broadcasting Act from becoming a producer itself, owning significant chunks of its largest suppliers might be the next best thing for the Channel from a purely commercial standpoint, allowing it to share in the financial success of those companies. The Channel had already announced that it would be signing deals with between twenty and forty 'key suppliers' who it would expect to make 'at least several programmes or a series' for it each year. The producers concerned would be offered more 'grown-up' contract terms. Where these moves might leave the idea of Channel Four as a publisher–broadcaster equally open to all-comers, the independent sector as a whole or the encouragement of real creative originality, democratic and cultural freedom of expression for different, unusual or unpopular voices, was, it seemed, no longer relevant.

Some high-profile independents had for some time been actively seeking partnerships with wealthy international entertainment corporations, often companies which also controlled or were controlled by overseas broadcasters, so as to enter into ongoing programme and rights deals. Such arrangements often involved the independents selling off significant stakes in their companies to these corporations. As a result, by 2000 seven of the most successful independents had lost their independent status under the rules governing qualification for the 25% independent quota. The companies concerned now began to proclaim that the rules governing the 25% quota were an out-dated anomaly. Actively supported by PACT and led by Café Productions, which had recently been bought by a Canadian broadcast company, Alliance Atlantis, and Peter Bazalgette, the boss of Bazal productions (suppliers of *Big Brother* and numerous long-running lifestyle series), which had been bought by the large Dutch producer, Endemol, which, in turn, had been taken over by the Spanish broadcaster Telefónica, they started a vociferous campaign to get the rules changed so that they could get their independent status back. Bazalgette argued that to relax the rules would stimulate investment: 'Foreign investment in our creative industries', he said, shrewdly chiming in with New Labour industrial policy, 'should be seen as no less beneficial than in car companies or chip manufacturers.' Their campaign suc-ceeded and eighteen months later the government agreed to change the rules so that Bazalgette and others could regain their independent status.[17]

The distance between small independents and large, and the increasingly entrenched attitudes of those who spoke for them, was highlighted again in August 2001 when PACT invited a group made up only of large independents to a meeting with officials at the Department of Culture, Media and Sport. When news of this got out and John McVay, the new Chief Executive of PACT, was asked why these independents had been invited in preference to any representa-tives of smaller companies, he told a *Broadcast* reporter: 'We chose these indies because they demonstrate the creativity and innovation and are the real driving force of UK programming.' The inference, conscious or not, seemed to be that PACT no longer considered that smaller independents did demonstrate these things. Challenged over the fact that some of the independents had used the occasion to ask DCMS officials to drop the BBC's 25% quota in favour of allowing producers to retain more rights in their programmes (the BBC's Director-General, Greg Dyke, had already announced that he was approaching the government over a reduction in the 25% quota of programmes the BBC was obliged to take from independents), McVay had admitted to *Broadcast* that the independents chosen to meet DCMS officials did either want 'to retain more rights or to get more value through repeats on digital channels'.[18]

*   *   *

On 12 December 2000, after three and a half years in office, the New Labour government published its long promised Communications White Paper – *A New Future for Communications*.[19] Its priorities were instantly clear. 'First, we will make the UK home to the most dynamic and competitive communications and media market in the world.' The second objective, although spelled out in a more rambling and confused manner, ended with a similarly ringing declaration: 'Creating a dynamic, growing consumer market, which leads the world in innovation, is vital if the UK's creative, software and communications industries are to maintain their strengths. It also makes the UK an attractive place for inward investment.' The White Paper confirmed that the New Labour government regarded broadcasting as little more than part of a wider communications market and infrastructure which included telephones, the internet and mobile communications: 'We want the UK to be the world's leading innovative market for convergent communications software, content and technology.' Public service broadcasting, the quality and diversity of programmes available to the public except as an assumed adjunct or consequence of competition, came well down the list of government priorities, making their first rather apologetic appearance as no more than a part of the White Paper's eighth objective: 'Our public service broadcasting television and radio is among the best in the world. We will make sure that our citizens can continue to rely on, and enjoy, public service broadcasting which is widely admired and enjoyed.'

The White Paper was the work of two separate Departments of State, the DTI and the DCMS. There seemed little doubt about which department had been the dominant partner – the DTI. Throughout stress was laid on the contribution that communications could make to the national and regional economies and on what the White Paper called the need to 'maintain the UK's competitive advantage' in 'the international marketplace'. To this end it was proposed that broadcasting should be subject to 'lighter touch' and even 'self-regulation'.

The White Paper's proposals were clearly posited on the expectation that the availability of digital and satellite services would accelerate and on the fervent desire of the Treasury to switch off the existing analogue services some time between 2006 and 2010, so that it could raise billions of pounds from selling off the vacated frequencies to commercial interests. It was mainly to this end that, at the start of the year, the BBC had been given a well above inflation licence fee increase with which to develop new digital services.

PACT, by its own lights, had played its White Paper hand well. In its lobbying it had concentrated on getting government recognition for 'the value of content creators', arguing that in the multi-channel age 'appealing content will be the main driver'. Therefore, it had argued, 'creating an environment in which makers of content can thrive' must be 'the top policy priority'.[20] PACT blamed the broadcasters' insistence on retaining all the rights in the programmes that they commissioned from independents for the fact that independent production companies were still failing to build up proper asset bases. The result was that independent production companies remained under-capitalised and had been unable to 'grow their businesses'. It was essential, PACT argued, to retain the independent production quota, as it provided 'the only protection for our members'. But quotas, on their own, PACT said, were not sufficient. What independents wanted was 'competition regulation', to ensure that the terms independents got from the ITV Network applied to all broadcasters. PACT suggested that Oftel, the telecoms industry regulator, offered a suitable model for a new broadcasting regulator which should take over the duties of both the ITC and the BBC Governors.

When it was published, not only did the White Paper indicate that the independent quota would be kept, it suggested that the rules limiting the level of cross-ownership between broadcasters and independents would be relaxed in more or less precisely the way that PACT had asked for. In places the White Paper's language actually seemed to echo PACT's own. However, once again the effect of PACT's successful lobbying appeared likely to advantage the few big producers rather than the mass of medium-sized and small independents who did not have the financial resources, nor often the desire, to take full advantage of the new terms. Supplying the high volumes of low-cost material that the broadcasters seemed increasingly likely to demand already often meant that the producer was paid less than the full cost of production in return for an increased share in the ongoing rights. The proposed new arrangements, successfully backed by PACT, seemed likely to increase this practice.

The White Paper's publication touched off a veritable plethora of articles, speeches and conferences, both inside the broadcasting industry and beyond. First off the mark was the ITC with a research paper,[21] published in January 2001, showing that the public wanted a continuation of public service broadcasting regulation. They wanted regulation strengthened rather than weakened, and did not believe that market forces alone would deliver diversity, high quality or innovative programming. This was felt as much by those who already subscribed to pay-TV services as by those who did not. Pundit followed pundit in slamming the White Paper's proposals, saying that they were too vague, gave too much power to the commercial operators, that the emphasis on market forces would push diversity to the margins and that the government's forecasts of the rate of digital take-up were wildly optimistic. At a conference at the Royal Society of Arts in January the broadcaster Jon Snow said that this was 'the defining moment, when Britain either sustains or abandons public service broadcasting'.[22] In June Lord Thomson, the former Chairman of the IBA, told an international conference that the Government's plans were 'primarily technology-driven to meet the demands of the global marketplace' and were not being put forward in the interests of public service broadcasting but to free up the UK's analogue frequencies 'to be sold by the state for non-broadcast activities and to meet the appetites of the Treasury'.

*   *   *

On 7 June 2001 the Blair government was, as expected, re-elected for a second term with a barely reduced majority. This was probably more a measure of the continuing shambles in the Conservative Party than of public admiration for New Labour's achievements in office. The overall election turn-out fell to less than 60%.

That August David Liddiment delivered the annual McTaggart Lecture at the start of the Edinburgh International Television Festival. Liddiment, ITV's Director of Channels, had charge of ITV's £740 million a year programme budget. As he himself freely admitted, he therefore bore a heavy responsibility for not only what was seen on ITV but, because of the knock-on effects of his decisions, for much of what had happened on the other channels as well. He declared that the industry had a suffered a loss of 'innate creativity', arising, he believed, from the broadcasters' obsession with ratings. Voicing what many in television thought but had until then been too much in awe of the prevailing consumerist orthodoxy to openly confront, he said: 'The soul of British television is in danger . . . Numbers now seem to be the only universal measure for excellence we have: how many, how much, how often. We are losing sight of the innate value of programmes in our fixation on the success that can be measured by profit, profile and performance . . . The relentless quest to find out what viewers want and then to give it to them has made for sameness.'[23] Predictably, he sought to shift much of the blame from ITV and place the major responsibility for rectifying matters on the BBC.

Two weeks later, on 11 September, Islamist terrorists hijacked four passenger aircraft in the United States and deliberately smashed them into the twin towers of the New York World Trade Center and the Pentagon in Washington, murdering some 3,000 people. The world suddenly darkened, appearing more riven and threatening than at any time for more than a generation. In response President George W. Bush declared a 'War on Terror' and less than a month later launched a full-scale assault on Afghanistan.

To those who still believed that television had a role beyond escapism or as a weapon in the armoury of the advertising industry, this new situation called for a response way beyond any mere pursuit of numbers or success measured by profit. It required not only news programmes, journalism and current affairs programmes that were fearless, comprehensive and fair, but drama, documentary and arts programmes worthy of the imaginations, intelligence and ideals of the public; it required schedulers who would not be content to dump serious or challenging programmes in the hours when no one would watch them or on channels where only a handful of viewers would see them, and regulators armed with the powers and possessing the will to enforce such decisions.

However, just two days after the attack on the World Trade Center, Peter Bazalgette, UK boss of the Dutch entertainment corporation Endemol, the purveyors of much of the reality television and many of the consumer make-over shows that had infected the schedules like a measles epidemic, delivered the prestigious Royal Television Society Huw Wheldon Memorial Lecture. For all the notice that he took of what had been said by Liddiment, or for that matter of the tragic events in America two days earlier, Bazalgette might have been living on another planet. Instead he used his lecture to argue that, far from the 1960s or 1970s having been television's golden age – 'Golden age be damned' – this was it. This dubious thesis he rested on the claim that because there were now more channels, more ordinary people appeared on them and the popular factual shows of 2001 attracted larger audiences than some of the factual programmes of the past, television was better than ever before. Far from 'television's soul' being in danger, we needed still more channels and still greater chunks of the airtime on them dedicated to programmes such as *Who Wants To Be a Millionaire?*, *EastEnders* and *The Weakest Link*. Bazalgette was having no truck with notions such as a programme's 'innate value'. He rejoiced in the idea that regulation was 'gradually passing from the state to the individual'. He derided Kingsley Amis's dictum that 'More means worse' and dismissed all those who disagreed with him as merely disappointed older programme makers who were no longer able to get their pet projects commissioned. He called on the industry to celebrate 'the opportunities we now have'.

Before quitting Channel Four for America, Michael Jackson had made a speech in which he had called public service broadcasting a 'pointless ju-ju stick', a term 'drained of all purpose and meaning'. Now, with the government clearly bent on reducing regulation and giving commercial competition ever more free rein, more and more of the industry's leading figures began picking up the same theme. A few months after Bazalgette's speech John Hambley, the chief executive of a tiny, struggling subscription channel, Artsworld, told journalists that rather than strive to find a new definition for the term 'public service broadcasting' it 'should be put in the bin'.[24] Cento Veljanovski, a free-market communications consultant who had advised the Peacock Committee, went still further. He claimed that as the number of channels grew, the reasons there had been for establishing the BBC in the first place were becoming ever weaker: 'The basic problem is that all the objectives of public service broadcasting have been breached by the BBC so it is hard to decide what (public service broadcasting) is now. No one's been prepared to take the logical step of going back to the drawing board and asking, why do we need non-commercial television in a digital age?'

* * *

In February 2002 the number of multi-channel viewers (those who could receive digital, satellite or cable channels, rather than only analogue channels) out-numbered terrestrial viewers for the first time, while the total fees paid by viewers to subscription services now topped £2 billion. At the same time, however, increasing numbers of those running these new services were finding the going hard and by the end of that year 104 of them had handed back their licences, while the overall hours of viewing on all channels had begun to fall by record amounts. That spring ITV Digital, into which the two biggest ITV companies, Carlton and Granada had reportedly sunk a billion pounds, finally collapsed.

A few days later, on 7 May, five years after taking office, the New Labour Government published its Draft Communications Bill.[25] Unswayed by all the dire warnings and doubts voiced in the previous eighteen months, the Draft Bill confirmed and reinforced the objectives and priorities of the White Paper. The first aim remained to create 'the most dynamic, competitive communications industry in the world' and make the UK 'one of the most attractive places for communications companies to do business', while the drive to deregulate seemed, if anything, stronger than ever. 'Across the economy, deregulation brings benefits for consumers and for businesses' (try telling that to people in rural areas threatened with losing their daily home delivery of post or who travelled regularly by train). 'Unnecessary regulations need to be removed wherever possible. By eliminating undue burdens on business we can drive innovation, increase investment, raise employment and bring better services to consumers.' In order to police this new broadcasting and communications landscape the Bill proposed to sweep away a plethora of separate regulators and replace them with one catch-all regulator, Ofcom. This body was to be responsible for everything from radio spectrum and communications networks to media ownership, TV licensing and broadcasting regulation. For the moment at least, there remained just one major element in broadcasting that would not be regulated by Ofcom, the BBC. The draft Bill also signalled a further relaxation in the ITV ownership rules, opening the way for the creation of a single ITV, possibly under foreign ownership, and for Rupert Murdoch's BSkyB to take over Channel 5. The new regime, the two Secretaries of State said in a joint summary of their proposals, 'will provide a clear set of rules that will give businesses the certainties they need to invest and expand'. This new regime would provide for 'more self-regulation and give commercial broadcasters greater freedom to set their own standards'.

The broadcasting industry's reaction to the Bill was what might kindly be called 'cautious'. Even those who had grave doubts seemed frightened of offending the government. David Liddiment, who had so recently warned that 'the soul of British television is in danger', and that we were 'losing sight' of television's innate value, now confined himself to telling an RTS seminar, held on the day after the Draft Bill was published, that the market environment it promoted 'can breed endless repetition'. The new Chief Executive of Channel Four, Mark Thompson's most severe criticism was that all the talk of encouraging diversity might 'end up meaning its reverse'.[26]

Robust public criticism of the government's proposals was left to media commentators, trade unions and people who no longer had a direct stake in broadcasting. Two days after the Draft Bill was published Janine Gibson wrote in the *Guardian*, 'The only way to protect what is good and worthwhile . . . is through *more* content regulation, not less.' Faced with 'the sort of bring and buy sale now envisaged by the Communications Bill' those who cared about broadcasting were going to have to fight for it.

But would they? It looked ominously as if they would not, or if they did, not effectively enough. The commercial broadcasters, faced with increased competition for audiences, were hardly likely to offer coherent opposition to measures that promised to free them of some or all of their remaining programme obligations. The BBC, charged after the 1996 Charter renewal with the task of quadrupling its commercial income within a decade, and already fearing that when next its Charter came up for renewal, in 2006, it might face a powerful commercial lobby demanding the abolition of the licence fee, was equally unlikely to risk antagonising the government by assaulting its plans. The independents, who had once prided themselves on being the champions of programme quality, had already shown that their efforts were now concentrated on enlisting Government support for improved business terms in their dealings with broadcasters. Accordingly PACT confined itself to saying that the Draft Bill contained 'much to praise' and welcoming the government's promise to retain the 25% quota while loosening the ownership rules governing who could qualify under it as an independent.

In contrast to such mealy-mouthed responses, that autumn the President of the actors' trade union Equity, Harry Landis, told the TUC conference in Blackpool that the Draft Bill threatened to undermine the quality and range of programmes available to the viewing public. 'Do you remember the days when television was worth watching? When did you last see a play that was not only entertaining but also informative and uplifting?' Already, Landis said, even the police series and soaps are at risk under the onslaught of gardening, cooking and reality shows and 'Some poor sod getting their front room painted mauve and orange.' The government's new, lighter-touch regulation and relaxation of the requirements determining the amounts and placing of specific genres of programmes were likely, Landis told the TUC, to leave companies 'free to put out a watered down version of any standards and we could get more cheap rubbish like *Wheel of Fortune* and *Changing Rooms*.' Following his speech, the TUC passed a motion committing it to lobby the Government to drop all dilution of regulation and relaxation of ownership controls.[27]

In June an equally powerful attack came from John Willis, a highly respected former Channel Four and ITV executive. He had quit ITV after the company for which he had worked, the south of England contractor United Broadcasting, was taken over by Granada. Willis had felt, like others before him, that Granada's 'one priority was profit, and programmes and people were irrelevant' and that his position had become untenable after 'they realised I wasn't a cost-cutting loyalist'.[28] In a valedictory article in the *Guardian*, before leaving Britain to take up a senior post with the largest public service broadcast station in the USA, Willis wrote that the television he was leaving behind in the UK was 'riddled with even more self-doubt than usual. Now', he said, 'the government is promising worse to come . . . The only way of ensuring quality on behalf of the viewers is to inflict significant regulation on the modern media company.' He went on, 'A giant regulator [Ofcom] starting from scratch and with much to learn looks like a thin line of defence.' Commenting on the government's decision to encourage overseas investment in British television, Willis said, 'Tessa Jowell and Patricia Hewitt (the Secretaries of State for Culture, Media and Sport and Trade and Industry) put out the welcome mat for US media companies, while broadcasters' doors in LA and New York remain firmly closed to British investors.' Some UK broadcasters might already be neglecting home-grown product for British viewers, 'but surely US owners will care even less. Moreover, if the US majors move in here, profits will be repatriated to America, not invested in the UK . . . US entry here, backed by huge global resources, will intensify competition for audiences, squeezing public broadcasters such as the BBC and C4 where it hurts. A combination of Sky and C5, with their capacity to buy up international rights plus their cross-promotional possibilities, could be lethal . . . The government's vandalism is commercial as well as cultural, risking jobs and export revenue as well as range and quality of production.'[29]

Even the ITC, the anaemic regulator widely held responsible for much of the loss of quality in ITV since the 1990 Broadcasting Act, flagged up grave concerns over the system of content regulation proposed in the Draft Bill. It pointed out that allowing the broadcasters to write their own annual policy statements and then restricting Ofcom to commenting on how well they had fulfilled those promises was likely to lead to an unacceptable delay in the time it would take to bring about any correction if companies failed to honour the promises they had made. Analysis of shortcomings 'could be three years out-of-date and may not provide relevant guidance as to the range and quality of available programmes'. The time-lag could be exacerbated still further because Ofcom was to be required to produce a comprehensive review of public service broadcasting only every three years and therefore, with programme commissioning lead times of up to two years 'there could be a gap of five years between Ofcom's ability to analyse a trend, apply its concern to a licensee's annual statement and remedial action'.

A week after the Draft Bill's publication Tessa Jowell addressed a group of some seventy anxious members of the Voice of the Listener and Viewer (VLV), representatives of talent unions and of voluntary organisations, in the Grand Committee Room of the House of Commons. Attempting to reassure them, the Secretary of State told them that the Content Board, the body which would in future be responsible for broadcasting quality and content, would be 'at the heart of Ofcom'. It would 'have teeth'. Trying to find positive reasons to justify the new regime of 'self-regulation', of broadcasters writing their own statements of programme policy and of Ofcom only reporting on their fulfilment of these 'performance remits' months or years after the event, Jowell called the new system 'a healthy move away from the box ticking that characterises so much of present regulation'. The new set-up would, she maintained, 'enable Channel 3 (ITV) to deliver high quality programming'.[30] Most of us who heard her remained unconvinced, aware that this was no better than a pious hope completely unsupported by experience. The older people among us had seen how, every time in the past when there had been a loosening of regulation, and no matter what the protestations and promises of government ministers, the result had been not better programmes but worse. We knew that television in Britain had only been as good as it had been because regulators had had real powers and had been encouraged to use them. A clutch of former regulators, people with long experience of both ITV and the BBC, were there to hear Jowell that evening. One said to me privately afterwards that the Bill was 'an absolute scandal'. Another that it was 'the most reactionary and right-wing thing this New Labour government has yet done'.

Many of the concerns of people worried by the draft legislation were put to a Joint Parliamentary Committee set up to scrutinise the Draft Bill during the summer of 2002, chaired by *Chariots of Fire* film producer David (since 1997 Lord) Puttnam. However, when the Puttnam Committee[31] reported in late July, while it reiterated some of these concerns, its recommendations were not couched in sufficiently robust terms to deflect the government. Indeed, far from forcing any major improvements to the legislation out of the government, the greatest effect of the Puttnam Committee's deliberations was, as the minister responsible for steering the Bill through Parliament later admitted, to take 'a lot of heat out of the Bill'.[32] The Committee's sharpest criticism centred on the danger of allowing overseas companies to take ownership of UK broadcasters. But Tessa Jowell responded immediately by making it clear that the government had no intention of budging.

In November John Willis returned to the attack. In a scathing article in the Royal Television Society's Journal he reported how, during his first four months of actually living with American television, of having 201 channels available on the television set in his Boston living room, the diet on offer to him was of almost unrelieved aridity and sameness. 'Of course, if you are a news junkie, or a golf addict or enjoy weather porn, there is a channel (or more) for you. But the network broadcast offerings are almost indistinguishable, the same shows spread amoeba-like via syndication so that *Friends* or *Cheers* is everywhere like McDonald's or Dunkin' Donuts. News productions, the breakfast programmes and talk shows are hard to tell apart.' American sit-coms, with which, Willis observed, British television industry pundits had recently 'become obsessed', exhibited the same tendencies. The new season's emerging hits are, Willis reported, 'old-fashioned and conventional. These network comedies are blessed with the same tone as if they were created by the same computer, full of families and groups of friends who are virtually interchangeable.' Willis pointed out that as channels multiply the need for safe financial returns in an ever more competitive market encourages the tendency in broadcasters to play safe. In the US the proliferation of channels, which supposedly provide the viewer with choice, in fact limits that choice, 'particularly for the 25% of the population who cannot afford or do not want cable TV'.

Willis warned that, as the number of new look-alike channels in Britain multiply, cross-media companies will be increasingly driven to 'promote their own programmes and channels, undermining their own journalistic independence by substituting promotion for news . . . I never realised I would miss the clarity and range of British news programmes so much. Once excellent news productions in the USA have now been reduced to a commodity, a McNews. Alongside them sit talk shows in which the dark realities of American life are repackaged as entertainment. As my predecessor at WGBH, Peter McGhee, put it: "Most television enters our people and our body politic not as food for thought, but as an embalming fluid." Yet this is the television culture the UK government seems hell bent on importing. The inevitable result, however carefully regulated, will be a diminution of our cultural identity and a reduction in the range and diversity for the British television viewer. Just ask the Canadians. Do US companies protect Canadian cultural identity? No. Are US programmes dumped on Canada? Yes.'

In American society, Willis said, 'despite the illusion of choice, the most disenfranchised citizens are the thoughtful, independent-minded viewers from all backgrounds'. For this group American television, upon which the British government seemed determined to model the future of the British system, 'is off their cultural radar, an irrelevance'.[33]

In the face of such dire predictions the government continued to assert that it would not work out like that here. In spite of the evidence to the contrary, Tessa Jowell repeated her faith that a healthy public service system could survive and prosper alongside and in competition with a market system without damaging or debasing the quality, variety or range of the programmes.

*　　*　　*

When the Communications Bill proper appeared in late November 2002, although it contained 120 out of the 146 changes proposed by the Puttnam Committee, in all the areas where it really mattered, including the ownership rules, it still remained essentially the same. It still provided for ITV companies to write and monitor their own statements of programme policy. It still offered the companies a get-out clause if they should fail to live up their own statements of programme policy on account of 'economic or market conditions'. Only after a broadcaster had failed to comply with its own statement of programme policy, after Ofcom had pointed out that failure and after the company had failed to rectify those failings, would Ofcom be able to 'vary that licence so as to replace self-regulation with detailed regulation'. Even then, no matter how extreme or persistent a franchise holder's failure to comply with its obligations, it still appeared that Ofcom would not have the power to revoke that broadcaster's franchise. The percentage of original production, volume of local programmes and proportion of programmes made in a franchise holder's local area were all left to what Ofcom considers to be 'appropriate' or 'suitable'. The same applied to the number of programmes that must be 'made outside the M25 area'. The IBA, which had had much greater powers than those proposed for Ofcom, had failed to act effectively when LWT and TV-am breached the programme terms in their contracts. With its greatly diminished powers, and with all the get-out clauses and means of delay open to the companies, there seemed almost no chance of Ofcom being able to act as an effective regulator, even it wanted to.

In the days that followed Jocelyn Hay, the Chairman of VLV, accused the government of naïvety: 'To impose such irreversible change is irresponsible. Why is the government rushing into this change? They can provide no evidence of benefits to listeners and viewers.' Lord McNally, the Liberal Democrat spokesman on the Bill, said that his party feared that once the new system was up and running the interests of the DTI and business would predominate over those of the DCMS and the viewer as citizen. Lord Puttnam warned that if the government tried to 'flannel' the Bill through the Lords it would encounter fierce opposition. But in the face of this barrage of criticism Tessa Jowell remained unrepentant: 'It doesn't bother me who owns our media companies. [It doesn't matter] whether it's a dollar, a Euro or a yen that's buying the programming as long as that programming is UK-originated, high quality and what people in the UK want to see.' She rejected suggestions that if US companies gained control over ITV they would dump trashy US programmes on British screens: 'In practice it would be very hard to find evidence of dumping. Why would an American company think that it was going to achieve commercial success by dumping low value, rubbish television on British screens, when by and large UK viewers are discerning and used to quality? They would simply not watch it.' She dismissed the evidence that showed that over the decade since lighter regulation had been introduced in the wake of the Tory 1990 Broadcasting Act the variety of programmes available on all channels had been massively reduced – on the BBC as much as on ITV.

The one change the government did readily agree to make to the Bill followed a report by the ITC which had found that independents were still at a disadvantage in negotiating contracts for programmes they supplied to the BBC and Channel Four. Accordingly the government introduced an amendment to the Bill that met PACT's lobbying demands and ensured that in future deals between independents and the BBC or Channel Four would incorporate terms over ownership of programme rights in line with those already operated by ITV. Ofcom was also given responsibility for measuring the 25% independent quota by both value and hours broadcast. At last, it seemed, independents were to get the contracts and system of quota measurement which Michael Peacock, I and a succession of other negotiators had tried to win for the sector for over twenty years. However, by now, with the changed priorities of the broadcasters, it was far from clear that this would in practice really be such an advantage to the majority of small- and medium-sized producers, rather than to just the few big ones. It seemed likely that the reaction of the broadcasters might be to try to recoup any loss of overseas and secondary rights income from independent programmes by cutting their total programme budgets or the amount they paid independents for producing programmes. If this was the result the chief beneficiaries were likely to be the handful of independent distributors and larger independent producers who made the kind of popular, high-volume material that was tailored to overseas markets, rather than the mass of smaller producers who concentrated primarily on making the kind of one-off programmes or short series which had characterised so much of British public service broadcasting.[34]

Major worries about the future quality of British broadcasting loomed ever larger as the Bill started its progress through Parliament. In late January 2003 some seventy people from VLV, voluntary organisations, talent unions and groups such as the Campaign for Quality Television filed into Portcullis House, the expensive new parliamentary office building by the Thames opposite Big Ben, for what was billed to be a 'seminar' on the Bill with the Secretary of State, Tessa Jowell. Jowell bustled in half an hour late, announced that she could give us thirty minutes and launched into a set-piece speech. Reiterating the main points of the government's case, Jowell claimed that we had already seen the value of increased competition in television and that the new digital channels were already providing greater choice and better programmes. She then said that she could take only a few questions before she had to leave.

Jowell's answers, when she provided any rather than simply repeating what had been asked and then avoiding the question altogether, satisfied almost none of us. When the Commissioning Editor for Children's Programmes at Channel Four asked for Ofcom to be given the power to require all five major terrestrial channels to provide high-quality children's programmes, he was told that children's programmes were adequately protected in the Bill and that where a channel failed to provide them Ofcom would be able to criticise the company concerned in its triennial review. When Ray Fitzwalter pointed to the decline in the volume and quality of regional programmes in ITV over the previous decade and suggested that if an amalgamated Carlton and Granada were taken over by an American company the quality and range of regional programmes would fall still further, Jowell responded that it was simply nonsense to continue to exclude American or Australian companies from owning ITV companies when EC companies could already do so and that in any case the powers of Ofcom would be sufficient to ensure effective regulation. She simply refused to engage with the idea, raised by me and many other questioners, that there had already been an unacceptable fall in the quality and range of programmes.

When I suggested that rather than a series of routine discrete reviews of public service broadcasting by Ofcom every three years, what was needed before any decisions were made over the BBC's Charter after 2006 was a full, dispassionate public inquiry into all aspects of broadcasting along the lines of the Annan Committee, she simply repeated that a review of public service broadcasting would be included as part of the BBC Charter review process. When I interrupted that, with the greatest respect that was simply not good enough, that the different parts of broadcasting all inter-reacted on each other, she said that Ofcom would have a duty to review public service broadcasting every three years.

Two weeks later a smaller group of us met for the first of a series of seminars with Richard Hooper, the Deputy Chairman of Ofcom and Chairman of its Content Board (fifteen years earlier he had given the star-turn at the by-now notorious Thatcher seminar on broadcasting in Number 10). Intended to explore how the Board might work, each seminar was attended by at least one other member of the Content Board in addition to Hooper himself, and a range of people with real knowledge and experience of broadcasting and its regulation. They included a former Director of the National Consumer Council, a former Chair of the Broadcasting Standards Commission, Professor Steve Barnett, compiler of the Campaign for Quality Television's devastating survey that had quantified the reduction in television current affairs and drama programmes, Colin Shaw, the former Secretary of the BBC, Director of Television at the IBA and first Director of the Broadcasting Standards Council, Professor Naomi Sargant, Channel Four's original Senior Commissioning Editor for Education, the Assistant Secretary of the Society of Authors and others like Peter Bazalgette. Although the discussions were full and well informed, the suspicion remained by the end that we had all been wasting our time. No matter that Hooper and his fellow members of the Content Board were well intentioned, they were not going to have the powers necessary to deal effectively with powerful broadcasters or act as a counterweight to the commercial forces that would be unleashed by the Bill.

Early in 2003 debate over the Communications Bill became overshadowed by the threat of war in Iraq and Tony Blair's evident determination to support President George W. Bush in mounting an attack over Saddam Hussein's alleged possession of weapons of mass destruction. On 15 February more than a million people took part in an anti-war march in London, the largest demonstration ever held in Britain. Millions of others marched in countries across the world. They made no difference. A month later Bush, supported by Blair but without the formal sanction of a United Nations resolution authorising the war, invaded Iraq.

With such deep divisions in the country over the war, broadcasters, and particularly the BBC, came under political pressure of a kind not experienced since the Falklands and the US bombing raids on Libya in the 1980s. The BBC was accused by the government and sections of the right-wing press of anti-war bias in its reporting. In this hostile climate an unholy alliance of the BBC's commercial competitors, and a few genuinely concerned experts who favoured the creation of a unified regulatory system to cover all broadcasting, increased calls for the BBC's wings to be clipped, its commercial clout curbed and for the regulatory functions of the BBC Governors to be handed over to Ofcom.

Then, on 29 May 2003, an event occurred which, because of the continuing controversy over the government's decision to go to war in Iraq and with the Communications Bill entering the last phase of its passage through Parliament, took on a significance which in more normal times it would probably not have merited. At seven minutes past six in the morning, in a live, unscripted interview on BBC Radio 4's *Today* programme, Andrew Gilligan, its defence correspondent, revealed that back in September 2002 the government had inserted a last-minute section in a dossier detailing evidence of Saddam Hussein's possession of weapons of mass destruction which claimed that Iraq could launch weapons of mass destruction within 45 minutes. Gilligan said that 'one of the senior officials in charge of drawing up the dossier' had told him that 'the government probably knew that the 45-minute figure was wrong, even before it decided to put it in'. He continued that the 45-minute claim had been added in the week before the dossier's publication in response to a Number 10 demand that the document be 'sexed up'. Although Gilligan's report had been modified in later items in the same programme, Downing Street reacted furiously and demanded a retraction from the BBC. The BBC refused and a huge row developed.

Meanwhile fresh warnings that the government's broadcasting plans were 'fundamentally flawed' continued to flow in. One came from Barry Diller, a former Hollywood studio boss and the man who had set up Murdoch's Fox Network, who told a broadcasters' conference that 'we need more regulation not less'. An influential US academic, Professor Michael Tracey, warned, 'Don't do it guys, it's fucking crazy.' The Communications Bill, he said, 'doesn't make sense in terms of how public broadcasting functions or in terms of how good TV is made and I've seen no economic analysis that shows it's worth doing'.[35]

Nevertheless, despite this and the much wider issues that the row over Gilligan's report on the government's WMD dossier should have brought to the fore, that summer, when the Communications Bill entered the House of Lords for the final phase of its passage through Parliament, debate over it, and most of the media interest in its outcome, narrowed down primarily to a tussle over the so-called 'Murdoch clause', the proposed changes to the media ownership rules that would end the restriction on owners of national newspapers buying Channel 5. The most obvious beneficiary of this change seemed likely to be Rupert Murdoch and his News International, already the owners of a slew of national newspapers and a large stake in satellite television through BSkyB. A coalition of 110 lords, including ex-BBC Chairman Lord (Marmaduke) Hussey, led by Lord Puttnam, succeeded in getting the Bill amended.

When the Bill finally received the Royal Assent, on 17 July 2003, all the sound and fury could be seen to achieved very little. The Act still opened the way for a massive deregulation of broadcasting and threatened the overall quality of public service broadcasting. It still ended restrictions on American media corporations buying ITV. Murdoch was not even barred from acquiring Channel 5, though, as a result of the action in the Lords, the Secretary of State had been empowered to ask Ofcom to consider the effect on choice and quality before making a decision on whether to allow takeovers to go ahead. Although some stipulations had been added to strengthen broadcasters' duty to supply children's programmes and provide drama other than soaps, Ofcom still lacked powers that would enable it to enforce quality requirements in a timely and effective manner. Ofcom was now charged with taking cognisance of viewers' interests as citizens in addition to their interests as consumers. However, this duty, while potentially important, seemed likely in practice to lay Ofcom open to expensive legal challenges by wealthy media corporations whenever they did not like any Ofcom decision which they chose to claim had the potential to benefit consumers. Even these limited changes to the Bill were criticised by Lord Currie, Ofcom's Chairman, and by its Chief Executive.

Notes

1. *Television Faces the New Reality*, speech by Michael Jackson to the Royal Television Society, reproduced in *Television*, the Royal Television Society Journal, April/May 1996.
2. *Guardian*, 23 March 2000.
3. The author of these précised 'confidential notes' has asked me not to acknowledge their source.

4. Notes jotted down in the reception area of Channel Four, Horseferry Road, Victoria, 16 November 2000.

5. *Evening Standard*, 27 September 2000.

6. Speech by Dawn Airey to an RTS dinner on 28 September 1999, reproduced in *Television*, the Royal Television Society Journal for November/December 1999.

7. Grade, *op. cit.*

8. Dominic Dromgoole, *The Full Room – an A–Z of Contemporary Playwriting*, Methuen Publishing Ltd, London, 2000.

9. David Hare, *John Osborne Memorial Lecture*, Hay-on-Wye Festival, June 2002.

10. It has recently been announced that *Correspondent* is to be replaced.

11. Lord Griffiths of Fforestfach, interviewed by the author in October 2000.

12. *Our Time Has Come, Broadcast*, 30 January 1998 and *And it's Goodbye from Him . . . , PACT Magazine*, January 1998.

13. David Frank, quoted in *Broadcast*, 14 September 2001.

14. Stephen Lambert, quoted in *Broadcast*, 31 May 2002.

15. The BBC and ITV had for some years operated a system of residual fees for directors. When one of their programmes was repeated, sold to another broadcaster or used in another medium, the director received an additional fee based on the fees he or she had originally been paid.

16. *Broadcast*, 31 May 2002.

17. Peter Bazalgette, quoted in *Televisual*, November 2000. On 1 March 2002 *Broadcast* reported that the Broadcasting Minister, Kim Howells, had written to Bazalgette saying, 'We do not want to see UK independent producers at a disadvantage compared to independent producers in other European countries.'

18. *Broadcast*, 3 August 2001.

19. *A New Future for Communications*, Cmnd. 5010, December 2000.

20. *Levelling the Playing Field* by PACT's Head of Public Affairs, *PACT Magazine*, August 2000.

21. *Public Service Broadcasting: What Viewers Want*, Independent Television Commission, January 2001.

22. Jon Snow, *Communications Reform for All*, called by the ITC and Public Voice, 16 January 2001.

23. McTaggart Lecture, the Guardian Edinburgh International Television Festival, 24 August 2001.

24. *Broadcast*, 25 January 2002.

25. *Draft Communications Bill*, Cmnd. 5508-I, II, III, May 2002

26. *Programmes and Public Service Broadcasting – Will the Communications Bill Help or Hinder Creativity?*, Royal Television Society, 8 May 2002.

27. Reported in *Equity*, Winter 2002.

28. John Willis, quoted in *Broadcast*, 24 October 2003.

29. John Willis, *The Sopranos Won't Save Us, Guardian*, 10 June 2002.

30. Tessa Jowell, speaking to a Voice of the Listener & Viewer Westminster seminar at the House of Commons, 14 May 2002.

31. House of Lords and House of Commons Joint Committee on the Draft Communications Bill, 25 July 2002. HL Paper 169-I/HC 876-I.

32. See *'My Year of Pain'*, report of a question and answer event with Kim Howells, MP, in *Television*, the journal of the Royal Television Society, September 2003.

33. John Willis, *The Real Cost of US Ownership* in *Television*, journal of the Royal Television Society, November 2002.

34. Late in 2003, when the new regulator Ofcom confirmed that in future independents were to be granted greater ongoing control over the rights in the programmes they produced, Mark Thompson, Chief Executive of Channel Four, announced that as a result the Channel was likely to cut its total programme budget.

35. Diller, quoted in *Guardian Unlimited*, 2 May 2003 and Tracey, quoted in *Broadcast*, 9 May 2003.

18

Time To Come Round Again? –
July 2003 and on . . .

'The social responsibility of companies is to make profits.
It is not a question of how, but of how much.'

Milton Friedman

What had persuaded the government to persist in pushing through its broadcasting policies in the face of all the warnings and predictions of disaster to come? Surely, its policy must have been based on something more substantial than a much remarked on over-adulation of big business or the desire to curry favour with media magnates?

Back in May 2001, when the Communications Act was still no more than a White Paper, Ray Snoddy, that best-informed and most prescient of media journalists, had addressed this question in a speech to the Royal Television Society. Making what he described as 'a very modest plea – that somehow a sense of reality should be allowed to intrude into the making of policy on media and broadcasting', he said that government policy was 'being driven by digital day-dreams and fantasies of an interactive always online world in which channels will disappear and everything will be available to everyone on demand'. As examples, Snoddy cited the over-optimistic forecasts about the rate of digital take-up, the government's 2010 target for analogue switch-off and the unrealistic expectations of commercial operators about the income they were likely to derive from an ever-expanding number of new digital and online services. 'Visions', Snoddy said, 'are best left to the Archbishop of Canterbury.' It would be better, he said, if politicians and everyone in the industry, especially the digital operators, 'were a bit more sceptical about their own myths'.[1]

A whole range of such myths had been bought into by the government, myths often propagated by one or more sections of the broadcasting industry for their own sectional ends. The first such myth was what might be called 'the employment myth', the idea that broadcasting will create tens of thousands of new, high-tech jobs. A survey carried out in 2000 by the joint industry training body Skillset found that 115,000 people worked in the UK television, film, video and related industries, more than the industry had previously thought. By 2002 that figure had reached 200,000. Findings like these appear to substantiate claims that the television industry is a great creator of employment. However, such claims need serious qualification. Of that 200,000 only about 40,000 are working at any one time in broadcast television – not much more than it was in the 1960s. Yet today we have five major terrestrial network channels in place of the three we had throughout the 1960s and 1970s, plus hundreds of local stations, cable, satellite and DTT channels. Whereas thirty years ago nearly all the jobs in television were well-paid, pension-able, permanent employment, on the industry census day in 2002 (which fell in June, when the number of people working could be expected to be at its greatest) almost a third of those in work were freelances. Behind these freelances lay tens of thousands more – perhaps two or three times as many – who were not working. These freelances represent a huge pool of people who are often frustrated, under- or un-employed. Even among those in permanent jobs many are ill-paid, insecure and far from highly skilled. Yet successive New Labour Ministers, from the Prime Minister down, continue to talk about the media being the industries which will 'deliver the growth, jobs and international success of the future'.

The second of these myths is that the proliferation of channels and consequent need for programmes to fill them will provide a great bonus for the UK's balance of trade. The truth, however, is that since the beginning of the 1990s and, particularly since content regulation was relaxed and the number of channels started to proliferate, our balance of trade in television programmes has gone heavily into the red, leaving Britain with a deficit of nearly £300 million. We now pay almost twice as much to import programmes as we earn from selling our own programmes overseas. This process seems set to continue for as long as the government continues to encourage the creation of more and more channels dependent on cheaper and cheaper programmes, and the established channels become steadily more cautious and reliant on sure-fire, already proven inter-national product. A graphic example of this can be found in programming for children. Since the 1960s the volume of programmes available for children and young people has multiplied many times over. However, during the same period, as the number of children's channels has grown and regulation has decreased, the proportion of imported children's and young people's programmes shown on

ITV has multiplied tenfold. On the non-terrestrial channels, other than those operated by the BBC, almost 90% of the programmes for children and young people are imported. This not only damages our balance of trade, it ill-serves our domestic audience and devalues the idea of television programmes as culturally specific creative products. Independent producers have long been as guilty as anyone else of encouraging false expectations about the export potential of British programmes and their impact on Britain's balance of trade. The independents, wholly dependent on selling their programmes and wanting the government to assist them in increasing their penetration of UK broadcasting, have had a vested interest in sustaining such false expectations.

The third myth for which the New Labour government seems to have fallen, as governments so often have in the past, is the technological one. 'We want to unleash the potential for these convergent communications technologies to extend choice, deepen democracy, enrich entertainment and enable learning', said the White Paper with a fine flourish. Since then not only has ITV Digital collapsed and major UK cable companies lost millions of pounds, around the world major international media corporations have gone bust, the over-inflated price of the mobile phone spectrum has crashed and even Rupert Murdoch has felt financial pain. Yet the government continues to look to a technological and creative industry sunrise on which Britain will build its future. Does it really know nothing of the industry's recent history? Of the multi-core cable revolution that we were promised was 'around the corner' in the 1970s? Of HDTV, the British high-tech satellite system D-MAC, British Satellite Broadcasting and the squarial? Each one was supposed to be going to sweep everything before it. Has it already forgotten the dot-com crash, the modern equivalent of the South Sea Bubble? Perhaps so – governments are notorious for listening to only those things which they want to hear.

*   *   *

The day after the Communications Act received the Royal Assent, 18 July 2003, Dr David Kelly was found dead. Three days earlier Kelly, a government weapons expert who had been a UN weapons inspector in Iraq, had been subjected to a harsh public grilling by the House of Commons Foreign Affairs Committee and then confirmed by the Department of Defence to have been the source referred to in Andrew Gilligan's controversial report in the BBC's *Today* programme about the disputed 45-minute WMD claim in the government's September 2002 dossier. The Prime Minister immediately ordered a public inquiry into the circumstances surrounding Kelly's death and through much of August and most of September anyone who might be able to throw light on the events leading up to the death, from the Prime Minister and Director-General of the BBC to members of Kelly's family and the ambulance crew who had gone to the scene, trooped into the Royal Courts of Justice to give evidence to Lord Hutton, a former lord chief justice of Northern Ireland, and be cross examined. By the end of it the public standing of many of those concerned, not least the government and the BBC, had been damaged.[2]

The threat to the BBC was obvious. The BBC Governors' immediate, unqualified defence of the Gilligan broadcast, although a refreshing change from the way in which their predecessors' had acted over the Zircon affair, the unseating of Alasdair Milne and the *Panorama* 'supergun' exposé, now seemed over-hasty or worse. Sensing blood, the BBC's enemies openly set about exploiting its discomfort, reiterating demands for its commercial activities to be curtailed, its size to be reduced and for the functions of the Governors to be handed over to Ofcom. Even some people claiming to be the Corporation's friends joined in. One of the first in the field was the House of Commons Media Select Committee which, days before Dr Kelly's death, attacked the BBC for publishing a 'gushing, Enron-style' Annual Report (Enron, one of America's largest companies, had gone spectacularly bust amid accusations of lying about its profits and concealing its debts). One MP described the Report as having been 'dipped in a big bucket of whitewash', adding that, while he would 'defend the BBC and the licence fee until the end of time', if the Governors would not curb the BBC's management then 'someone else will – and that will be Ofcom'. PACT's Chief Executive, John McVay, also piped up, accusing the BBC of being 'deeply arrogant' over the way that it had reported its failure to meet the independent's 25% quota in full. He called for Ofcom to institute sanctions against the BBC if it failed to meet the quota again. The BBC blamed the shortfall (4%) on the fact that some of its big independent suppliers, such as Endemol, had lost their independent status. As PACT had been actively campaigning for companies like Endemol to get their independent status back, it looked rather as if PACT was trying to have its cake and eat it.

Barry Cox, Channel Four's Deputy Chairman, who also headed the government's digital task force, went further still. He not only accused the Governors of acting as the BBC's 'champion' rather than as its regulators, calling for their regulatory duties to be taken over by Ofcom, he suggested that the licence fee should be done away with and in future the BBC should rely on voluntary subscriptions.

With open season on the BBC now well and truly declared, Tony Ball, the Chief Executive of BSkyB, used his Edinburgh International Television Festival McTaggart Lecture to accuse the BBC of being bloated with cash and call for it to be severely reined in. It should be made to stop buying US hit programmes and forced to auction off its own most popular programmes, such as *EastEnders*, to its commercial rivals. Although the majority of Ball's audience dismissed his speech as self-interested nonsense, some independent producers suggested that, on the contrary, he had not gone far enough. What was needed, PACT's John McVay told a reporter, was a debate about the BBC more or less ceasing to be a programme producer and becoming instead a publisher–broadcaster along the lines of Channel Four.

Three weeks later Tessa Jowell, having once again arrived late (her late arrivals had by now become the stuff of industry jokes), announced during a speech to the Royal Television Society's biennial Cambridge Convention a complete review of the BBC's role and purpose, as a precursor to the government's review of the BBC Charter, due to expire in 2006. With more and more people now piling into the BBC, the *Daily Telegraph* instigated what it called a 'Beebwatch'. Readers were invited to supply the paper with examples of what the *Telegraph* described as the BBC's usually unconscious, soft-left, liberal, anti-business, anti-American, anti-Iraq war bias. Meanwhile the Conservative Party had set up its own review of the BBC's funding and appointed David Elstein to chair it. Although Elstein insisted that he and the other members of his panel were strictly neutral and brought no pre-conceived ideas to the task, Elstein had already spoken publicly about changing the BBC licence system and reducing its funding. On top of this Elstein was reported to be trying to put together, with assistance from the American greetings card company Hallmark, a bid to buy ITV. If nothing else, one could not but admire his industry!

With the Communications Act safely on the statute book, ITV had started to seek reductions in its public service broadcasting obligations. Early in October ITV's Director of Programmes called for the number of hours of religious programmes broadcast by ITV to be cut, suggesting that the BBC and Channel Four should take on more of ITV's public service role. Channel 5 was reported to be lobbying to be allowed to drop its 7 p.m. news programme, and both ITV and

Channel Four bosses were arguing that, as public service broadcasters, they should share in the BBC's licence fee income. Meanwhile Channel Four seemed to be continuing in its shamelessly attention-seeking ways. In October it gave peak-time scheduling to Derren Brown playing Russian roulette with what was billed to be a live bullet and, a few days later, apparently anticipating that it would capture night-vision shots of teenage participants having unprotected sex, it rescheduled a teenage version of *Big Brother*, out of the daytime educational slot for which it had been commissioned, into a peak-time evening slot.

On 7 October, as expected, the DTI gave its blessing to the merger of ITV's two largest contractors, Granada and Carlton, subject only to their coming up with a plan within a month to satisfy the concerns of the Competition Commission over the way in which they sold advertising airtime. As the only franchises not now controlled by the new Granada–Carlton merged company were those covering Scotland, Northern Ireland and the Channel Islands, the result was to create, almost fifty years after it began, what was effectively a single ITV company. As David Plowright commented: 'ITV used to be an industry for programme production but has changed out of all recognition to one about profits above all else.'[3]

*   *   *

On the same day as the Communications Act received the Royal Assent, Hat Trick Productions, the independent production company started by Jimmy Mulville and Denise O'Donoghue, the young woman who had been recruited twenty-two years earlier from the city by Michael Peacock to become IPPA's first General Manager, sold 45% of its shares to Kleinwort Capital for £23 million.

However, while a few independents were becoming rich, many, probably the majority, were continuing to experience the narrowing of creative opportunities. By 2003 four out of the five people awarded Royal Television Society silver medals in 2000 for their role in the rise of the independent sector had taken decisions which meant that in future they would work primarily in areas other than broadcast television. David Graham, a first-class current affairs producer, had dropped out of producing programmes and re-directed his talents into media research. This, he said, was because 'anything that we could get commissioned were boring programmes'.[4] Sophie Balhetchet had established a company with the television writer Lynda La Plante to concentrate, in the first instance, on making films for the cinema. She had found the escalating degree of market-orientated interference in the creative process by commissioning editors and broadcast executives increasingly at odds with her wish to produce the best and most original work. Similarly, John Wyvver had found that commissions for the kind of distinctive broadcast television documentaries and arts programmes for which he and his company, Illuminations, had become celebrated in the first dozen years of Channel Four had now more or less dried up. As a result, he had increasingly moved away from conventional television. Instead he and his young team now concentrated much of their energy on specialised projects for new media and online channels. In this way he could 'still do work in the area that truly interests me and is genuinely creative'. Only Phil Redmond still worked regularly in television. His company, Mersey Television, still produced soaps such as Channel Four's *Hollyoaks* and *Brookside* (*Brookside* was scheduled to finish on Channel Four late in 2003, twenty-one years after it first began). As for me, I had reached an age when I would have been reducing the amount of time I spent working anyway. Yet I too now found that I was no longer interested in pitching projects to commissioning editors when I knew that the kind of programmes they wanted were no longer the kind of programmes that I wanted to make. Instead I am happy to devote my time to writing and working occasionally in the theatre or helping young film makers. In the theatre and among young film makers I still find the energy, commitment and enthusiasm that was once so abundant in television.

Teliesyn, the successful co-operative in which Colin Thomas had played a leading role, had decided to close its doors at the end of 2002, in spite of the fact that it had just enjoyed one of the most successful years in its twenty-year existence. Teliesyn had launched the careers of many of the best film and television programme makers in the country, including one who had been short-listed for an Oscar. But in 2002 its members had unanimously decided that 'in a period when maximising the size of the audience has precedence over every other criteria', rather than compromise their programme making values they would prefer to 'go out with a bang'.

Phillip Whitehead, one of the original campaigners who still made programmes, described today's successful businessman-programme producer to me like this: 'The businessmen looks at two things: where are the areas where we can pile it high and sell it cheap? And – how quickly can I increase the asset value of my business so that I can sell it on? In the old days the television barons, for all their faults, included people like Denis Forman who would go off and get *Jewel in the Crown* made. Today the people I make programmes for are all in hock to people who have nothing to do with making programmes. The last series we made was ultimately for people whose real interest is in increasing the profits of Seagram's Whisky. The terrible temptation is to pitch your programmes for something that will increase your audience, or to make something sensational. Something that will attract attention to the channel.'[5]

Programme maker after programme maker bemoaned the caution, amount of executive interference in the actual programme making process and commissioning editors' obsession with ratings. In the words of John Wyvver: 'Television commissioning editors, but people in other systems as well, are constantly looking for what they claim to be innovation, but I would argue that they are consistently looking for novelty. They are not looking for ways of sustaining and supporting thoughtful, radical engaged attempts to find new kinds of images and new kinds of ideas . . . [Television] is now significantly impoverished from what it was ten or fifteen years ago. It's ultra-cautious.'[6] Even programme heads inside the broadcasters are worried. Laurence Rees, a brilliant programme maker and head of one the BBC's most consistently excellent programme departments, the History Department, talking about the importance of maintaining the BBC as an independent institution committed to the values of public service broadcasting, told me that there was now 'a real danger of something that up until now I have never faced in my career, a bifurcation, of the market dividing into those who are making films that do have a commercial proposition and those that don't'. He said that if the BBC's award-winning 2000 series *The History of Britain* was being produced today in a commercial television environment its producers would probably be confronted by this kind of problem. Already, Rees told me, even inside the BBC, producers are likely to have to say things like: 'Oh, we will do the battle of Hastings because we know that that will get a bigger audience, but when we get to the Jacobite Rebellion you may say "Do we really need to do the Jacobite Rebellion? The South Sea Bubble?" ' Commercial criteria can come in on projects at the BBC because of the need to involve overseas co-producers and maximise overseas sales. Already, Rees said, there are a load of projects 'where you can point to the fact that the budgets are related to what they are worth commercially.'[7]

One of Ofcom's first tasks is to undertake a root and branch review of public service broadcasting as a whole, including not only ITV, Channel Four and Channel 5, but all the digital, cable and satellite channels as well. Its conclusions will be considered by the government in deciding about the BBC Charter after 2006. The manner in which Ofcom sets about this task will obviously be crucial to the whole future of broadcasting in Britain. It will also provide a good indication of how Ofcom intends to operate. The first clue can be found in who the government has appointed to run Ofcom. The chairman is Lord Currie, an academic economist with experience as a Treasury adviser and in regulation of the gas and electricity industries. Ed Richards, the senior Ofcom Partner responsible for Strategy and Market Development, was previously the senior media, telecoms and internet adviser to Tony Blair at Number 10. Richards is unusual among his senior Ofcom colleagues in that he does have some broadcasting experience – as a researcher at the independent company Diverse and more recently as John Birt's Controller of Corporate Strategy at the BBC. It is striking how many members of what Ofcom describes as its 'top team' were government advisers during the Communications Act's gestation, or worked either at the telephone regulator Oftel (the regulator whose market-driven agenda had caused it to get rid of the single Directory Inquiries system and replace it with a chaos of 118 numbers) or for John Birt at the BBC.

Ofcom's Chief Executive, Stephen Carter, is only 38. He started his career as a trainee in the British arm of the advertising company J. Walter Thompson, working his way up to be Chief Executive by 1997. In 2002 he moved on to run the bankrupt cable company NTL. During the Royal Television Society's Cambridge Convention in September 2003 Carter provided some pretty clear indications of how Ofcom will go about its review of public service broadcasting. He made it clear that despite the extra duties placed on Ofcom during the Communications Act's progress to the statute book, he believed that the Act remained what he called a 'liberalising piece of legislation. It enjoins us as a regulator to de-regulate.' Public service broadcasting will be subjected to what Carter described as 'detailed authorative research and analysis' and objective principles of cost-benefit analysis will be applied to its achievement. Carter is clearly dissatisfied with the rather nebulous definitions of what constitutes public service broadcasting which have sufficed since the BBC was founded with the duty to 'inform, educate and entertain' or woolly statements, such as that made by Gavyn Davies at the end of his team's deliberations on the BBC's future funding in 1999: 'When we each tried to define public service broadcasting . . . we decided that we may not be able to offer a tight new definition of public service broadcasting, but we nevertheless each felt we knew it when we saw it.' The fact that public service broadcasting, like health or education, has social benefits which most people who have thought about it believe make any sort of straight-forward financial valuation difficult if not meaningless does not appear to deter Carter. In Cambridge he briskly dismissed earlier descriptions or understandings about the nature of public service broadcasting: 'Surely soundbites from the 1930s will no longer suffice . . . As a country we have a cultural preference for opacity and vagueness.' He wanted 'a written constitution for public service broadcasting' and intended to extend the mechanisms of market trading to the fulfilment of public service obligations. So if ITV provides programmes for which advertisers won't cover the full cost then that could, under the system Ofcom seems to envisage, be balanced against the price that a franchisee pays for its licence: 'There is a trade-off, our review will make that trade-off explicit.' Asked if TV was 'special', Carter replied that, yes, he thought it was 'very special' but 'I just don't think it is as special as people who work in TV think.'

To someone of my generation Carter and Ofcom's approach, designed to liberate the commercial and competitive forces in broadcasting, sounds ominously rigid, particularly when they talk about the criteria they will apply to evaluating public service broadcasting. That the New Labour government has bought into the myths highlighted by Ray Snoddy in his Royal Television Society lecture should, of course, come as no surprise. A similar dedication to numerical targets has been long been evident in areas such as health, education and penal policy. Even in fields as intrinsically unsusceptible to numerical or fiscal evaluation as the arts and culture, Blair and New Labour have always tended to talk of their value more in terms their potential as earners of tourist income or sources of job creation rather than in terms of their intrinsic value or their role in achieving a civilised society.

One of the fundamental tenets of public service broadcasting is that for a simple flat licence fee the viewer gets a full service, a complete mix and range of culture and entertainment, news and sport, and has nothing else to pay. While the current licence fee system might usefully be improved by relating how much each household pays more closely to its ability to pay, and may need updating to take account of new systems of programme delivery such as broadband, the idea which underpins the licence fee principle, that once one has opted into the system it involves no further discrimination by ability or willingness to pay, remains uniquely valuable.

All the other systems cost the viewer extra money. Buying into even a fairly basic satellite or pay cable package means that a subscriber has to pay two, three or more times the cost of the licence fee on its own. For instance the latest offering from Rupert Murdoch's Sky starts at £160 a year for five TV channels delivered on digital, while the top of the range package, which includes sports and movie channels comes to a staggering £40 per month – some four times the licence fee. A subscriber pays extra on top of this if he opts to watch a pay-per-view movie or sports fixture. In 2002 fees paid to UK subscription channels totalled £2bn. But having paid all this money the people in the 50% of homes that can receive digital, cable or satellite services still spent almost 60% of their time watching the five terrestrial services that they could receive without paying anything at all beyond the cost of the licence fee. In the evening, when television makes its greatest impact because the greatest number of people are watching, some 80% of all viewers are watching programmes put out by the five terrestrial services. In the autumn of 2003, after Sky had been on the air for nearly fifteen years, ITV-1 and BBC-1 were each still attracting twelve or more times as many viewers as the highest rating satellite programme, while for hundreds of hours each month many of the digital channels were registering no viewers at all.

The government has recently encouraged the expectation that it will continue the licence fee system in some form. At the same time it continues to expect the BBC to play a major role in achieving its target of analogue switch off by 2010. So the BBC pours £280 million a year, money provided by all television viewers, into providing a raft of new digital terrestrial services which can be received by only that section of the audience which already pays for a basic satellite or cable package on top of its licence fee or has invested in equipment with which to receive the DTT signal direct. (As of the autumn of 2003, although some 50% of the UK population had access to multi-channel TV, the figures were still sharply skewed against the poorest and older sections of the community). So £24 million a year is poured into BBC *News 24* but it is watched by less than 0.3% of the audience. More than £40 million a year is poured into providing BBC-4, whose programmes are often watched by fewer than 20,000 viewers. That £40 million is too much to take out of the BBC's existing services but too little with which to run a whole high-quality channel, particularly one dedicated to arts programmes, serious or largely original work, with the result that BBC-4 is heavily dependent on repeats and cheap interview programmes. At best, as in November 2003 when a programme about the National Trust achieved an audience of 350,000 or when Ian Curteis's Falklands play was viewed by almost 200,000 in 2002, BBC-4 gets

0.2% of the total viewing audience.[8] Worse, and even harder to justify in terms of the BBC's public service remit (or on any other basis than perhaps a self-preserving determination to promote the New Labour government's digital agenda) is BBC-3. The Corporation devotes more than twice as much licence payers' money to BBC-3 as it does to BBC-4, to offering a schedule largely made up of downmarket fare and repeats (its most popular programme is *EastEnders*) to win just 0.55% of the multi-channel audience – £97 million for a weekly audience of 95,000 viewers. Of all the BBC's new digital channels, even the determinedly Reithian BBC-4, it is surely necessary to ask – is the money devoted to them the best or even a proper use of that money? Is funding BBC *News 24*, BBC-3, BBC-4 and all its other new digital services the best and fairest use for the £280 million which the Corporation spends on them? That money was, after all, provided by all the viewers not just the 1.4% of the total audience that watches them. For instance, might not BBC-4's £40 million be better and more equitably used to fund, say, a primetime weekly current affairs show on one of the BBC's main channels BBC-1 or BBC-2? That would leave money over to fund a regular mid-evening arts programme (such as the late lamented BBC-2 series *The Works*), plus some domestic one-off documentaries and low-cost single plays by young writers and directors on the BBC's main channels. To use the money in this way would offer something to all viewers and do much to restore the quality and range of these channels. It would also bolster the BBC's flagging reputation as the world's outstanding public service broadcaster.

Where does the proliferation of BBC channels lead us? At the end of the day are we really going to get ten, twelve or more BBC channels all for the price of two? No. Either the BBC is going to cost us more or the fare on its channels is going to be diluted. Probably both.

The government and its fellow proponents of a 'market shall be king', multi-channel future base their case on two propositions – the first being that the market is the best provider of what the public wants or needs. But, as we have seen, the evidence from places such as America points overwhelmingly not to an increase in the range and variety of programmes on offer to the public but to a decrease. Those who believe that because of our different history and tradition in broadcasting going over to a more market-driven system will not have the same effects here as in America perhaps need, as I tried to point out to Tessa Jowell during the VLV's session with her in January 2003, to pay more attention to what happened in countries which had broadcasting systems based on the British model, countries such as Australia, Canada and New Zealand, which went over to more market-driven systems. Despite the confident predictions and 'safeguards' promised by politicians, once-proud broadcasting institutions were reduced to threadbare shadows of their former selves, while the variety and distinctiveness of programmes was reduced to little beyond buy-ins and derivatives of those on offer in the USA.

Proponents of the market-as-best-provider future for British broadcasting, from Professor Peacock on, have had to admit to the probability of there being areas of 'market failure' under a more competitive and less regulated system. The Peacock Committee proposed a Public Service Broadcasting Council, operating along the lines of the Arts Council, which would dish out money to get desirable but uncommercial programmes made and transmitted. Stephen Carter and others close to Ofcom have indicated that using some of the BBC's licence money for this purpose is likely to be among the ideas that will be looked at during Ofcom's review of public service broadcasting.

The second key element in the champions of the market's case is posited on the right to free speech. In 1986 the Peacock Committee said that it was difficult to see how anyone who accepted the spirit of the 'First Amendment' to the American Constitution could be against the establishment of a full broadcasting market that gave multiplicity of choices to viewers, listeners and broadcasters. This is, indeed, a very attractive argument, at first sight unassailable. However, since 1986 people have become rather more leery about the efficacy of markets and their ability to provide genuine and unfettered free choice. They have noticed, as John Willis pointed out in his Royal Television Society Journal article in 2002, how in America giving free rein to a 'full broadcasting market' has led to the debasement of news values and their replacement with corporate promotion. They have become more aware of the range of hidden restraints and controls that exist in actual markets as opposed to the idealised markets of free-market economists' dreams. The difficulties are essentially the same as the difficulty raised by Phillip Whitehead when he whispered in my ear during the original Peter Jay lecture on the necessity of 'electronic publishing' at the Edinburgh International Television Festival in 1981. Phillip wanted to ask Jay why it was that the invention of the photocopier had not revolutionised publishing? He recognised, even if Jay and other champions of the free market did not, that in order to get your work seen you need not only a means of producing it and then access to a means of distribution, you also require the means to draw it to the attention of the audience and persuade them that it might be worth paying for. The Peacock Committee compared unfavourably the number of television channels then on offer with the tens of thousands of books published each year, suggesting that in the number of book titles the public was provided with a much greater choice of reading matter than of television. Leaving aside whether comparing the number of book titles with the number of television channels was really a proper comparison (a fairer comparison might have been between the number of book titles and the number of individual television programmes transmitted in a year, in which case the disparity between the number of books and the number television programmes is much less), a large question still remains. How many of these books are really available to any one reader or household in everyday practice rather than in theory? Not even the largest bookshops will display every one of these titles, nor will your public library.[9] Yes, you can go and ask for them, and today you can interrogate the world wide web, call them up and order them. But to do that you have to discover their existence, to know about them or, more likely, to have them brought to your attention. Then there is the question of what it is going to cost you to avail yourself of all these titles. Forty years ago the Pilkington Committee rejected the simple antithesis between 'giving the public what it wants' and 'giving the public what someone else thinks is good for it' as inadequate, pointing out that, Alice in Wonderland-like, when people say 'they know what they like, they mean that they like what they know'. Similar questions arise in respect of electronic programme publishing. These questions will remain even after the remaining technical difficulties have been resolved and a viewer has acquired the necessary equipment, range of channels and technical proficiency to view or download them. The PVR (personal video recorder) may eventually, as the pundits claim, make us each our own scheduler and put out of business the numerous channels which exist by playing out the same limited number of programmes time and time again at different times of the day. Electronic indexing may simplify exercising the act of choice when we are faced with hundreds of channels and other sources offering seemingly thousands of inadequately described programmes, and bring to our notice only those kinds of programmes which we already think we are interested in. Yet huge questions will remain over branding, the real range of choice, over cost and power in the marketplace.

Another difficulty in realising the electronic publishers' dreams is entry cost. Television programmes tend to cost a lot more to produce than books. Although costs are coming down all the time, few, if any, television programmes are ever likely to cost as little to produce as a book. Already the special interest channels rely overwhelmingly on the safe, on repeats of tried and trusted programmes bought in from mainstream broadcasters around the world. So, for instance, in Britain history channels have recently shown yet again *The World at War*, a series made by Thames thirty years ago and subsequently shown repeatedly on both the BBC and Channel Four. Or they depend on international co-productions, with the result that on the arts and performance channels you see endless re-runs of classic opera productions and ageing recordings of relays from the world's opera houses, arts films devoted to the safe canon of well-known painters and sculptors put together in such a way as to reduce the need for synchronous dialogue or interviews which might have to be subtitled or over-dubbed.

Proponents of the free market say that they want to increase the number of gateways into broadcasting and in so doing change the nature of its gatekeepers. Most profess to wishing eventually to do away with gatekeepers altogether. (Just how keen the government really is on that in practice as opposed to rhetorical theory may be doubted in view of its response to BBC reporting of the war in Iraq.) However, in practice, this side of some democratic and economic utopia, one seems likely simply to exchange one kind of gatekeeper for another. Instead of public service gatekeepers one is likely to wind up with a series of commercial gatekeepers.

As Alasdair Milne reminded Peter Jay during the Church House Peacock Committee debate in 1985, public service broadcasting, unlike any form of commercial undertaking, is akin to scattering seed far and wide and being prepared to wait and see what comes up. The point made by the Pilkington Committee forty years ago still holds good – it is not enough to give the public what it wants unless the public has also had a chance to sample all the possibilities – 'Broadcasting must be prepared to make mistakes, for if it does not, it will make no discoveries.'

A healthy society requires of television not only access for everyone to balanced, comprehensive and accurate news services but also access to the full range of that society's culture, to education, sport, entertainment, drama, music and the arts. On the face of it, the New Labour government accepts this. When I started in television in the 1960s it was common for people working in the medium to talk in terms of the quality of the television that we put into people's homes being as important as the quality of the water supply. Today such attitudes are widely derided as unduly patronising. As a result the government has pushed through a replacement of our established system with one whose primary aim is to make the UK 'one of the most attractive places for communications companies to do business'.

Perhaps the Red Guards of Blair's cultural revolution should heed the words of Albert Einstein: 'Not everything that counts can be counted, and not everything that can be counted counts.'

*   *   *

When I was a drama student in the north of England in the early 1950s as part of our training we ran and performed in a children's theatre, playing sometimes in big Victorian theatres, more often in community halls. One afternoon after a performance in a miners' hall in south Yorkshire we opened the curtains and came onto the stage to start preparing things for the evening performance. After a few moments someone noticed three boys, aged about ten, sitting in the middle of the auditorium chatting. A couple of us went down to ask them why they were still there. 'Oh,' they said cheerfully, 'we're waiting for it to come round again.' They saw our efforts as just like the local cinema. If they stayed in their seats the whole programme would come round again. In a sense they were paying us the greatest compliment. And in a sense, too, that is what I believe has to happen now if our television is not to be reduced to merely the sum of those things that can be counted. Those who care about the quality of our television are going to have to clear the stage and prepare for a fresh performance. That new performance will require a new script and will depend on mostly new players, although the things that happen during the performance are likely to bear some similarities to the old performance. The story? A new campaign, not simply to restore our television to the prestige it enjoyed before Mrs Thatcher and her acolytes got to work on it in the 1980s, but to lift it to new heights and allow it to achieve its full potential.

A new generation of campaigners can take heart from the fact that when our generation of campaigners set out in 1968 the situation confronting us also looked more or less hopeless. That generation, too, confronted what seemed like a broadcasting system already cast in legislative, institutional and commercial granite, together with a philistine government, more interested in business models and making sure that broadcasters did not embarrass it than in the needs of society. There were plenty of people who told us not to bother. To most of our contemporaries the 'sensible thing' to do would have been to settle down within the system, doing what one could to ameliorate some of its worst features, while exploiting whatever opportunities there were to produce worthwhile work. In some ways the broadcasting system of the 1960s, split between the twin edifices of the powerful ITV companies and an ever more centralised BBC, appeared even more impregnable than the system of today. Yet the campaigners of thirty years ago chose not simply to do 'the sensible thing'. In spite of pressures to keep their noses clean and to conform, in the face of threats to their livelihood and even intimidation, they set about challenging the broadcasting institutions of their day, exposing their failures, ridiculing their greed and hypocrisies, and working towards changing the mind of government. They realised that one of the first things that had to be done was to change the ground on which the whole public debate about broadcasting was conducted. A similar, perhaps even more fundamental shift in the grounds of debate will be one of the most urgent tasks facing a new generation of campaigners.

They will have to accept that change will not be effected quickly. It took that earlier group of campaigners more than fourteen years from the first tentative discussions that led from the creation of the Free Communications Group to the realisation on air of Channel Four. Even then the realisation was incomplete. However, there are grounds for optimism. Not all the good features of the old system are dead. Some of the politicians and executives who still pay lip-service to the values of our public service broadcasting culture actually believe what they say. There is still a residue of values and people upon which to build.

As Sir Paul Fox (a true champion of the values of public service broadcasting whatever his differences with the independents in the 1980s) told me when I interviewed him, the reason that we now have 'the most buggered-up television system in Europe' is because for too long the people within it were 'fighting from different corners'. There is no more reason to hope that people in television today will be any less inclined to fight 'from different corners' than they were in the past. So a new generation of campaigners will need, like their predecessors, to concentrate initially on bringing together all those individuals in each section of the industry who share their concerns. They will need to unite with all those journalists, idealistic young media professionals, people in the other arts and from the wider community who, like them, value the potential of broadcasting for reasons which are more enduring than profit, trade or employment.

Among the organisations inside the industry and beyond which would be likely to be sympathetic to such a campaign are the unions Equity and BECTU, organisations such as the Campaign for Quality Television and the Voice of the Listener and Viewer, plus various academics and university faculties which are interested in broadcasting. Unfortunately the independent sector as a whole, as opposed to some individuals and companies within it, having become more a part of broadcasting's disease rather than of any cure, seems likely to remain largely irrelevant. It pains me to say it, but the sector will remain irrelevant, or worse, to any concerted effort to improve the quality of broadcasting until such time as it begins to disavow the ethos of commerce and those who speak for it start to pay more than lip-service to their sector's idealistic roots.

Any new group of campaigners will need to remember that while it is not possible to regulate the good into existence (and that, even if it were, it might not be desirable, as there will always be a tendency for the result to be the predominance of one set of tastes or values over others – of either Mao Tse Tung's television or Rupert Murdoch's), it remains all too possible to legislate in such a way as to virtually ensure the exclusion of the good and its wholesale replacement by the mediocre. Conditions will need to be created that allow the widest possible plurality of programmes of every type, from high art, original drama and bold factual reporting to *Blind Date*, to become available to the widest possible audience without discrimination based on the ability to pay or on geography.

At some point those conducting any campaign will need to draw up some kind of list of the principles or purposes for which they are fighting. So here is my first tentative stab at a few of the things that I think ought to figure among the goals of the kind of new campaign I am advocating:

1. **The prime goal of broadcasting policy must be to sustain, enhance and extend the health and vigour of public service broadcasting so as to maximise its value in the cultural, social and political life of the country and of all its citizens.** Issues such as job creation, exports, business initiatives or driving digital take up can only ever be secondary to this central goal. The DTI must be kept out of broadcasting policy except for those areas which impinge on its proper concerns, such as frequency allocation or international trade agreements affecting the trade in programmes, formats etc. If need be the UK should learn from French cultural policies and be prepared to abrogate international trade agreements or EU rules where these conflict with the health of UK domestic public service broadcasting.

2. **The independence of the BBC must be guaranteed.** However, the

appointment of BBC governors should be made more open and subject to public scrutiny. The duties of the BBC's governors must not be taken over by Ofcom. It is important for the health of our democracy that there remain two separate and distinct systems of broadcasting regulation. However, the Governors should come to be less involved in the day-to-day running of the BBC and its editorial decision-making.

3. **The BBC licence fee must be retained, and no element of subscription or advertising revenue introduced to help pay for the BBC**. However, means should be found to equate the sum paid by households or individuals more nearly to their ability to pay. The level of the licence fee should cease to be set by the government and the task given to an independent body created for the purpose. Requirements on the BBC to maximise the proportion of income it generates from commercial activities should be relaxed and the BBC must not in future be used to drive government policies such as digital take up.

4. **ITV, Channels Four and Five and all other broadcasters, including satellite and cable channels, must be made subject to full public service regulation and the regulator given the requisite powers to undertake this**. These powers must include the regulatory authority having a duty to award licences on the basis of the quality of the service likely to be provided rather than the amount an applicant pays for a licence. The regulatory authority should have the duty to undertake detailed schedule approval and powers to exercise pre-transmission scrutiny of programmes.

5. It is now more than 25 years since there has been a full inquiry into broadcasting as a whole (Annan Committee 1974–7). Rather than more limited inquiries and investigations into discrete areas of broadcasting, such as those undertaken by the Peacock Committee or the government-sponsored 'consultations' and reviews carried out by ministers, government departments and statutory bodies during the run-up to 2003 Communications Act there should be a **full inquiry or Royal Commission into all aspects of broadcasting similar to those carried out by the Pilkington and Annan Committees**. Ofcom is not a suitable body to oversee such an inquiry as it would be one of the institutions being scrutinised by the inquiry.

6. **The 25% independent production quota must be reviewed to determine if it still serves any creative or cultural purpose. If not it should be phased out**. If a quota is retained it should apply only to programmes produced by UK companies, excluding subsidiaries of UK, EC or foreign broadcasters (terres-

trial, digital, satellite or cable), or companies owned or controlled in whole or part by any such broadcaster. The fulfilment of any quota must be assessed not only by the hours and value of programmes but by the range, variety and character of such programmes and the geographic spread of the organisations producing them. It defeats the objects of such a quota if, as now, it is met by just 5% of independents supplying 80% of the programmes or three companies make as many programmes as all the rest combined.

As we have seen, the blurring around the edges of the independent quota, of who qualified and who did not, of which programmes counted and the terms under which they could be made, indeed, the purpose of having an independent quota at all, had by 2002 all reached the point of almost total confusion. Back in 1987 at Mrs Thatcher's Downing Street seminar on broadcasting I told her that the 25% quota was needed as 'a runway of opportunity' so that the independents could 'get airborne' to compete with the broadcasters. After that, I said, it would not be needed. In the simplest sense, that runway has now served its purpose. Independent producers do provide the broadcasters' in-house production arms with competition and independents have played their part in bringing down production costs. As a specific means of injecting new blood into broadcasting and as a means of entry for those who were previously excluded, independent production is now of less and less relevance. Today the benefits of having a protective quota for independent producers may be outweighed by its disadvantages for the health of broadcasting as a whole. Independent producers, solely dependent on the sale of their programmes and format rights, tend to increase the pressure to commodify creativity, talent and programmes. So the time has come, if not to scrap the independents' 25% quota, to question it in its current form.

*   *   *

I have no doubt that the kind of passion still exists which is needed if the trends of the last decade are to be reversed and the quality and vigour of our broadcasting is to be lifted to new heights. I find it in the students I meet, in young people protesting about the environment and globalisation, in people working in the theatre and youngsters struggling to get their own films made. Nor do I doubt the continued commitment to public service values and creative courage of some of the older people who continue to work in television. My fears are about the climate in which they today find themselves. Dare they speak out or take creative risks in a climate of all-pervading commercialism, working on short-term contracts for the broadcast institutions or separated from each other in a myriad of independent production companies which are themselves terrified of doing anything that might lose them favour with the broadcasters? Dare they repudiate the morality of the market and the attitude that says broadcasting should be valued only according to the sum of those things that can be counted or measured?

This book opened with a favourite quotation of Robert Kennedy's, repeated by his brother Edward during the memorial service held after Robert's assassination in June 1968: 'Some men see things as they are and say why. I dream things that never were and say why not.' In 1968 a small group of film and television programme makers looked at the small, closed world of British television and they also said 'Why?' They began to dream of a better world and came to say, 'Why not.' In face of pressure and in spite of the odds stacked against them, they strove to bring about that better world. For a while, and to a limited extent, they achieved it. Then they began to lose their way. So it is that today's young programme makers, inside the institutions as much as the freelances, independents and aspirants outside them, face a renewed challenge. It is a challenge that everyone urgently needs them to take up because, while most of the things that politicians do make little impact on ordinary people's lives, what happens to broadcasting affects the psyche of the nation. And so, in closing, I throw down this challenge to today's programme makers: Can you see things as they are and say, why? Will you dream of a better world and dare to say, *Why Not!*

Notes

1. *Time for a Reality Check*, a speech delivered to a Royal Television Society dinner on 16 May 2001.
2. The Hutton Report, published as this book was going to press, almost completely exonerated the government and heaped blame on the BBC. In its immediate aftermath the BBC lost both its Chairman and its Director-General and was plunged into the gravest crisis in its eighty-year history.
3. *Guardian*, 13 October 2003.
4. David Graham, interviewed by the author in November 2000.
5. Phillip Whitehead, interviewed by the author in November 2000.
6. John Wyvver, interviewed by the author in August 2002.
7. Laurence Rees, interviewed by the author in March 2003.

8. In its best week BBC4 achieved a total of 0.6% of multi-channel viewers (those able to receive DTT, cable or satellite transmissions), which equates to about 0.3% of all viewers during the peak evening hours when BBC4 is broadcast.

9. At any one time something like a million books are in print. A similar number of television programmes might be available if you were to hunt around the airwaves, video shops and archives of the world. Since the Peacock Committee reported in 1986, there has been considerable consolidation in the book trade as international media companies have moved in on publishing and multiples have swallowed retail outlets, with the result that, while the number of titles has not decreased, the range of what is on offer has narrowed. The parallels with trends in broadcasting are striking.

Interviewees

Neal Ascherson

Sophie Balhetchet

Sir Bill Cotton

David Elstein

Sir Denis Forman

Sir Paul Fox

John Gau

Michael Grade

David Graham

Lord Griffiths of Fforestfach

Sir Jeremy Isaacs

Roy Lockett

Lord Macdonald of Tradeston

Alasdair Milne

Sir Alan Peacock

David Plowright

Colin Shaw

Greg Smith

Brian Tesler

Janet Walker

John Whitney

John Woodward

Colin Young

Joan Bakewell

Graham Benson

Charles Denton

Ray Fitzwalter

Christine Fox (Benson)

Nicholas Garnham

David Glencross

Roger Graef

James Graham

Jon Irvin

Michael Jackson

Michael Luckwell

Sir Donald Maitland

David Norris

Michael Peacock

Richard Price

Anthony Smith

Paul Styles

Colin Thomas

Phillip Whitehead

Shaun Williams

John Wyvver

In addition I picked the brains of many others including Mike Dibb, Bruce Page, Laurence Rees, Chris Rowley, Charles Stewart, Shaun Sutton and Rod Taylor.

Bibliography

Allen, Rod (ed.), *The Annan Debate: A Conference for Practitioners*, edited transcript of the proceedings, Broadcast Ltd, London, 1977

Annan, Lord, *The Politics of a Television Inquiry*, Ulster Television Ltd, Belfast, 1981

Baker, Kenneth, *The Turbulent Years: My Life in Politics*, Faber & Faber Ltd, London, 1993

Barnett, Steve, *The Battle for the BBC*, Aurum Press, 1994

Barnet, Steve & Seymour, Emily, *A Shrinking Iceberg Travelling South . . . : Changing Trends in British Television*, The Campaign for Quality Television Ltd, London, 1999

Benn, Tony, *Office Without Power: Diaries 1968–1972*, Century Hutchinson Ltd, London, 1988

Birt, John, *The Harder Path: The Autobiography*, Time Warner Books, London, 2002

Blanchard, Simon, & Morley, David (eds), *What's This Channel Fo(u)r?*, Comedia Publishing Group, London, 1982

Bolton, Roger, *Death on the Rock and Other Stories*, W. H. Allen & Co. Plc, London, 1990

Bonner, Paul with Aston, Lesley, *Independent Television in Britain, Volume 5, ITV and the IBA 1981–92: The Old Relationship Changes*, Independent Television Association and Independent Television Commission, Macmillan Press Ltd, Basingstoke, 1998

Bose, Mihir, *Michael Grade: Screening the Image*, Virgin Books, London, 1992

Briggs, Asa, *Governing the BBC*, British Broadcasting Corporation, London, 1979

——, *The History of Broadcasting in the United Kingdom, Volume V: Competition*, Oxford University Press, Oxford, 1995

BIBLIOGRAPHY

Butler, Ivan, *To Encourage the Art of the Film: The Story of the British Film Institute*, Robert Hale & Co., London, 1971

Cain, John, *The BBC: 70 Years of Broadcasting*, British Broadcasting Corporation, London, 1992

Carver, Robert (ed.), *Ariel at Bay: Reflections on Broadcasting and the Arts*, Carcanet Press Ltd, Manchester, 1990

Catteral, Peter (ed.), *The Making of Channel Four*, Frank Cass Publishers, London, 1999

Cotton, Bill, *Double Bill: 80 Years of Entertainment*, Fourth Estate Ltd, London, 2000

Crisp, C. G., *François Truffaut*, November Books Limited, London, 1972

Crossman, Richard, *Diaries of a Cabinet Minister, Volume Two*, Hamish Hamilton Ltd & Jonathan Cape Ltd, London, 1976

Curran, Charles, Young, Brian & Annan, Lord, *Television Today and Tomorrow*, The Granada Guildhall Lectures 1977, Granada Publishing Ltd, London 1977

Davies, Hunter, *The Grades: The First Family of British Entertainment*, George Weidenfeld and Nicolson Ltd, London, 1981

Day, Robin, *Television: A Personal Report*, Hutchinson & Co Ltd, London, 1961

Dickinson, Margaret (ed.), *Rogue Reels: Oppositional Film in Britain, 1945–90*, British Film Institute, London, 1999

Docherty, David, *Running the Show: 21 Years of London Weekend Television*, Boxtree Ltd, London, 1990

Docherty, David, Morrison, David E. & Tracey, Michael, *Keeping Faith? Channel Four and its Audience*, John Libbey & Co. Ltd, London 1988

Dromgoole, Dominic, *The Full Room: An A–Z of Contemporary Playwriting*, Methuen Publishing Limited, London, 2000

Dunn, Richard, *The 1990 Broadcasting Act: A Benefit or a Disaster?*, Peter Le Neve Foster Lecture delivered to the Royal Society for the Encouragement of Arts, Manufactures and Commerce on 16 November 1994, *RSA Journal*, Vol. 143, London, March 1995

Eberts, Jake & Ilott, Terry, *My Indecision Is Final: The Rise and Fall of Goldcrest Films*, Faber and Faber Limited, London, 1990

Forman, Denis, *Persona Granada: Some Memories of Sidney Bernstein and the Early Days of Independent Television*, André Deutsch Ltd, London, 1997

——, *British Television: Who Are the Masters Now?*, The Richard Dimbleby Lecture, July 1987, BBC Books, London, 1987

Frank, Thomas, *One Market under God: Extreme Capitalism, Market Populism, and the End of Economic Democracy*, Secker & Warburg, London, 2001

Frost, David, *David Frost, An Autobiography: Part One – From Congregations to Audiences*, HarperCollins Publishers, London, 1993

Garnham, Nicholas & Bakewell, Joan, *The New Priesthood, British Television Today*, Allen Lane, The Penguin Press, London, 1970

Garnham, Nicholas, *Structures of Television*, BFI Monograph, British Film Institute, London, 1973

Gilbert, Martin, *Challenge to Civilisation: A History of the 20th Century 1952–1999*, HarperCollins Publishers, London, 1999

Grade, Michael, *It Seemed Like a Good Idea at the Time*, Macmillan Publishers, London, 1999

Greene, Sir Hugh, *Third Floor Front: A View of Broadcasting in the Sixties*, Bodley Head, London, 1969

Griffiths, Brian, *Monetarism and Morality – A Response to the Bishops*, Centre For Policy Studies, London, 1985

Griffiths of Fforestfach, Lord, *The Business of Values*, The Hansen–Wessner Memorial Lecture, Service Master Corporation, USA, 1996

Heller, Caroline, *Broadcasting and Accountability*, British Film Institute Television Monograph 7, British Film Institute, London, 1978.

Hill, Lord (Charles H.), *Behind the Screen – The Broadcasting Memoirs of Lord Hill of Luton*, Sidgwick and Jackson Ltd, London, 1974

Horrie, Chris & Clarke, Steve, *Fuzzy Monsters, Fear and Loathing at the BBC*, Heinemann, London,1994

Horsman, Mathew, *Sky High: The Inside Story of BSkyB*, Orion Publishing Group Ltd, London, 1997

Hussey, Marmaduke, *Chance Governs All: A Memoir*, Macmillan, London, 2001

Isaacs, Jeremy, *Storm Over 4: A Personal Account*, George Weidenfeld & Nicolson Ltd, London, 1989

Lambert, Stephen, *Channel Four: Television with a Difference?*, British Film Institute, London, 1982

Lawson, Nigel, *The View from Number 11, Memoirs of a Tory Radical*, Bantam Press, London, 1992

Leadbeater, Charles & Oakley, Kate, *The Independents: Britain's New Cultural Entrepreneurs*, Demos, London, 1999

Leapman, Michael, *The Last Days of the Beeb*, Allen & Unwin, London, 1986

——, *Treachery? The Power Struggle at TV-am*, George Allen & Unwin Ltd, London, 1984

Madge, Tim, *Beyond the BBC: Broadcasters and the Public in the 1980s*, the Macmillan Press Ltd, London, 1989

Marwick, Arthur, *A Modern History of the British Isles 1914–1999*, Blackwell Publishers Ltd, Oxford, 2000

——, *The Sixties: Cultural Revolution in Britain, France, Italy and the United States, c.1958–c.1974*, Oxford University Press, Oxford, 1998

Miller, Nod & Norris, Cresta (eds.), *Life after the Broadcasting Bill: Proceedings of the 20th University of Manchester Broadcasting Symposium*, Manchester Monographs, Manchester, 1982

Milne, Alasdair, *DG: Memoirs of a British Broadcaster*, Hodder & Stoughton, London, 1988

Potter, Jeremy, *Independent Television in Britain, Volume 3, Politics and Control 1968–80*, Independent Broadcasting Authority & Independent Television Companies Association, Macmillan Press Ltd, London, 1989

——, *Independent Television in Britain, Volume 4, Companies and Programmes 1968–80*, Macmillan Academic & Professional Ltd, Basingstoke, 1990

Quicke, Andrew, *Tomorrow's Television*, Lion Publishing, Berkhamsted, 1976

Schumacher, E. F., *Small Is Beautiful: A Study of Economics as if People Mattered*, Blond & Briggs Ltd, London, 1973

Seglow, Peter, *Trade Unionism in Television*, Saxon House, Farnborough, England, 1978

Sendall, Bernard, *Independent Television in Britain, Volume 2, Expansion and Change 1958–68*, Independent Broadcasting Authority & Independent Television Companies Association, Macmillan Press Ltd, London, 1983

Shawcross, William, *Rupert Murdoch: Ringmaster of the Information Circus*, Chatto & Windus Ltd, London, 1992

Smith, Anthony, *The Shadow in the Cave, A Study of the Relationship between the Broadcaster, His Audience and the State*, George, Allen & Unwin Ltd, London, 1973

Smith, Anthony (ed.), *British Broadcasting*, David & Charles (Holdings) Ltd, Newton Abbott, 1974

Thatcher, Margaret, *The Downing Street Years*, HarperCollins Publishers, London, 1993

Tinker, Jack, *The Television Barons*, Quartet Books Ltd, London, 1980

Trethowan, Ian, *Split Screen*, Hamish Hamilton Ltd, London, 1984

Wenham, Brian (ed.), *The Third Age of Broadcasting*, Faber & Faber Ltd, London, 1982

Whitelaw, William, *The Whitelaw Memoirs*, Aurum Press Ltd, London, 1989

Williams, Raymond, *Britain in the Sixties: Communications*, Penguin Books Ltd, London, 1962

Windlesham, Lord, *Broadcasting in a Free Society*, Basil Blackwell Publisher, Oxford, 1980

Wyatt, Will, *The Fun Factory, A Life in the BBC*, Aurum Press Ltd, London, 2003

Wyvver, John, *A Decade of Independence*, unpublished paper commissioned by ORF, Austria, 1992

Young, Lord, *The Enterprise Years*, Headline, London, 1990

Parliamentary Papers, Reports from Government and statutory authorities, etc. (*Chronological order*)

Report of the Committee on Broadcasting, Chairman: Sir Harry Pilkington, presented to Parliament June 1962, Cmnd. 1753

Select Committee on Nationalised Industries. Report and Consultations, HCP 465, published 1 August 1972

Evidence to the Committee on the Future of Broadcasting under the Chairmanship of Lord Annan, Independent Broadcasting Authority, London, September, 1974

Submission to the Committee on the Future of Broadcasting by the Association of Independent Producers: On Co-Operation Between the Film and Television Industries, July 1976

Report of the Committee on the Future of Broadcasting, Chairman: Lord Annan, presented to Parliament, March 1977, Cmnd. 6753 and 6753–1

White Paper on Broadcasting, July 1978, Cmnd. 7294

Home Office: *Two Studies Concerning the British Broadcasting Corporation: 1. The BBC's Forward Planning*, HMSO, 1979

Broadcasting Bill: Bill 139 HMSO, Broadcasting Bill, published 6 February, 1980

Broadcasting Act 1980, Eliz.2 ch64, 1980

Report of the Inquiry into Cable Expansion and Broadcasting Policy, Chairman: Lord Hunt of Tamworth, October 1982, Cmnd. 8679

Report of the Committee on Financing the BBC, Chairman: Professor Alan Peacock, DSC, FBA, presented to Parliament, July 1986, Cmnd. 9824

House of Commons Home Affairs Committee Third Report: The Future of Broadcasting, Session 1987–8, HC262–I, HC262–II, HMSO, 1988

Broadcasting Act 1987

Broadcasting in the '90s: Competition, Choice and Quality, The Government's Plans for Broadcasting Legislation, November 1988, Cmnd. 517

Broadcasting Act 1990

Creative Industries UK Television Exports Inquiry – The Report of the Creative Industries Task Force Inquiry into Television Exports, chaired by Chris Smith, Secretary of State for Culture, Media And Sport, DCMS, 1999

A New Future for Communications, presented to Parliament by the Secretary of State for Trade and Industry and the Secretary of State for Culture, Media and Sport, December 2000, Cmnd. 5010

Culture and Communications, Perspectives on Broadcasting and the Information Society, Independent Television Commission, London, 2001

Public Service Broadcasting: What Viewers Want – An ITC Research Publication, Report by Jane Sancho, Independent Television Commission, London, 2001

Draft Communications Bill, presented to Parliament by the Secretary of State for the Department of Trade and Industry and the Secretary of State for Culture, Media and Sport, May 2002, Cmnd. 5508–I, II & III

Joint Committee on the Draft Communications Bill – Report Volume I, House of Lords and House of Commons, HL Paper 169–I & HC 876–I, 25 July 2002

Communications Bill, Bill 6 – I and II, HMSO, 19 November 2002

Communications Act, 2003

Selected Publications by pressure groups, etc.

(Specific quotations from publications by pressure groups are acknowledged in the text or footnotes)

Sound Choice: Local Radio Report, collected papers on local radio by the 76 Group, London, February 1971

The Purposes of Broadcasting, a paper by the Campaign for Quality Television Ltd, London, 1998

The Public Purposes of Broadcasting: Funding the BBC, University of Luton Press, Luton, 1999

Building a Global Audience: British Television in Overseas Markets, David Graham and Associates, for the Department of Culture, Media & Sport, 1999

Out of the Box, The Programme Supply Market in the Digital Age, a report for the Department of Culture, Media and Sport, David Graham Associates, Taunton, December, 2000

Index